Multiagent Systems
Introduction and Coordination Control

Magdi S Mahmoud
Distinguished Professor, Systems Engineering Department
King Fahd University of Petroleum and Minerals
Dhahran, Saudi Arabia

CRC Press is an imprint of the
Taylor & Francis Group, an **informa** business
A SCIENCE PUBLISHERS BOOK

CRC Press
Taylor & Francis Group
6000 Broken Sound Parkway NW, Suite 300
Boca Raton, FL 33487-2742

First issued in paperback 2021

Version Date: 20200116

ISBN 13: 978-0-367-50925-5 (pbk)
ISBN 13: 978-0-367-25536-7 (hbk)

Visit the Taylor & Francis Web site at
http://www.taylorandfrancis.com

and the CRC Press Web site at
http://www.crcpress.com

Publisher's Note
The publisher has gone to great lengths to ensure the quality of this reprint but points out that some imperfections in the original copies may be apparent.

This book is dedicated to my family. With tolerance, patience and wonderful frame of mind, they have encouraged and supported me for many years.

Preface

Multiagent system (MAS) is perhaps one of the most exciting and fastest growing domains in the intelligent resource management and agent oriented technology which deals with modeling of autonomous decision making entities. The field of multiagent dynamic systems is an inter-disciplinary research field that has become very popular in recent years, in parallel with the significant interest in the practical applications of such systems in various areas, including robotics.

Recent developments have produced very encouraging results in its novel approach to handle multi-player interactive systems. In particular, the multiagent system approach is adapted to model, control, manage or test the operations and management of several system applications, including multi-vehicles, microgrids and multi-robots, where agents represent individual entities in the network. Each participant is modeled as an autonomous participant with independent strategies and responses to outcomes. They are able to operate autonomously and interact proactively with their environment.

In recent publication, the problem of information consensus is addressed, where a team of vehicles must communicate with each other in order to agree on key pieces of information that enable them to work together in a coordinated fashion. The problem is particularly challenging because communication channels have limited range and experience fading and dropout. Along a parallel avenue, various topics regarding synchronization and consensus in multiagent systems were examined. The results demonstrated that the joint presentation of synchronization and consensus allows the reader to learn about the similarities and differences of both concepts. Cooperative control of multiagent dynamical systems interconnected by a communication network topology was also studied. Using the terminology of cooperative control, each system is endowed with its own state variable and dynamics. A fundamental problem in multiagent dynamical systems on networks is the design of distributed protocols that guarantee consensus or synchronization, in the sense that the states of all the systems reach the same value.

In view of the available results, it turns out that research avenues in multiagent systems offer great opportunities for further developments from theoretical, simulation and implementations standpoints. This volume provides "*system dynamics and control perspective*" of multiagent systems, with focus on mathematical modeling of multiagent systems and paying particular attention to the agent dynamics models available in the literature. We provide a number of problems on coordination and control of multiagent systems which have gained significant attention recently as well as various approaches to these problems. Looked at in this light, it has the following objectives:

1. It gathers together the theoretical preliminaries and fundamental issues related to multiagent systems.
2. It provides coherent results on adopting multiagent framework for critically examining problems in smart microgrid systems.
3. It presents advanced analysis of multiagent systems under cyber-physical attacks and develops resilient control strategies in order to guarantee safe operation.

October 2019 **Magdi S Mahmoud**

Acknowledgement

In writing this volume, I took the approach of referring within the text to papers and/or books which I believe taught me some concepts, ideas and methods. I further complemented this by adding some remarks and notes within and at the end of each chapter to shed some light on other related results.

A particular manifestation of our life is due the "interaction" with people in general and colleagues and friends. This is true in my technical career, where I benefited from listening, discussing and collaborating with several colleagues. Foremost, I would like to express my deep gratitude to Prof Yuanqing Xia, BIT, China, who has been a good supporter, but most importantly an example of a true friend. I owe him for his deep insight as well as for his trust and perseverance.

The process of fine tuning and producing the final draft was pursued at the Distributed Control Research Group (DCRG), Systems Engineering Department and special thanks must go to my colleague Dr Nezar M Alyazidi and graduate students Mojeed O Oyedeji and Bilal J Karaki for helpful comments, superb interactions and assistance throughout the writing of this book. The great effort by Dr Mutaz M Hamadan was instrumental in producing the last version of the book. Portions of this volume were developed and upgraded while offering the graduate courses *SCE-612-171, SCE-612-172, SCE-701-172, SCE-701-181, SCE-515-182* at KFUPM, Saudi Arabia.

It is a great pleasure to acknowledge the financial funding afforded by the deanship of scientific research (DSR) through project no. *BW 181006* and for providing a superb competitive environment and overall support of research activities at KFUPM.

I would appreciate any comments, questions, criticisms or corrections that readers may kindly provide to me at my emails:
msmahmoud@kfupm.edu.sa or magdisadekmahmoud@gmail.com.

Contents

Author Biography

Magdi S Mahmoud has been a Professor of Engineering since 1984. He is now a Distinguished Professor at King Fahd University of Petroleum and Minerals (KFUPM), Saudi Arabia. He was on the faculty at different universities worldwide, including Egypt (CU, AUC), Kuwait (KU), UAE (UAEU), UK (UMIST), USA (Pitt, Case Western), Singapore (Nanyang) and Australia (Adelaide). He lectured in Venezuela (Caracas), Germany (Hanover), UK ((Kent), USA (UoSA), Canada (Montreal) and China (BIT, Yanshan). He is the principal author of fiftyone (51) books, inclusive book-chapters and the author/co-author of more than 610 peer-reviewed papers. He is a fellow of the IEE, a senior member of the IEEE, the CEI (UK), and a registered consultant engineer of information engineering and systems (Egypt). He received the Science State Incentive Prize for outstanding research in engineering (1978, 1986), the *State Medal for Science and Arts, First Class* (1978), and the *State Distinction Award* (1986), Egypt. He awarded the *Abdulhameed Showman Prize for Young Arab Scientists in Engineering Sciences* (1986), Jordan. In 1992, he received the *Distinguished Engineering Research Award*, Kuwait University (1992), Kuwait. He is co-winner of the Most Cited Paper Award 2009, "Signal Processing", vol. 86, no. 1, 2006, pp. 140–152. His papers were selected among the 40 best papers in Electrical & Electronic Engineering by the Web of Science ISI in July 2012. He interviewed for "*People in Control*", IEEE Control Systems Magazine, August 2010. He served as Guest Editor for the special issue "Neural Networks and Intelligence Systems in Neurocomputing" and Guest Editor for the "2015 International Symposium onWeb of Things and Big Data (WoTBD 2015)" 18–20 October 2015, Manama, Bahrain. He is a Regional Editor (Middle East and Africa) of International Journal of Systems, Control and Communications (JSCC), INDERSCIENCE Publishers since 2007, member of the Editorial Board of the Journal of Numerical Algebra, Control and Optimization (NACO), Australia since 2010, an Associate Editor of the International Journal of Systems Dynamics Applications (IJSDA), since 2011, member of the Editorial Board of the Journal of

Engineering Management, USA since 2012 and an Academic Member of Athens Institute for Education and Research, Greece since 2015. Since 2016, He is an Editor of the Journal Mathematical Problems in Engineering, Hindawi Publishing Company, USA. He is currently actively engaged in teaching and research in the development of modern methodologies to distributed control and filtering, networked control systems, fault-tolerant systems, cyber-physical systems and information technology.

Chapter 1

Introduction

1.1 Overview

The field of coordinated multiagent dynamic systems, including swarms and swarm robotics, is a relatively new field that has become popular in recent years. Since the pioneering work [1] on simulation of a flock of birds in flight using a behavioral model based on a few simple rules and only local interactions, the field has witnessed many developments. Currently, there is significant interest in the applications of the field in various areas involving teams of manned or unmanned aerial, ground, space or underwater vehicles, robots and mobile sensors, to name a few [2]–[9].

Because of the interdisciplinary nature of the field, the literature on coordinated multiagent dynamic systems have a moderately wide spectrum of perspectives. This chapter focuses on the system dynamics and control perspective with the aim of presenting a short review on mathematical modeling, coordination and control of multiagent dynamical systems.

Integrator and double integrator models are the simplest abstraction, upon which a large part of results on consensus of multiagent systems have been based, see [34], [35], [36], [41], [42], [43]. To deal with more complex models, a number of recent papers are devoted to consensus of multiple LTI systems [37], [38], [39], [40], [44], [45], [46], [47], [48], [49], [50], [51]. These results keep most of the concepts provided by earlier developments, and provide new design and analysis techniques, such as LQR approach, low gain approach, $\mathcal{H}_\infty$ approach, parametrization and geometric approach, output regulation approach, and homotopy-based approach. However, most of these results [37], [38], [39], [40], [44], [46], [50], [51] mainly focus on fixed interaction topology, rather than time-varying topology. How do the switches of the interaction topology and agent dynamics jointly affect the collective behavior of the multiagent system? Attempts to understand this issue have been hampered by the lack of suitable analysis tools. The results of Scardovi et al. [45] and Ni et al. [40] are mentioned here, because of their contributions to dealing with switching topology in the setup of high-order agent model. However, when dealing with switching topology, [45] and [40] assumed that the system of each agent is neutrally stable; thus, it has no positive real parts eigenvalues. This assumption was widely assumed in the literature when the interaction topology is fixed or switching. Unfortunately, when the agent is stabilizable and detectable rather than neutrally stable, and when the interaction topology is switching, there is no result reported in the literature to investigate the consensus of these agents.

1.2 Elements of Graph Theory

In this section, some preliminary knowledge of graph theory [10] is introduced so as to facilitate the subsequent analysis. For a system of n connected agents, its network topology can be modeled as a directed graph.

A)) Let $\mathcal{G} = (\mathcal{V}, \mathcal{E}, \mathcal{A})$ be a weighted directed graph of order n, where $\mathcal{V} = 1, ..., n$ is the set of nodes; $\mathcal{E} \subseteq \mathcal{V} \times \mathcal{V}$ is the set of edges and $\mathcal{A} = [a_{ij}] \in \mathbf{R}^{n\times n}$ is the non-negative adjacency matrix. An edge of $\mathcal{G}$ is denoted by a pair of distinct nodes $(i, j) \in \mathcal{E}$, where node i and node j are called the child node and the parent node, respectively. A path in a directed graph is a sequence $i_0, i_1, ..., i_f$ if it consists of different nodes such that (i_{j-1}, i_j) is an edge for $j = 1, 2, ..., f, f \in \mathbf{Z}^+$. Denote $\mathcal{N}_i = j \mid (i, j) \in \mathcal{E})$ as the set of neighbors of node i. The adjacency matrix $\mathcal{A} = [a_{ij}] \in \mathbf{R}^{n\times n}$ is defined such that a_{ij} is the non-negative weight of edge (i, j).

B)) We assume $a_{ij} = 0$ if $(i, j) \notin \mathcal{E}$ and $a_{ii} = 0$ for all $i \in 1, ..., n$. The Laplacian matrix $\mathcal{L} = [l_{ij}] \in \mathbf{R}^{n\times n}$ is defined as $l_{ii} = \sum_{j=1, j\neq i}^{n} a_{ij}$ and $l_{ij} = -a_{ij} (i \neq j)$. A *directed tree* is a directed graph, in which there is exactly one parent for every node, except for a node called the root. A *directed spanning tree* is a directed tree, which consists of all of the nodes in $\mathcal{G}$. A directed graph contains a directed spanning tree if there exists a directed spanning tree as a subgraph of the graph. Let $G = (V, E, A)$ be a directed graph of order n, where $V = \{s_1, \ldots, s_n\}$ is the set of nodes, $E \subseteq V \times V$ is the set of edges, and $A = [a_{ij}] \in \Re^{n\times n}$ is a weighted adjacency matrix. The node indexes belong to a finite index set $I = \{1, 2, \ldots, n\}$. An edge of G is denoted by $e_{ij} = (s_i, s_j)$, where the first element s_i of the e_{ij} is said to be the tail of the edge and the other s_j to be the head. The adjacency elements associated with the edges are positive, that is, $e_{ij} \in E \Leftrightarrow a_{ij} > 0$. If a directed graph has the property that $a_{ij} = a_{ji}$ for any $i, j \in I$, the directed graph is called undirected. The Laplacian with the directed graph is defined as $L = \Delta - A \in \Re^{n\times n}$, where $\Delta = [\Delta_{ij}]$ is a diagonal matrix with $\Delta_{ii} = \sum_{j=1}^{n} a_{ij}$. An important fact of L is that all the row sums of L are zero and, thus, 1 is an eigenvector of

L associated with the zero eigenvalue. The set of neighbors of node s_i is denoted by $N_i = \{s_j \in V : (s_i, s_j) \in E\}$. A directed path is a sequence of ordered edges of the form $(s_{i1}, s_{i2}), (s_{i2}, s_{i3}), \ldots$, where $s_{ij} \in V$ in a directed graph. A directed graph is said to be strongly connected, if there is a directed path from every node to every other node. Moreover, a directed graph is said to have spanning trees, if there exists a node such that there is a directed path from every other node to this node.

Let Re(z),Im(z) and $\|z\|$ be the real part, the imaginary part and the modulus of a complex number z, respectively. Let $I_n(0_n)$ be the identity (zero) matrix of dimension n and 1_n be the $n \times 1$ column vector of all ones. Here, $\bigotimes$ represents the Kronecker product.

1.2.1 Basic results

Lemma 1.1 [32]
If the graph G has a spanning tree, then its Laplacian L has the following properties:

1. *Zero is a simple eigenvalue of L, and* $\mathbf{1_n}$ *is the corresponding eigenvector, that is* $L\mathbf{1_n} = \mathbf{0}$.
2. *The remaining* $n-1$ *eigenvalues all have positive real parts. In particular, if the graph G is undirected, then all these eigenvalues are positive and real.*

Lemma 1.2 [16]
Consider a directed graph G. Let $D \in \Re^{n\times|E|}$ *be the 01-matrix with rows and columns indexed by the nodes and edges of G, and* $E \in \Re^{|E|\times n}$ *be the 01-matrix with rows and columns indexed by the edges and nodes of G, such that*

$$D_{uf} = \begin{cases} 1 & if\ the\ node\ u\ is\ the\ tail\ of\ the\ edge\ f \\ 0 & otherwise \end{cases} \tag{1.1}$$

$$E_{fu} = \begin{cases} 1 & if\ the\ nodeu\ is\ the\ head\ of\ the\ edge\ f \\ 0 & otherwise \end{cases} \tag{1.2}$$

where $|E|$ *is the number of the edges. Let* $Q = diag\{q_1, q_2, \ldots, q_{|E|}\}$, *where* $q_p(p = 1, \ldots, |E|)$ *is the weight of the* pth *edge of G (i.e., the value of the adjacency matrix on the* pth *edge). Then the Laplacian of G can be transformed into* $L = DQ(D^T - E)$.

1.2.2 Laplacian spectrum of graphs

This section is a concise review of the relationship between the eigenvalues of a Laplacian matrix and the topology of the associated graph. We refer the reader to [11] for a comprehensive treatment of the topic. We list a collection of properties associated with undirected graph Laplacians and adjacency matrices, which will be used in subsequent sections of the paper.

A graph $\mathcal{G}$ is defined as

$$\mathcal{G} = (\mathcal{V}, \mathcal{A}) \tag{1.3}$$

where $\mathcal{V}$ is the set of nodes (or vertices) $\mathcal{V} = \{1, \ldots, N\}$ and $\mathcal{A} \subseteq \mathcal{V} \times \mathcal{V}$ the set of edges (i, j) with $i \in \mathcal{V}$, $j \in \mathcal{V}$. The degree d_j of a graph vertex j is the number of edges which start from j. Let $d_{\max}(\mathcal{G})$ denote the maximum vertex degree of the graph $\mathcal{G}$.

1.2.3 Properties of adjacency matrix

We denote $\mathbf{A}(\mathcal{G})$ by the (0, 1) adjacency matrix of the graph $\mathcal{G}$. Let $\mathbf{A}_{ij} \in \mathbb{R}$ be its i, j element, then $\mathbf{A}_{i,i} = 0$, $\forall i = 1, \ldots, N$, $\mathbf{A}_{i,j} = 0$ if $(i, j) \notin \mathcal{A}$ and $\mathbf{A}_{i,j} = 1$ if $(i, j) \in \mathcal{A}$, $\forall i, j = 1, \ldots, N$, $i \neq j$. We will focus on *undirected* graphs, for which the adjacency matrix is symmetric.

Let $\mathcal{S}(\mathbf{A}(\mathcal{G})) = \{\lambda_1(\mathbf{A}(\mathcal{G})), \ldots, \lambda_N(\mathbf{A}(\mathcal{G}))\}$ be the spectrum of the adjacency matrix associated with an undirected graph $\mathcal{G}$ arranged in non-decreasing semi-order.

- **Property 1:** $\lambda_N(\mathbf{A}(\mathcal{G})) \leq d_{\max}(\mathcal{G})$.

This property together with Proposition 1 implies

- **Property 2:** $\gamma_i \geq 0$, $\forall \gamma_i \in \mathcal{S}(d_{\max} I_N - \mathbf{A})$.

We define the Laplacian matrix of a graph $\mathcal{G}$ in the following way:

$$L(\mathcal{G}) = \mathbf{D}(\mathcal{G}) - \mathbf{A}(\mathcal{G}) \tag{1.4}$$

where $\mathbf{D}(\mathcal{G})$ is the diagonal matrix of vertex degrees d_i (also called the valence matrix). Eigenvalues of Laplacian matrices have been widely studied by graph theorists. Their properties are strongly related to the structural properties of their associated graphs. Every Laplacian matrix is a singular matrix. By Gershgorin theorem [15], the real part of each nonzero eigenvalue of $L(\mathcal{G})$ is strictly positive.

For undirected graphs, $L(\mathcal{G})$ is a symmetric, positive, semidefinite matrix, that only has real eigenvalues. Let $\mathcal{S}(L(\mathcal{G})) = \{\lambda_1(L(\mathcal{G})), \ldots, \lambda_N(L(\mathcal{G}))\}$ be the spectrum of the Laplacian matrix L associated with an undirected graph $\mathcal{G}$ arranged in non-decreasing semi-order. Then,

- **Property 3:**

1. $\lambda_1(L(\mathcal{G})) = 0$ with corresponding eigenvector of all ones, and $\lambda_2(L(\mathcal{G}))$ iff $\mathcal{G}$ is connected. In fact, the multiplicity of 0 as an eigenvalue of $L(\mathcal{G})$ is equal to the number of connected components of $\mathcal{G}$.

2. The modulus of $\lambda_i(L(\mathcal{G}))$, $i = 1, \ldots, N$ is less then N.

The second smallest Laplacian eigenvalue $\lambda_2(L(\mathcal{G}))$ of graphs is probably the most important information contained in the spectrum of a graph. This eigenvalue, called the algebraic connectivity of the graph, is related to several important graph invariants, and it has been extensively investigated.

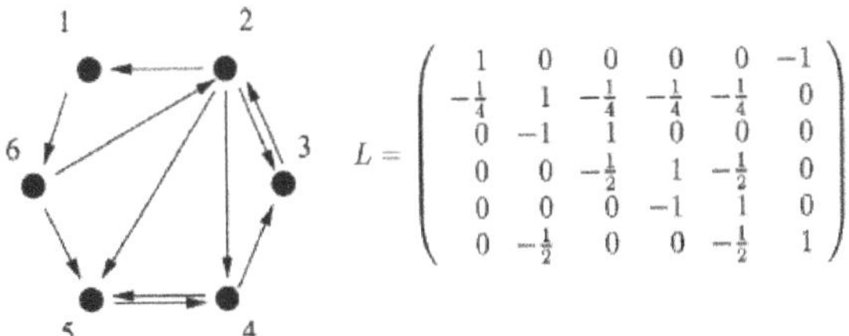

Figure 1.1: Sample graph and Laplacian

Let $L(\mathcal{G})$ be the Laplacian of a graph $\mathcal{G}$ with N vertices and with maximal vertex degree $d_{\max}(\mathcal{G})$. Then properties of $\lambda_2(L(\mathcal{G}))$ include

• **Property 4:**

1. $\lambda_2(L(\mathcal{G})) \leq (N/(N-1)) \min\{d(v), v \in \mathcal{V}\}$;
2. $\lambda_2(L(\mathcal{G})) \leq v(\mathcal{G}) \leq \eta(\mathcal{G})$;
3. $\lambda_2(L(\mathcal{G})) \geq 2\eta(\mathcal{G})(1-\cos(\pi/N))$;
4. $\lambda_2(L(\mathcal{G})) \geq 2(\cos\frac{\pi}{N} - \cos 2\frac{\pi}{N})\eta(\mathcal{G}) - 2\cos\frac{\pi}{N}(1-\cos\frac{\pi}{N})d_{\max}(\mathcal{G})$

where $v(\mathcal{G})$ is the vertex connectivity of the graph $\mathcal{G}$ (the size of a smallest set of vertices whose removal renders $\mathcal{G}$ disconnected) and $\eta(\mathcal{G})$ is the edge connectivity of the graph $\mathcal{G}$ (the size of a smallest set of edges whose removal renders $\mathcal{G}$ disconnected) [17].

Further relationships between the graph topology and Laplacian eigenvalue locations are discussed in [14] for undirected graphs. Spectral characterization of Laplacian matrices for directed graphs can be found in [15], see also Fig. 1.1.

A lemma about Laplacian L associated with a balanced digraph G is given hereafter:

Lemma 1.3

If G is balanced, then there exists a unitary matrix

$$V = \begin{bmatrix} \frac{1}{\sqrt{n}} & * & \dots & * \\ \frac{1}{\sqrt{n}} & * & \dots & * \\ \vdots & \vdots & & \vdots \\ \frac{1}{\sqrt{n}} & * & \dots & * \end{bmatrix} \in C^{m\times n} \tag{1.5}$$

such that

$$V^*LV = \begin{bmatrix} 0 & \\ & H \end{bmatrix} = \Lambda \in C^{n\times n}, \quad H \in C^{(n-1)\times(n-1)} \tag{1.6}$$

Moreover, if G has a globally reachable node, $H+H^*$ is positive definite.

Proof 1.1 Let $V = [\zeta_1, \zeta_2, \ldots, \zeta_n]$ be a unitary matrix where $\zeta_i \in C^n (i = 1, \ldots, n)$ are the column vectors of V and

$$\zeta_1 = (1/\sqrt{n})1 = (1/\sqrt{n}, 1/\sqrt{n}, \ldots, 1/\sqrt{n})^T$$

Notice that if G is balanced, it implies that $\zeta_1^* L = 0$. Then we have

$$\begin{aligned} V^* L V &= V^* L[\zeta_1, \zeta_2, \ldots, \zeta_n] \\ &= \begin{bmatrix} \zeta_1^* \\ \zeta_2^* \\ \vdots \\ \zeta_n^* \end{bmatrix} [0_n, L\zeta_2, \ldots, L\zeta_n] \\ &= \begin{bmatrix} 0 & 0_{n-2}^T \\ \bullet & H \end{bmatrix} \end{aligned}$$

Furthermore, if G has a globally reachable node, then $L + L^T$ is positive semi-definite, see *Theorem* 7 in [18]. Hence, $V^*(L + L^T)V$ is also positive semidefinite. Furthermore, we know that "zero" is a simple eigenvalue of L and, therefore, $H + H^*$ is positive definite.

As closing remarks, the Laplacian matrix satisfies the property $L = CC^T$. It is a well-known fact that this property holds regardless of the choice of the orientation of $\mathcal{G}$. Let x_i denote a scalar real value assigned to v_i. Then $x = [x_1, \ldots, x_n]^T$ denotes the state of the graph $\mathcal{G}$. We define the *Laplacian Potential* of the graph as follows

$$\Psi_{\mathcal{G}}(x) = \frac{1}{2} x^T L x \tag{1.7}$$

From this definition, the following property of the Laplacian potential of the graph follows:

Lemma 1.4

[33] The Laplacian potential of a graph is positive definite and satisfies the following identity:

$$x^T L x = \sum_{j \in N_i} (x_j(t) - x_i(t))^2 \tag{1.8}$$

Moreover, given a connected graph, $\Psi_{\mathcal{G}}(x) = 0$ *if and only if* $x_i = x_j, \forall i, j$.

It follows from 1.4, that the Laplacian potential of the graph $\Psi_{\mathcal{G}}(x)$ is a measure of the *total disagreement* among all nodes. If at least two neighboring nodes of $\Psi_{\mathcal{G}}$ disagree, then $\Phi_{\mathcal{G}} > 0$. Hence, minimizing $\Psi_{\mathcal{G}}$ is equivalent to reaching a consensus, which signifies a fundamental key in the design of consensus protocols.

Remark 1.1 *It well know that for a connected graph that is undirected, the following well-known property holds [10]:*

$$\min_{x \neq 0 1^t x = 0} \frac{x^t L x}{||x||^2} = \lambda_2(L) \tag{1.9}$$

The proof follows from a special case of **Courant–Fischer Theorem** *in [52]. A connection between $\lambda_2(\hat{L})$ with $\hat{L} = \frac{1}{2}(L + L^t)$, called the Fiedler eigenvalue of $(\hat{L})$ [53] and the performance (that is, worst case speed of convergence) of protocol (.) on digraphs is established in [11].* ▮

Remark 1.2 *Consider a simple digraph $G = (V, E, A)$ with $V = \{v_1, v_2, ..., v_n\}$ a nonempty finite set of nodes or vertices, a set of edges or arcs $E \subseteq V \times V$ and an adjacency matrix $A = [a_{ij}]$ with weights $a_{ij} > 0$ if $(v_j, v_i) \in E$ and $a_{ij} = 0$ otherwise. Let $(v_i, v_i) \notin = E \forall i$, with no self loops, and no multiple edges in the same direction between the same pairs of nodes. Thus, $a_{ii} = 0$. Define the in-degree of node v_i as the $i-th$ row sum of A, $d_{in}(v_i) = \sum_{j=1}^{n} a_{ij}$, and the out-degree of node v_i as the $i-th$ column sum of A, $d_{out}(v_i) = \sum_{j=1}^{n} a_{ij}$. The node of a digraph is balanced if and only if its in-degree and out-degree are equal, i.e., $d_{in}(v_i) = d_{out}(v_i)$. A graph G is called balanced if and only if all of its nodes are balanced. Define the diagonal in-degree matrix $D = diag\{d_{in}(v_i)\}$ and the graph Laplacian matrix $L = D - A$. The set of neighbours of a node v_i is $N_i = \{v_j : (v_j, v_i) \in E\}$, the set of nodes with edges incoming to v_i. A directed path is a sequence of nodes $v_1, v_2, ..., v_r$ such that $(v_i, v_{i+1}) \in E, i \in \{1, 2, ..., r-1\}$ A semipath is a sequence of nodes $v_1, v_2, ..., v_r$ such that $(v_i, v_{i+1}) \in E$, or $(v_{i+1}, v_i) \in E$, $i \in \{1, 2, ..., r-1\}$. Node v_i is said to be connected to node v_j if there is a directed path from v_i to v_j. Node v_i is called a root node if it has a directed path to all other nodes. Graph G is said to be strongly connected if there is a directed path from every node to every other node and weakly connected if any two different nodes are connected by a semipath. A subgraph of G is a digraph whose vertices and edges belong to V and E, respectively. A spanning subgraph of G is a subgraph of G with vertices V. A directed tree is a connected digraph where every node has in-degree equal to one, except for one with in-degree of zero. A spanning tree of a digraph is a directed tree formed by graph edges that connects all the nodes of the graph. A graph is said to have a spanning tree if a subset of the edges forms a directed tree. This is equivalent to saying that all nodes in the graph are reachable from a single (root) node.* ▮

1.2.4 Nonlinear stochastic dynamical systems

In multi-agent systems, the network topology among all vehicles plays a crucial role in determining consensus. The objective here is to explicitly identify necessary and/or sufficient conditions on the network topology, such that consensus can be achieved under properly designed algorithms.

It is often reasonable to consider the case when the network topology is deterministic under ideal communication channels. Accordingly, main research on the consensus problem was conducted under a deterministic fixed/switching network topology. That is, the adjacency matrix $\mathcal{A}(t)$ is deterministic. Some other times, when considering random communication failures, random packet drops, and communication channel instabilities inherited in physical communication channels, it is necessary and important to study consensus problem in the stochastic setting, where a network topology evolves according to some random distributions. That is, the adjacency matrix $\mathcal{A}(t)$ is stochastically evolving. In the deterministic setting, consensus is said to be achieved if all agents eventually reach agreement on a common state. In the stochastic setting, consensus is said to be achieved *almost surely* (respectively, *in mean-square* or in *probability*) if all agents reach agreement on a common state almost surely (respectively, in mean-square or in probability). Note that the problem studied in the stochastic setting is slightly different from that studied in the deterministic setting due to the different assumptions in terms of the network topology. Consensus over a stochastic network topology was perhaps first studied in [19], where some sufficient conditions on the network topology were given to guarantee consensus with probability one for systems with single-integrator kinematics. For consensus under a stochastic network topology, some results were reported in [20]–[28], where research efforts were conducted for systems with single-integrator kinematics [20, 21, 22, 23, 24, 25, 26, 27] or double-integrator dynamics [28]. Consensus for single-integrator kinematics under stochastic network topology has been extensively studied in particular, where some general conditions for almost-surely consensus were derived [22], [23], [26]. Loosely speaking, almost-surely consensus for single-integrator kinematics can be achieved, i.e., $x_i(t) - x_j(t) \to 0$ almost surely, if and only if the expectation of the network topology, namely, the network topology associated with expectation $E[\mathcal{A}(t)]$, has a directed spanning tree. It is worth noting that the conditions are analogous to that in [24], [25], but in the stochastic setting. In view of the special structure of the closed-loop systems concerning consensus for single-integrator kinematics, basic properties of the stochastic matrices play a crucial role in the convergence analysis of the associated control algorithms. Consensus for double-integrator dynamics was studied in [28], where the switching network topology is assumed to be driven by a Bernoulli process, and it was shown that consensus can be achieved if the union of all the graphs has a directed spanning tree. Apparently, the requirement on the network topology for double-integrator dynamics is a special case of that for single integrator kinematics due to the different nature of the final states (constant final states for single-integrator kinematics and possible dynamic final states for double-integrator dynamics) caused by the substantial dynamical difference. Whether some general conditions (corresponding to some specific algorithms) can be found for consensus with double-integrator dynamics is still an open question.

In addition to analyzing the conditions on the network topology, such that consensus can be achieved, a special type of consensus algorithm, the so-called gossip algorithm [29], [30], has been used to achieve consensus in the stochastic setting. The gossip algorithm can always guarantee consensus almost surely if the available pairwise communication channels satisfy certain conditions (such as a connected graph or a graph with a directed spanning tree). The way of network topology switching does not play any role in the consideration of consensus.

In what follows, we proceed to establish notation and definitions, then review some basic results for nonlinear stochastic dynamical systems ([356]; [364];[370]). Specifically, $\mathbb{R}$ denotes the set of real numbers, $\mathbb{R}^n$ denotes the set of $n \times 1$ real column vectors, and $\mathbb{R}^{n\times m}$ denotes the set of $n \times m$ real matrices. We write $||\cdot||$ for the Euclidean vector norm, $||\cdot||_F$ for the Frobenius matrix norm, $||\cdot||_1$ for the absolute sum norm, A^T for the transpose of the matrix A, and I_n or I for the $n\times n$ identity matrix. We define a complete probability space as $(\Omega, \mathcal{F}, \mathbb{P})$, where Ω denotes the sample space, $\mathcal{F}$ denotes a σ-algebra, and $\mathbb{P}$ defines a probability measure on the σ-algebra $\mathcal{F}$; that is, $\mathbb{P}$ is a nonnegative countably additive set function on $\mathcal{F}$ such that $P(\Omega) = 1$ ([356]). Furthermore, we assume that $w(\cdot)$ is a standard d-dimensional Wiener process defined by $(w(\cdot), \Omega, \mathcal{F}, \mathbb{P}^{w_0})$, where $\mathbb{P}^{w_0}$ is the classical Wiener measure ([370], p. 10), with a continuous-time filtration $\mathcal{F}_{t t\geq 0}$ generated by the Wiener process $w(t)$ up to time t. We denote a stochastic dynamical system by $\mathcal{G}$ generating a filtration $\mathcal{F}_{t t\geq 0}$ adapted to the stochastic process x : $\bar{\mathbb{R}}_+ \times \Omega \to \mathcal{D}$ on $(\Omega, \mathcal{F}, \mathbb{P}^{x_0})$ satisfying $\mathcal{F}_\tau \subset \mathcal{F}_t, 0\tau < t$, such that $\omega \in: x(t,\omega) \in \mathcal{B} \in \mathcal{F}_t, t \geq 0$, for all Borel sets $\mathcal{B} \subset \mathbb{R}^n$ contained in the Borel σ-algebra $\mathfrak{B}^n$. Here, we use the notation $x(t)$ to represent the stochastic process $x(t,\omega)$, omitting its dependence on ω.

Finally, we write $\text{tr}(\cdot)$ for the trace operator, $\otimes$ for the Kronecker product, $(\cdot)^{-1}$ for the inverse operator, $V^{'}(x) \triangleq \frac{\partial V(x)}{\partial x}$ for the Frchet derivative of V at $x, V^{''}(x) \triangleq \frac{\partial^2 V(x)}{\partial x^2}$ for the Hessian of V at x, and $\mathcal{H}_n$ $(resp., \mathcal{H}_[n \times m])$ for the Hilbert space of random vectors $x \in \mathbb{R}^n$ (resp., random matrices $X \in \mathbb{R}^[n \times m])$ with finite average power, that is, $\mathcal{H}_n x :\rightarrow \mathbb{R}^n : \mathbb{E}[x^T x] < \infty$ (resp., $\mathcal{H}_{n\times m} X :\rightarrow \mathbb{R}^{n\times m} : \mathbb{E}[||X||_F] < \infty$). Furthermore, we write $\lambda_{min}(A)(resp., \lambda_{max}(A))$ for the minimum (resp., maximum) eigenvalue of the Hermitian matrix A and $\underline{x}$ (resp., $\bar{x}$) for the lower bound (resp., upper bound) of a bounded signal x, that is, for $x(t) \in \mathcal{H}_n, t \geq 0, \underline{x} \leq ||x(t)||, t \geq 0$ (resp., $||x(t)|| a.s. \leq \bar{x}, t \geq 0$). For $y \in \mathbb{R}^n$ or $y(t) \in \mathcal{H}_n, t \geq 0$, $[y]_i$ denotes the ith component of y or $y(t)$, and for an open set $\mathcal{D} \subseteq \mathbb{R}^n, \mathcal{H}_n^{\mathcal{D}} \triangleq x \in \mathcal{H}_n : x : \Omega \to \mathcal{D}$ denotes the set of all the random vectors in $\mathcal{H}_n$ induced by $\mathcal{D}$. Similarly, for every $x_0 \in \mathbb{R}^n, \mathcal{H}_n x_0 \triangleq x \in \mathcal{H}_n : x = x_0$. Finally, C^2 denotes the space of real-valued functions $V : \mathcal{D} \to \mathbb{R}$ that are two-times continuously differentiable with respect to $x \in \mathcal{D} \subseteq \mathbb{R}^n$.

Consider now the nonlinear stochastic dynamical system $\mathbb{G}$ given by

$$dx(t) = f(x(t))dt + D(x(t))dw(t), x(t_0) a.s. = x_0, t \geq t0, \tag{1.10}$$

where, for every $t \geq 0$, $x(t) \in \mathcal{H}_n^{\mathcal{D}}$ is a Ft-measurable random state vector, $x(t_0) \in$ $Hnx0$, $D \subseteq \mathbb{R}^n$ is an open set with $0 \in \mathcal{D}$, $w(t)$ is a d-dimensional independent standard Wiener process (i.e., Brownian motion) defined on a complete filtered probability space $(\Omega, \mathcal{F}_{t_{t \geq t_0}}, \mathbb{P})$, $x(t_0)$ is independent of $(w(t) - w(t0)), t \geq t_0$, and $f : \mathcal{D} \to \mathbb{R}^n$ and $D : \mathcal{D} \to \mathbb{R}^{n \times d}$ are continuous functions and satisfy $f(x_e) = 0$ and $D(x_e) = 0$ for some $x_e \in \mathcal{D}$. Here, we assume that $f : \mathcal{D} \to \mathbb{R}^n andD : \mathcal{D} \to \mathbb{R}^{n \times d}$ satisfy the uniform Lipschitz continuity condition:

$$||f(x) - f(y)|| + ||D(x) - D(y)||_F \leq L||x - y||, \quad x,\ y \in \mathcal{D} \tag{1.11}$$

and the growth restriction condition

$$||f(x)||^2 + ||D(x)||_F^2 \leq L^2(1 + ||x||^2), x \in \mathcal{D}, \tag{1.12}$$

for some Lipschitz constant $L > 0$.

Hence, since $x(t_0) \in \mathcal{H}_n^{\mathcal{D}}$ and $x(t_0)$ is independent of $(w(t) - w(t_0)), t \geq t_0$, it follows that there exists a unique solution $x \in \mathcal{L}^2(\Omega, \mathcal{F}, \mathbb{P})$, where $\mathcal{L}^2(\Omega, F, P)$ denotes the set of equivalence class of measurable and square integrable $\mathbb{R}^n$ valued random processes on $(\Omega, \mathcal{F}, \mathbb{P})$ over the semi-infinite parameter space $[0, \infty)$, to (1.10) in the following sense. For every $x \in \mathcal{H}_n^{\mathcal{D}} \backslash \{0\}$ there exists $T_x > 0$ such that if $x_1 : [t_0, \tau_1] \times \Omega \to \mathcal{D}$ and $x_2 : [t_0, \tau_2] \times \Omega \to \mathcal{D}$ are two solutions of (1.10); that is, if $x_1, x_2 \in \mathcal{L}^2(\Omega, \mathcal{F}, \mathbb{P})$ with continuous sample paths almost surely solve (1), then $T_x \leq min\tau_1, \tau_2$ and $\mathbb{P}\Big(x_1(t) = x_2(t), t_0 \leq t \leq T_x\Big) = 1$. The following definition introduces the notions of boundedness and uniform ultimate boundednesss for stochastic dynamical systems.

Definition 1.1 ([376]; [383]): *The pathwise trajectory $x(t) \in \mathcal{H}_n^{\mathcal{D}}, t \geq 0$, of (1.10) in $(\Omega, \{\mathcal{F}_t\}_{t \geq t_0}, \mathbb{P}^{x_0}$) is bounded in probability if $\lim_{c \to \infty} \sup_{t \geq 0} P||x(t)|| > c = 0$. Furthermore, $x(t) \in \mathcal{H}_n^{\mathcal{D}}, t \geq 0$, is uniformly ultimately bounded in the pth moment if, for every compact subset $\mathcal{D}_c \subset \mathbb{R}^n$ and all $x(0) a.s. = x0 \in \mathcal{D}_c$, there exist $\varepsilon > 0$ and a finite-time $T = T(\varepsilon, x_0)$ such that $\mathbb{E}^{x_0}[||x(t)||^p] < \varepsilon$ for all $t > 0 + T$. If, in addition, $p = 2$, then we say that $x(t), t \geq 0$, is uniformly ultimately bounded in a mean square sense.*

The following lemma is needed for the main result of this section. First, however, recall that the infinitesimal generator $\mathcal{L}$ of $x(t), t \geq 0$, with $x(0) a.s. = x_0$, is defined by

$$\mathcal{L}V(x_0) \triangleq \lim_{t \to 0^+} \frac{\mathbb{E}^{x_0}[V(x(t))] - V(x_0)}{t}, x_0 \in \mathcal{D} \tag{1.13}$$

where $\mathbb{E}^{x_0}$ denotes the expectation with respect to the transition probability measure $\mathbb{P}^{x_0}(x(t) \in \mathcal{B}) \triangleq \mathbb{P}(t_0, x_0, t, \mathcal{B})$ ([370], Def. 7.7). If $V \in C^2$ and has a compact support, and $x(t), t \geq 0$, satisfies (1.10), then the limit in (1.13) exists for all

$x \in D$ and the infinitesimal generator $\mathcal{L}$ of $x(t), t \geq 0$, can be characterised by the system drift and diffusion functions, $f(x)$ and $D(x)$, defining the stochastic dynamical system (1.10) and is given in [370],

$$\mathcal{L}V(x) \triangleq \frac{\partial V(x)}{\partial x} f(x) + \frac{1}{2} trD^T(x) \frac{\partial^2 V(x)}{\partial x^2} D(x), x \in \mathcal{D}. \tag{1.14}$$

Lemma 1.5

([362]): Consider the nonlinear stochastic dynamical system $\mathcal{G}$ given by (1.10). If there exist a two-times continuously differentiable function $V : \mathbb{R}^n \rightarrow \mathbb{R}_+$, positive constants $\beta_1 > 0$ and $\beta_2 > 0$, and class $\mathcal{K}_\infty$ functions α_1: $[0,\infty) \rightarrow [0,\infty)$ and $\alpha_2 : [0,\infty) \rightarrow [0,\infty)$ such that

$$\alpha_1(||x||) \leq V(x) \leq \alpha_2(||x||), x \in \mathbb{R}^n, \tag{1.15}$$

$$\mathcal{L}V(x) \leq -\beta_1 V(x) + \beta_2, x \in \mathbb{R}^n, \tag{1.16}$$

then

$$\mathbb{E}^{x_0}[V(x(t))] \leq V(x(0))e^{-\beta_1 t} + \frac{\beta_2}{\beta_1}, t \geq 0. \tag{1.17}$$

Finally, we recall some basic notation from graph theory [10]. Specifically, $\mathfrak{G} = (\mathcal{V}, \mathcal{E}, \mathcal{A})$ denotes a weighted directed graph (or digraph) denoting the static network (or static graph) with the set of nodes (or vertices) $\mathcal{V} = 1, \ldots, N$ involving a finite nonempty set denoting the agents, the set of edges $\mathcal{E} \subseteq \mathcal{V} \times \mathcal{V}$ involving a set of ordered pairs denoting the direction of information flow between agents, and a weighted adjacency matrix $\mathcal{A} \in R^{N \times N}$ such that $\mathcal{A}_{(i,j)} = a_{ij} > 0, i, j = 1, \ldots, N, if (j,i) \in \mathcal{E}$, and $a_{ij} = 0$, otherwise. The edge $(j,i) \in \mathcal{E}$ denotes that agent i can obtain information from agent j, but not necessarily vice versa. Moreover, we assume that $a_{ii} = 0$ for all $i \in \mathcal{V}$.

Note that if the weights $a_{ij}, i, j = 1, \ldots, N$, are not relevant, then a_{ij} is set to 1 for all $(j,i) \in \mathcal{E}$. In this case, $\mathcal{A}$ is called a normalized adjacency matrix.

Every edge $l \in \mathcal{E}$ corresponds to an ordered pair of vertices $(i, j) \in \mathcal{V} \times \mathcal{V}$, where i and j are the initial and terminal vertices of the edge l. In this case, l is incident into j and incident out of i. Finally, we say that G is strongly (resp., weakly) connected if for every ordered pair of vertices $(i, j), i \neq j$, there exists a directed (resp., undirected) path, that is, a directed (resp., undirected) sequence of arcs leading from i to j.

The in-neighbours and out-neighbours of node i are, respectively, defined as $\mathcal{N}_{in}(i) \triangleq \{j \in \mathcal{V} : (j,i) \in \mathcal{E}\}$ and $\mathcal{V}_{out}(i) \triangleq \{j \in \mathcal{V} : (i, j) \in \mathcal{E}\}$. The in-degree $\deg_{in}(i)$ of node i is the number of edges incident into i and the out-degree $\deg_{out}(i)$ of node i is the number of edges incident out of i, that is, $\deg_{in}(i) \triangleq \sum_{j=1}^{N} a_{ji}$ and $\deg_{out}(i) \triangleq \sum_{j=1}^{N} a_{ji}$. We say that the node i of a digraph G is balanced if $\deg\ _{in}(i) = \deg_{in}(i)$, and a graph $\mathfrak{G}$ is called balanced if all of its nodes are balanced, that is, $\sum_{j=1}^{N} a_{ji} = \sum_{j=1}^{N} a_{ij}, i = 1,\ldots,N$. Furthermore, we define the graph Laplacian of $\mathfrak{G}$ by $L \triangleq \mathcal{D} - \mathcal{A}$, where $\mathcal{D} \triangleq \text{diag}[deg_{in}(1),\ldots,\text{deg}_{in}(N)]$.

A graph or undirected graph $\mathfrak{G}$ associated with the adjacency matrix $\mathcal{A} \in R^{N\times N}$ is a directed graph for which the arc set is symmetric, that is, $\mathcal{A} = \mathcal{A}^T$. In this case, $\mathcal{N}_{in}(i) = \mathcal{N}_{out}(i)\mathcal{N}(i)$ and $\text{deg}_{in}(i) = \text{deg}_{out}(i) \triangleq \text{deg}(i), i = 1,\ldots,N$. Furthermore, in this case, we say that G is connected if for every ordered pair of vertices $(i,j), i \neq j$, there exists a path, that is, a sequence of arcs, leading from i to j. Finally, the leader adjacency matrix Q =diag$[q_1,\ldots,q_N] \in R^{N\times N}$ is such that $q_i > 0$ when agent i has direct access to the leader and $q_i = 0$ otherwise. Furthermore, the set of nodes that do not have access to the leader information is denoted by $\mathcal{N}_I$, whereas the set of nodes with access to the leader information is denoted by $\mathcal{N}_{II}$. It is clear that $\mathcal{N}_I \cap \mathcal{N}_{II} = \emptyset and \mathcal{N}_I \cup \mathcal{N}_{II} = 1,\ldots,\mathcal{N}$.

1.2.5 Complex dynamical systems

As a direct extension of the study of the consensus problem for systems with simple dynamics, for example, with single-integrator kinematics or double-integrator dynamics, consensus with general linear dynamics was also studied recently, where research was mainly devoted to finding feedback control laws, such that consensus (in terms of the output states) can be achieved for general linear systems

$$\dot{x} = Ax_i + Bu_i, \quad y_i = Cx_i, \tag{1.18}$$

where A, B, and C are constant matrices with compatible sizes. Apparently, the well-studied single-integrator kinematics and double-integrator dynamics are special cases of (1.18) for properly choosing A, B and C. Consensus for complex systems has also been extensively studied. Here, the term consensus for complex systems is used for the study of consensus problem when the system dynamics are nonlinear or with nonlinear consensus algorithms. Examples of the nonlinear system dynamics studied in the consensus problem include:

- *Nonlinear oscillators.* The dynamics are often assumed to be governed by the Kuramoto equation

$$\dot{\theta} = \omega_i + \frac{K}{N}\sum_{j=1}^{N}\sin(\theta_j - \theta_i), \quad i = 1,2,\ldots,N \tag{1.19}$$

  where θ_i and ω_i are, respectively, the phase and natural frequency of the ith oscillator, N is the number of oscillators, and K is the control gain. Generally, the control gain K plays a crucial role in determining the synchronizability of the network.

- *Complex networks*. The dynamics are typically represented as

$$\dot{x}(t) = f(x_i(t)) + c \sum_{j=1, j\neq i}^{N} a_{ij}(t)\Gamma(x_j(t) - x_i(t)), \quad i = 1, 2, ..., N \quad (1.20)$$

where $x_i = (x_{i1}, x_{i2}, ..., x_{in})^T \in \mathbb{R}_n$ is the state vector of the ith node, $f : \mathbb{R}_n \to \mathbb{R}_n$ is a nonlinear vector function, c is the overall coupling strength, $A(t) = [a_{ij}(t)]$ is the outer coupling matrix with $a_{ij}(t) = 1$ if node i and node j are connected at time t, otherwise $a_{ij}(t) = 0$, with $a_{ii}(t) = k_i$ (degree of node i), and Γ is a general inner coupling matrix describing the inner interactions between different state components of agents. It is easy to see that model

$$\dot{x}_i(t) = u_i(t), \quad i = 1, ..., n, \quad (1.21)$$

with control input

$$u_i(t) = \sum_{j=1}^{n} a_{ij}(t)\,[x_j - x_i] \quad (1.22)$$

is a special case of (1.18) with $f = 0$.

- *Nonholonomic mobile robots*. The dynamics are described by

$$\dot{x} = u_i \cos\theta_i, \dot{y} = u_i \sin\theta_i, \dot{\theta}_i = \omega_i, i = 1, 2, ..., N, \quad (1.23)$$

where $[x_i, y_i]$ denotes the location of the ith agent, and u_i and ω_i denote, respectively, its translational and rotational velocity. Note that there are three states and two control inputs. Therefore, the dynamics for nonholonomic mobile robots are underactuated. This poses substantial difficulties in designing proper consensus algorithms with corresponding stability analysis.

- *Rigid bodies and the like*. One typical (but not unique) description of the dynamics is

$$M_i(q_i)\ddot{q}_i + C_i(q_i, \dot{q}_i)\dot{q}_i + g_i(q_i) = \tau_i, \quad i = 1, 2, ..., N, \quad (1.24)$$

where $q_i \in \mathbb{R}^p$is the vector of generalized coordinates, $M_i(q_i) \in \mathbb{R}^{p\times p}$ is the symmetric positive-definite inertia matrix, $C_i(q_i, \dot{q}_i)\dot{q}_i \in \mathbb{R}^p$ is the vector of Coriolis and centrifugal torques, $g_i(q_i)$ is the vector of gravitational torques, and $\tau_i \in \mathbb{R}^p$ is the vector of torques produced by the actuators associated with the ith agent. In practice, the dynamics of many mechanical systems are similar to (1.24). A notable property regarding the dynamics of rigid bodies is that $\dot{M}_i(qi) - 2C_i(q_i, \dot{q}_i)$ is skew-symmetric (i.e., $z^T\left[\dot{M}_i(qi) - 2C_i(q_i, \dot{q}_i)\right] z = 0$ for all $z \in \mathbb{R}^p$), which plays a crucial role in finding Lyapunov functions and the subsequent stability analysis.

One particular interesting topic is synchronization in complex networks, which has been widely investigated in the past decade. Mathematically, the definitions for synchronization in complex networks and consensus in multiagent systems are very similar, so in order to differentiate these two definitions and promote research exchanges in these two topics, their differences are briefly summarized below.

1. *Different Asymptotic States* (Nonlinear Dynamics versus Linear Dynamics). In the studies of synchronization in complex networks, researchers focus on synchronization with self-nonlinear dynamics, where each single system is unstable and, thus, the final asymptotic synchronization state is typically time-varying. However, in the investigations of multiagent systems, the individual self-dynamics on each system are usually linear or zero and, therefore, the asymptotic consensus state is usually a constant.

2. *Different Focuses* (Known Connectivity versus Time-Varying Distributed Protocol). In synchronization of complex networks, the aim is to reveal how the network structure, which is known *a priori*, affects the nonlinear collective dynamics, while the aim of consensus in multiagent systems is to figure out how the designed distributed local protocol concerning mobile time-varying network structure affects the consensus behavior.

3. *Different Approaches* (Lyapunov Method versus Stochastic Matrix Theory). Since both complex networks and multiagent systems are networked systems, algebraic graph theory is a common approach to use. Because of the nonlinear terms in synchronization of complex networks, Lyapunov function method is usually used together with matrix theory. In order to show consensus in multiagent systems with time-varying network structures, stochastic matrix theory and convex analysis are often applied.

4. *Different Inner Matrices* (Γ) (General Inner Matrix versus Particular Inner Matrix). In the typical simple consensus model, the inner matrices Γ are usually an identity matrix and a rank-one matrix

$$\begin{pmatrix} 0 & 1 \\ 0 & 0 \end{pmatrix}$$

for multiagent systems with single-integrator kinematics and double-integrator dynamics, respectively. In consensus models with higher–order dynamics, the inner matrix is similar. However, the inner matrix in system (1.20) is a general one.

Briefly stated, synchronization in complex networks focuses on nonlinear dynamics, while consensus in multiagent systems focuses on distributed cooperative control, thus, different approaches are utilized. The current research on consensus with complex systems focuses on fully-actuated systems although consensus for nonholonomic mobile robots, which are typical underactuated systems. Note that many mechanical devices are described by systems with underactuation. Therefore, it is important to develop appropriate consensus algorithms for underactuated systems.

1.2.6 Delay effects

Time delay appears in almost all practical systems for several reasons:

(1) limited communication speed when information transmission exists;

(2) extra time required by the sensor to get the measurement information;

(3) computation time required for generating the control inputs; and

(4) execution time required for the inputs being acted.

In general, time delay reflects an important property inherited in practical systems due to actuation, control, communication and computation.

Knowing that time delay might degrade the system performance or even destroy the system stability, studies have been conducted to investigate its effect on system performance and stability. A well-studied consensus algorithm for (1.21) is given in (1.22), where it is now assumed that time delay exists. Two types of time delays, *communication delay* and *input delay*, have been considered in the literature. Communication delay accounts for the time required in order to transmit information from origin to destination. More precisely, if it takes time T_{ij} for agent i to receive information from agent j, the closed-loop system of (1.21) using (1.22) under a fixed network topology becomes

$$\dot{x}_i(t) = \sum_{j=1}^{n} a_{ij}(t)\left[x_j(t-T_{ij}) - x_i(t)\right] \tag{1.25}$$

An interpretation of (1.25) is that at time t, agent i receives information from agent j and uses data $x_j(t-T_{ij})$ instead of $x_j(t)$ due to the time delay. Note that agent i can get its own information instantly, therefore, input delay can be considered as the summation of computation time and execution time. More precisely, if the input delay for agent i is given by T_i^p , then the closed-loop system of (1.21) using (1.22) becomes

$$\dot{x}_i(t) = \sum_{j=1}^{n} a_{ij}(t)\left[x_j(t - T_i^p) - x_i(t - T_i^p)\right] \tag{1.26}$$

Clearly, (1.25) refers to the case when only communication delay is considered. While (1.26) refers to the case when only input delay is considered. It should be emphasized that both communication delay and input delay might be time-varying and they might co-exist at the same time.

In addition to time delay, it is also important to consider packet drops in exchanging state information. Fortunately, consensus with packet drops can be considered as a special case of consensus with time delay, because re-sending packets after they were dropped can be easily done but with a time delay in the data transmission channels.

Thus, the main problem involved in consensus with time delay is to study the effects of time delay on the convergence and performance of consensus, referred to as *consensusability* [31].

1.2.7 Sampled-data framework

The foregoing subsections describe the main research work in the study of the consensus problem. The following introduces a few other aspects, namely, sampled-data framework, quantization, asynchronous effect, convergence speed, and finite-time convergence, that have been considered in the consensus problem as well. Among these topics, sampled-data framework, quantization, and asynchronous effects are considered due to some physical limitations in practical systems, while convergence speed and finite-time convergence are concerned with the performance for some proposed consensus algorithms.

Due to the limitations in the measurement and control units, it is often impossible to acquire information measurements at an arbitrarily fast speed and to execute the control inputs instantaneously. Accordingly, the closed-loop systems are modeled in a hybrid fashion. That is, the system plant is described in a continuous-time setting while the measurements and control inputs are described in a piecewise constant fashion. For instance, in a sampled-data setting, (1.22) becomes

$$u_i(t) = u_i(kT) = \sum_{j=1}^{n} a_{ij}(kT)\left[x_j(kT) - x_i(kT)\right] \tag{1.27}$$

for $kT \le t < (k+1)T$, where T is the sampling period and k is the discrete-time index. Essentially, (1.27) is a zero order- hold version of $u_i(t)$, in the sense that the control inputs remain unchanged during each sampling period. Under this circumstance, consensus is studied in a sampled-data framework, called *sampled-data consensus*, which reflects the limitations inherited in physical measurement and control units. Meanwhile, it is also important to point out that the sampled-data consensus algorithms require much less information exchange and computational power than the continuous-time consensus algorithms. Accordingly, consensus under the sampled-data framework deserves certain consideration.

It is natural to consider the sampled-data effect for consensus with general linear or nonlinear dynamics. In addition, it is meaningful to consider the case when all vehicles do not necessarily share the same sampling period or the sampling period is not necessarily constant. Accordingly, it is expected that a careful design of the sampling periods (associated with the proposed algorithms) might lead to the optimization of the closed-loop systems under the proposed algorithms, subject to certain cost functions, such as maximum convergence rate and minimum total information exchange. In other words, it is intriguing to move from analysis to design when investigating the consensus problem in a sampled-data framework.

1.3 Multiagent System Approach

By and large, a multiagent dynamic system can be defined as *a network of a number of loosely coupled dynamic units that are called agents*. Each agent can be a robot, a vehicle, or a dynamic sensor, to name a few. The main purpose of using multiagent systems is to collectively reach goals that are difficult to achieve by an individual agent or a monolithic system. When the main dynamic action of interest is *motion*, the terms *swarm* or sometimes *formation* are used in place of multiagent dynamic system. The term *swarm* is used for a collection of (physical) agents moving in real 2- or 3- dimensional space to fulfill certain mission requirements.

One should bear in mind that the distinction between the terms formation and swarm is not clearly formulated or stated in the systems and control literature, although in some places swarm is preferred to indicate that the corresponding collection of agents is less structured, the number of agents is larger, or the motion of each agent has higher uncertainty as opposed to formation, indicating a well-structured collection of a relatively small number of agents with more deterministic dynamics. Using this convention, a *swarm* can be thought of as a multiagent dynamic system that can form various types of formations. Throughout this book, we use both of these two terms interchangeably with the term multiagent dynamic systems without making any distinction. Typical examples are displayed below.

1.3.1 *Practical examples*

Typical examples of MAS are displayed in Fig. (1.4) for robot swarms and (1.4) for power systems.

The main elements of a swarm (or a formation) are the agents and the information (such ad sensing, control, and communication) links among these agents, assuming that the individual dynamics of the agents are uncoupled or loosely coupled. For formations where the individual agent dynamics are coupled, the dynamic interactions among the agents need to be considered as well.

1.3.2 Some relevant definitions

In what follows, we adopt the definition of an *agent* as merely *a software (or hardware) entity that is situated in some environment and is able to autonomously react to changes in that environment.* In this regard, the *environment* is simply everything external to the agent. In order to be situated in an *environment,* at least part of the *environment* must be observable to, or alterable by, the agent. The *environment*

- may be physical (such as, the power system), therefore, observable through sensors, or
- it may be the computing environment (such as, data sources, computing resources, and other agents), observable through system calls, program invocation, and messaging.

An agent may alter the *environment* by taking some action: Either physically (such as closing a normally-open point to reconfigure a network), or otherwise (such as storing diagnostic information in a database for others to access).

The separation of *agent* from *environment* means that agents are inherently distributable. An *agent* can operate usefully in any *environment* which supports the tasks that the *agent* intends to perform.

By extending the definition of *autonomy* to *flexible autonomy*, an *agent* which displays *flexible autonomy* is termed hereafter an *intelligent agent.* It has the following three characteristics.

- **Reactivity:** An *intelligent agent* is able to react to changes in its *environment* in a timely fashion, and takes some action based on those changes and the function it is designed to achieve.
- **Pro-activeness:** *Intelligent agents* exhibit goal-directed behavior. Goal-directed behavior connotes that an agent will dynamically change its behavior in order to achieve its goals. For example, if an agent loses communication with another agent whose services it requires in order to fulfill its goals, it will search for another agent that provides the same services.
- **Social ability:** *Intelligent agents* are able to interact with other intelligent agents. Social ability connotes more than the simple passing of data between different software and hardware entities, something many traditional systems do. It connotes the ability to negotiate and interact in

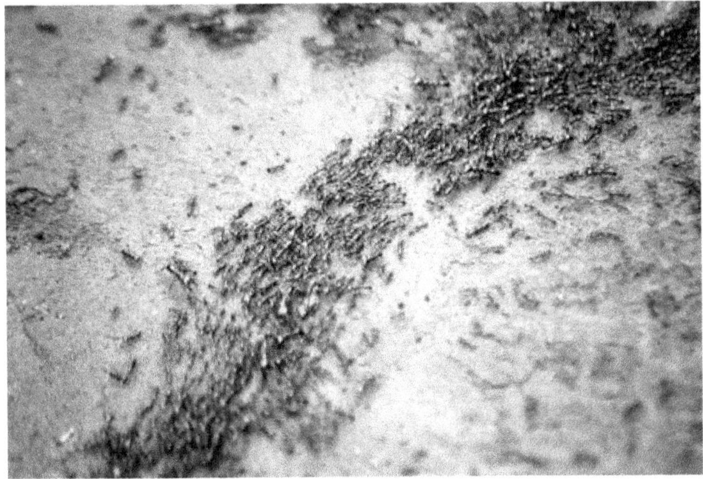

Figure 1.2: Ant swarm

Figure 1.3: Bird swarms

a cooperative manner. That ability is normally underpinned by an *agent communication language (ACL)*, which allows agents to converse rather than simply pass data.

It is worth emphasizing that multiagent systems are more than a systems integration method, they also provide a modeling approach. By offering a way of viewing the world, an agent system can intuitively represent a real-world situation of interacting entities, and give a way of testing how complex behaviors may emerge.

Figure 1.4: Robot swarms

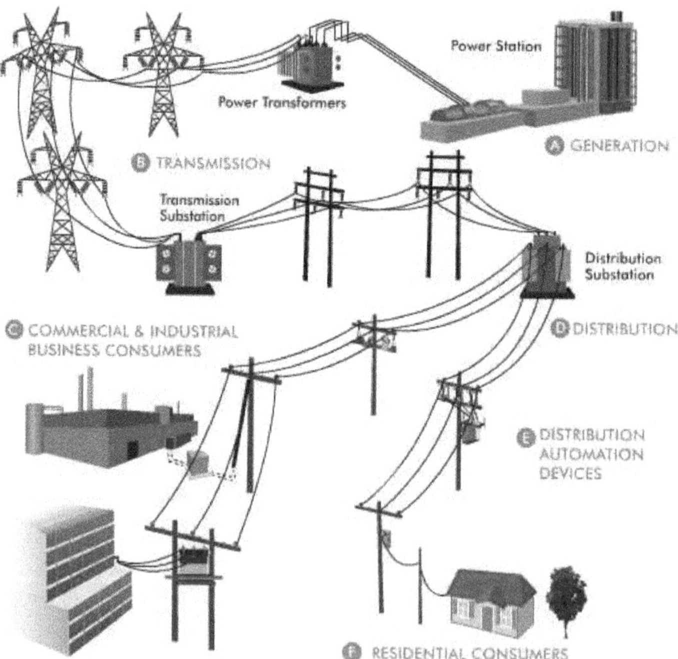

Figure 1.5: Power system networks

1.4 Mathematical Models for Agent Dynamics

In this section, we focus on a particular element among those, the agents and modeling of their dynamics. We briefly summarize some of the mathematical models for agent/vehicle dynamics considered in the systems and control literature on multiagent dynamic systems (or swarms). We consider a swarm consisting of N individuals/agents moving in an n-dimensional Euclidean space, and unless otherwise stated, denote with $x_i \in \Re^n$ the state vector and with $m_i \in \Re^m$, $m \leq n$ the control input of agent i. Depending on the context, the state vector x_i may denote (a collection of) the position, orientation, synchronization frequency, information to be agreed upon, etc. The dimensions of the state and control spaces (the values of n and m) change depending on the context as well.

1.4.1 Single integrator model

The simplest mathematical model considered in the literature for studying MAS or swarm behavior is the so-called higher-level or kinematic or single integrator model, in which the agent motions are given by

$$\dot{x}_i(t) = u_i(t), \quad i = 1, ..., N \tag{1.28}$$

where x_i is the state of agent i, u_i is its control input, and the dot represents the derivative (the change) with respect to time. As mentioned above, depending on the context, the state x_i can represent the position p_i, the orientation angle or synchronization frequency θ_i, or other variables (or collection of those).

We refer to this model as a higher-level or kinematic model, since it ignores the lower-level vehicle dynamics of the individual agents (e.g., robots). However, it is a relevant and useful model, because it can be used to study higher level algorithms independent of the agent/vehicle dynamics and to obtain "proof of concept" type results for swarm behavior. Moreover, in certain control tasks involving path planning, the trajectories generated using the higher-level agent models can be used as reference trajectories for the actual agents to track. Furthermore, (1.28) is a realistic simplified kinematic model for a class of omnidirectional mobile robots with so-called universal (or Swedish) wheels.

1.4.2 Double integrator model

Another dynamic model which is commonly used in the multi-agent coordination and control literature is the point mass or double integrator model, given by

$$\begin{aligned} \dot{p}_i(t) &= v_i(t), \\ \dot{v}_i(t) &= \frac{1}{m_i} u_i(t), \quad N \end{aligned} \tag{1.29}$$

where p_i is the position, v_i is the velocity, m_i is the mass of the agent, and u_i is the force (control) input (and the state of the systems can be defined as

$$x_i^T = [p_i^T, \; v_i^T]^T$$

The higher-level model in (1.28) can be viewed also as a special case of the point mass model (1.29), under the assumption that the motion environment is very viscous, that $mi \approx 0$ (as is the case for some bacteria), and the control input is taken as

$$u_i(t) = -k_v v_i + \bar{u}_i$$

with the velocity damping coefficient $k_v = 1$, and the control term $\bar{u}_i$ corresponding to u_i of (1.28). However, in general, this assumption is not satisfied for many biological and engineering systems and the point mass model in (1.29) becomes more relevant.

1.4.3 Uncertain fully actuated model

A more realistic model for agent/vehicle dynamics (compared to the higher-level and the point mass models) is the fully actuated model:

$$M_i(p_i)\ddot{p}_i + f_i(p_i, \dot{p}_i) = u_i(t), \quad 1 \leq i \leq N \tag{1.30}$$

where p_i represents the position or configuration (and note that $x_i^T = [p_i^T, v_i^T]^T$), $M_i(p_i) \in \mathbf{R}^{n \times n}$ is the mass or inertia matrix, $f_i(p_i, \dot{p}_i) \in \mathbf{R}^n$ represents the centripetal, Coriolis, gravitational effects and additive disturbances. It is a realistic model for fully actuated omni-directional mobile robots or for some fully actuated manipulators. What makes the model even more realistic, is that it is assumed that (1.30) contains uncertainties and disturbances. In particular, it is assumed that

$$f_i(p_i, \dot{p}_i) = f_i^k(p_i, \dot{p}_i) + f_i^u(p_i, \dot{p}_i), \quad 1 \leq i \leq N \tag{1.31}$$

where $f_i^k(p_i, \dot{p}_i)$ represents the known part and $f_i^u(p_i, \dot{p}_i)$ represents the unknown part. The latter is assumed to be bounded with a known bound, that is,

$$||f_i^u(p_i, \dot{p}_i)|| \leq \bar{f}_i(p_i, \dot{p}_i), \quad 1 \leq i \leq N \tag{1.32}$$

where $\bar{f}_i(p_i, \dot{p}_i)$, $\forall\, i$ are known. Moreover, besides the additive disturbances and uncertainties, it is assumed that for all i the mass/inertia matrix is unknown but is nonsingular and lower and upper bounded by known bounds. This means that, the matrices $M_i(p_i)$ satisfy

$$\underline{M}_i(p_i)\, ||y||^2 \leq y^T M_i(p_i)\, y \leq \overline{M}_i(p_i)\, ||y||^2, \quad 1 \leq i \leq N \tag{1.33}$$

where $y \in \mathbf{R}^n$ is arbitrary and $\underline{M}_i(p_i)$, $\overline{M}_i(p_i)$ are known and satisfy $0 < \underline{M}_i(p_i) < \overline{M}_i(p_i) < \infty$. These uncertainties provide an opportunity for developing algorithms that are robust with respect to above type of realistic uncertainties and disturbances.

1.4.4 Non-holonomic unicycle model

$$\begin{aligned}
\dot{p}_{ix}(t) &= v_i(t)\,\cos(\theta_i), \\
\dot{p}_{iy}(t) &= v_i(t)\,\sin(\theta_i), \\
\dot{\theta}_i(t) &= \omega_i(t), \\
\dot{v}_i(t) &= \frac{1}{m_i}\,F_i, \\
\dot{\omega}_i(t) &= \frac{1}{J_i}\tau_i(t),\ 1\,\leq\,i\,\leq\,N \qquad (1.34)
\end{aligned}$$

where p_{ix} and p_{iy} are the Cartesian (x and y, respectively) coordinates (on the 2- dimensional-motion space), θ_i is the steering angle (or orientation), v_i is the translational (linear) speed, and ω_{ix} is the rotational (angular) speed of each agent i. The quantities m_i and J_i are positive constants and represent the mass and the moment of inertia of each agent, respectively. The control inputs to the system are the force input F_i and the torque input τ_i. Many mobile robots used for experimentation in the laboratories (e.g., robots with one castor and two differentially driven wheels) obey the model in (1.34).

It must be emphasized that the main mathematical tools used to represent swarms, beside differential or difference equations describing agent dynamics, are directed and undirected graphs and their geometric representations in the particular motion space [10], see Section 1.2 for a concise introduction on these tools.

1.5 Coordination and Control Problems

From a control viewpoint, a multiagent system (MAS) is a group of independent systems working together through a communication network to perform joint tasks that cannot be executed by a single system.

In multiagent systems, the network topology among all vehicles plays a crucial role in determining consensus. The objective here is to explicitly identify necessary and/or sufficient conditions on the network topology such that consensus can be achieved under properly designed algorithms. It is often reasonable to consider the case when the network topology is deterministic under ideal communication channels. Accordingly, main research activities on the consensus problem were conducted under a deterministic fixed/switching network topology. That is, the adjacency matrix $\mathcal{A}(t)$ is deterministic.

Some other times, when considering random communication failures, random packet drops, and communication channel instabilities inherited in physical communication channels, it is necessary and important to study consensus problem in the stochastic setting where a network topology evolves according to

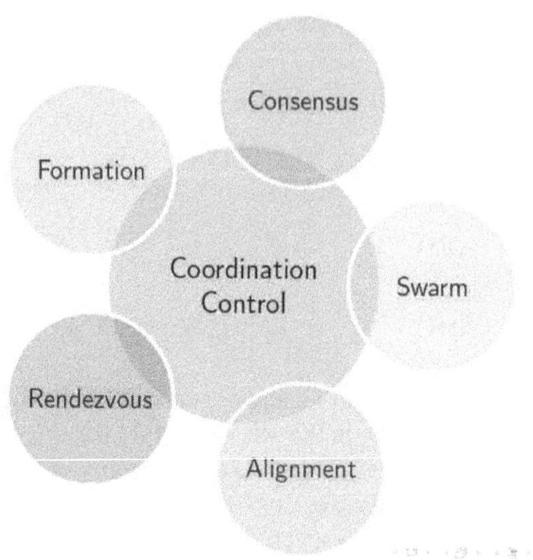

Figure 1.6: Elements of multiagent systems in nature

some random distributions. That is, the adjacency matrix $\mathcal{A}(t)$ is stochastically evolving.

There are a number of different MAS coordination and control tasks that have been investigated in the systems and control literature. With references to (1.6), we briefly present some of the main ones among these tasks, namely aggregation and foraging, flocking, rendezvous, formation stabilization, formation acquisition, formation reconfiguration, formation maintenance, agreement, cohesive motion and cooperation.

1.5.1 Aggregation and social foraging

Aggregation (or gathering together) is a basic behavior that many swarms in nature exhibit. Moreover, many of the collective behaviors seen in biological swarms and some behaviors to be possibly implemented in engineering multiagent dynamic systems emerge in aggregated swarms. Therefore, developing mathematical models for swarm aggregations and studying the dynamics and properties of these models are important.

Initial studies on mathematical modeling and simulation of aggregation in biological swarms were performed by biologists. Inspired by the work of biologists, recent studies provided a rigorous analysis of an artificial potential function based model of swarm aggregations and some corresponding convergence results, assuming discrete time swarm models with synchronous motion dynamics.

The asynchronous counterpart of the analysis and the results are also provided in [13].

Aggregation in biological swarms usually occurs during social foraging. Social foraging has many advantages, such as increasing probability of success for the individuals. Therefore, social foraging is an important problem since swarm studies in engineering may benefit from similar advantages. In social foraging, the environment affects the motion or behavior of the agents. The environment may have favorable regions (representing food or nutrients in biological swarms or targets or goals in engineering applications) to which the agents may want/need to move and unfavorable regions (representing toxic or hazardous substances in biological swarms or threads or obstacles in engineering applications) which the agents may want/need to avoid.

1.5.2 Flocking and rendezvous

Flocking, in general, can be defined as the collective motion behavior of a large number of interacting agents with a common group objective. The work by Reynolds [1] is the first extensive study in the literature on flocking. This work has proposed three simple rules to implement a flocking behavior, namely

(i) separation,

(ii) alignment, and

(iii) cohesion.

These rules have been used to develop realistic computer simulations of the flocking behavior of animal swarms. Subsequent studies showed that coordination (which is in the form of motion in a common direction) emerges from the local interactions of the agents in the swarm.

A mathematical analysis of achieving common orientation during the flocking behavior based on "nearest neighbor rules" is provided and some corresponding convergence results are established. Using potential functions for aggregation and alignment, several algorithms are proposed and analyzed with and without group objective and it is shown that, under certain conditions, flocking will be achieved and the flock will have a lattice-type structure [12]. In the subsequent chapters, all these concepts are discussed in detail.

1.5.3 Synchronization of coupled nonlinear oscillators

A good example of distributed synchronization (a type of distributed agreement) in nature is the synchronization of the flashing of fireflies. More generally, this phenomenon can be viewed as distributed synchronization of coupled oscillators, which is usually represented mathematically by:

$$\dot{x}_i(t) = \omega_i(t) + \sum_j u_{ij}(x_j(t) - x_i(t)) \tag{1.35}$$

where x_i is the oscillation phase of the ith individual and ω_i is the oscillation frequency. Moreover, researchers usually take

$$u_{ij}(x_j(t) - x_i(t)) = \frac{1}{N}\sin(x_j(t) - x_i(t))$$

Note that this model is a special case of the kinematic model (1.28) with the control input taken as

$$u_i(t) = \omega_i(t) + u_{ij}(x_j(t) - x_i(t)) \tag{1.36}$$

The control strategies or update rules that lead to agreement are usually called consensus protocols in the literature. Both continuous-time and discrete-time update rules or consensus protocols have been considered in the literature. The equation in (1.36) is an example of a continuous-time consensus protocol. Other examples are described below.

Continuous-Time Consensus Protocol. The model of the continuous-time consensus protocol considered in the literature can be summarized as

$$\dot{x}_i(t) = -\sum_{j\in\mathcal{N}_i(t)} \alpha_{ij}(x_i(t) - x_j(t)) \tag{1.37}$$

where $\mathcal{N}_i(t)$ represents the set of neighbors of agent i at time t or, basically, the set of agents whose information is available to agent i at time t and $\alpha_i > 0$ denote positive time-varying weighting factors. This means that the information state of each agent is driven toward the states of its (possibly time-varying) neighbors at each time. Note that some agents may not have any information exchange with other agents during some time intervals.

Discrete-Time Consensus Protocol. The discrete-time consensus protocol considered can be summarized as

$$x_i(t+1) = \sum_{j\in\mathcal{N}_i(t)\cup i} \beta_{ij}x_j(t) \tag{1.38}$$

where

$$\sum_{j\in\mathcal{N}_i(t)\cup i} \beta_{ij} = 1, \; \beta_{ij} > 0, \forall j \in \mathcal{N}_i(t)\cup i$$

This means that, the next state of each agent is updated as the weighted average of its current state and the current states of its (possibly time-varying) neighbors. Note that an agent simply maintains its current state if it has no information exchange with other agents at a certain time step.

1.6 Scope and Book Layout

From this perspective, this book has the following objectives:

1. It gathers together the theoretical preliminaries and fundamental issues related to multiagent systems;

2. It provides coherent results on adopting multiagent framework for critically examining problems in smart microgrid systems;

3. It presents advanced analysis of multiagent systems under cyber-physical attacks and develops resilient control strategies to guarantee safe operation.

- **Chapter 1:** (Introduction)

  This chapter provides a guided tour into the the key ingredients of cloud control systems and their prevailing features under normal operating environments and when subjected to cyber-physical attacks.

- **Chapter 2:** (Theoretical Background)

  The focus of this chapter is on the fundamental issues underlying the analysis, design and estimation methods of cloud control systems (CCS) with particular emphasis on workflow, security objectives under different attacks.

- **Chapter 3:** (Distributed Intelligence in Power Systems)

  This chapter critically examines the impact of distributed denial of service attacks in cyber-physical control systems (CPCS).

- **Chapter 4:** (Consensus for Heterogeneous Systems with Delays)

  This chapter further introduces the paradigm of cyber physical control systems and discusses several approaches.

- **Chapter 5:** (Secure Stabilization of Distributed Systems)

  This chapter examines the construction of stabilization methods that guaranteeing secure (sufficiently safe) operation of cyber-physical control systems (CPCS)

- **Chapter 6:** (Secure Control of Distributed Multiagent Systems)

  This chapter introduces some typical practical case studies.

- **Chapter 7:** (Cooperative Control of Networked Microgrid Systems)

  This chapter examines networked control systems in the presence attacks that prevent transmissions over the network. We characterize frequency and duration of the DoS attacks under which input-to-state stability (ISS) of the closed-loop system can be preserved. Then, a secure observer-based controller for discrete-time CPS, subject to both cyber and physical attacks, will be presented

- **Chapter 8:** (Dynamic Differential Games)

  In this chapter, couple-group consensus of multiagent systems under denial-of-service (DoS) attacks is studied. Specifically, we study a couple-group consensus problem involving DoS attack within subgroups.

The book includes an appendix of basic lemmas and theories needed throughout.

Chapter 2

Theoretical Background

2.1 Preliminaries of Distributed Systems

Recently, some great advances have been achieved in the cooperative control of multiagent systems. The research focus is mainly on communication environments which consequently require distributed control design. To this day, some control techniques have been proposed according to different communication conditions, such as time-varying networks [59], [69], subject to measurement noise [63], [66], time delays [62], [10], or disturbances [68], [72].

A future control design may equip agents with embedded micro-processors to collect information from neighboring agents so as to update the controller according to some pre-designed rules. Motivated by this observation, some protocols were proposed to deal with distributed algorithms of communication and controller actuation scheduling [57], [71], [73]. Since micro-processors are generally resource- and energy-limited, an event-triggered control was designed based on measurement errors for execution in [71]. A timing issue was investigated through the use of a distributed event-triggered feedback scheme in networked control systems in [73]. Very recently, some distributed event-triggered control strategies were proposed for multi-agent systems [56], [57], [67]. All these control design methods possess a common characteristic in that the controller is updated only when the measurement error magnitude exceeds a certain threshold.

In [57] and [56], centralized and decentralized event-triggered multiagent control protocols were developed for a first-order agreement problem, which were proven to be input-to-state stable (ISS) [65]. The centralized cooperative controller was actuated according to a global event-trigger rule while the decentralized one was updated at a sequence of separate event-times encoded by a local trigger function for each agent. Furthermore, a centralized event-triggered cooperative control was constructed for higher-dimensional multi-agent consensus with a weighted topology in [67], an event-triggered cooperative control was proposed for first-order discrete-time multi-agent systems in [58], and a neighbor-based tracking control together with a distributed estimation was proposed for leader-follower multi-agent systems in [61].

In what follows, we follow [54] and consider a distributed event-triggered tracking control problem for leader-follower multi-agent systems in a fixed directed network topology with partial measurements and communication delays. In collective coordination of a group of autonomous agents, the leader-follower problem has been considered for tracking a single or multiple leaders in [55], [61], [63], [64], [70].

In reality, some state information of the leader cannot be measured, therefore, a decentralized observer design plays a key role in the cooperative control of leader-follower multiagent systems. Within this context, an observer-based dynamic tracking control was proposed in order to estimate the unmeasurable state (i.e., velocity) of an active leader in [61] by collecting real-time measurements from neighbors. In this paper, inspired by the event-triggered scheduling strategy in multi-agent systems, we consider a dynamic tracking problem with event-triggered strategy involved in the control update. During the event-triggered tracking control process, we assume that every follower agent broadcasts its state information only if needed, which requires the follower agent to update its state only if some measure of its state error is above a specified threshold.

It is noted in the literature about event-triggered control of multi-agent systems that, event-triggered cooperative controllers often keep constant between two consecutive broadcasts. However, in this section, we concern ourselves with the scenario of an independent active leader that does not need the event-triggered control updates. Thus, a more sophisticated event-triggered strategy needs to be developed in order to continuously update every agent's partial control input, subject to its local computational resources availability. We adopt a decentralized event-triggered strategy in order to update the local controllers, and finally take into account the communication delays in the tracking control design.

2.1.1 Problem description

The multi-agent system under study is a group of n follower-agents (called followers for simplicity and labeled $1,...,n$) and one active leader-agent (called leader and labeled 0). The followers are moving based on the information exchange in their individual neighborhood while the leader is self-active, hence, moving independently. Thus, the information flow in the leader-follower multiagent system can be conveniently described by a directed graph $\bar{G}$. We recall the information about graph theory from [10] or Section 1.2.

The dynamics of the ith follower are assumed to be a first-order linear system:

$$\dot{x}_i(t) = u_i(t), \quad i = 1, \ldots., n \tag{2.1}$$

where $x_i(t) \in \Re^l$ and $u_i(t) \in \Re^l$ are, respectively, the state and the control input. The active leader is described by a second-order linear system with a partially unknown acceleration:

$$\begin{aligned} \dot{x}_0(t) &= v_0(t), \\ \dot{v}_0(t) &= u_0(t) + \delta(t) \\ y_0(t) &= x_0(t) \end{aligned} \tag{2.2}$$

where $x_0(t) \in \Re^l$, $v_0(t) \in \Re^l$ and $u_0(t) \in \Re^l$ are, respectively, the position, velocity and acceleration, the disturbance $\delta(t) \in \Re^l$ is bounded with an upper bound $\bar{\delta}$, and $y_0(t)$ is the only measured output.

Since only the position of the leader can be measured, each follower has to collect information from its neighbors and estimate the leader's velocity during the motion process. In [61], a distributed observer-based dynamic tracking control was proposed for each follower i:

$$\begin{aligned} \dot{v}_i(t) &= u_0(t) - \gamma k \left[\sum_{j \in \mathbf{N}_i} a_{ij}(x_i - x_j) + a_{i0}(x_i - x_0) \right] \\ u_i(t) &= v_i(t) - k \left[\sum_{j \in \mathbf{N}_i} a_{ij}(x_i - x_j) + a_{i0}(x_i - x_0) \right] \end{aligned} \tag{2.3}$$

where $v_i(t)$ is the "estimate" of the leader's velocity $v_0(t)$ and a_{i0} is the leader's adjacency coefficient. The dynamic tracking control (2.3) assumes that the relative position measurements $(x_i - x_0)$ are transmitted in continuous time.

In practice, however, communication (especially wireless communication) takes place over digital networks, therefore, information is transmitted at discrete time instants. When the follower finds that a local "error" signal exceeds a given threshold, it broadcasts its state information to all neighboring agents. In this scenario, the event-triggered dynamic tracking control is more preferable than that proposed in (2.3).

In the leader-follower problem under investigation, the active leader is independent and need not broadcast its information in any event-triggered fashion. However, follower i's control, $u_i(t)$, has to be designed based on the latest states received from its neighboring followers and also the sate $x_0(t)$ if it is linked to the leader. Therefore, a new control protocol needs to be designed in order to solve the leader-following problem with an event-triggered scheduling strategy. The event-triggered tracking problem is said to be solved if one can find a distributed event-triggered control strategy such that

$$||(x_i - x_j)|| \leq \xi, \quad i = 1, ..., n \tag{2.4}$$

for some constant $\xi = \xi(\bar{\delta})$ as $t \to \infty$.

2.1.2 Control design scheme

In consensus control, it turns out that the typical information available for a follower is its relative positions with the neighbors. It is usually assumed that the relative-position measurement

$$y_{ij}(t) = x_i(t) - -x_j(t) \tag{2.5}$$

is performed in continuous time, which implicitly implies that the multi-agent communication network bandwidth is unlimited or every agent has abundant energy.

However, when followers transmit their state information in discrete time, distributed tracking control needs to be redefined in order to take into account event-triggered strategies. In order to model the event-triggers for followers, assume that there are n monotone increasing sequences of event times

$$\tau_i(s)(s = 0, 1, \cdots\cdots, i = 1, \cdots, n)$$

Let $\hat{x}_i(t) = x_i(\tau_i(s)), \ t \in [\tau_i(s), \tau_i(s+1))$, be the measured state of follower i. The measured relative-position measurements $y_{ij}(t)$ depend on the measured states $\hat{x}_i(t)$ and $\hat{x}_j(t), \ j \in \mathbf{N}_i$, that is,

$$\hat{y}_{ij}(t) = \hat{x}_i(t) \ - - \ \hat{x}_j(t), \ \ i, \ j = 1, ..., n \tag{2.6}$$

It should be noted that the event times $\tau_i(s)$ are mutually independent among followers and may take different values, as illustrated by Fig. 2.1. Furthermore, if the communication between agent i and agent j (or the leader) has a time-varying delay $r(t)$, then the measured relative-position measurement is described by

$$\hat{y}_{ij}(t - r(t)) = \hat{x}_i(t - r(t))?\hat{x}_j(t(t) - r) \tag{2.7}$$

where $r(t)$ is a continuously differentiable function satisfying $0 < r(t) < \bar{r} < \infty$.

Due to unavailable measurement of the leader's velocity $v_0(t)$, each follower can have an estimate $v_i(t)$ by fusing the information obtained from its neighbors. When communication delay is not considered, the velocity estimate $v_i(t)$ is given with the measurements $\hat{y}_{ij}(t)$ and $y_{i0}(t)$, as follows:

$$\dot{v}_i(t) \ = \ u_0(t) - \gamma k \left[\sum_{j \in \mathbf{N}_i} a_{ij}\hat{y}_{ij}(t) + a_{i0}y_{i0}(t) \right] \tag{2.8}$$

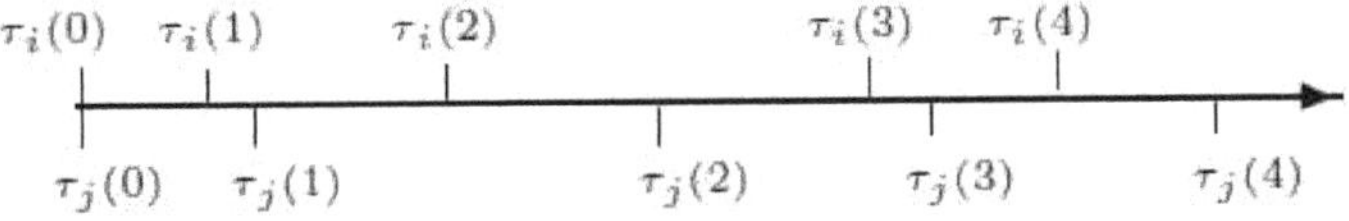

Figure 2.1: The event times for follower i and follower j

where a_{ij} denotes the adjacency coefficient between follower i and follower j, constant $0 < \gamma < 1$, and the gain k is to be designed. Moreover, an event-triggered tracking control is designed as follows:

$$u_i(t) \quad = \quad v_i(t) - k\left[\sum_{j\in\mathbf{N}_i} a_{ij}\hat{y}_{ij}(t) + a_{i0}y_{i0}(t)\right] \tag{2.9}$$

where the gain k is the same as above. It is noted that both the velocity estimate $v_i(t)$ and the control input $u_i(t)$ use the broadcasted measurements $\hat{y}_{ij}(t)$ from neighboring followers and the continuous-time measurement $y_{i0}(t)$ from the leader.

When communication delay is involved in the multi-agent coordination, a distributed event-triggered tracking control with time delays can be similarly formulated, as follows:

$$\begin{aligned} u_i(t) &= v_i(t) - k\left[\sum_{j\in\mathbf{N}_i} a_{ij}\hat{y}_{ij}(t-r) + a_{i0}y_{i0}(t-r)\right] \\ \dot{v}_i(t) &= u_0(t) - \gamma k\left[\sum_{j\in\mathbf{N}_i} a_{ij}\hat{y}_{ij}(t-r) + a_{i0}y_{i0}(t-r)\right] \end{aligned} \tag{2.10}$$

Next, we analyze the convergence of the tracking errors for all followers under distributed event-triggered control in both cases with and without communication delays.

2.1.3 Without communication delays

For simplicity in exposition, we define the error term

$$e_i(t) = \hat{x}_i(t) - x_i(t) \;=\; \hat{x}_i(\tau_i(s)) - x_i(t), \;\; t \in [\tau_i(s), \; \tau_i(s+1))$$

The event-time $\tau_i(s)$ is implicitly defined by an event-trigger, $f_i(e_i(t), e_j(t)|j \in \mathbf{N}_i) = 0$, which will be given below. Hence, $\hat{x}_i(t) = e_i(t) + x_i(t)$.

With this variable change, the control (2.9) together with the velocity estimation (2.8) is applied to system (2.1), which yields the following closed-loop system:

$$\begin{aligned}\dot{x} &= v - k\,(L+B)x + kB\mathbf{1}x_0 - k\,Le,\\ \dot{v} &= u_0\mathbf{1} - \gamma k\,(L+B)x + \gamma kB\mathbf{1}x_0 - \gamma kLe\end{aligned} \tag{2.11}$$

where

$$x = \begin{bmatrix} x_1 \\ x_2 \\ \vdots \\ x_n \end{bmatrix} \in \Re^n,\ v = \begin{bmatrix} v_1 \\ v_2 \\ \vdots \\ v_n \end{bmatrix} \in \Re^n,\ e = \begin{bmatrix} e_1 \\ e_2 \\ \vdots \\ e_n \end{bmatrix} \in \Re^n$$

respectively, denote the position, velocity estimation, measurement error of the leader-follower multi-agent system, $L = D?A \in \Re^{n\times n}$, $A = [a_{ij}] \in \Re^{n\times n}$, and $D \in \Re^{n\times n}$ are, respectively, the Laplacian matrix, adjacency matrix and degree matrix of the directed subgraph G. $B = diag\{a_{10}, ..., a_{n0}\}$ is a diagonal matrix representing the leader-follower adjacency relationship, and $\mathbf{1} = col[1, ..., 1] \in \Re^n$.

From the algebraic graph theory [10], it is known that L always has a zero eigenvalue associated with the right eigenvector $\mathbf{1}$. Moreover, if the subgraph G is balanced, L has a zero eigenvalue associated with the left eigenvector $\mathbf{1}$. This leads to

$$-(L+B)x + B\mathbf{1}x_0 = -(L+B)(x - x_0\mathbf{1}) := -H(x - x_0\mathbf{1})$$

It follows from Section II that

- vertex 0 is a globally reachable vertex of the directed graph $\bar{\mathcal{G}}$ and if its subgraph $\mathcal{G}$ is balanced, then

$$\lambda_* = \min\{\lambda : eigenvalues\ of\ (H+H^t)\} > 0 \tag{2.12}$$

- H is a stable matrix whose eigenvalues have negative real-parts;
- $\mathcal{G}$ is balanced and $(H+H^t)$ is a symmetric positive-definite matrix.

Proceeding to examine the stability of system (2.11), we introduce the change of variables:

$$\bar{x} = x - x_0\mathbf{1},\ \ \bar{v} = v - v_0\mathbf{1} \tag{2.13}$$

so that system (2.11) is expressed by

$$\begin{aligned}\dot{\bar{x}} &= \bar{v} - kH\bar{x} - k\,Le,\\ \dot{\bar{v}} &= -\gamma kH\bar{x} - \gamma k\,Le - \mathbf{1}\otimes\delta\end{aligned} \tag{2.14}$$

or in compact form:

$$\begin{aligned} \dot{\xi} &= \Xi\xi + \Gamma e + d, \;\; \xi = [\bar{x}^t, \; \bar{v}]^t, \\ \Xi &= \begin{bmatrix} -kH & I \\ -\gamma kH & 0 \end{bmatrix}, \Gamma = \begin{bmatrix} -kL \\ -\gamma kL \end{bmatrix}, d = \begin{bmatrix} 0 \\ \mathbf{1}\otimes\delta \end{bmatrix} \end{aligned} \tag{2.15}$$

Define a candidate ISS Lyapunov function

$$V(\xi) = \xi^t P\xi, \;\; P = \begin{bmatrix} I & -\gamma I \\ \bullet & I \end{bmatrix}, \;\; 0 < \gamma < 1$$

The main result is established by the following theorem:

Theorem 2.1
Assume that vertex 0 is a globally reachable vertex of the directed graph $\bar{\mathcal{G}}$, if its subgraph $\mathcal{G}$ is balanced and the gain k satisfies

$$k > \frac{1}{2\gamma(1-\gamma^2)\lambda_*} \tag{2.16}$$

Then, control (2.9) and estimation (2.8) solve the event-triggered tracking problem. Moreover, if the disturbance bound $\bar{\delta} = 0$, then $\lim_{t\to\infty}||\xi(t)|| = 0$.

Proof: Computing the derivative $\dot{V}(\xi)$ along the solutions of (2.15) yields

$$\begin{aligned} \dot{V}(\xi) &= \xi^t[P\Xi + \Xi^t P]\xi + 2\xi^t P\Gamma e + 2\xi^t Pd \\ &= -\xi^t Q\xi + 2\xi^t P\Gamma e + 2\xi^t Pd \end{aligned} \tag{2.17}$$

where

$$Q = \begin{bmatrix} k(1-\gamma^2)(H+H^t) & -I \\ \bullet & 2\gamma I \end{bmatrix}$$

With the help of Schur complements, it is easy to see that $Q > 0$ if k satisfies (2.16). Further computations show that the minimum eigenvalue of Q is given by

$$\sigma_* = \frac{1}{2}\left[(1-\gamma^2)k\lambda_* + 2\gamma - \sqrt{[(1-\gamma^2)k\lambda_* - 2\gamma] + 4}\right. \tag{2.18}$$

When k satisfies (2.16), then $\sigma_* > 0$. Since the eigenvalues of P are $1+\gamma$, $1-\gamma$, it follows that

$$(1-\gamma)||\xi||^2 \le V(\xi) \le (1+\gamma)||\xi||^2 \tag{2.19}$$

Taking advantage of (2.18) and (2.19), we get along the solutions of (2.15) that:

$$\begin{aligned}
\dot{V}(\xi) &\leq -\sigma_*||\xi||^2 + 2\xi^t P\Gamma e + 2\xi^t P d \\
&\leq -\sigma_*||\bar{x}||^2 - \sigma_*||\bar{v}||^2 - 2(1-\gamma^2)k\sum_i\sum_{j\in\mathbf{N}_i}\bar{x}(e_i - e_j) + 2(1+\gamma)||\xi||\bar{\delta} \\
&\leq -\sigma_*||\bar{v}||^2 - \sigma_*\sum_i\left[||\bar{x}_i||^2 - \frac{2(1-\gamma^2)k||\bar{x}||}{\sigma_*}\sum_{j\in\mathbf{N}_i}(||e_i|| - ||e_j||)\right] \\
&+ 2(1+\gamma)||\xi||\bar{\delta}
\end{aligned} \tag{2.20}$$

Enforcing the condition

$$\sum_{j\in\mathbf{N}_i}(||e_i|| + ||e_j||) \leq \varepsilon\frac{\sigma_*||\bar{x}_i||}{2(1-\gamma^2)k}, \quad 0 < \varepsilon < 1 \tag{2.21}$$

we have

$$\begin{aligned}
\dot{V}(\xi) &\leq -(1-\varepsilon)\sigma_*||\xi||^2 + 2(1+\gamma)||\xi||\bar{\delta} \\
&\leq -\frac{1}{2}(1-\varepsilon)\sigma_*||\bar{x}||^2 + 2\frac{(1+\gamma)^2\bar{\delta}^2}{(1-\varepsilon)\sigma_*}
\end{aligned} \tag{2.22}$$

Thus, for follower i, an event-trigger can be defined by

$$f_i(e_i(t), \{e_j(t)|j\in\mathbf{N}_i\}) = \sum_{j\in\mathbf{N}_i}(||e_i|| + ||e_j||) - \varepsilon\frac{\sigma_*||\bar{x}||}{(1-\gamma^2)k} \tag{2.23}$$

When the event-trigger $f_i(e_i(t), \{e_j(t)|j\in\mathbf{N}_i\}) = 0$, condition (2.21) is enforced. Given the event-trigger (2.23), then from (2.19) and (2.22) we have

$$\dot{V}(\xi) \leq -\frac{(1-\varepsilon)\sigma_*}{2(1+\gamma)}V(\xi) + \frac{2(1+\gamma)^2\bar{\delta}^2}{(1-\varepsilon)\sigma_*} \tag{2.24}$$

With $t_o = 0$, we obtain

$$V(\xi) \leq e^{-\frac{(1-\varepsilon)\sigma_*}{2(1+\gamma)}t}V(\xi(0)) + \frac{4(1+\gamma)^3\bar{\delta}^2}{(1-\varepsilon)^2\sigma_*^2} \tag{2.25}$$

which implies

$$\lim_{t\to\infty}||\xi|| \leq \psi, \quad \psi^2 = \frac{4(1+\gamma)^3\bar{\delta}^2}{(1-\varepsilon)^2\sigma_*^2}$$

Additionally, if $\bar{\delta} = 0$, then $\lim_{t\to\infty}||\xi|| = 0$, which completes the proof.

Remark 2.1 *For simplicity in the exposition, the event-trigger condition (2.21) can be replaced by a centralized one*

$$||e|| \leq \varepsilon\frac{\sigma_*||\xi||}{2(1-\gamma^2)||L||} \tag{2.26}$$

Evidently, the trigger condition (2.26) is conservative, however it helps in simulation experimentation. Suppose that this condition (2.26) is satisfied and $\bar{\delta} = 0$, then there exists at least one agent for which the next inter-event interval is bounded from below by a time τ_D, determined by

$$\begin{aligned} \tau_D &= \frac{1}{||\Xi|| - ||\Gamma||} \ln\left[\frac{1+\phi}{1+\frac{||\Gamma||}{||\Xi||}\phi}\right] \\ \phi(\tau_D, 0) &= \frac{\varepsilon\sigma_*}{2(1-\gamma^2)||L||} \\ \frac{||e||}{||\xi||} &\leq \phi(t,\phi_o), \;\; \phi_o = \phi(0,\phi_o) \end{aligned} \tag{2.27}$$

and $\phi(t,\phi_o)$ is the solution of

$$\dot{\phi} == ||\Xi||(1+\phi)\left[1+\frac{||\Gamma||}{||\Xi||}\phi\right] \tag{2.28}$$

■

2.1.4 With communication delays

In this case, we take into consideration model (2.10) along with $\hat{x}_i(t) = e_i(t) + x_i(t)$ and manipulate to obtain:

$$\begin{aligned} \dot{x}_(t) &= v(t) - k\,(L+B)x(t-r) + kB\mathbf{1}x_o(t-r) - kLe(t-r) \\ \dot{v}_i(t) &= u_0\mathbf{1} - \gamma k\,(L+B)x(t-r) + \gamma k\,B\mathbf{1}x_o(t-r) - kLe(t-r) \end{aligned} \tag{2.29}$$

Using the change of variables (2.13), algebraic manipulations yield a further simplified closed-loop system in the form of time-delayed differential equations:

$$\begin{aligned} \dot{\bar{x}} &= \bar{v} - k\,H\,\bar{x}(t-r) - k\,Le(t-r), \\ \dot{\bar{v}} &= -\gamma\,k\,H\,\bar{x}(t-r) - \gamma k\,Le(t-r) - \mathbf{1}\otimes\delta \end{aligned} \tag{2.30}$$

or in compact form:

$$\begin{aligned} \dot{\xi} &= \Xi_1\xi(t) + \Xi_2\xi(t-r) + \Gamma e(t-r) + d \\ \xi &= [\bar{x}^t,\; \bar{v}]^t,\; \Xi_1 = \begin{bmatrix} 0 & I \\ 0 & 0 \end{bmatrix}, \Xi_2 = \begin{bmatrix} -k\,H & 0 \\ -\gamma\,k\,H & 0 \end{bmatrix}, \\ \Gamma &= \begin{bmatrix} -k\,L \\ -\gamma\,k\,H \end{bmatrix}, d = \begin{bmatrix} 0 \\ \mathbf{1}\otimes\delta \end{bmatrix} \end{aligned} \tag{2.31}$$

Before proceeding further, the standard theorem of stability from the Appendix must be recalled. The main results can then be readily derived and left for the time being.

2.2 Networked Multiagent Systems

Consensus problems have a long history in computer science and form the foundation of the field of distributed computing [140]. Formal study of consensus problems in groups of experts originated in management science and statistics in 1960s [141] (and references therein). The ideas of statistical consensus theory reappeared two decades later in aggregation of information with uncertainty obtained from multiple sensors1 [142] and medical experts [143].

Distributed computation over networks has a tradition in systems and control theory, starting with the pioneering work of Borkar and Varaiya [144] and Tsitsiklis [145] and Tsitsiklis, Bertsekas, and Athans [146] on asynchronous asymptotic agreement problem for distributed decisionmaking systems and parallel computing [147].

In networks of agents (or dynamic systems), Bconsensus means to reach an agreement regarding a certain quantity of interest that depends on the state of all agents. A Bconsensus algorithm (or protocol) is an interaction rule that specifies the information exchange between an agent and all of its neighbors on the network.

The theoretical framework for posing and solving consensus problems for networked dynamic systems was introduced by Olfati-Saber and Murray in [148] and [149], building on the earlier work of Fax and Murray [150], [151]. The study of the alignment problem involving reaching an agreement without computing any objective functions V appeared in the work of Jadbabaie et al. [152]. Further theoretical extensions of this work were presented in [153] and [154], with a look toward treatment of directed information flow in networks, as shown in Fig. 1(a).

Note in Fig. 2.2 that each agent i in the network of integrator agents receives the state x_j of its neighbor, agent j, if there is a link (i, j) connecting the two nodes and (b) a network of interconnected dynamic systems in block diagram form, all with identical transfer functions $P(s) = 1/s$. The collective networked system has a diagonal transfer function corresponding to a multiple-input multiple-output (*MIMO*) linear system.

The common motivation behind the work in [144], [145], and [149] is the rich history of consensus protocols in computer science [140], whereas Jadbabaie et al. [152] attempted to provide a formal analysis of emergence of alignment in the simplified model of flocking by Vicsek et al. [155]. The setup in [149] was originally created with the vision of designing agent-based amorphous computers, [156], [157], for collaborative information processing in networks. Later, [149] was used in the development of flocking algorithms with guaranteed convergence and the capability to deal with obstacles and adversarial agents [158].

Graph Laplacians and their spectral properties [10, 159, 160, 161] are important graph-related matrices that play a crucial role in the convergence analysis of consensus and alignment algorithms. Graph Laplacians are an important point of focus of this paper. It is worth mentioning that the second smallest eigen-

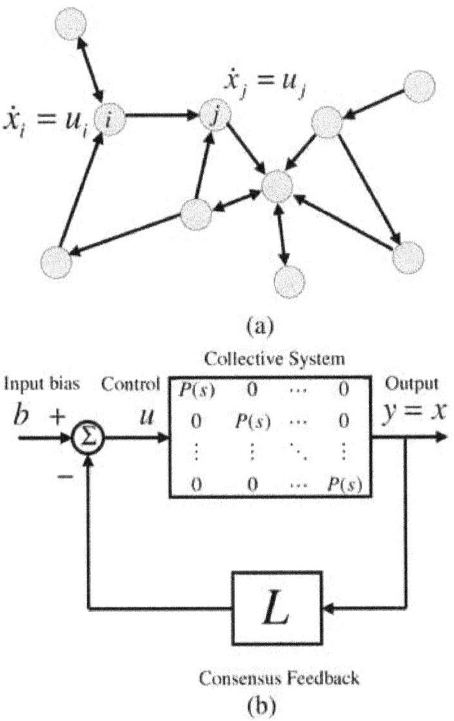

Figure 2.2: Two equivalent forms of consensus algorithms: (a) a network of integrator agents and (b) the block diagram for a network of interconnected dynamic systems

value of graph Laplacians, called algebraic connectivity, quantifies the speed of convergence of consensus algorithms. The notion of algebraic connectivity of graphs has appeared in a variety of other areas, including low-density parity-check codes (LDPC) in information theory and communications [162], Ramanujan graphs [163] in number theory and quantum chaos, and combinatorial optimization problems, such as the max-cut problem [160].

More recently, there has been a tremendous surge of interest among researchers from various disciplines of engineering and science in problems related to multiagent networked systems with close ties to consensus problems. This includes subjects such as consensus [164]–[170], collective behavior of flocks and swarms [158], [171]–[175], sensor fusion [176, 177, 178], random networks [179], [180], synchronization of coupled oscillators [180]–[184], algebraic connectivity3 of complex networks [185, 186, 187], asynchronous distributed algorithms [168], [188], formation control for multirobot systems [189]–[197], optimization-based cooperative control [198]– [201], dynamic graphs [202]–[204], complexity of coordinated tasks [205]–[208], and consensus-based belief propagation in Bayesian networks [209], [210]. A detailed discussion of selected applications will be presented shortly.

In what follows, we focus on the work described in five key works, [152], [149], [151], [153] and [154], that have been instrumental in paving the way for more recent advances in the study of self-organizing networked systems, or swarms. These networked systems are comprised of locally interacting mobile/static agents equipped with dedicated sensing, computing, and communication devices. As a result, we now have a better understanding of complex phenomena, such as flocking [158], or design of novel information fusion algorithms for sensor networks that are robust to node and link failures [176], [209]–[213].

Gossip-based algorithms, such as the push-sum protocol [214], are important alternatives in computer science to Laplacian-based consensus algorithms in this paper. Markov processes establish an interesting connection between the information propagation speed in these two categories of algorithms proposed by computer scientists and control theorists [215].

2.2.1 Consensus in networks

The interaction topology of a network of agents is represented using a directed graph $G = (V,E)$ with the set of nodes $V = 1,2,\ldots,n$ and edges $E \subseteq V \times V$. The neighbors of agent i are denoted by $N_i = j \in V : (i,j) \in E$. According to [149], a simple consensus algorithm to reach an agreement regarding the state of n integrator agents with dynamics $\dot{x}_i = u_i$ can be expressed as an nth-order linear system on a graph

$$\dot{x}_i(t) = \sum_{j \in N_i} (x_j(t) - x_i(t)) + b_i(t), x_i(0) = z_i \in \mathbb{R}, b_i(t) = 0 : \tag{2.32}$$

The *collective* dynamics of the group of agents following protocol (1) can be written as

$$\dot{x} = -Lx \tag{2.33}$$

where $L = [l_{ij}]$ is the graph Laplacian of the network and its elements are defined as follows:

$$l_{ij} = \begin{cases} -1, j \in N_i \\ |N_i|, j = i \end{cases}. \tag{2.34}$$

Here, $|N_i|$ denotes the number of neighbors of node i (or out-degree of node i). Figure 2.2 shows two equivalent forms of the consensus algorithm in (2.32) and (2.34) for agents with a scalar state. The role of the input bias b in Fig. 2.2(b) is defined later.

According to the definition of graph Laplacian in (1.10), all row-sums of L are zero because of $\sum_j l_{ij} = 0$. Therefore, L always has a zero eigenvalue $\lambda_1 = 0$.

This zero eigenvalues corresponds to the eigenvector $1 = (1,\ldots,1)^T$ because 1 belongs to the null-space of $L(L1 = 0)$. In other words, an equilibrium of system (1.11) is a state in the form $x^* = (\alpha,\ldots,\alpha)^T = \alpha 1$ where all nodes agree. Based on analytical tools from algebraic graph theory [10], we later show that $x^*$is a unique equilibrium of (1.11) (up to a constant multiplicative factor) for connected graphs. One can show that, for a connected network, the equilibrium $x^* = (\alpha,\ldots,\alpha)^T$ is globally exponentially stable. Moreover, the consensus value is $\alpha = 1 = n\pi z_i$, which is equal to the average of the initial values. This implies that, irrespective of the initial value of the state of each agent, all agents reach an asymptotic consensus regarding the value of the function $f(z) = 1/n\sum_i z_i$. While the calculation of $f(z)$ is simple for small networks, its implications for very large networks are more interesting. For example, if a network has $n = 10^6$ nodes and each node can only talk to $\log_{10}(n) = 6$ neighbors, finding the average value of the initial conditions of the nodes is more complicated. The role of protocol (1.10) is to provide a systematic consensus mechanism in such a large network in order to compute the average. There are a variety of functions that can be computed in a similar fashion using synchronous or asynchronous distributed algorithms (see [149], [166], [168], [210] and [213]).

2.2.2 The f-consensus problem

To understand the role of cooperation in performing coordinated tasks, we need to distinguish between unconstrained and constrained consensus problems. An unconstrained consensus problem is simply the alignment problem in which it suffices that the state of all agents asymptotically be the same. In contrast, in distributed computation of a function $f(z)$, the state of all agents has to asymptotically become equal to $f(z)$, meaning that the consensus problem is constrained. We refer to this constrained consensus problem as the f-consensus problem. Solving the f-consensus problem is a cooperative task and requires willing participation of all the agents. To demonstrate this fact, suppose a single agent decides not to cooperate with the rest of the agents and keep its state unchanged. Then, the overall task cannot be performed despite the fact that the rest of the agents reach an agreement. Furthermore, there could be scenarios in which multiple agents that form a coalition do not cooperate with the rest and removal of this coalition of agents and their links might render the network disconnected. In a disconnected network, it is impossible for all nodes to reach an agreement (unless all nodes initially agree which is a trivial case). From the above discussion, cooperation can be informally interpreted as "giving consent to providing one's state and following a common protocol that serves the group objective."

One might think that solving the alignment problem is not a cooperative task. The justification is that, if a single agent (called a leader) leaves its value unchanged, all others will asymptotically agree with the leader according to the consensus protocol and an alignment is reached. However, if there are multiple leaders where two of whom are in disagreement, then no consensus can be asymptotically reached. Therefore, alignment is, in general, a cooperative task as well. Formal analysis of the behavior of systems that involve more than one type of agent is more complicated, particularly, in the presence of *adversarial agents* in noncooperative games [216], [217]. The focus of this paper is on cooperative multi-agent systems.

2.2.3 Iterative consensus and Markov chains

It is shown previously how an iterative consensus algorithm that corresponds to the discrete-time version of system (2.32) is a Markov chain

$$\pi(k+1) = \pi(k)P \tag{2.35}$$

with $P = I - \varepsilon L$ and a small $\varepsilon > 0$. Here, the ith element of the row vector $\pi(k)$ denotes the probability of being in state i at iteration k. It turns out that, for any arbitrary graph G with Laplacian L and a sufficiently small ε, the matrix P satisfies the property $\sum_j p_{ij} = 1$ with $p_{ij} \geq 0, \forall i, j$. Hence, P is a valid transition probability matrix for the Markov chain in (2.35). The reason matrix theory [218] is so widely used in analysis of consensus algorithms [149], [151, 152, 153, 154], [202] is primarily due to the structure of P in (2.35) and its connection to graphs. There are interesting connections between this Markov chain and the speed of information diffusion in gossip-based averaging algorithms [214], [215]. One of the early applications of consensus problems was dynamic load balancing [219] for parallel processors with the same structure as system (2.35). To date, load balancing in networks proves to be an active area of research in computer science.

2.3 Applications

Many seemingly different problems that involve interconnection of dynamic systems in various areas of science and engineering happen to be closely related to consensus problems for multi-agent systems. In this section, we provide an account of the existing connections.

2.3.1 Synchronization of coupled oscillators

The problem of synchronization of coupled oscillators has attracted numerous scientists from diverse fields, including physics, biology, neuroscience, and mathematics [220, 221, 222, 223]. This is partly due to the emergence of synchronous oscillations in coupled neural oscillators. Let us consider the generalized Kuramoto model of coupled oscillators on a graph with dynamics

$$\theta_i = \kappa \sum_{j \in N_i} sin(\theta_j - \theta_i) + \omega_i \tag{2.36}$$

where θ_i and ω_i are the phase and frequency of the ith oscillator. This model is the natural nonlinear extension of the consensus algorithm in (2.32) and its linearization around the aligned state $\theta_1 = \cdots = \theta_n$ is identical to system (1.11) plus a nonzero input bias $b_i = (\omega_i - \bar{\omega})/\kappa$ with $\bar{\omega} = 1/n \sum_i \omega_i$ after a change of variables $x_i = (\theta_i - \bar{\omega}t)/\kappa$.

In [181], Sepulchre et al. show that if the number of oscillators n is sufficiently large then for a network with all-to-all links, synchronization to the aligned state is globally achieved for all initial states. Recently, synchronization of networked oscillators under variable time-delays was studied in [183]. We believe that the use of convergence analysis methods that utilize the spectral properties of graph Laplacians will shed light on the performance and convergence analysis of self-synchrony in oscillator networks [180].

2.3.2 Flocking theory

Flocks of mobile agents equipped with sensing and communication devices can serve as mobile sensor networks for massive distributed sensing in an environment [224]. A theoretical framework for design and analysis of flocking algorithms for mobile agents with obstacle-avoidance capabilities was developed by Olfati-Saber [158]. The role of consensus algorithms in particle-based flocking is for an agent to achieve velocity matching with respect to its neighbors. In [158], it is demonstrated that flocks are networks of dynamic systems with a dynamic topology. This topology is a proximity graph that depends on the state of all agents and is determined locally for each agent, i.e., the topology of flocks is a state-dependent graph. The notion of state-dependent graphs was introduced by Mesbahi [202] in a context that is independent of flocking.

2.3.3 Fast consensus in small-worlds

In recent years, network design problems for achieving faster consensus algorithms has attracted considerable attention from a number of researchers. In Xiao and Boyd [225], the design of the weights of a network is considered and solved using semi-definite convex programming. This leads to a slight increase in algebraic connectivity of a network that is a measure of speed of convergence of consensus algorithms. An alternative approach is to keep the weights fixed and design the topology of the network in such a way as to achieve a relatively high algebraic connectivity. A randomized algorithm for network design is proposed by Olfati-Saber [185], based on the random rewiring idea of Watts and Strogatz [226] that led to the creation of their celebrated small-world model. The random rewiring of existing links of a network gives rise to considerably faster consensus algorithms. This is due to a multiple orders of magnitude increase in algebraic connectivity of the network in comparison to a lattice-type nearest-neighbor graph.

2.3.4 Rendezvous in space

Another common form of consensus problems is rendezvous in space [227], [228]. This is equivalent to reaching a consensus in position by a number of agents with an interaction topology that is position induced (i.e., a proximity graph). We refer the reader to [229] and references therein for a detailed discussion. This type of rendezvous is an unconstrained consensus problem that becomes challenging under variations in the network topology. Flocking is somewhat more challenging than rendezvous in space because it requires both inter-agent and agent-to-obstacle collision avoidance.

2.3.5 Distributed sensor fusion in sensor networks

The most recent application of consensus problems is distributed sensor fusion in sensor networks. This is done by posing the various distributed averaging problems required to implement a Kalman filter [176], [177], approximate Kalman filter [211], or linear least-squares estimator [212] as average-consensus problems. Novel low-pass and highpass consensus filters that dynamically calculate the average of their inputs in sensor networks are also developed [177], [230].

2.3.6 Distributed formation control

Multi-vehicle systems are an important category of networked systems due to their commercial and military applications. There are two broad approaches to distributed formation control: i) representation of formations as rigid structures [191], [231] and the use of gradient-based controls obtained from their structural potentials [190] and ii) representation of formations using the vectors of relative positions of neighboring vehicles and the use of consensus-based controllers with input bias. We discuss the latter approach here. A theoretical framework for design and analysis of distributed controllers for multi-vehicle formations of type ii) was developed by Fax and Murray [151]. Moving in formation is a cooperative task and requires the consent and collaboration of every agent in the formation. In [151], graph Laplacians and matrix theory were extensively used, which makes one wonder whether relative-position-based formation control is a consensus problem. The answer is yes. To see this, consider a network of self-interested agents whose individual desire is to minimize their local cost $U_i(x) = \sum_{\in N_i} ||x_j - x_i - rij||^2$ via a distributed algorithm. (x_i) is the position of vehicle i with dynamics $\dot{x}_i = u_i$ and r_{ij} is a desired inter-vehicle relative-position vector). Instead, if the agents use gradient-descent algorithm on the collective cost $\sum_{i=1}^{n} U_i(x)$ using the following protocol:

$$\dot{x}_i = \sum_{j \in N_i} (x_j - x_i - r_{ij}) = \sum_{j \in N_i} (x_j x_i) + b_i \tag{2.37}$$

with input bias $b_i = \sum_{j \in N_i} rji$ [see Fig. 2.2(b)], the objective of every agent will be achieved. This is the same as the consensus algorithm in (2.32) up to the nonzero bias terms b_i. This nonzero bias plays no role in the stability analysis of system (1.15). Thus, distributed formation control for integrator agents is a consensus problem. The main contribution of the work by Fax and Murray is to extend this scenario to the case where all agents are multiinput multioutput linear systems $x_i = Ax_i + Bu_i$.

2.4 Information Consensus

Consider a network of decision-making agents with dynamics $\dot{x}_i = u_i$ interested in reaching a consensus via local communication with their neighbors on a graph $G = (V, E)$. By reaching a consensus, we mean asymptotically converging to a one-dimensional agreement space characterized by the following equation:

$$x_1 = x_2 = \cdots = x_n.$$

This agreement space can be expressed as $x = \alpha 1$, where $1 = (1, \ldots, 1)^T$ and $\alpha \in R$ is the collective decision of the group of agents. Let $A = |a_{ij}|$ be the adjacency matrix of graph G. The set of neighbors of agent i is N_i and defined by

$$N_i = j2V : a_{ij} \neq 0; V = 1, \ldots, n.$$

Agent i communicates with agent j if j is a neighbor of i (or $a_{ij} \neq 0$). The set of all nodes and their neighbors defines the edge set of the graph as $E = (i, j) \in V \times V : a_{ij} \neq 0$. A dynamic graph $G(t) = (V, E(t))$ is a graph in which the set of edges $E(t)$ and the adjacency matrix $A(t)$ are time-varying. Clearly, the set of neighbors $N_i(t)$ of every agent in a dynamic graph is a time-varying set as well. Dynamic graphs are useful for describing the network topology of mobile sensor networks and flocks [158]. It is shown in [149] that the linear system

$$\dot{x}_i(t) = X \sum_{N_i} a_{ij}(x_j(t) - x_i(t)) \tag{2.38}$$

is a distributed consensus algorithm, i.e., guarantees convergence to a collective decision via local interagent interactions. Assuming that the graph is undirected

($a_{ij} = a_{ji}$ for all i, j), it follows that the sum of the state of all nodes is an invariant quantity, or $\sum_i \dot{x}_i = 0$. In particular, applying this condition twice at times t = 0 and $t = \infty$ gives the following result

$$\alpha = \frac{1}{n}\sum_i x_i(0).$$

In other words, if a consensus is asymptotically reached, then it follows that the collective decision is equal to the average of the initial state of all nodes. A consensus algorithm with this specific invariance property is called an average-consensus algorithm [148] and has broad applications in distributed computing on networks (e.g., sensor fusion in sensor networks). The dynamics of system (1.16) can be expressed in a compact form as

$$\dot{x} = -Lx \tag{2.39}$$

where L is known as the graph Laplacian of G. The graph Laplacian is defined as

$$L = D - A \tag{2.40}$$

where $D = diag(d_1, \ldots, d_n)$ is the degree matrix of G with elements $d_i = \sum_{j \neq i} a_{ij}$ and zero off-diagonal elements. By definition, L has a right eigenvector of 1 associated with the zero eigenvalue because of the identity $L[1...1] = 0$. For the case of undirected graphs, graph Laplacian satisfies the following sum-of-squares (SOS) property:

$$x^T Lx = \frac{1}{2}\sum_{(i,j)\in E} a_{ij}(x_j - x_i)^2. \tag{2.41}$$

By defining a *quadratic disagreement* function as

$$\rho = \frac{1}{2}x^T Lx \tag{2.42}$$

It becomes apparent that algorithm (2.32) is the same as

$$\dot{x} = \nabla\rho(x)$$

or the gradient-descent algorithm. This algorithm globally asymptotically converges to the agreement space, provided that two conditions hold: 1) L is a positive semidefinite matrix, 2) the only equilibrium of (7) is $\alpha 1$ for some α. Both of these conditions hold for a connected graph and follow from the SOS property of graph Laplacian in (2.41). Therefore, an average-consensus is asymptotically reached for all initial states. This fact is summarized in the following lemma.

Lemma 2.1

Let G be a connected undirected graph. Then, the algorithm in (2.32) asymptotically solves an average consensus problem for all initial states.

2.4.1 Algebraic connectivity and spectral properties

Spectral properties of Laplacian matrix are instrumental in analysis of convergence of the class of linear consensus algorithms in (2.32). According to Gershgorin theorem [218], all eigenvalues of L in the complex plane are located in a closed disk centered at $\Delta + 0j$ with a radius of $\Delta = max_i d_i$, i.e., the maximum degree of a graph. For undirected graphs, L is a symmetric matrix with real eigenvalues and, therefore, the set of eigenvalues of L can be ordered sequentially in an ascending order as

$$0 = \lambda_1 \leq \lambda_2 \leq \cdots \leq \lambda_n \leq 2\Delta. \tag{2.43}$$

The zero eigenvalue is known as the trivial eigenvalue of L. For a connected graph G, $\lambda_2 > 0$ (i.e., the zero eigenvalue is isolated). The second smallest eigenvalue of Laplacian λ_2 is called algebraic connectivity of a graph [159]. Algebraic connectivity of the network topology is a measure of performance/speed of consensus algorithms [149].

Simulation example 1 Fig. 2.3 shows two examples of networks of integrator agents with different topologies. Both graphs are undirected and have 0-1 weights. Every node of the graph in Fig. 2.3(a) is connected to its 4 nearest neighbors on a ring. The other graph is a proximity graph of points that are distributed uniformly at random in a square. Every node is connected to all of its spatial neighbors within a closed ball of radius $r > 0$. Here are the important degree information and Laplacian eigenvalues of these graphs

$$\begin{aligned} &a)\lambda_1 = 0, \lambda_2 = 0.48, \lambda_n = 6.24, \Delta = 4 \\ &b)\lambda_1 = 0, \lambda_2 = 0.25, \lambda_n = 9.37, \Delta = 8. \end{aligned} \tag{2.44}$$

In both cases, $\lambda_i < 2\Delta$ for all i.

2.4.2 Convergence analysis for directed networks

The convergence analysis of the consensus algorithm in (1.16) is equivalent to proving that the agreement space characterized by $x = \alpha 1, \alpha \in \mathbb{R}$ is an asymptotically stable equilibrium of system (1.16). The stability properties of system (1.16) are completely determined by the location of the Laplacian eigenvalues of the network. The eigenvalues of the adjacency matrix are irrelevant to the stability analysis of system (1.16), unless the network is k-regular (all of its nodes have the same degree k). The following lemma combines a well-known rank property of graph Laplacians with Gershgorin theorem to provide spectral characterization of Laplacian of a fixed directed network G. Before stating the *lemma*, we need to define the notion of strong connectivity of graphs. A graph is strongly connected (SC) if there is a directed path connecting any two arbitrary nodes s, t of the graph.

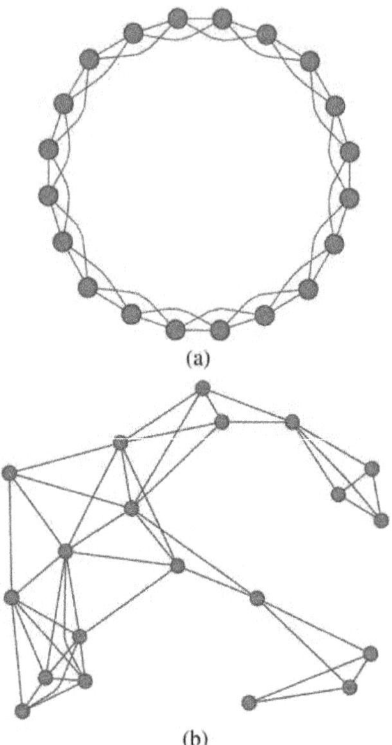

Figure 2.3: Examples of networks with $n = 20$ nodes: (a) a regular network with 80 links and (b) a random network with 45 links

Lemma 2.2

(spectral localization) Let G be a strongly connected digraph on n nodes. Then $rank(L) = n-1$ *and all nontrivial eigenvalues of L have positive real parts. Furthermore, suppose G has* $c \geq 1$ *strongly connected components, then* $rank(L) = n-c$.

Proof: The proof of the rank property for digraphs is given in [149]. The proof for undirected graphs is available in the algebraic graph theory literature [10]. The positivity of the real parts of the eigenvalues follow from the fact that all eigenvalues are located in a Gershgorin disk in the closed right-hand plane that touches the imaginary axis at zero. The second part follows from the first part after relabeling the nodes of the digraph so that its Laplacian becomes a block diagonal matrix.

Remark 2.2 Lemma 2.2 holds under a weaker condition of existence of a directed spanning tree for G. G has a directed spanning tree if there exists a node r (a root) such that all other nodes can be linked to r via a directed path. This type of condition on existence of directed spanning trees has appeared in [152, 153, 154]. The root node is commonly known as a leader [152]. The essential results regarding convergence and decision value of Laplacian-based consensus algorithms for directed networks with a fixed topology are summarized in the following theorem. Before stating this theorem, we need to define an important class of digraphs that appear frequently throughout this section. ■

Definition 2.1 (balanced digraphs [149]) A digraph G is called balanced if $\sum_{j\neq i} a_{ij} = \sum_{j\neq i} a_{ji}$ for all $i \in V$. In a balanced digraph, the total weight of edges entering a node and leaving the same node are equal for all nodes. The most important property of balanced digraphs is that $w = 1$ is also a left eigenvector of their Laplacian (or $1^T L = 0$).

Theorem 2.2

Consider a network of n agents with topology G applying the following consensus algorithm

$$\dot{x}_i(t) = \sum_{j \in N_i} a_{ij}(x_j(t) - xi(t)), x(0) = z: \tag{2.45}$$

Suppose G is a strongly connected digraph. Let L be the Laplacian of strongly connected digraph G. Let L be the satisfying $\gamma^T L = 0$. *Then*

1. *a consensus is asymptotically reached for all initial states,*
2. *the algorithm solves the f-consensus problem with the linear function* $f(z)(\gamma^T z/\gamma^T 1)$, *i.e., the group decision is* $\alpha = \sum_i w_i z_i$ *with* $\sum_i w_i = 1$,
3. *if the digraph is balanced, an average-consensus is asymptotically reached and* $\alpha = (\sum_i x_i(0))/n$.

Proof: The convergence of the consensus algorithm follows from Lemma 2. To show part ii), note that the collective dynamics of the network is $\dot{x} = -Lx$. This means that $y = \gamma^T x$ is an invariant quantity due to $\dot{y} = -\gamma^T Lx = 0, \forall x$. Thus, $\lim_{t\to\infty} y(t) = y(0)$, or $\gamma^T(\alpha 1) = \gamma^T x(0)$ that implies the group decision is $\alpha = (\gamma^T z) = \sum_i \gamma_i$. Setting $w_i = \gamma_i / \sum_i$, we get $\alpha = w^T z$. Part iii) follows as a special case of the statement in part ii) because for a balanced digraph $\gamma = 1$ and $w_i = 1 = /, \forall i$.

Remark 2.3 In [149], it is shown that a necessary and sufficient condition for L to have a left eigenvector of $\gamma = 1$ is that G must be a balanced digraph. ■

A challenging problem is to analyze the convergence of a consensus algorithm for a dynamic network with a switching topology $G(t)$ that is time-varying.

Various aspects of this problem have been addressed by several groups during recent years [149], [152, 153, 154] and will be discussed in detail.

2.4.3 Consensus in discrete-time

An iterative form of the consensus algorithm can be stated as follows in discrete-time:

$$x_i(k+1) = x_i(k) + \varepsilon \sum_{j \in N_i} a_{ij}(x_j(k) - x_i(k)) \tag{2.46}$$

The discrete-time collective dynamics of the network under this algorithm can be written as

$$x(k+1) = Px(k) \tag{2.47}$$

with $P = I - \varepsilon L$ (I is the identity matrix) and $\varepsilon > 0$ is the step-size. In general, $P = exp(-\varepsilon L)$ and the algorithm in (2.46) is a special case that only uses communication with first-order neighbors. We refer to P as the *Perron matrix* of a graph G with parameter ε.

Three important types of *nonnegative matrices* are irreducible, stochastic, and primitive (or ergodic) matrices [218]. A matrix A is *irreducible* if its associated graph is strongly connected. A nonnegative matrix is called row (or column) *stochastic* if all of its row-sums (or column-sums) are 1. An irreducible stochastic matrix P is primitive if it has only one eigenvalue with maximum modulus.

Lemma 2.3
Let G be a digraph with n nodes and maximum degree $\Delta = max_i(\sum_{j \neq i} a_{ij})$. *Then, the Perron matrix P with parameter* $\varepsilon \in (0; 1/\Delta]$ *satisfies the following properties.*

1. *P is a row stochastic nonnegative matrix with a trivial eigenvalue of 1;*
2. *All eigenvalues of P are in a unit circle;*
3. *If G is a balanced graph, then P is a doubly stochastic matrix;*
4. *If G is strongly connected and* $0 < \varepsilon < 1/\Delta$, *then P is a primitive matrix.*

Proof: Since $P = I\varepsilon L$, we get $P1 = 1\varepsilon L1 = 1$, which means the row sums of P is 1. Moreover, 1 is a trivial eigenvalue of P for all graphs. To show that P is nonnegative, notice that $P = I\varepsilon D + \varepsilon A$ due to definition of Laplacian $L = D - A$. εA is a nonnegative matrix. The diagonal elements of $I\varepsilon D$ are $1 - \varepsilon d_i \geq 1 - d_i/\Delta \geq 0$, which implies $I\varepsilon D$ is nonnegative. Since the sum of two nonnegative matrices is a nonnegative matrix, P is a nonnegative row stochastic matrix. To prove part ii), one notices that all eigenvectors of P and L are the same. Let λ_j be the jth eigenvalue of L. Then, the jth eigenvalue of P is

$$\mu_j = 1 - \varepsilon\lambda_j \tag{2.48}$$

Based on Gershgorin theorem, all eigenvalues of L are in the disk $|s - \Delta| \leq \Delta$. Defining $z = 1 - s/\Delta$, we have $|z| \leq 1$ which proves part ii). If G is a balanced digraph, then 1 is the left eigenvector of L, or $1^T L = 0$. This means that $1^T P = 1T - \varepsilon 1^T L = 1^T$, which implies the column sums of P are 1. This combined with the result in part i) gives part iii). To prove part iv), note that, if G is strongly connected, then P is an irreducible matrix [218]. To prove that P is primitive, we need to establish that it has a single eigenvalue with maximum modulus of 1. For all $0 < \varepsilon < 1/\Delta$, the transformation $\mu = 1\varepsilon s$ maps the circle $|s - \Delta| = \Delta$ into a circle that is located strictly inside a unit disk passing through the point $\mu = 1$. This means that only a single eigenvalue at $\mu_1 = 1$ can have a modulus of 1.

Remark 2.4 The condition $\varepsilon < 1/\Delta$ in part iv) is necessary. If an incorrect step-size of $\varepsilon = 1/\Delta$ is used. Then, P would no longer be a primitive matrix because it could have multiple eigenvalues of modulus 1. The counterexample is a directed cycle of length n with a Laplacian that has n roots on the boundary of the Gershgorin disk $|s - \Delta| \leq \Delta$. With the choice of $\varepsilon = 1/\Delta = 1$, one gets a Perron matrix that is irreducible but has n eigenvalues on the boundary of the unit circle. This is a common mistake that is repeated by some of the researchers in the past. The convergence analysis of the discrete-time consensus algorithm relies on the following well-known lemma in matrix theory. ▮

Lemma 2.4

(Perron-Frobenius, [218]) Let P be a primitive nonnegative matrix with left and right eigenvectors w and v, respectively, satisfying $Pv = v, w^T P = w^T$ and $v^T w = 1$. Then $\lim_{k\to\infty} P^k = vw^T$. The convergence and group decision properties of iterative consensus algorithms x Px with row stochastic Perron matrices are stated in the following result. It turns out that this discrete-time convergence result is almost identical to its continuous-time counterpart.

Theorem 2.3

Consider a network of agents $x_i(k+1) = x_i(k) + u_i(k)$ with topology G applying the distributed consensus algorithm

$$x_i(k+1) = x_i(k)\varepsilon \sum_{j\in N_i} a_{ij}(x_j(k) - x_i(k)) \tag{2.49}$$

Table 2.1: Continuous-time versus discrete-time consensus

	CT	DT
Dynamics	$\dot{x} = -Lx$	$x(k+1) = Px(k)$
Key Matrix	L(Laplacian)	$P = I - \varepsilon L$ (Perron)
Connected G	converges	converges
Decision (general)	$\sum_i w_i x_i(0)$	$\sum_i w_i x_i(0)$
Decision (balanced)	$\sum_i x_i(0)/n$	$\sum_i x_i(0)/n$

where $0 < \varepsilon < 1/\Delta$ and Δ is the maximum degree of the network. Let G be a strongly connected digraph. Then,

1. *A consensus is asymptotically reached for all initial states;*
2. *The group decision value is $\alpha = \sum_i w_i x_i(0)$ with $\sum_i w_i = 1$;*
3. *If the digraph is balanced (or P is doubly stochastic), an average-consensus is asymptotically reached and $\alpha = (\sum_i x_i(0))/n$.*

Proof: Considering that $x(k) = P^k x(0)$, a consensus is reached in discrete-time, if the limit $\lim_{k\to\infty} P^k$ exists. According to Lemma 2.4, this limit exists for primitive matrices. Based on part iv) of Lemma 2.3, P is a primitive matrix. Thus, $\lim_{k\to\infty} x(k) = v(w^T x(0))$ with $v = 1$, or $x_i \to \alpha = w^T x(0)$ for all i as $k \to 1$. Hence, the group decision value is $\alpha = \sum_i w_i x_i(0)$ with $\sum_i w_i = 1$ (due to $v^T w = 1$). If the graph is balanced, based on part iii) of Lemma 2.3, P is a column stochastic matrix with a left eigenvector of $w = (1/n)1$. The group decision becomes equal to $\alpha = (1/n)1^T x_i(0)$ and average-consensus is asymptotically reached.

So far, we have presented a unified framework for analysis of convergence of consensus algorithms for directed networks with fixed topology in both discrete-time and continuous-time. A comparison between the two cases of continuous-time and discrete-time consensus are listed in Table 2.1.

2.4.4 Performance of consensus algorithms

The speed of reaching a consensus is the key in design of the network topology as well as analysis of performance of a consensus algorithm for a given network. Let us first focus on balanced directed networks that include undirected networks as a special case. This is primarily due to the fact that the collective dynamics of the network of agents applying a continuous- or discrete-time consensus algorithm in this case has an invariant quantity $\alpha = (\sum_i x_i)/n$. To demonstrate this in discrete-time, note that $1^T P = 1^T$ and

$$\alpha(k+1) = \frac{1}{n} 1^T x(k+1) = \frac{1}{n}(1^T P)x(k) = \alpha(k)$$

which implies α is invariant in at iteration k. Let us define the disagreement vector [149]

$$\delta = x - \alpha 1 \tag{2.50}$$

and note that $\sum_i \delta_i = 0$, or $1^T\delta = 0$. The consensus algorithms result in the following disagreement dynamics:

$$\begin{aligned} CT &: \dot{\delta}(t) = -L\delta(t) \\ DT &: \delta(k+1) = P\delta(k). \end{aligned} \tag{2.51}$$

Based on the following lemma, one can readily show that $\Phi(\delta) = \delta^T\delta$ is a valid Lyapunov function for the CT system that quantifies the collective disagreement in the network.

Theorem 2.4

(algebraic connectivity of digraphs) Let G be a balanced digraph (or undirected graph) with Laplacian L with a symmetric part $L_s = (L+L^T)/2$ and Perron matrix P with $P_s = (P+P^T)/2$. Then,

1. $\lambda_2 = min_{1^T\delta=0}(\delta^T L\delta/\delta^T\delta)$ *with* $\lambda_2 = \lambda_2(L_s)$, *i.e*

$$\delta^T L\delta \geq \lambda_2 k\delta||\delta||^2$$

for all disagreement vectors δ;

2. $\mu_2 = max 1^T\delta = 0(\delta^T P\delta/\delta^T\delta)$ *with* $\mu_2 = 1 - \varepsilon\lambda_2$, *i.e.,*

$$\delta^T P\delta \leq \mu_2||\delta||^2$$

for all disagreement vectors δ.

Proof: Since G is a balanced digraph, $1^TL = 0$ and $L1 = 0$. This implies that Ls is a valid Laplacian matrix because of $L_s1 = (L1 + L^T1)/2 = 0$. Similarly, P_s is a valid Perron matrix which is a nonnegative doubly stochastic matrix. Part i) follows from a special case of Courant Fisher theorem [218] for a symmetric matrix Ls due to

$$min_{1^T\delta=0}\frac{\delta^T L\delta}{\delta^T\delta} = min_{1^T\delta=0}\frac{\delta^T L_s\delta}{\delta^T\delta}\lambda_2(L_s).$$

To show part ii), note that for a disagreement vector δ satisfying $1^T\delta = 0$, we have

$$\begin{aligned} max_\delta\frac{\delta^T P\delta}{\delta^T\delta} &= max_\delta\frac{\delta^T P\delta}{\delta^T\delta} = max_\delta\frac{\delta^T P\delta - \varepsilon\delta^T L\delta}{\delta^T\delta} \\ &= 1 - \varepsilon min_\delta\frac{\delta^T L\delta}{\delta^T\delta} = 1 - \varepsilon\lambda_2(L_s) \\ &= \mu_2(P_s) \end{aligned} \tag{2.52}$$

Corollary 2.1

A continuous-time consensus is globally exponentially reached with a speed that is faster or equal to $\lambda_2 = \lambda_2(L_s)$with $L_s = (L+L^T)/2$ for a strongly connected and balanced directed network.

Proof: For CT consensus, we have

$$\Phi = -2\delta^T L\delta \leq -2\lambda_2\delta^T\delta = -2\lambda_2\Phi$$

Therefore, $\Phi(\delta) = ||\delta||^2$ exponentially vanishes with a speed that is at least $2\lambda_2$. Since $||\delta|| = \Phi^{1/2}$, the norm of the disagreement vector exponentially vanishes with a speed of at least λ_2.

Recently in [185], it was shown that quasi-random small-world networks have extremely large λ_2 values compared to regular networks with nearest neighbor communication, such as the one in Fig. 2(a). For example, for a network with n = 1000 nodes and uniform degree di = 10;8i, the algebraic connectivity of a small-world network can become more than 1500 times of the λ_2 of a regular network [185].

According to Theorem 2.4, 2.3 is the second largest eigenvalue of P_s—the symmetric part of the Perron matrix P. The speed of convergence of the iterative consensus algorithm is provided in the following result.

Corollary 2.2

A discrete-time consensus is globally exponentially reached with a speed that is faster or equal to $\mu_2 = 1 - \varepsilon\lambda_2(L)$ for a connected undirected network

Proof: Let $\Phi(k) = \delta(k)^T\delta(k)$ be a candidate Lyapunov function for the discrete-time disagreement dynamics of $\delta(k+1) = P\delta(k)$. For an undirected graph $P = P^T$ and all eigenvalues of P are real. Calculating $\Phi(k+1)$, one gets

$$\begin{aligned}\Phi(k+1) &= \delta(k+1)^T\delta(k+1) \\ &= ||P\delta(k)||^2 \leq \mu_2^2||\delta(k)||^2 \\ &= \mu_2^2\Phi_k\end{aligned} \tag{2.53}$$

with $/0 < \mu_2 < 1$, due to the fact that P is primitive. Clearly, $||\delta(k)||$ exponentially vanishes with a speed faster or equal to μ_2.

Remark 2.5 The proof of Corollary 2.2 for balanced digraphs is rather detailed and beyond the scope of this paper. ■

2.4.5 Alternative forms of consensus algorithms

In the context of formation control for a network of multiple vehicles, Fax and Murray [151] introduced the following version of a Laplacian-based system on a graph G with $0-1$ weights:

$$\dot{x}_i = \frac{1}{|N_i|}\sum_{j\in N_i}(x_j - x_i) \tag{2.54}$$

This is a special case of a consensus algorithm on a graph G^* with adjacency elements $a_{ij} = 1/|N_i| = 1/d_i$ for $j \in N_i$ and zero for j 62 Ni. According to this form, $d_i = \sum_{j\neq i} a_{ij} = 1$ for all i, which means the degree matrix of G^* is $D^* = I$ and its adjacency matrix is $A^* = D^{-1}A$, provided that all nodes have nonzero degrees (e.g., for connected graphs/digraphs). In graph theory literature, A^* is called normalized adjacency matrix. Let Q be the key matrix in the dynamics of (2.54), i.e., $\dot{x} = -Qx$. Then, an alternative for of graph Laplacian is

$$Q = I - D^{-1}A \tag{2.55}$$

This is identical to the standard Laplacian of the weighted graph G^* due to $L^* = D^* - A^* = I - D^{-1}A$. The convergence analysis of this algorithm is identical to the consensus algorithm presented earlier. The Perron matrix associated with Q is in the form $P = I\varepsilon L^*$ with $0 < \varepsilon < 1$. In explicit form, this gives the following iterative consensus algorithm:

$$x(k+1) = [(1-\varepsilon)I + \varepsilon D^{-1}Ax]x(k).$$

The aforementioned algorithm for $\varepsilon = 1$ takes a rather simple form $x(k+1) = D^{-1}Ax(k)$ that does not converge for digraphs such as cycles of length n. Therefore, this discretization with $\varepsilon = 1$ is invalid. Interestingly, the Markov process

$$\pi(k+1) = \pi(k)P \tag{2.56}$$

with transition probability matrix $P = D^{-1}A$ is known as the process of random walks on a graph [232] in graph theory and computer science literature with close connections to gossip-based consensus algorithms [215]. Keep in mind that, based on algorithm (2.54), if graph G is undirected (or balanced), the quantity

$$\alpha = \left(\sum_i d_i x_i\right) / \left(\sum_i d_i\right)$$

is invariant in time and a weighted-average consensus is asymptotically reached. The weighting $w_i = d_i/(\sum_i d_i)$ is specified by node degree $d_i = |N_i|$. Only for regular networks (i.e., $d_1 = d_2 = \cdots = d_n$), (2.54) solves an average consensus problem. This is a rather restrictive condition because most networks are not regular. Another popular algorithm proposed in [152] (also used in [153], [154]) is the following discrete-time consensus algorithm for undirected networks:

$$x_i(k+1) = \frac{1}{1+|N_i|}\left(x_i(k) + \sum_{j\in N_i} x_j(k)\right) \tag{2.57}$$

which can be expressed as

$$x(k+1) = (I+D)^{-1}(I+A)x(k).$$

Note that the stochastic Perron matrix $P = (I+D)^{-1(I+A)}$ is obtained from the following normalized Laplacian matrix with $\varepsilon = 1$:

$$Q_l = I - (I+D)^{-1(I+A)}. \tag{2.58}$$

This Laplacian is a modification of (2.55) and has the drawback that it does not solve average-consensus problem for general undirected networks. Now, we demonstrate that algorithm (2.57) is equivalent to (2.55) (and, thus, a special case of (1.16)). Let G be a graph with adjacency matrix A and no self-loops, i.e., $a_{ii} = 0, \forall i$. Then, the new adjacency matrix $A_l = I + A$ corresponds to a graph G_l that is obtained from G by adding n self-loops with unit weights $(a_{ii} = 1, \forall i)$. As a result, the corresponding degree matrix of G_l is $D_l = I + D$. Thus, the normalized Laplacian of G_l in (2.58) is $Q_l = I - D_l^{-1}A_l$. In other words, the algorithm proposed by Jadbabaie et al. [152] is identical to the algorithm of Fax and Murray [151] for a graph with n self-loops. In both cases $\varepsilon = 1$ is used to obtain the stochastic nonnegative matrix P.

Remark 2.6 ▮

Remark 5: A undirected cycle is not a counterexample for discretization of $\dot{x} = -Q_l x$ with $\varepsilon = 1$. Since the Perron matrix $P_l = (I+D)^{-1}(I+A)$ is symmetric and primitive.

Simulation example 2 In this example, we clarify that why $P = D^{-1}A$ can be an unstable matrix for a connected graph G, whereas $P_l = (I+D)^{-1}(I+A)$ remains stable for the same exact graph. for doing so, let us consider a bipartite graph G with $n = 2m$ nodes and adjacency matrix

$$\begin{bmatrix} 0_m & J_m \\ J_m & 0_m \end{bmatrix} \tag{2.59}$$

where 0_m and J_m denote the $m \times m$ matrices of zeros and ones, respectively. Note that $D = mI_n$ and $P = D^{-1}A = (1/m)A$. On the other hand, the Perron matrix of G with n self-loops is

$$P_l = (I_n + D)^{-1}(I_n + A) = \frac{1}{m+1}\begin{bmatrix} I_m & J_m \\ J_m & I_m \end{bmatrix}.$$

Let $v = 1_{2m}$ be the vector of ones with $2m$ elements and $w = col(1_m, -1_m)$. Both v and w are eigenvectors of P associated with eigenvalues 1 and -1, respectively, due to $Pv = v$ and $Pw = -w$. This proves that P is not a primitive matrix and the limit $lim_{k\rightarrow\infty}P^k$ does not exist (since P has two eigenvalues with modulus 1).

Table 2.2: Forms of Laplacians

Source	Laplacian L	Perron P	ε
[149]	$D-A$	$I-\varepsilon L$	$(0,\Delta^{-1})$
[151]	$I-D^{-1}A$	$D^{-1}A$	1
[152]	$I-(I+D)^{-1}(I+A)$	$(I+D)^{-1}(I+A)$	1

In contrast, P_l does not suffer from this problem because of the n nonzero diagonal elements. Again, v is an eigenvector of P_l associated with the eigenvalue 1, but $P_l w = -(m-1)/(m+1)w$ and due to $(m-11)/(m+1) < 1$ for all $m \geq 1, -1$ is no longer an eigenvalue of P_l.

Table 2.2 summarizes three types of graph Laplacians used in systems and control theory. The alternative forms of Laplacians in the second and third rows of Table 2 are both special cases of $L = D - A$ that are widely used as the standard definition of Laplacian in algebraic graph theory [10]. The algorithms in all three cases are in two forms

$$\dot{x} = -Lx \tag{2.60}$$

$$x(k+1) = Px(k) \tag{2.61}$$

Based on Simulation example 2, the choice of the discrete-time consensus algorithm is not arbitrary. Only the first and the third row of Table 2.2 guarantee stability of a discrete-time linear system for all possible connected networks. The second type requires a further analysis in order to verify whether P is stable, or not.

2.4.6 Weighted-average consensus

The choice of the Laplacian for the continuous-time consensus depends on the specific application of interest. In cases where reaching an average-consensus is desired, only $L = D - A$ can be used. In case of weighted-average consensus with a desired weighting vector $\gamma = (\gamma_i, \cdots, \gamma_n)$, the following algorithms can be used:

$$K\dot{x} = -Lx \tag{2.62}$$

with $K = diag(\gamma_1, \cdots, \gamma_n)$ and $L = D - A$. This is equivalent to a node with a variable rate of integration based on the protocol

$$\gamma_i \dot{x}_i = \sum_{j \in N_i} a_{ij}(x_j - x_i)$$

In the special case the weighting is proportional to the node degrees, or $K = D$, one obtains the second type of Laplacian in Table 2.2, or $\dot{x} = -D^{-1}Lx = -(I - D^{-1})x$.

2.4.7 Consensus under communication time-delays

Suppose that agent i receives a message sent by its neighbor j after a time-delay of τ. This is equivalent to a network with a uniform one-hop communication time-delay. The following consensus algorithm:

$$\dot{x}_i(t) = \sum_{j \in N_i} a_{ij}(x_j(t-\tau) - x_i(t-\tau)) \tag{2.63}$$

was proposed in [149] in order to reach an average-consensus for undirected graphs G.

Remark 2.7 Keep in mind that the algorithm

$$\dot{x}_i(t) = \sum_{j \in Ni} a_{ij}(x_j(t-\tau) - x_i(t)) \tag{2.64}$$

does not preserve the average $\bar{x} = (1/n)\sum_i x_i(t)$ in time for a general graph. The same is true when the graph in (2.63) is a general digraph. It turns out that for balanced digraphs with $0-1$ weights, $\bar{x}(t)$ is an invariant quantity along the solutions of (2.63). ▮

The collective dynamics of the network can be expressed as

$$\dot{x}_(t) = -Lx(t-\tau)$$

Rewriting this equation after taking Laplace transform of both sides, we get

$$x(s) = \frac{H(s)}{s}x(0) \tag{2.65}$$

with a proper MIMO transfer function $H(s) = (I_n + (1/s)exp(-s\tau)L)^{-1}$. One can use Nyquist criterion to verify the stability of $H(s)$. A similar criterion for stability of formations was introduced by Fax and Murray [151]. The following theorem provides an upper bound on the time delay such that the stability of the network dynamics is maintained in the presence of time-delays.

Theorem 2.5
(Olfati-Saber and Murray, 2004) The algorithm in (2.63) asymptotically solves the average consensus problem with a uniform one-hop time-delay for all initial states if and only if $0 \leq \tau < \pi/2\lambda_n$.

Proof: See the proof of Theorem 10 in [149]. Since $\lambda_n < 2\Delta$, a sufficient condition for convergence of the average-consensus algorithm in (2.63) is that $\tau < \pi/4\Delta$. In other words, there is a trade-off between having a large maximum degree and robustness to time delays. Networks with hubs (having very large degrees) that are commonly known as scale-free networks [233] are fragile to time-delays. In contrast, random graphs [234] and small-world networks [185], [226] are fairly robust to timedelays since they do not have hubs. In conclusion, construction of engineering networks with nodes that have high degrees is not a good idea for reaching a consensus.

2.5 Consensus in Switching Networks

In many scenarios, networked systems can possess a dynamic topology that is time-varying due to node and link failures/creations, packet-loss [178], [235], asynchronous consensus [179], state-dependence [202], formation reconfiguration [191], evolution [233], and flocking [158], [236]. Networked systems with a dynamic topology are commonly known as switching networks. A switching network can be modeled using a dynamic graph $G_{s(t)}$ parametrized with a switching signal $s(t) : \mathbb{R} \to J$ that takes its values in an index set $J = 1, \cdots, m$. The consensus mechanism on a network with a variable topology becomes a linear switching system

$$\dot{x} = -L(G_k)x; \tag{2.66}$$

with the topology index $k = s(t) \in J$ and a Laplacian of the type $D - A$. The set of topologies of the network is $\Gamma = G_1, G_2, \cdots, G_m$. First, we assume at any time instance, the network topology is a balanced digraph (or undirected graph) that is strongly connected. Let us denote $\lambda_2((L+L^T)/2)$ by $\lambda_2(G_k)$ for a topology dependent Laplacian $L = L(G_k)$. The following result provides the analysis of average-consensus for dynamic networks with a performance guarantee.

Theorem 2.6

(Olfati-Saber and Murray, 2004) Consider a network of agents applying the consensus algorithm in (2.66) with topologies $G_k \in \Gamma$. Suppose every graph in Γ is a balanced digraph that is strongly connected and let $\lambda_2^* = min_{k \in J} \lambda_2(G_k)$. Then, for any arbitrary switching signal, the agents asymptotically reach an average-consensus for all initial states with a speed faster or equal to λ_2^*. Moreover, $\Phi(\delta) = \delta^T \delta$ is a common Lyapunov function for the collective dynamics of the network.

Proof: See the proof of Theorem 9 in [149].

Note that Γ is a finite set with at most $n(n-1)$ elements and this allows the definition of λ_2^*. Moreover, the use of normal Laplacians does not render the average $\bar{x} = (1/n)\sum_i x_i$ invariant in time, unless all graphs in Γ are d-regular (all of their nodes have degree d). This is hardly the case for various applications

The following result on consensus for switching networks does not require the necessity for connectivity in all time instances and is due to Jadbabaie et al. [152]. This weaker form of network connectivity is crucial in analysis of asynchronous consensus with performance guarantees (which is currently an open problem). We need to rephrase the next result for the purpose of compatibility with the notation used in this paper.

Consider the following discrete-time consensus algorithm:

$$x_{k+1} = P_{sk} x_k; t = 0, 1, 2, \ldots \tag{2.67}$$

with $s_k \in J$. Let$P = P_1, \ldots, P_m$ denote the set of Perron matrices associated with a finite set of undirected graphs Γ with n self-loops. We say a switching network with the set of topologies Γ is periodically connected with a period $N > 1$ if the unions of all graphs over a sequence of intervals $[j, jN)$ for $j = 0, 1, 2, \ldots$ are connected graphs, i.e., $\mathcal{G}_j = \cup_{k=j}^{N-1}$ is connected for $j = 0, 1, 2, \ldots$.

Theorem 2.7

(Jadbabaie, Lin and Morse, 2003) Consider the system in (2.67) with $P_{s_k} \in \mathcal{P}$ for $j = 0, 1, 2, \ldots$. Assume the switching network is periodically connected. Then, $\lim_{k \to \infty} x_k = \alpha 1$, or an alignment is asymptotically reached.

Proof: See the proof of Theorem 2.3 in [152].

The solution of (2.67) can be explicitly expressed as

$$x_t = \left(\prod_{k=0}^{t} P_{s_k} \right) x_0 = \Lambda_t x_0$$

with $\Lambda_t = Ps_t \ldots P_{s_2} P_{s_1}$. the convergence of the consensus algorithm in (2.67) depends on whether the infinite product of nonnegative stochastic matrices $Ps_t \ldots P_{s_2} P_{s_1}$ has a limit. The problem of convergence of infinite product of stochastic matrices has a long history and has been studied by several mathematicians, including Wolfowitz [237]. The proof in [152] relies on Wolfowitzs lemma:

Lemma 2.5

(Wolfowitz, 1963) Let $\mathcal{P} = P_1, P_2, \ldots, P_m$ be a finite set of primitive stochastic matrices such that for any sequence of matrices $Ps_1, Ps_2, \ldots, Ps_k \in \mathcal{P}$ with $k \geq 1$, the product $Ps_k \ldots P_{s_2} P_{s_1}$ is a primitive matrix. Then, there exists a row vector w such that

$$\lim_{k \to \infty} P_{s_k} \ldots P_{s_2} P_{s_1} = 1w. \tag{2.68}$$

According to Wolfowitz's lemma, we get $\lim_{k\to\infty} x_k = 1(wx_0) = \alpha 1$ with $\alpha = wx_0$. The vector w depends on the switching sequence and cannot be determined *a priori*.

Thus, an alignment is asymptotically reached and the group decision is an undetermined quantity in the convex hull of all initial states.

Remark 2.8 Since normal Perron matrices in the form $(I+D)^{-1}(I+A)$ are employed in [152], the agents (in general) do not reach an average-consensus. The use of Perron matrices in the form $I-\varepsilon L$ with $0<\varepsilon<1/(1+max_{k\in J}\Delta(G_k))$ resolves this problem. ▮

Recently, an extension of Theorem 6 with connectivity of the union of graphs over an infinite interval has been introduced by Moreau [153] (also, an extension is presented in [154] for weighted graphs). Here, we rephrase a theorem due to Moreau and present it based on notation. First, let us define a less restrictive notion of connectivity of switching networks compared to periodic connectivity. Let Γ be a finite set of undirected graphs with n self-loops. We say a switching networks with topologies in Γ is ultimately connected if there exists an initial time k0 such that over the infinite interval [1/2–0]; 1+ the graph $\mathcal{G} = \cup_{k=k_0}^{\infty} G_{s_k}$ with $s_k \in J$ is connected.

Theorem 2.8

(Moreau, 2005) Consider an ultimately connected switching network with undirected topologies in Γ and dynamics (2.67). Assume $Ps_k \in \mathcal{P}$, where $\mathcal{P}$ is the set of normal Perron matrices associated with Γ. Then, a consensus is globally asymptotically reached.

Proof: See the proof of Proposition 2 in [153]. Similarly, the algorithm analyzed in Proposition 2 of [153] does not solve the f-consensus problem. This can be resolved by using the first form of Perron matrices in Table 2.2. The proof in [153] uses a nonquadratic Lyapunov function and no performance measures for reaching a consensus are presented.

2.6 Cooperation in Networked Control Systems

This section provides a system-theoretic framework for addressing the problem of cooperative control of networked multivehicle systems using distributed controllers. On one hand, a multivehicle system represents a collection of decision-making agents that each have limited knowledge of both the environment and the state of the other agents. On the other hand, the vehicles can influence their own state and interact with their environment according to their dynamics, which

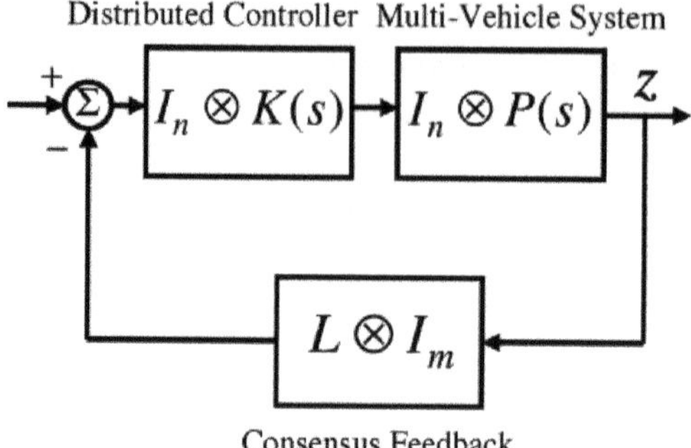

Figure 2.4: The block diagram of cooperative and distributed formation control of networked multivehicle systems. The Kronecker product $\otimes$ is defined in (2.69)

determines their behavior. The design goal is to execute tasks cooperatively, exercising both the decision-making and control capabilities of the vehicles. In real-life networked multivehicle systems, there are a number of limitations, including limited sensing capabilities of the vehicles, network bandwidth limitations, as well as interruptions in communications due to packet-loss [178], [235] and physical disruptions to the communication devices of the vehicle. The system framework we analyze is presented in a schematic form in Fig. 2.4. The Kronecker product $\otimes$ between two matrices $P = [p_{ij}]$ and $Q = [q_{ij}]$ is defined as

$$P \otimes Q = [p_{ij}Q] \tag{2.69}$$

This is a block matrix with the ijth block of $p_{ij}Q$. The dynamics of each vehicle, represented by $P(s)$, are decoupled from the dynamics of other vehicles in the network, thus, the system transfer function $I_n \otimes P(s)$. The output of $P(s)$ represents observable elements of the state of each vehicle. Similarly, the controller of each vehicle, represented by $K(s)$, is decoupled from the controller of others, thus, the controller transfer function $I_n \otimes K(s)$. The coupling occurs through cooperation via the consensus feedback. Since all vehicles apply the same controller, they form a cooperative team of vehicles with consensus feedback gain matrix $L \otimes I_m$. This cooperation requires sharing of information among vehicles, either through inter-agent sensing, or explicit communication of information.

2.6.1 Collective dynamics of multivehicle formation

Let us consider a group of n vehicles, whose (identical) linear dynamics are denoted by

$$\dot{x}_i = Ax_i + Bu_i \tag{2.70}$$

where $x_i \in \mathbb{R}^m, u_i \in \mathbb{R}^p$ are the vehicle states and controls, and $i \in V = 1, \ldots, n$ is the index for the vehicles in the group. Each vehicle receives the following measurements:

$$y_i = C_1 x_i \tag{2.71}$$

$$z_{ij} = C_2(x_i - x_j), j \in N_i \tag{2.72}$$

Thus, $y_i \in \mathbb{R}^k$ represents internal state measurements, and $z_{ij} \in \mathbb{R}^l$ represents external state measurements relative to other vehicles. We assume that $N_i \neq \oslash$, meaning that each vehicle can sense at least one other vehicle. Note that a single vehicle cannot drive all the z_{ij} terms to zero simultaneously; the errors must be fused into a single signal error measurement

$$z_i = \frac{1}{|N_i|} \sum_{j \in N_i} z_{ij} \tag{2.73}$$

where $|N_i|$ is the cardinality of the set N_i. We also define a distributed controller K which maps y_i, z_i to u_i and has internal states $v_i \in \mathbb{R}^s$, represented in state-space form by

$$\begin{aligned} \dot{v}_i &= F v_i + G_1 y_i + G_2 z_i \\ u_i &= H v_i + D_1 y_i + D_2 z_i. \end{aligned} \tag{2.74}$$

Now, we consider the collective system of all n vehicles. For dimensional compatibility, we use the Kronecker product to assemble the matrices governing the formation behavior. The collective dynamics of n vehicles can be represented as follows:

$$\begin{pmatrix} \dot{x} \\ \dot{v} \end{pmatrix} = \begin{pmatrix} M_{11} & M_{12} \\ M_{21} & M_{22} \end{pmatrix} \begin{pmatrix} x \\ v \end{pmatrix}. \tag{2.75}$$

where the M_{ij}'s are block matrices defined as a function of the normalized graph Laplacian L (i.e., the second type in Table 2) and other matrices as follows:

$$\begin{aligned} M_{11} &= I_n \otimes (A + BD_1C_1) + (I_n \otimes BD_2C_2)(L \otimes I_m) \\ M_{12} &= I_n \otimes BH \\ M_{21} &= I_n \otimes G_1C_1 + (I_n \otimes G_2C_2)(L \otimes I_m), \\ M_{22} &= I_n \otimes F. \end{aligned} \tag{2.76}$$

2.6.2 Stability of relative dynamics

The main stability result on relative-position-based formations of networked vehicles is due to Fax and Murray [151] and can be stated as follows:

Theorem 2.9

(Fax and Murray, 2004) A local controller K stabilizes the formation dynamics in (2.75) if and only if it stabilizes all the n systems

$$\begin{aligned} \dot{x}_i &= Ax_i + Bu_i \\ y_i &= C_1 x_i \\ z_i &= \lambda_i C_2 x_i \end{aligned} \tag{2.77}$$

where $\lambda_{ii=1}^{n}$ is the set of eigenvalues of the normalized graph Laplacian L. Theorem 2.9 reveals that a formation of identical vehicles can be analyzed for stability by analyzing the stability of a single vehicle with the same dynamics, modified by only a scalar, representing the interconnection, that takes values according to the eigenvalues of the interconnection matrix.

The zero eigenvalue of L can be interpreted as the un-observability of absolute motion of the formation in the measurements z_i. A prudent design strategy is to close an inner loop around *yi* such that the internal vehicle dynamics are stable, and then to close an outer loop around z_i which achieves desired formation performance. For the remainder of this section, we concern ourselves solely with the outer loop. Hence, we assume from now on that C_1 is empty and that A has no eigenvalues in the open right half plane. We do not wish to exclude eigenvalues along the $j\omega$ axis because they are characteristic of vehicle systems, representing the directions in which motion is possible. The controller K is also presumed to be stable. If K stabilizes the system in (2.77) for all λ_i other than the zero eigenvalue, we say that it stabilizes the relative dynamics of a formation.

Let us refer to the system from u_i to y_i as P, its transfer function as $P(s)$, and that of the controller from y_i to ui as $K(s)$. For single-input single-output (SISO) systems, we can state a second version of Theorem 2.9 which is useful for stability and robustness analysis.

Theorem 2.10

(Fax and Murray, 2004) Suppose P is a SISO system. Then, K stabilizes the relative dynamics of a formation if and only if the net encirclement of $-1/\lambda_i$ *by the Nyquist plot of* $-K(s)P(s)$ *is zero for all nonzero* λ_i.

2.7 Simulation Studies

In this section, we present the simulation results for three applications of consensus problems in networked systems.

2.7.1 Consensus in complex networks

In this experiment, we demonstrate the speed of convergence of consensus algorithm (2.9) for three different networks with n = 100 nodes in Fig. 2.5. The initial

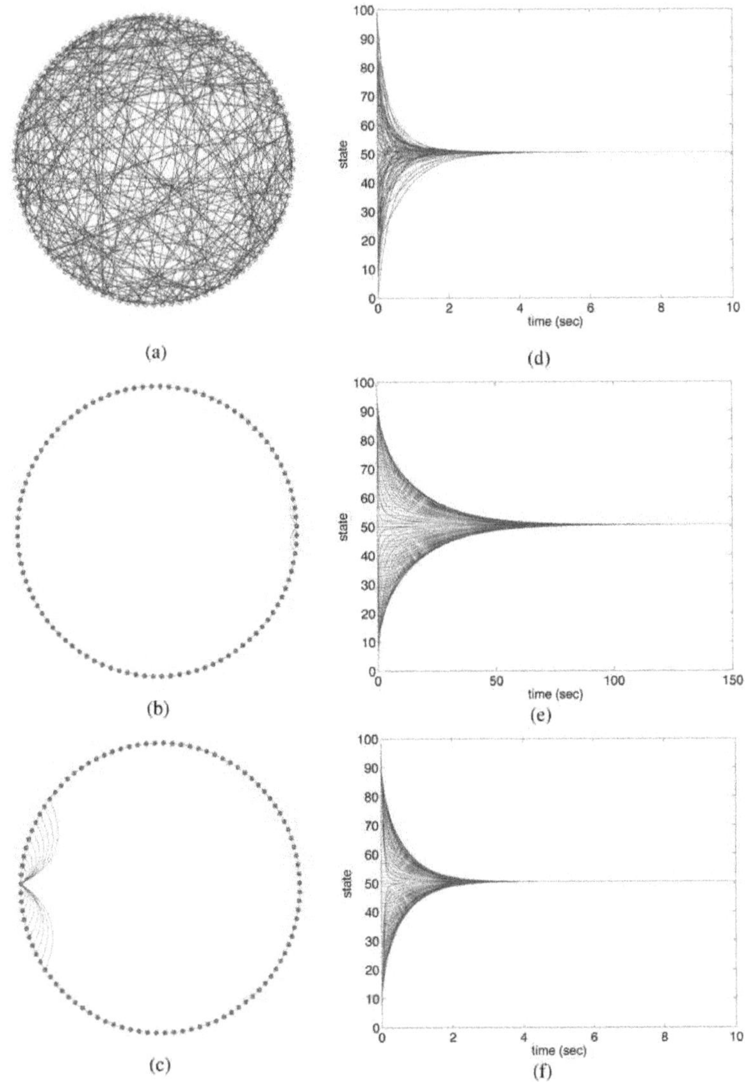

Figure 2.5: (a) A small-world with 300 links, (b) a regular lattice with interconnections to $k = 3$ nearest neighbors and 300 links, (c) a regular lattice with interconnections to $k = 10$ nearest neighbors and 1000 links; (d), (e), (f) the state evolution corresponding to networks in (a), (b), and (c), respectively. [Note: Only the links of a single node are depicted in parts (b) and (c)]

state is set to $x_i(0) = i for i = 1, \ldots, 100$. In Fig. 2.5(a) and (c), the network has 300 links and on average each node communicates with

$$\bar{d} = 6 \tag{2.78}$$

neighbors. Apparently, the group with a small-world network topology reaches an average-consensus more than $\lambda_2(G_a)/\lambda_2(G_c) \approx 22$ times faster. To create a regular lattice with comparable algebraic connectivity, every node has to communicate with 20 other nodes on average in order to gain an algebraic connectivity $\lambda_2(G_e)/\lambda_2(G_a) \approx 1.2$ that is close to that of the small world network. Of course, the regular network in Fig. 2.5(e) has 3.33 times as many links as the small-world network. For further information on small-world networks, we refer the reader to [185], [226], and [239].

2.7.2 Multivehicle formation control

Consider a system of the form $P(s) = e^{-sT}/s^2$, modeling a second-order system with time-delay and suppose this system has been stabilized with a proportional derivative (PD) controller. Figure 2.6 shows a formation graph and the Nyquist plot of $K(s)P(s)$ with the location of Laplacian eigenvalues. The "o" locations correspond to the eigenvalues of the graph defined by the solid arcs in Fig. 2.6, and the $'\times'$ locations are for eigenvalues of the graph when the dashed arc is included as well. This example clearly shows the effect the formation has on stability margins. The standard Nyquist plot reveals a system with reasonable stability margins V about 8dB and 45. When one accounts for the effects of the formation, however, one sees that for the "o" formation, the stability margins are substantially degraded, and for the "$\times$" formation, the system is in fact unstable. Interestingly, the formation is rendered unstable when additional information (its position relative to vehicle 6) is used by vehicle 1. This is primarily due to the fact that changing the topology of a network directly effects the location of eigenvalues of the Laplacian matrix. This example clarifies that the stability analysis of formations of networked vehicles with directed switching topology in presence of time-delays is by no means trivial.

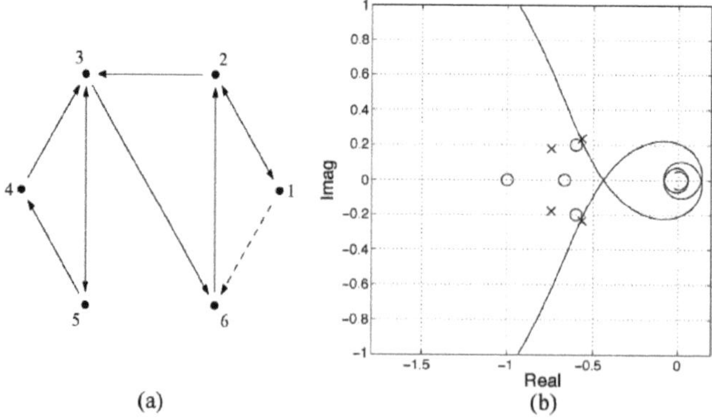

Figure 2.6: (a) Interconnection graph of a multi-vehicle formation and (b) the Nyquist plot

2.8 Notes

A theoretical framework was provided for analysis of consensus algorithms for networked multi-agent systems with fixed or dynamic topology and directed information flow. The connections between consensus problems and several applications were discussed, this including synchronization of coupled oscillators, flocking, formation control, fast consensus in small-world networks, Markov processes and gossip-based algorithms, load balancing in networks, rendezvous in space, distributed sensor fusion in sensor networks, and belief propagation. The role of B cooperation in distributed coordination of networked autonomous systems was clarified and the effects of lack of cooperation was demonstrated with an example. It was demonstrated that notions such as graph Laplacians, nonnegative stochastic matrices, and algebraic connectivity of graphs and digraphs play an instrumental role in analysis of consensus algorithms. We proved that algorithms introduced in [151], [152] are identical for graphs with n self-loops and are both special cases of the consensus algorithm of [11]. The notion of Perron matrices was introduced as the discrete-time counterpart of graph Laplacians in consensus protocols. A number of fundamental spectral properties of Perron matrices were proved. This led to a unified framework for expression and analysis of consensus algorithms in both continuous-time and discrete-time. Simulation results for reaching a consensus in small-worlds versus lattice-type nearest-neighbor graphs and cooperative control of multivehicle formations were presented.

Chapter 3

Distributed Intelligence in Power Systems

3.1 Introduction to MAS Technology

Multiagent system (MAS) is perhaps one of the most exciting and the fastest growing domains in agent-oriented technology which deals with the modeling of autonomous decision-making entities. This paper presents an application of MAS for distributed energy resource (DER) management in a microgrid. Microgrids can be defined as low voltage distributed power networks comprising various distributed generators (DG), storage and controllable loads, which can be operated interconnectedly or as islands from the main power grid. By representing each element in the microgrid as an autonomous intelligent agent, multi agent modeling of a microgrid is designed and implemented. JADE framework is proposed for the modeling, and the reliability of the microgrid is confirmed with Power World Simulator. Further, the FIPA contract net coordination between the agents is demonstrated through software simulation. As a result, this paper provides a microgrid modeling which has the communication and coordination structure necessary in order to create a scalable system. The optimized Microgrid management and operations can be developed on it in future.

The power system grid is highly nonlinear with fast varying dynamics [75]. The traditional electrical grid is a multi-manifold network with several components, like generation units, transmission lines, transformers and active loads. The frequent blackouts occur due to various economical and physical constraints, including unbalanced demand-generation conditions, large power drops in distributed networks, and extreme swings in power flow dispatch. In turn, power systems networks are pushed to the maximum operation levels, threatening the grid reliability. Distributed energy resources (DERs) or Microgrids (MG) represent a reliable solution to many issues in the power system networks, while at the same time introducing other operational and technical challenges [79].

Microgrids are constructed to supply the local loads in remote areas, which decreases the power drop during the power transmission. Moreover, microgrids reduce the need to have new distribution lines and new power generation units, and keep the carbon emissions at minimum levels [75]–[76]. Though, the microgrid has to optimize its operation, to improve the quality of the output voltage and frequency delivery, in addition to the overall efficiency [77]. A microgrid can work in both tied mode and standalone modes. Transitions between these two modes create severe frequency and voltage control degradation [81]. These challenges were tackled by researchers throughout the last decade. Controlling a large number of distributed generations is even more challenging due to the conflict among the operation objectives and the communication issues [78].

Electrical switches are used to alternate between the different modes of operation of the micrgrids [80]. During the islanded mode, the microgrid delivers power and regulates the output voltage. The microgrid's controller should be able to regulate the changes due to the disturbances in the active load demand [82]. A control structure for an autonomous microgrid with a local load is developed in [87]. A servomechanism regulator for an autonomous microgrid is introduced in [88]. This approach used optimal control-based design to guarantee the robustness of the proposed control system. Multi-level control structure (primary, secondary, and tertiary control levels) is proposed for microgrids in [83]. A pseudo-decentralized control architecture is used to optimize the wireless communication network with the help of a global supervisory controller and local regulators in [84]. A networked control scheme based on system of systems is developed for microgrids, where a distributed generated system is treated as system of systems and an output feedback control scheme is considered in [85]. A two-level control scheme has been used for islanded MG in [86].

Herein, adaptive critics-based controller is proposed to control an autonomous microgrid. Approximate Dynamic Programming (ADP) will be used to solve the optimal control problem of the microgrid. Approximate Dynamic Programming (ADP) is used to solve the Dynamic Programming (DP) problems and it is classified into four types; Heuristic DP (HDP), Dual Heuristic DP (DHP), Action-Dependent HDP (ADHDP), and Action-Dependent Dual HDP (ADDHP) [94]. A Reinforcement Learning (RL) allows the development of online algorithms to solve the optimal control problems for dynamic systems [94], [92]. A large number of problems in Artificial Intelligence can be mapped to decision processes. RL involves two approaches, Value Iteration (VI) and Policy Iteration (PI) [92], [93].

In the sequel, a novel approach is proposed to control an autonomous microgrid using Reinforcement Learning techniques. The controller is implemented using partial knowledge about the microgrid's dynamics. Adaptive critics are used to implement the Value Iteration solution. Actor-Critic Neural Networks (NN) are used to approximate the optimal policies and the value functions respectively.

3.1.1 Autonomous microgrid system

The autonomous or islanded mode of MG can be driven by the network's faults/failures in the utility grid, scheduled maintenance, and the economical or management constraints [93]. In this paper, the dynamic model of an autonomous microgrid in [87, 88] is considered in order to carry out the analysis. The schematic single-line diagram of a coupled MG model is shown in Fig. 3.1. A point of common coupling (PCC) is used to isolate the MG from main grid and vice versa [80]. The system consists of inverter-based DG units, feeding an active load (RLC mesh structure), through series filter and transformer. The DC voltage source works as the generating unit and R_t and L_t are the series filter/ transformer equivalent components. The model parameters are given in Table 1. During the islanded operation, the main duty of the microgrid is to deliver quality power by regulating any disturbances caused by the continuous change in the active load demand. The microgrid and its control structure should be able to maintain the load voltage level at the desired set point.

3.1.2 A state-space model

Let the system in Fig. 3.1 be balanced, then the governing dynamical equations of the MG are given by

$$\begin{aligned} I_{t,abc} &= C\frac{dV_{abc}}{dt} + \frac{1}{R}V_{abc} + I_{L,abc} \\ V_{t,abc} &= V_{abc} + L_t\frac{dI_{t,abc}}{dt} + R_t I_{t,abc} \, , \\ V_{abc} &= L\frac{dI_{L,abc}}{dt} + R_l I_{L,abc} \end{aligned} \tag{3.1}$$

where these dynamical equations are in the abc-frame, and $V_{t,abc}$, $I_{t,abc}$, $I_{L,abc}$, and V_{abc} are three phase vectors.

The system is under balanced situations, each of the three-phase quantities x_{abc} can be transformed to a fixed $\alpha\beta$-reference frame using the subsequent transformation

$$x_{\alpha\beta} = x_a e^{j0} + x_b e^{j\frac{2\pi}{3}} + x_c e^{j\frac{4\pi}{3}}, \tag{3.2}$$

where $x_{\alpha\beta} = x_\alpha + jx_\beta$.

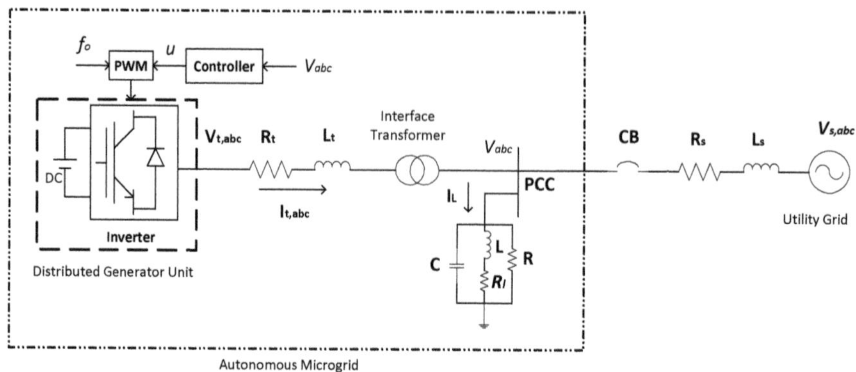

Figure 3.1: Single-line diagram of a coupled microgrid electrical model

Table 3.1: System parameters

Quantity	Value
R_t	1.5 m Ω
L_t	300 μ H
V_{dc}	1500 V
$PWM\ Carrier\ Frequency$	1980 Hz
Load Parameters	
R	76 Ω
L	111.9 mH
C	62.855 μ F
R_l	0.3515 Ω
Grid Parameters	
R_s	1 Ω
L_s	10 μ H
Nominal Frequency f_o	60 Hz
Nominal Voltage (rms)	13.8 kV
Interface Transformer Parameters	
Type	Wye/Delta
Rating	2.5 MVA
Voltage Ratio (n)	0.6/13.8 kV

Using the $\alpha\beta$-frame, the dynamical model can be given by

$$\begin{aligned}
\frac{dI_{t,\alpha\beta}}{dt} &= -\frac{R_t}{L_t}I_{t,\alpha\beta} - \frac{V_{\alpha\beta}}{L_t} + \frac{V_{t,\alpha\beta}}{L_t} \\
\frac{dV_{\alpha\beta}}{dt} &= \frac{1}{C}I_{t,\alpha\beta} - \frac{1}{RC}V_{\alpha\beta} - \frac{1}{C}I_{L,\alpha\beta} \, , \\
\frac{dI_{L,\alpha\beta}}{dt} &= \frac{1}{L}V_{\alpha\beta} - \frac{R_l}{L}I_{L,\alpha\beta}
\end{aligned} \tag{3.3}$$

This can be transformed into the dq-reference frame using the subsequent transformation

$$x_{\alpha\beta} = x_{dq}e^{j\theta} = (x_d + jx_q e^{j\theta}), \tag{3.4}$$

where $\theta = arctan(\frac{x_\beta^{ref}}{x_\alpha^{ref}})$ is the phase-angle of an arbitrary reference vector.

$V_{\alpha\beta}$ is taken as a reference vector such that $V_q = 0$. In the isolated mode, the system frequency is regulated in an open-loop structure such that, the Voltage Source Converter (VSC) generates three-phase voltages at frequency ω_0, by employing internal oscillator of constant frequency of $\omega_0 = 2\pi f_0$. Moreover, the steady state voltage and current signals are evaluated at frequency ω_0 if the load is passive. Therefore, the dq state variables are given by

$$\begin{aligned}
\frac{dI_{td}}{dt} &= -\frac{R_t}{L_t}I_{td} + \omega_0 I_{tq} - \frac{1}{L_t}V_d + \frac{1}{L_t}V_{td} \\
\frac{dI_{tq}}{dt} &= \omega_0 I_{td} - \frac{R_l}{L}I_{tq} - 2\omega_0 I_{Ld} + (\frac{R_l C\omega_0}{L} - \frac{\omega_0}{R})V_d \\
\frac{dI_{Ld}}{dt} &= \omega_0 I_{tq} - \frac{R_l}{L}I_{Ld} + (\frac{1}{L} - \omega_0^2 C)V_d \\
\frac{dV_d}{dt} &= \frac{1}{C}I_{td} - \frac{1}{C}I_{Ld} - \frac{1}{RC}V_d
\end{aligned},$$

where

$$V_{tq} = L_t[2\omega_0 I_{td} + (\frac{R_t}{L_t} - \frac{R_l}{L})I_{tq} - 2\omega_0 I_{Ld} + (\frac{R_l\omega_0 C}{L} - \frac{\omega_0}{R})V_d \tag{3.5}$$

Thus, the foregoing autonomous MG system can be mathematically modeled by a standard state-space representation such that

$$\dot{x}(t) = A_c x(t) + B_c u(t),\, y(t) = C_c x(t),\, u(t) = v_{td}. \tag{3.6}$$

where $x^T = \begin{bmatrix} I_{td}^T & I_{tq}^T & I_{Ld}^T & V_d^T \end{bmatrix}$ is the state vector,

$$A_c = \begin{bmatrix} -\frac{R_t}{L_t} & \omega_0 & 0 & -\frac{1}{L_t} \\ \omega_0 & -\frac{R_l}{L} & -2\omega_0 & \frac{R_l C\omega_0}{L} - \frac{\omega_0}{R} \\ 0 & \omega_0 & -\frac{R_l}{L} & \frac{1}{L} - \omega_0^2 C \\ \frac{1}{C} & 0 & -\frac{1}{C} & -\frac{1}{RC} \end{bmatrix},\, B_c = \begin{bmatrix} \frac{1}{L_t} \\ 0 \\ 0 \\ 0 \end{bmatrix},\, C_c = \begin{bmatrix} 0 \\ 0 \\ 0 \\ 1 \end{bmatrix}.$$

In the following setup, the system (3.6) will be discretized.

3.1.3 Heuristic dynamic programming

In the sequel, *value iteration algorithm* based on Heuristic Dynamic Programming (HDP) is proposed, the simplest but powerful form to minimize a performance index. The microgrid applies a control policy to its environment and this policy is assessed and, hence, rewarded or punished based on the associated utility or the cost function. Consequently, the microgrid will decide a better policy based on the assessed cost function. This is known as action-based learning [90, 91], [95].

Heuristic Dynamic Programming (HDP) uses value function approximation to solve the Dynamic Programming problems. This involves solving the respective temporal difference structures. Thus, in order to propose the Value Iteration algorithm, Bellman equation is introduced for the autonomous microgrid.

3.1.4 Discrete-time Bellman equation

Herein, the analysis of the optimal control problem is based on Bellman equation.

The discrete-time system model of (3.6) is given by

$$x_{k+1} = Ax_k + Bu_k. \tag{3.7}$$

where k is the time-step, $x_k \in \mathbb{R}^n$ are the states, and $u_k \in \mathbb{R}^m$.

Assume that the model (3.7), is stabilizable into some set $\Omega \in \mathbb{R}^n$.

Definition 3.1 *Stabilizable System: A system is said to be stabilizable on a set $\Omega \in \mathbb{R}^n$, if there exists a policy $u \in \mathbb{R}^m$ such that, the closed loop system is asymptotically stable on Ω.*

Let $h(\cdot) : \mathbb{R}^n \rightarrow \mathbb{R}^m$ be a mapping function that relates the control policy to the states x_k such that $u_k = h(x_k)$. The goal is to select the control policy $u(x_k)$ which minimizes the following performance index

$$V(x_k) = \sum_{i=k}^{\infty} \frac{1}{2}(x_k^T Q x_k + u_k^T R u_k), \tag{3.8}$$

where $Q = Q^T > 0 \in \mathbb{R}^{n\times n}$ and $R = R^T > 0 \in \mathbb{R}^{m\times m}$.

Definition 3.2 *Admissible Control Policy: A control law $u_k = h(x_k)$ is considered to be admissible if it stabilizes the system (3.7) and has finite value $V(x_k)$ [99].*

The summation form (3.8), can be written using the following difference form

$$V(x_k) \quad = \quad \frac{1}{2}(x_k^T Q x_k + u_k^T R u_k) + V(x_{k+1}), \tag{3.9}$$

Therefore, using the current control policy u_k, the cost function V can be evaluated by solving the above difference equation 3.9. This equation is known as Bellman equation. Applying Bellman optimality principles [100], yields the optimal value function and the optimal policy such that

$$V^*(x_k) = \min_{u_k}[\frac{1}{2}(x_k^T Q x_k + u_k^T R u_k) + V^*(x_{k+1})], \tag{3.10}$$

$$u_k^* = -R^{-1}B^T\nabla V^*(x_{k+1}). \tag{3.11}$$

This leads to Bellman optimality equation such that

$$V^*(x_k) = \frac{1}{2}(x_k^T Q x_k + u_k^{*T} R u_k^*) + V^*(x_{k+1}). \tag{3.12}$$

Remark 3.1 *Solving Bellman optimality equation (3.12), would result in a solution for the underlying optimal control problem. Moreover, in order to solve for $V(x_k)$, the policy u_{k+1} is first evaluated, which is a dynamic programming scheme.* ∎

In the sequel, value iteration algorithm is proposed in order to solve for the optimal policy u_k^* and the value function $V(x_k)$. This technique does not require initial stabilizing policy.

3.1.5 Value iteration algorithm

A value iteration algorithm is developed to control the autonomous microgrid system (3.7). This algorithm solves Bellman optimality equation (3.12) and finds the optimal policy (3.11).

Algorithm 1 (Value Iteration Algorithm for The Autonomous Microgrid)

1. **Initialization:** *Initial u_k^o and $V^o(x_k)$*

2. **Value Update:** *Solve for $V^{\ell+1}(x_k)$*

$$V^{\ell+1}(x_k) = \frac{1}{2}(x_k^T Q x_k + u_k^{\ell T} R u_k^{\ell}) + V^{\ell}(x_{k+1}) \tag{3.13}$$

   where ℓ is the iteration index.

3. **Policy Update:** *Calculate the policy u_k^{l+1}*

$$u_k^{\ell+1} = -R^{-1}B^T \bigtriangledown V(x_{k+1})^{\ell+1} \tag{3.14}$$

   where $\bigtriangledown V(x_{k+1}) = \dfrac{\partial V(x_{k+1})}{\partial x_{k+1}}$.

4. **Convergence:** *The above steps are repeated until $\|V(x_k)^{\ell+1} - V(x_k)^{\ell}\|$ converges.*

Remark 3.2 *The value iteration algorithm depends on the solution of the recursive equation (3.12), which is easy to compute and it is named partial backup in RL. Value Iteration successfully mixes one sweep of value evaluation and one sweep of policy improvement.* ∎

3.1.6 Adaptive critics implementation

Adaptive Critics are used to implement the Value Iteration *Algorithm 1*. This is done using two feed forward and feedback approximation structures. Figure 3.2 shows the adaptive critics structure [96]. The actor and critic neural networks are used to approximate the control action and the value function, respectively. The actor applies a control value (action) to the surrounding environment and the quality of the taken action is assessed by the critic structure [94].

The actor's mathematical expression can be viewed as a mapping, which has the state x_{k+1} and the improved value function $V^l(x_{k+1})$ as inputs. The dynamics of the system is a part of the assessed environment. During the learning process, the actor does not need the desired control signals to be known and available. RL techniques are successful with complex systems with partially unknown dynamics. The actor-critic networks are tuned consecutively, using the data observed along the trajectory of system. The process is repeated until both actor and critic networks weights converge [97].

The actor network provides the control policy to minimize the value function. For each iteration, the output of actor network is a series of control signals in feedforward mode and in feedback mode it adjusts the internal network weights. Critic network establishes a relationship between the control signals and value function. After learning the relationship, the critic network provides a proper feedback to the actor, in order to generate the desired control policy. The operation of critic is two-fold, in the feedforward mode, it predicts the value function for an initial set of control signals and in the feedback mode, it assists the actor network to generate a control policy which minimizes the cost function. The value iteration algorithm starts with assuming random initial control signals (not necessarily admissible). The training process is divided into critic network training and actor network training [98]. The performance function (3.8) is approximated by a critic NN and the control law (3.13) is approximated by an actor

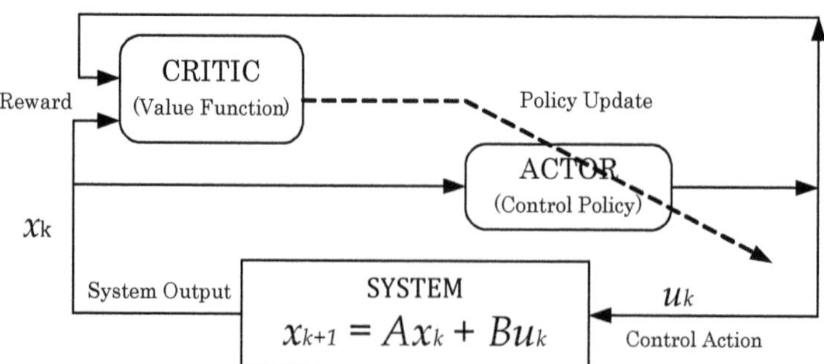

Figure 3.2: Actor-critic dynamic environment

NN such that

$$\hat{V}_k(W_c) = \frac{1}{2}x_k^T W_c^T x_k, \tag{3.15}$$

where $W_c \in \mathbb{R}^{n\times n}$ denote the critic weights.

$$\hat{u}_k(W_a) = W_a^T x_k, \tag{3.16}$$

where $W_a \in \mathbb{R}^{n\times m}$ denote the actor weights.
The approximation error of the policy is given by

$$\zeta_{u_k}^{V(x_k)} = \hat{u}_k(W_a) - u_k, \tag{3.17}$$

Thus, the control policy in (3.10) is given by

$$u_k = -R^{-1}B^T \nabla\hat{V}(x_{k+1}). \tag{3.18}$$

The desired policy in terms of the critic approximation is given by

$$u_k = -R^{-1}B^T W_c^T x_k. \tag{3.19}$$

The squared approximation error is given by $\frac{1}{2}(\zeta_{u_k}^{V(x_k)})^T \zeta_{u_k}^{V(x_k)}$, the variations in the actor weights are given by the gradient descent such that

$$W_a^{(l+1)T} = W_a^{lT} - \lambda_a[(W_a^{lT} x_k - u_k^l)(x_k)^T], \tag{3.20}$$

where $0 < \lambda_a < 1$ is the actor learning rate.

Let $\psi_{x_k}^{V(x_k)}$ be the target value of critic network and the value function is updated using (3.13). Therefore,

$$\psi_{x_k}^{V(x_k)} = \frac{1}{2}[(x_k^T Q x_k + u_k^{lT} R u_k^l)] + \hat{V}_{k+1}(W_c). \tag{3.21}$$

The network approximation error of the critic is given by $\zeta_{x_k}^{V(x_k)} = \psi_{x_k}^{V(x_k)} - \hat{V}_k(W_c)$. Similarly, the squared approximation error is given by $\frac{1}{2}(\zeta_{x_k}^{V(x_k)})^T \zeta_{x_k}^{V(x_k)}$. The variations in the critic weights are given by gradient descent method such that

$$W_c^{(l+1)T} = W_c^{lT} - \lambda_c[\psi_{x_k}^{V(x_k)} - x_k^T W_c^{lT} x_k] x_k x_k^T, \tag{3.22}$$

where $0 < \lambda_c < 1$ denotes the critic learning rate.

3.1.7 Actor-critic implementation

The following **Algorithm 2** is used to implement the adaptive critic-based controller. It is noted that, the knowledge of all the autonomous microgrid dynamics is not required. In this algorithm, random initial states, value function approximation weights, and actor approximation weights are used to guarantee sufficient exploration during the tuning process.

Algorithm 2 (Actor-Critic Implementation of Algorithm 1)

1. *Randomly Initialize* W_a *and* W_c.
2. ***Loop-1*** *(for q iterations) Start with random initial states* $x(0)$. ***Loop-2*** *(for* ℓ *iterations)*
   (a) *Evaluate* $\hat{u}_k^{\ell}(W_a) = W_a^{\ell T} x_k$.
   (b) *Evaluate* x_{k+1}^{ℓ}.
   (c) *Evaluate* $\hat{V}_{k+1}^{\ell}(W_c)$.
   (d) *Update the critic weights using*
   $W_c^{(l+1)T} = W_c^{lT} - \lambda_c[\psi_{x_k}^{V(x_k)} - x_k^T W_c^{lT} x_k] x_k x_k^T$
   (e) *Update the actor weights using*
   $W_a^{(l+1)T} = W_a^{lT} - \lambda_a[(W_a^{lT} x_k - u_k^l)(x_k)^T]$
   (f) *On convergence of the actor-critic weights end loop-2*
3. *Calculating the difference* $\hat{V}(x_k)^{\ell+1} - \hat{V}(x_k)^{\ell}$
4. *On convergence of* $\|\hat{V}(x_k)^{\ell+1} - \hat{V}(x_k)^{\ell}\|$ *end loop-2.*
5. *Transfer the actor-critic weights to the next iteration. On convergence end loop-1*

3.1.8 Simulations results

In this section, the adaptive critics-based controller is tested using the autonomous microgrid shown in Fig. (3.1). The microgrid system is simulated using the SimPowerSystems library in the MATLAB/Simulink, as shown in Fig. (3.3). An IGBT inverter is used as the converter and the Simulink model is built using *Table 1*. A parallel *RLC* load is supplied by both the utility grid and the microgrid unit. The performance criteria of the proposed controller is the output voltage regulation. The learning rates are selected such that $\mu_a = 0.01, \mu_c = 0.01$ and the weighting matrices are given by $Q = 10I_{4\times4}, R = I$.

3.1.9 Actor-critic tuning results

The controller is designed using ***Algorithms 1 & 2***. Starting with random initial values for system's states and the actor-critic weights, ***Algorithm 2*** tunes the actor-critic weights to search for the optimal value and control function. This control signal is fed to the gating signal generator of the VSC for generation of firing pulses. Figures (3.4)–(3.6) show the actor-critic tuning simulation results of ***Algorithm 2***. Figures (3.4) and (3.5) represent the tuning of actor weights and critic weights, respectively. Figure (3.6) shows the dynamics of the microgrid system. It is shown that, after 100 iteration steps, the weights of actor and critic

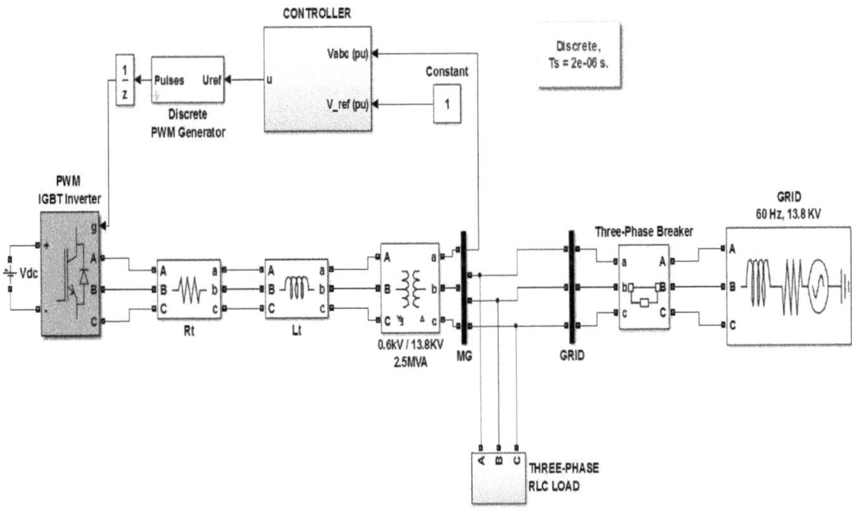

Figure 3.3: Simulink implementation for the autonomous microgrid model and the controller

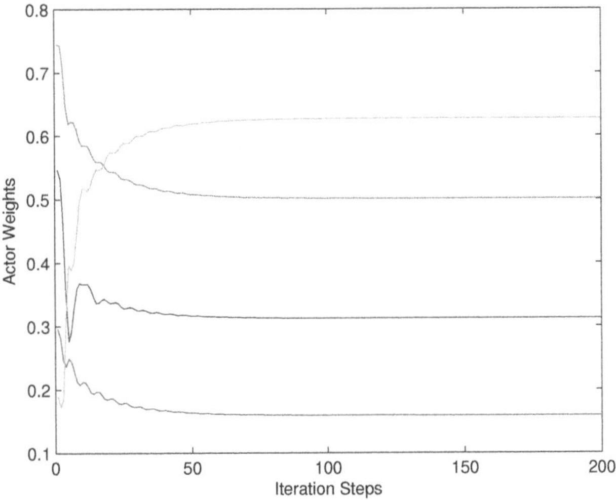

Figure 3.4: Update of the actor's weights

networks converge. Using these weights, the dynamics of the autonomous microgrid is shown to be asymptotically stable. To test the robustness of the proposed controller, a pulse disturbance is injected into the system states at t=0.2 s. By observing the response in Fig. (3.7), it can be concluded that ***Algorithms 1 & 2*** yield asymptotic stability.

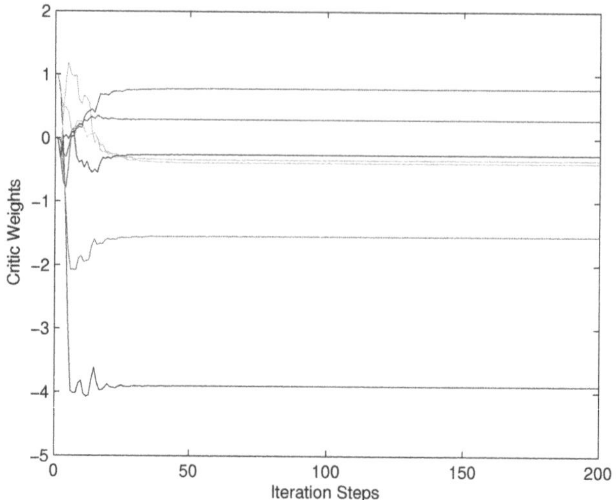

Figure 3.5: Update of the critic's weights

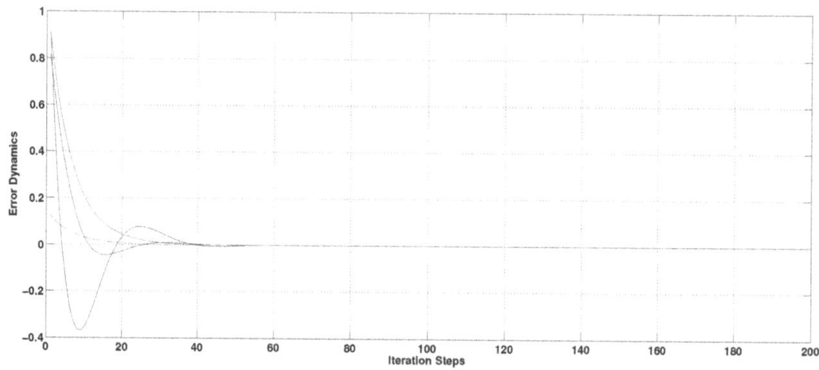

Figure 3.6: The microgrid's dynamics

3.1.10 Robustness of the proposed controller

Two simulation cases are considered in order to show the robustness of the proposed controller. First, the microgrid is isolated from the main grid and operated in the islanded mode. Second, the microgrid starts to operate in islanded mode, and a load disturbance is incorporated into its environment.

At $t = 0.2$ seconds, the circuit breaker (CB) is opened, and, at the same time, the control strategy is changed from conventional i_d/i_q controller used in [87] to the proposed RL-based controller. The control policy u_k generated by the

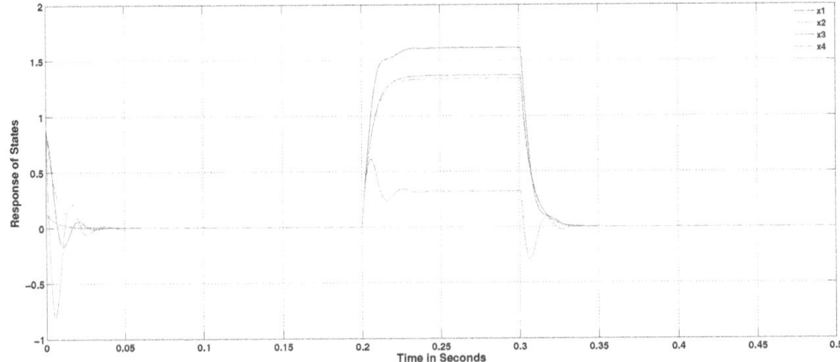

Figure 3.7: Response to pulse disturbances

Algorithm-2 is fed into the gating signal generator. Figure (3.8) shows the instantaneous three-phase voltage at Point of Common Coupling (PCC) and the respective control effort. At $t = 0.2$ seconds, transients can be seen, this distortion in the waveform is due to disconnecting the microgrid from the main grid. The voltage at PCC is brought back to desired reference value of 1 p.u. The system is now completely isolated from the grid. The microgrid is supplying the load, using its own control structure (autonomous mode). To verify the robustness of proposed controller, another experiment is carried out on the system. The microgrid's system is tested against active local load disturbance. The disturbance is *RLC* disturbance, and it is applied to the local active load supplied by the microgrid. At $t = 0.4$ seconds, an additional parallel *RLC* load of $R = 42.8\Omega, L = 0.2119H, C = 10\mu F$ is added to the local active load of the microgrid. Due to application of this load disturbance, transients can be seen in PCC voltage, as shown in Fig. (3.9). These transients can degrade the output voltage from its rated value, and causes degradation of the power supplied. This figure shows also the applied control effort by the proposed control scheme to regulate the output voltage to its desired value. From this figure, within few cycles, the proposed controller acts and brings back the load voltage to the desired reference value of 1 p.u.

3.2 Operation in Islanded Mode

The concept of Microgrid (MG) was originally introduced in [101]; it can be operated in Autonomous mode or can be connected to the utility grid. MG concept has evolved to a great extent in terms of both modeling and control. An overview of the different methods of modeling and control is reported in [81]. The defini-

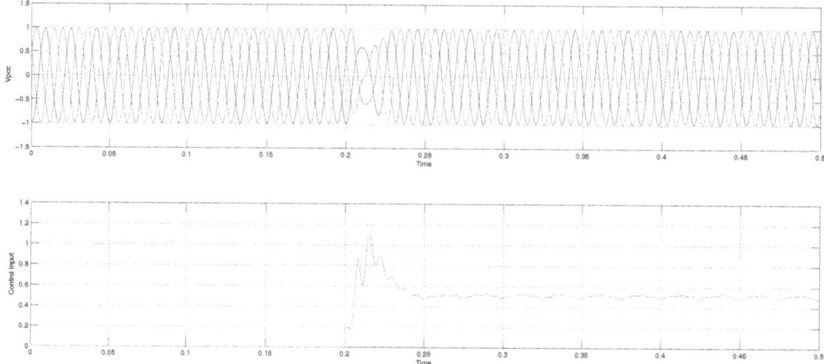

Figure 3.8: Islanded mode: dynamic response of the microgrid

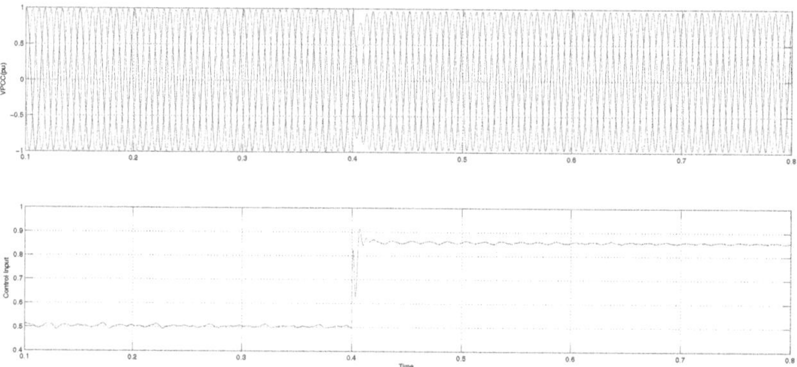

Figure 3.9: Dynamic response of the microgrid under load disturbances

tion of microgrid is evolving into the smart microgrid within the context of smart grids. The definition of "smart grid" is quite flexible and its framework varies with individual vision [102].

A networked microgrid is termed as *"smart microgrid"* [103]; Fig. (3.10) shows its simple architecture. It will have high penetration of Distributed Generation (DG) units which, when integrated alone, raises a number of issues [104]. It also makes use of renewable energy resources, making it cost effective and environmentally friendly. The most vital aspect of smart MG is *Distributed/Decentralized* control using communication network. In other words, it will employ Networked Control System (NCS) so that we can have a network of DG units exchanging information. Control is the key point here which will be implemented in a distributed fashion, contrary to the centralized control in

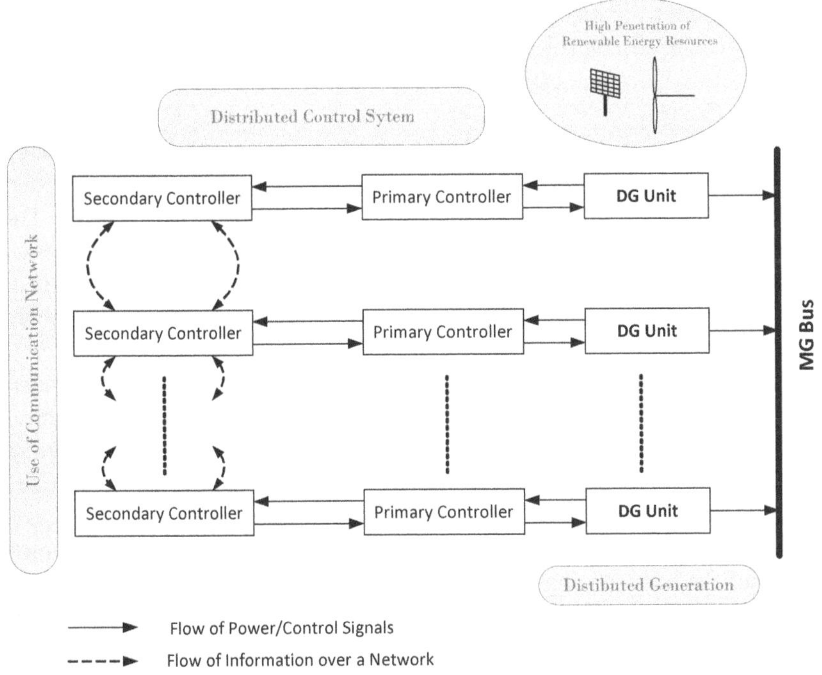

Figure 3.10: Architecture of smart autonomous microgrid

several conventional techniques which can be seen in the literature [105], [106]. This will ensure stability of the system, power balancing, proper load sharing and voltage and frequency regulation.

One of the most widely-used and crucial control techniques is the "Multi-level Control" [107]–[83]. There are three main control levels, each taking care of particular responsibilities. Primary Control level ensures the proper load sharing between the converters. Secondary Control removes any steady state error introduced by primary control. Tertiary Control deals with global responsibilities, like energy transfer to and from the grid. Tertiary control comes into the picture only when the MG is connected to the utility grid. Tertiary control is a decentralized control level responsible for global optimization of the MG. Since autonomous operation of an MG does not involve the tertiary control level, we will be focusing only on the primary and secondary control levels of an MG.

The primary control, which is the first level, makes use of the Droop-based control techniques for its operation. However, due to various reasons discussed in next sections, the primary level alone is not sufficient for the overall stable operation of an MG. For global controllability, a secondary control level is often used. This concept has already been used for a long time in large electrical power systems [108] and has recently been adopted in the MG concept.

Secondary control strategies using NCS have been proposed in literature. A pseudo-decentralized control architecture which can be used for the optimization of Wireless Communication Network (WCN) with the help of a Global Supervisory Control (GSC) and local controllers is proposed in [84]. In [109], NCS strategy was applied to a parallel inverter system in order to achieve superior load sharing and good robustness. Investigation of the centralized secondary controller in a MG with primary voltage droops is carried out in [110]. This controller regulates the voltage at pilot points in the MG. In [111], a networked controlled parallel multi-inverter system is proposed in order to achieve precise load sharing among each module, a centralized controller is used here along with the local controllers.

Most of the works in the literature are based on the *Centralized* secondary control, where all the *DG's* in the MG are supervised by a common centralized secondary control. This controller is often termed as a MicroGrid Central Controller (MGCC), wherein all DG units measure signals and send them to a centralized single controller which, in turn, produces suitable control signals and sends them to the primary control of DG units. It makes use of the communication channel for both sensing the measurements and to send the control signal. [112, 113, 114, 115].

MGCC is relatively slow in functioning. Any fault in the MGCC can result in failure of secondary control action for all the DG units [116]. This single point failure is somewhat unreliable and can be a result of bad functioning of the whole system. Depending on only one central control unit for the proper operation is a big drawback in itself.

A distributed secondary controller based on averaging algorithms is proposed in [117]. The controller, which is also termed as Distributed Averaging Proportional Integral (*DAPI* controller), regulates the system frequency under time varying loads. Recently, a new method of implementing secondary control in a distributed fashion using the Networked Control Systems (NCS) approach was proposed in [118]. This concept has proved to be better, as both the primary and secondary control are implemented in a distributed way, resulting in individual secondary control for each DG unit.

However, the proposed controller in [118] is based on fixed PI gains which may perform well under some operating conditions, but not all. The gains of the secondary controller were randomly tuned and lacked a proper defined procedure. Consequently, improper tuning of the controller results in poor adaptation to varying operating conditions. Moreover, proportional-plus-integral (PI) controllers are not robust enough to accommodate the variations in the load. It is preferable to have an intelligent PI-type controller, which can self-tune its controller gain when the load changes [119, 120].

In this section, a neural-network-based distributed secondary controller which can operate over a wide range of operating points is proposed. Using *Differential Evolution* (DE), the optimized gains of the secondary controller are obtained and serve as a training pattern for the artificial neural network. The salient features of the proposed controller are listed below:

- Each DG has its own local secondary controller and, hence, obviates the requirement for a central controller.
- Neural network learns by example and, hence, avoids traditional programming algorithms and procedures.
- Better performance as the training set and controller parameters are optimized values.
- Use of trained neural network enhances the adaptability of the controller.
- The proposed controller can react faster to load changes and can operate over a wide range of operating points.
- Increased robustness and reliability.

Although the concept of using NN approach to replace traditional PI controller exists in the literature, it has not been used in the field of microgrid systems. The voltage and frequency regulation, load sharing performance of the controller are demonstrated using Matlab/Simulink simulations. A performance comparison between the proposed controller and fixed-gain controller is also performed. The simulation results show that the proposed secondary control ensures stable operation of the system under varying loads.

3.2.1 Autonomous microgrid

Autonomous mode operation of MG is also know as *Islanded* MG, which can be caused by two reasons. One is due to any network fault or some failure in the utility grid and the other is due to performance of maintenance at planned intervals. An electrical switch will disconnect the MG from main utility grid and result in the autonomous operation of the MG [80]. As explained in [121], without loss of generality, the prime mover can be replaced with a *DC* source because they both essentially serve the same purpose. This simplification allows us to study the behavior of inverter-based generators without actually using a prime mover.

In this section, an *MG* involving only inverter-interfaced *DG* units is considered. Figure 3.11 shows the block diagram of an inverter- based DG unit. It consists of an inverter that is connected to a primary DC source (e.g., wind system, PV array etc), control loops containing power, voltage and current controllers. Due to their ride through capability and improved power quality [116, 122] , voltage source inverters (VSI) are used. Load is connected through an *LC* filter and coupling inductance. The power, voltage and current controllers constitute

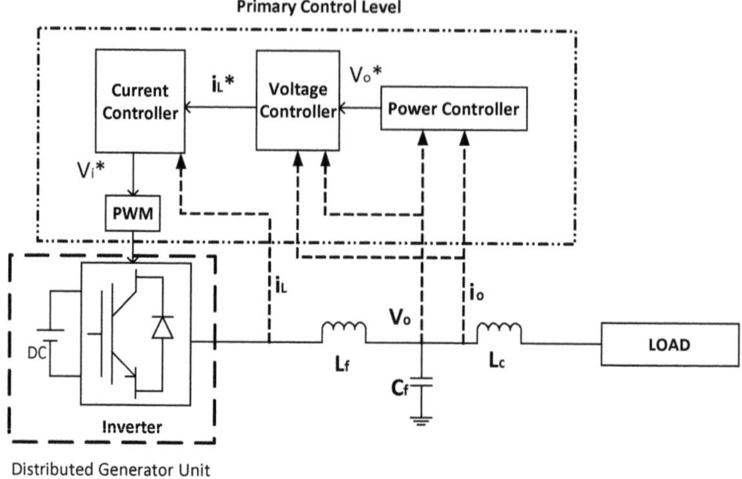

Figure 3.11: Block diagram of inverter-based DG unit

the primary control level of any individual DG unit. Small signal modeling of each of the part of *MG* can be carried out by following the procedure outlined in [123] and [124].

As mentioned in [123], d-q reference frame was used to formulate the non-linear dynamics of DG units. The reference frame of one DG is considered as the common reference frame with frequency ω_{com}. The angle δ between an individual reference frame and common reference frame satisfies the following equation.

$$\dot{\delta} = \omega - \omega_{com}$$

3.2.2 Primary control

The control technique used at this level is known as *Droop*-based control [125, 126]. This type of control makes use of local measurements and does not need any communication medium for its operation. Droop control is a decentralized strategy which ensures proper load sharing. Its main purpose is to share active and reactive powers among DG units, while at the same time maintaining the output levels of voltage and frequency within limits. In droop technique, there is a desired relationship between the active power P and angular frequency ω and between reactive power Q and voltage V, as given below:

$$\omega = \omega_n - m_p P, \quad V = V_n - n_q Q$$

where V_n and ω_n are the nominal values of output voltage and angular frequency, respectively. P and Q are the real and reactive powers, respectively. m_p and n_q

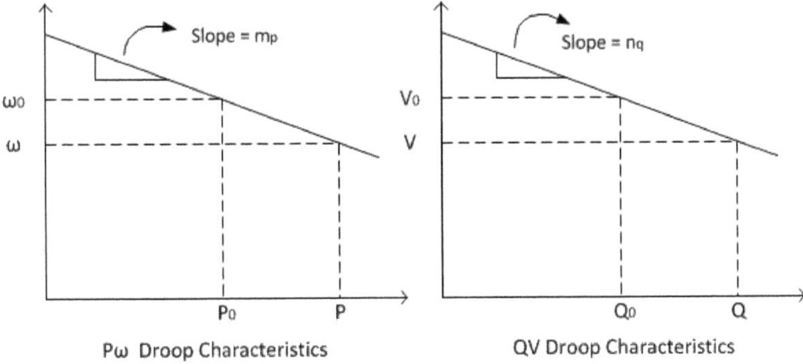

Figure 3.12: Droop characteristics

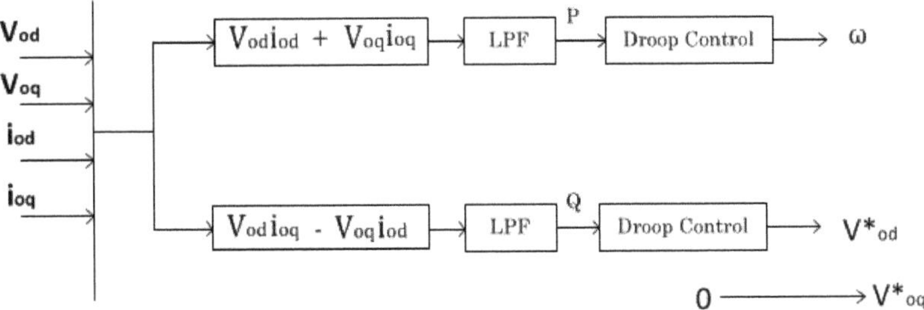

Figure 3.13: Block diagram of power controller

are the real and reactive power droop gains, respectively. The frequency ω is set according to the droop gain m_p and output voltage V is set as per droop gain n_q.

Therefore, the output frequency/voltage is decreased when there is an increase in the load real/reactive power and vice versa. The $P\omega$ and QV droop characteristics are shown in Fig. 3.12.

The primary control level can be divided into three different parts, namely power, voltage and current controller. The power controller, shown in Fig. 3.13, sets the inverter output voltage magnitude and frequency with the help of "Droop" characteristics. Basically, it mimics the operation of a synchronous generator which will change the frequency of the output voltage if any change in load is sensed. First, the instantaneous powers are calculated using output voltages and currents, by filtering these instantaneous values with a low pass filter (LPF) we get the average real and reactive powers. These average values are passed through their respective droop gains in order to obtain the angular frequency and voltage [127]. The control strategy is chosen such that the output voltage magnitude reference is aligned to the d-axis of the inverter reference frame and q-axis reference is set to zero.

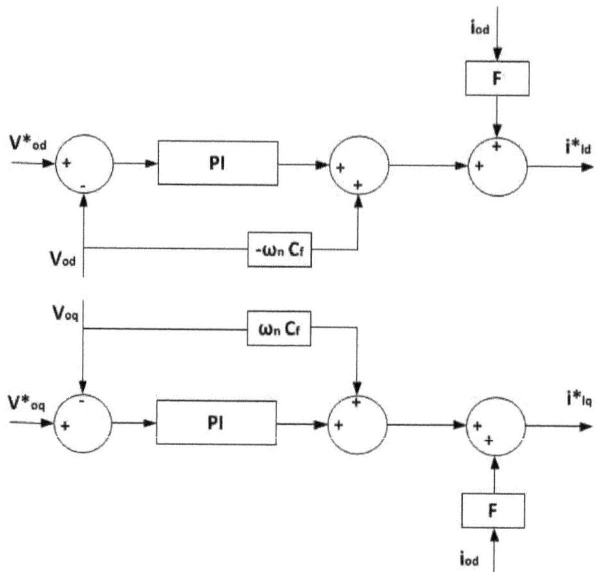

Figure 3.14: Block diagram of voltage controller

The block diagram of voltage controller is shown in Fig. 3.14, a PI controller is used to achieve the output voltage control. The corresponding state equations are given by

$$\dot{\phi}_d = v_{od}^* - v_{od}, \quad \dot{\phi}_q = v_{oq}^* - v_{oq}$$

where ϕ_d and ϕ_q are the d-q axis state variables of the voltage controller (integrator states), respectively.

$$\begin{aligned} i_{ld}^* &= Fi_{od} - \omega_n C_f v_{oq} + K_{pv}(v_{od}^* - v_{od}) + K_{iv}\phi_d \\ i_{lq}^* &= Fi_{oq} + \omega_n C_f v_{od} + K_{pv}(v_{oq}^* - v_{oq}) + K_{iv}\phi_q \end{aligned}$$

The block diagram of Current controller is shown in Fig. 3.15, a PI controller is used to achieve the output filter inductor current. The corresponding state equations are given by

$$\dot{\gamma}_d = i_{ld}^* - i_{ld}, \quad \dot{\gamma}_q = i_{lq}^* - i_{lq}$$

where γ_d and γ_q are the d-q axis state variables of the current controller (integrator states), respectively.

$$\begin{aligned} v_{id}^* &= -\omega_n L_f i_{lq} + K_{pc}(i_{ld}^* - i_{ld}) + K_{ic}\gamma_d \\ v_{iq}^* &= \omega_n L_f i_{ld} + K_{pc}(i_{lq}^* - i_{lq}) + K_{ic}\gamma_q \end{aligned}$$

The main purpose of voltage and current controllers is to reject the high frequency disturbances and damp the output filter in order to avoid any resonance

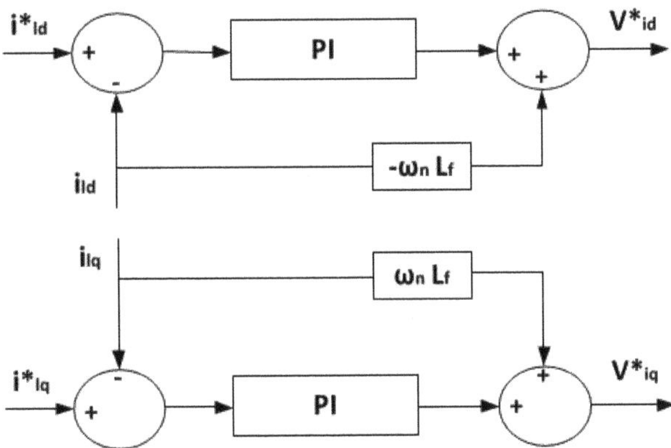

Figure 3.15: Block diagram of current controller

with the external network. The PI controller provides zero steady state error and stabilizes the system. As can be seen in figures, additional feedforward gain and decoupling terms are also used. These PI controllers make use of the local measurements to perform the control action. Detailed analysis on modeling and behavior of this system can be found in [123].

Due to virtual impedance and virtual inertias within the primary control, deviations are produced inside the *MG* which can be observed during its transient behavior. These deviations can make the output voltage and frequency levels go out of the specified range and, hence, can cause the destabilization of the system. The main advantage of primary control is that it is fast, does not need any communication medium and makes use of local measurements.

Primary control is a tradeoff between voltage regulation and power sharing. Good sharing of power is achieved at the expense of errors in output voltage and vice versa. Poor transient performance, lack of robustness and steady state error are its main drawback. Therefore, a secondary control level which brings back the output voltage frequency within the allowable limits is deployed.

3.2.3 Fixed gain distributed secondary control

The block diagram of a distributed secondary controller is shown in Fig. 3.16. This controller ensures zero steady state error and regulates the deviations produced in output frequency and voltage due to load change towards zero. The control law at the secondary level is given as follows

$$\delta\omega = K_{p\omega}(\omega_n - \omega_{avg}) + K_{i\omega}\int(\omega_n - \omega_{avg})dt \quad (3.23)$$

$$\delta V = K_{pv}(V_n - V_{avg}) + K_{iv}\int(V_n - V_{avg})dt \quad (3.24)$$

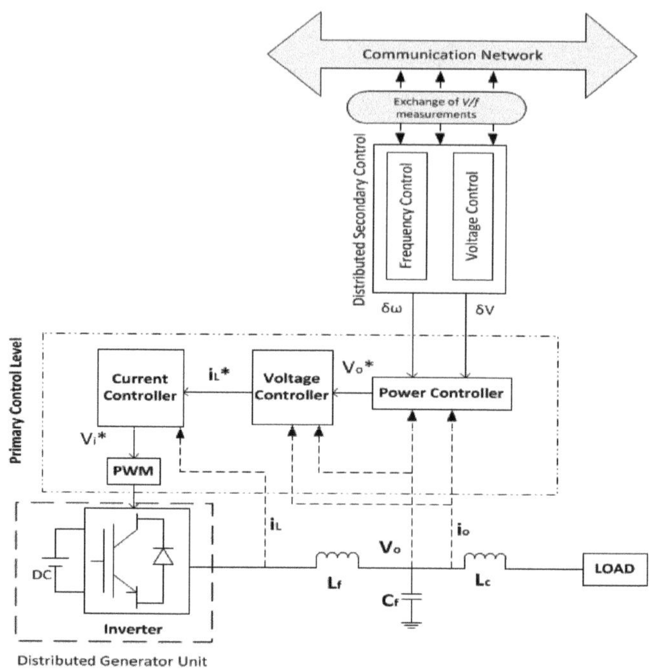

Figure 3.16: Distributed secondary controller

where $K_{p\omega}$, $K_{i\omega}$ are the PI controller parameters for frequency control, K_{pv}, K_{iv} are the PI controller parameters for voltage control, ω_n and V_n are the frequency and voltage set points, ω_{avg} and V_{avg} are the average values of frequency and voltage, respectively, and $\delta\omega$ and δV are the control signals produced by the secondary controller.

At each sample time, each DG unit measures their respective output voltage and frequency and sends this information to other DG units by means of a communication network. DG units average the frequency/voltage measurements and compare them with the reference values in order to produce an error signal. The secondary control then processes this error signal in order to produce control signals. Because the deviations are produced by the *Droop* Control, these control signals are sent to the primary control level so as to remove the steady state error. The output voltage and frequency are restored to their nominal values, as follows:

$$\omega = \omega_n - m_p P + \delta\omega, \quad V = V_n - n_q Q + \delta V$$

$\delta\omega$ and δV are the control signals received by the primary control from the secondary control to restore the output frequency and voltage, respectively, to their nominal values.

3.2.4 Neural network distributed secondary control

The controller discussed above is based on the fixed-gain PI scheme. Under certain operating points or conditions, this fixed-gain scheme may work fine, but its performance degrades at other operating conditions. Also, suitable PI gains are obtained using time-consuming trial-and-error methods. Poor tuning of gains deteriorates the system performance. To increase the robustness and adaptability of the fixed-gain secondary controller, in this section we propose a neural-network-based secondary controller, which solves the robustness and adaptability problem of the PI controller, maintaining its simplicity, reliability and feasibility.

Over the past few years, artificial neural networks have been widely used in the field of control systems for various purposes, like non linear modeling, tuning controller parameters, system identification, etc., [128]. A trained neural network has the remarkable ability of being able to analyze and derive meaning from the given data; it is self-organizing and adaptive in nature.

Figure 3.17 illustrates the block diagram of a neural-network-based secondary controller. This controller can self-tune the PI gains as per various operating conditions. A trained artificial neural network provides optimal gains to the secondary controller whenever the load changes, i.e., input to the NN is the load value and its output is the corresponding PI gains. The secondary controller then produces a control signal as per the control law given by expression in (1) and (2). The control signals produced are sent to the primary control level of the respective DG unit in order to compensate for the errors. This way, the proposed secondary controller dynamically regulates the output voltage and frequency for time varying load.

The following are the stages required to design the proposed neural-network-based distributed secondary controller. Each stage has its own importance and all are discussed in the following sections.

3.2.5 Stage 1: Selection of training data

Before using the NN for self tuning, it has to be trained offline with a learning (or training) process. Training is effective only if the network output matches the desired output for each training pattern. For this purpose, a training set, which is a set of input and desired output data, is required. It is very important to have a proper training set, otherwise the accuracy of the NN can be affected [129]. Therefore, *Evolutionary* computational technique, known as *Differential Evolution* (DE), is used to obtain a proper training set. For each load value (operating point), *DE* is employed in order to perform the optimization process and to provide the optimized values of PI gains which will give the proper regulation of output voltage and frequency.

Most of the problems related to engineering science cannot be solved using analytical methods, in particular, global optimization problems are solved using

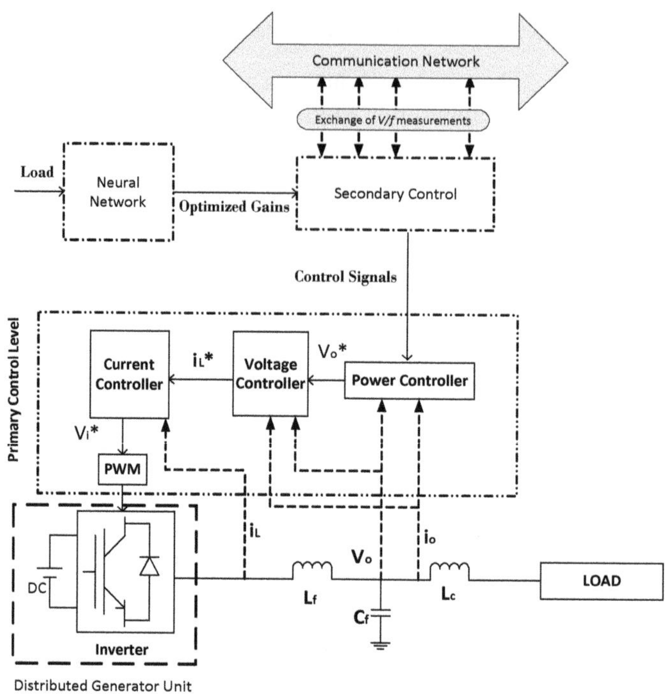

Figure 3.17: Neural-network-based distributed secondary control

Evolutionary Algorithms [130]. These algorithms are used to find the near optimal solution for a wide range of problems. *Differential Evolution* (DE) is one such novel evolutionary algorithm and uses a simple population-based stochastic search for optimizing functions with real value parameters [131].

DE produces a new vector by adding perturbation of two vectors to a third vector. This process is the main differential and is termed as *Mutation*. The new vector produced is combined with pre-defined parameters in accordance with a set of rules. This process is called *Crossover*. This operation is performed to enhance the searching process. Thereafter, an operator that compares the fitness function of two competing vectors to determine who can survive for the next generation is applied. This process is known as *Selection* process [132, 133].

The objective function (or performance index) used is the Integral of Time Multiply Squared Error (ITSE), defined as follows

$$J_{ITSE} = \int te^2(t)dt$$

where e is the error which is equal to $(\omega_n - \omega_{avg})$ for frequency control and $(V_n - V_{avg})$ for voltage control. The optimization problem is defined as

$$\min[\max(J_{ITSE})]$$

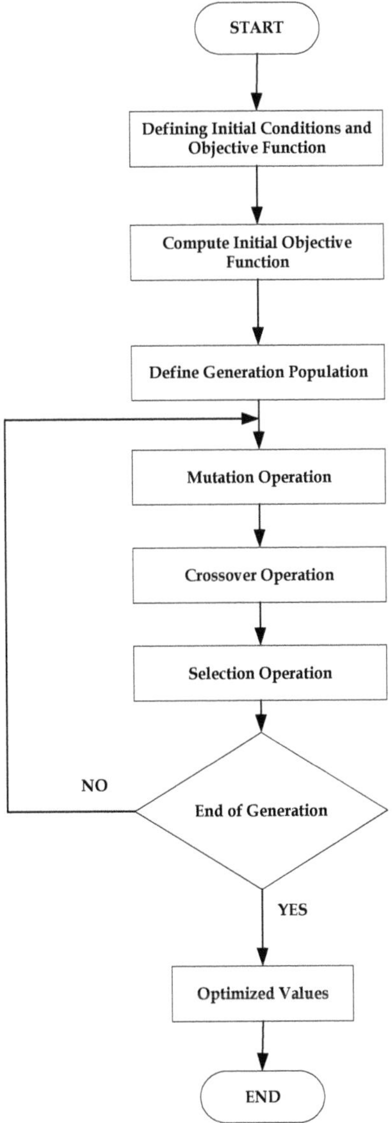

Figure 3.18: Flow chart of differential evolution

DE algorithm is coded in MATLAB/Simulink and implemented on-line in order to minimize the integral error and to obtain the optimal PI gains of the secondary controller. DE specifications and the final optimized gains are shown in Fig. 3.19. With the help of a flowchart, the DE process is explained in detail in Fig. 3.18.

Specifications	No. of Iterations	Initial Population	Mutation Factor	Crossover Factor	ODE Solver
Value	100	20	0.5	0.6	ODE45

Optimized Values / Load Value	Frequency Control		Voltage Control	
	Proportional Gain	Integral Gain	Proportional Gain	Integral Gain
4500 Watts	7.4072	10.8121	10.5367	10.7784

Figure 3.19: Optimization details

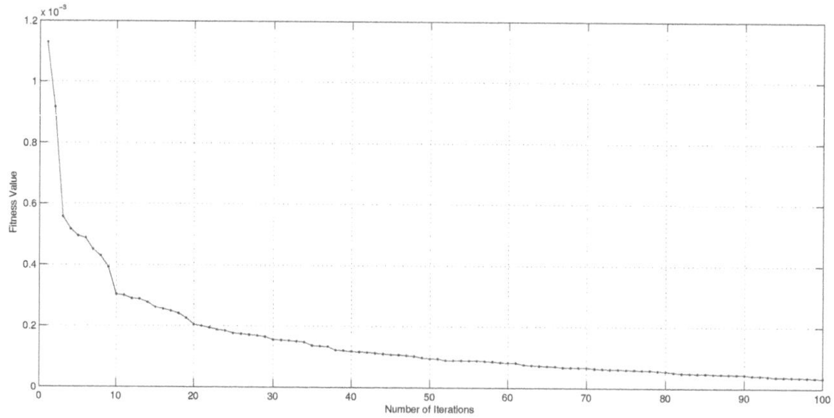

Figure 3.20: Fitness vs iteration curve

The fitness vs. number of iterations graph for frequency control corresponding to above optimization details is shown in Fig. 3.20, where the fitness corresponds to ITSE. It can be seen that the fitness gradually reduces, which in turn reduces the steady state error.

To obtain the optimal PI gains for one operating condition, approximately 1 hour was required. To reduce the collection time of training set, only 37 operating points were considered. From 100 Watts to 7500 Watts, the above optimization process was repeated for 37 different load values with an interval of approximately 200 Watts. For each load value, optimal PI gains were obtained for both frequency and voltage control. The load values and their corresponding optimized controller gains form the *Training Set* for the neural network.

3.2.6 Stage 2: Selection of artificial neural network

The next stage is the selection of the NN structure and its properties. Neural Network (NN) consists of *Neurons* which are simple computational units. A neuron is a building block of an NN and it resembles the information processing model

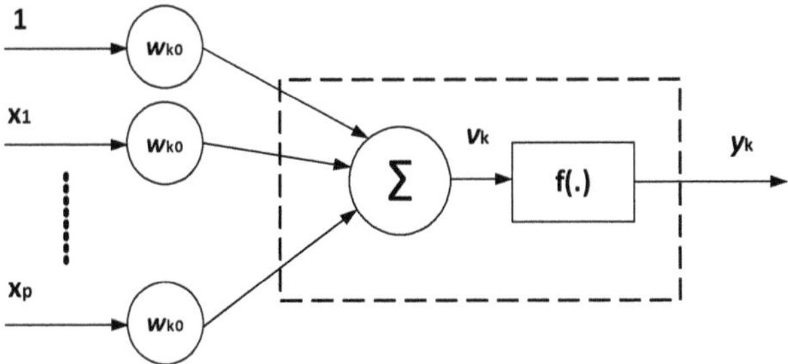

Figure 3.21: Artificial neuron model

of the human brain. The structure of a neuron is shown in Fig. (3.21). Any k-th neuron can be defined mathematically as [134]

$$v_k = \sum_{j=1}^{p} w_{kj}x_j + w_{ko}, \quad y_k = f(v_k)$$

where $x_1, x_2 ... x_p$ denotes inputs signals, $w_{k1}, w_{k2} ... w_{kp}$ denotes the synaptic weights of k-th neuron, w_{k0} is the bias, v_k denotes the linear combiner output, $f(.)$ is the activation function and y_k denotes the output of the neuron.

In this study, the neural network used is of feedforward type, as shown in Fig. (3.22). It consists of input, hidden and output layers. As can be seen, the flow of signal is unidirectional, i.e., the output of each neuron is connected to the input of a neuron in the next layer. Depending on the activity level at the input of a neuron, the activation function defines its output [135].

To design and train an artificial neural network, the *Neural Network Toolbox* [136], available in Matlab/Simulink, is used. The command "*nntool*" opens the Network/Data Manager window, which allows the user to import, create, use, and export neural networks. Figure 3.23 illustrates the Matlab/Simulink architecture of the NN. It consists of 1 input node and 4 output nodes and 10 nodes in the hidden layer.

3.2.7 Stage 3: Neural network training

The next stage is training of the *Neural Network*. NNs resemble adaptive control, since they learn from a set of example data rather than having to be programmed in a conventional way [137], therefore, a set of data called *Training Set* is required in order to train the NN and adjust its synaptic weights and thresholds. The training data was obtained from the DE optimization algorithm explained in the previous section.

To train the neural network, the Levenberg-Marquardt backpropagation [138] algorithm was used. It is a type of back propagation algorithm [139] mostly used

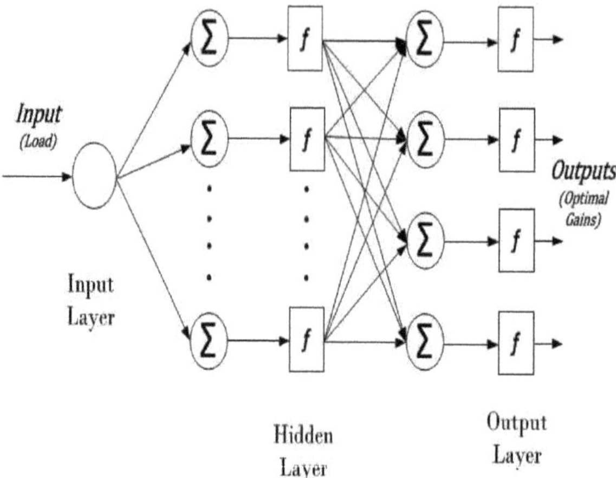

Figure 3.22: Structure of feedforward neural network

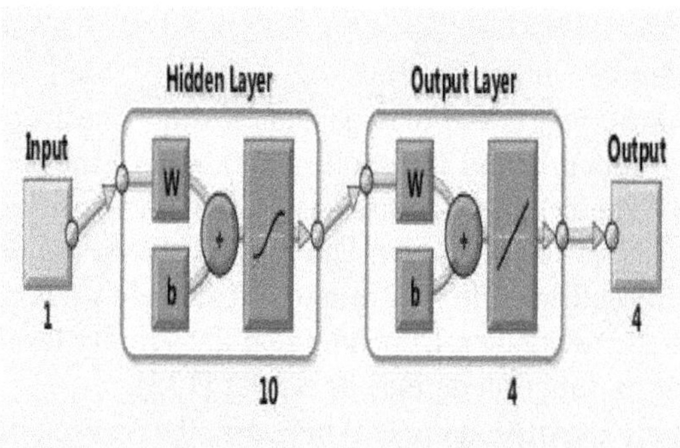

Figure 3.23: Architecture of neural network

for approximation of function, mode identification and classification, data compression, and so on. The other details of neural network training are tabulated in Table I. The neural network inputs are the load values R_L and the outputs generated by the neural network are the corresponding optimal secondary control parameters.

3.2.8 Simulation results I

The simulations were performed in MATLAB/Simulink environment. A non-linear model of the multiple *DG* units is designed using *SimPowerSystems* Library. Figure (3.24) shows an autonomous MG system developed in the Simulink. There are a total number of 3 *DG* units connected to the a three

Table 3.2: Neural network training details

S.No.	Network Property
1	Adaption Learning Function :
	Gradient descent with momentum weight and bias learning function
2	Performance Function:
	Mean squared normalized error
3	Transfer Function in hidden layer:
	Hyperbolic tangent sigmoid transfer function
4	Transfer Function in output layer:
	Linear transfer function

Table 3.3: System parameters

Symbol	Quantity	Value
L_f	Filter Inductance	1.35 mH
r_f	Filter Resistance	0.1 Ω
C_f	Filter Capacitance	50 μ F
L_c	Coupling Inductance	0.35 mH
r_c	Coupling Resistance	0.03 Ω
V_n	Nominal Voltage	381v
ω_n	Nominal Frequency	314 rad/sec
ω_c	Cutoff Frequency of Low Pass Filter	31.4 rad/sec
f_s	Switching Frequency	8 Khz
m_p	Real Power Droop Gain	9.4×10^{-5}
n_q	Reactive Power Droop Gain	1.3×10^{-3}
K_{pv}	Proportional gain of Voltage Controller	0.05
K_{iv}	Integral gain of Voltage Controller	390
K_{pc}	Proportional gain of Current Controller	10.5
K_{ic}	Integral gain of Current Controller	16000
F	Feedforward gain of Voltage Controller	0.75

phase load by means line impedance, given by $R_{l1} = 0.23\Omega$, $L_{l1} = 31.8\mu H$, $R_{l2} = 0.35\Omega$, $L_{l2} = 184.7\mu H$ and $R_{l3} = 0.18\Omega$, $L_{l3} = 0.0022$. The other parameters of the system and their values are given in Table II.

Initially, the MG system is operated without secondary control level under no load conditions with only primary control enabled. After 5 seconds, a load of 4.5 KW is applied to the system. The response of output frequency and voltage from no load condition to sudden application of load is illustrated in Figs. 3.25 and 3.26, respectively. As a result of sudden application of load, transients can be seen at t = 5 seconds in both output voltage and frequency. These transients result in the steady state error which deviates the output values from their nominal values. This steady state error is also a result of the poor quality of power.

By observing the above figures, it can also be concluded that a major part of the transient is taken up by the DG-3 unit, whereas DG-1 and DG2 responded more slowly. This is because the load is closely located to DG-3, which implies

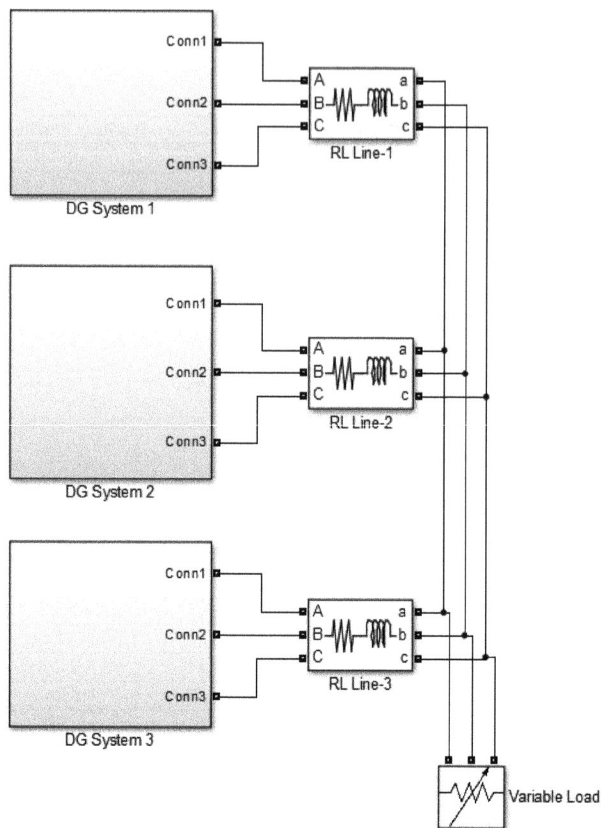

Figure 3.24: Simulink model of three DG system

that during large load changes, DGs located nearer to load can be overloaded and may trip out.

To regulate the output voltage and frequency to their nominal values and to eliminate the steady state error, secondary control is enabled. To demonstrate the effectiveness of the proposed controller, a comparative analysis between the fixed-gain secondary control and neural-network based secondary control is performed. Figures 3.27–3.29 summarize the performance comparison between the fixed-gain distributed secondary control and neural-network-based distributed secondary control. These figures illustrate comparative analysis for output voltage regulation, output frequency regulation and load sharing capability, respectively, of the two controllers.

By observing the comparison results, it can be seen that proposed controller is superior than the conventional one in responding to the load changes. Its response is much quicker and, therefore, has better performance. The proposed controller

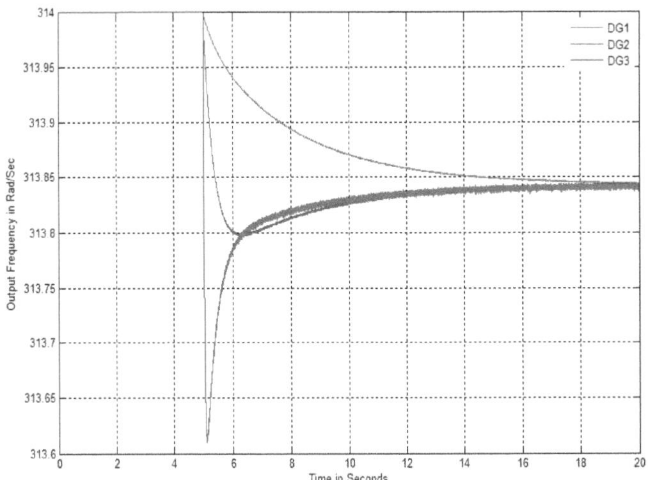

Figure 3.25: Frequency response under sudden application of load

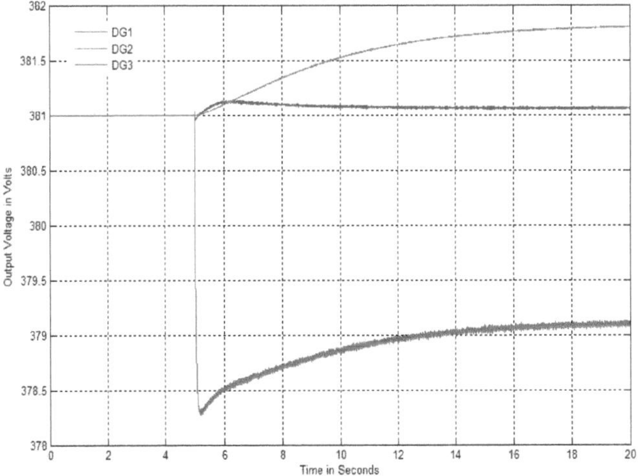

Figure 3.26: Voltage response under sudden application of load

eliminates the error faster, which indicates the controller parameters are well optimized and work more effectively than the conventional one.

To demonstrate the robustness and adaptability of the proposed controller under varying loads, the system is subjected to different load changes with respect to time. One load change indicates one operating point of the system.

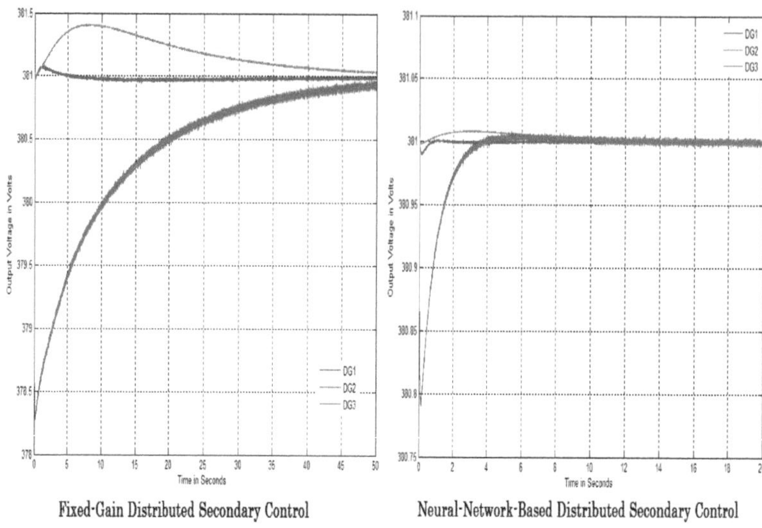

Figure 3.27: Performance comparison for voltage regulation

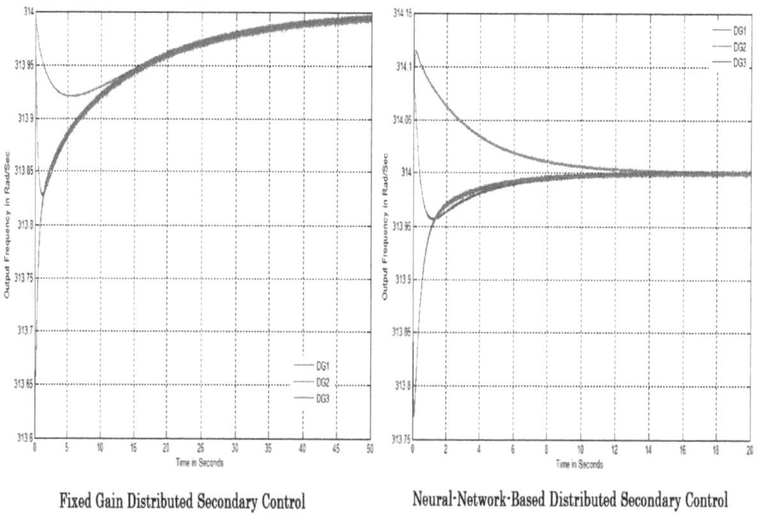

Figure 3.28: Performance comparison for frequency regulation

As can be seen in Fig. 3.30, the system is subjected to change in load after each 20 seconds, indicating 5 different operating points. Transients can be observed at the instant when the load is applied on the system. As can be seen, DG-1 and DG-2 reacted slowly to the load change compared to DG-3, which shared the major part after every change in load. The controller is able to share the load

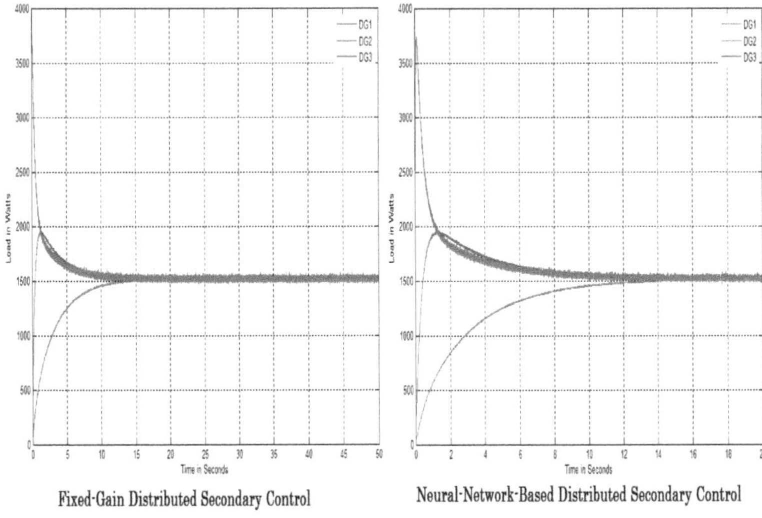

Figure 3.29: Performance comparison for load sharing

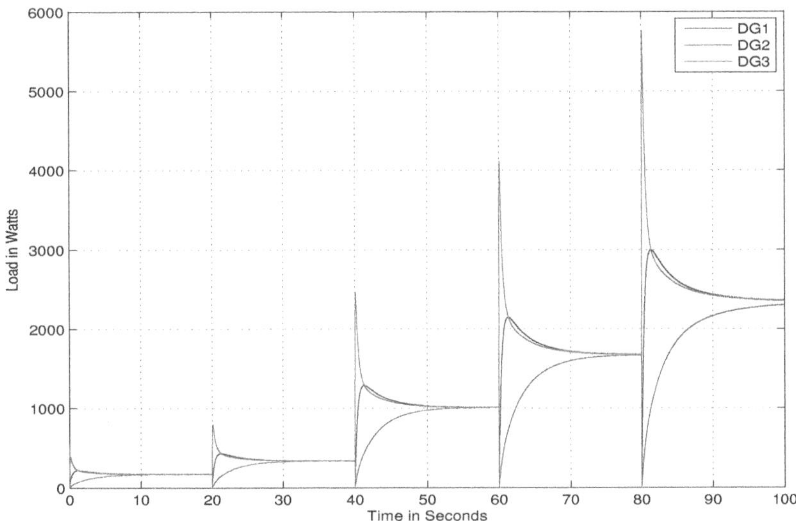

Figure 3.30: Output Frequency under varying load

equally among the DG units within a considerable amount of time. Therefore, proper load balancing is also achieved.

The corresponding response of output frequency and voltage under the same load change pattern is illustrated in Figs. (3.31) and (3.32). Because the load change at each interval is the same, the transients in these figures are in coher-

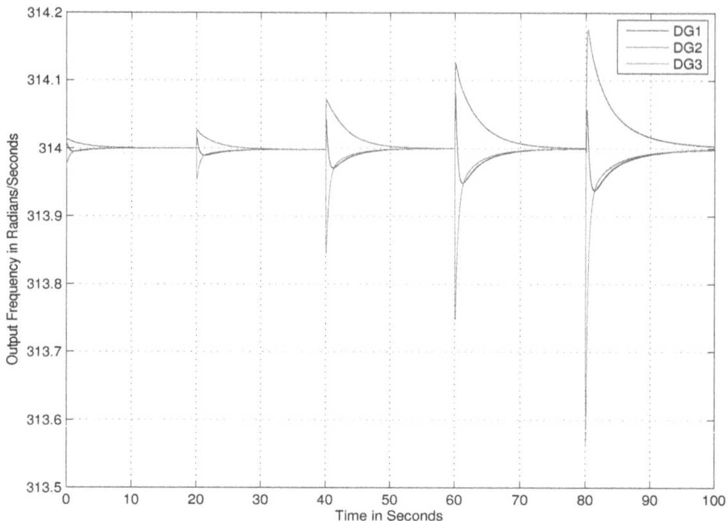

Figure 3.31: Output Voltage under varying load

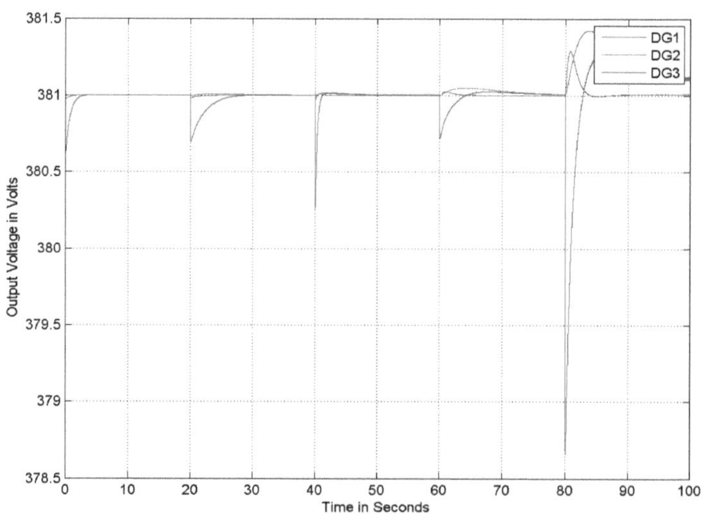

Figure 3.32: Load sharing among the DG units

ence. It can be seen that the deviations in output frequency and voltage after every load change are regulated towards zero by the controller so that output voltage and frequency are restored to their nominal values. Proper regulation of output voltage and frequency is achieved and, hence, the proposed controller is more adaptive and has a faster response.

3.3 Multiagent Coordination for Distributed Energy Resources

Multiagent technology is one of the most exciting fields in the intelligent resource management sector. Recent developments [240], [241] have produced very encouraging results in its novel approach to handling multi-player interactive systems. In particular, the multi-agent system approach is adapted to model, control, manage or test the operations and management of microgrid. Agents represent individual entities in the network. Each participant is modeled as an autonomous participant with independent strategies and responses to outcomes. They are able to operate autonomously and interact pro-actively with their environment. Such characteristics of agents are best employed in situations like microgrid modeling.

The deregulated energy environment [242], [243] has favored a gradual transition from centralized power generation to distributed generation (DG), where sources are connected at the distribution network. These DG sources comprise several technologies, like diesel engines, micro turbines, fuel cells, wind turbines and photovoltaic. The capacity of the DG sources varies from a few kWs to a few MWs. Distributed systems can also bring electricity to remote communities not connected to a main grid. Such communities can create a microgrid of power generation and distribution.

3.3.1 *Introduction*

The common communication structure and distributed control of DG sources, together with controllable loads and storage devices, such as flywheels, energy capacitors and batteries, is central to the concept of microgrids [240]. A microgrid can operate as interconnected to the main distribution grid, or as islanded if disconnected from the main distributed grid. From the grid's point of view, a microgrid can be regarded as a controlled entity within the power system that can be operated as a single aggregated load and as a small source of power or ancillary service supporting the network. From the customers' point of view, microgrids similar to traditional LV distribution networks service thermal and electricity needs. In addition, microgrids enhance local reliability, reduce emissions, improve power quality by supporting voltage and potentially lower the cost of energy supply.

The literature shows a variety of applications of MAS in power systems, especially in microgrids. The optimization of interconnected microgrid operation [244] was done by optimizing production of the local DGs and power exchanges with the main distribution grid. In the application of microgrid control, research work of [245] shows how the local intelligence and the social ability of the agents may provide solutions in the optimal and effective control. Authors in [246] invented the new concept for a distributed power system with agent technology as (Intelligent Distributed Autonomous Power Systems) IDAPS, which is a specialized microgrid for coordinating customer-owned DERs. In addition, MAS has also been successfully applied in the other power system operations. For instance, switching and restoration [247] in power system.

This paper provides multi agent modeling of a microgrid, which can be extended easily to perform microgrid management and control operations. A simple *PoolCo market simulation* [248]–[251] illustrates the implementation of coordination between agents in the microgrid modeling.

3.3.2 Advantages of MAS approach

Multiagent (MAS) technology has recently been successfully applied to power systems management and operations. Each power source and load in the system is represented as an autonomous agent that provides a common communication interface for all the other agents representing the other components in the network.

The basic element of MAS is the agent, which can be described as a piece of software with some characteristics. Some of the important characteristics of agents in the microgrid are;

1. Agents are capable of acting in the environment, which means the agent is capable of changing its environment by its actions. For instance, an agent that controls a storage unit and intends to store energy, rather than to inject it, alters the decision and the behavior of other agents.

2. Agents communicate with each other. This is a part of their ability to act in the environment. For instance, agents controlling micro sources communicate with the market operator (MO) and the other agents in order to negotiate for the internal microgrid market.

3. Agents have a certain level of autonomy. This means that they can make decisions driven by a set of tendencies without a central controller or commander. The autonomy of each agent is related to its resources. For example, the available fuel, in the case of a production unit.

4. Agents represent the environment partially or fully. Each agent not only knows the status of the unit but also informs via conversation with the other agents about the status of the neighboring agents or sub systems.

5. Agents have certain behaviors and tend to satisfy certain objectives using their resources, skills and services. For instance, one skill could be the ability to produce or store energy and a service could be to sell power in a market. The way that the agent uses its resources, skills and services defines its behaviors. As a consequence, the behaviors of each agent are formed by its goals. An agent that controls a battery system aiming to provide uninterruptible supply to a load has a different behavior than a

similar battery system. On the whole, the behaviors of MAS are formed by the system goal, which is to maximize benefits of system managerial operations.

It turns out that the MAS approach has several advantages over the traditional approaches for management and control of microgrid. Some of the important advantages of the MAS approach are;

1. Unit autonomy: Depending on the goals of the unit owners, the various units in a microgrid can behave mostly autonomously in a cooperative or competitive environment. This is a basic characteristic of an agent.
2. Reduced need for large data manipulation: The agent-based approach suggests that the information should be processed locally and the agents should exchange knowledge. In this way, the amount of information exchanged is limited and so is the demand for an expensive communication network. This feature is common to the traditional distributed computing. Moreover, the multi agent system is characterized by the fact that agents have partial or no representation of the environment. In our application, the agent of a unit only knows the active power level of its own bus and, based on this, it can estimate what is happening at other buses, but it has no information about the whole microgrid.
3. Increased reliability and robustness of the control system: In case one of the controllers fails, other agents may adapt and continue the system function.
4. Openness of the system: Multi agent system allows any manufacturer of DER units or loads to embed a programmable agent in the controller of his equipment according to some rules. In this way, the required plug and play capability for installing future DER units and loads can be provided.

Distributed coordination for DER, a potential method to realize these benefits, can be implemented by using multi agent technology.

3.3.3 Agent platform

Agent platform is a software environment where software agents run. JADE (Java Agent DEvelopment) framework [252] is an agent platform proposed for this project. JADE develops multi-agent systems and applications conforming to FIPA standards for intelligent agents.

JADE is a middleware, which is a software platform that provides another layer of separation between the software and operating system. In this implementation, the underlying operating system is the Java Virtual Machine, the middleware is JADE and the application is the code for the agents written in Java.

JADE is also the runtime environment in which agents execute, and therefore hides from the agents the underlying complexity of the operating system or network. Agents can span multiple computers or be on one computer, yet for the implementation, the code for sending and receiving messages is the same. The JADE runtime manages the agent's life cycle, queuing and sending of messages, and interaction with the directory services. The JADE runtime, in turn, executes within a Java Virtual Machine.

Every agent is in a container and a collection of containers make up a platform. There can be multiple containers on a computer, but containers cannot span computers. A platform encompasses all the containers within an agent system and, therefore, can span multiple computers.

The simulation takes advantage of the administration services provided by the JADE runtime, primarily the directory service. The directory services and other administration services are hosted on the Main Container, which is the first container launched in the platform, but are duplicated on the other containers for robustness.

JADE platform provides a set of functions and classes to implement agent functionality, such as agent management service, directory facilitator and messaging passing services, which all are specified by FIPA [253] standards. Agent management service (AMS) is responsible for managing the agent platform which maintains a directory of AIDs (Agent Identifiers) and agent states. AMS provides White page and life cycle services. Directory facilitator (DF) provides the default yellow page services in the platform, which allows the agents to discover the other agents in the network based on the services they wish to offer or to obtain. Finally, the message transport service (MTS) is responsible for delivering messages between agents.

3.3.4 Software system analysis

The ultimate goal of the project is to develop an agent-based solution for managing and controlling distributed energy sources in the microgrid. The scalability and robustness are the main key attractive features of this software development.

The system allows for scalability in terms of adding any number of agents to the system at any time. Through a common directory service, each agent registers their abilities. As the system grows, there could potentially be network congestion. Because of the fast processors available today and the large bandwidth over networks, it seems that system size scaling should not be a problem. There are no limits within JADE to how many agents can be registered on the same platform.

The system robustness is another property to analyze. Each agent can be run on a separate computer, so the failure of one computer will only remove one agent and the system can continue to function, with a performance loss of the physical capability of that failed device. By using the backup features of JADE, the directory service can be duplicated on every computer. Only one container with administrative services is active at a time; with the failure of that container, JADE is able to migrate essential administrative services to other computers in order to create a fully distributed system that is inherently robust. With the design based on contact net, at every contract net cycle new agents are included in the process and missing agents are no longer considered. However, if an agent is removed while currently fulfilling a contract, then that contract is left unfilled and there will be shortfall somewhere. Because the contracts are short in length, this does not affect the system dramatically.

The created simulation is fully distributed. The agents in an energy node configuration can be run on any number of machines without changing the functionality of the system. The same configuration can be used with all agents on a single machine and with agents running on separate machines. Because of the Java-based tools used, the system is platform independent and has been run with a mix of Windows-based and Linux-based agents.

3.3.5 Distributed control system

It is very important to emphasize that the integration of the micro sources into the LV grids, and their relationship with the MV network upstream will contribute to optimizing the general operation of the system [245], [258].

Distributed control of microgrid has three levels, distribution network operator (DNO) and market operator (MO) at the level of the medium voltage, microgrid central controller (MGCC) and local controllers (LC), which could be either micro source controllers or load controllers.

The DNO is responsible for the technical operation in a medium and low voltage area, where the microgrid exists. The MO is responsible for the market operation of the area.

The main interface between the DNS/MO and the microgrid is the microgrid Central Controller (MGCC). The MGCC is primarily responsible for the optimization of the microgrid operation, or alternatively, it simply coordinates the local controllers, which assume the main responsibility for this optimization. The lower level of control consists of the LC. The LCs control the Distributed Energy Resources, production and storage units, and some of the local loads. Depending on the mode of operation, they have certain level of intelligence, in order to take decisions locally. For example, for voltage control, the LCs do not need the coordination of the MGCC, and all necessary calculations are performed locally.

There are several levels of decentralization that can be applied, ranging from centralized control to a fully decentralized approach. According to the fully decentralized approach, the main responsibility is given to the DER controllers, which compete to maximize their production in order to satisfy the demand and probably provide the maximum possible export to the grid, taking into account current market prices. Furthermore, LCs should take all the appropriate decisions to ensure safe and smooth operation of the DER that they are controlling.

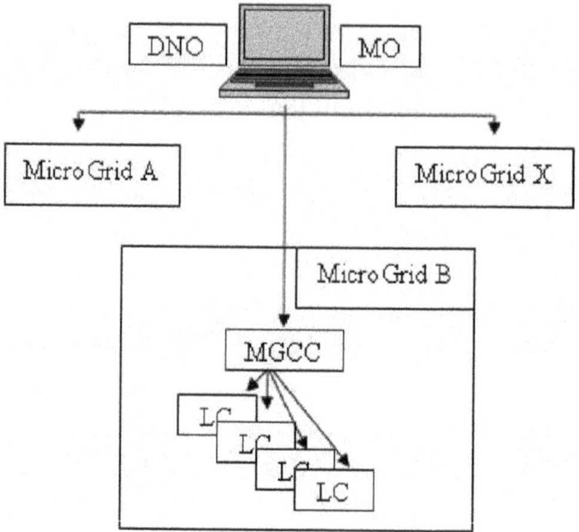

Figure 3.33: Microgrid control architecture

3.3.6 Simulation studies I

In order to demonstrate the multiagent coordination for DER in a microgrid based on contract net approach [253], a simulation system with specific agents to visualize each element interacting with others in a common environment must be created. A specific implementation has been coded to demonstrate an instance of microgrid management operations: PoolCo market operation. The main task of this market algorithm is to centrally dispatch and schedule DER in the microgrid. The operating mechanism of the PoolCo model is described below.

In the PoolCo market operation, generators and loads submit their bids to pool, in order to sell power to the pool or buy power from the pool. All the generators have the right to sell power to the pool, but never specify customers. If generator agents' bids are too high, they have low possibility to sell power. On the other hand, loads compete for buying power. If load agents' bids are too low, they may not be getting any power at all. In such a model, low cost generators and high demanded loads would essentially be rewarded.

During PoolCo operation, each player will submit their bids to the pool which is handled by MGCC. The MGCC sums up these bids and matches the demand and supply. The MGCC will implement the economic dispatch and produce a single spot price for electricity, giving participants a very clear signal of the market forces. This is called the market clearing price (MCP). The MCP is the highest price in the selected bids in PoolCo. Winning generators are paid the MCP for their successful bids while successful bids of loads are obliged to purchase electricity at MCP.

The simulation will run through five sequences of stages, starting from agent world creation and initialization. Then, clearing of the market, scheduling the

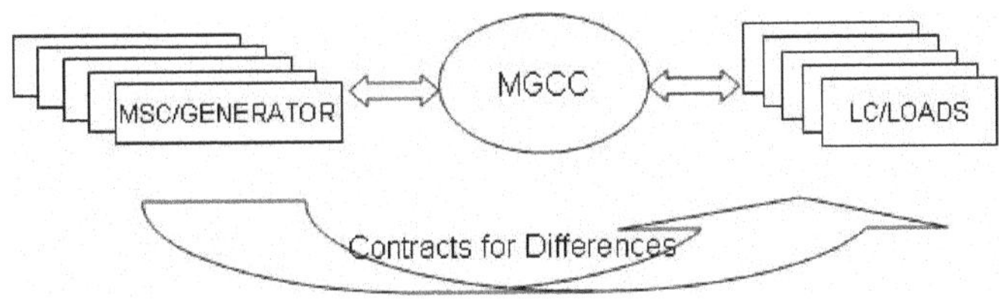

Figure 3.34: PoolCo model

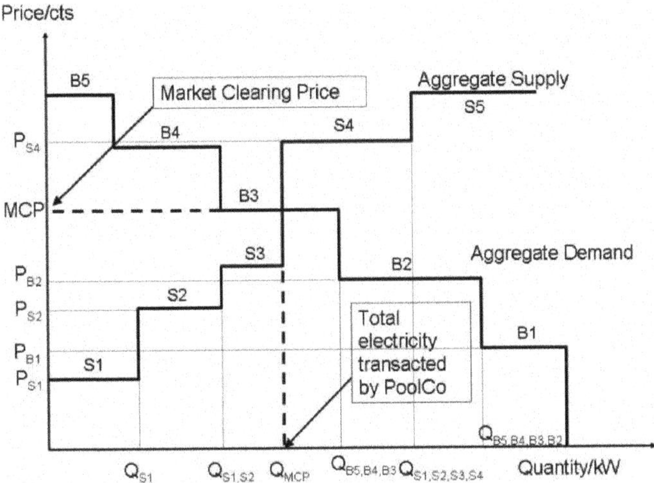

Figure 3.35: PoolCo market clearing

DER and checking congestion and reliability will follow. Finally, the system will finalize and seal the contracts. The general flow of the programming is shown in Fig. 4.

The multiagent system can be started up via the agent launch pad. The system consists of its administrative agents, and agents representing generators, loads, storage, local controllers and other power system elements. All the agents are created and launched as static agents in a local machine. Then, they execute their own thread of initialization. The initialization of generators and loads consists of their generation capacities, load requirements and bidding price by obtaining from a database in the simulation environment. When all the parameters of the agent are properly initialized, each agent will autonomously register themselves with the DF as their first task.

As soon as the agents register themselves with the DF, the agents will query the DF for a complete listing of agents and their services on the network using a certain search constraint. These search constraints are usually queries to the DF for agents with a certain type of service or agents with certain types of names.

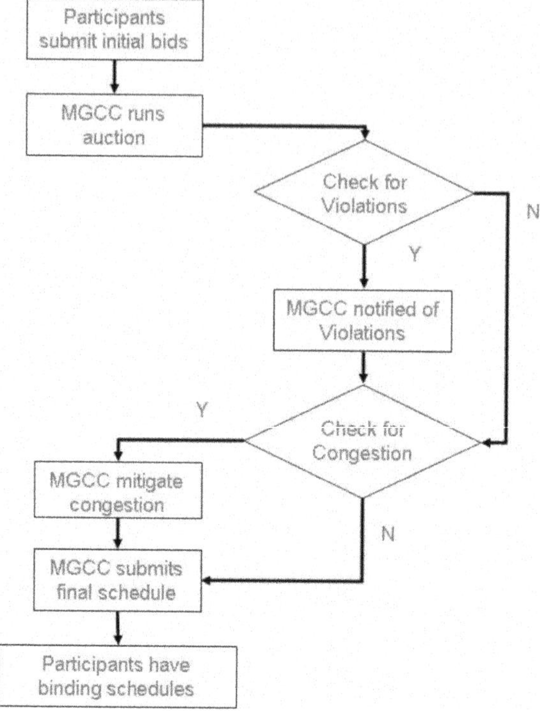

Figure 3.36: General flow of simulation

Generators will send a query to the DF on all other Loads agents and MGCC. Loads will send a query to the DF on all other Generators agents and MGCC. The DF will reply to these requests with a listing of all agents that match their search constraints and all the physical addresses of these agents.

3.3.7 Coordination between agents

The coordination between agents is an important issue in the MAS modeling. In this paper, the agents coordinate among themselves in order to satisfy the energy demand of the system and accomplish the distributed control of the system. The coordination strategy defines the common communication framework for all interactions between agents. Simple contract net coordination [253] was chosen because it is one of the simplest coordination strategies. All discussions between agents are started simply by a requesting agent asking the other agents for a proposed contract to supply some commodity, and then awarding contracts from the returned proposals in a fashion that minimizes cost or fulfills some other goal. The disadvantage of simple contract net coordination is that it only enables simple negotiation without allowing for counter proposals. Effectively, the ini-

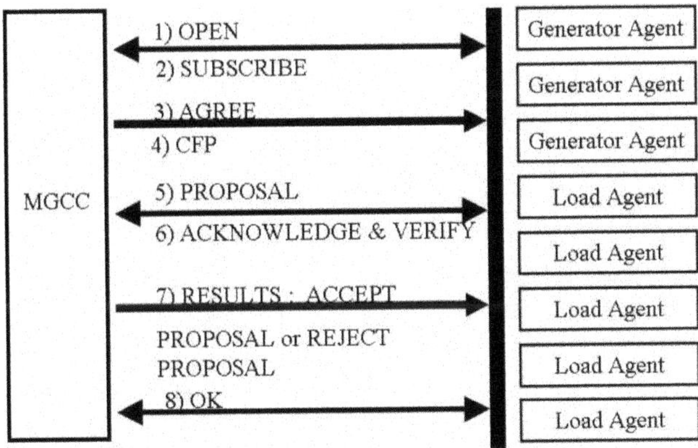

Figure 3.37: Communication between agents: Contract-Net protocol

tiating agent has to pick from the presented contracts and cannot negotiate the price. The advantage of contract net is that it distributes computing, allowing the specific agent that started a contract net process to be responsible for evaluating bids and deciding, based on its own rules, which contracts to accept. It also separates internal agent information from one another, since agents only communicate through the defined contract net protocol and all calculations are done internally to each agent. Since the agents can change at every contract net cycle, there is no dependence on a specific agent. A system with more complex negotiation might lead to lower costs for the system; however, simple contract net is sufficient to demonstrate a distributed coordination framework.

Another factor in having a fully distributed system is the use of a directory service. A directory service allows agents to register themselves and publish their capabilities. By using a directory service, agents do not have to be aware of the other agents. For example, a load agent will look up sources in the directory every time it wants to secure a new supply contract. This allows for agents to be added or removed from the system at any time, since agents are included in contract net negotiations once they register themselves with the directory service.

The coordination layer that the approach defines is the strategic layer above the real time layer. Because of the time required for a contract net interaction to complete, and since contracts are assigned in discrete time intervals, this coordination layer cannot address real time issues. The coordination layer allows for the distributed agents to plan how resources should be applied in order to satisfy demand. The actual operation of the system components self regulates through negative feedback since the system cannot produce more energy than is consumed. Figure 5 shows the proposed contract-net message flowing.

3.3.8 Checking reliability

Once the market is simulated, and before the scheduling is proposed, the reliability of the microgrid is checked with PowerWorld Simulator [254] in order to ensure that the scheduling does not undermine the reliability of the microgrid.

PowerWorld simulator is a commercial power system simulation package based on a comprehensive, robust power flow solution engine capable of efficiently solving a system of up to 100000 buses, implementing the full Newton-Raphson method, the fast decoupled power flow and a DC power flow. It also allows the user to visualize the system through the use of animated diagrams, proving good graphical information about the technical and economic aspects of the transmission network. It has several optional add-ons. OPF and SimAuto add-ons are used for this project.

The OPF provides the ability to optimally dispatch the generation in an area or group of areas, while simultaneously enforcing the transmission line and interface limits. Simulator OPF can then calculate the marginal price (LMP) to supply electricity to a bus, while taking into account transmission system congestion. The advantages of the Simulator OPF over other commercially available Optimal Power Flow packages are the ability to display the OPF results on system one-line diagrams and contour the results for ease of interpretation and the fact that users can export the OPF results to a spreadsheet, a text file, or a PowerWorld AUX file for added functionality.

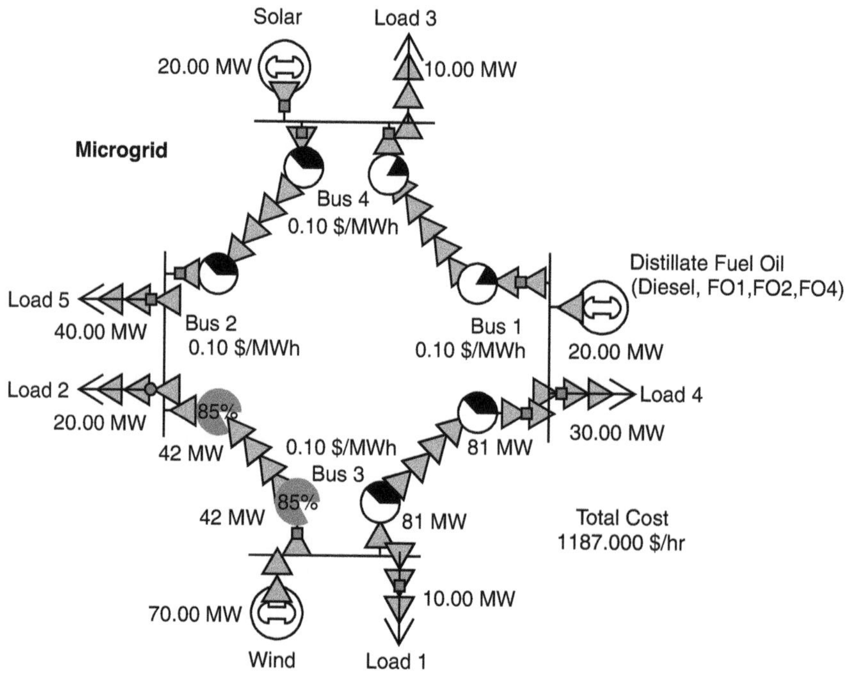

Figure 3.38: PowerWorld simulator snapshot

SimAuto [254] is an automated server (COM interface), enabling the user to access the functionalities from a program written externally by COM server. Even though Java does not have COM compatibility, Java platform integrates Java Native Interface (JNI), which is a standard programming interface for writing Java native methods and embedding the Java virtual machine into a native application. The IBM Development Tool for Java-COM Bridge [255] is chosen to build a communication layer between Java and the Power World automation server.

Suppose the scheduling is congested, the MGCC would employ the use of the PowerWorld Simulator OPF to mitigate congestion. The purpose of the OPF is to minimize the cost function by changing system controls and taking into account both equality and inequality constraints, which are used to model the power balance constraints and various operating limits. It functionally combines the power flow with economic dispatch. In PowerWorld, the optimal solution is being determined using the primal approach of linear programming. Once congestion has been mitigated, the new network schedule and relevant network information will be extracted.

3.3.9 Simulation results II

An agent-based approach for coordinating DER, using contract net as the coordination technique, has been developed and demonstrated by software simulation. Some portions of the output of the programming are given here in order to show that the contract net protocol is successfully implemented.

Furthermore, the different scenarios of double-sided bidding PoolCo market are simulated and results are given in the Table 3.5. Scenario 1 has excess demand and scenario 2 has excess supply at the MCP and supply and demand are matched at the MCP for scenario 3. The excess demand and excess supply at MCP for corresponding scenarios are indicated with bolded numbers.

3.4 Notes

An adaptive learning controller is proposed to regulate the voltage of an autonomous microgrid. The optimal control strategy is selected based on a value iteration adaptive learning technique and it was implemented using means of adaptive critics. Actor-Critic neural networks implementation provides an optimal solution for the microgrid's Bellman optimality equation, hence, finds the optimal control policies. The proposed controller doesn't require knowledge of all the system's dynamics, only the input control matrix is required. The developed control structure showed to be robust against the power system disturbances, in the dynamics and the active load demands.

Table 3.4: Algorithm

StartAgent NUS-ELESHC:1099/JADE: is launched. Power1 is created. Load1 is created. Power1 started and registered with DF as Power Generator Load1 started and registered with DF as Load Power1: The list of Load in the network: Load1 Load2 Load3 Load4 Load5 MGCC is created. Load1: The list of pGen in the network: Power1 Power2 Power3 MGCC started and registered with DF as MGCC Agent Load1: The list of MGCC agents in the network: MGCC Load1: Sent to MGCC: SUBSCRIBE Power1: The list of MGCC agents in the network: MGCC Power1: Sent to MGCC: SUBSCRIBE MGCC: The list of pGen in the network: Power1 Power2 Power3 MGCC: The list of Load in the network: Load1 Load2 Load3 Load4 Load5 MGCC: Message received: Load1: SUBSCRIBE MGCC: Message received: Power1: SUBSCRIBE Load1: Message received: MGCC: AGREE Power1: Message received: MGCC: AGREE Load1: Message received: MGCC: CFP Power1: Message received: MGCC: CFP MGCC: Message received: Load1: PROPOSE MGCC: Message received: Load1: Bid Owner: Load1 Quantity: 10.0MW Price: 11.0cts MGCC: Message received: Power1: PROPOSE MGCC: Message received: Power1: Bid Owner: Power1 Quantity: 70.0MW Price: 10.5cts MGCC: Sent RESULTS: Power1 Load1: Message received: REJECT-PROPOSAL Load1: Message received: Unsuccessful at bidding! Power1: Message received: ACCEPT-PROPOSAL Power1: Successful bid at: Bid Owner: Power1 Quantity: 70.0MW

Table 3.5: Inputs and outputs of simulations

AGENTS	SCENARIO 1				SCENARIO 2				SCENARIO 3			
	INPUT		OUTPUT		INPUT		OUTPUT		INPUT		OUTPUT	
	P	Q	P	Q	P	Q	P	Q	P	Q	P	Q
PGen1	11	70	11	70	11	70	11	65	11	70	12	70
PGen2	12	20	NA	NA	12	20	NA	NA	12	20	NA	NA
PGen3	10	25	11	25	10	35	11	35	10	20	12	20
Load1	11	10	11	5	11	10	11	10	11	10	NA	NA
load2	12	20	11	20	12	20	11	20	12	20	12	20
Load3	10	10	NA	NA	10	10	NA	NA	10	10	NA	NA
load4	14	30	11	30	14	30	11	30	14	30	12	30
load5	13	40	11	40	13	40	11	40	13	40	12	40

A neural-network-based distributed secondary control scheme for an autonomous smart microgrid system has been designed. In this scheme, the controller is constructed to act dynamically to load changes and the associated optimized gains have been evaluated using differential evolution optimization procedure. Performance comparison between the proposed controller with traditional fixed-gain controller is also shown. The controller performance when subjected to time varying load is also summarized. The ensuing results have emphasized that the proposed controller has been able to restore the output voltage and frequency to their nominal values, by eliminating the transients, whenever there is a change in load. Proper load sharing among the generating units has also been achieved. The simulation results show that the proposed controller is much faster, with greater adaptability and robustness when operating point changes and, therefore, ensures superior performance in comparison to a traditional one.

In the next section, Distributed energy resource can be made scalable and robust with a coordination strategy that allows for easily adding or removing energy resources. An energy node can expand as demand increases and can change configuration easily. Distributed coordination, a potential method to realize these benefits, can be implemented by using multi-agent technology. The software simulation demonstrates that it is possible to apply a distributed coordination approach to coordinating distributed energy systems at the strategic level. The distributed system is also self-organizing, allowing agents to be added or removed at any time, without any dependency on a specific agent. By using the appropriate software architecture, distributed coordination seems like a likely strategy to realize the benefits of distributed energy systems. Ultimately, the concept of multiagent-based distributed coordination will need to be connected with an actual hardware implementation to demonstrate a complete agent-based solution for distributed energy resources management. In order to achieve it, the future research will be focused on intelligent microgrid operations, such as load forecasting, forecasting of RES power production, economic resource scheduling and demand side management (DSM), which can be added on this microgrid modeling in the future.

The main focus of the next section is to present a distributed algorithm that will allow the agents to learn and adapt to the environment based on reinforcement learning. The main characteristic is that the agents are capable to learn and to solve a problem that requires planning for the future in a stochastic and complicated environment without the existence of a central controller. Another important feature is that the agents learn to cooperate. The final solution, although not guaranteed to be optimal, provides a good solution. One key parameter of this approach is the proper formulation of the reward function. However, the main goal of the intelligent system is to provide an answer to the question "What do we want to do? rather than "How to do it?, like in the traditional control algorithm. In this sense, we should consider the reward function as a means to explain to the agents what we really want them to do.

Chapter 4

Consensus for Heterogeneous Systems with Delays

4.1 Introduction

Recent technological advances in communications and computation have spurred a broad interest in control law architectures involving the monitoring, coordination, integration, and operation of sensing, computing, communication and actuation components that tightly interact with the physical processes that they control. These systems are known as cyber-physical systems (see [354] and the references therein) and even though they are transforming the way in which we interact with the physical world, they introduce several grand research challenges. In particular, due to the use of open computation and communication platform architectures, controlled cyber-physical systems are vulnerable to adversarial attacks. The pervasive security and safety challenges underlying cyber-physical systems place additional burdens on standard adaptive control methods. Cyberphysical security involving information security and detection in adversarial environments has been considered in the literature ([357], [359], [361], [363], [365], [369], [371], [373], [374]).

Multiagent systems comprise an important subclass of cyberphysical systems that involve communication and collaboration between interacting agents that locally exchange information. In particular, leader-follower consensus has a wide application in areas such as surveillance, formation control, and search and rescue. In such systems, the system-state information of different agents is exchanged through communication channels represented by a given graph communication topology, and local actuators of each agent utilize the information received from its neighbours for the control design protocol. For the leader-follower consensus problem, most of the results in the literature assume that at least a subset of the followers have access to the exact leader state information ([358], [372], [375], [377], [378], [381], [382]). However, in realistic situations, the leader state information measured or received by the follower agents may be corrupted due to an attack on the communication channel. Consequently, each follower, which has a communication link with the leader, may measure or receive erroneous leader state information. In other words, every follower agent may have inexact state information for the leader.

In this section, we build on the solid foundation of adaptive control theory and multiagent systems theory in order to develop a new distributed adaptive control architecture that can foil malicious sensor and actuator attacks in the face of exogenous stochastic disturbances. Specifically, for a class of linear multiagent systems with an undirected communication graph topology, we develop a new structure of the neighborhood synchronization error for the distributed adaptive control protocol design of each follower in order to account for time-varying multiplicative sensor attacks on the leader state. In addition, the proposed framework accounts for time-varying multiplicative actuator attacks on the followers that do not have a communication link with the leader. Moreover, our framework addresses time-varying additive actuator attacks on all the follower agents in the network. The proposed controller guarantees uniform ultimate boundedness in probability of the state tracking error for each follower agent in a mean-square sense. Finally, to show the efficacy of our adaptive control architecture, we provide a numerical illustrative example, involving the lateral directional dynamics of an aircraft group of agents subject to state-dependent atmospheric drag disturbances as well as sensor and actuator attacks.

4.2 Multiagent Leader-Follower Consensus Problem

Consider a leader-follower networked multiagent system consisting of N-follower agents with the dynamics of agent $i \in 1,\dots,N$ given by

$$\begin{aligned} dx_i(t) &= [Ax_i(t)+Bu_i(t)]dt \\ &+ x_i(t)g^T dw(t), x_i(0) a.s. = x_{i0}, t \geq 0 \end{aligned} \tag{4.1}$$

where, for $t \geq 0$ and $i \in 1,\dots,N, x_i(t) \in \mathcal{H}_n$ is the state of the ith follower agent, $u_i(t) \in \mathcal{H}_m$ is the uncorrupted control input to the ith follower agent, $A \in \mathbb{R}^{n \times n}$ and $B \in \mathbb{R}^{n \times m}$ are system matrices,$w(\cdot)$ is a d-dimensional independent standard Wiener process (i.e., Brownian motion) defined on a complete filtered probability space $(\Omega, F, \mathcal{F}_{t_{t \geq 0}}, \mathbb{P})$, and $g \in \mathbb{R}^d$. Furthermore, we assume that $u_i(t) \in \mathcal{H}_m$ satisfies sufficient regularity conditions such that (4.58) has a unique solution forward in time. Specifically, we assume that the control process $u_i(\cdot)$ in (4.5) is restricted to the class of admissible controls consisting of measurable functions $u_i(\cdot)$ adapted to the filtration $\mathcal{F}_{t_{t\geq 0}}$ such that $u_i(t) \in \mathcal{H}_m$ and, for all $t \geq s, w(t) - w(s)$ is independent of $u_i(\tau), w(\tau), \tau s, and x_0(0)$, and hence, $u_i(\cdot)$ is non-anticipative. In addition, we assume that $u_i(\cdot)$ takes values in a compact metrisable set, and hence, it follows from Theorem 2.2.4 of [355] that there exists a unique path-wise solution to (14) in $(\Omega, \{\mathcal{F}_t\}_{t\geq 0}, \mathbb{P}^{x_{i0}})$ for every $i \in 1,\ldots,N$.

Furthermore, we assume that the control input of the ith follower agent with $i \in \mathcal{N}_I$ is compromised and is given by

$$\tilde{u}_i(t) = \triangle_i(t)u_i(t) + d_i(t), i \in \mathcal{N}_I, \tag{4.2}$$

where, for $t \geq 0 and i \in \mathcal{N}_I, \tilde{u}_i(t) \in \mathcal{H}_m$ denotes the compromised control command signal,$\triangle_i(t) = diag[\delta_{i1}(t),\ldots,\delta_{im}(t)] \in \mathbb{R}^{m\times m}, where \delta_{ik}(t) \in \mathbb{R}, k \in 1,\ldots,m$, represents a multiplicative actuator attack, such that $0 < \delta_{ik,min} \leq \delta_{ik}(t)\delta_{ik,max}$ with $\delta_{ik,min}$ and $\delta_{ik,max}$ denoting upper and lower bounds, respectively, and $d_i(t) \in \mathbb{R}^m$ denotes an additive actuator attack. Moreover, the control input of the ith follower agent with $i \in \mathcal{N}_{II}$ is compromised and is given by

$$\tilde{u}_i(t) = u_i(t) + d_i(t), i \in \mathcal{N}_{II}, \tag{4.3}$$

where, for $t \geq 0$ and $i \in \mathcal{N}_{II}, d_i(t) \in \mathbb{R}^m$ represents an additive actuator attack. Note that (4.2) and (4.3) can be combined as

$$\tilde{u}_i(t) = \triangle_i(t)u_i(t) + d_i(t), i = 1,\ldots,N, \tag{4.4}$$

where, for $i \in \mathcal{N}_{II}$, we take $\triangle_i(t) \equiv I_m$. Now, the compromised controlled system is given by

$$\begin{aligned} dx_i(t) &= [Ax_i(t) + B\tilde{u}_i(t)]dt \\ &+ x_i(t)g^T dw(t), x_i(0) a.s. = x_{i0}, i = 1,\ldots,N, t \geq 0. \end{aligned} \tag{4.5}$$

Next, the leader dynamics are given by

$$\begin{aligned} dx_0(t) &= [Ax_0(t) + Br_0(t)]dt \\ &+ x_0(t)g^T dw(t), x_0(0) a.s. = x_{00}, t \geq 0, \end{aligned} \tag{4.6}$$

where, for $t \geq 0, x_0(t) \in \mathcal{H}_n$ is the leader state and $r_0(t) \in \mathbb{R}^m$ is a bounded continuous reference input. Here, we assume that $r_0(\cdot)$ satisfies sufficient regularity conditions such that (4.6) has a unique solution forward in time. In the literature, the leader-follower consensus problem formulation typically assumes a relative state information between neighboring agents in order to derive the ith agent controller. Specifically, for $i \in 1,\ldots,N$, the neighborhood synchronization error ([358], [372], [375], [377], [378], [381], [382]) is given by

$$\bar{e}_i(t) = \sum_{j\in N_{in}(i)} \mathcal{A}_{(i,j)}[x_i(t) - x_j(t)] + q_i[x_i(t) - x_0(t)] \tag{4.7}$$

Note that the structure of the neighborhood synchronization error given by (4.7) assumes exact measurement of the leader information $x_0(t), t \geq 0$, by the ith follower agent for every $i \in \mathcal{N}_{II}$. However, this may not always be the case in practice. Specifically, in the case where we have communication channel attacks or when the sensors measuring the leader state are under attack, the leader state information $x_0(t), t \geq 0$, may not be accurately available to the agents. A more realistic scenario is, thus, the case where $x0i,m(t) a.s. \neq x_0(t), where\ x0i,m(t), t \geq 0$, is the leader state information measured or received by the ith follower agent for $i \in \mathcal{N}_{II}$. In this case, for $i \in \mathcal{N}_{II}$, the compromised leader measurement by the ith agent is given by

$$x_{0i,m}(t) = \Theta_i(t) x_0(t) \tag{4.8}$$

where $\Theta_i(t) = diag[\theta_{i1}(t), \ldots, \theta_{in}(t)] \in \mathbb{R}^{n \times n} with \theta_{ik}(t) = 0, k \in 1, \ldots, n$, and all $t \geq 0$. Note that, for generality, we assume $x0i,m(t) a.s. = x_{0j,m}(t), i, j \in \mathcal{N}_{II}, i = j$. For agent $i \in \mathcal{N}_I, q_i = 0$, which implies that agent i does not have access to the leader information, and hence, $\Theta_i(t), t \geq 0$, is set to $\Theta_i(t) \equiv I_n$. The following assumptions are necessary for the main results of this section.

Assumption 1 *The undirected communication graph topology $\mathfrak{G}$ is connected and at least one follower agent is connected to the leader.*

Remark 4.1 Assumption 1 implies that $L+Q$ is symmetric and positive definite ([367], [377], [378]). ▮

Assumption 2 *For $t \geq 0$ and $i \in 1, \ldots, N$, there exist unknown scalars $\bar{r}_0, \bar{x}_0, \bar{d}_i, \bar{\Theta}_{j,-1}, j \in \mathcal{N}_{II}, \bar{\dot{\Theta}}_{j,-1}, j \in \mathcal{N}_{II}, \bar{\Delta}_j, j \in \mathcal{N}_I, and \bar{\bar{\Delta}}_j, j \in \mathcal{N}_I$, such that $||r_0(t)|| \leq \bar{r}_0, ||x_0(t)|| \leq \bar{x}_0, ||d_i(t)|| \leq \bar{d}_i, ||\Theta_j^{-1}(t)||_F \leq \Theta_{j,-1}, j \in \mathcal{N}_{II}, ||\dot{\Theta}_j^{-1}||_F \leq \bar{\dot{\Theta}}_{j,-1}, j \in \mathcal{N}_{II}, ||\Delta_j(t)||_F \leq \bar{\Delta}_j, j \in \mathcal{N}_I$, and $||\dot{\Delta}_j(t)||_F \leq \bar{\bar{\Delta}}_j, j \in \mathcal{N}_I$.*

4.3 Distributed Adaptive Control Design

In this section, we develop a distributed adaptive control architecture for the stochastic multiagent system given by (4.58) and (4.6). The control action for the ith follower agent is given by

$$u_i(t) = \hat{\Delta}_i^{-1}(t) u_{i0}(t), \tag{4.9}$$

$$u_{i0}(t) = -cKe_i(t), \tag{4.10}$$

where $c > 0$ is a design constant, $K \in R^{m \times n}$ is a control gain to be determined, $\hat{\Delta} i(t) \equiv Im, i \in \mathcal{N}_{II}$, and $\hat{\Delta}_i(t) \in \mathcal{H}^{m \times m}, i \in \mathcal{N}_I, t \geq 0$, are the estimates of $\Delta_i(t), i \in \mathcal{N}_I, t \geq 0$. In light of the fact that we do not assume an exact measurement for the leader information by the follower agents that are in direct communication with the leader, we formulate a new neighborhood synchronization error $e_i(t), i \in 1, \ldots, N, t \geq 0$, given by

$$e_i(t) = \sum_{j \in \mathcal{N}_{in}(i)} \mathcal{A}_{(i,j)}[x_i(t) - x_j(t)] + q_i[x_i(t) - \hat{\Upsilon} i(t) x0i, m(t)], \qquad (4.11)$$

where $\hat{\Upsilon}_i(t) \equiv In, i \in \mathcal{N}_I$, and $\hat{\Upsilon}_i(t) \in \mathcal{H}_{n \times n}, i \in \mathcal{N}_{II}, t \geq 0$, is the estimate of $\Theta_i^{-1}(t), i \in \mathcal{N}_{II}, t \geq 0$.

The update laws $\hat{\Upsilon}_i(t) \in \mathcal{H}_{n \times n}, i \in \mathcal{N}_{II}, t \geq 0, and \hat{\Delta}_i(t) \in \mathcal{H}_{m \times m}, i \in \mathcal{N}_I, t \geq 0$, are given by

$$\begin{aligned}
d\hat{\Upsilon}_i(t) &= -[n_{\Upsilon_i} K^T K e_i(t) x_{0i}^T, m(t) \\
&+ n_{\Upsilon_i} q_i K^T K \hat{\Upsilon}_i(t) x_{0i,m}(t) x_{0i}^T, m(t) + \sigma_{\Upsilon_i} \hat{\Upsilon}_i(t)] dt, \\
\hat{\Upsilon}_i(0) a.s. &= \hat{\Upsilon}_{i0}, i \in \mathcal{N}_{II}, t \geq 0, \qquad (4.12) \\
d\hat{\delta}_{ik}(t) &= \begin{cases} 0, \hat{\delta}_i k = \delta_{ik,min}, and \phi_{ik}(t) < 0; \\ \phi_{ik}(t) dt, otherwise, \end{cases} \\
\hat{\delta}_{ik}(0) a.s. &= \hat{\delta}_{ik0} > \delta_{ik,min}, i \in \mathcal{N}_I, k = 1, \ldots, m, t \geq 0, \qquad (4.13)
\end{aligned}$$

where $\phi_{ik}(t) \triangleq n_{\Delta_i}[e_i^T(t) K^T] k [u_i(t)]_k - \sigma_{\Delta_i} \hat{\delta}_{ik}(t)$, $[\cdot]_k$ denotes the kth component of a vector $[\cdot], n_{\Upsilon_i} > 0, i \in \mathcal{N}_{II}, ni > 0, i \in \mathcal{N}_I, \sigma_{\Upsilon_i} > 2, i \in \mathcal{N}_{II}, and \sigma_{\Delta_i} > 1, i \in \mathcal{N}_I$, are design gains. Note that

$$\begin{aligned}
e_i(t) &= \sum_{j \in \mathcal{N}_{in}(i)} \mathcal{A}_{(i,j)}[x_i(t) - x_j(t)] + q_i[x_i(t) - \hat{\Upsilon}_i(t) x_{0i,m}(t)] \\
&= \sum_{j \in \mathcal{N}_{in}(i)} \mathcal{A}_{(i,j)}[x_i(t) - x_j(t)] + q_i[x_i(t) - x_0(t)] \\
&+ q_i[\Theta_i^{-1}(t) - \hat{\Upsilon}_i(t)] x_{0i,m}(t) \\
&= \sum_{j \in \mathcal{N}_{in}(i)} \mathcal{A}_{(i,j)}[x_i(t) - x_j(t)] + q_i[x_i(t) - x_0(t)] \\
&- q_i \tilde{\Upsilon}_i(t) x_{0i,m}(t) \\
&:= \bar{e}_i(t) - q_i \tilde{\Upsilon}_i(t) x_{0i,m}(t), \qquad (4.14)
\end{aligned}$$

where $\tilde{\Upsilon}_i(t) \hat{\Upsilon}_i(t) - \Theta_i^{-1}(t), i \in \mathcal{N}_{II}$. By definition $\tilde{\Upsilon}_i(t) \equiv 0$ when $q_i = 0, i \in \mathcal{N}_I$, and hence, in this case $e_i(t) = \bar{e}_i(t) = \sum_{j \in \mathcal{N}_{in}(i)} \mathcal{A}_{(i,j)}[x_i(t) - x_j(t)]$.

Next, it follows from (4.9) that

$$\begin{aligned}
\Delta_i(t) u_i(t) &= \hat{\Delta}_i(t) \hat{\Delta}_i^{-1}(t) u_{i0}(t) \\
&- \hat{\Delta}_i(t) \hat{\Delta}_i^{-1}(t) u_{i0}(t) + \Delta_i(t) u_i(t) \\
&= u_{i0}(t) - \tilde{\Delta}_i(t) u_i(t), i = 1, \ldots, N, \qquad (4.15)
\end{aligned}$$

where $\tilde{\triangle}_i(t) \triangleq \hat{\triangle}_i(t) - \triangle_i(t)$. Furthermore, by definition $\tilde{\triangle}_i(t) \equiv 0, i \in \mathcal{N}_{II}$. Now, defining the tracking error $\varepsilon_i(t) \triangleq x_i(t) - x_0(t)$ and using (4.9) and (4.10), the dynamics for the tracking error of the ith agent is given by

$$\begin{aligned} d\varepsilon_i(t) &= [A\varepsilon_i(t) - cBKe_i(t) - B\tilde{\triangle}_i(t)u_i(t) \\ &+ B(d_i(t) - r_0(t))]dt + \varepsilon_i(t)g^T dw(t), \varepsilon_i(0) a.s. = \varepsilon_{i0}, t \geq 0. (4.16) \end{aligned}$$

For the statement of the next result, sgn denotes the sign operator, that is, $\text{sgn}(\alpha)\frac{\alpha}{|\alpha|}, \alpha \neq 0$, and $\text{sgn}(0) \triangleq 0$. Furthermore, by Assumption 2, there exist constants $d_{i1}, i \in 1,\ldots,N$, such that $||d_i(t) - r_0(t)|| \leq d_{i1}, i \in 1,\ldots,N, t \geq 0$, and, for every finite $K \in \mathbb{R}^{m\times n}$, there exist constants $d_{i2} > 0, i \in \mathcal{N}_{II}$, such that $|tr[K^T K\Theta_i^{-1}(t)x_{0i,m}(t)x_{0i,m}^T(t)]| \leq d_{i2}, i \in \mathcal{N}_{II}, t \geq 0$. Finally, by definition, $\Theta_{i,-1} = 1, i \in \mathcal{N}_I, \bar{\hat{\Theta}}_{i,-1} = 0, i \in \mathcal{N}_I, \bar{\triangle}_i = 1, i \in \mathcal{N}_{II}$, and $\bar{\hat{\triangle}}_i = 0, i \in \mathcal{N}_{II}$.

Theorem 4.1

Consider the stochastic multiagent system given by (4.58) and (4.6) with actuator and sensor attacks given by (4.4) and (4.8), respectively. Assume Assumptions 1 and 2 hold, and, for a given positive-definite matrix $R \in \mathbb{R}^{n\times n}$, assume there exists a positive-definite matrixP $\in \mathbb{R}^{n\times n}$ such that

$$\tilde{A}^T P + P\tilde{A} - 2(c - \gamma_1)\lambda_{min}(L+Q)PBB^T P + R = 0, \tag{4.17}$$

where $\tilde{A} \triangleq A + \frac{1}{2}||g||^2 I_n$. Then, with the controller given by (4.9) and (4.10), adaptive laws given by (4.12) and (4.13), and control gain $K = B^T P$, the closed-loop system given by (4.12), (4.13), and (4.16) satisfies

$$\begin{aligned} &\lim_{t\to\infty} sup\mathbb{E}^{\varepsilon_{i0}}[||x_i(t) - x_0(t)||^2] \\ &\leq \frac{c_0}{c_1\lambda_{min}((L+Q)\otimes P)}, i = 1,\ldots,N, \end{aligned} \tag{4.18}$$

where

$$\begin{aligned} c_0 &\triangleq \sum_{i=1}^{N} \frac{(1-sgn(q_i))\sigma_{\triangle_i}}{n_{\triangle_i}}\bar{\triangle}_i^2 + \sum_{i=1}^{N} \frac{1-sgn(q_i)}{n_{\triangle_i}}\bar{\hat{\triangle}}_i^2 \\ &+ \sum_{i=1}^{N} \frac{q_i c\sigma_{\Upsilon_i}}{n_{\Upsilon_i}}\Theta_{i,-1}^2 + \sum_{i=1}^{N} \frac{q_i c}{n_{\Upsilon_i}}\Theta_{i,-1}^2 + \sum_{i=1}^{N} \frac{1}{\gamma} d_{i1}^2 \\ &+ \sum_{i=1}^{N} q_i^3 c n_{\Upsilon_i} d_{i2}^2 \end{aligned}$$

and

$$\begin{aligned} c_1 \triangleq min\Big\{ &\sigma_{\Upsilon_1} - 2,\ldots,\sigma\Upsilon_N - 2, \sigma_{\triangle_1} - 1, \\ &\ldots, \sigma\triangle_N - 1, \frac{\lambda_{min}(L+Q)\lambda_{min}(R)}{\lambda_{max}((L+Q)\otimes P)}\Big\}. \end{aligned}$$

Furthermore, the adaptive estimates $\hat{\Upsilon}_i(t), i \in \mathcal{N}_{II}, t \geq 0$, *and* $\hat{\triangle}_i(t), i \in \mathcal{N}_I, t \geq 0$, *are ultimately uniformly bounded in a mean-square sense.*

Proof: To show ultimate boundedness of the closed-loop system, consider the Lyapunov-like function given by

$$\begin{aligned} V(\varepsilon, \tilde{\triangle}\tilde{\Upsilon}) &= \varepsilon^T[(L+Q)\otimes P]\varepsilon + \sum_{i=1}^{N} \frac{1-sgn(q_i)}{n_{\triangle_i}} Tr(\tilde{\triangle}_i^2) \\ &+ \sum_{i=1}^{N} \frac{q_i c}{n_{\Upsilon_i}} Tr(\tilde{\Upsilon}_i^T \tilde{\Upsilon}_i), \end{aligned} \tag{4.19}$$

where $Tr(.)$ is the trace operator, $\varepsilon = [\varepsilon_1^T, \ldots, \varepsilon_N^T]^T \in \mathbb{R}^{nN}, \tilde{\triangle} =$ block-diag $[\tilde{\triangle}_1, \ldots, \tilde{\Upsilon}_N] \in \mathbb{R}^{nN \times nN}, \tilde{\Upsilon} = block-diag[\tilde{\Upsilon}_1, \ldots, \tilde{\Upsilon}_N] \in \mathbb{R}^{nN \times nN}$, and P satisfies (4.17). Note that if $i \in \mathcal{N}_I$, then $q_i = 0$, and hence, $\frac{1-sgn(q_i)}{n_{\triangle_i}} Tr(\tilde{\triangle}_i^2) = \frac{1}{n_{\triangle_i}} Tr(\tilde{\triangle}_i^2)$. In addition, $\frac{q_i c}{n_{\Upsilon_i}} Tr(\tilde{\Upsilon}_i^T \tilde{\Upsilon}_i) = 0$. Alternatively, if $i \in \mathcal{N}_{II}$, then $q_i > 0$, and hence, $\frac{1-sgn(q_i)}{n_{\triangle_i}} Tr(\tilde{\triangle}_i^2) = 0$. In this case, $\frac{q_i c}{n_{\Upsilon_i}} tr(\tilde{\Upsilon}_i^T \tilde{\Upsilon}_i) \neq 0$.

Now, the infinitesimal generator $\mathcal{L}V(\varepsilon, \tilde{\triangle}\tilde{\Upsilon})$ of the closed loop system (4.12), (4.13), and (4.16) is given by

$$\begin{aligned} & \mathcal{L}V\big(\varepsilon, \tilde{\triangle}, \tilde{\Upsilon}\big) \\ = \; & 2\varepsilon^T[(L+Q)\otimes PA - c(L+Q)^2 \otimes PBB^T P]\varepsilon \\ + \; & 2c\sum_{i=1}^{N} e_i^{-T} PBB^T P q_i \tilde{\Upsilon} ix0i,m + 2\sum_{i=1}^{N} e_i^{-T} PB(d_i - r_0) \\ - \; & 2\sum_{i=1}^{N} e_i^{-T} PB\tilde{\triangle}_i u_i + Tr(g\varepsilon^T((L+Q)\otimes P)\varepsilon g^T) \\ + \; & \sum_{i=1}^{N} \frac{2(1-sgn(q_i))}{n_{\triangle_i}} Tr(\tilde{\triangle}_i(n_{\triangle_i} u_i e_i^T PB - \sigma_{\triangle_i}\hat{\triangle}_i - \dot{\triangle}_i)) \\ + \; & \sum_{i=1}^{N} \frac{2q_i c}{n_{\Upsilon_i}} Tr(\tilde{\Upsilon}_i^T(-n_{\Upsilon_i} PBB^T P e_i x_{0i,m}^T - n_{\Upsilon_i} q_i PBB^T P\hat{\Upsilon}_i x_{0i,m} x_{0i,m}^T \\ - \; & \sigma_{\Upsilon_i}\hat{\Upsilon}_{ik} - \dot{\Theta}_i^{-1})), \quad (\varepsilon, \tilde{\triangle}, \tilde{\Upsilon}) \in \mathbb{R}^{Nn} \times \mathbb{R}^{Nm \times Nm} \times \mathbb{R}^{Nn \times Nn}. \end{aligned} \tag{4.20}$$

For $\gamma_1 > 0$, we observe that

$$
\begin{aligned}
& 2\sum_{i=1}^{N} e_i^{-}TPB(d_i - r_0) \\
\leq\ & \sum_{i=1}^{N} \gamma_1 \bar{e}_i^{-T} PBB^T P\bar{e}_i + \sum_{i=1}^{N} \frac{1}{\gamma_1}(d_i - r_0)^T(d_i - r_0) \\
\leq\ & \sum_{i=1}^{N} \gamma_1 \bar{e}_i^{-T} PBB^T P\bar{e}_i + \sum_{i=1}^{N} \frac{1}{\gamma_1} d_{i1}^2 \\
=\ & \gamma_1 \varepsilon^T [(L+Q)\otimes I_n](I_N \otimes PBB^T P)[(L+Q)\otimes I_n]\varepsilon + \sum_{i=1}^{N} \frac{1}{\gamma_1} d_{i1}^2 \\
=\ & \gamma_1 \varepsilon^T [(L+Q)^2 \otimes PBB^T P]\varepsilon + \sum_{i=1}^{N} \frac{1}{\gamma_1} d_{i1}^2.
\end{aligned}
\tag{4.21}
$$

On using the first part of (4.13) we have,

$$
\tilde{\delta}_{ik} \leq 0, \quad n_{\triangle_i}[e_i^T PB]_k [u_i]_k < \sigma_{\triangle_i}\hat{\delta}_{ik}, i \in \mathcal{N}_I, k = 1, \ldots, m
$$

and hence,

$$
-2[e_i^T PB]_k [u_i]_k \tilde{\delta}_{ik} < -\frac{2\sigma_{\triangle_i}(1 - sgn(q_i))}{n_{\triangle_i}} \tilde{\delta}_{ik}\hat{\delta}_{ik}. \tag{4.22}
$$

Alternatively, using the second part of (4.13) we have

$$
-2sum_{i=1}^{N} e_i^{-T} PB\tilde{\triangle}_i u_i = -\sum_{i=1}^{N} \frac{2(1 - sgn(q_i))}{n_{\triangle_i}} Tr\left(\tilde{\triangle}_i n_{\triangle_i} u_i e_i^T PB\right). \tag{4.23}
$$

Furthermore, we note that

$$
\begin{aligned}
& 2c\sum_{i=1}^{N} e_i^{-T} PBB^T Pq_i \tilde{\Upsilon}_i x0i,m \\
=\ & 2c\sum_{i=1}^{N} (e_i + q_i \tilde{\Upsilon}_i x_{0i,m})^T PBB^T Pq_i \tilde{\Upsilon}_i x_{0i,m} \\
=\ & 2c\sum_{i=1}^{N} e_i^T PBB^T Pq_i \tilde{\Upsilon}_i x_{0i,m} \\
+\ & 2c\sum_{i=1}^{N} (q_i \tilde{\Upsilon}_i x_{0i,m})^T PBB^T Pq_i \tilde{\Upsilon}_i x_{0i,m}.
\end{aligned}
\tag{4.24}
$$

Invoking the trace properties, it turns out that $Tr(Q^T vy^T) = Tr(Q^T vy^T)^T = v^T Qy$ for every $Q \in \mathbb{R}^{m\times n}, v \in \mathbb{R}^m$, and $y \in \mathbb{R}^N$. Therefore, it can be shown that

$$2c\sum_{i=1}^{N} e_i^T PBB^T Pq_i\tilde{\Upsilon}_i x0i,m = \sum_{i=1}^{N} \frac{2q_i c}{n_{\Upsilon_i}} tr\left(\tilde{\Upsilon}_i^T n_{\Upsilon_i} PBB^T Pe_i x_{0i,m}^T\right) \tag{4.25}$$

and

$$\begin{aligned}
& 2c\sum_{i=1}^{N}(q_i\tilde{\Upsilon}_i x_{0i,m})^T PBB^T Pq_i\tilde{\Upsilon}_i x_{0i,m} \\
= & \sum_{i=1}^{N} \frac{2q_i c}{n_{\Upsilon_i}} Tr\left(\tilde{\Upsilon}_i^T n_{\Upsilon_i} q_i PBB^T P\hat{\Upsilon}_i x_{0i,m} x_{0i,m}^T\right) \\
- & \sum_{i=1}^{N} \frac{2q_i c}{n_{\Upsilon_i}} Tr\left(\tilde{\Upsilon}_i^T n_{\Upsilon_i} q_i PBB^T P\Theta_i^{-1} x_{0i,m} x_{0i,m}^T\right) \\
\leq & \sum_{i=1}^{N} \frac{2q_i c}{n_{\Upsilon_i}} Tr\left(\tilde{\Upsilon}_i^T n_{\Upsilon_i} q_i PBB^T P\hat{\Upsilon}_i x_{0i,m} x_{0i,m}^T\right) \\
+ & \sum_{i=1}^{N} \frac{q_i c}{n_{\Upsilon_i}} Tr\left(\tilde{\Upsilon}_i^T \tilde{\Upsilon}_i\right) + \sum_{i=1}^{N} q_i^3 c n_{\Upsilon_i} d_{i2}^2.
\end{aligned} \tag{4.26}$$

Proceeding further, we have

$$\begin{aligned}
- & \sum_{i=1}^{N} \frac{2q_i\sigma_{\Upsilon_i} c}{n_{\Upsilon_i}} Tr(\tilde{\Upsilon}_i^T \hat{\Upsilon}_i) \\
= & -\sum_{i=1}^{N} \frac{2q_i\sigma_{\Upsilon_i} c}{n_{\Upsilon_i}} Tr[\tilde{\Upsilon}_i^T(\tilde{\Upsilon}_i + \Theta_i^{-1})] \\
\leq & -\sum_{i=1}^{N} \frac{2q_i\sigma_{\Upsilon_i} c}{n_{\Upsilon_i}} Tr(\tilde{\Upsilon}_i^T \tilde{\Upsilon}_i) + \sum_{i=1}^{N} \frac{q_i\sigma_{\Upsilon_i} c}{n_{\Upsilon_i}} tr(\tilde{\Upsilon}_i^T \tilde{\Upsilon}_i) \\
+ & \sum_{i=1}^{N} \frac{q_i\sigma_{\Upsilon_i} c}{n_{\Upsilon_i}} Tr(\Theta_i^{-2}) \\
= & -\sum_{i=1}^{N} \frac{q_i\sigma_{\Upsilon_i} c}{n_{\Upsilon_i}} Tr(\tilde{\Upsilon}_i^T \tilde{\Upsilon}_i) + \sum_{i=1}^{N} \frac{q_i\sigma_{\Upsilon_i} c}{n_{\Upsilon_i}} Tr(\Theta_i^{-2})
\end{aligned} \tag{4.27}$$

and

$$\begin{aligned} & - \sum_{i=1}^{N} \frac{2q_i c}{n_{\Upsilon_i}} Tr(\tilde{\Upsilon}_i^T \dot{\Theta}_i^{-1}) \\ & \leq \sum_{i=1}^{N} \frac{q_i c}{n_{\Upsilon_i}} Tr(\tilde{\Upsilon}_i^T \tilde{\Upsilon}_i) + \sum_{i=1}^{N} \frac{q_i c}{n_{\Upsilon_i}} tr(\dot{\Theta}_i^{-2}), \end{aligned} \tag{4.28}$$

Now, it follows that

$$\begin{aligned} & - \sum_{i=1}^{N} \frac{2q_i c}{n_{\Upsilon_i}} Tr\left(\tilde{\Upsilon}_i^T (\sigma_{\Upsilon_i} \hat{\Upsilon} ik + \dot{\Theta}_i^{-1}) \right) \\ & \leq -\sum_{i=1}^{N} \frac{q_i c(\sigma_{\Upsilon_i} - 1)}{n_{\Upsilon_i}} tr(\tilde{\Upsilon}_i^T \tilde{\Upsilon}_i) + \sum_{i=1}^{N} \frac{q_i c \sigma_{\Upsilon_i}}{n_{\Upsilon_i}} Tr(\Theta_i^{-2}) \\ & + \sum_{i=1}^{N} \frac{q_i c}{n_{\Upsilon_i}} Tr(\dot{\Theta}_i^{-2}). \end{aligned} \tag{4.29}$$

Using (4.29) and a similar construction as above for bounding the term

$$-\sum_{i=1}^{N} \frac{2(1 - sgn(q_i))}{n_{\Delta_i}} Tr[\tilde{\Delta}_i (\sigma_{\Delta_i} \hat{\Delta}_i + \dot{\Delta}_i)]$$

as well as recalling the fact that

$$Tr(g\varepsilon^T ((L+Q) \otimes P)\varepsilon g^T) = ||g||^2 \varepsilon^T [(L+Q) \otimes P]\varepsilon$$

with some algebraic manipulation, it can be shown that (4.20) yields

$$\begin{aligned} & \mathcal{L}V(\varepsilon, \tilde{\Delta}, \tilde{\Upsilon}) \\ \geq \; & \leq 2\varepsilon^T [(L+Q) \otimes PA - (c - \gamma_1)(L+Q)^2 \otimes PBB^T P \\ + \; & g2(L+Q) \otimes P]\varepsilon - \sum_{i=1}^{N} \frac{q_i c(\sigma_{\Upsilon_i} - 2)}{n_{\Upsilon_i}} Tr(\tilde{\Upsilon}_i^T \tilde{\Upsilon}_i) \\ - \; & \sum_{i=1}^{N} \frac{(1 - sgn(q_i))(\sigma_{\Delta_i} - 1)}{n_{\Delta_i}} Tr(\tilde{\Delta}_i^2) + c_0, \\ & (\varepsilon, \tilde{\Delta}, \tilde{\Upsilon}) \in \mathbb{R}^{Nn} \times \mathbb{R}^{Nm \times Nm} \times \mathbb{R}^{Nn \times Nn}, \end{aligned} \tag{4.30}$$

where

$$\begin{aligned} c_0 &= \sum_{i=1}^{N} \frac{(1-sgn(q_i))\sigma_{\triangle_i}}{n_{\triangle_i}} \bar{\triangle}_i^2 + \sum_{i=1}^{N} \frac{1-sgn(q_i)}{n_{\triangle_i}} \bar{\bar{\triangle}}_i \\ &+ \sum_{i=1}^{N} \frac{q_i \sigma_{\Upsilon_i} c}{n_{\Upsilon_i}} \bar{\Theta}_i^2 + \sum_{i=1}^{N} \frac{q_i c}{n_{\Upsilon_i}} \bar{\Theta}_{i,-1}^2 \\ &+ \sum_{i=1}^{N} \frac{1}{\gamma_1} d_i^2 + \sum_{i=1}^{N} q_i^3 c n_{\Upsilon_i} d_{i2}^2. \end{aligned} \tag{4.31}$$

Now, since $L+Q$ is positive definite, there exists an orthogonal matrix $T \in \mathbb{R}^{N\times N}$such that $T^T(L+Q)T = diag[\lambda_1,\ldots,\lambda_N]$, where $\lambda_i, i \in \{1,\ldots,N\}$, are the eigenvalues of $L+Q$. Defining $\xi \triangleq (T^T \otimes I_n)\varepsilon$, it follows from (4.30) that

$$\begin{aligned} &\mathcal{L}V(\varepsilon,\tilde{\triangle},\tilde{\Upsilon}) \\ \leq\ & \sum_{i=1}^{N} \lambda_i \xi_i^T [P\tilde{A} + \tilde{A}^T P - 2(c-\gamma_1)\lambda_{min}(L+Q)PBB^T P]\xi_i \\ -\ & \sum_{i=1}^{N} \frac{q_i c(\sigma_{\Upsilon_i}-2)}{n_{\Upsilon_i}} Tr(\tilde{\Upsilon}_i^T \tilde{\Upsilon}_i) \\ -\ & \sum_{i=1}^{N} \frac{(1-sgn(qi))(\sigma_{\triangle_i}-1)}{n_{\triangle_i}} Tr(\tilde{\triangle}_i^2) + c_0, \\ \leq\ & -\lambda_{min}(L+Q)\lambda_{min}(R)\varepsilon^T\varepsilon \\ -\ & \sum_{i=1}^{N} \frac{(1-sgn(q_i))(\sigma_{\triangle_i}-1)}{n_{\triangle_i}} Tr(\tilde{\triangle}_i^2) \\ -\ & \sum_{i=1}^{N} q_i c(\sigma_{\Upsilon_i}-2) n_{\Upsilon_i} Tr(\tilde{\Upsilon}_i^T \tilde{\Upsilon}_i) + c_0, \\ & (\varepsilon,\tilde{\triangle},\tilde{\Upsilon}) \in \mathbb{R}^{Nn} \times \mathbb{R}^{Nm\times Nm} \times \mathbb{R}^{Nn\times Nn}. \end{aligned} \tag{4.32}$$

Next, defining

$$c_1 \triangleq min\{\sigma_{\Upsilon_1}-2,\ldots,\sigma_{\Upsilon_N}-2,\sigma_{\triangle_1}-1,\ldots,\sigma_{\triangle_N}-1,\frac{\lambda_{min}(L+Q)\lambda_{min}(R)}{\lambda_{max}((L+Q)\otimes P)}\}$$

it follows from (4.32) that

$$\begin{aligned} &\mathcal{L}V\left(\varepsilon,\tilde{\triangle},\tilde{\Upsilon}\right) \leq -c_1 V\left(\varepsilon,\tilde{\triangle},\tilde{\Upsilon}\right) + c_0, \\ &(\varepsilon,\tilde{\triangle},\tilde{\Upsilon}) \in \mathbb{R}^{Nn} \times \mathbb{R}^{Nm\times Nm} \times \mathbb{R}^{Nn\times Nn}. \end{aligned} \tag{4.33}$$

Recalling standard stability results, it follows from (4.33) that

$$\begin{aligned} 0 &\leq \mathbb{E}^{\varepsilon_0}[V(\varepsilon(t),\tilde{\Delta}(t),\tilde{\Upsilon}(t))] \\ &\leq V(\varepsilon(0),\tilde{\Delta}(0),\tilde{\Upsilon}(0))e^{-c_1 t}+\frac{c_0}{c_1}, t\geq 0, \end{aligned} \tag{4.34}$$

and hence, all the signals of the closed-loop system are uniformly ultimately bounded in probability in a mean-square sense. Finally, noting that

$$\begin{aligned} &\lim_{t\to\infty} sup\mathbb{E}^{\varepsilon_0}[\varepsilon^T(t)((L+Q)\otimes P)\varepsilon(t)] \\ \leq &\lim_{t\to\infty} sup\mathbb{E}^{\varepsilon_0}[V(\varepsilon(t),\tilde{\Delta}(t),\tilde{\Upsilon}(t))]\leq \frac{c_0}{c_1}, \end{aligned} \tag{4.35}$$

it follows that, for every $i \in \{1,\ldots,N\}$,

$$\lim_{t\to\infty} \mathbb{E}^{\varepsilon_{i0}}[||x_i(t)-x_0(t)||^2] \leq \frac{c_0}{c_1\lambda_{min}((L+Q)\otimes P)}, \tag{4.36}$$

which implies that the path-wise trajectory of the state tracking error for each agent of the closed-loop system associated with the plant dynamics is uniformly ultimately bounded in a mean–square sense.

Remark 4.2 In the absence of any sensor attacks on the follower agents that measure or receive leader state information, we have $x_{0i,m}(t) = \Theta_i(t)x_0(t), i \in \mathcal{N}_{II}$, with $\Theta_i(t) \equiv I_n, t \geq 0$. In this case, the estimation error $\tilde{\Upsilon}_i(t) = \hat{\Upsilon}_i(t) - \Theta_i^{-1}(t), i \in \mathcal{N}_{II}$, vanishes, and hence, c_0 in Theorem 4.1 reduces to

$$c_0 \triangleq \sum_{i=1}^{N} \frac{(1-sgn(q_i))\sigma_{\Delta_i}}{n_{\Delta_i}}\bar{\Delta}_i^2 + \sum_{i=1}^{N} \frac{1-sgn(q_i)}{n_{\Delta_i}}\dot{\Delta}_i^2 + \sum_{i=1}^{N} \frac{1}{\gamma_1} d_{il}^2$$

■

Remark 4.3 ■

Note that $n_{\Upsilon_i}, i \in \mathcal{N}_{II}$, and $n_{\Delta_i}, i \in \mathcal{N}_I$, are design gain parameters used in the adaptive laws (4.14) and (4.15), respectively, and thus, selecting large values of these parameters can introduce transient oscillations in the update law estimates of $\hat{\Upsilon}_i(t), t \geq 0$, and $\hat{\Delta}_i(t), t \geq 0$. This can be remedied by adding a modification term in the update laws to filter out the high frequency content in the control signal while preserving uniform ultimate boundedness in a mean-square sense. This architecture is developed in [379].

4.4 Illustrative Example

To illustrate the key ideas presented in what follows, consider the multiagent system representing the controlled lateral dynamics of four follower aircrafts and one leader aircraft, with a communication topology shown in Fig. 4.1. Node x_0 represents the leader aircraft and nodes 1 through 4 represent the follower aircrafts. For the leader aircraft, the dynamical system representing the lateral directional dynamics of an aircraft ([366]) are given by (4.6), where $x_0(t) \triangleq [\beta(t), p(t), r(t)]^T, \beta(t)$ is the sideslip angle in deg, $p(t)$ is the roll rate in deg/sec, and $r(t)$ is the yaw rate in deg/sec. Here, we take $x_{00} = [1, -2, 1]^T$ and $g = [1, 1]^T$. The state-dependent disturbance is used to capture perturbations in atmospheric drag ([368]). Furthermore, the system matrices are given by

$$
\begin{aligned}
A &= \begin{bmatrix} -0.025 & 0.104 & -0.994 \\ 574.7 & 0 & 0 \\ 16.20 & 0 & 0 \end{bmatrix}, \\
B &= \begin{bmatrix} 0.122 & -0.276 \\ -53.61 & 33.25 \\ 195.5 & -529.4 \end{bmatrix}
\end{aligned}
\tag{4.37}
$$

with reference input

$$
r_0(t) = \begin{bmatrix} 2.4056 & 0.0765 & -0.0613 \\ -4.3701 & -0.1086 & 0.1485 \end{bmatrix} x0(t). \tag{4.38}
$$

The follower aircraft dynamics are given by (4.58), where, for $t \geq 0$ and $i \in 1,2,3,4, x_1(t) \triangleq [\beta_1(t), p_1(t), r_1(t)]^T, x_{10} = [2, -3, -1]^T$, $x_2(t) \triangleq [\beta_2(t), p_2(t), r_2(t)]^T, x_{20} = [3, 0, 1]^T, x_3(t) \triangleq [\beta_3(t), p_3(t), r_3(t)]^T, x_{30} =$ $[2, -1, -1]^T$, and $x_4(t) \triangleq [\beta_4(t), p_4(t), r_4(t)]^T, x_{40} = [1, -1, 1.5]^T$.

We assume that the leader information received by Agent 1 is given by

$$
\begin{aligned}
& x_{01,m}(t) \\
&= \begin{bmatrix} 1+0.1(1-e^{-0.5t}) & 0 & 0 \\ 0 & 1+0.2(1-e^{-0.8t}) & 0 \\ 0 & 0 & 1+0.4(1-e^{-0.1t}) \end{bmatrix} x_0(t).
\end{aligned}
\tag{4.39}
$$

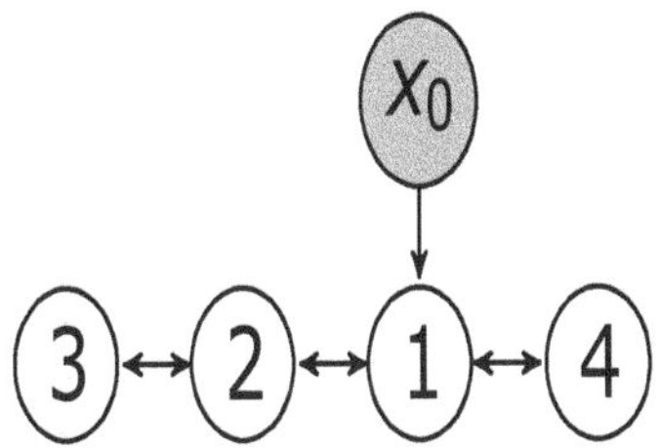

Figure 4.1: Communication topology of $\mathcal{G}$

The uncorrupted control inputs for the follower agents $u_i(t) \triangleq [\delta_{ail,i}(t), \delta r_{ud,i}(t)]^T, i \in \{1,2,3,4\}$, involve the aileron command in deg and the rudder command in deg, respectively. The actuator attacks are characterized as

$$d_1(t) = \begin{bmatrix} 0.1(1-e^{-10.1t}) \\ 0.08(1-e^{-0.15t}) \end{bmatrix}, d_2(t) = \begin{bmatrix} 0.2(1-e^{-0.1t}) \\ 0.1(1-e^{-0.15t}) \end{bmatrix}, \tag{4.40}$$

$$d_3(t) = \begin{bmatrix} 0.15(1-e^{-10.1t}) \\ 0.1(1-e^{-0.15t}) \end{bmatrix}, d_4(t) = \begin{bmatrix} 0.2(1-e^{-0.1t}) \\ 0.12(1-e^{-0.15t}) \end{bmatrix}, \tag{4.41}$$

$$\triangle_2(t) = \begin{bmatrix} 0.2+0.2e^{-0.2t} & 0 \\ 0 & 0.85+0.15e^{-0.11t} \end{bmatrix}, \tag{4.42}$$

$$\triangle_3(t) = \begin{bmatrix} 0.8+0.2e^{-0.15t} & 0 \\ 0 & 0.85+0.15e^{-0.15t} \end{bmatrix}, \tag{4.43}$$

$$\triangle_4(t) = \begin{bmatrix} 0.8+0.2e^{-0.2t} & 0 \\ 0 & 0.85+0.15e^{-0.2t} \end{bmatrix}, \tag{4.44}$$

Note that at $t = 0, \triangle_i(0) = I_2, i \in \{2,3,4\}$, and $d_i(0) = [0,0]^T, i \in \{1,2,3,4\}$, which implies that initially the actuator is uncompromized and is gradually compromised over time. To design a distributed adaptive controller, we use Theorem 4.1 with

$$P = \begin{bmatrix} 56.7970 & 0.1292 & -0.0348 \\ 0.1292 & 0.0411 & 0.0033 \\ -0.0348 & 0.0033 & 0.0031 \end{bmatrix} \tag{4.45}$$

and control design parameters $c = 2, \gamma_1 = 0.1, n_{\triangle_i} = 1, i \in \{2,3,4\}, \sigma_{\triangle_i} = 2, i \in \{2,3,4\}, n_{\Upsilon_1} = 1$, and $\sigma_{\Upsilon_1} = 3$. The system performance of the controller given by (4.9) and (4.10) with the proposed adaptive scheme is shown in Figs. 4.2-4.5 for the ith follower agent, where $i \in \{1,2,3,4\}$. Specifically, Figs. 4.2-4.5 show a sample trajectory along with the standard deviation of the state tracking error $\varepsilon_i(t) = x_i(t) - x_0(t)$ for agent $i \in \{1,2,3,4\}$ versus time for 10 sample paths. The mean control profile is also plotted in Figs. 4.7-4.5. It follows from Theorem 4.1, that the state tracking error for each agent is guaranteed to be uniformly ultimate bounded in a mean-square sense.

4.5 Tracking and Coordination Using Sensor Networks

Recently, we have been witnessing dramatic advances in micro-electromechanical sensors (MEMS), digital signal processing (DSP) capabilities, computing, and

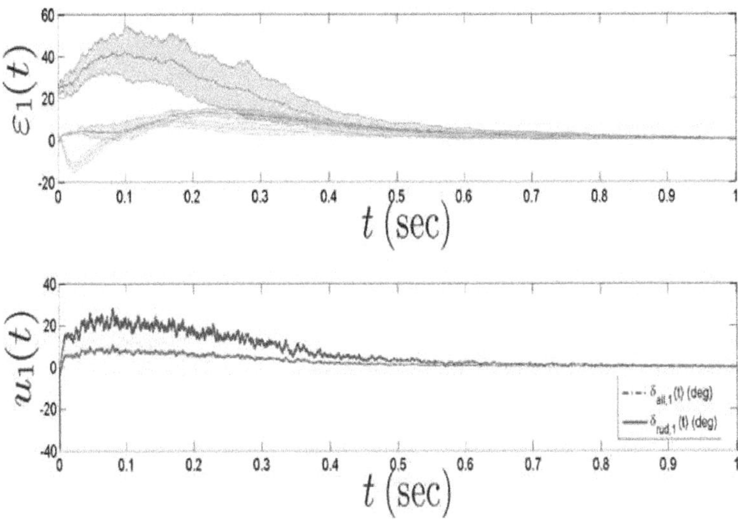

Figure 4.2: (Colour online) Agent1 sample average of the state tracking error profile along with the sample standard deviation of the closed-loop nominal system trajectories versus time; $\beta_1(t) - \beta(t)$ in blue , $p_1(t) - p(t)$ in red, and $r_1(t) - r(t)$ in green. The control profile is plotted as the mean of the 10 sample runs

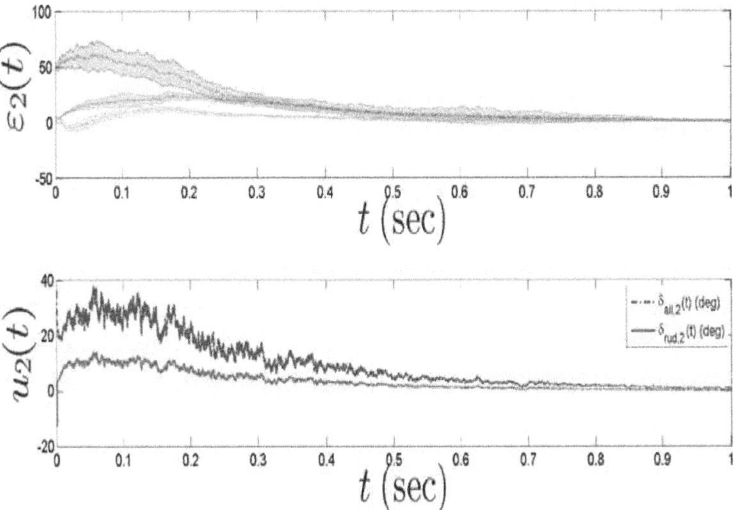

Figure 4.3: (Colour online) Agent–sample average of the state tracking error profile along with the sample standard deviation of the closed-loop nominal system trajectories versus time; $\beta_2(t) - \beta(t)$ in blue, $p_2(t) - p(t)$ in red, and $r_2(t) - r(t)$ in green. The control profile is plotted as the mean of the 10 sample runs

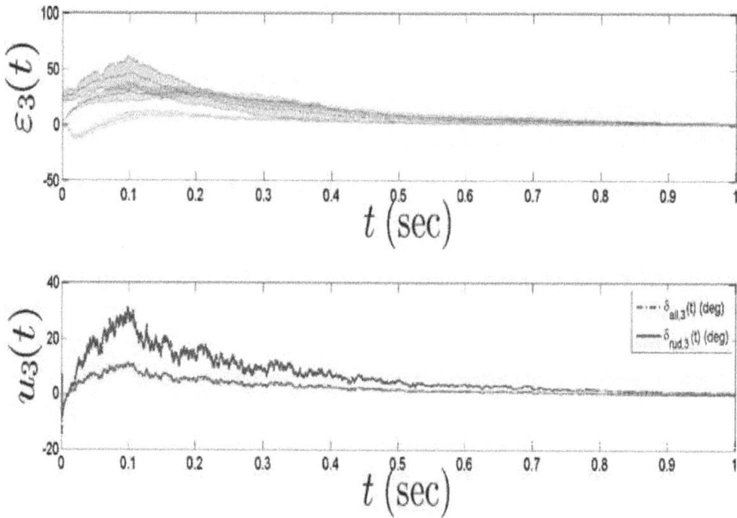

Figure 4.4: (Colour online) Agent 3 sample average of the state tracking error profile along with the sample standard deviation of the closed-loop nominal system trajectories versus time; $\beta_3(t) - \beta(t)$ in blue, $p_3(t) - p(t)$ in red, and $r_3(t) - r(t)$ in green. The control profile is plotted as the mean of the 10 sample runs

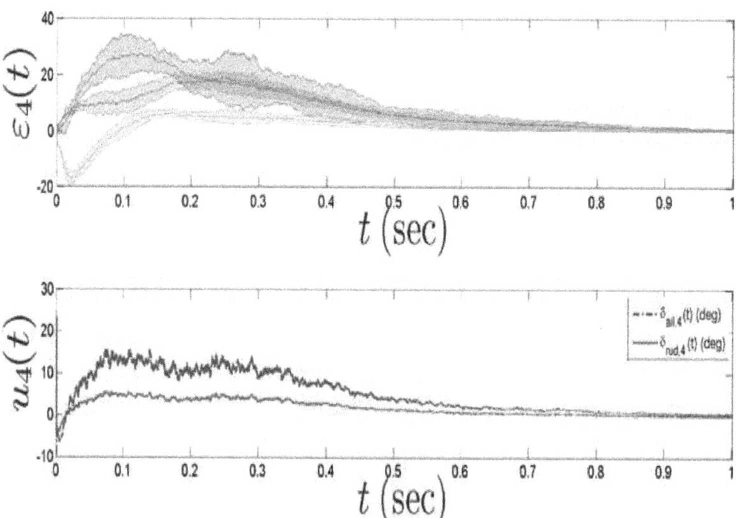

Figure 4.5: (Colour online) Agent 4 sample average of the state tracking error profile along with the sample standard deviation of the closed-loop nominal system trajectories versus time; $\beta_4(t) - \beta(t)$ in blue, $p_4(t) - p(t)$ in red, and $r_4(t) - r(t)$ in green. The control profile is plotted as the mean of the 10 sample runs

low-power wireless radios which are revolutionizing our ability to build massively distributed, easily deployed, self-calibrating, disposable, wireless sensor networks [384, 385, 386]. Soon, the fabrication and commercialization of inexpensive millimeter-scale autonomous electromechanical devices containing a wide range of sensors, including acoustic, vibration, acceleration, pressure, temperature, humidity, magnetic, and biochemical sensors, will be readily available [387]. These potentially mobile devices [388] can communicate with neighboring sensor nodes via low-power wireless communication to form a wireless ad-hoc sensor network with up to 100 000 nodes [389], [390]. Sensor networks can offer access to an unprecedented quantity of information about our environment, bringing about a revolution in the amount of control an individual has over his environment. The ever-decreasing cost of hardware and steady improvements in software will make sensor networks ubiquitous in many aspects of our lives [391], such as building comfort control [392], environmental monitoring [393], traffic control [394], manufacturing and plant automation [395], service robotics [396], and surveillance systems [397], [398].

In particular, wireless sensor networks are useful in applications that require locating and tracking moving targets and real-time dispatching of resources. Typical examples include search-and-rescue operations, civil surveillance systems, inventory systems for moving parts in a warehouse, and search-and-capture missions in military scenarios. The analysis and design of such applications are often reformulated within the framework of pursuit evasion games (PEGs), a mathematical abstraction which addresses the problem of controlling a swarm of autonomous agents in the pursuit of one or more evaders [399], [400]. The locations of moving targets (evaders) are unknown and their detection is typically accomplished by employing a network of cameras or by searching the area using mobile vehicles (pursuers) with on-board high resolution sensors. However, networks of cameras are rather expensive and require complex image processing to properly fuse their information. On the other hand, mobile pursuers with their on-board cameras or ultrasonic sensors with a relatively small detection range can provide only local observability over the area of interest. Therefore, a time-consuming exploratory phase is required [401], [402]. This constraint makes the task of designing a cooperative pursuit algorithm harder, because partial observability results in suboptimal pursuit policies [see Fig. 4.6(a)]. An inexpensive way to improve the overall performance of a PEG is to use wireless ad-hoc sensor networks [403]. With sensor networks, global observability of the field and long distance communication are possible [see Fig. 4.6(b)]. Global pursuit policies can then be used to efficiently find the optimal solution, regardless of the level of intelligence of the evaders. Also, with a sensor network, the number of pursuers needed is a function exclusively of the number of evaders and not the size of the field.

Now, we consider the problem of pursuit evasion games (PEGs), where the objective of a group of pursuers is to chase and capture a group of evaders in the

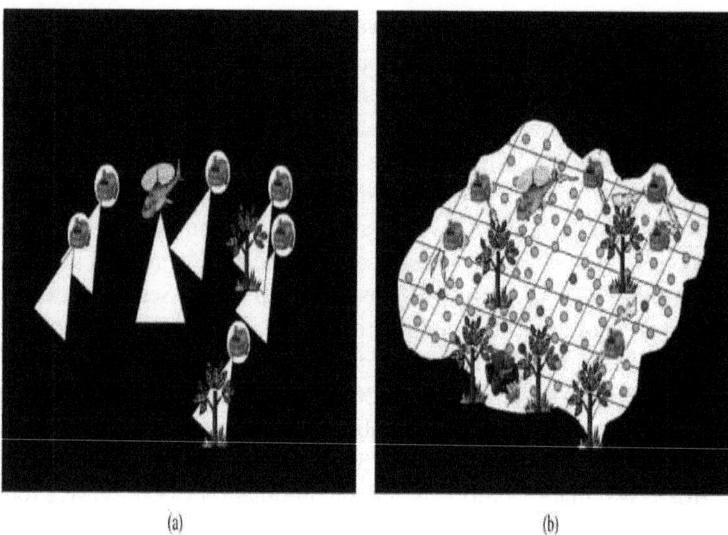

(a) (b)

Figure 4.6: (a) Sensor visibility in PEGs without sensor network. (b) Sensor visibility in PEGs with sensor network. Dots correspond to sensor nodes, each provided with a vehicle detection sensor. Courtesy of [403]

least amount of time with the aid of a sensor network. The evaders can either move randomly to model moving vehicles in search-and-rescue and traffic control applications, or can adopt evasive maneuvers to model search-and-capture missions in military scenarios.

While sensor networks provide global observability, they cannot provide high quality measurements in a timely manner due to packet loss, communication delay, and false detections. This has been the main challenge in developing a real-time control system using sensor networks. In this paper, we address this challenge by developing a real-time hierarchical control system called LochNess (Large-scale on-time collaborative heterogeneous Networked embedded systems). LochNess decouples the estimation of evader states from the control of pursuers via multiple layers of data fusion. Although a sensor network generates noisy, inconsistent, and bursty measurements, the multiple layers of data fusion convert raw sensor measurements into fused measurements in a compact and consistent representation and forward the fused measurements to the pursuers controllers in a timely manner.

- A multisensor fusion algorithm that combines noisy and inconsistent sensor measurements locally. The algorithm produces coherent evader position reports and reduces the communication load on the network.

- A multitarget tracking algorithm that tracks an unknown number of targets (or evaders). The algorithm is a hierarchical extension of the Markov chain Monte Carlo data association (MCMCDA) [404] algorithm for sensor networks to add scalability. MCMCDA is a true approximation scheme for the optimal Bayesian filter; i.e., when run with unlimited resources, it converges to the Bayesian solution [405]. MCMCDA is computationally efficient and robust against measurement noise and inconsistency (including packet loss and communication delay) [406]. In addition, MCMCDA operates with no or incomplete classification information, making it suitable for sensor networks. In fact, the performance of the algorithm can be improved given additional measurements to help identify the targets.

- A multiagent coordination algorithm that assigns one pursuer to one evader, such that the estimated time to capture the last evader is minimized based on the estimates computed by the multitarget tracking algorithm.

4.6 Target Tracking in Sensor Networks

One of the main applications of wireless ad-hoc sensor networks is surveillance. However, considering the resource constraints on each sensor node, the well-known multitarget tracking algorithms, such as joint probabilistic data association filter (JPDAF) [410] and multiple hypothesis tracker (MHT) [411], [412], are not feasible for sensor networks due to their exponential time and space complexities. As a result, many new tracking algorithms have been developed recently.

Most of the algorithms developed for sensor networks are designed for single-target tracking [397], [398], [407, 408, 409], [413, 414, 415, 416, 417, 418, 419] and some of these algorithms are applied to track multiple targets using classification [398], [413], [419] or heuristics, such as the nearest-neighbor filter (NNF)[1] [397]. A few algorithms are designed for multitarget tracking [420, 421, 422], where the complexity of the data association problem[2] inherent to multitarget tracking is avoided by classification [420], [422] or heuristics [421]. When tracking targets of a similar type or when reliable classification information is not available, the classification-based tracking algorithm behaves as the NNF. Considering the fact that the complexity of the data association problem is NP-hard

[1]The NNF [410] processes the new measurements in some predefined order and associates each with the target whose predicted position is closest, thereby selecting a single association. Although effective under benign conditions, the NNF gives order-dependent results and breaks down under more difficult circumstances.

[2]In multitarget tracking, the associations between measurements and targets are not completely known. The data association problem is to work out which measurements were generated by which targets; more precisely, we require a partition of measurements such that each element of a partition is a collection of measurements generated by a single targetor clutter [423].

[424], [425], a heuristic approach breaks down under difficult circumstances. Furthermore, the measurement inconsistencies common in sensor networks, such as false alarms and missing measurements (due to missing detection or packet loss), are not fully addressed in many algorithms. On the contrary, the multitarget tracking algorithm developed in this paper is based on a rigorous probabilistic model and based on a true approximation scheme for the optimal Bayesian filter.

Tracking algorithms for sensor networks can be categorized according to their computational structure: Centralized [398], [407], [416], hierarchical [417], [418], or distributed [397], [408], [409], [413, 414, 415], [419, 420, 421]. However, since each sensor has only local sensing capability and its measurements are noisy and inconsistent, measurements from a single sensor and its neighboring sensors are not sufficient to initiate, maintain, disambiguate, and terminate tracks of multiple targets in the presence of clutter; it requires measurements from distant sensors. Considering the communication load and delay when exchanging measurements between distant sensors, a completely distributed approach to solve the multitarget tracking problem is not feasible for real-time applications. On the other hand, a completely centralized approach is neither robust not scalable. In order to minimize the communication load and delay while being robust and scalable, a hierarchical architecture is considered in this paper.

4.7 Control System Architecture

We now consider the problem of pursuing multiple evaders over a region of interest (or the surveillance region). Evaders (or targets) arise at random in space and time, persist for a random length of time, and then cease to exist. When evaders appear, a group of pursuers is required to detect, chase and capture the group of evaders in minimum time with the aid of a sensor network. In order to solve this problem, we propose a hierarchical real-time control system, LochNess, which is shown in Fig. 2. LochNess is composed of seven layers: The *sensor network*, the *multisensor fusion (MSF)* module, the *multitarget tracking (MTT)* modules, the *multitrack fusion (MTF)* module, the *multiagent coordination (MAC)* module, the path planner module, and the path follower modules.

Sensors are spread over the surveillance region and form an ad-hoc network. The sensor network detects moving objects in the surveillance region and the MSF module converts the sensor measurements into target position estimates (or reports) using spatial correlation. This paper considers a hierarchical sensor network. In addition to regular sensor nodes Tier-1 nodes, we assume the availability of nodes which have long-distance wireless links and more processing power. We assume that each Tier-2 node can communicate with its neighboring Tier-2 nodes. Examples of a Tier-2 node include high bandwidth sensor nodes, such as iMote and BTnode [426], gateway nodes, such as Stargate, Intrinsyc Cerfcube, and PC104 [426], and the Tier-2 nodes designed for our experiment [427].

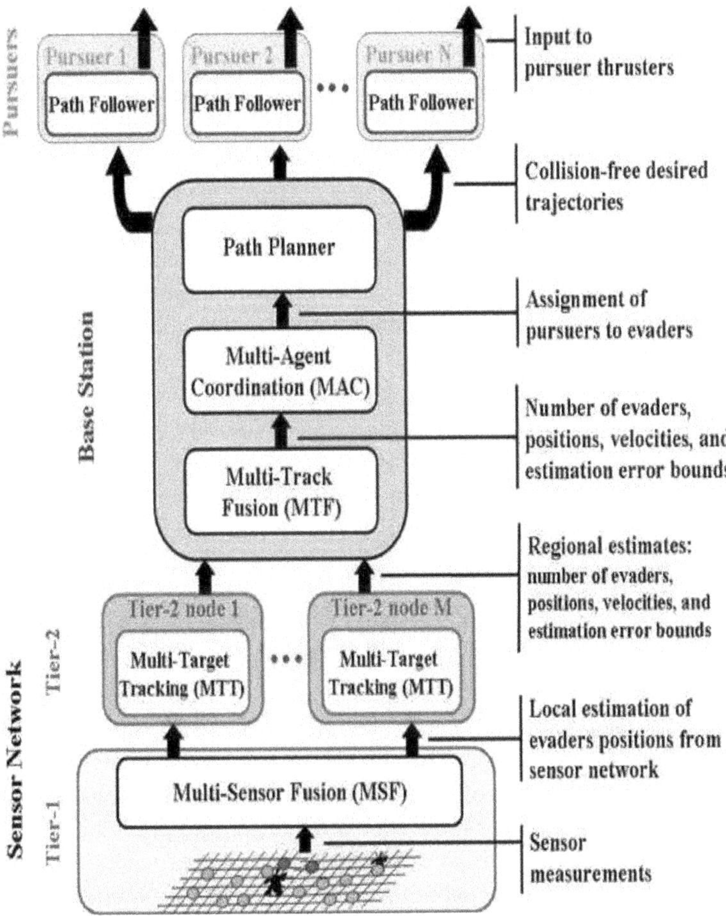

Figure 4.7: LochNess: A hierarchical real-time control system architecture using sensor networks for multitarget tracking and multiagent coordination

Each Tier-1 node is assigned to its nearest Tier-2 node and the Tier-1 nodes are grouped by Tier-2 nodes. We call the group of sensor nodes formed around a Tier-2 node an enquotetracking group. When a node detects a possible target, it listens to its neighbors for their measurements and fuses the measurements to forward to its Tier-2 node. Each Tier-2 node receives the fused measurements from its tracking group and the MTT module in each Tier-2 node estimates the number of evaders, the positions and velocities of the evaders, and the estimation error bounds. Each Tier-2 node communicates with its neighboring Tier-2 nodes when a target moves away from the region monitored by its tracking group. Finally, the tracks estimated by the Tier-2 nodes are combined hierarchically by the MTF module at the base station.

The estimates computed by the MTF module are then used by the MAC module to estimate the expected capture times of all pursuer-evader pairs. Based on these estimates, the MAC module assigns one pursuer to one evader by solving the bottleneck assignment problem [428] such that the estimated time to capture the last evader is minimized. Once the assignments are determined, the path planner module computes a trajectory for each pursuer to capture its assigned evader in the least amount of time without colliding into other pursuers. Then, the base station transmits each trajectory to the path following controller of the corresponding pursuer. The path following controller modifies the pursuers trajectory on the fly in order to avoid any obstacles sensed by the pursuers on-board sensors. The path planning and path follower modules can be implemented using dynamic programming [429] or model predictive control [430]. In the paper, we focus on MSF, MTT, MTF, and MAC modules and they are described in Section IV. In the remainder of this section, we describe the sensor network model and the problem formulations of multitarget tracking and multiagent coordination.

4.7.1 Sensor network and models

In this section, we deal with the models describing the sensing, the signal-strength and binary sensor as well as the sensor network model to considered hereinafter. A signal-strength sensor reports the range to a nearby target, while a binary sensor reports only a binary value indicating whether an object is detected near the reporting sensor. The signal-strength sensor model is used for the development and analysis of our system, while the binary sensor model is used in our experiments. While the signal-strength sensors provide better accuracy, our evaluation of the sensors developed for the experiments showed that the variability in the signal strength of the sensor reading prohibited extraction of ranging information. However, we found that the sensors were still effective as binary sensors. We also found that binary sensors were much less sensitive to time synchronization errors than signal-strength sensors.

Let N_s be the number of sensor nodes, including both Tier-1 and Tier-2 nodes, deployed over the surveillance region $\mathcal{R} \subset \mathbb{R}^2$. Let $s_i \in \mathcal{R}$ be the location of the ith sensor node and let $S = \{s_i : 1 \leq I \leq N_s\}$. Let $N_{ss} \ll N_s$ be the number of Tier-2 nodes and let $s_s^j \in S$ be the position of the jth Tier-2 node, for $j = 1;\ldots,N_{ss}$.

Signal-Strength Sensor Model: Let $R_s \in \mathbb{R}$ be the sensing range. If there is an object at $x \in \mathcal{R}$, a sensor can detect the presence of the object. Each sensor records the sensors signal strength

$$z_i = \begin{cases} \frac{\beta}{1+\gamma\|s_i - x\|^{\alpha}} + \omega_s^i, & if\ \|s_i - x\| \leq R_s \\ \omega_s^i, & if\ \|s_i - x\| > R_s \end{cases} \tag{4.46}$$

where α, β, and γ are constants specific to the sensor type, and we assume that z_i are normalized such that ω_s^i has the standard Gaussian distribution. This signal-strength based sensor model is a general model for many sensors available in sensor networks, such as acoustic and magnetic sensors, and has been used frequently [397], [408], [409], [422].

Binary Sensor Model: For each sensor i, let R_i be the sensing region of i. R_i can have an arbitrary shape but we assume that it is known to the system. Let $z_i \in \{0,1\}$ be the detection made by sensor i, such that sensor i reports $z_i = 1$ if it detects a moving object in R_i, and $z_i = 1$ otherwise. Let p_i be the detection probability and qi be the false detection probability of sensor i.

Sensor Network Model: Let $G = (S,E)$ be a communication graph such that $(s_i, s_j) \in E$ if and only if node i can communicate directly to node j. Let $g : \{1,...,N_s\} \rightarrow \{1,...,N_{ss}\}$ be the assignment of each sensor to its nearest Tier-2 node such that $g(i) = j$ if $\left\| s_i - s_S^j \right\| = min_{k=1,...,N_{ss}} \left\| s_i - s_S^j \right\|$. For a node i, if $g(i) = j$, the shortest path from s_i to $s_s j$ in G is denoted by $sp(i)$. In this paper, we assume that the length of $sp(i)$, i.e., the number of communication links from node i to its Tier-2 node, is smaller when the physical distance between node i and its Tier-2 node is shorter. If his is not the case, we can assign a node to the Tier-2 node with the fewest communication links between them.

Local sensor measurements are fused by the MSF module described in Section IV-A. Let $\hat{z}_i$ be a fused measurement originated from node i. Node i transmits the fused measurement $\hat{z}_i$ to the Tier-2 node $g(i)$ via the shortest path $sp(i)$. A transmission along an edge (s_i, s_j) on the path fails independently with probability p_{te} and the message never reaches the Tier-2 node. Transmission failures along an edge (s_i, s_j) may include failures from retransmissions from node i to node j. We can consider transmission failure as another form of a missing observation. If k is the number of hops required to relay data from a sensor node to its Tier-2 node, the probability of successful transmission decays exponentially as k increases. To overcome this problem, we use k independent paths to relay data if the reporting sensor node is k hops away from its Tier-2 node. The probability of successful communication p_{cs} from the reporting node i to its Tier-2 node $g(i)$ can be computed as $p_{cs}(p_{te}, k) = 1 - \left((1 - p_{te})^k\right)^k$, where $k = |sp(i)|$ and $|sp(i)|$ denotes the cardinality of the set $sp(i)$.

We assume each node has the same probability p_{de} of delaying a message. If d_i is the number of (additional) delays on a message originating from the sensor i, then d_i is distributed as

$$p(d_i = d) = \begin{bmatrix} |sp(i)| + d - 1 \\ d \end{bmatrix} (1 - p_{de})^{sp(i)} (p_{de})^d \tag{4.47}$$

We are modeling the number of (additional) delays by the negative binomial distribution. A negative binomial random variable represents the number of failures before reaching a fixed number of successes from Bernoulli trials. In our case, it is the number of delays before $|sp(i)|$ successful delay-free transmissions.

If the network is heavily loaded, the independence assumptions on transmission failure and communication delay may not hold. However, the model is realistic under moderate conditions and we have chosen it for its simplicity.

4.7.2 Multitarget tracking

The MTT and MTF modules of *LochNess* estimate the number of targets, positions and velocities of targets, and estimation error bounds. Since the number of targets is unknown and time-varying, we need a general formulation of the multitarget tracking problem. This section describes the multitarget tracking problem and two possible solutions.

Let $T_s \in \mathbb{Z}^+$ be the duration of surveillance. Let K be the number of targets that appear in the surveillance region $\mathcal{R}$ during the surveillance period. Each target k moves in $\mathcal{R}$ for some duration $\left[t_i^k, t_f^k\right] \subset [1, T_s]$. Notice that the exact values of K and $\left\{t_i^k, t_f^k\right\}$ are unknown. Each target arises at a random position in $\mathcal{R}$ at t_k^i , moves independently around $\mathcal{R}$ until t_k^f , and disappears. At each time, an existing target persists with probability $1 - p_z$ and disappears with probability p_z. The number of targets arising at each time over $\mathcal{R}$ has a Poisson distribution with a parameter $\lambda_b V$, where λ_b is the birth rate of new targets per unit time, per unit volume, and V is the volume of $\mathcal{R}$. The initial position of a new target is uniformly distributed over $\mathcal{R}$.

Let $F_k : \mathbb{R}^{n_x} \rightarrow \mathbb{R}^{n_x}$ be the discrete-time dynamics of the target k, where n_x is the dimension of the state variable, and let $x^k(t) \in \mathbb{R}^{n_x}$ be the state of the target k at time t for $t = 1, ..., T_s$. The target k moves according to

$$x^k(t+1) = F^k\left(x^k(t)\right) + \omega^k(t), fort = t_i^k, ..., t_f^k - 1 \tag{4.48}$$

where $\omega^k(t) \in \mathbb{R}^{n_x}$ are white noise processes. When a target is present, a noisy observation (or measurement)[3] of the state of the target is measured with a detection probability p_d. Notice that, with probability $1 - p_d$, the target is not detected and we call this a missing observation. There are also false alarms and the number of false alarms has a Poisson distribution with a parameter $\lambda_f V$, where λ_f is the false alarm rate per unit time, per unit volume. Let $n(t)$ be the number of observations at time t, including both noisy observations and false alarms. Let $y^j(t) \in \mathbb{R}^{n_y}$ be the jth observation at time t for $j = 1, ..., n(t)$, where n_y is the dimension of each observation vector. Each target generates a unique observation at each sampling time if it is detected. Let $H_j : \mathbb{R}^{n_y} \rightarrow \mathbb{R}^{n_y}$ be the observation model. Then, the observations are generated as follows:

$$y^j(t) = \begin{cases} H^j\left(x^k(t)\right) + v^j(t), & \text{if } y^j(t) \text{ is from } x^k(t) \\ u_f(t), & \text{otherwise} \end{cases} \tag{4.49}$$

[3]Note that the terms observation and measurement are used interchangeably in this paper.

where $v^j(t) \in \mathbb{R}^{n_x}$ are white noise processes and $u_f(t) \sim \mathrm{Unif}(\mathcal{R})$ is a random process for false alarms. We assume that the targets are indistinguishable in this paper, but if observations include target type or attribute information, the state variable can be extended to include target type information, as done in [431].

The main objective of the multitarget tracking problem is to estimate K, $\left\{t_i^k, t_f^k\right\}$ and $\left\{x^k(t) : t_i^k \leq t \leq t_f^k\right\}$, for $k = 1, ..., K$, from noisy observations.

Let $Y(t) = \{y^t(t) : j = 1, ..., n(t)\}$ be all measurements at time t and $Y = \{Y(t) : 1 \leq t \leq T_s\}$ be all measurements from $t = 1$ to $t = T_s$. Let Ω be a collection of partitions of Y such that, for $\omega \in \Omega, \omega = \{\tau_0, \tau_1, ..., \tau_k\}$, where τ_0 is a set of false alarms and τ_k is a set of measurements from target k for $k = 1, ..., K$. Note that Ω is also known as a joint association event in literature. More formally, Ω is defined as follows.

1. $\omega = \{\tau_0, \tau_1, ..., \tau_k\}$
2. $\bigcup_K^{k=0} \tau_k = Y$ and $\tau_i \cap \tau_j = \emptyset$ for $i \neq j$;
3. τ_0 is a set of false alarms;
4. $|\tau_k \cap Y(t)| \leq 1$ for $k = 1, ..., K$ and $t = 1, ..., T_s$;
5. $|\tau_k| \geq 2$ for $k = 1, ..., K$.

An example of a partition is shown in Fig. 4.8. Here, K is the number of tracks for the given partition $\omega \in \Omega$. We call τ_k a track when there is no confusion, although the actual track is the set of estimated states from the observations τ_k. This is because we assume there is a deterministic function that returns a set of estimated states, given a set of observations. A track is assumed to contain at least two observations, since we cannot distinguish a track with a single observation from a false alarm, assuming $\lambda_f > 0$. For special cases, in which $p_d = 1$ or $\lambda_f = 0$, the definition of Ω can be adjusted accordingly.

Let $n_e(t-1)$ be the number of targets at time $t-1$, $n_e(t)$ be the number of targets terminated at time t and $n_c(t) = n_e(t-1) - n_z(t)$ be the number of targets from time $t-1$ that have not terminated at time t. Let $n_b(t)$ be the number of new targets at time t, $n_d(t)$ be the number of actual target detections at time t and $n_u(t) = n_c(t) + n_b(t) - n_d(t)$ be the number of undetected targets. Finally, let $n_f(t) = n(t) - n_d(t)$ be the number of false alarms. Using the Bayes rule, it can be shown that the posterior of ω is [405]

$$\begin{aligned} P(\omega \mid Y) &\propto P(\omega) \cdot P(Y \mid \omega) \\ &\propto \prod_{t=1}^{T_s} p_z^{n_z(t)} (1-p_z)^{n_c(t)} p_d^{n_d(t)} (1-p_d)^{n_u(t)} \\ &\times \prod_{t=1}^{T_s} (\lambda_b V)^{n_b(t)} (\lambda_f V)^{n_f(t)} \cdot P(Y \mid \omega) \end{aligned} \tag{4.50}$$

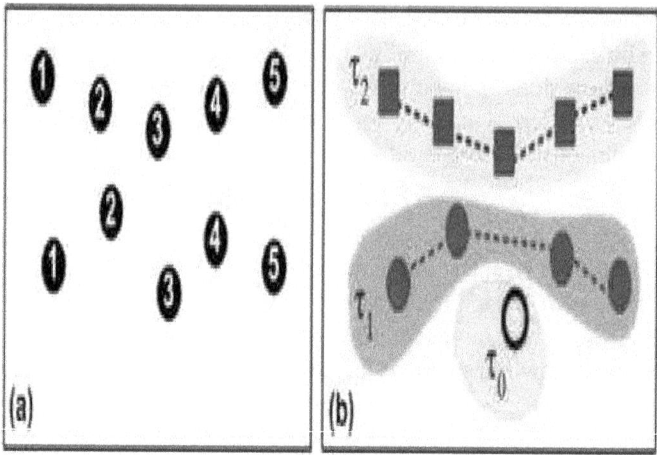

Figure 4.8: (a) An example of observations Y (each circle represents an observation and numbers represent observation times). (b) An example of a partition ω of Y

where $P(Y \mid \omega)$ is the likelihood of observations Y given ω, which can be computed based on the chosen dynamic and measurement models.[4] For example, the computation of $P(Y \mid \omega)$ for the linear dynamic and measurement models can be found in [404].

There are two major approaches to solve the multitarget tracking problem [405]:

- Maximum a posteriori (MAP) approach, where one seeks to find a partition of observations such that $P(\omega \mid Y)$ is maximized and estimates the states of the targets based on this partition.

- Bayesian approach or minimum mean square error (MMSE) approach, where one seeks to find an estimate which minimizes the expected square error. For instance, $\mathbb{E}(x^k(t) \mid Y)$ is the MMSE estimate for the state $x^k(t)$ of target k. However, when the number of targets is not fixed, a unique labeling of each target is required in order to find $\mathbb{E}(x^k(t) \mid Y)$ under the MMSE approach.

For convenience in the sequel, we take the MAP approach to the multitarget tracking problem.

[4]Our formulation of (5) is similar to MHT [432] and the derivation of (5) can be found in [433]. The parameters p_z, p_d, λ_b and λ_f have been widely used in many multitarget tracking applications [410], [432]. Our experimental and simulation experiences show that our tracking algorithm is not sensitive to changes in these parameters, in most cases. In fact, we used the same set of parameters for all our experiments.

4.7.3 Agent dynamics and coordination objective

In a situation where multiple pursuers and evaders are present, several assignments are possible and some criteria need to be chosen in order to optimize performance. In this work, we focus on minimizing the time to capture all evaders. However, other criteria might be possible, such as minimizing the pursuers energy consumption while guaranteeing capture of all evaders or maximizing the number of captured evaders within a certain amount of time. Since the evaders motions are not known, an exact time to capture a particular evader is also not known. Therefore, we need to define a metric to estimate the time to capture the evaders. Let us define the state vector of a vehicle as $x = [x_1, x_2, \dot{x}_1, \dot{x}_2]^T$, where (x_1, x_2) and $(\dot{x}_1, \dot{x}_2)$ are the position and the velocity components of the vehicle along the x and y axes, respectively. We denote by x_p and x_e the state of a pursuer and an evader, respectively. We will use the following definition of time-to-capture:

Definition 3.1 (Time-to-Capture): Let $x_e(t_0)$ be the position and velocity vector of an evader in a plane at time t_0, and $x_p(t)$ be the position and velocity vector of a pursuer at the current time $t \geq t_0$. We define the (constant speed) *time-to-capture* as the minimum time T_c necessary for the pursuer to reach the evader with the same velocity, assuming that the evader will keep moving at a constant velocity, that is,

$$T_c \min[T \mid x^P(t+T) = x^e(t=T)]$$

where $x^e_{1,2}(t+T) = x^e_{1,2}(t_0) + (t+T-t_0)\dot{x}^e_{1,2}(t_0), \dot{x}^e_{1,2}(t+T) = \dot{x}^e_{1,2}(t_0)$, and the pursuer moves according to its dynamics.

This definition allows us to quantify the time-to-capture in an unambiguous way. Although an evader can change trajectories over time, it is a more accurate estimate than, for example, some metric based on the distance between an evader and a pursuer, since the time-to-capture incorporates the dynamics of the pursuer.

Given Definition 3.1 and the constraints on the dynamics of the pursuer, it is possible to calculate explicitly the time-to-capture T_c, as well as the optimal trajectory $x^{e*}(t)$ for the pursuers as shown in Section IV-C.

We assume the following dynamics for both pursuers and evaders:

$$x(t+\delta) = A_\delta x(t) + G_\delta u(t) \tag{4.51}$$

$$\eta(t) = x(t) + v(t) \tag{4.52}$$

where δ is the sampling interval, $u = [u_1, u_2]^T$ is the control input vector, $\eta(t)$ is the estimated vehicle state provided by the MTF module, $v(t)$ is the estimation error, and

$$A_\delta = \begin{bmatrix} 1 & 0 & \delta & 0 \\ 0 & 1 & 0 & \delta \\ 0 & 0 & 1 & 0 \\ 0 & 0 & 0 & 1 \end{bmatrix} \quad G_\delta = \begin{bmatrix} \frac{\delta^2}{2} & 0 \\ 0 & \frac{\delta^2}{2} \\ \delta & 0 \\ 0 & \delta \end{bmatrix}$$

which correspond to the discretization of the dynamics of a decoupled planar double integrator. Although this model appears simplistic for modeling complex motions, it is widely used as a first approximation in path-planning [434, 435, 436]. Moreover, there exist methodologies to map such a simple dynamic model into a more realistic model via consistent abstraction, as shown in [437], [438]. Finally, any possible mismatch between this model and the true vehicle dynamics can be compensated for by the path-follower controller implemented on the pursuer [430].

The observation vector $\eta = [\eta_1, \eta_2, \dot{\eta}_1, \dot{\eta}_1]$ is interpreted as a measurement, although in reality it is the output from the MTF module shown in Fig. 4.7. The estimation error $v_t = [v_0, v_2, \dot{v}_1, \dot{v}_2]^T$ can be modeled as a Gaussian noise with zero mean and covariance Q or as an unknown but bounded error, i.e., $|v_1| < V_1, |v_2| < V_2, |\dot{v}_1| < \dot{V}_1, |\dot{v}_2| < \dot{V}_2$, where $V_1, V_2, \dot{V}_1$ and $\dot{V}_2$ are positive scalars that are possibly time-varying. Both modeling approaches are useful for different reasons. Using a Gaussian noise approximation enables a closed-form optimal filter solution, such as the well-known Kalman filter [439]. On the other hand, using the unknown but bounded error model allows for the design of a robust controller, such as the robust minimum time control of pursuers proposed in Section IV-C.

We also assume that the control input to a pursuer is bounded, i.e.,

$$|u_1^P| \le U_P, \quad |u_2^P| \le U_P \tag{4.53}$$

where $U_P > 0$. We consider two possible evader dynamics

$$u_1^e \sim \mathcal{N}(0, q_e), \quad u_2^e \sim \mathcal{N}(0, q_e) \quad \text{(random motion)} \tag{4.54}$$

$$|u_1^e| \le U_e, \quad |u_2^e| \le U_e \quad \text{(evasive motion)} \tag{4.55}$$

where $\mathcal{N}(0, q_e)$ is a Gaussian distribution with zero mean and variance $q_e \in \mathbb{R}^+$. Equation (9) is a standard model for the unknown motion of vehicles, where the variation in a velocity component is a discrete-time white noise acceleration [440]. Equation (10) allows for evasive maneuvers but places bounds on the maximum thrust. The multiagent coordination scheme proposed in Section IV-C is based on dynamics (10), as pursuers choose their control actions to counteract the best possible evasive maneuver of the evader being chased. However, in our simulations and experiments, we test our control architecture using the dynamics (4.54) for evaders, where we set $q_e = 2U_e$.

Since the definition of the time-to-capture is related to relative distance and velocity between the pursuer and the evader, we consider the state space error $\xi = x^P - x^e$ which evolves according to the following error dynamics:

$$\begin{aligned} \xi(t+\delta) &= A_\delta \xi(t) + G_\delta u^p(t) - G_\delta u^e(t) \\ \eta^\xi(t) &= \xi(t) + v^\xi(t) \end{aligned} \tag{4.56}$$

where the pursuer thrust $u^p(t)$ is the only controllable input, while the evader thrust $u^e(t)$ acts as a random or unknown disturbance, and $v^\xi(t)$ is the measurement error which takes into account the uncertainties on the states of both the pursuer and the evader. According to the definition above, an evader is captured if and only if $\xi(t) = 0$, and the time-to-capture T_c corresponds to the time necessary to drive $\xi(t)$ to zero, assuming $u^e(t) = 0$ for $t \geq t_0$ t0. However, this assumption is relaxed in Section IV-C.

According to the aforementioned definition of time-to-capture and the error dynamics (4.3), given the positions and velocities of all the pursuers and evaders, it is possible to compute the time-to-capture matrix $C = [c_{ij}] \in \mathbb{R}^{N_p \times N_e}$, where N_p and N_e are the total number of pursuers and evaders, respectively, and the entry c_{ij} of the matrix C corresponds to the expected time-to-capture between pursuer i and evader j. When coordinating multiple pursuers to chase multiple evaders, it is necessary to assign pursuers to evaders. Our objective is to select an assignment that minimizes the expected time-to-capture of all evaders, which correspond to the *global worst case time-to-capture*. In this paper, we focus on a scenario with the same number of pursuers and evaders, i.e., $N_p = N_e$. When there are more pursuers than evaders, then, only a subset of all the pursuers can be dispatched and the others are kept on alert in case more evaders appear. Alternatively, more pursuers can be assigned to a single evader. When there are more evaders than pursuers, one approach is to minimize the time to capture the N_p closest evaders. Obviously, many different coordination objectives can be formulated as they are strongly application-dependent. We have chosen the definition of global worst case time-to-capture as it enforces strong global coordination in order to achieve high performance.

4.8 Control System Implementation

4.8.1 Multisensor fusion module

1. *Signal-Strength Sensor Model:* Consider the signal-strength sensor model described in Section III-A. Recall that z_i is the signal strength measured by node i. For each node i, if $z_i \geq \theta$, where θ is a threshold set for appropriate values of detection and false-positive probabilities, the node transmits z_i to its neighboring nodes, which are, at most, $2R_s$ away from s_i, and listens to incoming messages from neighboring nodes within a $2R_s$ radius. We

assume that the communication range of each node is larger than a $2R_s$. For a node i, if z_i is larger than all incoming messages, $z_{i1},...,z_{i-k}$, and $z_{ik} = z_i$, then the position of an object is estimated by

$$\hat{z}_i = \frac{\sum_{j=1}^{k} Z_{i_j} S_{i_j}}{\sum_{j=1}^{k} Z_{i_j}} \tag{4.57}$$

The estimate $\hat{z}_i$ corresponds to a center of mass of the node locations weighed by their measured signal strengths. Node i transmits $\hat{z}_i$ to the Tier-2 node $g(i)$. If z_i is not the largest compared to the incoming messages, node i simply continues sensing. Although each sensor cannot give an accurate estimate of the objects position, as more sensors collaborate, the accuracy of the estimates improves, as shown in Fig. 4.9.

2. *Binary Sensor Model:* In order to obtain finer position reports from binary detections, we use spatial correlation among detections from neighboring sensors. The idea behind the fusion algorithm is to compute the likelihood of detections, assuming there is a single target. This is only an approximation, since there can be more than one target. However, any inconsistencies caused by this approximation are fixed by the tracking algorithm described in Section IV-B using spatio-temporal correlation.

   Consider the binary sensor model described in Section III-A. Let x be the position of an object. For the purpose of illustration, suppose that there are two sensors, sensor 1 and sensor 2, and $R_1 \cap R_2 = \theta$; [see Fig. 4.5(a)].

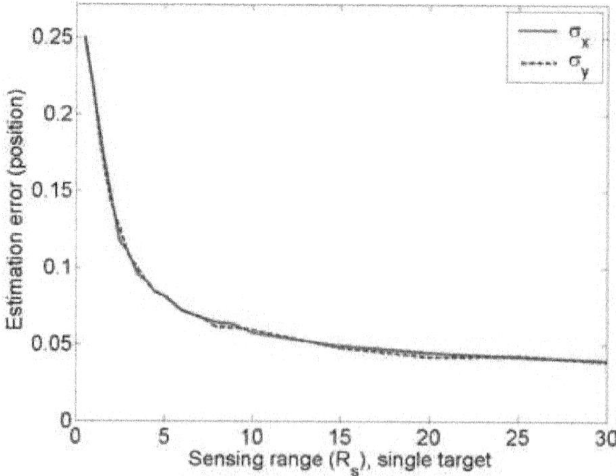

Figure 4.9: Single target position estimation error as a function of sensing range. See Section IV-B3 for the sensor network setup used in simulations (Monte Carlo simulation of 1000 samples, unity corresponds to the separation between sensors)

The overall sensing region $R_1 \cup R_2$ can be partitioned into a set of nonoverlapping cells (or blocks), as shown in Fig. 4.5(b). The likelihoods can be computed as follows:

$$\begin{aligned} P(z_1, z_2 \mid x \in S_1) &= p_1^{z_1}(1-p_1)^{1-z_1} q_2^{z_2}(1-q_2)^{1-z_2} \\ P(z_1, z_2 \mid x \in S_2) &= p_1^{z_1}(1-p_1)^{1-z_1} q_2^{z_2}(1-q_2)^{1-z_2} \\ P(z_1, z_2 \mid x \in S_3) &= p_1^{z_1}(1-p_1)^{1-z_1} q_2^{z_2}(1-q_2)^{1-z_2} \end{aligned} \tag{4.58}$$

where $S_1 = R_1 \setminus R_2$, $S_2 = R_2 \setminus R_1$, and $S_3 = R_1 \cap R_2$ [see Fig. 4.10(b)]. Hence, for any deployment we can first partition the surveillance region into a set of nonoverlapping cells. Then, given detection data, we can compute the likelihood of each cell, as shown in the previous example.

An example of detections of two targets by a 10×10 sensor grid is shown in Fig. 4.11. In this example, the sensing region is assumed to be a disk with radius of $7.62m(10ft)$. We have assumed $p_i = 0.7$ and $p_i = 0.05$ for all i. These parameters are estimated from measurements made with the passive infrared (PIR) sensor of an actual sensor node described in Section V. From the detections shown in Fig. 4.11, the likelihood can be computed using equations similar to (13) for each nonoverlapping cell (see Fig. 4.12). Notice that it is a time-consuming task to find all nonoverlapping cells for arbitrary sensing region shapes and sensor deployments. Hence, we quantized the surveillance region and the likelihoods are computed for a finite number of points as shown in Fig. 4.12.

There are two parts in this likelihood computation: The detection part (terms involving p_i) and the false detection part (terms involving q_i). Hereafter, we call the detection part of the likelihood the detection-likelihood and the false detection part of the likelihood the false-detection likelihood. Notice that the computation of the false detection- likelihood

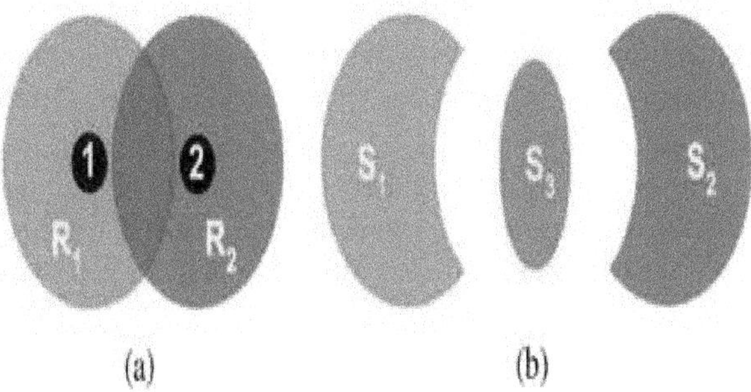

Figure 4.10: (a) Sensing regions of two sensors 1 and 2. R_i is the sensing region of sensor i. (b) A partition of the overall sensing region $R_1 \cup R_2$ into nonoverlapping cells S_1, S_2 and S_3, where $S_1 = R_1 \setminus R_2$, $S_2 = R_2 \setminus R_1$, and $S_3 = R_1 \cap R_2$

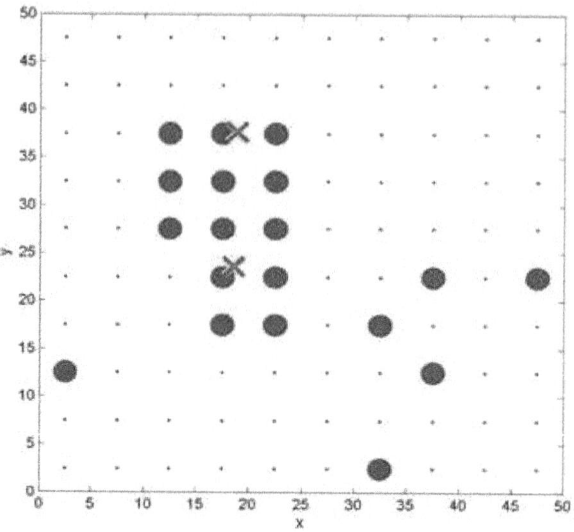

Figure 4.11: Detections of two targets by a 10×10 sensor grid (targets in $\times$, detections in disks, and sensor positions in small dots)

requires measurements from all sensors. However, for a large wireless sensor network, it is not feasible to exchange detection data with all other sensors. Instead, we use a threshold test to avoid computing the false-detection-likelihood and distribute the likelihood computation. The detection-likelihood of a cell is computed if there are at least θ_d detections, where θ_d is a user-defined threshold. Using $\theta_d = 3$, the detection likelihood of the detections from Fig. 4.11 can be computed as shown in Fig. 4.13. The computation of the detection likelihood can be done in a distributed manner. Assign a set of non-overlapping cells to each sensor such that no two sensors share the same cell and each cell is assigned to a sensor whose sensing region includes the cell. For each sensor i, let $\{S_{i_1},...,S_{i_{m(i)}}\}$ be a set of nonoverlapping cells, where $m(i)$ is the number of cells assigned to sensor i. Then, if sensor i reports a detection, it computes the likelihoods of each cell in $\{S_{i_1},...,S_{i_{m(i)}}\}$ based on its own measurements and the measurements from neighboring sensors. A neighboring sensor is a sensor whose sensing region intersects the sensing region of sensor i. Notice that no measurement from a sensor means no detection. Based on the detection-likelihoods, we compute target position reports by clustering. Let $\mathcal{S} = \{S_i,...,S_m\}$ be a set of cells whose detection-likelihoods are computed, i.e., the number of detections for each S_i is at least θ_d. First, randomly pick S_j from $\mathcal{S}$ and remove S_j from $\mathcal{S}$. Then, cluster around S_j the remaining cells in $\mathcal{S}$ whose set distance to S_j is less than the sensing ra-

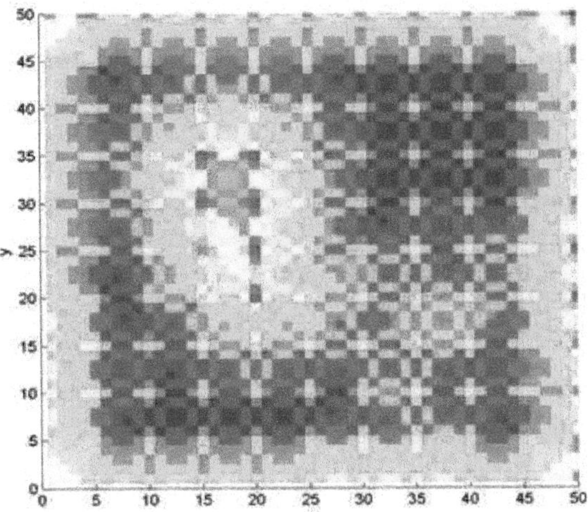

Figure 4.12: Likelihood of detections from Fig. 4.11

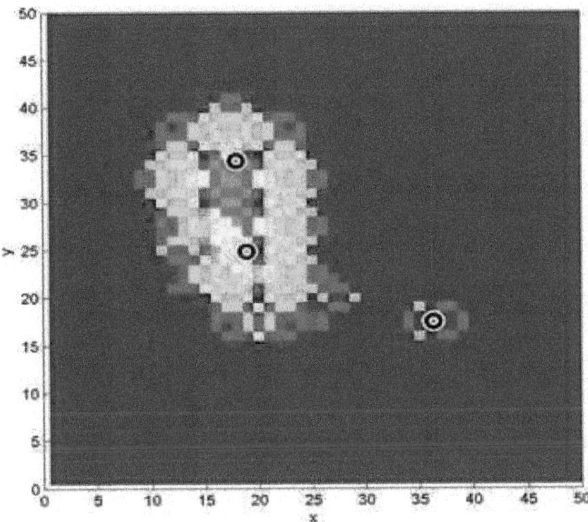

Figure 4.13: Detection-likelihood of detections from Fig. 6 with threshold $\theta_d = 3$. Estimated positions of targets are shown in circles

dius. The cells clustered with S_j are then removed from $\mathcal{S}$. Now repeat the procedure until $\mathcal{S}$ is empty. Let $\{C_k :\leq k \leq K_{cl}\}$ be the clusters formed by this procedure, where K_{cl} is the total number of clusters. For each cluster C_k, its center of mass is computed in order to obtain a fused position report, i.e., an estimated position of a target. An example of position reports is shown in Fig. 4.13.

The multisensor fusion algorithm described above runs on two levels: Algorithm 4.1 on the Tier-1 nodes and Algorithm 4.3 on the Tier-2 node. Each Tier-1 node combines detection data from itself and neighboring nodes using Algorithm 4.1 and computes detection-likelihoods. The detection-likelihoods are forwarded to its Tier-2 node and the Tier-2 node generates position reports from the detection-likelihoods using Algorithm 2. The position reports are then used by the MTT module, described in Section IV-B, to track multiple targets.

Algorithm 4.1
DontPrintSemicolon
SetAlgoLined
SetKwInOutInputInput
SetKwInOutOutputOutput
Inputdetections from sensor i and its neighbors
Outputdetection-likelihoods
BlankLine

Algorithm 4.2
FOReach S_{i_j}, $j = 1,...,m(i)$ *IFnumber of detections for* $S_{i_j} \geq \theta_d$ *STATE compute detection-likelihood* $\hat{z}_i(j)$ *of* S_{i_j}; *STATE forward* $\hat{z}_i(j)$ *to Tier-2 node* $g(i)$; *ENDIF ENDFOR*

4.8.2 Multitarget tracking and multitrack fusion modules

Our tracking algorithms are based on MCMCDA [404]. We first describe the MCMCDA algorithm and then describe the MTT and MTF modules of LochNess.

Algorithm 4.3
DontPrintSemicolon SetAlgoLined SetKwInOutInputInput SetKwInOutOutputOutput
Inputdetection-likelihoods $\mathcal{Z} = \{\hat{z}_i(j)\}$ *received from its tracking group Outputposition reports y BlankLine*

Algorithm 4.4
STATE $S = \{S_{i_j} : \hat{z}_i(j) \in \mathcal{Z}\}$; *STATE* $y = \phi$; *STATE find clusters* $\{C_k : 1 \leq k \leq K_{cl}\}$ *from S as described in the text; FOR*C_k, $k = 1,...,K_{cl}$ *STATE compute the center of mass* y_k *of* C_k; *STATE* $y = y \cup y_k$ *ENDFOR*

Markov chain Monte Carlo (MCMC) plays a significant role in many fields, such as physics, statistics, economics, and engineering [441]. In some cases, MCMC is the only known general algorithm that finds a good approximate solution to a complex problem in polynomial time [442]. MCMC techniques have been applied to complex probability distribution integration problems, counting problems such as #P-complete problems, and combinatorial optimization problems [441], [442].

MCMC is a general method to generate samples from a distribution π on a space Ω by constructing a Markov chain $\mathcal{M}$ with states $\omega \in \Omega$ and stationary distribution $\pi(\omega)$. We now describe an MCMC algorithm known as the Metropolis-Hastings algorithm [443]. If we are at state $\omega \in \Omega$, we propose $\omega' \in \Omega$, following the proposal distribution $q(\omega, \omega')$. The move is accepted with an acceptance probability $A(\omega, \omega')$, where

$$A(\omega, \omega') = min\left(1, \frac{\pi(\omega')q(\omega', \omega)}{\pi(\omega)q(\omega, \omega')}\right) \tag{4.59}$$

otherwise, the sampler stays at ω, so that the detailed balance is satisfied. If we make sure that $\mathcal{M}$ is irreducible and aperiodic, then $\mathcal{M}$ converges to its stationary distribution by the ergodic theorem [444].

The MCMC data association (MCMCDA) algorithm is described in Algorithm 4.5. MCMCDA is an MCMC algorithm whose state space is ω, as described in Section III-B, and whose stationary distribution is the posterior (5). The proposal distribution for MCMCDA consists of five types of moves (a total of eight moves). They are: 1) a birth/death move pair; 2) a split/merge move pair; 3) an extension/ reduction move pair; 4) a track update move; 5) a track switch move. The MCMCDA moves are illustrated in Fig. 4.14. We index each move by an integer, such that $m = 1$ for a birth move, $m = 2$ for a death move and so on. The move m is chosen randomly from the distribution $q_K^m(m)$, where K is the number of tracks of the current partition ω. When there is no track, we can only propose a birth move, so we set $q_0^m(m = 1) = 1$ and $q_0^m(m = m') = 0$ for $m' > 1$. When there is only a single target, we cannot propose a merge or track switch move, so $q_1^m(m = 4) = q_1^m(m = 8) = 0$. For the other values of K and m, we assume $q_K^m > 0$. For a detailed description of each move, see [404]. The inputs for MCMCDA are the set of all observations Y, the number of samples n_{mc}, the initial state ω_{init}, and a bounded function $X : \Omega \to \mathbb{R}^n$. At each step of the algorithm, ω is the current state of the Markov chain. The acceptance probability $A(\omega, \omega')$ is defined in (4.59), where $\pi(\omega) = P(\omega \mid Y)$ from (4.49). The output $\hat{X}$ approximates the MMSE estimate $\mathbb{E}_\pi X$ and $\hat{\omega}$ approximates the MAP estimate argmax $P(\omega \mid Y)$. The computation of $\hat{\omega}$ can be considered as simulated annealing at a constant temperature. Notice that MCMCDA can provide both MAP and

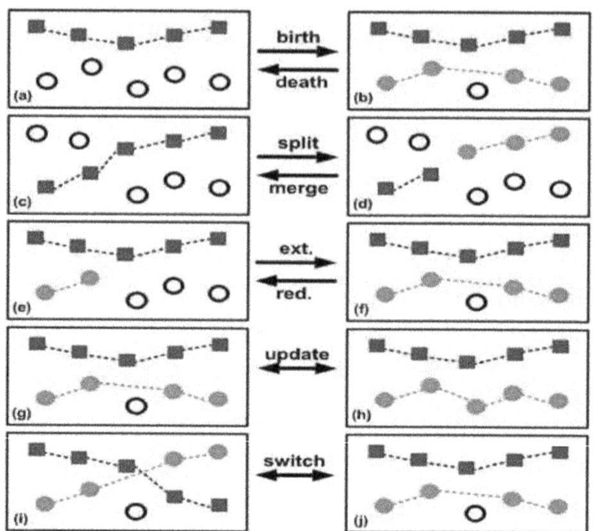

Figure 4.14: Graphical illustration of MCMCDA moves (associations are indicated by dotted lines and hollow circles are false alarms). Each move proposes a new joint association event ω' which is a modification of the current joint association event ω. The birth move proposes ω' by forming a new track from the set of false alarms $((a) \to (b))$. The death move proposes ω' by combining one of the existing tracks into the set of false alarms $((b) \to (a))$. The split move decomposes a track from ω' into two tracks $((c) \to (d))$ while the mergemove combines two tracks in ω' into a single track $((d) \to (c))$. The extension move extends an existing track in $\omega((e) \to (f))$ and the reduction move reduces an existing track in $\omega((f) \to (e))$. The track update move chooses a track in ω and assigns different measurements from the set of false alarms $((g) \to (h))$. The track switch move chooses two track from ω and switches some measurement-to-track associations $((i) \to (j))$

MMSE solutions to the multitarget tracking problem. In this paper, we use the MAP estimate $\hat{\omega}$ to estimate the states of the targets.[5]

Algorithm 4.5
DontPrintSemicolon SetAlgoLined SetKwInOutInputInput SetKwInOutOutputOutput
InputY, n_{mc}, ω_{init}, $X : \Omega \to \mathbb{R}^n$ *Output*$\hat{\omega}$,$\hat{X}$

Algorithm 4.6
STATE $\omega = \omega_{init}$; $\hat{\omega} = \omega_{init}$; $\hat{X} = 0$; *FORn* $= 1$ *to* n_{mc} *STATE propose* $\hat{\omega}$ *based on* ω*(see text); STATE sample Ufrom Unif*$[0,1]$; *STATE* $\omega = \hat{\omega}$, *if* $U < A(\omega, \hat{\omega})$; *STATE*

[5]The states of the targets can be easily computed by any filtering algorithm since, given $\hat{\omega}$, the associations between the targets and the measurements are completely known.

$\hat{\omega} = \omega$, *if* $p(\omega \mid Y)/p(\hat{\omega} \mid Y) > 1$; *STATE* $\hat{X} = (n/(n+1))\hat{X} + (1/(n+1))X(\omega)$
ENDFOR

It has been shown that MCMCDA is an optimal Bayesian filter in the limit [405]. In addition, in terms of time and memory, MCMCDA is more computationally efficient than MHT and outperforms MHT with heuristics (i.e., pruning, gating, clustering, N-scan-back logic and k-best hypotheses) under extreme conditions, such as a large number of targets in a dense environment, low detection probabilities, and high false alarm rates [404].

1. *Multitarget Tracking Module:* At each Tier-2 node, we implement the online MCMCDA algorithm with a sliding window of size ws using Algorithm 4.5 [404]. This online implementation of MCMCDA is suboptimal because it considers only a subset of past measurements. But since the contribution of older measurements to the current estimate is much less than recent measurements, it is still a good approximation. At each time step, we use the previous estimate to nitialize MCMCDA and run MCMCDA on the observations belonging to the current window. Each Tier-2 node maintains a set of observations $Y = \{y^j(t) : 1 \leq j \leq n(t), t_{curr} - w_s + 1 \leq t \leq t_{curr}\}$, where t_{curr} is the current time. Each $y^j(t)$ is either a fused measurement $\hat{z}_i$ from some signal-strength sensor i or an element of the fused position reports y from some binary sensors. At time $t_{curr} + 1$, the observations at time $t_{curr} - w_s + 1$ are removed from Y and a new set of observations is appended to Y. Any delayed observations are inserted into the appropriate slots. Then, each Tier-2 node initializes the Markov chain with the previously estimated tracks and executes Algorithm 4.5 on Y. Once a target is found, the next state of the target is predicted. If the predicted next state belongs to the surveillance area of another Tier-2 node, the targets track information is passed to the corresponding Tier-2 node. These newly received tracks are then incorporated into the initial state of MCMCDA for the next time step. Finally, each Tier-2 node forwards its track information to the base station.

2. *Multitrack Fusion Module:* Since each Tier-2 node maintains its own set of tracks, there can be multiple tracks from a single target maintained by different Tier-2 nodes. To make the algorithm fully hierarchical and scalable, the MTF module performs the track-level data association at the base station to combine tracks from different Tier-2 nodes. Let ω_j be the set of tracks maintained by Tier-2 node $j \in \{1, ..., N_{ss}\}$. Let $Y_c = \{\tau_i(t) \in \omega_j : 1 \leq t \leq t_{curr}, 1 \leq i \leq |\omega_j|, 1 \leq j \leq N_{ss}\}$ be the combined observations only from the established tracks. We form a new set of tracks ω_{init} from $\{\tau_i \in \omega_j : 1 \leq i \leq |\omega_j|, 1 \leq j \leq N_{ss}\}$ while making sure that the constraints defined in Section III-B are satisfied. Then, we run Algorithm 4.5 on this combined observation set Y_c with the initial state ω_{init}.

An example in which the multitrack fusion corrects mistakes made by Tier-2 nodes due to missing observations at the tracking group boundaries is given in Section IV-B3.

The algorithm is autonomous and shown to be robust against packet loss, communication delay and sensor localization error. In simulation, there is no performance loss up to an average localization error of 0.7 times the separation between sensors, and the algorithm tolerates up to 50% lost-to-total packet ratio and 90% delayed-to-total packet ratio [406].

3. *An Example of Surveillance Using Sensor Networks:* Here, we give a simulation example of surveillance using sensor networks. The surveillance region $\mathcal{R} = [0,100]^2$ was divided into four quadrants and sensors in each quadrant formed a tracking group, where a Tier-2 node was placed at the center of each quadrant. The scenario is shown in Fig. 4.15(a). We assumed a 100×100 sensor grid, in which the separation between sensors was normalized to 1. Thus, the unit length in simulation was the length of the sensor separation. For MCMCDA, $n_{mc} = 1000$ and $w_s = 10$. The signal-strength sensor model was used with parameters $\alpha = 2, \gamma = 1$, $\theta = 2$, and $\beta = 3(1+\gamma R_s^\alpha)$. In addition, $p_{te} = .3$ and $p_{de} = .3$. The surveillance duration was $T_s = 100$.

   The state vector of a target is $x = [x_1, x_2, \dot{x}_1, \dot{x}_2]^T$ as described in Section III-C. The simulation used the dynamic model in (4.51) and the evader control inputs were modeled by the random motion (4.1), with $q_e = .15^2$ and Q set according to Fig. 4.9. Since the full state is not observable, the measurement model (4.52) was modified as follows:

$$y(t) = Dx(t) + v(t), \quad whereD = \begin{bmatrix} 1 & 0 & 0 & 0 \\ 0 & 1 & 0 & 0 \end{bmatrix} \tag{4.60}$$

and y is a fused measurement computed by the MSF module in Section IV-A.

Figure 4.15(b) shows the observations received by the Tier-2 nodes. There were a total of 1174 observations, of which 603 were false alarms. A total of 319 packets out of 1174 packets were lost due to transmission failures and 449 packets out of 855 received packets were delayed. Figure 4.15(c) shows the tracks estimated locally by the MTT modules on the Tier-2 nodes while Fig. 4.15(d) shows the tracks estimated by the MTF module using track-level data association. Figure 4.15(d) shows that the MTF module corrected mistakes made by Tier-2 nodes due to missing observations at the tracking group boundaries. The algorithm is written in C++ and MATLAB and run on PC with a 2.6-GHz Intel Pentium 4 processor. It takes less than 0.06 seconds per Tier-2 node, per simulation time step.

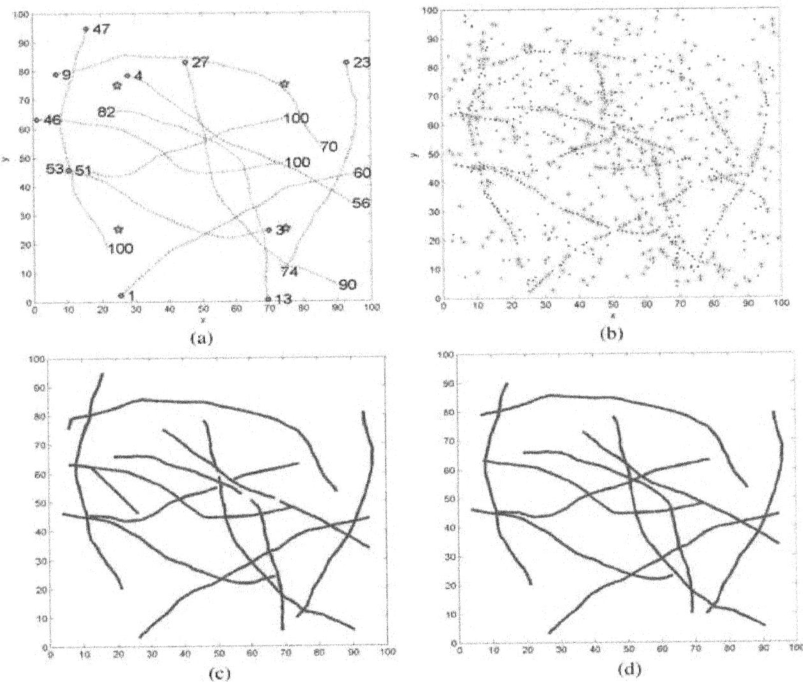

Figure 4.15: (a) Tracking scenario, where the numbers are target appearance and disappearance times, the initial positions are marked by circles, and the stars are the positions of Tier-2 nodes. (b) Accumulated observations received by Tier-2 nodes with delayed observations circled.(c) Tracks estimated locally by the MTT modules at Tier-2 nodes, superimposed. (d) Tracks estimated by the MTF module

4.8.3 Multiagent coordination module

The time-to-capture is estimated using the abstract model of pursuer and evader dynamics given in Section III-C. Let us consider the error between the pursuer and the evader $\xi = \left[\xi_1, \xi_2, \dot{\xi}_1, \dot{\xi}_1\right]^T$ whose dynamics is given in (4.3). The time-to-capture problem is equivalent to the following optimization problem:

$$min_{u_1^P(t),u_2^P(t)} \quad T \quad \text{subject to} \begin{cases} \xi(t+\delta) = A_\delta \xi(t) + G_\delta u^P(t) \\ \left|u_1^P(t)\right| \leq U)P, \left|u_2^P(t)\right| \leq U)P \\ \xi(t+T) = 0 \end{cases} \tag{4.61}$$

Recently, Gao et al. [445] solved the previous problem as an application of minimum-time control for the discretized double integrator. An extension to minimum-time control for the discretized triple integrator is also available [446]. Despite its simplicity and apparent efficacy, minimum time control is rarely used in practice, since it is highly sensitive to small measurement errors and external disturbances. Although, in principle, minimum-time control gives the best performance, it needs to be modified to cope with practical issues such as the quantization of inputs, measurement and process noise, and modeling errors. We propose an approach that adds robustness while preserving the optimality of minimum-time control.

Since the state error dynamics is decoupled along the x- and y-axes, the solution of the optimization problem (4.61) can be obtained by solving two independent minimum-time problems along each axis. When $\delta \to 0$ in (4.3), the minimum-time control problem restricted to one axis reduces to the well-known minimum-time control problem of a double integrator in continuous time, which can be found in many standard textbooks on optimal control such as [447], [448]. The solution is given by a bang-bang control law and can be written in state feedback form, as follows:

$$u_1^P = \begin{cases} -U_P, & \text{if} \;\; 2U_P\xi_1 > -\dot{\xi}_1 \left|\dot{\xi}_1\right| \\ +U_P, & \text{if} \;\; 2U_P\xi_1 < -\dot{\xi}_1 \left|\dot{\xi}_1\right| \\ -U_P sign(\xi_1), & \text{if} \;\; 2U_P\xi_1 = -\dot{\xi}_1 \left|\dot{\xi}_1\right| \\ 0, & \text{if} \;\; \dot{\xi}_1 = \xi_1 = 0 \end{cases} \tag{4.62}$$

The minimum time required to drive ξ_1 to zero in the x-axis can be also written in terms of the position and velocity error, as follows:

$$T_{c,1} = \begin{cases} \frac{-\dot{\xi}_1 + \sqrt{2\dot{\xi}_1^2 - 4U_P\xi_1}}{U_P}, & \text{if} \;\; 2U_P\xi_1 \geq -\dot{\xi}_1 \left|\dot{\xi}_1\right| \\ \frac{\dot{\xi}_1 + \sqrt{2\dot{\xi}_1^2 + 4U_P\xi_1}}{U_P}, & \text{otherwise} \end{cases} \tag{4.63}$$

Figure 4.16 shows the switching curve $2U_P\xi_1 \geq -\dot{\xi}_1 \left|\dot{\xi}_1\right|$ and the level curves of the time-to-capture Tc for different values.

Similar equations can be written for the control u_2^P along the y-axis. Therefore, the minimum time-to-capture is given by

$$T_c = max(T_{c,1}, T_{c,2}). \tag{4.64}$$

According to the previous analysis, given the state error $\xi(t)$ at current time t, we can compute the corresponding constant velocity time-to-capture T_c, the optimal input sequence $u^{p*}(t')$ and the optimal trajectory $\xi^*(t')$ for $t' \in [t, t+T_c]$.

However, the optimal input (4.62) is the solution when $\delta \to 0$ in (4.3) with no measurement errors and no change in the evaders trajectory. In order to add robustness, to take into account the quantization in the digital implementation, the measurement errors, and the evasive maneuvers of the evader, we analyze how the time-to-capture can be affected by these terms. Let us first rewrite the error dynamics given by (4.3) explicitly for the x-axis

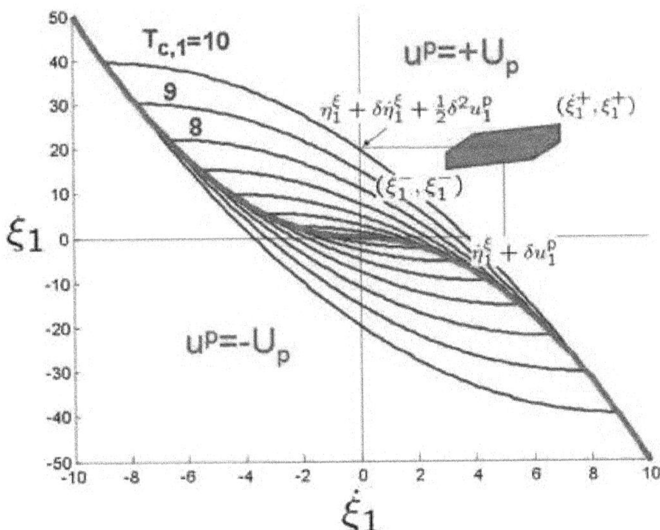

Figure 4.16: Optimal switching curve for the continuous minimum-time control of the double integrator (thick solid line) and curves of constant time-to-capture (thin solid lines) in the phase space $(\xi_1, \dot{\xi}_1)$. The hexagon represents the set of all possible locations of the true error state $(\xi_1(t+\delta), \dot{\xi}_1(t+\delta))$ at the next time step $t+\delta$ given measurement $(\eta_1, \dot{\eta}_1)$ and pursuer control input u_1^p at time t

$$\xi_1(t+\delta) = \xi_1(t) + \delta\dot{\xi}_1(t) + \tfrac{1}{2}\delta^2 u_1^e(t) + \tfrac{1}{2}\delta^2 u_1^P(t)$$

$$\dot{\xi}_1(t+\delta) = \dot{\xi}_1(t) + \delta u_1^P(t) + \delta u_1^e(t)$$

$$\eta_1^{\xi}(t) = \xi_1(t) + v_1^{\xi}(t)$$

$$\dot{\eta}_1^{\xi}(t) = \dot{\xi}_1(t) + \dot{v}_1^{\xi}(t)$$

If we substitute the last two equations into the first two we get

$$\xi_1(t+\delta) = \eta_1^{\xi}(t) + \dot{\eta}_1^{\xi}(t) + \frac{1}{2}\delta^2 u_1^P(t) - v_1^{\xi}(t) - \delta\dot{v}_1^{\xi}(t) + \frac{1}{2}\delta^2 u_1^e(t) \tag{4.65}$$

$$\dot{\xi}_1(t+\delta) = \dot{\eta}_1^{\xi}(t) + \delta u_1^P(t) + \dot{v}_1^{\xi}(t) + \delta u_1^e(t) \tag{4.66}$$

where $(\eta_1, \dot{\eta}_1)$ are output estimates from the MTF module, u_1^P is the controllable input, and $(u_1^e, v_1^{\xi}, \dot{v}_1^{\xi})$ play the role of external disturbances. Our goal now is to choose u_1^P , i.e., the thrust of the pursuer, in such a way as to minimize the time-to-capture under the worst possible choice of $(u_1^e, v_1^{\xi}, \dot{v}_1^{\xi})$, which are not known in advance but are bounded. Figure 4.16 illustrates this approach graphically: The hexagon in the figure represents the possible position of the true state error $(\xi_1, \dot{\xi}_1)$ at the next time step $(t+\delta)$, which accounts for all possible evasive maneuvers of the evader, i.e., $|u_1^e| < U_e$, and accounts for the estimation errors on the position and velocity of the pursuer and the evader, i.e., $\left|v_1^\xi\right| < V_1, \left|\dot{v}_1^\xi\right| < \dot{V}_1$, for a given choice of u_1^P. Since the center of the hexagon $(\eta_1^\xi + \delta\dot{\eta}_1^\xi + (1/2)\delta^2 u_1^P, \dot{\eta}_1^\xi + \delta u_1^P)$ depends on the pursuer control u_1^P, one could try to choose u_1^P in such a way that the largest time-to-capture $T_{c,1}$ of the hexagon is minimized. This approach is common in the literature for non–cooperative games [449]. More formally, the feedback control input will be chosen based on the following min-max optimization problem:

$$u_1^{P^*}(t) = \arg \min_{\left|u_1^P\right| \le U_P} \left(\max_{\left|v_1^\xi\right| \le V_1, \left|\dot{v}_1^\xi\right| \le \dot{V}_1, \left|u_1^e\right| \le U_e} T_{c,1}(\xi_1(t+\delta), \dot{\xi}_1(t+\delta)) \right) \quad (4.67)$$

This is, in general, a nonlinear optimization problem. However, thanks to the specific structure of the time-to-capture function $T_{c,}$, it is possible to show that (4.67) is equivalent to

$$u_1^{P^*} = \arg \min_{\left|u_1^P\right| \le U_P} \max\left(T_{c,1}\left(\xi_1^+, \dot{\xi}_1^{\ +}\right), T_{c,1}\left(\xi_1^-, \dot{\xi}_1^{\ -}\right)\right) \xi_1^\pm$$

$$\eta_1^\xi + \delta\dot{\eta}_1^\xi \pm V_1 \pm \delta\dot{V}_1 \pm \frac{1}{2}\delta^2 U_e + \frac{1}{2}\delta^2 u_1^P \quad (4.68)$$

$$\dot{\xi}_1^\pm$$

$$\dot{\eta}_1^\xi \pm \dot{V}_1 \pm \delta U_e + \delta u_1^P \quad (4.69)$$

i.e., it is necessary to compute only the time-to-capture of the top right and the bottom left corner of the hexagon in Fig. 4.16, since all points inside the set always have smaller values of $T_{c,1}$. Once the expected minimum time-to-capture control input $u^{P*}(t')$, $t' \in [t, t+T_c]$ is computed, the corresponding optimal trajectory for the pursuer $x^{P*}(t')$, $t' \in [t, t+T_c]$ can easily be obtained by substituting $u^{P*}(t')$ into the pursuer dynamics (4.51). The robust minimum-time path planning algorithm is summarized in Algorithm 4.7.

Algorithm 4.7

DontPrintSemicolon
SetAlgoLined
SetKwInOutInputInput
SetKwInOutOutputOutput
Inputx$^P(t), x^e(t)$*, and bounds* $V_1, V_2, \dot{V}_1, \dot{V}_2, U_e, U_P$ *Outputoptimal trajectoryx*$^{P*}(t'), t' \in [t, t+T_c]$ *BlankLine*

Algorithm 4.8
STATE compute $u^{P*}(t'),t' \in [t,t+T_c]$ using (4.68); STATE compute $x^{P*}(t'),t' \in [t,t+T_c]$ given $u^{P*}(t')$ using (4.51)

Figure 4.17 shows the performance of the proposed robust minimum time-to-capture control feedback for a scenario where the evader moves with random motion and the evader's position and velocity estimates are noisy. It is compared with the discrete-time minimum-time controller proposed in [446] and [445]. Our controller feedback design outperforms the discrete-time minimum-time controller since the latter one does not take into account process and measurement noises. Note how both controllers do not direct pursuers toward the actual position of evader, but to the estimated future location of the evader in order to minimize the time-to-capture.

As introduced in Section III-C, given the positions and velocities of all pursuers and evaders and bounds on the measurement error and evader input, it is possible to compute the expected time-to-capture matrix $C = [c_{ij}] \in \mathbb{R}^{N_p \times N_e}$ using the solution to the optimal minimum-time control problem. The entry c_{ij} of the matrix C corresponds to the expected time for pursuer i to capture evader j, $T_c(i,j)$, that can be computed as described in (4.10) and (4.11). As motivated in Section III-C, we assume the same number of pursuers as the number of evaders, i.e., $N_p = N_e = N$.

An assignment can be represented as a matrix $\Phi = [\o_{ij}] \in \mathbb{R}^{N\times N}$, where the entry $\o_{ij}$ of the matrix Φ is equal to 1 if pursuer i is assigned to evader j, and equal to 0 otherwise. The assignment problem can, therefore, be written formally as follows:

$$\begin{bmatrix} \min_{\o_{ij}} & \max_{i,j=1,\ldots,N}(c_{ij}\cdot\phi_{ij}) \\ \text{subject to} & \sum_{i=1}^{N}\phi_{ij} = 1, \forall i \\ & \sum_{j=1}^{N}\phi_{ij} = 1, \forall j \end{bmatrix} \tag{4.70}$$

As formulated in (4.70), the assignment problem is a combinatorial optimization problem.

The optimization problem given in (4.16) can be reformulated as a linear bottleneck assignment problem and can be solved by any of the polynomial-time algorithms based on network flow theory. Here, we give a brief description of one algorithm and we direct the interested reader to the survey [428] for a detailed review of these algorithms. For our implementation, we use a randomized threshold algorithm that alternates between two phases. In the first phase, we list the cost elements c_{ij} in increasing order and we choose a cost element c_*, i.e., a threshold. Then we construct the matrices $\bar{C}(c^*) = [\bar{c}_{ij}] \in \mathbb{R}^{N\times N}$ and $C_{Tutte}(c^*) = [\bar{c}_{ij}] \in \mathbb{R}^{2N\times 2N}$ as follows:

$$\bar{c}_{ij} = \begin{cases} a_{ij}, & \text{if} \quad c_{ij} > c^* \\ 0, & \text{if} \quad c_{ij} \leq c^* \end{cases}, \quad C_{Tutte} = \begin{bmatrix} 0 & \bar{C} \\ -\bar{C} & 0 \end{bmatrix} \tag{4.71}$$

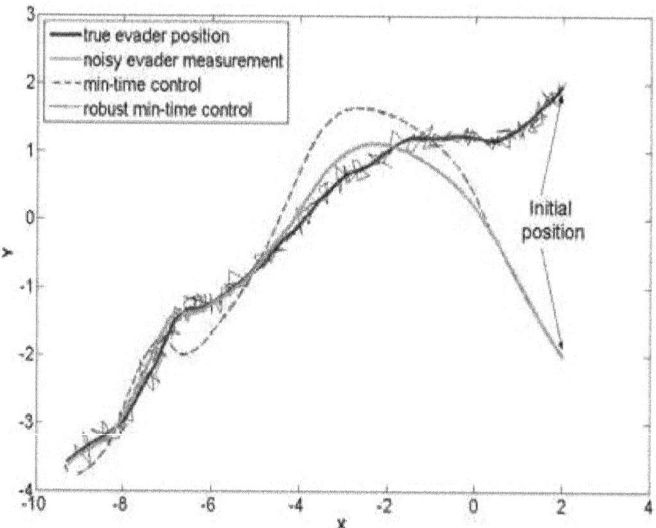

Figure 4.17: Trajectories of pursuers and evaders on the x-y plane. The feedback control is based on noisy measurements (thin solid line) of the true evader positions (thick solid line). The robust minimum time-to-capture feedback proposed in this paper (dot-solid line) is compared with the discrete-time minimum time-to-capture feedback (dashed line) proposed in [446]

where $a'_{ij}s$ are independent random numbers sampled from a uniform distribution in the interval $[0,1]$, i.e., $a_{ij} \sim \mathcal{U}([0,1])$. Using Tuttes Theorem [428], it is possible to show that if $\det C_{Tutte}(c^*) \neq 0$, then there exists an assignment that achieves c^*.[6] Therefore, we search for the smallest c^*_{min} in the ordered list of costs c_{ij} which guarantees an assignment. Once we find c^*_{min}, we find the pursuer-evader pair corresponding to that cost. Then, we remove its row and column from the cost matrix C and repeat the procedure until all pursuers are assigned. The assignment algorithm is summarized in Algorithm 4.9.

It is important to note that an assignment based on the solution to the global optimization problem described above is necessary for good performance. For example, let us consider the *greedy assignment* algorithm. This algorithm looks for the smallest time-to-capture entry in the matrix C, assigns the corresponding pursuer-evader pair, and removes the corresponding row and column from the matrix C. The dimensions of the resulting matrix C become $(N-1)\times(N-1)$ and the algorithm repeats the same process until each pursuer is assigned to an evader. This algorithm is very simple and can be implemented in a fully distributed fashion. However, it is a suboptimal algorithm since there are cases where the

[6]In reality, since the algorithm is randomized, there is a small probability equal to $(1/N)^r$ that there exists a feasible assignment if $\det C_{Tutte} = 0$ for r random Tuttes matrices C_{Tutte}. In the rare cases when this event happens, the algorithm simply gives a feasible assignment with a higher cost to capture.

greedy assignment finds the worst solution. Consider the time-to-capture matrix $c = \begin{bmatrix} 1 & 2 \\ 3 & 100 \end{bmatrix}$. The optimal assignment that minimizes the time-to-capture of all evaders for this matrix is $1 \rightarrow 2$ and $2 \rightarrow 1$, which gives $T_{c,max} = 3$, where Tc;max is the time-to-capture of all evaders. The greedy assignment would instead assign pursuer 1 to evader 1 and pursuer 2 to evader 2, with the time-to-capture of all evaders equal to $T_{c,max} = 100$.

Algorithm 4.9
DontPrintSemicolon SetAlgoLined SetKwInOutInputInput SetKwInOutOutputOutput
Input$x_i^P, x_j^e, i, j, = 1, ..., N$ *Outputassignment* $i \rightarrow j$*fori* $- 1, .., N$

Algorithm 4.10
STATE compute matrix $C = [c_{ij}], c_{ij} = T_c(i, j)$; *FOR*$n = 1$ *to N STATE* $[i^*, j^*] = \arg\min_{ij} \{c_{ij} \mid det(C_{Tutte}(c_{ij}) \neq 0)\}$, *using(4.17); STATE assign pursuer* i^* *to evader* j^*, *i.e.,*$i^* \rightarrow j^*$; *STATE* $C \leftarrow \{C \mid$ *remove row* i^* *and column* $j^*\}$; *ENDFOR*

4.9 Experimental Results

Multitarget tracking and a pursuit evasion game using the control system LochNess were demonstrated at the Defense Advanced Research Projects Agency (DARPA) Network Embedded Systems Technology (NEST) final experiment on August 30, 2005. The experiment was performed in warm, sunny conditions on a large-scale, long-term, outdoor sensor network testbed deployed on a short grass field at U.C. Berkeleys Richmond Field Station (see Fig. 4.18). A total of 557 sensor nodes were deployed and 144 of these nodes were allotted for the tracking and PEG experiments. However, six out of the 144 nodes used in the experiment were not functioning on the day of the demo, reflecting the difficulties of deploying large-scale, outdoor systems. The 144 nodes used for the tracking and PEG experiments were deployed at approximately 5 meter spacing in a 12×12 grid (see Fig. 4.19). Each node was elevated using a camera tripod to prevent the PIR sensors from being obstructed by grass and uneven terrain [see Fig. 4.18(a)]. The locations of the nodes were measured during deployment using differential GPS and stored in a table at the base station for reference and for generating Fig. 4.19. However, in the experiments, the system assumed the nodes were placed exactly on a 5-m spacing grid in order to highlight the robustness of the system with respect to localization error.

The deployment of *LochNess* contained some modifications to the architecture described in Section III. Due to the time constraint, the Tier-2 nodes were not fully functional on the day of the demo. Instead, we used a mote connected to

(a) (b)

Figure 4.18: Hardware for the sensor nodes. (a) Trio sensor node on a tripod. On top is the microphone, buzzer, solar panel, and user and reset buttons. On the sides are the windows for the passive infrared sensors. (b) A live picture from the 2 target PEG experiment. The targets are circled

Figure 4.19: Sensor network deployment (not all deployed sensor nodes are shown). The disks and circles represent the positions of the sensor nodes. The network of 144 nodes used in the multitarget tracking and PEG experiments is highlighted

a personal computer as the Tier-2 node. Only one such Tier-2 node was necessary in order to maintain connectivity to all 144 nodes used for the tracking experiment. In the experiment, simulated pursuers were used since it was difficult to navigate a ground robot in the field of tripods.

4.9.1 Platform

A new sensor network hardware platform, called the Trio mote, was designed by Dutta et al. [427] for the outdoor testbed. The Trio mote is a combination of the designs of the Telos B mote, eXtreme Scaling Mote (XSM) sensor board [450], and Prometheus solar charging board [451], with improvements. Figure 15 shows the Trio node components and Fig. 4.20(a) shows the assembled Trio node in a waterproof enclosure sitting on a tripod.

The Telos B mote [452] is the latest in a line of wireless sensor network platforms developed by U.C. Berkeley for the NEST project. It features an 8 MHz Texas Instruments MSP430 micro-controller with 10 kB of RAM and 48 kB of program flash and a 250 kbps, 2.4GHz, IEEE 802.15.4 standard compliant, Chip-con CC2420 radio. The Telos *B* mote provides lower power operation than previous motes (5.1μA sleep, 19 mA on) and a radio range of up to 125 meters (m), making it the ideal platform for large-scale, long-term deployments.

The Trio sensor board includes a microphone, a piezoelectric buzzer, x-y axis magnetometers, and four PIR motion sensors. For the multitarget tracking application, we found that the PIR sensors were the most effective at sensing human subjects moving through the sensor field.

The magnetometer sensor had limited range even detecting targets with rare earth magnets and the acoustic sensor required complex signal processing to pick out the various acoustic signatures of a moving target from background noise. The PIR sensors provided an effective range of approximately 8 m, with sensitivity varying depending on weather conditions and time of day. The variability in the signal strength of the PIR sensor reading prohibited extraction of ranging information from the sensor, so the PIR sensors were used as binary detectors.

The software running on the sensor nodes are written in NesC [453] and run on TinyOS [454], an event-driven operating system developed for wireless embedded sensor platforms. The core sensor node application is the *DetectionEvent* module, a multimode event generator for target detection and testing node availability. The sensor node application relies on a composition of various TinyOS subsystems and services that facilitate management and interaction with the network (see Fig. 4.21).

The *Detection Event* module provides four modes of event generation from the nodeVevents generated periodically by a timer, events generated by pressing a button on the mote, events generated by the raw PIR sensor value crossing a threshold, and events generated by a three-stage filtering, adaptive threshold, and windowing detection algorithm for the PIR sensor signal developed by the University of Virginia [458]. The timer generated events ere parsed and displayed at the base station in order to help visualize which nodes in the network were alive. The three-stage PIR detection filter code was used during the development cycle. While it had potential to be more robust to different environmental conditions,

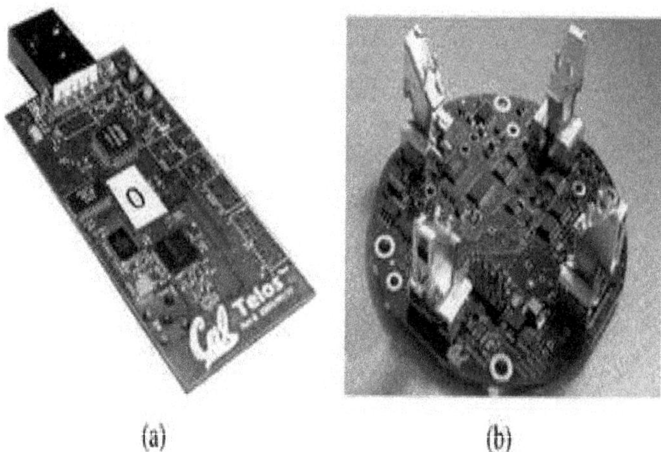

Figure 4.20: (a) Telos B. (b) Trio sensor board, based off the XSM sensor board and Prometheus solar power circuitry. See [427] for details

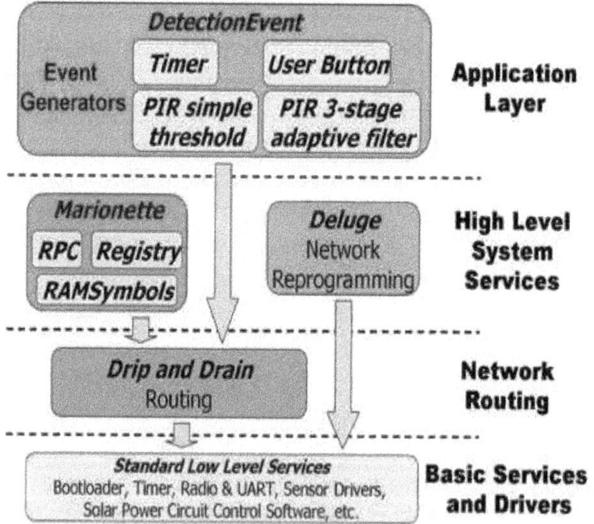

Figure 4.21: Software services on the sensor network platform. The core network management services are Deluge for network reprogramming [455] and Marionette for fast reconfiguration of parameters on the nodes [456]. The Detection Event application relies on the Drip and Drain routing layer for insemination of commands and collection of data [457]. For more details on the software architecture used in the outdoor testbed, see [427], [456]

during the day of the demo, we reverted to the simple threshold PIR detector because the simple threshold detector was easy to tune and performed well.

The algorithms for the MSF, MTT, MTF, and MAC modules are all written in MATLAB and C++ and run on the base station in real-time. The same implementation of the tracking algorithm and the robust minimum time controller used in the simulations shown in Figs. 4.15 and 4.17 are used in the experiments. The data was timestamped at the base station.

4.9.2 *Live demonstration*

The multitarget tracking algorithm was demonstrated on one, two, and three human targets, with targets entering the field at different times. In all three experiments, the tracking algorithm correctly estimated the number of targets and produced correct tracks. Furthermore, the algorithm correctly disambiguated crossing targets in the two and three target experiments without classification labels on the targets, using the dynamic models and target trajectories before crossing to compute the tracks.

Figure 4.22 shows the multitarget tracking results with three targets walking through the field. The three targets entered and exited the field around time

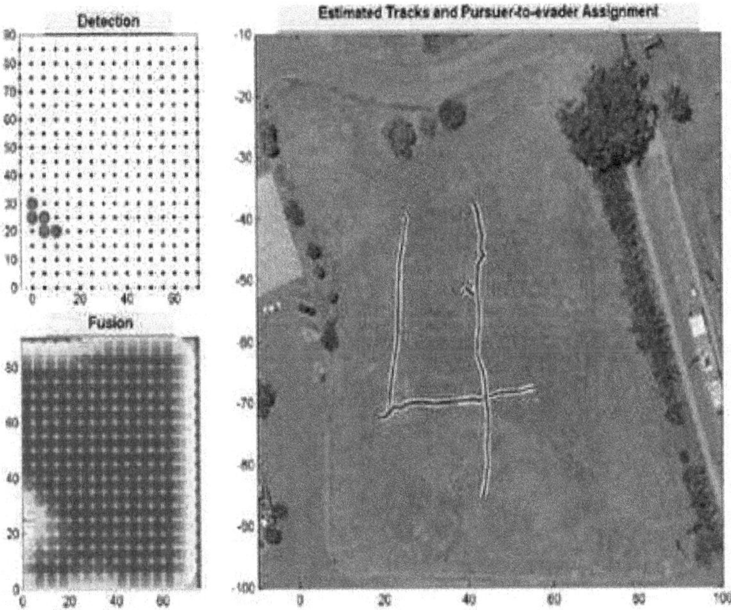

Figure 4.22: Estimated tracks of targets at time 70 from the experiment with three people walking in the field. (upper left) Detection panel. Sensors are marked by small dots and detections are shown in large disks. (lower left) Fusion panel shows the fused likelihood. (right) Estimated Tracks and Pursuer-to-evader Assignment panel shows the tracks estimated by the MTT module, estimated evader positions (stars) and pursuer positions (squares)

10 and 80, respectively. During the experiment, the algorithm correctly rejected false alarms and compensated for missing detections. There were many false alarms during the span of the experiments, as can be seen from the false alarms before time 10 and after time 80 in Fig. 4.23. Also, though not shown in the figures, the algorithm dynamically corrected previous track hypotheses as it received more sensor readings. Figure 4.23 also gives a sense of the irregularity of network traffic. The spike in traffic shortly after time 50 was approximately when two of the targets crossed. It shows that the multitarget tracking algorithm is robust against missing measurements, false measurements, and the irregularity of network traffic.

In the last demonstration, two simulated pursuers were dispatched to chase two crossing human targets. The pursuer-to-target assignment and the robust minimum time-to-capture control law were computed in real-time, in tandem with the real-time tracking of the targets. The simulated pursuers captured the human targets, as shown in Fig. 4.24. In particular, note that the MTT module is able to correctly disambiguate the presence of two targets [right panel of Fig. 4.24(a)] using past measurements, despite the fact that the MSF module reports the detection of a single target [upper left panel of Fig. 4.24(a)]. A live picture of this experiment is shown on the right of Fig. 4.18.

In order to coordinate multiple pursuers, the MAC module is developed. The assignments of pursuers to evaders are chosen such that the time to capture all evaders is minimized. The controllers for the pursuers are based on minimum-time control but were designed to account for the worst-case evader motions and

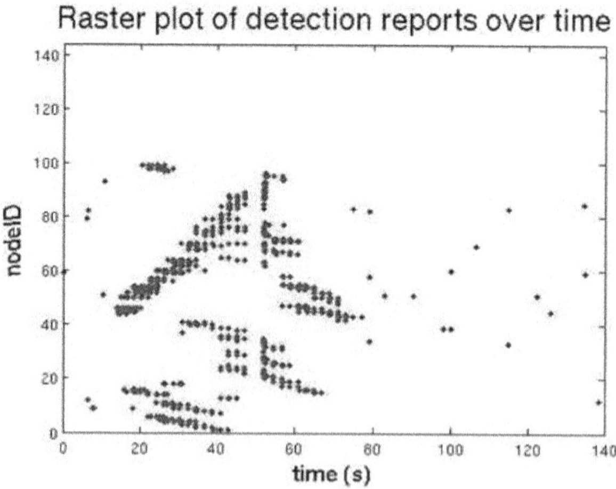

Figure 4.23: Raster plot of the binary detection reports from the three target tracking demo. Dots represent detections from nodes that were successfully transmitted to the base station

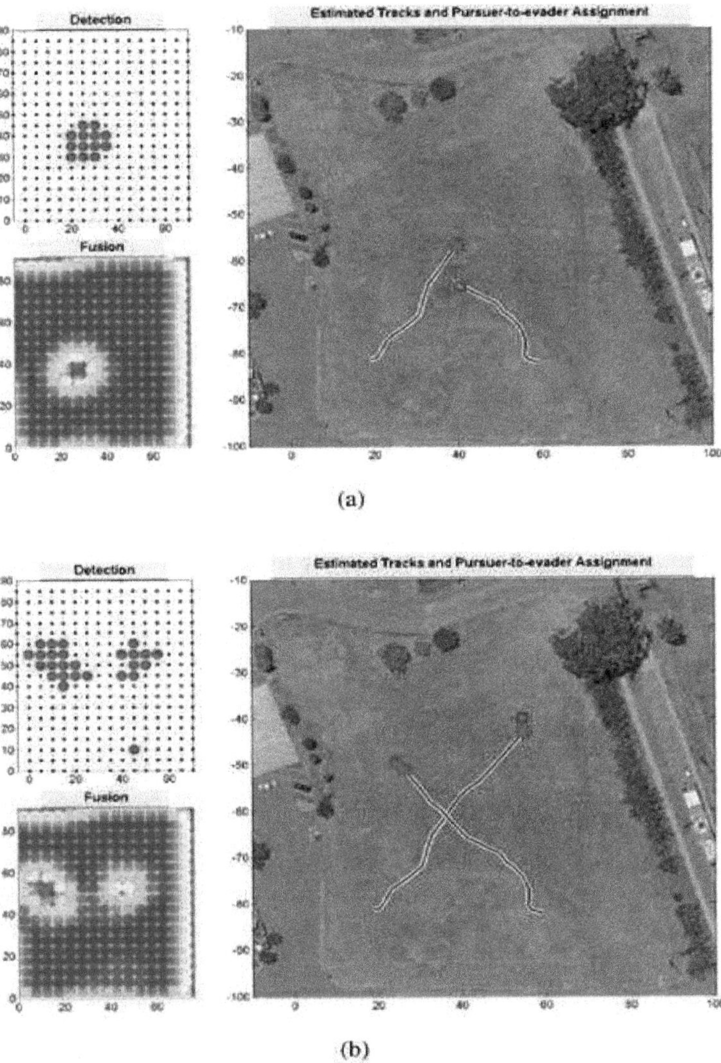

Figure 4.24: Estimated tracks of evaders and pursuer positions from the pursuit evasion game experiment. (a) Before crossing. (b) After crossing

to add robustness to the quantization of inputs, measurement and process noises, and modeling errors.

Simulation and experimental results have shown that *LochNess* is well suited to solving real-time control problems using sensor networks and that a sensor network is an attractive solution for the surveillance of a large area.

In this section, we assumed a stationary hierarchy, i.e., the Tier-2 nodes and base station are fixed. However, a stationary hierarchy is not robust against malicious attacks. In our future work, we will address this issue by introducing redundancy, distributing the coordination tasks among Tier-2 nodes, and dynamically managing the hierarchy of the system. Our immediate goal is to quantify the robustness of the system against false measurements and packet loss and to identify the sensor network parameters, such as maximum delay rate, maximum packet loss rate, and maximum false detection rate, necessary for seamless operation of the control system.

4.10 Notes

In this paper, we developed a distributed adaptive control framework for the control design of a class of multiagent systems in the presence of exogenous stochastic disturbances and actuator and sensor attacks. In particular, we address the problem of time-varying multiplicative and additive actuator attacks on the follower agents. The proposed adaptive controller architecture guarantees uniform ultimate boundedness in probability of the state tracking errors for each agent in a mean-square sense. In future research, we will extend the proposed framework to develop reliable hybrid-adaptive control architectures for multiagent as well as cyber-physical systems involving system nonlinearities and system modelling uncertainty, with integrated verification and validation, for providing robust system performance and reconfigurable system operation in the presence of system uncertainties, component failures, and adversarial attacks. Optimality considerations along the lines of [380] and [382] in the face of sensor and actuator attacks can also be considered.

Following this is a hierarchical real-time control system for sensor networks. LochNess is applied to pursuit evasion games, in which a group of evaders are tracked using a sensor network and a group of pursuers are coordinated to capture the evaders. Although sensor networks provide global observability, they cannot provide high quality measurements in a timely manner due to packet loss, communication delay, and false detections. These factors have been the main challenge to developing a real-time control system using sensor networks.

The foregoing section proposes a possible solution for closing the loop around wireless ad-hoc sensor networks. The hierarchical real-time control system LochNess decouples the estimation of evader states from the control of pursuers by using multiple layers of data fusion, including the multisensor fusion (MSF) module, the multitarget tracking (MTT) module, and the multitrack fusion (MTF) module. While a sensor network generates noisy, inconsistent, and bursty measurements, the three layers of data fusion convert raw sensor measurements into fused measurements in a compact and consistent representation and forward the fused measurements to the pursuers controllers in a timely manner.

Chapter 5

Secure Control of Distributed Multiagent Systems

5.1 Introduction

In the last few years, the consensus problem of multi-agent systems has received compelling attention in the control and system community due to its broad applications in many areas, such as unmanned vehicles [459], formation control [461] and flocking [468]. The basic objective of consensus is to design protocols, based on local information of agents, which guarantee that the states of all agents converge to a common value. The consensus protocol was initially designed for systems of first-order agents [469] and then extended to systems of second-order dynamics; see, e.g., [476], [472], [478] and references therein.

It has been shown that the first-order consensus can always be reached if certain connectivity conditions are satisfied; however, the second-order consensus relies not only on the connectivity of the communication topology but also on the parameters (or gains) of consensus protocols [476]. As a result, one critical issue in the second-order consensus problem is the characterization of the parameters of consensus protocols, i.e., finding all possible parameters which guarantee the consensus. [472] gave a sufficient condition on parameters which depends only on the real parts of the eigenvalues of the Laplacian matrix. Based on this, [478] further derived some necessary and sufficient conditions with the same second-order consensus protocol. By using the Hurwitz stability criteria, [480] studied a more general second-order consensus protocol which includes several existing protocols, such as the protocol of [478], as special examples. In this work, all of the gains which guarantee the consensus were obtained and the design method for protocols was constructively provided; different consensus modes can be realized by altering gains. However, the Hurwitz stability criteria may result in a comparatively complicated calculation in the analysis of the stability of complex coefficient polynomials.

On the other hand, time delays may arise naturally, which are usually the key factors that influence the stability of multiagent systems. The delay effects in multi-agent systems with first-order agents by using a frequency domain approach were studied by [469]. For the second-order consensus problem, the delay sensitivity of protocols is an important issue as well. [478] extended the delay sensitivity analysis of [469] to systems of double integrators by using a similar method. Other important works include [476] for the consensus with diverse input delays and [467] for the consensus with both input and communication delays. Note that, in the literature related to the delay sensitivity analysis in the consensus problem, usually protocols with particular forms are analyzed. To the best of the authors knowledge, up to now, however, there have been few results available for certain eneral protocol with which the delay sensitivity analysis can be constructively given.

This chapter focuses on the general consensus protocol proposed by [480] with input delays. The major differences between this work and [480] are listed as follows:

- In what follows, we impose a constraint on the state trajectories of agents; under the necessary and sufficient condition on protocol parameters obtained in this paper, not only is the consensus guaranteed but also the agents states are not exponentially diverging. This constraint is from Assumption 1 of [475], under which the oscillatory and the unbounded states are allowed while the exponentially unstable ones are not allowed.

- Compared to [480], where the Hurwitz stability criteria was used to indirectly analyze the stability of complex coefficient polynomials, we adopt a different method to study the parameter condition, which comparatively reduces the analysis complexity.

- [480] studied the general consensus protocol without delays. In this paper, we further analyze the robustness of the protocol to input delays. The proof idea is mainly from [478]. However, as the delay sensitivity analysis hereinafter is based on the general protocol, the results include several existing ones as special cases. By analyzing the closed-loop poles of the system, the maximal allowable upper bound of the delay is obtained.

5.2 Problem Formulation

Let $\mathcal{G} = (\mathcal{V}, \mathcal{E}, \mathcal{A})$ be a weighted directed graph of order n, where $\mathcal{V} = 1, ..., n$ is the set of nodes; $\mathcal{E} \subseteq \mathcal{V} \times \mathcal{V}$ is the set of edges and $\mathcal{A} = [a_{ij}] \in \mathbf{R}^{n\times n}$ is the non-negative adjacency matrix. An edge of $\mathcal{G}$ is denoted by a pair of distinct nodes $(i, j) \in \mathcal{E}$, where node i and node j are called the child node and the parent node, respectively. A path in a directed graph is a sequence $i_0, i_1, ..., i_f$ if of different nodes such that (i_{j-1}, i_j) is an edge for $j = 1, 2, ..., f, f \in \mathbf{Z}^+$. Denote $\mathcal{N}_i = j \mid (i, j) \in \mathcal{E})$ as the set of neighbors of node i. The adjacency matrix $\mathcal{A} = [a_{ij}] \in \mathbf{R}^{n\times n}$ is defined such that a_{ij} is the non-negative weight of edge (i, j).

We assume $a_{ij} = 0$ if $(i, j) \notin \mathcal{E}$ and $a_{ii} = 0$ for all $i \in 1, ..., n$. The Laplacian matrix $\mathcal{L} = [l_{ij}] \in \mathbf{R}^{n\times n}$ is defined as $l_{ii} = \sum_{j=1, j\neq i}^{n} a_{ij}$ and $l_{ij} = -a_{ij}(i \neq j)$. A *directed tree* is a directed graph, in which there is exactly one parent for every node except for a node called the root. A *directed spanning tree* is a directed tree, which consists of all of the nodes in $\mathcal{G}$. A directed graph contains a directed spanning tree if there exists a directed spanning tree as a subgraph of the graph.

Let $\text{Re}(z)$,$\text{Im}(z)$ and $\|z\|$ be the real part, the imaginary part and the modulus of a complex number z, respectively. Let $I_n(0_n)$ be the identity (zero) matrix of dimension n and 1_n be the $n \times 1$ column vector of all ones. Here, $\bigotimes$ represents the Kronecker product.

Now, consider a network of agents with double-integrator dynamics. The dynamics of each agent is

$$\dot{x}_i(t) = v_i(t), \quad \dot{v}_i(t) = u_i(t), \tag{5.1}$$

where $i = 1, ..., n$, $x_i(t) \in \mathbf{R}^m$, $v_i(t) \in \mathbf{R}^m$ and $u_i(t) \in \mathbf{R}^m$ are the position-like state, the velocity-like state and the control input of agent i, respectively. Without loss of generality, in this paper, we let $m = 1$ for notational simplicity.

Definition 2.1. [472]. *System (5.1) is said to reach consensus if there exists a distributed protocol $u_i(t)$, $i = 1, ..., n$, such that for any initial conditions, the states of agents satisfy*

$\lim_{t\to\infty} \|x_i(t) - x_j(t)\| = 0$, and $\lim_{t\to\infty} \|v_i(t) - v_j(t)\| = 0, \forall i, j = 1, ..., n.$

The following general consensus protocol was studied in [480]:

$$u_i(t) = -k_0 x_i(t) - k_1 v_i(t) - \sum_{j\in\mathcal{N}_i} a_{ij}[k_2(x_i(t) - x_j(t)) + k_3(v_i(t) - v_j(t))], \tag{5.2}$$

where $k_0 \in \mathbf{R}, k_1 \in \mathbf{R}, k_2 \in \mathbf{R}$ and $k_3 \in \mathbf{R}$ are the parameters. Using the notation

$$x(t) = [x_1(t), ..., x_n(t)]^T, \quad v(t) = [v_1(t), ..., v_n(t)]^T, \quad \xi(t) = [x(t)^T, v(t)^T]^T$$

Under protocol (5.2), system (5.1) can be written as

$$\begin{aligned} \dot{x}_i(t) &= v_i(t), \\ \dot{v}_i(t) &= -k_0 x_i(t) - k_1 v_i(t) \\ &- \sum_{j\in\mathcal{N}_i} a_{ij}[k_2(x_i(t) - x_j(t)) + k_3(v_i(t) - v_j(t))] \end{aligned} \tag{5.3}$$

which has the following matrix form:

$$\dot{\xi}(t) = \tilde{\mathcal{L}}\xi(t), \tag{5.4}$$

where $\tilde{\mathcal{L}} = \begin{bmatrix} 0_n & I_n \\ -k_0 I_n - k_2\mathcal{L} & -k_1 I_n - k_3\mathcal{L} \end{bmatrix}$ and $\mathcal{L}$ is the Laplacian matrix associated with $\mathcal{G}$.

We now focus on the following model with input delays:

$$\begin{aligned} \dot{x}_i(t) &= v_i(t), \\ \dot{v}_i(t) &= -k_0 x_i(t-\tau) - k_1 v_i(t-\tau) \\ &- \sum_{j\in\mathcal{N}_i} a_{ij}[k_2(x_i(t-\tau) - x_j(t-\tau)) + k_3(v_i(t-\tau) - v_j(t-\tau))] \end{aligned} \tag{5.5}$$

where $\tau \geq 0$ represents the constant delay.

The matrix form of (5.5) is written as

$$\dot{\xi}(t) = \tilde{\mathcal{L}}_1\xi(t) + \tilde{\mathcal{L}}_2\xi(t-\tau), \tag{5.6}$$

where $\tilde{\mathcal{L}}_1 = \begin{bmatrix} 0_n & I_n \\ 0_n & 0_n \end{bmatrix}$ and $\tilde{\mathcal{L}}_2 = \begin{bmatrix} 0_n & 0_n \\ -k_0 I_n - k_2\mathcal{L} & -k_1 I_n - k_3\mathcal{L} \end{bmatrix}$

Lemma 2.1 [473]. *Let $\mathcal{L}$ be the Laplacian matrix corresponding to a directed graph $\mathcal{L}$. Here $\mathcal{L}$ has exactly one zero eigenvalue and all other eigenvalues have positive real parts if and only if the directed graph $\mathcal{L}$ contains a directed spanning tree.*

Henceforth, we assume the network topology of the agents contains a directed spanning tree. According to **Lemma 2.1**, $\mathcal{L}$ has exactly one zero eigenvalue and all other eigenvalues have positive real parts. Denote the eigenvalues of $\mathcal{L}$ by $\mu_i, i-1,\ldots,n$. Without loss of generality, we assume $\mu_i = 0$.

5.3 Main Results

In this section, we first derive a parameter condition and then study the delay sensitivity of the protocol based on the condition obtained. To study the parameter condition, we consider system (5.1) under protocol (5.2). The Laplacian transform of (5.4) is

$$s\Xi(s) - \xi(0) = \tilde{\mathcal{L}}\Xi(s), \longrightarrow (sI_{2n} - \tilde{\mathcal{L}})\Xi(s) = \xi(0)$$

The closed-loop poles of system (5.4) satisfy

$$\begin{aligned}\det(sI_{2n}-\tilde{\mathcal{L}}) &= \det\begin{pmatrix} sI_n & -I_n \\ k_0I_n+k_2\mathcal{L} & sI_n+k_1I_n+k_3\mathcal{L}\end{pmatrix} \\ &= \det[(s^2I_n)+s(k_1I_n+k_3\mathcal{L})+(k_0I_n+k_2\mathcal{L})] \\ &= \prod_{i=1}^{n}[s^2+(k_1+k_3\mu_i)s+k_0+k_2\mu_i]=0.\end{aligned} \tag{5.7}$$

As a result, we have

$$\begin{aligned} s_{i1} &= \frac{-(k_1+k_3\mu_i)+\sqrt{(k_1+k_3\mu_i)^2+4(k_0+k_2\mu_i)}}{2}, \\ s_{i2} &= \frac{-(k_1+k_3\mu_i)-\sqrt{(k_1+k_3\mu_i)^2+4(k_0+k_2\mu_i)}}{2}, \\ & \qquad i=1,...,n, \end{aligned} \tag{5.8}$$

where s_{i1} and s_{i2} are the roots of $s^2+(k_1+k_3\mu_i)s+k_0+k_2\mu_i=0$.

Denote $\eta_i(t)=[x_i(t),v_i(t)]^T$ and $\eta_i(t)=[\eta_1(t^T,...,\eta_n(t)^T]^T$. Then the matrix form of system (5.1) under protocol (5.2) can be written as

$$\dot{\eta}(t)=(I_n\otimes A+\mathcal{L}\otimes B)\eta(t), \tag{5.9}$$

where $A=\begin{bmatrix}0 & 1\\ -k_0 & -k_1\end{bmatrix}$ and $B=\begin{bmatrix}0 & 0\\ -k_2 & -k_3\end{bmatrix}$

It is obvious that (5.9) is equivalent to (5.4).

Lemma 3.1 [480]. *System (5.1) under protocol (5.2) reaches consensus if and only if* $Re(s_{ij})<0, i=2,...,n, j=1,2$.

If the consensus is reached, we have that the synchronizing state is given by

$$\lim_{t\to\infty}\eta_i(t)=(p^T\otimes e^{At})\begin{bmatrix}\eta_1(0)\\ \cdot\\ \cdot\\ \cdot\\ \eta_n(0)\end{bmatrix}, \tag{5.10}$$

where p is the left eigenvector of $\mathcal{L}$ associated with eigenvalue 0 satisfying $p^T 1_n=0$.

Lemma 3.2. *System (5.1) under protocol (5.2) reaches consensus without exponentially diverging state trajectories if and only if* $Re(s_{ij})<0, i=2,...,n, j=1,2$ *and* $Re(s_{1j})\le 0, j=1,2$.

Proof: Sufficiency. By **Lemma 3.1**, it can be seen that system (5.1) under protocol (5.2) reaches consensus if $Re(s_{ij})<0, i=2,...,n, j=1,2$. From (5.10), it is seen that the consensus mode is decided by A. If $Re(s_{ij}) < 0, i = 2, ..., n, j = 1, 2$, is guaranteed and all of the eigenvalues of A lie in the closed left half-plane, we can conclude that the consensus is reached and the agent trajectories are not exponentially diverging. As det $(sI_2 - A) = s^2 + k_1 s + k_0$, it follows that if $Re(s_{ij}) < 0, i = 2, ..., n, j = 1, 2$, and the roots of $s^2 + k_1 s + k_0 = 0$ lie in the closed left half complex plane, system (5.1) under protocol (5.2) reaches consensus without exponentially diverging state trajectories.

Necessity. We can prove the necessity in a similar manner and the proof is omitted here.

Lemma 3.3 [470]. *The complex coefficient polynomial* $g(s) = s^2 + as + b$ *is stable if and only if* $Re(a) > 0$ *and* $Re(a)Im(a)Im(b) + Re2(a)Re(b) - Im^2(b) > 0$, *where a and b are complex numbers.*

Extending on [480] with a constraint on the state trajectories, we provide the parameter condition by the following lemma:.

Lemma 3.4. *System (5.1) under protocol (5.2) reaches consensus without exponentially diverging state trajectories if and only if the protocol parameters satisfy*

$$k_0 \geq 0, \tag{5.11}$$

$$k_1 \geq 0, \tag{5.12}$$

$$k_1 + k_3 Re(\mu_i) > 0, \tag{5.13}$$

$$(k_1 + k_3 Re(\mu_i))k_2 k_3 Im^2(\mu_i) + (k_1 + k_3 Re(\mu_i))^2 (k_0 + k_2 Re(\mu_i)) > k_2^2 Im^2(\mu_i), \quad i = 2, ..., n \tag{5.14}$$

Proof: The roots of $s^2 + k_{1s} + k_0 = 0$ lie in the closed left half complex plane if and only if $k_0 \geq 0$ and $k_1 \geq 0$. From **Lemma 3.3**, it is followed that $Re(s_{ij}) < 0, i = 2, ..., n, j = 1, 2$, if and only if both (5.13) and (5.14) hold. According to **Lemma 3.2**, we can conclude that system (5.1) under protocol (5.2) reaches consensus without exponentially diverging state trajectories if and only if the parameters satisfy (5.11)(5.14). It is easy to see that (5.13) and (5.14) are equivalent to (39) and (40) of [480], respectively. By using the stability theory of the complex coefficient polynomial, the analysis complexity is comparatively reduced.

Based on **Lemma 3.4**, we study the delay sensitivity of system (5.5) and have the following theorem.

Theorem 3.1: *Suppose that (5.11)(5.14) are satisfied and* k_0 *and* k_1 *are not simultaneously zero. If the parameters are given as* $k_0 > 0$ *and* $k_1 = 0$, *system (5.5) reaches equi-amplitude periodic consensus if and only if* $\tau = 0$. *In other cases, system (5.5) reaches consensus without exponentially diverging states if*

$$\tau < \tau_1 = \min_{1 \leq i \leq n} \{\theta_i / \phi_i\} \tag{5.15}$$

where $\theta_i \in [0, \pi)$ *satisfies*

$$
\begin{aligned}
sin\theta_i &= \frac{k_1\phi_i^2 + k_3 Re(\mu_i)\phi_i^2 + k_2 Im(\mu_i)}{\phi_i^2}, \\
cos\theta_i &= \frac{k_0 + k_2 Re(\mu_i) + k_3 Im(\mu_i)\phi_i}{\phi_i^2},
\end{aligned} \tag{5.16}
$$

and $\phi_i > 0$ *satisfies*

$$
\begin{aligned}
\phi_i^4 &= \left[(k_1 + k_3 Re(\mu_i))^2 + k_3^2 Im^2(\mu_i)\right]\phi_i^2 + 2Im(\mu_i)(k_2k_1 - k_3k_0)\phi_i \\
&+ \left[(k_0 + k_2 Re(\mu_i))^2 + k_2^2 Im^2(\mu_i)\right]
\end{aligned} \tag{5.17}
$$

Proof: The closed-loop poles of system (5.5) satisfy

$$
\begin{aligned}
det(sI_{2n} - \tilde{\mathcal{L}}_1 - e^{-s\tau}\tilde{\mathcal{L}}_2) &= det\begin{pmatrix} sI_n & -I_n \\ e^{-s\tau}(k_0 I_n + k_2\mathcal{L}) & sI_n + e^{-s\tau}(k_1 I_n + k_3\mathcal{L}) \end{pmatrix} \\
&= det\left[s^2 I_n + se^{-s\tau}(k_1 I_n + k_3\mathcal{L}) + e^{-s\tau}(k_0 I_n + k_2\mathcal{L})\right] \\
&= \prod_{i=1}^{n}\left[s^2 + (k_1 + k_3\mu_i)se^{-s\tau} + (k_0 + k_2\mu_i)e^{-s\tau}\right] = 0.
\end{aligned} \tag{5.18}
$$

Let $p_i(s, e^{-st}) = s^2 + (k_1 + k_3\mu_i)se^{-st} + (k_0 + k_2\mu_i)e^{-st}$, $i = 1, ..., n$, and $p(s, e^{-st}) = \prod_{i=1}^{n} p_i(s, e^{-st})$. According to Lemma 3.4, system (5) reaches consensus without exponentially diverging states when $\tau = 0$, where all of the roots of $\prod_{i=2}^{n}\left[s^2 + (k_1 + k_3\mu_i) + (k_0 + k_2\mu_i)\right] = 0$ are located in the open left half plane and the roots of $s^2 + k_1 s + k_0 = 0$ are located in the closed left half plane. Note that the roots of $p(s, e^{-st}) = 0$ are continuous with respect to τ.

Next we find the minimum value of τ such that $p(s, e^{-st}) = 0$ has some purely imaginary roots.

In the case where $k_0 > 0$ and $k_1 = 0$, the roots of $s^2 + k_1 s + k_0 = 0$ are $\pm j\sqrt{k_0}$. As a result, $p(s, e^{-st}) = 0$ has some purely imaginary roots when $\tau = 0$. It is easy to see that for any $\tau > 0$, the agents states are of exponentially diverging; system (5.5) reaches equi-amplitude periodic consensus if and only if $\tau = 0$.

In other cases, we consider the following equation:

$$
s^2 + (k_1 + k_3\mu_i)se^{-s\tau} + (k_0 + k_2\mu_i)e^{-s\tau} = 0, i = 1, ..., n. \tag{5.19}
$$

Let $s = j\omega(\omega \neq 0)$ By (5.19), we have

$$
\begin{aligned}
\omega^2 &= e^{-j\omega\tau}[j\omega(k_1 + k_3 Re(\mu_i) + jk_3 Im(\mu_i)) \\
&+ (k_0 + k_2 Re(\mu_i) + jk_2 Im(\mu_i))] \\
&= e^{-j\omega\tau}[(k_0 + k_2 Re(\mu_i) - k_3 Im(\mu_i)\omega) \\
&+ j(k_1\omega + k_3 Re(\mu_i)\omega + k_2 Im(\mu_i))] \\
&= (cos\,\omega\tau - jsin\,\omega\tau)[(k_0 + k_2 Re(\mu_i) - k_3 Im(\mu_i)\omega) \\
&+ j(k_1\omega + k_3 Re(\mu_i)\omega + k_2 Im(\mu_i))]
\end{aligned} \tag{5.20}
$$

It follows from (5.20) that

$$\begin{aligned}
\omega^4 &= (k_0 + k_2Re(\mu_i) - k_3Im(\mu_i)\omega)^2 \\
&+ (k_1\omega + k_3Re(\mu_i)\omega + k_2Im(\mu_i))^2, \qquad (5.21)\\
\omega^2 &= (k_0 + k_2Re(\mu_i) - k_3Im(\mu_i)\omega)cos\omega\tau \\
&+ (k_1\omega + k_3Re(\mu_i)\omega + k_2Im(\mu_i))sin\,\omega\tau \qquad (5.22)\\
0 &= (k_1\omega + k_3Re(\mu_i)\omega + k_2Im(\mu_i))cos\,\omega\tau \\
&- (k_0 + k_2Re(\mu_i) - k_3Im(\mu_i)\omega)sin\,\omega\tau. \qquad (5.23)
\end{aligned}$$

By (5.21)–(5.22), we readily obtain

$$\sin\,\omega\tau = \frac{(k_1\omega + k_3Re(\mu_i)\omega + k_2Im(\mu_i))}{\omega^2}, \qquad (5.24)$$

$$\cos\,\omega\tau = \frac{(k_0 + k_2Re(\mu_i) + k_3Im(\mu_i))\omega}{\omega^2}, \qquad (5.25)$$

Further manipulation of (5.21) yields

$$\begin{aligned}
\omega^4 &= \left[(k_1 + k_3Re(\mu_i))^2\right]\omega^2 + 2Im(\mu_i)(k_2k_1 + k_3k_0)\omega \\
&+ \left[(k_0 + k_2Re(\mu_i))^2 + k_2^2Im^2(\mu_i)\right] \qquad (5.26)
\end{aligned}$$

which calls for further discussions. We first consider the case $\omega > 0$.

For $i = 1$, we have $\omega^4 = k_1^2\omega^2 + k_0^2$. As k_0 and k_1 are not simultaneously zero and $\omega > 0$, there exists a single $\phi_1 > 0$ such that $\phi_1^4 = k_1^2\phi_1^2 + k_0^2$.

For $i = 2, ..., n$, by (5.13), we have $(k_1 + k_3Re(\mu_i))^2 + k_3^2Im^2(\mu_i) > 0$. Note that $(k_0 + k_2Re(\mu_i))^2 + k_2^2Im^2(\mu_i) = 0$ if and only if $k_0 = k_2 = 0(Im(\mu_i) \neq 0)$ or $k_0 + k_2Re(\mu_i) = 0(Im(\mu_i) = 0)$. If $k_0 = k_2 = 0$, (5.14) is not satisfied, which results in a contradiction. Similarly, if $k_0 + k_2Re(\mu_i) = 0$ and $Im(\mu_i) = 0$, (5.14) is not satisfied, which results in a contradiction. Thus, we have $(k_0 + k_2Re(\mu_i))^2 + k_2^2Im^2(\mu_i) > 0$. As $(k_1 + k_3Re(\mu_i))^2 + k_3^2Im_2\mu_i) > 0$, $(k_0 + k_2Re(\mu_i))^2 + k_2^2Im^2(\mu_i) > 0$ and $\omega > 0$, we can conclude that there exists a single $\phi_i > 0$ such that (5.17) is satisfied. Let $\theta_i \in [0, 2\pi)$, which satisfies (5.16). Then, we have that $p(s, e^{-st}) = 0$ has purely imaginary roots if and only if

$\tau \in \Omega = \{(2l\pi + \theta_i)/\phi_i \mid i = 1, ..., n, l = 0, 1, 2, ...\}$

As $\theta_i \in [0, 2\pi)$, the minimum value of τ such that the first root crosses the imaginary axis is at $l = 0$ and is given by $\tau_1 = min_{1 \leq i \leq n}\{\theta_i/\phi_i\}$. It follows that, for any $\tau \in [0, \tau_1)$, system (5.5) reaches consensus without exponentially diverging state trajectories.

Similar conclusions can be drawn for the case ror $\omega < 0$ and it is left to the reader to get it.

Remark 3.1. *When $k_0 > 0$ and $k_1 = 0$, all of the eigenvalues of A lie on the imaginary axis and system (5.1) under protocol (5.2) reaches periodic consensus. [480] studied the periodic consensus when $k_2 = 0$. However, from* **Lemma 3.2** *and* **Lemma 3.4**, *it can be seen that $k_2 = 0$ is not a necessary condition for the periodic consensus; system (5.1) under protocol (5.2) reaches periodic consensus if and only if $k_0 > 0, k_1 = 0, k_3 > 0$ and $k_2k_3^2Re(\mu_i)Im^2(\mu_i) + k_3^2Re(\mu_i)^2(k_0 + k_2Re(\mu_i)) > k_2^2Im^2(\mu_i), i = 2\ldots,n$.*

Remark 3.2. *When $k_0 = k_1 = 0$, it is the case discussed by [478], where the results are based on the assumption that $k_2 > 0$ and $k_3 > 0$ (where k_2 and k_3 are called the coupling strengths). However,* **Lemma 3.4** *shows that the condition that $k_2 > 0$ and $k_3 > 0$ is necessary for the consensus.*

Remark 3.3. *The proof idea of* **Theorem 3.1** *is based on that of Theorem 2 of [478]. However, as the case where $k_0 = k_1 = 0$ was discussed in [478], only consider the cases where k0 and k1 are not simultaneously zero.*

5.4 Illustrative Examples

In this section, we provide numerical examples to illustrate the effectiveness of the theoretical results.

Example 4.1. Consider a group of four agents with the communication topology shown in Fig. 5.1. The Laplacian matrix $\mathcal{L}$ corresponding to the graph is

$$\begin{bmatrix} 1 & 0 & -1 & 0 \\ -1 & 1 & 0 & 0 \\ 0 & -1 & 1 & 0 \\ -1 & 0 & 0 & 1 \end{bmatrix}$$

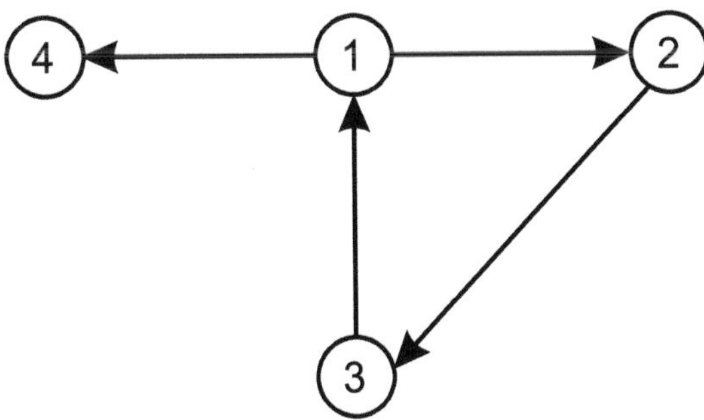

Figure 5.1: Communication topology of four agents

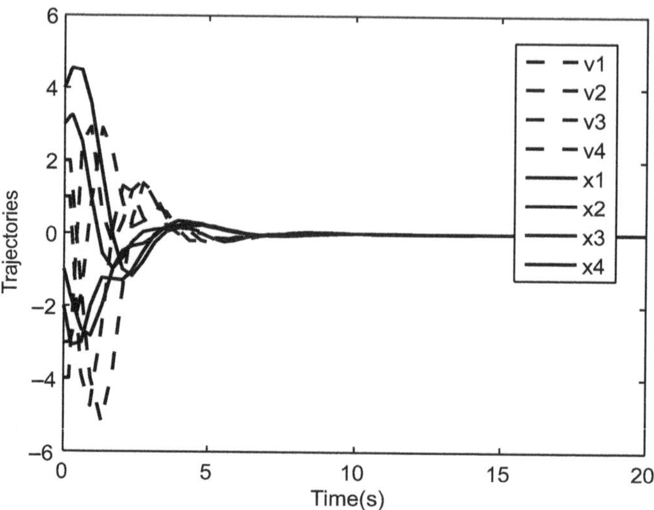

Figure 5.2: $k_0 = k_1 = k_2 = k_3 = 1$ and $\tau = 0.2(s)$

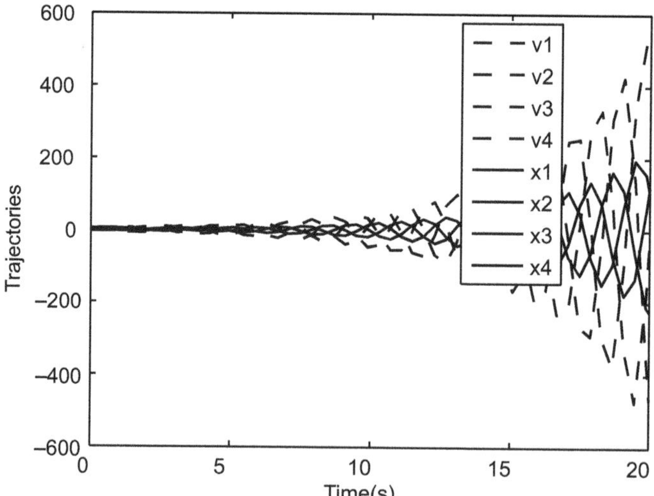

Figure 5.3: $k_0 = k_1 = k_2 = k_3 = 1$ and $\tau = 0.4(s)$

The eigenvalues of $\mathcal{L}$ are $\mu_1 = 0, \mu_2 = 1, \mu_3 = 1:5 - j0.866$ and $\mu_4 = 1.5 + j0.866$. The initial conditions are given as $x_1(0) = 3, x_2(0) = -2, x_3(0) = -1, x_4(0) = 4, v_1(0) = 1, v_2(0) = -4, v_3(0) = -3$ and $v_4(0) = 2$.

Let $k_0 = 1, k_1 = 1, k_2 = 1$ and $k_3 = 1$. It is easy to check that (5.11)(5.14) are satisfied. By Theorem 3.1, we obtain $\tau_1 = 0:3188(s)$. When delays are given as $\tau = 0:2(s)$ and $\tau = 0:4(s)$, the trajectories of the agents are shown in Figs. 5.2 and 5.3.

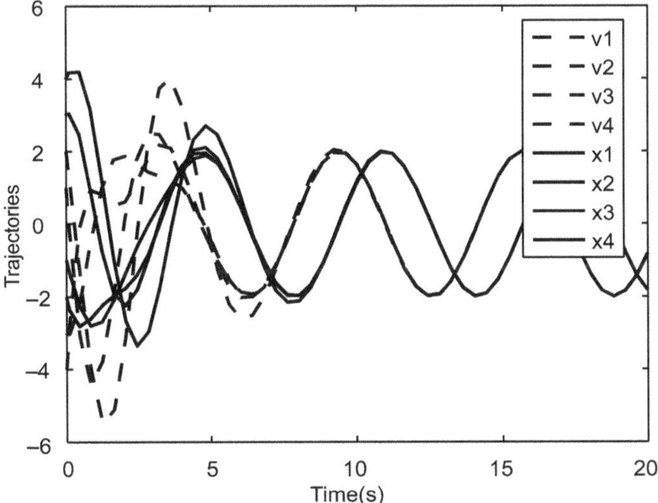

Figure 5.4: $k_1 = 1, k_0 = k_2 = k_3 = 1$ and $\tau = 0(s)$

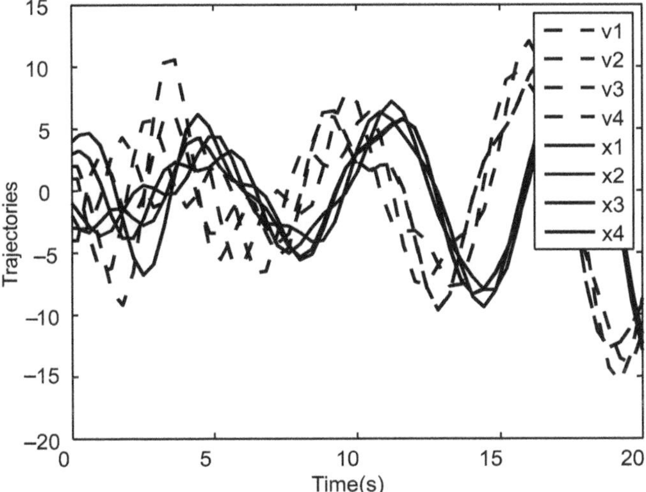

Figure 5.5: $k_1 = 1, k_0 = k_2 = k_3 = 1$ and $\tau = 0.2(s)$

Let $k_0 = 1, k_1 = 0, k_2 = 1$ and $k_3 = 1$. It is easy to check that (5.11)(5.14) are satisfied. By Theorem 3.1, we have that the system reaches equi-amplitude periodic consensus if and only if $\tau = 0$. When delays are given as $\tau = 0(s)$ and $\tau = 0.2(s)$, the trajectories of the agents are shown in 5.4 and 5.5.

Let $k_0 = 0, k_1 = 1, k_2 = 1$ and $k_3 = 1$. It is easy to check that (5.11)(5.14) are satisfied. By Theorem 3.1, we get $\tau 1 = 0.3778(s)$. When delays are given as $\tau = 0.3(s)$ and $\tau = 0.5(s)$, the trajectories of the agents are shown in Figs. 5.6 and 5.7.

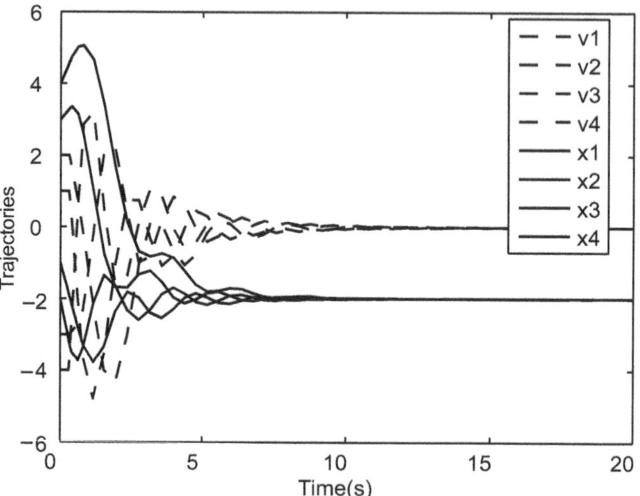

Figure 5.6: $k_1 = 1, k_0 = k_2 = k_3 = 1$ and $\tau = 0.3(s)$

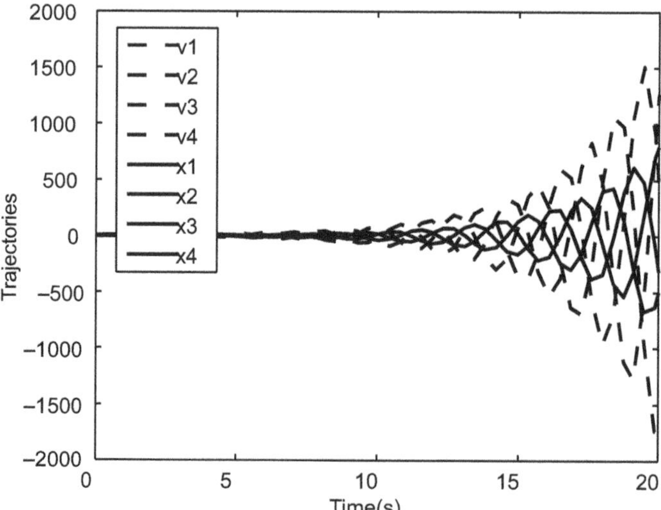

Figure 5.7: $k_1 = 1, k_0 = k_2 = k_3 = 1$ and $\tau = 0.5(s)$

5.5 Notes

A general consensus protocol for directed networks of double integrators with input delays has been analyzed. A necessary and sufficient condition on protocol parameters, under which not only the consensus is reached but also the agents states are not exponentially diverging, has been given. Based on this condition, the robustness of the protocol to input delays has been discussed. The maximal allowable upper bound of the delay has been obtained. Simulation results have been presented to illustrate the effectiveness of the theoretical results. Future work includes studying the general second-order consensus protocol with both input and communication delays:

$$\begin{aligned} u_i &= -k_0 x_i(t-\tau) - k_1 v_i(t-\tau) - \sum_{j\in\mathcal{N}_i} a_{ij}[k_2(x_i(t-\tau) - x_j(t-\tau_1-\tau_2)) \\ &+ k_3(v_i(t-\tau) - v_j(t-\tau_1-\tau_2))] \end{aligned} \tag{5.27}$$

where τ_1 and τ_2 are input and communication delays, respectively. [467] studied the consensus with both input and communication delays. Extending the results of [467] to the general second-order consensus protocol (5.27) is an interesting line of future research.

Chapter 6

Advanced Consensus Algorithms

6.1 Event-Triggered Control for Multiagent Systems

Recent years have witnessed the increasing interest in the study of the coordination problem for multiagent systems (MASs). In this area, the consensus of MASs is a basic and important problem that has had many applications in the fields of biology, computer science and control engineering ([608], [615], [605]). During the past decades, the study of the consensus problem has attracted much attention for systems of single-integrator kinematics ([605], [612]), double-integrator dynamics ([611], [610], [623]), fractional-order dynamics ([596], 2010) and high-order dynamics ([616]) based on the continuous-time models ([595], [611]) or discrete-time models ([596], [602]). At the same time, several scenes have also been addressed, such as networks with switching topologies and time-varying delays ([614]; [622]), asynchronous consensus ([598], [617]), finite-time consensus ([601]) and so on (see, for example, [606] and the references therein). More notably consensus with a dynamic leader is called a consensus tracking problem ([604]). The tracking control has been widely used in many practical applications, such as unmanned aerial vehicle formation, target tracking in sensor networks and so on ([600]).

6.1.1 Introduction

Decentralized consensus control for MASs is currently facilitated by recent technological advances on computing and communication resources. Each agent can be equipped with a small embedded microprocessor that will be responsible for collecting the information from neighboring nodes and actuating the controller updates according to some ruling ([597]). However, the embedded processors are usually resource-limited. So, one of the most important aspects in the implementation of decentralized consensus algorithms is the communication and control actuation schemes. In order to reduce the communication burden, while at the same time saving the communication resource for the network, the data-sampled control for continuous time MASs has been investigated by [619, 618], in which the sampled signals of the agents should be instantly transmitted through the network. It has been shown that the data-sampled control has many advantages over the continuous time control, such as reducing the required broad bandwidth of networks, having advantages in control accuracy, control speed and so on. Although the data-sampled control has some advantages, as mentioned above, it might be conservative in terms of finding a conservative constant sampling period to guarantee the stability of the network in the worst case. However, as stated in [621], the worst cases are seldom encountered in practical systems, therefore, this kind of sampled control method will lead to the sending of many unnecessary signals to the controller or to the network, which may cause a large waste of the communication bandwidth. In order to overcome the conservatism of data-sampled control, a novel control strategy has been given increased attention in recent years, where the sampled signals of the agents, whether or not to be instantly transmitted to their neighbours or to the controller, are determined by certain events that are triggered depending on some rulings. This approach is called event-triggered control strategy ([597], [609]) and provides a useful way of determining when the sampled signal is sent out. For instance, the distributed control design in [597] forced each agent to update its control law whenever a certain error measurement threshold was violated, as well as when the control law of its neighbours was updated. In [613], the control actuation is updated whenever a certain error becomes large enough to overtake the norm of the state.

In what follows, we focus our attention on the design of a reasonable discrete event-triggered communication scheme and its application to the tracking control design of discrete-time MASs in order to save the limited resource and reduce the communication burden while preserving the desired performance. During the event-triggered tracking control process, it is assumed that every agent (or the leader) release its state information to its neighbours only when the state error is above a specified threshold and each agent's local controller is updated by using the latest information received from neighbouring agents. The main contributions of this paper can be summarized as follows:

(1) Most existing works which have used the event-triggered control strategy mainly focus on the continuous-time models for MASs ([597], [609]). To the best of the authors' knowledge, the tracking problem of discrete-time MASs making use of the event-triggered control method has not been addressed before.

(2) Different from the time-triggered periodic communication scheme ([596]), the proposed scheme given hereafter is a discrete event-triggered scheme, where the sampled state signal of each agent that should be transmitted to its neighbors is determined by the error between the current sampled state and the latest transmitted one. Although both schemes mentioned above can guarantee the desired tracking performance, the number of the transmitted state signals through the multi-agent network is reduced by using the event-triggered scheme proposed in this paper. Thus, the communication resources embedded in the agents can be saved and the communication burden can be reduced.

(3) Compared with [609], some special dynamic thresholds presented by some discretetime exponential functions are used in this paper, which can guarantee that the tracking errors for all agents can be ultimately bounded by a smaller positive bound than when using the discrete-time counterpart of the dynamic thresholds proposed in [609].

Note in the sequel that, to realize the tracking control, the reference state is available to only a subset of the agents followed, and only the communication between the agent and its local neighbours is needed, therefore, the designed control is essentially distributed.

6.1.2 System model and problem statement

Suppose that agent i takes the following dynamics:

$$x_i[k+1] = x_i[k] + Tu_i[k], i = 1, 2, \cdots, n, \tag{6.1}$$

where the integer k is the discrete-time index, T is the sampling period which is assumed to be given a priori, and $x_i[k] \in R$ and $u_i[k] \in R$, respectively, represent the agent's state and the control input of the ith agent at time $t = kT$. In what follows, the consensus tracking problem will be considered, where the time-varying reference state is denoted by $x^r[k]$. If the ith agent can access the leader's state information, then $a_{(i,n+1)} > 0$, otherwise, $a_{(i,n+1)} = 0$.

Throughout this section, for simplicity, we use $[k]$ to represent (kT), for example, $x_i[k] = x_i(kT), x^r[k] = x^r(kT)$, etc.

Definition 6.1 ([620]) *We say the solution of a dynamic system is uniformly ultimately bounded (UUB), if for a compact set U of R^n and for all $x(t_0) = x_0 \in U$ there exists an $\varepsilon > 0$ and a number $T(\varepsilon, x_0)$ such that $||x(t)|| < \varepsilon$ for all $t > t_0 + T$.*

Assumption 3 *The communication graph between the agents and the leader is fixed and directed.*

Assumption 4 *No data loss and transmission delay occur in the network communication.*

For the system (6.1), the consensus tracking problem was investigated in Cao et al. (2009) based on the assumption that the sampled states of the agents should be instantly transmitted through the network, which means that the time-triggered scheme was used there. The following consensus algorithm was shown to be able to guarantee the tracking of states of agents (6.1) with a time-varying reference state $x^r[k]$:

$$\begin{aligned} u_i[k] &= \frac{1}{T\sum_{j=1}^{n+1} a_{(i,j)}} \sum_{j=1}^{n} a_{(i,j)}(x_j[k]-x_j[k-1]-T\gamma\{x_i[k]-x_j[k]\}) \\ &+ \frac{a_{(i,n+1)}}{T\sum_{j=1}^{n+1} a_{(i,j)}}(x^r[k]-x^r[k-1]-T\gamma\{x_i[k]-x_r[k]\}), \end{aligned} \tag{6.2}$$

where γ is a positive gain.

Remark 6.1 In Cao et al. (2009), *The tracking controller (6.2) is assumed to be realized based on a time-triggered scheme with a given sampling period T, which means that the state sampled at the current time kT for each agent i and the leader should be transmitted to its neighbours in order to realize the algorithm (6.2). In many real systems, however, the dynamics may change smoothly during a bounded time interval. Therefore, the time-triggered scheme may produce many useless messages if the current sampled signal has not significantly changed in contrast to the previous sampled signal, which then leads to a conservative usage of the communication bandwidth. In order to save the communication energy of the multi-agent network, in the following section, the event-triggered scheme is first introduced to realize the tracking controller (6.2), where the events are triggered for each agent i when the norm of the measurement errors exceeds certain dynamic thresholds presented by some trigger functions.* ▮

The realizing process for the algorithm with the tracking controller (6.2) under an event-triggered scheme can be illustrated as follows: First, all agents compute their trigger functions based on the past and current sampled signals; if the trigger condition is fulfilled for one agent, the agent will broadcast its actual measurement value to its neighbours. The time when the agent sends the measurement value of the state out to its neighbours is called the release time. Each agent's controller $u_i[k]$ is updated by evaluation using the latest information from its neighbours. In order to model the event-triggers for agents, here we denote the release times for the ith agent and its neighbours by s_m^i and $s_m^j(m=0,1,2,\cdots;j\in N_i)$ and for the leader by $s_m^r(m=0,1,2,\cdots)$. The broadcasted states for agents and the leader can be described by the following piecewise constant functions:

$$\tilde{x}_i[k]=x_i[s_m^i], k\in[s_m^i,s_{m+1}^i), \tag{6.3}$$

$$\tilde{x}r[k]=xr[s_m^r], k\in[s_m^r,s_{m+1}^r), \tag{6.4}$$

where $s^i_m - s^i_{m+1}$ is an integer and $s^i_m T - s^i_{m+1} T$ is a multiple of T.

In the sequel, we define the trigger functions for agent i as $f_i(\cdot), i = 1, 2, \cdots, n$, and the trigger function for the leader as $g(\cdot)$. For agent i, the states $x_j[k], j \in N_i$, are unknown; only $x_i[k]$ and $\tilde{x}_i[k]$, and the broadcasted values $\tilde{x}_j[k]$ of the neighbours $j \in N_i$ are available. An event for agent i about the state is triggered only when the trigger condition

$$f_i(k, x_i[k], \tilde{x}_i[k]) < 0, i = 1, 2, \cdots, n \tag{6.5}$$

is violated while the state of the leader is triggered as soon as

$$g(k, x^r[k], \tilde{x}^r[k]) < 0 \tag{6.6}$$

is violated. The consensus algorithm with the tracking controller (6.2) under an event-triggered scheme, called event-triggered consensus algorithm or event-triggered tracking control in the following, can be described as

$$\begin{aligned} u_i[k] &= \frac{1}{T\sum_{j=1}^{n+1} a_{(i,j)}} \sum_{j=1}^{n} a_{(i,j)} (\tilde{x}_j[k] - \tilde{x}_j[k-1] - T\gamma\{\tilde{x}_i[k] - \tilde{x}_j[k]\}) \\ &+ \frac{a_{(i,n+1)}}{T\sum_{j=1}^{n+1} a_{(i,j)}} (\tilde{x}^r[k] - \tilde{x}^r[k-1] - T\gamma\{\tilde{x}_i[k] - \tilde{x}^r[k]\}) \end{aligned} \tag{6.7}$$

$$\begin{aligned} &= \frac{1}{T\sum_{j=1}^{n+1} a_{(i,j)}} \sum_{j=1}^{n} a_{(i,j)} (x_j[s^j_{m_j}(k)] - xj[s^j_{m_j}(k-1)] \\ &- T\gamma xi[s^i_m] - xj[s^j_{m_j}(k)]) \\ &+ \frac{a_{(i,n+1)}}{T\sum_{j=1}^{n+1} a_{(i,j)}} (x^r[s^r_{n(k)}] - x^r[s^r_{n(k-1)}] \\ &+ T\gamma\{x_i[s^i_m] - x^r[s^r_n(k)]\}), \quad k \in [s^i_m, s^i_{m+1}), \end{aligned} \tag{6.8}$$

where

$$\begin{aligned} m_j(k) &\triangleq arg \min_{p \in N: s^j_p \le k} \{k - s^j_p\}, \\ n(k) &\triangleq arg \min_{q \in N: s^r_q \le k} \{k - s^r_q\}, \quad k \in [s^i_m, s^i_{m+1}) \end{aligned}$$

and $N = \{1, 2, 3, \cdots\}, \{s^j_p, p \in Z^+\}$ represents the set of release times for the jth agent before time k and $\{s^r_q, q \in Z^+\}$ represents the set of release times for the leader before time k.

Remark 6.2 *In this section, $s^i_{m+1} - s^i_m$ in (6.8) may be larger than T. Moreover, in the time interval $[s^i_m, s^i_{m+1})$, the events triggered by the neighbors of the ith agent and the leader may occur, which means that $s^j_{m_j(k)}$ and $s^r_{n(k)}$ may change for $k \in [s^i_m, s^i_{m+1})$. Therefore, $u_i[k]$ in (6.8) may be time-varying for $k \in [s^i_m, s^i_{m+1})$ depending on the variations of $s^j_{m_j(k)}$ and $s^r_{n(k)}$.* ■

6.1.3 Design tracking results

In this section, the tracking problem for system (6.1) under the event-triggered consensus algorithm (6.8) will be investigated. Before we obtain the main result, some arrangement is needed. Define the state error between the current sampled time and the last release time of the ith agent and the leader, respectively, as

$$e_i[k] = x_i[s^i_m] - x_i[k], k \in [s^i_m, s^i_{m+1}), e_j[k] = x_j[s^j_m] - x_j[k], k \in [s^j_m, s^j_{m+1}) \quad (6.9)$$

and

$$e^r[k] = x^r[s^r_m] - x^r[k], k \in [s^r_m, s^r_{m+1}), \quad (6.10)$$

where $m = 0, 1, \cdots$. Then, $u_i[k]$ in (6.8) can be rewritten as

$$\begin{aligned} u_i[k] &= \frac{1}{T\sum_{j=1}^{n+1} a_{(i,j)}} \sum_{j=1}^{n} a_{(i,j)}(x_j[k] + e_j[k] - x_j[k-1] - e_j[k-1] \\ &- T\gamma x_i[k] + e_i[k] - x_j[k] - e_j[k]) \\ &+ \frac{a_{(i,n+1)}}{T\sum_{j=1}^{n+1} a_{(i,j)}} (x^r[k] + e^r[k] - x^r[k-1] - e^r[k-1] \\ &- T\gamma\{x_i[k] + e_i[k] - x_r[k] - e^r[k]\}). \end{aligned} \quad (6.11)$$

Furthermore, define the tracking error between the ith agent and the leader as $\delta_i[k] \triangleq x_i[k] - x^r[k]$; then

$$x_i[k+1] - x_i[k] = \delta_i[k+1] + x^r[k+1] - \delta_i[k] - x^r[k] \quad (6.12)$$

and

$$\begin{aligned} u_i[k] &= \frac{1}{T\sum_{j=1}^{n+1} a_{(i,j)}} \sum_{j=1}^{n} a_{(i,j)}(\delta_j[k] + x^r[k] + e_j[k] - \delta_j[k-1] \\ &- x^r[k-1] - e_j[k-1] \\ &- \gamma\{\delta_i[k] + x^r[k] + e_i[k] - \delta_j[k] - x^r[k] - e_j[k]\}) \\ &+ \frac{a_{(i,n+1)}}{T\sum_{j=1}^{n+1} a_{(i,j)}} (x^r[k] + e^r[k] - x^r[k-1] - e^r[k-1] \\ &- T\gamma\{\delta_i[k] + e_i[k] - e^r[k]\}). \end{aligned} \quad (6.13)$$

Substituting (6.12) and (6.13) into (6.1) and making some arrangements, we obtain, for $k \in [s^i_m, s^i_{m+1})$,

$$\begin{aligned} \delta_i[k+1] &= 2x^r[k] - x^r[k+1] - x^r[k-1] \\ &+ \frac{a_{(i,n+1)}}{\sum_{j=1}^{n+1} a_{(i,j)}} \{e^r[k] + T\gamma e^r[k] - e^r[k-1]\} + (1 - T\gamma)\delta_i[k] - T\gamma e_i[k] \\ &+ \frac{1}{\sum_{j=1}^{n+1} a_{(i,j)}} \sum_{j=1}^{n} a_{(i,j)}[(1 + T\gamma)(\delta_j[k] + e_i[k]) \\ &- \delta_j[k-1] - e_j[k-1]]. \end{aligned} \quad (6.14)$$

To proceed further, we introduce the following matrix and augmented variable definitions as

$$\begin{aligned}
B &= diag\{a_{(1,n+1)},\cdots,a_{(n,n+1)}\}, \\
D &= diag\{\sum_{j=1}^{n+1} a_{(1,j)},\cdots,\sum_{j=1}^{n+1} a_{(n,j)}\}, \\
\triangle[k+1] &= (\delta_1[k+1],\cdots,\delta_n[k+1])^\top, \\
e[k] &= (e_1[k],\cdots,e_n[k])^\top, \\
\theta^r[k] &= 2x^r[k]-x^r[k+1]-x^r[k-1], \\
\beta^r[k] &= e^r[k]+T\gamma e^r[k]-e^r[k-1].
\end{aligned}$$

Therefore, (6.14) can be rewritten as

$$\begin{aligned}
\triangle[k+1] &= \theta^r[k]1_n+D^{-1}B\beta^r[k]1n+(1-T\gamma)I_n\triangle[k]-T\gamma e[k] \\
&+ D^{-1}A(1+T\gamma)\triangle[k]+D^{-1}A(1+T\gamma)e[k] \\
&- D^{-1}A\triangle[k-1]-D^{-1}Ae[k-1] \qquad (6.15)
\end{aligned}$$

and, subsequently, we reach

$$\begin{aligned}
\begin{bmatrix} \triangle[k+1] \\ \triangle[k] \end{bmatrix} &= \tilde{A}\begin{bmatrix} \triangle[k] \\ \triangle[k-1] \end{bmatrix}+\tilde{B}+\tilde{C} \\
\tilde{A} &= \begin{bmatrix} (1-T\gamma)I_n+(1+T\gamma)D^{-1}A-D^{-1}A & -D^{-1}A \\ I_n & 0 \end{bmatrix} \\
\tilde{B} &= \begin{bmatrix} (1+T\gamma)D^{-1}A-T\gamma In-D^{-1}A & -D6-1A \\ 0 & 0 \end{bmatrix} \\
\tilde{C} &= \begin{bmatrix} I_n & D^{-1}B \\ 0 & 0 \end{bmatrix} \qquad (6.16)
\end{aligned}$$

Defining the following augmented variables as

$$Y[k]=\begin{bmatrix} \triangle[k] \\ \triangle[k-1] \end{bmatrix},\omega[k]=\begin{bmatrix} e[k] \\ e[k-1] \end{bmatrix},z[k]=\begin{bmatrix} \beta^r[k]1_n \\ \theta^r[k]1_n] \end{bmatrix},$$

we have that (6.16) becomes

$$Y[k+1]=\tilde{A}Y[k]+\tilde{B}\omega[k]+\tilde{C}z[k], \qquad (6.17)$$

where

$$\begin{aligned}
\tilde{A} &= \begin{bmatrix} (1-T\gamma)I_n+(1+T\gamma)D^{-1}A & -D^{-1}A \\ I_n & 0 \end{bmatrix}, \\
\tilde{B} &= \begin{bmatrix} (1+T\gamma)D^{-1}A-T\gamma I_n & -D^{-1}A \\ 0 & 0 \end{bmatrix},\tilde{C}=\begin{bmatrix} I_n & D^{-1}B \\ 0 & 0 \end{bmatrix}. \qquad (6.18)
\end{aligned}$$

By using the iterative approach, the solution of (6.17) can be obtained as

$$Y[k] = \tilde{A}^k Y[0] + \sum_{s=1}^{k} \tilde{A}^{k-s}\{\tilde{B}\omega[s-1] + \tilde{C}z[s-1]\}. \tag{6.19}$$

In the following, the convergence analysis of (6.17) will be carried out based on (6.19. For use in the analysis, the following lemma ([596]) is needed.

Lemma 6.1

Assume that the leader has a directed path to all agents from 1 to n and let λ_i be the eigenvalue of $D^{-1}A$. Then $\tau_i > 0$ holds, where $\tau_i \triangleq 2|1-\lambda_i|2\{2[1-Re(\lambda_i)] - |1-\lambda_i|2\}/(|1-\lambda_i|^4 + 4[Im(\lambda_i)]^2)$, and $Re(\cdot)$ and $Im(\cdot)$ denote, respectively, the real and imaginary parts of a number. If positive scalars T and γ satisfy

$$T\gamma < min\{1, \min_{i=1,\ldots,n} \tau_i\}, \tag{6.20}$$

then $\tilde{A}$, defined in (6.18), has all eigenvalues within the unit circle.

In the following, a discrete-time counterpart of the event-triggered scheme proposed in [609] for continuous-time MASs is introduced. The bound for the tracking error is estimated under the control (6.8) with the event-triggered scheme.

Theorem 6.1

Assume that the leader has a directed path to all agents from 1 to n and its states $x^r[k]$ satisfy $|(x^r[k] - x^r[k-1])/T| \leq \bar{\xi}$ (i.e., the changing rate of $x^r[k]$ is bounded), and

$$|e_i[s]| \leq \alpha_1 + c_1 e^{-\beta_1 sT}, i = 1, 2, \cdots, n, \tag{6.21}$$

$$|e^r[s]| \leq \alpha_2 + c_2 e^{-\beta_2 sT}, \tag{6.22}$$

where $\alpha_j \geq 0, \beta_j \geq 0, c_j \geq 0, j = 1, 2$, are some constants, $s \in Z^+$. If positive scalars γ and T satisfy (6.20), under the control algorithm (6.8), the infinite norm of the solution of (6.17) is UUB by

$$\begin{aligned} ||Y[k]||_\infty \; & \leq \; [2\alpha_1(1+T\gamma) + 2c_1(1+T\gamma)e^{-\beta_1 T} + b_1] \\ & \times \; ||(I_{2n} - \tilde{A})^{-1}||_\infty, (k \to \infty), \end{aligned} \tag{6.23}$$

where $b_1 = max\{2T\bar{\xi}, (2+T\gamma)(\alpha_2 + c2e^{-\beta_2 T})\}$.

Proof. From the definition of $||\cdot||_\infty$, it can be seen from the condition (6.22) that

$$||\omega[s]||_\infty \leq \alpha_1 + c_1 e^{-\beta_1}(s-1)T \tag{6.24}$$

Furthermore, it is easy to see from the definitions of $\tilde{B}, \tilde{C}$ and $z[s]$ that

$$||\tilde{B}||_\infty \leq 2(1+T\gamma),$$

and

$$||\tilde{C}z[s]||_\infty \leq max\{2T\xi, (2+T\gamma)(\alpha_2 + c_2 e^{-\beta_2 T})\} \triangleq b_1 \tag{6.25}$$

Under the assumptions of this theorem, it follows from Lemma 1 that $\tilde{A}$ has all eigenvalues within the unit circle. According to [599], there exists a matrix norm $|||\cdot|||$ such that $|||\tilde{A}||| < 1$. Therefore, the following relation can be deduced

$$\lim_{k\to\infty} ||\sum_{s=0}^{k-1} \tilde{A}^s||_\infty \leq ||(I_{2n} - \tilde{A})^{-1}||_\infty. \tag{6.26}$$

Then, combining (6.19), (6.22) and (6.24-6.26) and according to ([596], proof of Theorem 3.1), it can be concluded that

$$\begin{aligned}
||Y[k]||_\infty &\leq ||\tilde{A}^k Y[0]||_\infty + ||\sum_{s=1}^{k} \tilde{A}^{k-s}\tilde{B}\omega[s-1]||_\infty + ||\sum_{s=1}^{k} \tilde{A}^{k-s}\tilde{C}z[s-1]||_\infty \\
&\leq ||\tilde{A}^k Y[0]||_\infty + (\alpha_1 + c1e^{-\beta_1 T})||\tilde{B}||_\infty ||\sum_{s=1}^{k} \tilde{A}^{k-s}||_\infty + b_1 ||\sum_{s=1}^{k} \tilde{A}^{k-s}||_\infty \\
&\leq ||\tilde{A}^k||_\infty ||Y[0]||_\infty + 2(1+T\gamma)(\alpha_1 + c1e^{-\beta_1 T})||\sum_{s=1}^{k} \tilde{A}^{k-s}||_\infty + b_1 ||\sum_{s=1}^{k} \tilde{A}^{k-s}||_\infty \\
&\leq [2\alpha_1(1+T\gamma) + 2c_1(1+T\gamma)e^{-\beta_1 T} + b_1]||(I_{2n} - \tilde{A})^{-1}||_\infty, (k \to \infty)
\end{aligned}$$

which ends the proof.

Remark 6.3 *From the definition of* $||\cdot||_\infty$ *and the inequality (6.23), it yields*

$$|\delta_i[k]| \leq [2\alpha_1(1+T\gamma) + 2c_1(1+T\gamma)e^{-\beta_1 T} + b_1]||(I_{2n} - \tilde{A})^{-1}||_\infty$$

as $k \to \infty, i = 1, 2, \cdots, n$*, which means the tracking error between the ith agent and the leader is ultimately bounded.* ∎

Remark 6.4 *For all agents and the leader, we define the event-triggered functions, respectively, as*

$$f_i(s, |e_i[s]|) \triangleq |e_i[s]| - (\alpha_1 + c1e^{-\beta_1 sT}), i = 1, 2, \cdots, n, \tag{6.27}$$

$$g(s, |e^r[s]|)|e^r[s]| - (\alpha_2 + c_2 e^{-\beta_2 sT}). \tag{6.28}$$

The events are triggered for the ith agent and the leader when $f_i(s,|e_i[s]|) > 0$ and $g(s,|e^r[s]|) > 0$, respectively. Under the above event-triggered schemes, the conditions in (6.21-6.22) can be guaranteed for all $s \in Z^+$, which can be concluded from the following analysis: For agent i, $\forall s \in Z^+$, there exists one interval $[s_l^i, s_{l+1}^i)$, such that $s \in [s_l^i, s_{l+1}^i)$, and in the time interval (s_l^i, s_{l+1}^i) no event has occurred. ■

Case 1: $s = s_p^i$, i.e., event is triggered for agent i at time s. According to equation (6.9), it can be obtained that $e_i[s] = 0$, so the condition in (6.21) is guaranteed. Case 2: $s \in (s_l^i, s_{l+1}^i)$. Because no event has occurred in this time interval, it can be concluded that the trigger function in (6.27) satisfies $f_i(s, e_i[s]) < 0$. So the condition in (6.21) can be guaranteed. Also, (6.22) can be guaranteed by using a similar analysis method as above. From the structure of event-triggers (6.27) and (6.28), it can also be seen that the triggered mechanism used in each agent is decentralized and, therefore, realizable.

Remark 6.5 *It is significant to note that the discrete exponentially decreasing threshold $\alpha + ce^{-\beta kT}$ provides a very flexible event-triggered control strategy for MASs. The parameter α can be used to adjust the state errors' convergence region. Parameter c can be tuned in such a way that the events are not too dense for small times kT. Parameter βcan be used to determine the speed of convergence. For small times kT, the event times depend dominantly on c, so the density of events does not increase with decreasing α. For larger times kT, the density does not increase with decreasing c either ([609]).* ■

In **Theorem** 6.1, the parameters β_1 and β_2 in (6.22) and (6.23), respectively, are assumed to be constant. In the following, revised versions of (6.22) and (6.23) are proposed by settingβ_1 and β_2 as time-varying functions which can lead to a smaller upper bound for $||Y[k]||_\infty$ compared with that in **Theorem** 6.1. To show this fact, we recall the following lemma [594].

Lemma 6.2

If function $f(k) = kC_k^m a^{k-m}$ where $0 < a < 1$, and m is a finite positive integer, then $\lim_{k\to+\infty} f(k) = 0$.

Theorem 6.2

Assume that the leader has a directed path to all agents from 1 to n and its state $x^r[k]$ satisfies $|(x^r[k] - x^r[k-1])/T| \le \xi$ (i.e., the changing rate of $x^r[k]$ is bounded), and

$$|e_i[s]| \le \alpha_1 + c_1 e^{-\beta_1(s)sT}, i = 1, 2, \cdots, n, \tag{6.29}$$

$$|e^r[s]| \le \alpha_2 + c_2 e^{-\beta_2(s)sT}, \tag{6.30}$$

where

$$\beta_1(s) = -\frac{ln\rho(\tilde{A})s}{sT}, \beta_2(s) = -\frac{ln\rho(\tilde{A})s}{sT}, \tag{6.31}$$

and $\alpha_j \geq 0, c_j \geq 0, j = 1,2$, *are some constants,* $s \in Z^+$. *If positive scalars* γ *and* T *satisfy (6.20), under the control algorithm (6.8), the infinite norm of the solution of (12) is UUB by*

$$||Y[k]||_\infty \leq [2\alpha_1(1+T\gamma)+b2]||(I_{2n}-\tilde{A})^{-1}||_\infty, (k \to \infty), \tag{6.32}$$

where $b_2 = max\{2T\bar{\xi}, \alpha_2(2+T\gamma)\}$.

Proof. It follows from (6.19) that

$$||Y[k]||_\infty \leq ||\tilde{A}^k Y[0]||_\infty + ||\sum_{s=1}^{k} \tilde{A}^{k-s}\tilde{B}\omega[s-1]||_\infty + ||\sum_{s=1}^{k} \tilde{A}^{k-s}\tilde{C}z[s-1]||_\infty.$$

Using the conditions in (6.29-6.31), we can easily show that

$$||\omega[s-1]||_\infty \leq \alpha_1 + c_1\rho(\tilde{A})^{s-1}$$

and

$$||\tilde{C}z[s-1]||_\infty \leq max\{2T\bar{\xi}, (2+T\gamma)(\alpha_2 + c_2\rho(\tilde{A})^{s-1})\} \triangleq b(s). \tag{6.33}$$

Following ([596], proof of Theorem 3.1), it can be concluded that

$$\begin{aligned} ||Y[k]||_\infty \quad \leq \quad & ||\tilde{A}^k||_\infty ||Y[0]||_\infty + \alpha_1 ||\tilde{B}||_\infty || \sum_{s=1}^{k} \tilde{A}^{k-s}||_\infty \\ + \quad & c_1||\tilde{B}||_\infty \sum_{s=1}^{k} ||\tilde{A}^{k-s}||_\infty \rho(\tilde{A})^{s-1} + ||\sum_{s=1}^{k} \tilde{A}^{k-s} b(s)||_\infty. \end{aligned} \tag{6.34}$$

As shown in [603], there exists an invertible matrix P such that $\tilde{A}$ is similar to a Jordan canonical matrix J, i.e. $P^{-1}\tilde{A}P = J = diag\{J_1, J_2, \cdots, J_l\}$, where $J_s, s = 1,2,\cdots,l$, are upper triangular Jordan blocks, whose principal diagonal elements are the eigenvalues of $\tilde{A}$. Then, for the third term in the right-hand side of inequality (6.34), we have

$$
\begin{aligned}
& c_1||\tilde{B}||_\infty \sum_{s=1}^{k} ||\tilde{A}^{k-s}||_\infty \rho(\tilde{A})^{s-1} \\
\leq\ & 2(1+T\gamma)\sum_{s=1}^{k} ||\tilde{A}^{k-s}||_\infty \rho(\tilde{A})^{s-1} \\
=\ & 2(1+T\gamma)\sum_{s=1}^{k} ||(PJP^{-1})^{k-s}||_\infty \rho(\tilde{A})^{s-1} \\
\leq\ & 2(1+T\gamma)\cdot c\sum_{s=1}^{k} ||J||_\infty^{k-s} \rho(\tilde{A})^{s-1} \\
\leq\ & 2c(1+T\gamma)\sum_{s=1}^{k} [\rho(\tilde{A})^{k-s} + C_{k-s}^{1}\rho(\tilde{A})^{k-s-1} + \cdots \\
+\ & C_{k-s}^{m}\rho(\tilde{A})^{k-s-m+1}]\rho(\tilde{A})^{s-1} \\
\leq\ & 2c(1+T\gamma)[k\rho(\tilde{A})^{k-1} + kC_k^1\rho(\tilde{A})^{k-2} + \cdots + kC_k^m\rho(\tilde{A})^{k-m}],
\end{aligned}
$$

where $c \triangleq ||P||_\infty \cdot ||P-1||_\infty$, and m is the maximum order of $J_s, s = 1, 2, \cdots, l$. According to **Lemma** 6.2 and the above analysis, it can be easily obtained that

$$
c_1||\tilde{B}||_\infty \sum_{s=1}^{k} ||\tilde{A}_\infty^{k-s} \rho(\tilde{A})^{s-1} \to 0, (k \to \infty). \tag{6.35}
$$

By a similar proof process for (6.35) and using (6.26), the following relation can be deduced

$$
||\sum_{s=1}^{k} \tilde{A}^{k-s} b(s)||_\infty \leq b_2||(I_{2n} - \tilde{A})^{-1}||_\infty, (k \to \infty), \tag{6.36}
$$

where $b_2 = max\{2T\bar{\xi}, \alpha_2(2+T\gamma)\}$.

Since all the eigenvalues of $\tilde{A}$ are within the unit circle as stated in **Lemma** 6.1, we can obtain that $\lim_{k\to\infty}\tilde{A}^k = 0_{2n\times 2n}$. Combining (6.34-6.36), we can obtain that

$$
||Y[k]||_\infty \leq [2(1+T\gamma)\alpha_1 + b_2]||(I_{2n} - \tilde{A})^{-1}||_\infty, (k \to \infty). \tag{6.37}
$$

This completes the proof.

Remark 6.6 *Define the trigger functions for each agent i and the leader, respectively, as follows:*

$$
f_i(s, |e_i[s]|) \triangleq |e_i[s]| - (\alpha_1 + c_1 e^{-\beta_1(s)sT}), i = 1, 2, \cdots, n, \tag{6.38}
$$

$$g(s, |e^r[s]|) \triangleq |e^r[s]| - (\alpha_2 + c_2 e^{-\beta_2(s)sT}). \tag{6.39}$$

Similarly to the statements in **Remark** *6.5, it is known that, under the event-triggered schemes with trigger functions above, the conditions in (6.29) and (6.30) can be guaranteed for all* $s \in Z^+$. ▮

Remark 6.7 *Similarly to* **Remark** *6.3 and from the inequality (6.32), it yields*

$$|\delta_i[k]| \leq 2[(1+T\gamma)\alpha_1 + b_2]||(I_{2n} - \tilde{A})^{-1}_{\infty}$$

as $k \to \infty, i = 1, 2, \cdots, n$. *Obviously, under the new event-triggered scheme, the resulting upper bound for the tracking error* $\delta_i[k]$ *is smaller than that under the event-triggered scheme in* **Remark** *6.5. However, since the introduction of the time-varying parameters* β_1 *and* β_2*, the relatively heavier computation is needed when using the event-triggered scheme in* **Remark** *6.7.* ▮

Remark 6.8 *On choosing* $\alpha_i = 0, c_i = 0, (i = 1, 2)$ *in* **Theorems** *6.1 and 6.2, the event-triggered communication scheme proposed heretofore reduces to the time-triggered scheme which was studied in [596], and the upper bound of tracking errors between agents and the leader is* $2T\bar{\xi}||(I_{2n} - \tilde{A})^{-1}||_{\infty}$. ▮

6.1.4 Numerical example

In this section, a numerical example with four agents and a time-varying reference satisfying the same communication graph as in [596] is employed in order to validate the main results of this section; see Fig. 6.1. If agent j is a neighbor of agent i, we let $a_{(i,j)} = 1$, otherwise $a_{(i,j)} = 0$. Then, for this example, the corresponding adjacency matrix

$$A = \begin{bmatrix} 0 & 1 & 0 & 0 \\ 1 & 0 & 1 & 0 \\ 1 & 0 & 0 & 0 \\ 0 & 1 & 1 & 0 \end{bmatrix}$$

Since the agent 3 can have access to the leader, $a_{(3,5)} = 1, a_{(1,5)} = 0, a_{(2,5)} = 0$ *and* $a_{(4,5)} = 0$. The reference state is chosen as $x^r[k] = \sin(kT) + kT$. This example was studied in [596] by using the synchronous communication scheme. In the following, we will study this example by using the asynchronous communication scheme, that is by using the proposed event-triggered scheme.

The initial states of the four agents are chosen as: $[x_1[0], x_2[0], x_3[0], x_4[0]] = [2, 1, -1, -3]$. Without loss of generality, suppose that

$$[x_1[-1], x_2[-1], x_3[-1], x_4[-1]] = [0, 0, 0, 0]$$

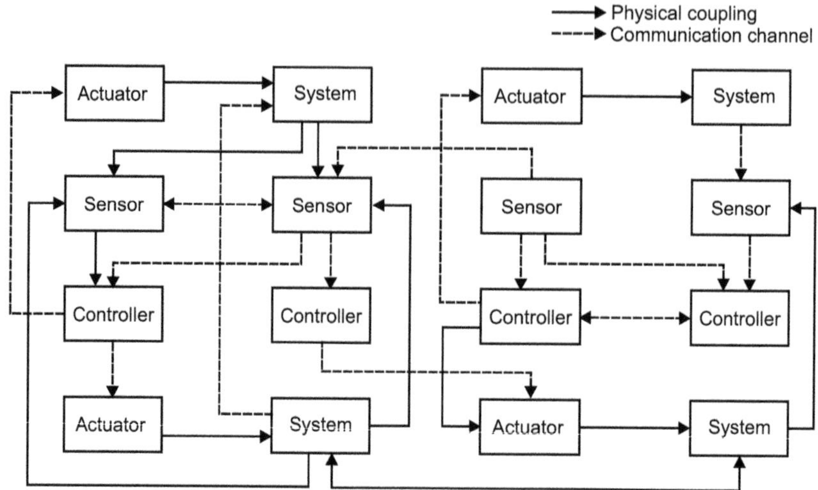

Figure 6.1: Directed graph for four agents with a leader

Let $T = 0.1$ and $\gamma = 3$. By simple computation, it can be seen that the condition (6.20) holds.

In the following simulation, two cases for the selection of α_j, c_j and $\beta_j (j = 1,2)$ will be considered, which correspond to different types of triggered thresholds.

Case 1: $\alpha_1 = 0.01, \alpha_2 = 0.04, c1 = 0.1, c2 = 0.5, \beta_1 = 0.5, \beta_2 = 0.5$. Under the tracking control (6.8) with the event-triggered schemes in **Remark** 6.5, the dynamic responses for the states $x_i[k]$ and the tracking errors $\delta_i[k] = x_i[k] - x^r[k], i = 1, \cdots, 4$, are shown in Figs. 6.2 and 6.3, respectively. By simple computation according to Table 6.2, we can obtain that only 80.68% of sampled states of all agents and the leader are needed to be sent out to their neighbours.

Case 2: α_j and $c_j (j = 1,2)$ are the same as in Case 1, but the parameters β_1 and β_2 are chosen as $\beta_1(s) = -ln\rho(\tilde{A})s/0.1s, \beta_2(s) = -ln\rho(\tilde{A})s/0.1s, s \in Z^+$ and $\rho(\tilde{A}) = 0.9405$. Under the tracking control (6.8) with the event-triggered schemes in **Remark** 6.7, the dynamic responses for the states $x_i[k]$ and the tracking errors $\delta_i[k] = x_i[k] - x^r[k], i = 1, \cdots, 4$, are shown in Figs. 6.4 and 6.5, respectively. By simple computation according to Table 6.2, we can obtain that only 79.84% of sampled states of all the agents and the leader are needed to be sent out to their neighbours.

Case 3: $\alpha_j = 0$ and $c_j = 0 (j = 1,2)$. Under the tracking control (6.2) with the time-triggered scheme, the dynamic responses for the states $x_i[k]$ and the tracking errors $\delta_i[k] = x_i[k] - x^r[k], i = 1, \cdots, 4$, are shown in Figs. 6.6 and 6.7, respectively. As obtained above, only around 80% of sampled states of all agents and the leader need to be transmitted through the network for Cases 1 and 2 in order to guarantee the tracking performance. Therefore, around 20% of commu-

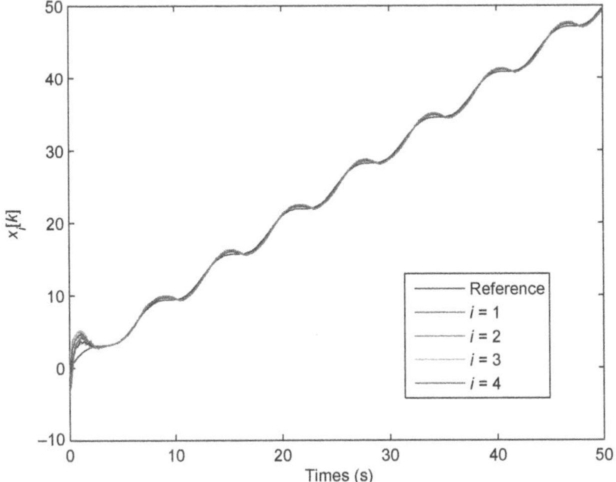

Figure 6.2: State responses of system (6.1) in Case 1

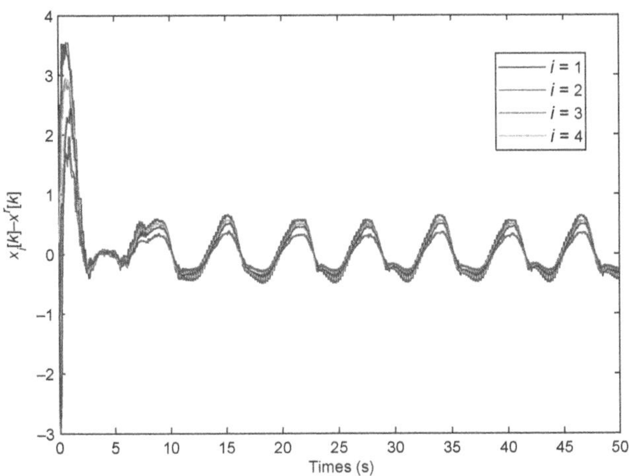

Figure 6.3: Tracking errors in Case 1

nication resource is saved. According to the simulation, when the time is larger than 30s, it can be computed that the bound of the tracking error for Case 1 is 0.6497 and for Case 2 is 0.6396. It is clear that $0.6396 < 0.6497$, which is consistent with the analysis in **Remark** 6.8 and validates the developed theoretical results.

Table 6.1: Sample and release time for Case 1

	Leader	Agent 1	Agent 2	Agent 3	Agent 4
Sample times	500	500	500	500	500
Release times	354	411	416	427	409

Table 6.2: Sample and release time for Case 2

	Leader	Agent 1	Agent 2	Agent 3	Agent 4
Sample times	500	500	500	500	500
Release times	356	412	409	420	399

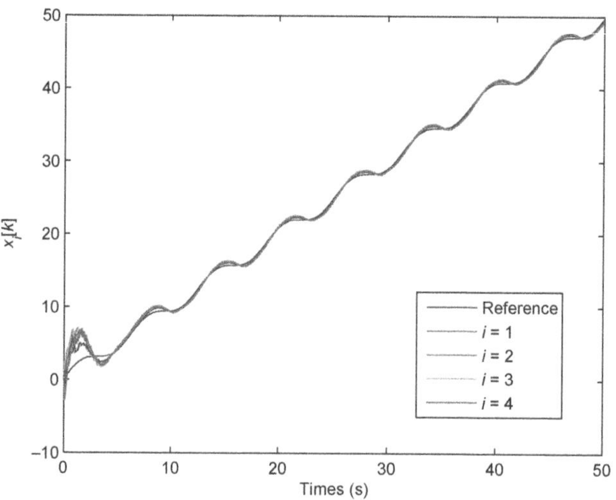

Figure 6.4: State responses of system (6.1) in Case 2

6.2 Pinning Coordination Control of Networked Systems

In the past decade, the consensus problem in the cooperative control community has been extensively studied. A theoretical explanation for the consensus behavior of the Vicsek model by using graph theory and matrix theory was given in [494]. The work of [501] solved the average consensus problem for the directed balanced network. In [505], it was shown that under certain assumptions consensus can be reached asymptotically under dynamically changing interaction topologies if the union of the collection of interaction graphs across some time intervals has a spanning tree frequently enough. Similar results were obtained by [496]. The spanning tree requirement is a more relaxed condition and is, there-

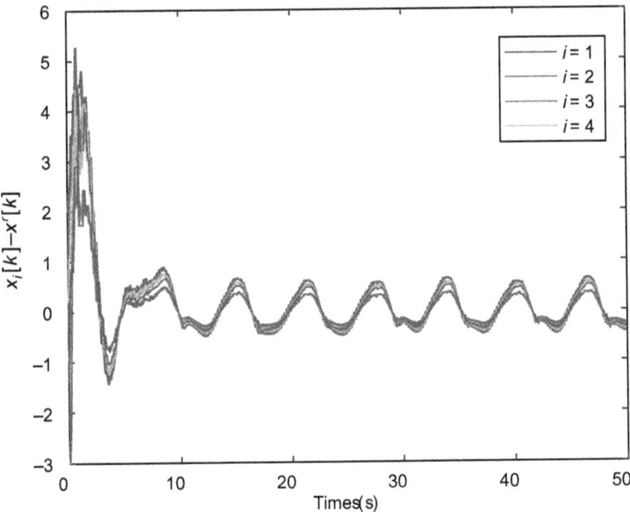

Figure 6.5: Tracking errors in Case 2

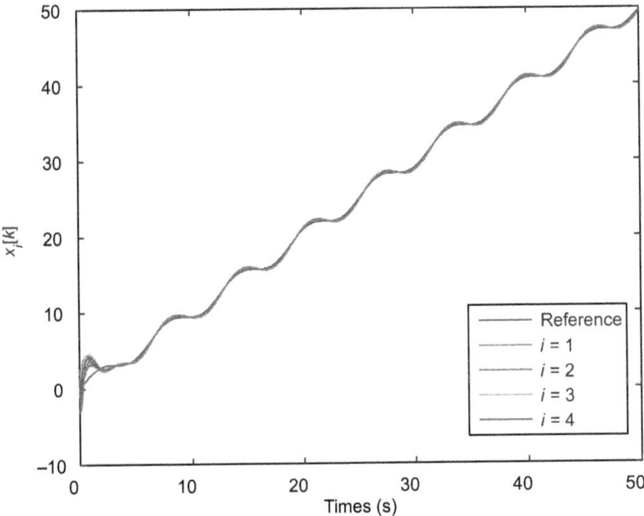

Figure 6.6: State responses of system (6.1) in Case 3

fore, suitable for practical application. With the development of this issue, many new consensus protocols and analysis methods appeared. [499] used a set-valued Lyapunov approach to address the consensus problem with unidirectional time-dependent communication links. In [484], a Lyapunov-based approach was used to consider the stability of consensus synchronization of passive systems for balanced and weakly connected communication topology. [498] extended the exist-

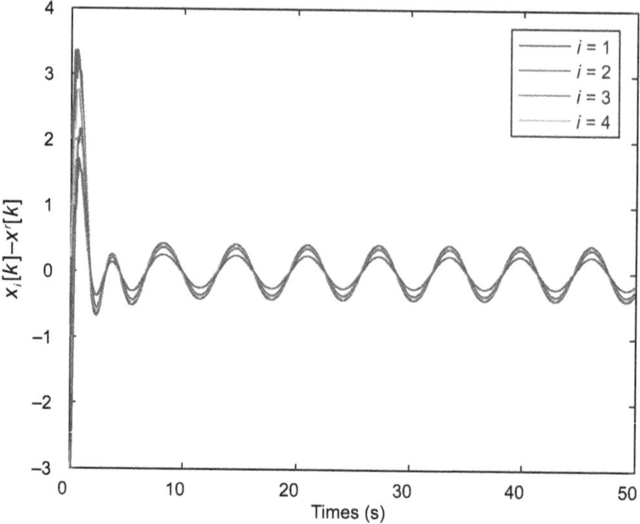

Figure 6.7: Tracking errors in Case 3

ing results for single consensus variables to include the case of forced consensus and multiple consensus variables separated by hard constrains. [481] proposed a continuous-time and a discrete-time bilinear trust update scheme for trust consensus. More profound theoretical results have been established for distributed consensus of networked dynamic systems ([5], [486], [503]). The extensions of the consensus algorithm to second-order dynamics have been studied in [489], [490], [491], [495], [497], [504], [510], and [511].

Pinning control is an important control scheme for the networked system since it can realize the control objective by controlling part of the nodes instead of all the nodes in the network. In [488], pinning control of spatio-temporal chaos, which has numerous applications to turbulence, instabilities in plasma and multi-mode lasers, was discussed. The stabilization problem for a scale-free dynamical network via pinning control was investigated in [507] and it was found that the pinning control based on highest connection degree has better performance than totally randomly pinning.

It is worth noting that the above research on pinning control is mainly concerned with the undirected communication topology or directed topology which has a root node. The motivation of this section is to consider a more general case that the communication digraph of the networked multi-vehicle systems is weakly connected and has two or more zero in-degree and strongly connected subgraphs, i.e., there exist two or more leader groups. Based on the previous works on consensus and pinning control, we study the second-order controlled consensus problem. We present a necessary and sufficient condition to achieve the second-order controlled consensus for multi-vehicle systems with two or more zero-in-degree and strongly connected subgraphs in the weakly connected communication topology. We also discuss how to design the pinning controller and how to choose the pinned vehicles. The proposed method allows us to extend several existing results for undirected graphs to directed balanced graphs. Furthermore, we study the case of variable topology.

6.2.1 Networked multi-vehicle systems

We consider a group of n vehicles. The dynamics of vehicle i is described by

$$\begin{aligned} \dot{x}_i &= v_i, \\ \dot{v}_i &= u_i, \qquad i = 1,2,...,n, \end{aligned} \tag{6.40}$$

where $x_i \in R$ and $v_i \in R$ denote the position and the velocity of the $i-th$ vehicle, respectively, and $u_i \in R$ is the interaction input. To avoid obscuring the essentials, here we take the vehicle states as scalars. If they are vectors, all the following development can be easily modified by introducing the Kronecker product terms as appropriate. For agent i, a neighbor-based coupling rule can be expressed as follows:

$$u_i = \sum_{j \in N_i} g_{ij}[b(x_j - x_i) + \eta b(v_j - v_i)], \tag{6.41}$$

where $b > 0$ denotes stiffness gain, $\eta > 0$ is the ratio of damping gain to stiffness gain and g_{ij} denotes the weighting factor of communication or sensing link from vehicle j to i. Let $x = [x_1, x\,2\,, ..., x_n]^T$ and $v = [v_1, v_2, ..., v_n]^T$. According to protocol (6.41), (6.40) can be written in matrix form as

$$\begin{aligned} \begin{bmatrix} \dot{x} \\ \dot{v} \end{bmatrix} &= \Gamma \begin{bmatrix} x \\ v \end{bmatrix} \\ \Gamma &= \begin{bmatrix} 0_{n\times n} & I_n \\ -bL & -\eta bL \end{bmatrix}. \end{aligned} \tag{6.42}$$

To avoid distraction from the main issues being introduced, the following discussion is mainly based on the case of fixed topologies. The case of time-varying topologies is discussed in Section 5.

Focusing on fixed topologies, we note some relations between Γ and L [498] and [506]:

Property 1: Γ has $2m$ zero eigenvalues if and only if $-L$ has m zero eigenvalues.

A necessary and sufficient condition to achieve second-order consensus for (6.42) is given as follows:

Lemma 3.1([5]): Consensus protocol (6.41) achieves second-order consensus asymptotically, i.e., $|x_i - x_j| \to 0$ and $|v_i - v_j| \to 0\ \forall i \neq j$, as $t \to \infty$, if and only if matrix Γ has exactly two zero eigenvalues and all the other eigenvalues have negative real parts.

Remark 6.9 *By appropriately choosing information states on which consensus is reached, the protocol (6.41) has applications in many areas, including synchronization, flocking and formation control. For example, a variant of protocol (6.41) is to guarantee* $\lim_{t\to\infty}|v_i - v_j| = 0$*and* $\lim_{t\to\infty}|x_i - x_j| = 0$ *for* $i, j \in 1,2,...,n$*, where* δ_{ij} *is the desired offset between agent i and agent j. Letting* $\delta_{ij} \in R$ *be constant, we design the control input*

$$u_i = b\sum_{j\in N_i} g_{ij}[(x_j - \delta_j) - (x_i - \delta_i) + (v_i - v_j)] \tag{6.43}$$

to guarantee $x_j - \delta_j \to x_i - \delta_i$ *and* $v_i \to v_j$*. Therefore,* δ_i *can be chosen such that the desired offsets between vehicles can be guaranteed.* ▮

The following preliminary results, which are needed in subsequent sections.

Definition 1 ([503]): *Matrix* $L = [l_{ij}] \in R^{n\times n}$ *is diagonally dominant if, for all* $i, l_{ii} \geq \sum_{j\neq i}|l_{ii}|$*. It is strictly diagonally dominant if these inequalities are all strict. L is strongly diagonally dominant if at least one of the inequalities is strict. L is irreducibly diagonally dominant if it is irreducible and at least one of the inequalities is strict.*

Lemma 3.2 ([509], [503]): *Let L be strictly diagonally dominant or irreducibly diagonally dominant. Then L is nonsingular. If in addition, the diagonal elements of L are all positive real numbers, then* $Re\lambda_i(L) > 0, 1 \leq i \leq n$*.*

Definition 2: *We call a subgraph zero-in-degree if there is no information flowing into it, i.e., it has no incoming edges.*

Lemma 3.3 ([505]): *Graph G has a spanning tree if and only if* $Rank(L) = n-1$.

The next result generalizes **Lemma 3.3** to the case of more than one leader group.

Lemma 3.4: *Suppose graph G is weakly connected. Then* $Rank(L) = n-k$ *if and only if G contains* $k(k \geq 1)$ *zero-in-degree and strongly connected subgraphs.*

Proof:

Sufficiency: Denote the k zero-in-degree and strongly connected subgraphs by $G_1 = (V_1, E_1), G_2 = (V_2, E_2), ..., G_k = (V_k, E_k)$, with $V_i \subseteq V, E_i \subseteq E$, separately, where the node set is indexed in such a way that the first numbers are given to V_1, the following numbers are given to $V_2, V_3, ...,$ and V_k in turn. The last numbers are given to the left nodes $V - \{V_1, V_2, ..., V_k\}$. Notice that the subgraph $G_i(1 \geq i \geq k)$ has zero-in-degree. Thus, the Laplacian matrix L of graph G can be written as a lower block triangular matrix, i.e.,

$$L = \begin{bmatrix} L_{11} & 0 & \cdots & 0 & & \cdots & 0 \\ 0 & L_{22} & \ddots & 0 & & & 0 \\ \vdots & \ddots & \ddots & \ddots & \ddots & \ddots & \vdots \\ 0 & 0 & \ddots & Lkk & \ddots & \ddots & \vdots \\ F_{k+1,1} & F_{k+1,2} & \cdots & F_{k+1,k} & F_{k+1,k+1} & \ddots & 0 \\ \vdots & & \cdots & & \cdots & \ddots & 0 \\ F_{k+r,1} & & \cdots & \cdots & F_{k+r,k+r-1} & F_{k+r,k+r} & \end{bmatrix} \tag{6.44}$$

where $r \geq 1$; $L_{ii}(1 \neq i \neq k)$ is the Laplacian matrix associated with subgraph G_i; since the number of zero-in-degree and strongly connected subgraphs is k, for $i > k$, there exists $j < i$ such that $F_{ij} \neq 0$. Noticing that the graph G is weakly connected, for $j \leq k$, we know that there exists $i > k$ such that $F_{ij} \neq 0$. With these in mind, we get that $F_{k+m,k+m}(1 \neq m \neq r)$ is irreducibly diagonally dominant. Applying Lemma 3.2, we get that $F_{k+m,k+m}(1 \neq m \neq k)$ is nonsingular. Since $L_{ii}(1 \neq m \neq k)$ is the Laplacian matrix associated with the strongly connected subgraph Gi, from **Lemma 3.3**, one can get that $Rank(L_{ii}) = |V_i| - 1$, where $|V_i|$ denotes the cardinality of V_i. Thus, there exist $n-k$, and no more than $n-k$, rows of L are linearly independent. Therefore, $Rank(L) = n-k$.

Necessity: Since the case of $k = 1$ is given in **Lemma 3.3**, we only consider the case $k > 1$. Noticing that G is weakly connected, if the number of zero-in-degree and strongly connected subgraphs contained in G is not k, one can get at least one $j < k$ such that $F_{kj} \neq 0$ or at least for row k+1, $F_{k+1,i} = 0\,(1 \leq i \leq k)$. In both cases, $Rank(L) \neq n-k$.

The block triangular matrix (6.44) is called k-reducible in [509]. We call the first k subgraphs in (6.44) "leader graphs". If graph G is weakly connected and contains two or more leader graphs, according to Property 1 and **Lemma 3.1** and **Lemma 3.4**, we know that consensus protocol (6.41) cannot achieve second-order consensus. Of particular interest is to show the evolution of states in the system $\dot{x} = -Lx$. To this end, we introduce the following lemmas.

Lemma 3.5 ([505]): *Let L denote the Laplacian matrix of graph G with* $L\underline{1} = 0, w_l^T L = 0$ *and* $w_l^T \underline{1} = 1$. *Then, for the system* $\dot{x} = -Lx$, *the consensus is achieved, i.e.,* $\lim_{t\to\infty} x(t) = \underline{1} w_l^T x(0)$, *if and only if G has a spanning tree.*

The following result is in the core of consensus theory ([509], [506]). It is proved here for completeness and also because the proof gives some insight into the structure of the leader group of a graph.

Lemma 3.6: *Let graph G contain a spanning tree. Then,* $\lambda_1 = 0$ *is a simple eigenvalue with right eigenvector* $\underline{1}$ *and a nonnegative left eigenvector* $w_l^T = \{\gamma_1, \gamma_1, \ldots, \gamma_n\}$. *Moreover, the entry* γ_1 *is positive for any node* v_i *which has a directed path to all other nodes, and zero for all other nodes.*

Proof: The graph Laplacian matrix L can be brought by a permutation matrix T to the lower block triangular Frobenius canonical form ([509], [503])

$$F = TLT^T = \begin{bmatrix} F_{11} & 0 & \cdots & 0 \\ F_{21} & F_{22} & \cdots & 0 \\ \vdots & \vdots & \ddots & \vdots \\ F_{p1} & F_{p2} & \cdots & F_{pp} \end{bmatrix} \text{ where } F_{ii} \text{ is square and irreducible.}$$

There exists a spanning tree if and only if L has a simple eigenvalue $\lambda_1 = 0$, equivalently, in every row i there exists at least one $j < i$ such that $F_{ij} \neq 0$. Then, there is only one leader group, which has nodes corresponding to F_{11}. Therefore, F_{11} has a simple eigenvalue $\lambda_1 = 0$ with right eigenvector $\underline{1}$ and left eigenvector $w_1 > 0$.

Since $F_{ii}, i \geq 2$, are irreducibly diagonally dominant, according to Lemma 3.2, we know that $F_{ii}, i \geq 2$, are nonsingular.

Now introduce

$$\begin{pmatrix} w_1^T & w_2^T & \cdots & w_p^T \end{pmatrix} = \begin{bmatrix} F_{11} & 0 & \cdots & 0 \\ F_{21} & F_{22} & \cdots & 0 \\ \vdots & \vdots & \ddots & \vdots \\ F_{p1} & F_{p2} & \cdots & F_{pp} \end{bmatrix}$$

where w_i are vectors of appropriate dimension. Therefore, we have

$$\begin{aligned} w_p^T F_{pp} &= 0 \\ w_{p-1}^T F_{(p-1)(p-1)} + w_{p-1}^T F_{p(p-1)} &= \\ &\vdots \\ w_1^T F_{11} + w_2^T F_{21} + \cdots + w_p^T F_{p1} &= 0 \end{aligned}$$

Since $F_{ii}, i \geq 2$, are nonsingular, this implies $w_i = 0, i \geq 2$ and $w_1^T F_{11} = 0$ with $w_i > 0$.

It should be noted that **Lemmas 3.5** and **3.6** show that all nodes converge to a weighted average of the initial conditions of all the root nodes. They only hold for a graph containing a single leader group. The next Lemma generalizes these results to the case of more than one leader group.

Lemma 3.7: *Suppose that graph G is weakly connected and contains $k(k \leq 1)$ zero-in-degree and strongly connected subgraphs. For the system $\dot{x}_= - Lx$ (L is given in (6.44)), the nodes in different leader groups converge to independent consensus values, i.e., $\lim_{t\to\infty} x_i(t) \triangleq x_i^* = \underline{1} w_{i,1}^T x_i(0), 1 \leq i \leq k$, where $wi,1$ satisfies $w_{i,1}^T L_{ii} = 0$, and $w_{i,1}^T \underline{1}, 1 \leq i \leq k$. Moreover, the nodes which are not in leader graphs converge to a weighted average consensus values of the leader graphs, i.e., $\lim_{t\to\infty} x_{k+m} \triangleq x_{k+m}^* = F_{k+m,k+m}^{-1}(\sum_{i=1}^{k+m-1} F_{k+m,i} x_i^*), 1 \leq m \leq r$.*

Proof: Ordering the nodes as in **Lemma 3.4**, the overall dynamics are given by

$$\begin{aligned} \dot{x}_i &= -L_{ii}x_i, \quad 1 \leq i \leq k; \\ \dot{x}_{k+m} &= -(F_{k+m,1}x_1 + F_{k+m,2}x_2 + \cdots + F_{k+m,k+m}x_{k+m}), \quad 1 \leq m \leq r \end{aligned} \tag{6.45}$$

Notice that $L_{ii}(1 \leq i \leq k)$ is irreducible. According to **Lemma 3.5**, we have $\lim_{t\to\infty} x_i(t) \triangleq x_i^* = \underline{1} w_{i,1}^T x_i(0), 1 \leq i \leq k,$. In what follows, we will discuss the convergence properties of the states $x_{k+m}, 1 \leq m \leq r$. First, we consider the dynamics corresponding to x_{k+m}

$$\dot{x}_{k+1} = -(F_{k+m,1}x_1 + F_{k+m,2}x_2 + \cdots + F_{k+1,k+1}x_{k+1}) \tag{6.46}$$

The change of variables

$$\dot{e}_1 = -(F_{k+m,1}x_1 + F_{k+m,2}x_2 + \cdots + F_{k+1,k+1}x_{k+1})$$

yields

$$\dot{e}_1 = -F_{k+1,k+1}e_1 - F_{k+1,1}L_{11}x_1 - \cdots - F_{k+1,k}L_{kk}x_k \tag{6.47}$$

Since $F_{k+1,k+1}$ is irreducibly diagonally dominant, according to **Lemma 3.2**, we know that the origin of the nominal system $\dot{e}_1 = -F_{k+1,k+1}e_1$ is globally exponential stable. Along similar lines, the other terms on the right side of (6.47) exponentially converge to zero since the first k subgraphs reach consensus exponentially. Thus, the origin is exponential stable, which implies that

$$\lim_{t\to\infty} x_{k+1} \triangleq x_{k+1}^* = -F_{k+1,k+1}^{-1}\left(\sum_{i=1}^{k} F_{k+1,i}x_i^*\right)$$

Now, we consider the dynamics corresponding to x_{k+2}

$$\dot{x}_{k+2} = -(F_{k+2,1}x_1 + F_{k+2,2}x_2 + \cdots + F_{k+2,k+2}x_{k+2})$$

Similarly, the change of variables

$$\dot{e}_2 = -F_{k+2,1}x_1 + F_{k+2,2}x_2 - \cdots + F_{k+2,k+2}x_{k+2}$$

yields

$$\dot{e}_2 = -F_{k+2,k+2}e_2 - F_{k+2,1}L_{11}x_1 - \cdots - F_{k+2,k+1}e_1$$

Employing a similar analysis method as that for the states x_{k+1}, we arrive at

$$\lim_{t\to\infty} x_{k+2} \triangleq x_{k+2}^* = -F_{k+2,k+2}^{-1}\left(\sum_{i=1}^{k+1} F_{k+2,i}x_i^*\right)$$

By applying the same procedure, one can get

$$\lim_{t\to\infty} x_{k+j} \triangleq x^*_{k+j} = -F^{-1}_{k+j,k+j}\left(\sum_{i=1}^{k+j-1} F_{k+j,i}x^*_i\right), \quad 2 < j \leq r$$

Lemma 3.7 shows that if the weakly connected graph contains two or more zero-in-degree and strong connected subgraphs, the networked nodes cannot achieve consensus. Thus, we introduce the pinning control strategy in the next section.

6.2.2 Fixed communication topology

The key idea behind pinning control is to control a small fraction of the nodes instead of all nodes in the network, that is, to control the network by pinning part of the nodes. In this section, we will adopt this idea to solve the cooperative control problem for multi-vehicle systems with two or more zero-in-degree and strongly connected subgraphs in the weakly connected communication topology; that is, systems with more than one leader group. Different from general leader-following consensus control, the pinning controller is constructed by using a virtual nodes information. It is not required to change the original topology.

Suppose that the networked multi-vehicle systems (6.42) are required to track a desired trajectory described by

$$\dot{x}_0 = v_0, \tag{6.48}$$

where v_0 is the desired constant velocity. To achieve this goal, we apply the pinning control strategy on a small fraction of the vehicles. The pinning controllers are designed as follows:

$$\begin{aligned} u_i &= \sum_{j\in N_i} g_{ij}\left[b(x_j - x_i) + \eta b(v_j - v_i)\right] + \bar{u}_i, \\ \bar{u}_i &= q_i s(x_0 - x_i) + q_i \eta s(v_0 - v_i), \quad i = 1,2,...,n, \end{aligned} \tag{6.49}$$

where q_i is equal to one for pinned nodes and zero otherwise; s is the pinning control gain. Position offsets can be introduced as in (6.43). Then, one could select $\bar{u}_i = q_i s(x_0 - (x_i - \delta_i)) + q_i \eta s(v_0 - v_i)$. Here we only consider a simple case with desired constant velocity. In fact, the corresponding results can be easily extended to the time-varying velocity case if we assume that the vehicle can get its neighbours' acceleration information. In practical applications, the acceleration of the vehicle can be calculated by numerical differentiation of the velocities.

$\xi = \underline{1} \otimes x_0, \zeta = v - \underline{1} \otimes v_0, Q = diag\{q_1, q_2, ..., q_n\}$, and $\bar{u} = (\bar{u}_1, \bar{u}_2, ..., \bar{u}_n)^T$. Equation (6.49) can be written in matrix form as

$$\bar{u} = \begin{bmatrix} -sQ & -\eta sQ \end{bmatrix} \begin{bmatrix} \xi \\ \zeta \end{bmatrix} \tag{6.50}$$

With (6.42) and (6.50), the closed-loop system can be written as

$$\begin{bmatrix}\dot{\xi}\\ \dot{\zeta}\end{bmatrix} = \Gamma\begin{bmatrix}\xi\\ \zeta\end{bmatrix} + \begin{bmatrix}0\\ \bar{u}\end{bmatrix} = \begin{bmatrix}0_{n\times n} & I_n\\ -(bL+sQ) & -\eta(bL+sQ)\end{bmatrix}\begin{bmatrix}\xi\\ \zeta\end{bmatrix} \triangleq \bar{\Gamma}\begin{bmatrix}\xi\\ \zeta\end{bmatrix} \qquad (6.51)$$

In contrast to the definition of second-order consensus given in **Lemma 3.1**, we present the following concept.

Definition 3: *We say second-order controlled consensus is achieved if* $\lim_{t\to\infty}\xi(t) = 0$ *and* $\lim_{t\to\infty}\zeta(t) = 0$.

Remark 2: *It is obvious that we introduce extra control inputs (6.50) without changing the structure of either the network G or the local protocol (6.41). For the second-order consensus protocol (6.41), the consensus value depends on the initial conditions of node states and cannot be arbitrarily controlled. However, the second-order controlled consensus approach can overcome this limitation. The work in [491] considered the coordination problem of a multiagent system with jointly connected leader-follower topologies. The graph formed by the followers are undirected topologies. The work in [504] mainly considered the connected graph with a spanning tree.*

In the sequel, we consider the case that the graph is weakly connected, which implies that the involved control strategy would be different from the previous work.

6.2.3 Case of general graphs

In this section, we show how to use pinning control to achieve consensus in graphs that may not have a spanning tree. That is, there may be more than one leader group.

Lemma 4.1: *Assume that graph G is weakly connected and contains* $k (k \geq 1)$ *zero-in-degree and strongly connected subgraphs. The eigenvalues of* $\check{L} = bL + sQ$ *are in the open right-half complex plane if and only if there exists at least one pinned node for each zero-in-degree and strongly connected subgraph.*

Proof:

Necessity: It is easily shown by counterexample that the eigenvalues of $\check{L}$ are not in the open right-half complex plane if there exists an unpinned zero-indegree and strongly connected subgraph.

Sufficiency: Assume that there exists at least one pinned node for each zero-in-degree and strongly connected subgraph in G. Suppose that the nodes are indexed as in **Lemma 3.4**. The matrix $\check{L}$ can be written as

$$\breve{L} = \begin{bmatrix} F_{11} & 0 & \cdots & 0 & & \cdots & 0 \\ 0 & F_{22} & \ddots & 0 & & \cdots & 0 \\ \vdots & \ddots & \ddots & \ddots & \ddots & \ddots & \vdots \\ 0 & 0 & \ddots & F_{kk} & \ddots & \ddots & \vdots \\ K_{k+1,1} & K_{k+1,2} & \cdots & K_{k+1,k} & K_{k+1,k+1} & \ddots & 0 \\ \vdots & & \cdots & & \cdots & \ddots & 0 \\ F_{k+r,1} & & \cdots & & \cdots & k_{k+r,k+r-1} & k_{k+r,k+r} \end{bmatrix}$$

where F_{ii}, $1 \leq i \leq k+r$, are square and irreducible, and for $i > k$, there exists $j < i$ such that $F_{ij} \neq 0$. Since the pinning controllers are injected into each zero-in-degree and strongly connected subgraph, thus F_{ii}, $1 \leq i \leq k$,, are irreducibly diagonally dominant. According to **Lemma 3.2**, we know that $Re\lambda_i(F_{ii}) > 0$, $1 \leq i \leq k$. Noticing that, for $i > k$, there exists $j < i$ such that $F_{ij} \neq 0$, we get that $F_{k+m,k+m}$, $1 \leq m \leq r$, are also irreducibly diagonally dominant. Thus, $Re\lambda_i(F_{k+m,k+m}) > 0$, $1 \leq m \leq r$. Therefore, all the eigenvalues of $\breve{L} = bL + sQ$ are in the open right-half complex plane.

It is readily seen that, the nodes in the graph are indexed in a special way. Usually, the nodes are indexed in a natural way. In this case, it is required to find the zero-in-degree and strongly connected subgraphs in the communication topology before injecting the pinning controllers into the network. In what follows, we give an algorithm to find all the zero-in-degree and strongly connected subgraphs in the communication topology.

For binary matrices, define the Boolean operations multiplication and addition, respectively, as logical and and logical or, denoted by $(\bullet, \oplus)$. E represents the edge matrix, which has 1 as entry (i, j) when a_{ij} is positive, and zero elsewhere. Let k_1 be such that $(I \oplus E)^{k_1} = (I \oplus E)^{k_1 - 1}$, where operations are carried out in the Boolean matrix algebra, and define the binary reachability matrix as $R_0 = (I \oplus E)^{k_1}$. This matrix has an entry of 1 in position (i, j) if there is a directed path from node j to node i, i.e., node i is reachable from node j.

Lemma 4.2: *Define the matrix $M = R_0 \cap R_0^T$ with $\cap$ the elementwise logical and operation. Then, the node set of zero-in-degree and strongly connected subgraphs is composed of the nodes corresponding to those rows which are identical in M and R_0. Furthermore, the node set of zero-in-degree and strongly connected subgraphs can be partitioned into a group of sub node sets, each corresponding to a zero-in-degree and strongly connected subgraph.*

Proof: The non-zero entries in the i-th column of R_0 correspond to those nodes reachable from node i. The non-zero entries in the i-th row of R_0, that is i-th column of R_0^T , correspond to those nodes that can reach (are antecedent to) node i. The i-th row of $M = R_0 \cap R_0^T$ yields the intersection of the reachable set of node i and the antecedent set of node i. It is known that the node set of zero-in-degree and strongly connected subgraphs is the set of nodes having their antecedent set equal to the intersection of their reachable set and antecedent set ([508]). Notice that the connectivity property for the nodes corresponding to each zero-in-degree and strongly connected subgraph is preserved during the Boolean operations. Thus, according to connectivity, the node set can be partitioned into several disjoint sub node sets, each sub node set corresponding to a zero-in-degree and strongly connected subgraph.

6.2.4 Example 6.1

We apply **Lemma 4.2** to find the root nodes of the digraph shown in Fig. 6.8. For Fig. 6.8, the edge matrix

$$E = \begin{bmatrix} 0 & 0 & 1 & 1 & 0 & 0 & 0 & 1 & 1 & 0 \\ 0 & 0 & 0 & 0 & 0 & 1 & 1 & 0 & 0 & 0 \\ 0 & 0 & 0 & 0 & 0 & 0 & 1 & 0 & 0 & 0 \\ 0 & 0 & 1 & 0 & 1 & 0 & 0 & 0 & 0 & 0 \\ 0 & 0 & 0 & 0 & 0 & 0 & 0 & 1 & 0 & 0 \\ 0 & 0 & 0 & 0 & 0 & 0 & 0 & 0 & 1 & 1 \\ 0 & 0 & 0 & 0 & 0 & 0 & 0 & 0 & 1 & 0 \\ 0 & 0 & 0 & 0 & 1 & 0 & 0 & 0 & 0 & 0 \\ 0 & 0 & 1 & 0 & 0 & 0 & 0 & 0 & 0 & 0 \\ 0 & 1 & 0 & 0 & 0 & 0 & 0 & 0 & 0 & 0 \end{bmatrix}$$

Through the iterative operations carried out in the Boolean matrix algebra, we get that

$$R_0 = (I \oplus E)^6 = (I \oplus E)^5 = \begin{bmatrix} 1 & 0 & 1 & 1 & 1 & 0 & 1 & 1 & 1 & 0 \\ 0 & 1 & 1 & 0 & 0 & 1 & 1 & 0 & 1 & 1 \\ 0 & 0 & 1 & 0 & 0 & 0 & 1 & 0 & 1 & 0 \\ 0 & 0 & 1 & 1 & 1 & 0 & 1 & 1 & 1 & 0 \\ 0 & 0 & 0 & 0 & 1 & 0 & 0 & 1 & 0 & 0 \\ 0 & 1 & 1 & 0 & 0 & 1 & 1 & 0 & 1 & 1 \\ 0 & 0 & 1 & 0 & 0 & 0 & 1 & 0 & 1 & 0 \\ 0 & 0 & 0 & 0 & 1 & 0 & 0 & 1 & 0 & 0 \\ 0 & 0 & 1 & 0 & 0 & 0 & 1 & 0 & 1 & 0 \\ 0 & 1 & 1 & 0 & 0 & 1 & 1 & 0 & 1 & 1 \end{bmatrix}$$

Furthermore, one can get

$$M = R_0 \cap R_0^T = \begin{bmatrix} 1 & 0 & 0 & 0 & 0 & 0 & 0 & 0 & 0 & 0 \\ 0 & 1 & 0 & 0 & 0 & 1 & 0 & 0 & 0 & 1 \\ 0 & 0 & 1 & 0 & 0 & 0 & 1 & 0 & 1 & 0 \\ 0 & 0 & 0 & 1 & 0 & 0 & 0 & 0 & 0 & 0 \\ 0 & 0 & 0 & 0 & 1 & 0 & 0 & 1 & 0 & 0 \\ 0 & 1 & 0 & 0 & 0 & 1 & 0 & 0 & 0 & 1 \\ 0 & 0 & 1 & 0 & 0 & 0 & 1 & 0 & 1 & 0 \\ 0 & 0 & 0 & 0 & 1 & 0 & 0 & 1 & 0 & 0 \\ 0 & 0 & 1 & 0 & 0 & 0 & 1 & 0 & 1 & 0 \\ 0 & 1 & 0 & 0 & 0 & 1 & 0 & 0 & 0 & 1 \end{bmatrix}$$

We find that the identical rows in M and R_0 are $3,5,7,8$ and 9. This obviously reveals two disjoint node sets $\{3,7,9\}$ and $\{5,8\}$ corresponding to two zero-in-degree and strongly connected subgraphs. It can also be observed from a more descriptive form given in Fig. 6.9.

Before giving our main results, we introduce the following Lemma.

Lemma 4.3 ([511]): *Consider the equation*

$$\lambda^2 - \eta\mu\lambda - \mu = 0, \tag{6.52}$$

where $\eta \in R$ and $\mu \in \mathbb{C}$. Assume $Re(\mu) > 0$. Then the roots of (6.52) lie in the open left-half complex plane if and only if $\eta > \frac{|Im(\mu)|}{|\mu|\sqrt{-Re(\mu)}}$.

The following result is provided

Theorem 4.4: *Suppose that the communication topology for the multi-vehicle systems is weakly connected and contains $k(k \geq 1)$ zero-in-degree and strongly*

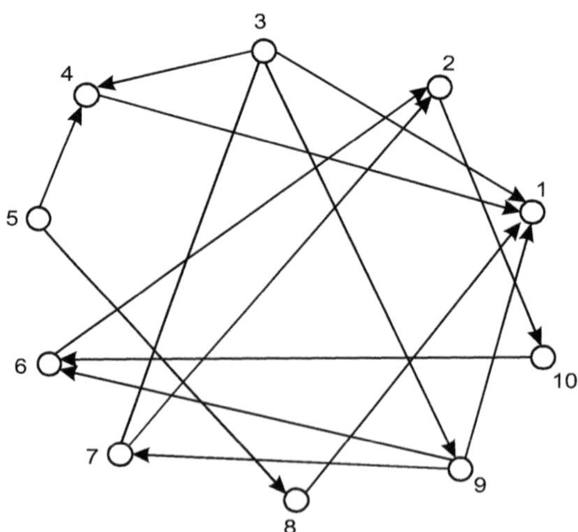

Figure 6.8: A digraph consisting of 10 nodes

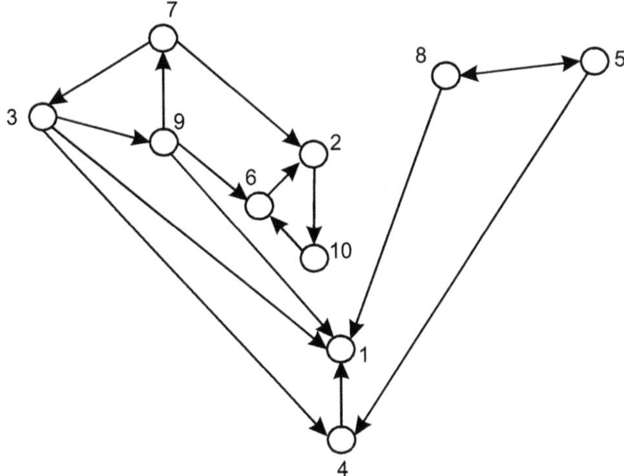

Figure 6.9: Illustration of the digraph

connected subgraphs. The second-order controlled consensus is achieved if and only if there is at least one pinned node for each zero-in-degree and strongly connected subgraph in the topology and $\eta > max_{1\leq i\leq n}\eta > \frac{|Im(\mu_i)|}{|\mu_i|\sqrt{-Re(\mu_i)}}$, *where* $\mu_i, i = 1,2,...,n$ *are the eigenvalues of* $-(bL+s\mathcal{Q}) = -\check{L}$.

Proof: From (6.51), we know that secondorder controlled consensus is achieved if and only if all the eigenvalues of $\bar{\Gamma}$ lie in the open left-half complex plane. To get the eigenvalues of $\bar{\Gamma}$, we first compute the characteristic polynomial of $\bar{\Gamma}$. Denote the eigenvalues of $-\check{L}$ by $\mu_1, \mu_2, ..., \mu_n$. Some simple computations lead to

$det(\lambda I_{2n} - \bar{\Gamma}) = det(\lambda^2 I_n + (1+\eta\lambda)\check{L}) = \prod_{i=1}^{n}(\lambda^2 - \eta\mu_i\lambda - \mu_i)$

The eigenvalues of $\bar{\Gamma}$ can be obtained by solving $\lambda^2 - \eta\mu_i\lambda - \mu_i = 0$, $i = 1,2,...,n$. Suppose that there exists an unpinned zero-in-degree and strongly connected subgraph in the communication topology, in light of Lemma 3.4, we know that $\check{L}$ has one zero eigenvalue. Thus, $\bar{\Gamma}$ has two zero eigenvalues. Therefore, to pin at least one node for each zero-in-degree and strongly connected subgraph in the topology is a necessary condition to guarantee that all the eigenvalues of $\bar{\Gamma}$ lie in the open left-half complex plane. Furthermore, in light of **Lemmas 4.1** and **4.3**, the claim follows.

6.2.5 Strongly connected and balanced graphs

In this section, we assume the graph is strongly connected and balanced. The strongly connected and balanced graphs allow us to determine the relationship among the pinning control gain, the stiffness gain, the number of pinned nodes and the Fiedler eigenvalue of the mirror graph. [502] studied pinning-controllability of undirected and first-order networks. We extend the corresponding results to directed balanced networks with second-order consensus. Before proceeding, we need the following Lemmas.

Lemma 4.5 *([492]): Consider a symmetric matrix*

$$B = \begin{bmatrix} A & C \\ C^T & F \end{bmatrix}$$

where A and F are square. Then B is positive definite if and only if both A and $F - C^T A^{-1} C$ are positive definite.

Definition 4 ([493]): *Let $G = (V, E, A)$ be a weighted digraph. Let $\tilde{E}$ be the set of reverse edges of G obtained by reversing the order of nodes of all the pairs in E. The mirror graph of G denoted by G_m is an undirected graph in the form $G_m = (V, E_m, A_m)$ with the same set of nodes as G, the set of edges $E_m = E \cup \tilde{E}$, and the symmetric adjacency matrix $A_m = [\hat{a}_{ij}]$ with elements $\hat{a}_{ij} = \hat{a}_{ji} = \frac{a_{ij}+a_{ji}}{2}$.*

Lemma 4.6 ([493]): *Let G be a graph with Laplacian L. Then $\hat{L} = \frac{L+L^T}{2}$ is a valid Laplacian matrix for G_m if and only if G is balanced.*

Lemma 4.7 ([493], [502]): *If $A \in R^{m\times m}$ is a symmetric matrix and $y \in R^n$, the following bound on the smallest eigenvalue of $A + yy^T$ holds*

$$\lambda_{min}(A + yy^T) \geq \lambda_{min}(A) + \frac{1}{2}(\gamma + \|y\|^2) - \frac{1}{2}\sqrt{(\gamma + \|y\|^2)^2 - 4\gamma(v_1^T(A)y)^2},$$

where $\gamma = \lambda_2(A) - \lambda_{min}(A)$

Lemma 4.8 ([492]): *Let $A, B \in R^n$ be symmetric and let eigenvalues $\lambda_i(A)$, $\lambda_i(B)$, and $\lambda_i(A+B)$ be arranged in increasing order. For each $k = 1, 2, \ldots, n$, we have $\lambda_k(A) + \lambda_1(B) \leq \lambda_k(A+B) \leq \lambda_k(A) + \lambda_n(B)$.*

Theorem 4.9: *If m pinning controllers are injected into the balanced and strongly connected multi-vehicle systems and the pinning control gain s satisfies*

$$\frac{bms\lambda_2(\hat{L})}{bms\lambda_2(\hat{L}) + smn} > \frac{1}{4(1 - \frac{1}{\eta^2})}, \tag{6.53}$$

where $\eta > 1, \hat{L} = \frac{L+L^T}{2}$, b is the stiffness gain, and L is the Laplacian matrix of the communication graph, then the second-order controlled consensus is achieved, i.e., the error dynamic system (6.51) is globally asymptotically stable about the origin.

Proof: Define a Lyapunov candidate as follows

$$V = (\xi^T \quad \zeta^T)P(\xi^T \quad \zeta^T)^T$$

where $P = \begin{bmatrix} I & \frac{1}{\eta}I \\ \frac{1}{\eta}I & I \end{bmatrix}$, which is positive definite due to $\eta > 1$.

According to (6.51), the derivative of V is given by

$$\dot{V} = (\xi^T \quad \zeta^T)(\bar{\Gamma}^T P + P\bar{\Gamma})(\xi^T \quad \zeta^T)^T \triangleq -(\xi^T \quad \zeta^T)U(\xi^T \quad \zeta^T)^T$$

where

$$u = \begin{bmatrix} \frac{1}{\eta}(b(L+L^T)+2sQ) & (b(L+L^T)+2sQ)-I \\ (b(L+L^T)+2sQ)-I & \eta(b(L+L^T)+2sQ)-\frac{2}{\eta}I \end{bmatrix}$$

Setting

$$\begin{aligned} R &= \eta(b(L+L^T)+2sQ)-\frac{2}{\eta}I \\ &- (\eta-\eta(b(L+L^T)+2sQ)^{-1})((b(L+L^T)+2sQ)-I) \\ &= (2\eta-\frac{2}{\eta})I-\eta(b(L+L^T)+2sQ)^{-1} \end{aligned}$$

Then, if

$$\lambda_{min}(b\hat{L}+sQ) > \frac{\eta^2}{4(\eta^2-1)}, \tag{6.54}$$

one can see that R is positive definite. Thus, by recalling **Lemma 4.5**, one can verify the positive definiteness of U. Assuming that there are m pinned nodes, we get

$$\lambda_{min}(b\hat{L}+sQ) = \lambda_{min}\left(b\hat{L}+s\textstyle\sum_{i=1}^{n}\sigma_i\theta_i\theta_i^T\right) \tag{6.55}$$

subject to $\sigma_i \in 0,1$ for $i = 1,2,...,n$ and $\sum_{i=1}^{n}\sigma_i = m,\theta_i$ is the n-dimensional vector with all entries equal to zero, but the i-th that is equal to 1.

Recalling **Lemma 4.8**, one can get

$$\lambda_{min} = \left(b\hat{L}+s\textstyle\sum_{i=1}^{n}\sigma_i\theta_i\theta_i^T\right) \geq \displaystyle\sum_{i=1}^{m}\lambda_{min}\left(\frac{b\hat{L}}{m}+s\theta_i\theta_i^T\right) \tag{6.56}$$

Applying **Lemma 4.7** to $\lambda_{min}(\frac{b\hat{L}}{m}+s\theta_i\theta_i^T)$ and noticing the fact that $\|\theta_i\| = 1, \lambda_{min}(\hat{L}) = 0$ and $v_i(\hat{L}) = \frac{1}{\sqrt{n}1_n}$, we obtain

$$\lambda_{min}\left(\frac{b\hat{L}}{m}+s\theta_i\theta_i^T\right) \geq \phi(s), \tag{6.57}$$

where
$\phi(s) = \frac{1}{2m}\left(b\lambda_2(\hat{L}) + ms - \sqrt{(b\lambda_2(\hat{L}) + ms)^2 - b\lambda_2(\hat{L})\frac{4ms}{n}}\right)$
Notice that for positive s,

$$\phi(s) \geq \frac{bs\lambda_2(\hat{L})}{bn\lambda_2(\hat{L}) + smn}. \tag{6.58}$$

Substituting (6.57) into (6.56) and applying (6.58), one can obtain $\lambda_{min}(b\hat{L} + sQ) \geq \frac{bms\lambda_2(\hat{L})}{bn\lambda_2(\hat{L})+smn}$. By imposing condition (6.53), one can get $\dot{V} < 0$. Thus, the claim follows.

6.2.6 Selection of the pinned nodes

Assume in what follows that the graph G is strongly connected and balanced. The Laplacian matrix of the mirror graph G_m (see **Definition 4**) is $\hat{L} = \frac{L+L^T}{2}$. If G is balanced, then $\lambda_2(\hat{L}) > 0$. As in [502], define

$$\varphi(s) = \lambda_{min}(b\hat{L} + sQ) \geq \frac{bms\lambda_2(\hat{L})}{bn\lambda_2(\hat{L}) + smn}$$

the network relative connectivity

$$\chi = \frac{\lambda_2(\hat{L})}{n}$$

and the fraction of pinned nodes $\rho = \frac{m}{n}$. Thus, $\varphi(s)$ can be rewritten as

$$\varphi(s) = \left(\frac{1}{\rho s} + \frac{1}{b\chi}\right) \tag{6.59}$$

For the mirror graph G_m of G, one has the lower bound on the Fiedler eigenvalue given by [485]:

$$\lambda_2\hat{L} \geq \frac{1}{D_m \text{ vol } G_m} \tag{6.60}$$

where the distance between two nodes is the number of edges in shortest path joining the two nodes, the diameter D_m is the maximum distance between any two nodes of G_m, and $volG_m$ denotes the volume of the graph G_m given by the sum of the in-degrees vol $G_m = \sum_i d_{in}(v_i)$. Equations (6.59) and (6.60) show that as the diameter and/or volume of the mirror graph decreases, i.e., the Fiedler eigenvalue increases, and the fraction of pinned nodes increases, the smaller pinning control gain and stiffness gain may be sufficient for the pinning control.

It is now desired to find out which nodes are most effectively pinned. Observe from (6.54) that it is desirable to have large $\lambda_{min}(b\hat{L} + sQ)$ so that the second-order controlled consensus can be achieved for the small ratio η of damping gain to stiffness gain. It can also be shown that convergence speed is faster if $\lambda_{min}(b\hat{L}+s\mathcal{Q})$ is larger. In [507] and Li et al. (2004), a simulation-based analysis for undirected graphs reveals that $\lambda_{min}(b\hat{L}+s\mathcal{Q})$ is bigger when the pinned nodes have higher degrees. In what follows, we will provide a theoretical explanation for this phenomenon for digraphs. First, we present a result on the determinant of $(b\hat{L}+s\mathcal{Q})$.

Theorem 4.10: *Suppose there are n nodes in the strongly connected and balanced graph G, among which, k nodes are pinned, i.e.,* $q_l \neq 0, \forall l \in \{i_1, i_2, ..., i_k\}$, *and* $q_l = 0$ *otherwise. Define* $\mathcal{Q}_k = diag q_l$ *and* $\bar{L} = b\hat{L}$. *Then, the determinant of* $\tilde{L}_k \triangleq \bar{L} + s\mathcal{Q}_k$ *is given by*

$$\left|\tilde{L}_k\right| = \left|\bar{L}\right| + \sum_{j=1}^{k} \sum_{1\leq s_1<s_2<\cdots<s_j\leq k} s^j \cdot \prod_{l=1}^{j} q_{i_{s_l}} \cdot \bar{L}\begin{pmatrix} i_{s1}i_{s2}...i_{sj} \\ i_{s1}i_{s2}...i_{sj} \end{pmatrix}, \tag{6.61}$$

where $\bar{L}\begin{pmatrix} i_{s1}i_{s2}...i_{sj} \\ i_{s1}i_{s2}...i_{sj} \end{pmatrix}$ *denotes the minor of* $\bar{L}$ *obtained by striking out the j rows and columns* $(i_{s1}i_{s2}...i_{sj})$.

Proof: The proof is by induction. First, we consider the case where there is only one injection node for graph G, i.e., $k = 1$. Then one has by a well-known determinant identity ([487])

$$\begin{aligned}
\left|\tilde{L}\right| = \left|\bar{L}+s\mathcal{Q}_1\right| \quad &= \begin{vmatrix}
\bar{L}_{11} & \bar{L}_{12} & \cdots & \bar{L}_{1i_{s1}} & \cdots & \bar{L}_{1n} \\
\bar{L}_{21} & \bar{L}_{22} & \cdots & \bar{L}_{2i_{s1}} & \cdots & \bar{L}_{2n} \\
\vdots & \vdots & \ddots & \cdots & & \\
\bar{L}_{i_{s1}1} & \bar{L}_{i_{s1}2} & \cdots & sq_{i_s1}\bar{L}_{i_{s1}i_{s1}} & & \vdots \\
\vdots & \vdots & & \ddots & & \\
\bar{L}_{n1} & \bar{L}_{n2} & & \cdots & & \bar{L}_{nn}
\end{vmatrix} \\
&= \begin{vmatrix}
\bar{L}_{11} & \bar{L}_{12} & \cdots & \bar{L}_{1i_{s1}} & \cdots & \bar{L}_{1n} \\
\bar{L}_{21} & \bar{L}_{22} & \cdots & \bar{L}_{2i_{s1}} & \cdots & \bar{L}_{2n} \\
\vdots & \vdots & \ddots & \cdots & & \\
\bar{L}_{i_{s1}1} & \bar{L}_{i_{s1}2} & \cdots & \bar{L}_{i_{s1}i_{s1}} & & \vdots \\
\vdots & \vdots & & \ddots & & \\
\bar{L}_{n1} & \bar{L}_{n2} & & \cdots & & \bar{L}_{nn}
\end{vmatrix} \\
&\quad + \begin{vmatrix}
\bar{L}_{11} & \bar{L}_{12} & \cdots & 0 & \cdots & \bar{L}_{1n} \\
\bar{L}_{21} & \bar{L}_{22} & \cdots & 0 & \cdots & \bar{L}_{2n} \\
\vdots & \vdots & \ddots & \cdots & & \\
\bar{L}_{i_{s1}1} & \bar{L}_{i_{s1}2} & \cdots & sq_{i_s1} & & \vdots \\
\vdots & \vdots & & \ddots & & \\
\bar{L}_{n1} & \bar{L}_{n2} & 0 & & & \bar{L}_{nn}
\end{vmatrix}
\end{aligned}$$

$$= \quad |\bar{L}| + sq_{i_s 1}\bar{L}\left(\tfrac{i_{s1}}{i_s 1}\right). \tag{6.62}$$

It is readily seen that (6.61) is true for $k = 1$. Assume that the result is true for $k = p$. For the case $k = p+1$, we have:

$$
\begin{aligned}
|\bar{L}_{p+1}| &= |\bar{L} + s\mathcal{Q}_{p+1}| \\
&= \begin{vmatrix}
\bar{L}_{11} & \cdots & \bar{L}_{1i_{s_1}} & \cdots & & \cdots & \bar{L}_{1i_{s_{p+1}}} & & \bar{L}_{1n} \\
\vdots & \ddots & & & & & & & \\
\bar{L}_{i_{s_1}1} & \ddots & sq_{i_{s_1}} + \bar{L}_{i_{s_1}i_{s_1}} & & & \ddots & & & \\
\vdots & \ddots & & \ddots & & & & & \vdots \\
\bar{L}_{i_{s_p}1} & & \ddots & & sq_{i_{s_p}} + \bar{L}_{i_{s_p}i_{s_p}} & & & & \\
\vdots & & & & & \ddots & & & \vdots \\
\bar{L}_{i_{s_{p+1}}1} & & & \ddots & & & sq_{i_{s_{p+1}}} + \bar{L}_{i_{s_{p+1}}i_{s_{p+1}}} & & \\
\vdots & & & & & & & \ddots & \\
\bar{L}_{n1} & \cdots & \bar{L}_{ni_{s_1}} & & & \cdots & & & \bar{L}_{nn}
\end{vmatrix} \\
&= \begin{vmatrix}
\bar{L}_{11} & \cdots & \bar{L}_{1i_{s_1}} & \cdots & & \cdots & \bar{L}_{1i_{s_{p+1}}} & & \bar{L}_{1n} \\
\vdots & \ddots & & & & & & & \\
\bar{L}_{i_{s_1}1} & \ddots & sq_{i_{s_1}} + \bar{L}_{i_{s_1}i_{s_1}} & & & \ddots & & & \\
\vdots & \ddots & & \ddots & & & & & \vdots \\
\bar{L}_{i_{s_p}1} & & \ddots & & sq_{i_{s_p}} + \bar{L}_{i_{s_p}i_{s_p}} & & & & \\
\vdots & & & & & \ddots & & & \vdots \\
\bar{L}_{i_{s_{p+1}}1} & & & \ddots & & & \bar{L}_{i_{s_{p+1}}i_{s_{p+1}}} & & \\
\vdots & & & & & & & \ddots & \\
\bar{L}_{n1} & \cdots & \bar{L}_{ni_{s_1}} & & & \cdots & & & \bar{L}_{nn}
\end{vmatrix} \\
&+ \begin{vmatrix}
\bar{L}_{11} & \cdots & \bar{L}_{1i_{s_1}} & \cdots & & \cdots & 0 & & \bar{L}_{1n} \\
\vdots & \ddots & & & & & & & \\
\bar{L}_{i_{s_1}1} & \ddots & sq_{i_{s_1}} + \bar{L}_{i_{s_1}i_{s_1}} & & & \ddots & 0 & & \\
\vdots & \ddots & & \ddots & & & 0 & & \vdots \\
\bar{L}_{i_{s_p}1} & & \ddots & & sq_{i_{s_p}} + \bar{L}_{i_{s_p}i_{s_p}} & & & & \\
\vdots & & & & & \ddots & & & \vdots \\
\bar{L}_{i_{s_{p+1}}1} & & & \ddots & & & sq_{i_{s_{p+1}}} & & \\
\vdots & & & & & & & \ddots & \\
\bar{L}_{n1} & \cdots & \bar{L}_{ni_{s_1}} & & & \cdots & 0 & & \bar{L}_{nn}
\end{vmatrix}
\end{aligned}
$$

$$
\begin{aligned}
&= \left|\tilde{L}_p\right| + sq_{i_{s_{p+1}}} \tilde{L}_p \left(\frac{i_{s_{p+1}}}{i_{s_{p+1}}}\right) \\
&= |\bar{L}| + \sum_{j=1}^{p} \sum_{1\le s_1 < s_2 < \cdots < s_j \le p} s^j \cdot \prod_{l=1}^{j} q_{i_{s_l}} \cdot \bar{L}\left(\frac{i_{s1} i_{s2} \ldots i_{sj}}{i_{s1} i_{s2} \ldots i_{sj}}\right) \\
&+ sq_{i_{s_{p+1}}} \bar{L}\left(\frac{i_{s_{p+1}}}{i_{s_{p+1}}}\right) + sq_{i_{s_{p+1}}} \sum_{j=1}^{p} \sum_{1\le s_1 < s_2 < \cdots < s_j \le p} s^j \cdot \prod_{l=1}^{j} q_{i_{s_l}} \\
&\cdot \bar{L}\left(\frac{i_{s1} i_{s2} \ldots i_{sj} i_{s_{p+1}}}{i_{s1} i_{s2} \ldots i_{sj} i_{s_{p+1}}}\right) |\bar{L}| \\
&+ \sum_{j=1}^{p+1} \sum_{1\le s_1 < s_2 < \cdots < s_j \le p} s^j \cdot \prod_{l=1}^{j} q_{i_{s_l}} \cdot \bar{L}\left(\frac{i_{s1} i_{s2} \ldots i_{sj}}{i_{s1} i_{s2} \ldots i_{sj}}\right)
\end{aligned}
$$

which, by the principle of induction, proves the desired result.

The following Lemma shows the relationship between the determinant $\left|\tilde{L}_k\right|$ and $\lambda_{min}(\tilde{L}_k)$.

Lemma 4.11: *Define $\tilde{L}_k = \bar{L} + s\mathcal{Q}_k$. Then*

$$
\lambda_{min}(\tilde{L}_k) \geq \frac{\left|\tilde{L}_k\right|}{(sn+)bn \max\{d_{out}(v_i)\}^{n-1}} \tag{6.63}
$$

Proof: Denote $\lambda_i(\tilde{L}_k), 1 \leq i \leq n$, as the eigenvalues of $\tilde{L}_k$. According to the relationship between the determinant and the eigenvalues for matrix $\tilde{L}_k$, one has ([483])

$$
\left|\tilde{L}_k\right| = \prod_{j=1}^{n} \lambda_i(\tilde{L}_k)
$$

Noting that all the eigenvalues of Lk are real and positive, one further gets

$$
\left|\tilde{L}_k\right| \leq \lambda_{min}(\tilde{L}_k)\lambda_{min}^{n-1}(\tilde{L}_k)
$$

Since $\tilde{L}_k$ is a real and symmetric matrix, its nonnegative eigenvalue is also a singular value. Thus

$$
\lambda_{min}(\tilde{L}_k) = \sigma_{max}(\tilde{L}_k)
$$

Using the fact

$$
\sigma_{max}(\tilde{L}_k) \leq \left\|\tilde{L}_k\right\|_1 \tag{6.64}
$$

from ([483]), it yields

$$
\left|\tilde{L}_k\right| \leq \lambda_{min}(\tilde{L}_k) \left\|\tilde{L}_k\right\|_1^{n-1}
$$

Notice that $\left\|\tilde{L}_k\right\|_1$ is related to the maximum absolute column sum. The graph is balanced, so $d_{in}(v_i) = d_{out}(v_i)$. Then, we get

$$
\left\|\tilde{L}_k\right\|_1 \leq sn + 2bn \max\{d_{out}(v_i)\}.
$$

Finally, **Theorem 4.10** and **Lemma 4.11** clearly show the importance of the out-degree of the nodes in selecting the pinning control nodes. For example, in the case where a single injection node is 1 (6.62), the determinant of $\tilde{L}_1$ is increased by $sq_{i_{s_l}}\bar{L}\left(\frac{i_{s_l}}{i_{s_l}}\right)$. Striking out a column i_{s_l} of $\bar{L}$ with entry $-ba_{li_{s1}}$ effectively increases the diagonal dominance of row 1 in the remaining matrix by $ba_{li_{s1}}$. To obtain the largest value of the minor $\bar{L}\left(\frac{i_{s_l}}{i_{s_l}}\right)$, which means to get the largest $\lambda min\tilde{L}_1$, one should strike out the column (and row) corresponding to the node i_{s_l} that influences the greatest number of other nodes, with the largest weights $ba_{li_{s1}}$. Then, the corresponding rows l in the remaining matrix have strict diagonal dominance, so that the remaining portion of $\bar{L}$ is the most diagonally dominant. This adds to the degree of diagonal dominance of $\bar{L}$, the out-degree (column sum) $bd_{out}(v_i) = \sum_{l=1}^{n} ba_{li_{s1}}$ of the struck out i_{s_l}-th column. [482] have equated the outdegree with the "social standing" of a node. The nodes with large out-degree have more influence in determining consensus values in the networks.

6.2.7 Pinning control with variable topology

In this section, we suppose that the communication topology is time-varying. In this case, the original multi-vehicle network is described by

$$\begin{aligned}\begin{bmatrix}\dot{x}\\ \dot{v}\end{bmatrix} &= \Gamma_{\sigma(t)}\begin{bmatrix}x\\ v\end{bmatrix}\\ \Gamma_{\sigma(t)} &= \begin{bmatrix}0_{n\times n} & I_n\\ -bL_{\sigma(t)} & -\eta_{\sigma}(t)bL_{\sigma(t)}\end{bmatrix}\end{aligned} \tag{6.65}$$

where

$$\sigma : [0,\infty) \to \Omega = \{1,2,...,N\}$$

is a switching signal that determines the coupling topology and N denotes the total number of all possible directed graphs. The following assumption is made for the switching instants.

Assumption 1: *There exists a dwell time* $\tau > 0$ *such that the switching instants* $\{t_s = 1,2,...\}$ *satisfy* $inf_s(t_{s+1} - t_s) \geq \tau_0, t_s \in R^+$.

Note that the switching sequence may or may not be infinite. In what follows, we consider a general case of the following infinite switching sequences.

Assumption 2: *The switching sequences* $S_0, S_1, ...,$ *where*

$$\begin{aligned}S_0 &= (t_0,\omega_0),(t_1,\omega_1),...,(t_{n_0-1},\omega_{n_0-1})\\ S_1 &= (t_{n_0},\omega_{n_0}),(t_{n_0+1},\omega_{n_0+1}),...,(t_{n_0+n_1-1},\omega_{n_0+n_1-1})\\ \vdots &= \vdots\end{aligned}$$

satisfies $\forall j \in Z^+, \bigcup_{\alpha}^{n_j-1} \omega_{n_{j-1}+\alpha} = \Omega$ *where* $n_{-1} = 0$. *The interval union* T_j *of a strictly increasing sequence of time* $t_{n_{j-1}}, t_{n_{j-1}+1}, \ldots, t_{n_{j-1}+n_{j-1}}$ *is the set* $T_j = \bigcup_{\alpha=0}^{n_j-2} \left[t_{n_{j-1}+\alpha}, t_{n_{j-1}+\alpha+1}\right]$.

Theorem 5.1: *Assume that the switching sequences satisfy* ***Assumptions 1*** *and* ***2***. *If the pinning controllers are injected into each zero-in-degree and strongly connected subgraph of multi-vehicle communication topology* $\omega_i (i \in Z^+)$ *and*

$$\eta_i > \max_{1 \le r \le n} \frac{|Im(\mu_r)|}{|u_r| \sqrt{-Re(\mu_r)}} \tag{6.66}$$

where μ_r, $r = 1, 2, \ldots, n$ *are the eigenvalues of* $-(bL_i + s_i \mathcal{Q}_i)$, *then the second-order controlled consensus is achieved.*

Proof: If inequality (6.66) is true, we know that all eigenvalues of

$$\Gamma_i = \begin{bmatrix} 0_{n \times n} & I_n \\ -(bL_i + s_i \mathcal{Q}_i) & -\eta_i (bL_i + s_i \mathcal{Q}_i) \end{bmatrix}$$

have negative real parts following the proof of Theorem 4.4. Thus, there exists Lyapunov function $V_i = (\xi^T \zeta^T) P_i (\xi^T \zeta^T)^T$ with the positive definite matrix P_i such that $\dot{V}_i < 0$.

Define $V_{max}^j \triangleq max_{t \in T_j} \{V_{\omega j}(t)\}$. Suppose $V_{max}^j = V_{\omega_p}(t_j'), t_j' \in T_j$. We have $V_{max}^{j+1} = V_{\omega_l}(t_{j+1}') < V_{\omega_l}(t_j'') \le V_{\omega_p}(t_j') = V_{max}^j,$, where $t_j'' \in T_j$ is a switching instant when ω_l is active. Therefore, $\lim_{j \to \infty} V_{max}^j \to 0$. Thus, the claim follows.

6.2.8 Simulation examples

In this section, some numerical simulation examples will be presented in order to illustrate the effectiveness of the pinning control method discussed in the previous sections. Consider a multiple unicycle robot network. Each unicycle robot has the dynamics model as follows:

$$\dot{x} = v_i cos(\theta_i), \quad \dot{y} = v_i sin(\theta_i), \quad \dot{\theta}_i = \omega_i, \quad \dot{v} = \frac{f_i}{m_i}, \quad \dot{\omega}_i = \frac{\tau_i}{J_i} \tag{6.67}$$

where (x_i, y_i) is the Cartesian position of the robot centre,θ_i is the steering angle, v_i is the transition speed, ω_i is the rotation speed, mi represents the mass, J_i denotes the moment of inertia, f_i is the force input and τ_i is the torque input. To avoid the nonholonomic constraint introduced by the equation, define

$$\begin{bmatrix} x_{i1} \\ y_{i1} \end{bmatrix} = \begin{bmatrix} x_i + d_i cos(\theta_i) \\ y_i + d_i sin(\theta_i) \end{bmatrix}$$

where (x_{i1}, y_{i1}) is a position off the wheel axis of the i-th robot by a distance d_i. The robot model (6.67) can be feedback linearized to

$$\begin{bmatrix} \dot{x_{i1}} \\ \dot{y_{i1}} \end{bmatrix} = \begin{bmatrix} v_{i1} \\ v_{i12} \end{bmatrix}, \quad \begin{bmatrix} \dot{v_{i1}} \\ \dot{v_{i2}} \end{bmatrix} = \begin{bmatrix} u_{i1} \\ u_{i12} \end{bmatrix} \tag{6.68}$$

with

$$\begin{bmatrix} f_i \\ \tau_i \end{bmatrix} = \begin{bmatrix} \frac{1}{m_i}cos(\theta_i) & -\frac{d_i}{J_i}sin(\theta_i) \\ \frac{1}{m_i}sin(\theta_i) & \frac{d_i}{J_i}cos(\theta_i) \end{bmatrix}^{-1} \times \begin{bmatrix} u_{i1} + v_i\omega_i sin(\theta_i) & d_i\omega_i^2 cos(\theta_i) \\ u_{i2} - v_i\omega_i cos(\theta_i) & d_i\omega_i^2 sin(\theta_i) \end{bmatrix}$$

In what follows, we consider the formation control problem of a network consisting of six unicycle robots. Suppose that the robots are required to keep the square shape, as depicted in Fig. 6.10, and the square center is required to move along the trajectory

$$\begin{pmatrix} \dot{x_0} \\ \dot{y_0} \end{pmatrix} = \begin{pmatrix} 0.5 \\ 1 \end{pmatrix}$$

The first example demonstrates the fixed topology case. Suppose that the interaction topology G_a for the robots is given in Fig. 6.11 with 01 weights and the neighbor-based protocols are described by

$$\begin{aligned} u_{i1} &= \sum_{j\in N_i} [(x_{j1}-\delta_j)-(x_{i1}-\delta_i)+\eta(v_{j1}-v_{i1})], \\ u_{i2} &= \sum_{j\in N_i} [(y_{j1}-\varepsilon_j)-(y_{i1}-\varepsilon_i)+\eta(v_{j2}-v_{i2})], \quad i=1,2,...,6, \end{aligned} \tag{6.69}$$

where $\delta_1 = \delta_6 = 1$, $\delta_2 = \delta_5 = 0$, $\delta_3 = \delta_4 = -1$, $\varepsilon_1 = \varepsilon_2 = \varepsilon_3 = 1$, $\varepsilon_4 = \varepsilon_5 = \varepsilon_6 = -1$. Define $x_{i2} = x_{i1} - \delta_i$ and $y_{i2} = y_{i1} - \varepsilon_i$, $i = 1,2,...,6$. Now, (6.69) can be rewritten as

$$u_{i1} = \sum_{j\in N_i} [(x_{j2}-x_{i2})+\eta(v_{j1}-v_{i1})],$$

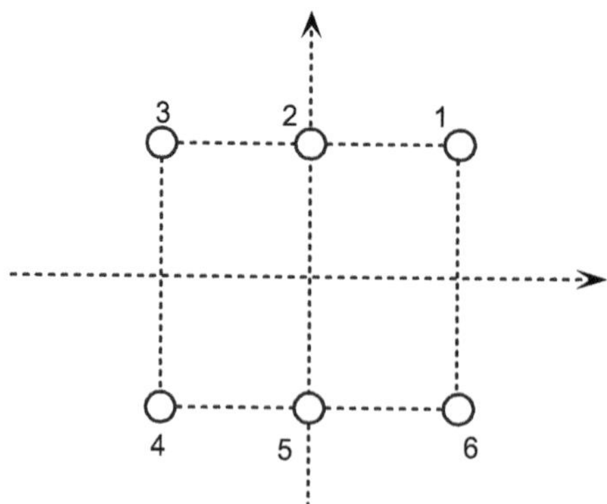

Figure 6.10: The expected square shape consisting of six nodes

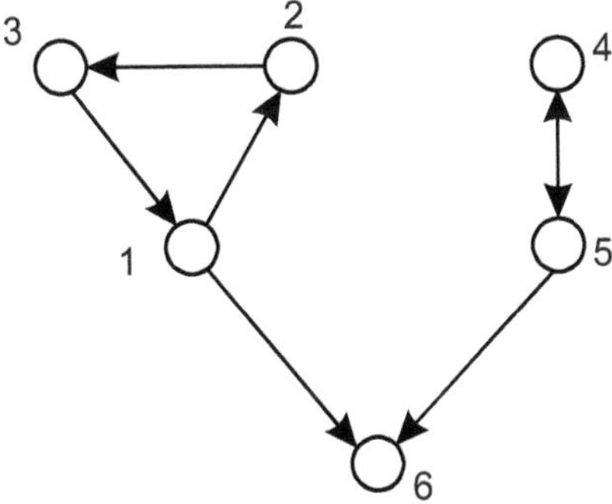

Figure 6.11: The interaction topology G_a

$$u_{i2} = \sum_{j \in N_i} [(y_{j2} - {}_{i1}) + \eta(v_{j2} - v_{i2})]$$

The pinning controllers are injected into the robots 1 and 5 and designed as

$$\begin{aligned} \bar{u}_{i1} &= s(x_0 - x_{i2}) + \eta s(0.5 - v_{i1}), \\ \bar{u}_{i2} &= s(y_0 - {}_{i1}) + \eta s(1 - v_{i2}), \quad i = 1,5 \end{aligned}$$

Selecting $s = 1$ and $\eta = 1.5$. All robots' initial positions $(x_{i1}, y\ i1\ )$ are randomly chosen from box $[-1,1] \times [-1,1]$. All robots initial velocities are zero. Figure 6.12 shows that the position errors and the velocity errors asymptotically converge to zero.

In the second example, the variable topology is considered. Suppose that there exist the other three possible topologies shown in Fig. 6.13, which are referred to as G_b, G_c and G_d, respectively. The system starts at G_a and switches every $t = 1s$ to the next topology as shown in Fig. 6.14, that is, $G_a \rightarrow G_b \rightarrow G_c \rightarrow G_d \rightarrow G_a$, and so on. For G_a, robots 1 and 5 are pinned. For topologies G_b, G_c and G_d, robots 2 and 4 are pinned with $s = 1$, $\eta = 1$. From Fig. 6.15, it is clearly observed that both position errors and velocity errors asymptotically converge to zero in spite of the topology changes.

6.3 Distributed Consensus Control

In what follows, we are concerned with the consensus of a network of agents with general linear or linearized dynamics, whose communication topology contains a directed spanning tree. An observer-type consensus protocol based on the relative outputs of the neighboring agents is adopted. The notion of consensus region is introduced, as a measure for the robustness of the protocol and as a basis for the

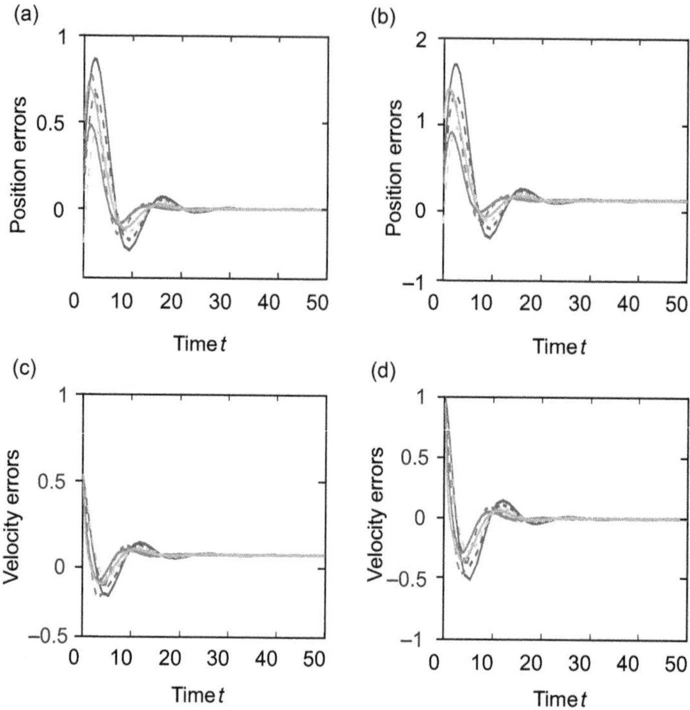

Figure 6.12: Formation-keeping errors in the fixed topology: (a) Position errors with respect to the x-axis, (b) position errors with respect to the y-axis, (c) velocity errors with respect to the x-axis and (d) velocity errors with respect to the y-axis

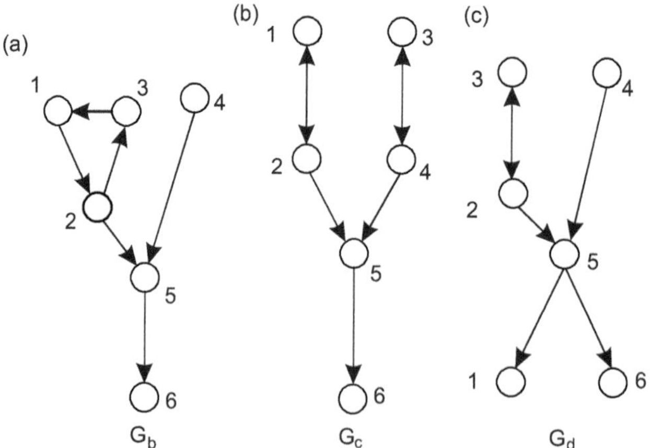

Figure 6.13: Three examples of weakly connected graphs

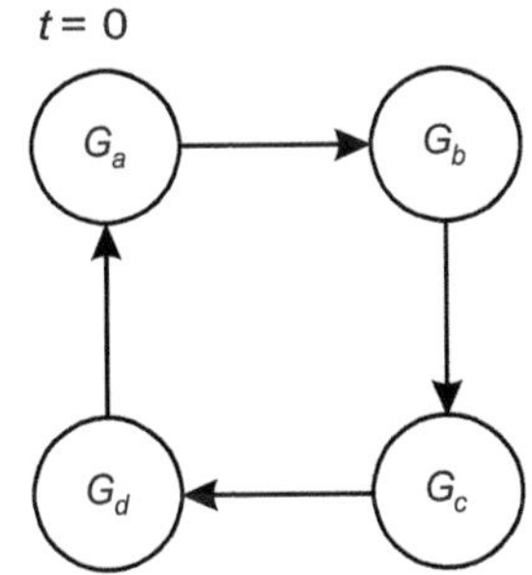

Figure 6.14: Switching topologies

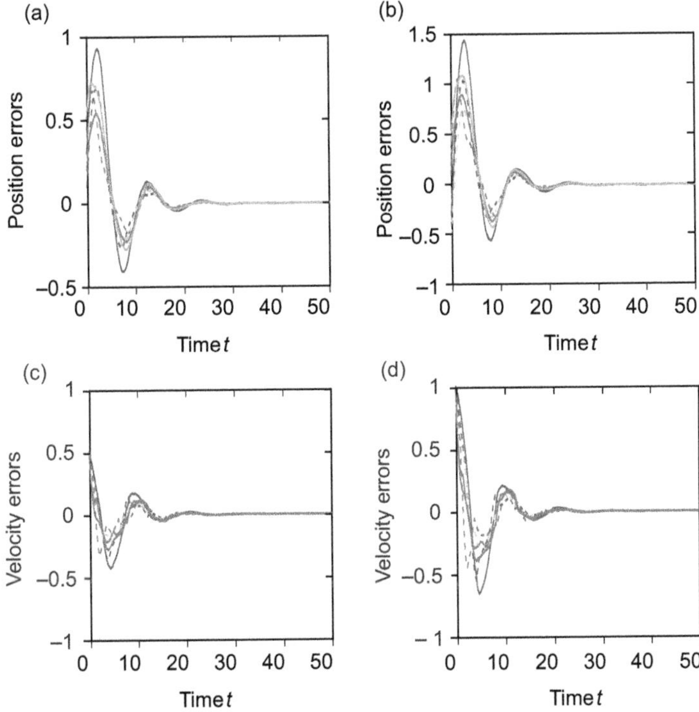

Figure 6.15: Formation-keeping errors in the variable topology: (a) Position errors with respect to the x-axis, (b) position errors with respect to the y-axis, (c) velocity errors with respect to the x-axis and (d) velocity errors with respect to the y-axis

protocol design. For neutrally stable agents, it is shown that there exists a protocol achieving consensus together with a consensus region that is the entire open right-half plane if and only if each agent is stabilizable and detectable. An algorithm is further presented for constructing such a protocol. For consensus with a prescribed convergence speed, a multi-step protocol design procedure is given, which yields an unbounded consensus region and at the same time maintains a favorable decoupling property. Finally, the consensus algorithms are extended to solve the formation control problems.

The consensus of networks of identical agents with linear or linearized dynamics whose communication topology contains a directed spanning tree is of particular interest. An observer-type using only the relative outputs of the neighboring agents is adopted here. A decomposition approach is utilized to cast the consensus problem of the multiagent system into the stability of a set of matrices that have the same dimension as that of a single agent.

Suppose that there are m nodes in the graph. The adjacency matrix $A \in \Re^{m\times m}$ is defined by $a_{ii} = 0$, and $a_{ij} > 0$ if $(j,i) \in E$ but 0 otherwise. The Laplacian matrix $L \in \Re^{m\times m}$ is defined as $L_{ii} = \sum_{j\neq i} a_{ij}, L_{ij} = -a_{ij}$ for $i \neq j$. It follows immediately that 0 is an eigenvalues of L with 1 as the corresponding right eigenvector and all the non-zero eigenvalues have positive real parts. For a directed graph, 0 is a simple eigenvalue of L if and only if the graph has a directed spanning tree.

6.3.1 Consensus with observer-type protocol

Consider a network of N identical agents with linear or linearized dynamics, where the dynamics of the ith agent are described by

$$\begin{aligned} \dot{x}_i &= Ax_i + Bu_i \\ y_i &= Cx_i. \end{aligned} \tag{6.70}$$

where $x_i \in \Re^n$ is the state, $u_i \in \Re^p$ is the control input, $y_i \in \Re^q$ is the measured output and A, B and C are constant matrices with compatible dimensions.

The communication topology among agents is represented by a directed graph $G = (V, E)$, where $V = \{1, \ldots, N\}$ is the set of nodes (i.e., agents), and $E \subset V \times V$ is the set of edges. An edge (i, j) in graph G means that agent j can obtain information from agent i, but not conversely.

At each time instant, the information available to agent i is the relative measurements of other agents with respect to i itself, given by

$$\zeta_i = \sum_{j=1}^{N} a_{ij}(y_i - y_j) \tag{6.71}$$

where $(a_{ii})N \times N$ is the adjacency matrix of graph G. The consensus protocol takes the following observer-type form:

$$\begin{aligned} \dot{v}_i &= (A+BK)v_i + cL\left(\sum_{j=1}^{N} a_{ij}C(v_i - v_j) - \zeta_i\right) \\ u_i &= Kv_i \end{aligned} \tag{6.72}$$

where $v_i \in \Re^n$ is the protocol state, $i = 1,2,\ldots,N, c > 0$ denotes the coupling strength, $L \in \Re^{q\times n}$ and $K \in \Re^{p\times n}$ are feedback gain matrices to be determined. In (6.72), the term $\sum_{j=1}^{N} a_{ij}C(v_i - v_j)$ denotes the information exchanges between the protocol of agent i and those of its neighboring agents. It is observed that the protocol in (6.72) maintains the same communication topology of the agents in (6.70).

Let $z_i = [x_i^T, v_i^T]^T$. Then, systems (6.70) and (6.72) together can be written as

$$\dot{z}_i = \mathcal{A}z_i + c\sum_{j=1}^{N} L_{ij}Hz_j, \quad i = 1,2,\ldots,N \tag{6.73}$$

where $L = (L_{ij})N \times N$ is the Laplacian matrix of graph G, and

$$\mathcal{A} = \begin{bmatrix} A & BK \\ 0 & A+BK \end{bmatrix}, \quad H = \begin{bmatrix} 0 & 0 \\ -LC & LC \end{bmatrix}$$

6.3.2 Dynamic consensus

We start by introducing the concept of dynamic consensus

Definition 6.2 *Given agents (6.70), the protocol (6.72) is said to solve the dynamic consensus problem if the states of system (6.73) satisfy*

$$\lim_{t\to\infty} \|z_i(t) - z_j(t)\| = 0, \quad \forall i,j = 1,2,\ldots,N \tag{6.74}$$

Let $r \in \Re^N$ be such that $r^T L = 0$ and $r^T\mathbf{1} = \mathbf{1}$

Remark 6.10 *Introduce a new variable*

$$\begin{aligned} \delta(t) &= z(t) - ((\mathbf{1}r^T)\otimes I_{2n})z(t) \\ &= ((I_N - \mathbf{1}r^T) - I_{2n})z(t) \end{aligned} \tag{6.75}$$

where $z = [z_1^T,\ldots,z_N^T]^T$ and $\delta \in \Re^{2Nn\times 2Nn}$ satisfies

$$(r^T \otimes I_{2n})\delta = 0$$

By similarity to [18], δ is referred to as the disagreement vector. It is easy to see that 0 is a simple eigenvalue of $I_N - \mathbf{1}r^T$ with $\mathbf{1}$ as the right eigenvector, and 1 is another eigenvalue with multiplicity $N-1$. ▌

It follows from (6.75) that $\delta = 0$ if and only if $z_1 = \cdots = z_N$, that is, the dynamic consensus problem can be recast into the asymptotic stability of vector δ, which evolves according to the following dynamics

$$\dot{\delta} = (I_N \otimes A + cL \otimes H)\delta \tag{6.76}$$

In the sequel, we provide a decomposition approach to the dynamic consensus problem.

Theorem 6.3

For the communication topology G containing a directed spanning tree, protocol (6.72) solves the dynamic consensus problem if and only if all the matrices

$$A + BK, \ A + c\lambda_i LC, i = 2, 3, \ldots, N$$

are Hurwitz, where $\lambda_i, i = 2, 3, \ldots, N$, are the non-zero eigenvalues of the Laplacian matrix L.

In the sequel, we let $Y_1 \in \Re^{N\times(N-1)}$, $Y_2 \in \Re^{(N-1)\times N}$, $T \in \Re^{N\times N}$, and an upper-triangular matrix $\Delta \in \Re^{(N-1)\times(N-1)}$ be such that

$$\begin{aligned} T &= \begin{bmatrix} 1 & Y_1 \end{bmatrix}, \quad T^{-1} = \begin{bmatrix} r^T \\ Y_2 \end{bmatrix}, \\ T^{-1}LT &= \Lambda = \begin{bmatrix} 0 & 0 \\ 0 & \Delta \end{bmatrix} \end{aligned} \tag{6.77}$$

where the diagonal entries of Δ are the non-zero eigenvalues of L. Then, (6.76) can be rewritten in terms of ξ, where $\xi = (T^{-1} \otimes I_{2n})\delta$ with $\xi = [\xi_1^T, \ldots, \xi_N^T]^T$, as follows

$$\dot{\xi} = (I_N \otimes A + c\Lambda \otimes H)\xi \tag{6.78}$$

As to ξ_1, it can be seen from (6.75) that

$$\xi_1 = (r^T \otimes I_{2n})\delta = 0 \tag{6.79}$$

Note that the elements of the state matrix of (6.78) are either block diagonal or block upper triangular. Hence, $\xi_i, i = 2, \ldots, N$, converge asymptotically to zero, if and only if the $N-1$ subsystems

$$\dot{\xi}_i = (A + c\lambda_i H)\xi_i, \quad i = 2, 3, \ldots, N \tag{6.80}$$

are asymptotically stable, which leads to the assertion by noting that matrices $A + \lambda_i H$ are similar to $\begin{bmatrix} A + \lambda_i LC & 0 \\ -\lambda_i LC & A + BK \end{bmatrix}, i = 2, \ldots, N.$

Remark 6.11 *The significance of* **Theorem** *6.3 lies in the fact that it converts the consensus of the multiagent system under the dynamic protocol (6.72) to the stability of a set of matrices with the same low dimensions as a single agent. The effects of the communication topology on the consensus are characterized by the eigenvalues of the corresponding Laplacian matrix L. Moreover, protocol (6.72) is based only on relative output measurements between neighboring systems.* ■

Lemma 6.3

Consider network (6.73) whose communication topology G has a directed spanning tree. If protocol (6.72) satisfies **Theorem** *6.3, then*

$$\begin{aligned} x_i(t) &\rightarrow \varpi(t) \triangleq (r^T \otimes e^{At}) \begin{bmatrix} x_1(0) \\ \vdots \\ x_N(0) \end{bmatrix} \\ v_i(t) &\rightarrow 0, \quad i = 1, 2, \ldots, N, \text{ as } t \rightarrow \infty \end{aligned} \tag{6.81}$$

where $r \in \Re^N$ is such that $r^T L = 0$ and $r^T 1 = 1$.

From (6.81), it follows that agents (6.70) are excluded from having poles in the open right-half plane; otherwise, the consensus value reached by the states of (6.70) will tend to infinity exponentially. On the other hand, if matrix A is Hurwitz, then the agents will reach consensus onto 0. Therefore it is critical for matrix A in (6.70) to have eigenvalues along the imaginary axis, so that the systems can reach consensus on a non-zero value, a special case of which is that matrix A is neutrally stable.

6.3.3 Consensus region

Given a protocol of the form (6.72), the dynamic consensus problem can be cast into analyzing the system

$$\dot{\varsigma} = (A + \sigma H)\varsigma \tag{6.82}$$

where $\varsigma \in \Re^{2n}, \sigma \in C$. The stability of system (6.82) depends on the parameter σ, based on which the notion of consensus region is introduced:

Definition 6.3 The region S of the complex parameter σ, such that (6.82) is asymptotically stable, is called the consensus region of network (6.73).

It follows from **Theorem** 6.3 that consensus is reached if and only if

$$c(\alpha_k + i\beta_k) \in S, \quad k = 2, 3, \ldots, N$$

where $i = \sqrt{-1}, \alpha_k = Re(\lambda_k)$ and $\beta_k = Im(\lambda_k)$. For an undirected communication graph, its consensus region S is an interval or a union of several intervals on the real axis. However, for a directed graph, where the eigenvalues of L are generally complex numbers, its consensus region S is a region or a union of several regions on the complex plane, which can be bounded or unbounded.

Remark 6.12 *It should be noted that the consensus region serves, in a certain sense, as a measure for the robustness of the protocol (6.72) to parametric uncertainties of its feedback gain matrix L and the communication topology. Given a consensus protocol, the consensus region should be large enough for the protocol to maintain a desirable robustness margin.* ∎

6.3.4 Consensus with neutrally stable matrix

In this subsection, for the case when matrix A is neutrally stable, it is shown that an unbounded consensus region in the form of the open right-half plane can be achieved. A constructive design algorithm for protocol (6.72) is then presented.

Lemma 6.4
A complex matrix $A \in C^{n\times n}$ is Hurwitz if and only if there exist a positive definite matrix $Q = Q^H$ and a matrix $C \in C^{m\times n}$ such that (A,C) is observable and $A^H Q + QA = -C^H C$.

Lemma 6.5
For matrices $S \in \Re^{n\times n}, H \in \Re^{m\times n}$, where S is skew-symmetric and (S,H) is observable, the matrix $S-(x+iy)H^T H$ is Hurwitz for any $x > 0, y \in R$.

Proof: Let $\tilde{S} = S-(x+iy)H^T H$. Then

$$\begin{aligned} \tilde{S}+\tilde{S}^H &= S-(x+iy)H^T H + S^T - (x-iy)H^T H \\ &= -2xH^T H \leq 0, \quad \forall x > 0 \end{aligned} \tag{6.83}$$

Obviously, $(\tilde{S},H)$ is observable, for (S,H) is observable. By **Lemma** 6.4, (6.83) directly leads to the assertion.

A constructive algorithm for protocol (6.72) is now presented, which will be used later.

Algorithm 6.1
Given that $A \in \Re^{n\times n}$ is neutrally stable and that the pair (A,B,C) is stabilizable and detectable, the dynamic protocol (6.72) can be constructed as follows:

1. *Let K be such that $A+BK$ is Hurwitz.*

2. *Choose* $U \in \Re^{n\times n_1}$ *and* $W \in \Re^{n\times(n-n_1)}$ *such that*

$$\begin{bmatrix} U & W \end{bmatrix}^{-1} A \begin{bmatrix} U & W \end{bmatrix} = \begin{bmatrix} S & 0 \\ 0 & X \end{bmatrix} \tag{6.84}$$

where $S \in \Re^{n_1\times n_1}$ *is skew-symmetric and* $X \in R^{(n-n_1)\times(n-n_1)}$ *is Hurwitz.*

3. *Let* $L = -UU^TC^T$.

4. *Select the coupling strength* $c > 0$.

In the above algorithm, note that matrices U and W can be derived by rendering matrix A into the real Jordan canonical form.

Theorem 6.4
Given that $A \in \Re^{n\times n}$ *is neutrally stable and that G has a directed spanning tree, there exists a distributed protocol in the form of (6.72) that solves the dynamic consensus problem and, meanwhile, yields an unbounded consensus region* $(0,\infty)\times(-\infty,\infty)$, *if and only if* (A,B,C) *is stabilizable and detectable*

Proof: $\Longrightarrow$ Follows **Theorem** 6.3.

$\Longleftarrow$ Let the related variables be defined as in Algorithm 6.1. Construct the protocol (6.72) by Algorithm 6.1, and let $H = CU$. Then, (S,H) is observable for (A,C) is detectable. Let $U^\dagger \in \Re^{n_1\times n}$ and $W^\dagger \in \Re^{(n-n_1)\times n}$ be such that $\begin{bmatrix} U^\dagger \\ W^\dagger \end{bmatrix} = \begin{bmatrix} U & W \end{bmatrix}^{-1}$, where $U^\dagger U = I, W^\dagger W = I, U^\dagger W = 0$ and $W^\dagger U = 0$. It can be verified by some algebraic manipulations that

$$\begin{aligned} &\begin{bmatrix} U & W \end{bmatrix}^{-1} (A+(x+iy)LC) \begin{bmatrix} U & W \end{bmatrix} \\ &= \begin{bmatrix} S+(x+iy)U^\dagger LCU & (x+iy)U^\dagger LCW \\ (x+iy)W^\dagger LCU & X+(x+iy)W^\dagger LCW \end{bmatrix} \\ &= \begin{bmatrix} S-(x+iy)H^TH & -(x+iy)H^TSW \\ 0 & X \end{bmatrix} \end{aligned} \tag{6.85}$$

which implies that matrix $A+(x+iy)LC$ is Hurwitz for all $x > 0$ and $y \in R$, because by **Lemma** 6.3, matrix $S-(x+iy)H^TH$ is Hurwitz for any $x > 0$ and $y \in R$. Hence, by **Theorem** 6.3, the protocol given by **Algorithm** 6.1 solves the dynamic consensus problem with an unbounded consensus region $(0,\infty)\times(-\infty,\infty)$.

Remark 6.13 *The consensus region* $(0,\infty)\times(-\infty,\infty)$ *achieved by the protocol constructed by Algorithm 6.1 means that such a protocol can reach consensus for any communication topology containing a directed spanning tree and for* *any positive coupling strength. However, the communication topology and the coupling strength do affect the performances of consensus, for example, the convergence speed. A general case of dynamic consensus protocol based on relative measurements of the neighboring agents are investigated here, containing the static protocol case. Moreover, the method leading to* **Theorem** *6.4 here is indeed comparatively much simpler.* ▮

6.3.5 Consensus with prescribed convergence speed

For the general case where matrix A has no eigenvalues in the open right-half plane, the protocol (6.72) is designed in this subsection to achieve consensus with a prescribed convergence speed. Previous works along this line include [15, 17, 18], where the convergence speed of consensus for networks of integrators was analyzed.

It turns out, from the proof of **Theorem** 6.3, that the convergence speed of N agents in (6.70) reaching consensus under protocol (6.72) is equal to the minimal decay rate of the $N-1$ systems in (6.80). The decay rate of system $\dot{x} = Ax$ is defined as the maximum of negative real parts of the eigenvalues of matrix A. Thus, the convergence speed of agents (6.70) reaching consensus can be manipulated by properly assigning the eigenvalues of matrices

$$A+BK, \quad A+c\lambda_i LC, \quad i=2,3,\ldots,N$$

We know from matrix theory that the decay rate of system $\dot{x} = Ax$ is larger than $\alpha > 0$, if and only if there exists a matrix $Q > 0$ such that

$$A^TQ+QA+2\alpha Q<0$$

Hence, we provide the following result

Proposition 6.1
Given the agents (6.70), there exists a matrix L such that $A+(x+iy)LC$ is Hurwitz with a decay rate larger than a for all $x \in [1,\infty)$, $y \in (-\infty,\infty)$, if and only if there exists a matrix $Q = Q^T > 0$ such that

$$A^TQ+QA-2C^TC+2\alpha Q<0 \tag{6.86}$$

Proof: $\Longleftarrow$ By **Lemma** 6.5, there exists a matrix L such that $A+LC$ is Hurwitz with a decay rate larger than a if and only if there exists a matrix $Q = Q^T > 0$ such that

$$(A+LC)^TQ+Q(A+LC)+2\alpha Q<0$$

Let $QL = V$. Then, the above inequality becomes

$$A^TQ+QA+VC+C^TV^T+2\alpha Q<0$$

By Finsler's Lemma, there exists a matrix V satisfying the above inequality if and only if there exists a scalar $\tau > 0$ such that

$$A^TQ + QA - \tau C^TC + 2\alpha Q < 0 \tag{6.87}$$

Without loss of generality, letting $\tau = 2$ in (6.87) leads to (6.86). Take $V = -C^T$, that is, $L = -Q^{-1}C^T$. By the above inequalities, one has

$$\begin{aligned}(A &+ (x+iy)LC)^HQ + Q(A+(x+iy)LC) + 2\alpha Q \\ &= (A+(x-iy)LC)^TQ + Q(A+(x+iy)LC) + 2\alpha Q \\ &= AQ + QA^T - 2xC^TC + 2\alpha Q < 0\end{aligned}$$

for all $x \geq 1$, that is, $A + (x+iy)LC$ is Hurwitz, with a decay rate larger than a for all $x \in [1,\infty), y \in (-\infty,\infty)$.

$\Longrightarrow$ Follows by letting $x = 1, y = 0$.

Combining **Proposition** 6.1 and **Theorem** 6.3 lead to the following result:

Theorem 6.5

For network (6.73) with G containing a directed spanning tree, there exists a protocol (6.72) that solves the consensus problem with a convergence rate larger than a and yields an unbounded consensus region $[1,\infty)\times(-\infty,\infty)$, if and only if there exist matrices K and L such that both $A+BK$ and $A+LC$ are Hurwitz, with a decay rate larger than α.

Algorithm 6.2

For graph G containing a directed spanning tree, a protocol (6.72) solving the dynamic consensus problem with a convergence speed larger than a can be constructed as follows:

1. *Obtain the feedback gain matrix K, for example, by using the Ackermann's formula, such that the poles of matrix $A+BK$ lie in the left-half plane of $x = -\alpha$.*

2. *Choose the feedback gain matrix $L = -Q^{-1}C^T$, where $Q > 0$ is one solution to (6.86).*

3. *Select the coupling strength c larger than the threshold value c_{th} given by*

$$c_{th} = \frac{1}{\min_{i=2,\ldots,N} Re(\lambda_i)} \tag{6.88}$$

where $\lambda_i, i = 2,\ldots,N$, are the non-zero eigenvalues of matrix L.

The following remarks stand out:

Remark 6.14 **Algorithm** *6.2 has a favorable decoupling feature. To be specific, steps 1 and 2 deal only with the agent dynamics and the feedback gain matrices of the consensus protocol, leaving the communication topology of the multiagent network to be handled in step 3 by manipulating the coupling strength. The protocol designed by* **Algorithm** *6.2 for one communication graph is applicable to any other graph with larger minimum real parts of eigenvalues and, thereby, is robust in this sense to the communication topology. For the case where the agent number N is large, for which the eigenvalues of the corresponding Laplacian matrix are hard to determine or even troublesome to estimate, one only needs to choose the coupling strength to be large enough.* ∎

Remark 6.15 *Compared to the consensus when A is neutrally stable, where the coupling strength can be chosen as any positive scalar, for the case where A is critically unstable or a prescribed convergence speed is desired, the coupling strength generally has to be larger than a threshold value, which is related to the specific communication topology. This is consistent with the intuition that unstable behaviors are more difficult to synchronize than stable behaviors.* ∎

Remark 6.16 *One sufficient condition satisfying* **Theorem** *6.5 is that (A,B,C) is controllable and observable. Under such a condition, the protocol achieving consensus with a convergence speed larger than an arbitrary given positive value can be constructed by* **Algorithm** *6.2. However, larger a implies higher feedback gains in protocol (6.72). Thus, a trade-off has to be made between the convergence speed and the cost of the consensus protocol.* ∎

6.3.6 Illustrative example 6.2

The agent dynamics are given by (6.70), with

$$A = \begin{bmatrix} 0 & -1 & 0 \\ 1 & 0 & 0 \\ 0 & 1 & 0 \end{bmatrix}, \quad B = \begin{bmatrix} 1 \\ 0 \\ 0 \end{bmatrix}, \quad C = \begin{bmatrix} 0 & 0 & 1 \end{bmatrix}$$

Obviously, matrix A is neutrally stable, and (A,B,C) is controllable and observable. A third-order consensus protocol is in the form of (6.72).

Simple computation shows that the feedback gain matrix K of (6.72) is given as $K = \begin{bmatrix} \% & -4.5 & -5.5 & -3 \end{bmatrix}$ such that the poles of $A+BK$ are $-1, -1.5, -2$. The matrix U, such that $U^{-1}AU = J$ is of the real Jordan canonical form, is

$$U = \begin{bmatrix} 0 & 0.5774 & 0 \\ 0 & 0 & -0.5774 \\ 1 & -0.5774 & 0 \end{bmatrix}, \quad J = \begin{bmatrix} 0 & 0 & 0 \\ 0 & 0 & 1 \\ 0 & -1 & 0 \end{bmatrix}$$

By **Algorithm** 6.1, the feedback gain L of (6.72) is obtained as $L = \begin{bmatrix} 0.3333 & 0 & -1.3333 \end{bmatrix}^T$. By **Theorem** 6.4, the agents under this protocol can reach consensus with respect to any communication graph containing a spanning tree and for any positive coupling strength. One such graph with 6 nodes is shown in Fig. 6.16, whose non-zero eigenvalues are 3 and 1 with multiplicity 4. Select the coupling strength $c = 1$ for simplicity. It can be verified that the convergence speed in this case equals 0.0303.

Next, protocol (6.72) is redesigned in order to achieve consensus with a specified convergence speed larger than 1. The feedback gain K is chosen the same as above. Solving linear matrix Inequality (LMI) (6.86) with $a = 1$ by using Sedumi toolbox [36] gives $L = \begin{bmatrix}\% & -8.5763 & -15.2128 & -5.6107 \end{bmatrix}^T$. For the graph in Fig. 6.16, the threshold value for the coupling strength is $c_{th} = 1$ by (6.88). Select $c = 1$, the same as before. The consensus errors $x_i - x_1, i = 2, \ldots, 6$, for the graph in Fig. 6.16 under the protocols generated by Algorithms 6.1 and by Algorithm 6.2 with $\alpha = 1$, are depicted in Figs. 6.17a and 6.17b, respectively. It can be observed that the consensus process of the former case is indeed much slower than the latter.

6.3.7 Consensus with static protocols

In this section, a special case where the relative states between neighboring agents are available is considered. For this case, a distributed static protocol is proposed as

$$u_i = cF \sum_{j=1}^{N} a_{ij}(x_i - x_j) \tag{6.89}$$

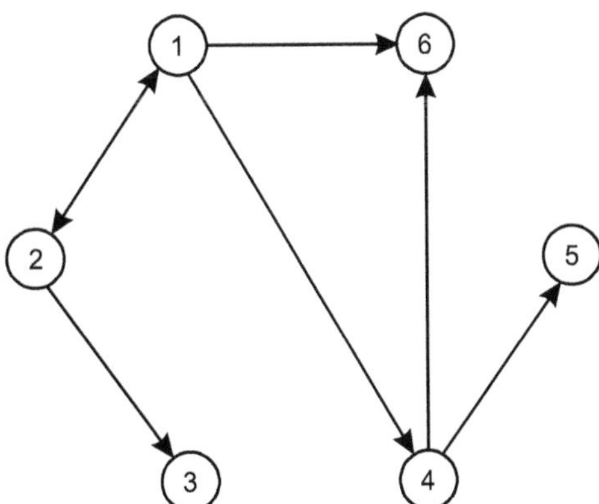

Figure 6.16: Communication graph

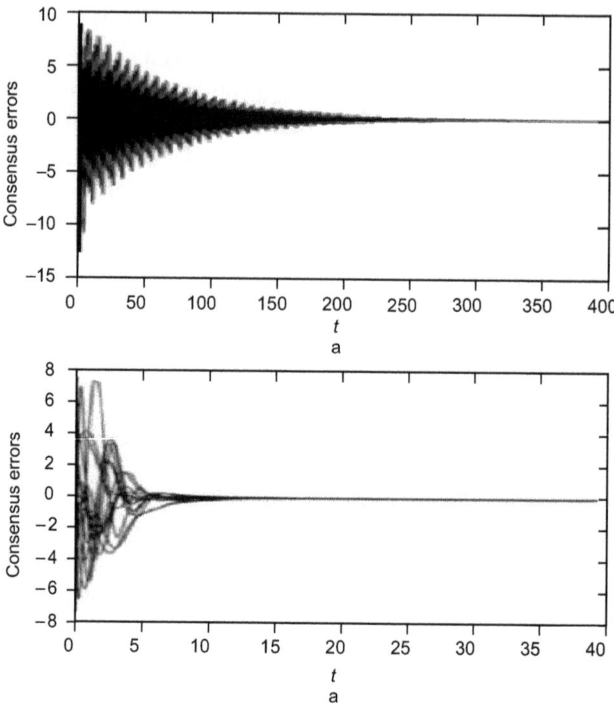

Figure 6.17: Consensus errors (a) **Algorithm** 1 (b) **Algorithm** 2 with $\alpha = 1$

where $c > 0$ and a_{ij} are the same as those defined in (6.72), and $F \in \Re^{p\times n}$ is the feedback gain matrix to be determined. For protocol (6.89), the dynamic consensus problem studied earlier reduces to the following static consensus problem.

Definition 6.4 *Protocol (6.89) is said to solve the (static) consensus problem if the states of agents (6.70) with (6.89) satisfy*

$$\lim_{t\to\infty} \|x_i(t) - x_j(t)\| = 0, \quad \forall i, j = 1, 2, \ldots, N \tag{6.90}$$

The following results are direct consequence of **Theorem** 6.3 in the static case.

Corollary 6.1

For graph G containing a directed spanning tree, there exists a protocol (6.89) solving the consensus problem if and only if all the matrices $A + c\lambda_i BF, i = 2, 3, \ldots, N$, are Hurwitz, where $\lambda_i,\ i = 2, 3, \ldots, N$, are the same as in **Theorem** *6.3. For the case where matrix A is neutrally stable, one has the following.*

Corollary 6.2
Given that $A \in \Re^{n\times n}$ is neutrally stable and that G has a directed spanning tree, there exists a protocol (6.89) solving the consensus problem and yielding a consensus region $(0,\infty)\times(-\infty,\infty)$, if and only if (A,B) is stabilizable.

A necessary and sufficient condition is obtained here as a consequence of **Theorem** 6.4. The method for constructing the protocol (6.89) is similar to **Algorithm** 6.1, therefore, it is omitted for brevity.

The design procedure for the protocol (6.89) solving consensus with a specification on the convergence speed is now presented.

Algorithm 6.3
For a controllable pair (A,B), a protocol (6.89) solving the consensus problem with a convergence speed larger than a can be constructed as follows:

1. *Choose the feedback gain matrix $F = -B^T P^{-1}$, where $P > 0$ is a solution to*

$$AP + PA^T - 2BB^T + 2\alpha P < 0$$

2. *Select the coupling strength $c \geq c_{th}$, with c_{th} given by (6.88).*

6.3.8 Formation control

In this section, the consensus algorithms are modified to solve formation control problems of multiagent systems.

Let $\tilde{H} = (h_1, h_2, \ldots, h_N) \in \Re^{n\times N}$ describe a constant formation structure of the agent network in a reference coordinate frame, where $h_i \in R_n$, is the formation variable corresponding to agent i. Then, variable $h_i - h_j$ can be used to denote the relative formation vector between agents i and j, which is independent of the reference coordinate. For the agents (6.70), a distributed formation protocol is proposed as

$$\begin{aligned} v_i^+ &= (A+BK)v_i + cL\Bigg(\sum_{j=1}^{N} d_{ij}C(v_i - -v_j) \\ &- \sum_{j=1}^{N} d_{ij}(y_i - y_j - C(h_i - h_j))\Bigg) \qquad (6.91) \\ u_i &= Kv_i \end{aligned}$$

where the variables are the same as those in (6.72). It should be noted that (6.91) reduces to the consensus protocol (6.72), when $h_i - h_j = 0,\ \forall\ i,j = 1,2,\ldots,N$.

Definition 6.5 *The agents (6.70) under protocol (6.91) achieve a given formation* $\tilde{H} = (h_1, h_2, \ldots, h_N)$, *if*

$$\lim_{t\to\infty} \|(x_i(t) - h_i) - (x_j(t) - h_j)\| \to 0, \quad \forall\ i, j = 1, 2, \ldots, N \tag{6.92}$$

Theorem 6.6

For graph G containing a directed spanning tree, the agents (6.70) reach the formation $\tilde{H}$ *under protocol (6.91) if all the matrices*

$$A + BK, \ A + c\lambda_i LC, \ \ i = 2, \ldots, N$$

are Hurwitz, and $Ah_i = 0$, $\forall\ i = 1, 2, \ldots, N$, *where* $\lambda_i, i = 2, 3, \ldots, N$, *are the non-zero eigenvalues of matrix L.*

Proof: Let $\tilde{x}_i = x_i - h_i$ and $\tilde{z}_i = [\tilde{x}_i^T, v_i^T]^T, i = 1, 2, \ldots, N$. Then, systems (6.70) and (6.91) together can be written as

$$\dot{\tilde{z}}_i = A\tilde{z}_i + c\sum_{j=1}^{N} L_{ij} H\tilde{z}_j + \begin{bmatrix} Ah_i \\ 0 \end{bmatrix} \quad , i = 1, 2, \quad , N \tag{6.93}$$

where matrices A and H are defined in (6.73). Note that the formation $\tilde{H}$ is achieved if system (6.93) reaches consensus, which, by (6.75), implies that $Ah_i = 0, \ \ i = 1, 2, \ldots, N$. The rest is similar to the proof of **Theorem** 6.3.

Remark 6.17 *Note that not all kinds of formation structure can be achieved for the agents (6.70) by using protocol (6.91) . The achievable formation structures have to satisfy the constraints* $Ah_i = 0$, $\forall\ i = 1, 2, \ldots, N$. *One should observe that* h_i *can be replaced by* $h_i - h_1, \ \ i = 2, \ldots, N$, *in order to be independent of the reference coordinate, by simply choosing* h_1 *corresponding to agent 1 as the origin. The formation protocol (6.91) satisfying* **Theorem** *6.6 can be constructed by using* **Algorithm** *6.1 or 6.2. Interestingly enough* **Theorem** *6.6 generalizes previous results.* ∎

6.3.9 *Illustrative example 6.3*

Consider a network of six double integrators, described by

$$\begin{aligned} \dot{x}_i &= v_i \\ \dot{v}_i &= u_i \\ y_i &= x_i, \quad i = 1, 2, \quad , 6 \end{aligned}$$

where $x_i \in \Re^2$, $\tilde{v}_i \in \Re^2$, $y_i \in \Re^2$ and $u_i \in R^2$ are the position, velocity, measured output and acceleration input of agent i, respectively.

The objective is to design a dynamic protocol (6.91) such that the agents will evolve to form a regular hexagon with edge length 4. Taking into consideration that the spacecraft's dynamics in deep space can be modeled as a double integrator, this example may have possible applications in deep-space formation flying missions.

In this case, choose

$$\begin{aligned} h_1 &= \begin{bmatrix} 0 & 0 & 0 & 0 \end{bmatrix}^T, \ h_2 = \begin{bmatrix} 4 & 0 & 0 & 0 \end{bmatrix}^T, \\ h_3 &= \begin{bmatrix} 6 & 2\sqrt{3} & 0 & 0 \end{bmatrix}^T, \ h_4 = \begin{bmatrix} 4 & 4\sqrt{3} & 0 & 0 \end{bmatrix}^T \\ h_5 &= \begin{bmatrix} 0 & 4\sqrt{3} & 0 & 0 \end{bmatrix}^T, \ h_6 = \begin{bmatrix} -2 & 2\sqrt{3} & 0 & 0 \end{bmatrix}^T \end{aligned}$$

We take

$$K = \begin{bmatrix} -1.5 & -2.5 \end{bmatrix} \otimes I_2$$

in (6.91), such that matrix

$$\lambda(A+BK) := \{-1, \ -1.5\}$$

By solving LMI (6.86) with $\alpha = 1$, one obtains

$$L = \begin{bmatrix} -3.6606 & -4.8221 \end{bmatrix}^T \otimes I_2$$

By **Theorem** 6.6 and **Algorithm** 6.2 , the six agents under protocol (6.91) with K, L given as above, and $c = 1$ will form a regular hexagon with a convergence rate larger than 1 for the communication topology given in Fig. 6.16. The state trajectories of the six agents are depicted in Fig. 6.18.

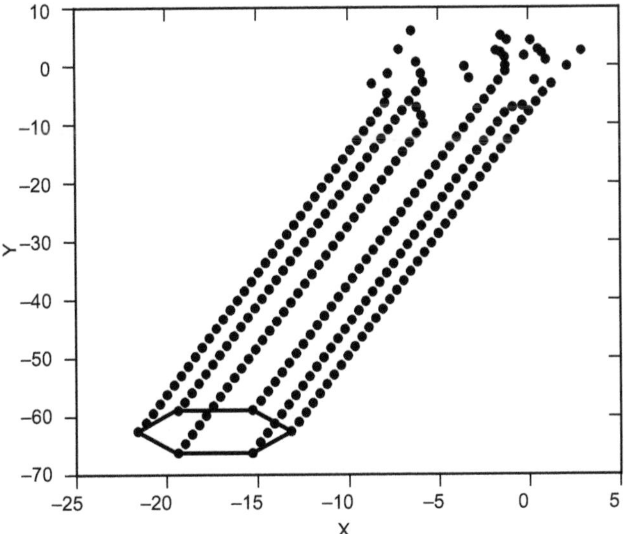

Figure 6.18: Six agents form a hexagon

6.4 Consensus Control for Time-Delay Systems

Time-delays resulting from interconnection links have been paid much attention regarding multiagent systems because of the practical background. A necessary and sufficient condition for a time-delay consensus problem was presented for the agents with first-order dynamics and undirected interconnection graph in [18]. Consensus problems for multiple agents with interconnection time delays are discussed. Local controller for each agent is neighbor-based, as was done in many references related to agent-based control systems.

6.4.1 Problem formulation

In this section, a consensus problem will be formulated mathematically for a leaderless multiagent system with double-integrator dynamics and time-varying interconnection delays. Then, we introduce some basic concepts and notations in algebraic graph theory and functional differential equations that will be used [10].

Consider a group of n identical agents move in an m- dimensional space and the agents are indexed by $1,\ldots,n$. A continuous-time model of the $i$xth agent is described by a second-order differential equation, as follows.

$$\begin{cases} \dot{x}_i = v_i, \\ \dot{v}_i = u_i \end{cases} \tag{6.94}$$

where $x_i \in \Re^m$ can be the position (or angle) of agent $i, v_i \in \Re^m$ its velocity (or angular velocity) and $u_i \in \Re^m$ its interconnection control inputs for $i = 1,\ldots,n$.

In the sequel, a free consensus problem of system (6.94) is solved if $x_i = x_j, v_i = v_j$ for all $i, j \in I = \{1,\ldots,n\}$. In order to enable the agents to achieve consensus along with interconnection delays, consensus control schemes have to be constructed for all mobile agents. The design of neighbor-based feedback $u_i(t)$ usually depends on $x_j(t), v_j(t)$ for some $j \in N_i$, which denotes the index set of the neighbors of agent i. However, in practice, there may be interconnection delays, and each agent cannot instantly obtain the information from others. Thus, the feedback $u_i(t)$ should be constructed based on the information of $x_j(t-r(t))$ and $v_j(t-r(t))$ for some $j \in N_i$ and time-varying delay $r(t) > 0$, a continuously differentiable function satisfying

$$0 < r(t) < \tau \tag{6.95}$$

To deal with this consensus problem for system (6.94), we propose the following local control scheme

$$u_i(t) \;=\; k^2\Bigg(\sum_{j \in N_i(\sigma)} a_{ij}(x_j(t-r) - x_i(t-r))$$

$$+k\sum_{j\in N_i(\sigma)} a_{ij}(v_j(t-r)-v_i(t-r))\Bigg), \quad k>0 \tag{6.96}$$

where $\sigma:[0,\infty)\to I_\Gamma=\{1,\ldots,N\}$ (N denotes the total number of all possible interconnection topologies). If the system (6.94) is free of time delay (i.e., $r\equiv 0$), then the consensus control (6.96) becomes

$$u_i(t)=k^2\left(\sum_{j\in N_i(\sigma)} a_{ij}(x_j(t)-x_i(t))+k\sum_{j\in N_i(\sigma)} a_{ij}(v_j(t)-v_i(t))\right)$$

which is consistent with the consensus rules in [5].

If each agent is regarded as a node, then the interconnection topology associated with the agents is conveniently described by a simple graph, see [18]. Let $G=(V,E,A)$ be a weighted digraph of order n with the set of nodes $V=\{1,2,\ldots,n\}$, set of arcs $E\subseteq V\times V$ and a weighted adjacency matrix $A=[a_{ij}]\in\Re^{n\times n}$ with non-negative elements. The node indexes belong to a finite index set $I=\{1,2,\ldots,n\}$. An arc of G is denoted by (i,j), which starts from i and ends on j when agent j is a neighbor of agent i. The element a_{ij} associated with the arc of the digraph is positive, that is $a_{ij}>0\Leftrightarrow(i,j)\in E$. Moreover, we assume $a_{ii}=0$ for all $i\in I$. The index set of neighbors of node i is denoted by $N_i=\{j\in V:(i,j)\in E\}$. If $\sum_{j\in N_i(\sigma)}a_{ij}=\sum_{j\in N_i(\sigma)}a_{ji}$ for all $i=1,\ldots,n$, the digraph G is called balanced. A cluster is any subset J,V of the nodes of the digraph. The set of neighbors of a cluster J is defined by $N_J=\cup_{i\in J}N_i=\{j\in V:i\in J,(i,j)\in E\}$. A path in a digraph is a sequence $i_0,i_1,\ldots,i_f$ of distinct nodes such that (i_{j-1},i_j) is an arc for $j=1,2,\ldots,f, f\in Z^+$. If there exists a path from node i to node j, we say that j is reachable from i. A digraph G is strongly connected if any two distinct nodes are reachable from each other. A strong component of a digraph is an induced subgraph that is maximal, subject to being strongly connected. If a node i is reachable from every other node in G, then we say it is globally reachable, which is much weaker than strong connectedness.

A diagonal matrix $D=diag\{d_1,\ldots,d_n\}\in R^{n\times n}$ is a degree matrix of G, whose diagonal elements $d_i=\sum_{j\in N_i}a_{ij}$ for $i=1,\ldots,n$. Then the Laplacian of the weighted digraph is defined as

$$L=D-A$$

The next lemma shows an important property of Laplacian L associated with G [18].

Lemma 6.6

L has least one zero eigenvalue with $1\in\Re^n$ as its eigenvector, and all the non-zero eigenvalues of L have positive real parts. Laplacian L has a simple zero eigenvalue if and only if G has a globally reachable node.

Let $S_1, S_2, \ldots, S-p$ be the strong components of $G = (V, \varepsilon, A)$ and N_{S_i} be the neighbor sets for $S_i, i = 1, \ldots, p, p > 1$.

Lemma 6.7

A digraph $G = (V, E, A)$ has a globally reachable node if and only if every pair of S_i, S_j satisfies $N_{S_i} \cup N_{S_j} \neq \emptyset$. Moreover, if the graph is strongly connected, then each node is globally reachable from every other node.

In the sequel, the interconnection topologies will be discussed in two cases. A fixed topology, described by a digraph, is considered first, and then variable topologies described by balanced digraphs are analyzed. To model varying interconnection topology, we introduce a function $\sigma : [0, \infty) \to I_\Gamma = \{1, \ldots, N\}$, which is a switching signal to show the sequence of the switched interconnection topologies over time. The set $\Gamma = \{G_1, \ldots, G_N\}$ is a finite collection of graphs with a common node set V. If σ is a constant function, then the corresponding interconnection topology is fixed. In addition, $N_i(\sigma)$ is the index set of neighbors of agent i in the digraph g_σ, whereas $a_{ij}(i, j = 1, \ldots, n)$ are elements of the adjacency matrix of g_σ.

Introducing

$$x = \begin{bmatrix} x_1 \\ x_2 \\ \vdots \\ x_n \end{bmatrix} \in \Re^{mn}, \quad v = \begin{bmatrix} v_1 \\ v_2 \\ \vdots \\ v_n \end{bmatrix} \in \Re^{mn},$$

$$u = \begin{bmatrix} u_1 \\ u_2 \\ \vdots \\ u_n \end{bmatrix} \in \Re^{mn}$$

Then, with the control scheme (6.96), the closed-loop system (6.94) can be rewritten in the following form

$$\begin{cases} \dot{x} = v \\ \dot{v} = u = -k^2(L_\sigma \otimes I_m)(x(t-r) + kv(t-r)) \end{cases} \tag{6.97}$$

where $\otimes$ denotes the Kronecker product [10].

Before the consensus stability of system (6.97) is analyzed, we refer the reader to Section 9.1 in the Appendix where the stability notions of time-delay systems were treated.

In the sequel, we will analyze the consensus stability of multiagent systems with time delays under controller (6.96).

6.4.2 Fixed interconnection topology

In this section, we will focus on the convergence analysis of the system (6.97) when the switching signal is constant (or equivalently, the interconnection topology is fixed). Then, the subscript σ is dropped, for simplicity, and the system (6.97) can be expressed with the following linear delayed differential equations

$$\begin{cases} \dot{x} = v \\ \dot{v} = -k^2(L \otimes I_m)(x(t-r) + kv(t-r)) \end{cases} \tag{6.98}$$

To solve the consensus problem of the system (6.98), we recall the following result.

Lemma 6.8

For Laplacian L associated with digraph G, then there exists a non-singular matrix

$$U = \begin{pmatrix} 1 & * & \dots & * \\ 1 & * & \dots & * \\ \vdots & \vdots & & \vdots \\ 1 & * & \dots & * \end{pmatrix} \in \Re^{n \times n} \tag{6.99}$$

such that

$$\begin{aligned} U^{-1}LU &= \begin{pmatrix} 0 & \alpha^T \\ 0_{n-1} & H \end{pmatrix} = \Lambda \in \Re^{n \times n}, \quad \alpha \in \Re^{n-1}, \\ & H \in \Re^{(n-1) \times (n-1)} \end{aligned} \tag{6.100}$$

According to **Lemma** 6.8, with a coordinate transformation

$$\bar{x} = (U^{-1} \otimes I_m)x, \quad \bar{v} = (U^{-1} \otimes I_m)v \tag{6.101}$$

the system (6.98) becomes

$$\begin{cases} \dot{\bar{x}} = \bar{v} \\ \dot{\bar{v}} = -k^3(\Lambda \otimes I_m) - k^2(\Lambda \otimes I_m)\bar{x}(t-r) \end{cases}$$

or equivalently

$$\begin{cases} \dot{\bar{x}}_1 = \bar{v}_1 \\ \dot{\bar{v}}_1 = -k^3(\alpha^T \otimes I_m)\bar{v}_2(t-r) - k^2(\alpha^T \otimes I_m)\bar{x}_2(t-r) \end{cases} \tag{6.102}$$

and

$$\begin{cases} \dot{\bar{x}}_2 = \bar{v}_2 \\ \dot{\bar{v}}_2 = -k^3(H \otimes I_m)\bar{v}_2(t-r) - k^2(H \otimes I_m)\bar{x}_2(t-r) \end{cases} \tag{6.103}$$

where

$$\bar{x} = \begin{pmatrix} \bar{x}_1 \\ \bar{x}_2 \end{pmatrix}, \quad \bar{v} = \begin{pmatrix} \bar{v}_1 \\ \bar{v}_2 \end{pmatrix}, \quad \bar{x}_1, \bar{v}_1 \in \Re^m,$$

$$\bar{x}_2, \bar{v}_2 \in \Re^{m(n-1)}$$

for the subsystem (6.103), let $\varepsilon = (\bar{x}_2^T, \bar{v}_2^T)^T \in \Re^{2m(n-1)}$. Then, we have a compact form

$$\dot{\varepsilon} = B\varepsilon(t) + E\varepsilon(t-r) \tag{6.104}$$

where

$$\begin{aligned} B &= \begin{pmatrix} O_{(n-1)\times(n-1)} & I_{n-1} \\ 0_{(n-1)\times(n-1)} & 0_{(n-1)\times(n-1)} \end{pmatrix} \otimes I_m, \\ E &= \begin{pmatrix} O_{(n-1)\times(n-1)} & 0_{(n-1)\times(n-1)} \\ -k^2 H & -k^3 H \end{pmatrix} \otimes I_m \end{aligned}$$

Remark 6.18 *From* **Lemmas** *6.6 and 6.8, if graph G has a globally reachable node, the real parts of all the eigenvalues of $H \in \Re^{(n-1)\times(n-1)}$ are positive, or equivalently, $-H$ is Hurwitz stable. Therefore, there exist a positive-definite matrix $\bar{P} \in \Re^{(n-1)\times(n-1)}$ such that*

$$\bar{P}H + H^T\bar{P} = I_{n-1} \tag{6.105}$$

Let $\bar{\lambda}_l$ (or λ) denote the minimum (or maximum) eigenvalue of $-P$ and μ the maximum eigenvalue of $H^T\bar{P}^T\bar{P}H$. Let $\lambda_{\min}$ be the minimum eigenvalue of $-(PF+F^TP)$ with $F = B+E$. Then, a result can be obtained for system (6.98). ▮

Theorem 6.7

For system (6.98), take

$$k > k_1^* = \max\left\{\sqrt{\frac{1}{2}\lambda + 1}, \frac{\mu}{\bar{\lambda}} + 1\right\} \tag{6.106}$$

and assume that

$$\tau \le \tau_1^* = \frac{\lambda_{\min}}{k^4 + k^6 + \|PE^2P^{-1}E^{2^T}P\| + 2q(k+1)\lambda} \tag{6.107}$$

where $q > 1$. Then, the free consensus problem of the system (6.98) is solved if and only if G has a globally reachable node.

Proof: $\Longleftarrow$ Since G has a globally reachable node, zero is a simple eigenvalue of Laplacian L, whereas other eigenvalues have positive real parts, see **Lemma** 6.6. By **Lemma** 6.8, there exists a nonsingular matrix U, given in (6.99), such that L can be transformed to (6.100), where H has eigenvalues with positive real parts. Then, there is a positive-definite matrix $\bar{P}$ satisfying (6.105).

For system (6.104), take a Lyapunov–Razumikhin function

$$V(\varepsilon) = \varepsilon^T P \varepsilon \tag{6.108}$$

where

$$P = \begin{pmatrix} k\bar{P} & \bar{P} \\ \bar{P} & k\bar{P} \end{pmatrix} \otimes I_m$$

is positive definite since $k > 1$.

Furthermore, by Leibniz–Newton formula

$$\begin{aligned} \varepsilon(t-r) &= \varepsilon(t) - \int_{-r}^{0} \dot{\varepsilon}(t+s)ds \\ &= \varepsilon(t) - B\int_{-r}^{0} \varepsilon(t+s)ds - E\int_{-r}^{0} \varepsilon(t-r+s)ds \end{aligned}$$

Therefore, (6.104) can be rewritten as

$$\dot{\varepsilon} = F\varepsilon - EB\int_{-r}^{0} \varepsilon(t+s)ds - E^2\int_{-r}^{0} \varepsilon(t-r+s)ds \tag{6.109}$$

for arbitrary initial function on $[-2\tau, 0]$. If the zero solution of (6.109) is asymptotically stable, then the zero solution of (6.104) is asymptotically stable, since (6.104) is a special case of (6.109) with continuous initial function $\tilde{\varphi}(s)$ given by $\tilde{\varphi}(s)$ arbitrary for $s \in [-2\tau, -\tau - r(0)]$, $\tilde{\varphi}(s) = \varphi(s + r(0))$, $-\tau - r(0) \leq s \leq -r(0)$, and $\tilde{\varphi}(s) = \varepsilon(t+s)$, $-r(0) \leq s \leq 0$ where $\varepsilon(t)$ is the solution of (6.104) with initial function φ on $[-\tau, 0]$.

Setting $\eta_1 = \varepsilon(t), \eta_2 = \varepsilon(t+s), \eta_3 = E^{2^T}P\varepsilon(t-r+s), \eta_4 = \varepsilon(t-r+s), M_1 = PEB = Y_1, M_2 = I_{2m(n-1)} = Y_2, X_1 = k^4(1+k^2)I_{2m(n-1)}, X_2 = P^{-1}$ and $Z_1 = Z_2 = P$. Invoking a standard bounding inequality, [74] gives (6.106), and leads to

$$\begin{aligned} \dot{V} &= \varepsilon^T(F^TP + PF)\varepsilon - 2\int_{-r}^{0} \varepsilon^T PEB\varepsilon(t+s)ds \\ &\quad -2\int_{-r}^{0} \varepsilon^T PE^2\varepsilon(t-r+s)ds \\ &\leq \varepsilon^T(FTP + PF)\varepsilon + rk^4(1+k^2)\varepsilon^T\varepsilon \\ &\quad + \int_{-r}^{0} \varepsilon^T(t+s)P\varepsilon(t+s)ds + r\varepsilon^T PE^2P^{-1}E^{2^T}P\varepsilon \\ &\quad + \int_{-r}^{0} \varepsilon^T(t-r+s)P\varepsilon(t-r+s)ds \end{aligned}$$

Take $\phi(s) = qs$ for some constant $q > 1$. In the case of

$$V(\varepsilon(t+\theta)) \leq qV(\varepsilon(t)), \quad -2\tau \leq \theta \leq 0 \tag{6.110}$$

we have, with **Remark** 6.18,

$$\dot{V} \leq -\varepsilon^T Q\varepsilon + r\varepsilon^T((k^4 + k^6)I_{2m(n-1)} + PE^2P^{-1}E^{2^T} + 2qP)\varepsilon$$

where

$$Q = -(F^T P + PF) = \begin{pmatrix} k^2 I_{n-1} & k^3 I_{n-1} - k\bar{P} \\ k^3 I_{n-1} - k\bar{P} & k^4 I_{n-1} - 2\bar{P} \end{pmatrix} \otimes I_m$$

Q is positive definite if k satisfies (6.106), according to Schur complements [60]. Let $\lambda_{\min}$ denote the minimum eigenvalues of Q. If we take the upper bound τ_1^* in (6.107), then $\dot{V}(\varepsilon) \leq -\eta \varepsilon^T \varepsilon$ for some $\eta > 0$. By the Lyapunov–Razumikhin Theorem, we conclude that $\bar{x}_2 \to 0_{m(n-1)}, \bar{v}_2 \to 0_{m(n-1)}$ as $t \to \infty$.

On the other hand, for the system (6.102), let $\bar{x}_1(0), \bar{v}_1(0)$ be the initial values of $\bar{x}_1(t), \bar{v}_1(t)$ and take a variable of change $\tilde{x}_1 = \bar{x}_1 - (\bar{v}_1(0)t + \bar{x}_1(0)), \tilde{v}_1 = \bar{v}_1 - \bar{v}_1(0)$. Then, the solution can be given by the following integral equation

$$\begin{pmatrix} \tilde{x}_1 \\ \tilde{v}_1 \end{pmatrix} = \int_0^t \begin{pmatrix} I_m & (t-s)I_m \\ 0_m & I_m \end{pmatrix} \times \begin{pmatrix} 0_m \\ -k^3(\alpha^T \otimes I_m)\bar{v}_2(s-r) - k^2(\alpha^T \otimes I_m)\bar{x}_2(s-r) \end{pmatrix} ds \quad (6.111)$$

As discussed before, the system (6.103) is uniformly asymptotically stable, which implies its exponential stability according to **Lemma** 5.3 of [60]. Thus, solution (6.111) has a exponential decay term with respect to time t and so, it is convergent to zero as $t \to \infty$. Consequently, we have

$$\begin{aligned} \begin{pmatrix} \bar{x}_1 \\ \bar{x}_2 \end{pmatrix} &- \begin{pmatrix} \bar{v}_1(0)t + \bar{x}_1(0) \\ 0_{m(n-1)} \end{pmatrix} \to 0_{mn}, \begin{pmatrix} \bar{v}_1 \\ \bar{v}_2 \end{pmatrix} \\ &\to \begin{pmatrix} \bar{v}_1(0) \\ 0_{m(n-1)} \end{pmatrix}, \text{as } t \to \infty \end{aligned}$$

From transformation (6.101), we have

$$\begin{aligned} x &- (U \otimes I_m) \begin{pmatrix} \bar{v}_1(0)t + \bar{x}_1(0) \\ 0_{m(n-1)} \end{pmatrix} \\ &= x - \mathbf{1} \otimes (\bar{v}_1(0)t + \bar{x}_1(0)) \to 0_{mn} \\ v &= (U \otimes I_m)\bar{v} \to (U \otimes I_m) \begin{pmatrix} \bar{v}_1(0) \\ 0_{m(n-1)} \end{pmatrix} = \mathbf{1} \otimes \bar{v}_1(0) \end{aligned}$$

Therefore, $x_i - x_j \to 0_{mn}, v_i - v_j \to 0_{mn}$ for all $i, j \in I$ as $t \to \infty$. The conclusion follows.

$\Longrightarrow$ It will be proved by contradiction. If G has no globally reachable node, then, from **Lemma** 6.7, there are at least two strong components of G having no neighbor sets. Thus, we renumber the nodes of G and L can be transformed to the following form

$$L = \begin{pmatrix} L_{11} & 0 & 0 \\ 0 & L_{22} & 0 \\ L_{31} & L_{32} & L_{33} \end{pmatrix} \quad (6.112)$$

where 0 denotes some zero matrices with appropriate dimensions and $L_{11} \in \Re^{k_1 \times k_1}, L_{22} \in R^{k_2 \times k_2} (k_1 + k_2 < n)$ are the Laplacians associated with two strong components, respectively.

Then, the system (6.98) can be expressed as

$$\begin{cases} \dot{x}_1 = v_1, \\ \dot{v}_1 = -k^3(L_{11} \otimes I_m)v_1(t-r) - k^2(L_{11} \otimes I_m)x_1(t-r) \end{cases} \tag{6.113}$$

$$\begin{cases} \dot{x}_2 = v_2, \\ \dot{v}_2 = -k^3(L_{22} \otimes I_m)v_2(t-r) - k^2(L_{22} \otimes I_m)x_2(t-r) \end{cases} \tag{6.114}$$

$$\begin{cases} \dot{x}_3 = v_3, \\ \dot{v}_3 = -k^3([L_{31}\ L_{32}\ L_{33}] \otimes I_m)v(t-r) \\ \qquad -k^2([L_{31}\ L_{32}\ L_{33}] \otimes I_m)x(t-r) \end{cases} \tag{6.115}$$

where

$$x = \begin{pmatrix} x_1 \\ x_2 \\ x_3 \end{pmatrix}, v = \begin{pmatrix} v_1 \\ v_2 \\ v_3 \end{pmatrix}, \quad x_1, v_1 \in \Re^{mk_1},$$
$$x_2, v_2 \in \Re^{mk_2}, \quad x_3, v_3 \in \Re^{m(n-k_1-K_1)}$$

Similar to the proof of sufficient condition, it is not hard to obtain that $x_1 - 1_{k_1} \otimes (\nu_1 t + \delta_1) \to 0_{mk_1}, v_1 \to 1_{k_1} \otimes \nu_1$ and $x_2 - 1_{k_2} \otimes (\nu_2 t + \delta_2) \to 0_{mk_2}, v_2 \to 1_{k_2} \otimes \nu_2$ for some constants $\nu_1, \delta_1, \nu_2, \delta_2$ as $t \to \infty$. Since ν_1, δ_1 and ν_2, δ_2 can be set arbitrarily, the system (6.98) cannot reach a consensus, which leads to a contradiction.

Remark 6.19 *During the derivations of the bounds on k_1^* and τ_1^*, high-order inequalities and the bounds on matrix function need to be solved, many zoom techniques have to be applied and, hence, the results may be very conservative.* ▌

6.4.3 Switched interconnection topology

We now consider the convergence of time-delay system (6.97) for the switched interconnection topology. Since it is hard to do this for switched interconnection topologies described by general digraphs, a special class of digraphs, that is, balanced digraphs, are considered in the subsequent stability analysis, see the Appendix.

With a coordinate transformation

$$x = (V^* \otimes I_m)x, \quad \bar{v} = (V^* \otimes I_m)v \tag{6.116}$$

the system (6.97) becomes

$$\begin{cases} \dot{\bar{x}}_1 = \bar{v}_1 \\ \dot{\bar{v}}_1 = 0_m \end{cases} \tag{6.117}$$

$$\begin{cases} \dot{\bar{x}}_2 = \bar{v}_2, \\ \dot{\bar{v}}_2 = -k^3(H_\sigma \otimes I_m)\bar{v}_2(t-r) - k^2(H_\sigma \otimes I_m)\bar{x}_2(t-r) \end{cases} \tag{6.118}$$

where $\bar{x}_1, \bar{v}_1 \in C^m, \bar{x}_2, \bar{v}_2 \in C^{m(n-1)}$.

Consider (6.118), or equivalently

$$\dot{\varepsilon} = B\varepsilon(t) + E_\sigma \varepsilon(t-r) \tag{6.119}$$

where

$$B = \begin{pmatrix} 0_{(n-1)\times(n-1)} & I_{n-1} \\ 0_{(n-1)\times(n-1)} & 0_{(n-1)\times(n-1)} \end{pmatrix} \otimes I_m,$$

$$E_\sigma = \begin{pmatrix} 0_{(n-1)\times(n-1)} & 0_{(n-1)\times(n-1)} \\ -k^2 H_\sigma & -k^3 H_\sigma \end{pmatrix} \otimes I_m$$

Based on **Lemma** 1.3 and the fact that the set I_Γ is finite, if the balanced digraph G_σ has a globally reachable node

$$\begin{aligned} \tilde{\lambda} &= \min\{\text{eigenvalues of} H_\sigma + H_\sigma^*\} > 0 \\ \tilde{\mu} &= \max\{\text{eigenvalues of} H_\sigma H_\sigma^*\} > 0 \end{aligned}$$

can be well defined. Let $F_\sigma = B + E_\sigma$ and $\tilde{\lambda}_{\min}$ denotes the minimum eigenvalue of all possible $-(\tilde{P}F_\sigma + F_\sigma \tilde{P})$.

A result of the switched system (6.97) with time-varying delay is given as follows:

Theorem 6.8

For system (6.97) with balanced interconnection topology G_σ, take

$$k > k_2^* = \max\left\{\sqrt{\frac{1}{2\tilde{\lambda}} + 1}, \tilde{\mu} + 1\right\} \tag{6.120}$$

and assume that

$$\tau < \tau_2^* = \frac{\tilde{\lambda}_{\min}}{k^4 + k^6 + (k^{13} + k^{11})\tilde{\mu}^2 + 2q(k+1)} \tag{6.121}$$

with $q > 1$. Then the free consensus problem of the system (6.97) is solved if G_σ has a globally reachable node.

Proof: To obtain the result, we first consider (6.118). Take a Lyapunov–Razumikhin function

$$V(\varepsilon) = \varepsilon^* \tilde{P} \varepsilon \tag{6.122}$$

where

$$\tilde{P} = \begin{pmatrix} kI_{n-1} & I_{n-1} \\ I_{n-1} & kI_{n-1} \end{pmatrix} \otimes I_m$$

is positive definite for $k > 1$.

Similar to the proof of **Theorem** 6.7, we can obtain

$$\begin{aligned} \dot{V}|_{(33)} &= \varepsilon^T(F_\sigma^T \tilde{P} + \tilde{P} F_\sigma)\varepsilon - 2\varepsilon^T \tilde{P} E_\sigma B \int_{-r}^{0} \varepsilon(t+s)ds \\ &\quad -2\varepsilon^T \tilde{P} E_\sigma^2 \int_{-r}^{0} \varepsilon(t-r+s)ds \end{aligned}$$

By a standard bounding inequality [74], it follows that

$$\begin{aligned} \dot{V}|_{(33)} &\leq \varepsilon^T(F_\sigma^T \tilde{P} + \tilde{P} F_\sigma)\varepsilon + r(k^4+k^6)\varepsilon^*\varepsilon \\ &\quad + \int_{-r}^{0} \varepsilon^*(t+s)\tilde{P}\varepsilon(t+s)ds \\ &\quad + r\varepsilon^T \tilde{P} E_\sigma^2 \tilde{P}^{-1} E_\sigma^{2^T} \tilde{P}\varepsilon \\ &\quad + \int_{-r}^{0} \varepsilon^*(t-r+s)\tilde{P}\varepsilon(t-r+s)ds \end{aligned}$$

Set $\phi(s) = qs$ for some constant $q > 1$. In the case of

$$V(\varepsilon(t+\theta)) < qV(\varepsilon(t)), \quad -2\tau \leq \theta \leq 0 \tag{6.123}$$

we have

$$\begin{aligned} \dot{V} &\leq -\varepsilon^T Q_\sigma \varepsilon + r\varepsilon^T((k^4+k^6)I_{2m(n-1)} \\ &\quad + \tilde{P} E_\sigma^2 \tilde{p}^{-1} E_\sigma^2 \tilde{p} + 2q\tilde{p})\varepsilon \end{aligned}$$

where

$$\begin{aligned} Q_\sigma &= -(F_\sigma^T \Phi + \Phi F_\sigma) \\ &= \begin{pmatrix} k^2(H_\sigma^* + H_\sigma) & k^3(H_\sigma^* + H_\sigma) - kI_{n-1} \\ k^3(H_\sigma^* + H_\sigma) - kI_{n-1} & k^4(H_\sigma^* + H_\sigma) - 2I_n \end{pmatrix} \otimes I_m \end{aligned}$$

Clearly, Q_σ is positive definite and then $\dot{V}(\varepsilon)$ is negative definite if k is taken as (6.120) and

$$r < \tau \leq \tau_2^*$$

where τ_2^* is defined in equation (6.121). Thus, the subsystem (6.118) converges to $0_{2m(n-1)}$ according to the Lyapunov–Razumikhin Theorem, see the Appendix. On the other hand, for the system (6.117),

$$\bar{x}_1 = \bar{v}_1(0)t + \bar{x}_1(0), \quad \bar{v}_1 = \bar{v}_1(0)$$

with

$$\bar{x}_1(0) = (1/\sqrt{n})\sum_{i=1}^{n} x_i(0), \quad \bar{v}_1(0) = (1/\sqrt{n})\sum_{i=1}^{n} v_i(0)$$

Then, with the transformation (6.116), we have

$$\begin{aligned} x & - (V\otimes I_m)\begin{pmatrix} \bar{v}_1(0)t+\bar{x}_1(0) \\ 0_{m(n-1)} \end{pmatrix} \\ &= x - 1\otimes \frac{1}{n}\sum_{i=1}^{n} x_i(0) \to 0_{mn} \end{aligned} \tag{6.124}$$

$$v \to (V\otimes I_m)\begin{pmatrix} \bar{v}_1(0) \\ 0_{m(n-1)} \end{pmatrix} = 1\otimes \frac{1}{n}\sum_{i=1}^{n} v_i(0) \tag{6.125}$$

which concludes the proof.

Remark 6.20 *In* **Theorem** *6.8, when we consider the stability of second-order time-delay system, by saying G_σ has a globally reachable node, we mean that every possible graph in the interconnection evolution has a globally reachable node. This is stronger than the usual requirement. There is $T \geq 0$, such that for all $t_0 > 0$ there is a node connected to all other nodes across $[t_0, t_0+T]$, that is, the opposite graph, which is formed by changing the orientation of each arc of $g([t_0,t_0+T]) = (V, \cup_{t\in[t_0,t_0+T]} E(t))$, has a globally reachable node.* ▮

Remark 6.21 *In fact, with balanced graphs, the position x_i and the velocity v_i of agent $i(i=1,\ldots,n)$ in the considered multiagent system converge to the average values of initial positions (that is, $(1/n)\sum_{i=1}^{n} x_i(0)$) and initial velocities (that is, $(1/n)\sum_{i=1}^{n} v_i(0)$), respectively, because of (6.124) and (6.125).* ▮

In the following section, some numerical examples are provided to illustrate the theoretical results in order.

6.4.4 Illustrative example 6.4

Consider different number of agents are moving in a plane (i.e., $m = 2$) with ring-shaped interconnection G_1 and G_2, respectively (see Figs. 6.19a and b).

It is not difficult to obtain two Laplacians associated with G_1 and G_2 as follows

$$L_1 = \frac{1}{4}\begin{pmatrix} 1 & -1 & 0 & 0 \\ 0 & 1 & -1 & 0 \\ 0 & 0 & 1 & -1 \\ -1 & 0 & 0 & 1 \end{pmatrix}$$

$$L_2 = \frac{1}{4}\begin{pmatrix} 1 & -1 & 0 & 0 & 0 \\ 0 & 1 & -1 & 0 & 0 \\ 0 & 0 & 1 & -1 & 0 \\ 0 & 0 & 0 & 1 & -1 \\ -1 & 0 & 0 & 0 & 1 \end{pmatrix}$$

Then, for the two interconnection topologies G_1, G_2, we can obtain $k_1^* = 1.5000, k_2^* = 2.0170$ and the upper bounds $\tau_1^* = 0.0104, \tau_2^* = 0.0011$, which shows that k^* will increase and τ^* will decrease as the number of agents become large.

6.4.5 Illustrative example 6.5

Consider the interconnection topology is switching between G_1 and G_3 (see Figs. 6.19 and 6.20) while four agents are moving in a plane. Suppose that the time varying interconnection delay is given by $r(t) = 0.01|\cos(t)|$ and the switching signal $\sigma(t) = \{G_1, G_3, G_1, G_3, \ldots\}$. The initial positions and velocities are given as follows

$$\begin{aligned} x(0) &= [0;1;0;0;1;0;1;1]^T; \\ v(0) &= [-1;1;2:5;-1.5;-2;-1;1;2]^T \end{aligned}$$

By using the proposed consensus algorithm (6.96) for four agents with time delay $r(t)$, the simulation results are shown in Figs. 6.21 and 6.22. It can be seen that all the agents will reach consensus while the interconnection is dynamically changing and there exist time-varying delays in the local interactions between agents from Fig. 6.21. From Fig. 6.22, we also find that the velocity of each agent

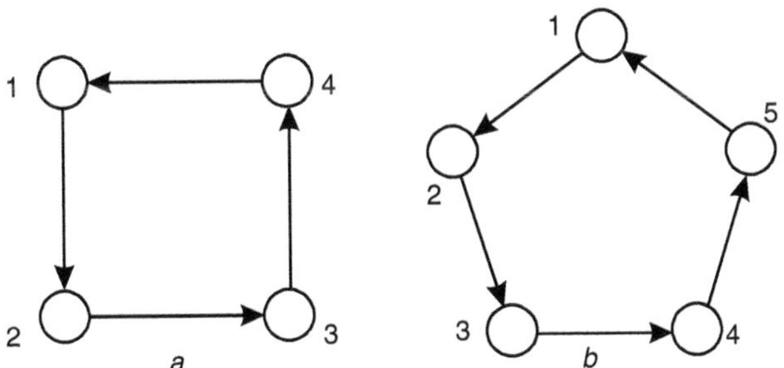

Figure 6.19: Interconnection topologies

a G_1 for four agents

b G_2 for five agents

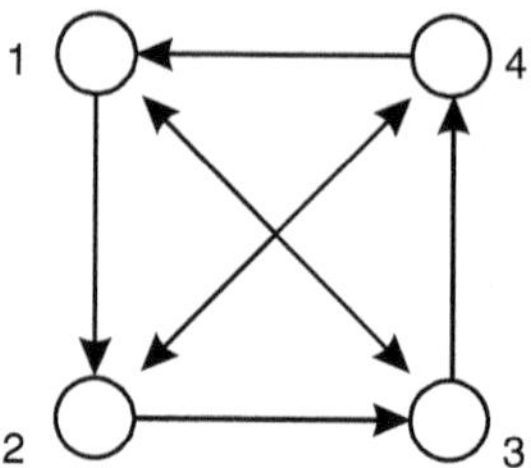

Figure 6.20: Interconnection topology G_3 for four agents

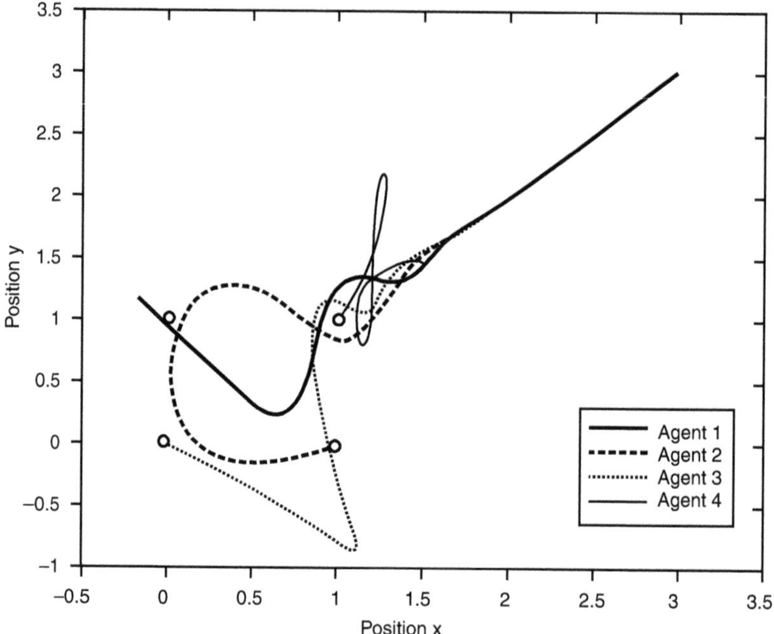

Figure 6.21: Position evolutions

will approach the average of the initial values, that is, $v_i(t) \to 1/4\sum_{j=1}^{4} v_j(0) = v^* = [0.125, 0.125]^T$ as $t \to \infty$.

6.5 Robust Consensus of Multiagent Systems

We are concerned here with consensus problems for a class of multiagent systems with second-order dynamics. Some dynamic neighbor-based rules are adopted for the agents with the consideration of parameter uncertainties and external disturbances. Sufficient conditions are derived to make all agents asymptotically reach consensus while satisfying desired H_∞ performance. Finally, numerical simulations are provided in order to show the effectiveness of our theoretical results.

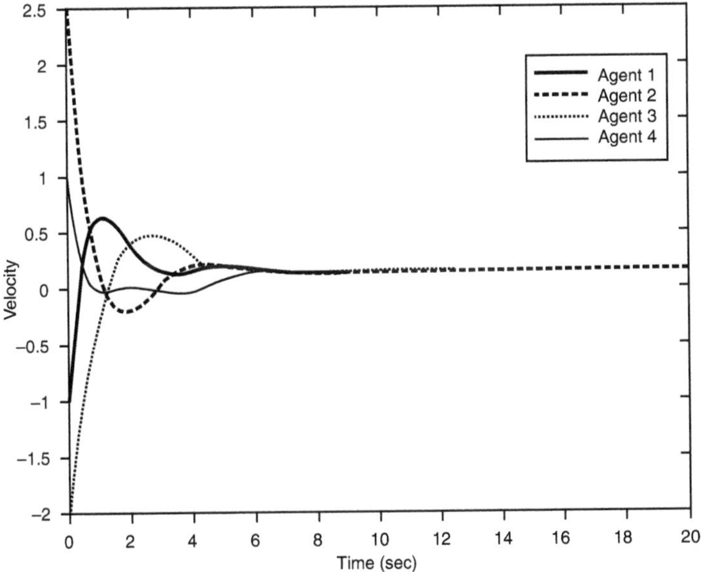

Figure 6.22: Velocity evolutions

6.5.1 Problem description

Suppose that the multiagent system under consideration consists of n agents that may be birds, airplanes, robots and so on. Each agent is regarded as a node in a directed graph G. Each edge $(s_j, s_i) \in E$ corresponds to an available information channel from the agent s_i to the agent s_j. Moreover, each agent updates its current state based upon the information received from its neighbors.

Suppose the dynamics of the ith agent $(i \in I)$ is

$$\begin{aligned} \dot{x}_i(t) &= v_i(t) \\ \dot{v}_i(t) &= u_i(t) \end{aligned} \tag{6.126}$$

where $x_i(t) \in R$ is the position state, $v_i(t) \in R$ is the velocity state and $u_i(t) \in R$ is the control input (or protocol).

Given the dynamical system in (6.126), we say the protocol u_i asymptotically solves the consensus problem, if the states of agents satisfy

$$\lim_{t \to +\infty} [x_i(t) - x_j(t)] = 0, \quad \lim_{t \to +\infty} [v_i(t) - v_j(t)] = 0 \tag{6.127}$$

for all $i, j \in I$.

In practical applications, the multiagent systems often suffer from various disturbances, such as actuator bias, measurement/ calculation errors and the variation of the communication topology. The existence of disturbances might lead to oscillation or divergence of the multiagent systems. It is of significance to investigate their effects on the behavior of the multiagent systems and find appropriate protocols to make the multiagent systems robust to disturbances. In this section, we are interested in investigating the robust H_∞ performance of system

(6.126) using the following consensus protocol

$$\begin{aligned} u_i(t) &= k_0 v_i + k_1 \sum_{s_j \in N_i} (a_{ij} + \Delta a_{ij}(t))(x_j(t) - x_i(t)) \\ &\quad + k_2 \sum_{s_j \in N_i} (a_{ij} + \Delta a_{ij}(t))(v_j(t) - v_i(t)) + w_i(t) \end{aligned} \tag{6.128}$$

where $k_1 > 0, k_2 > 0$ and k_0 are protocol parameters

$$|\Delta a_{ij}(t)| = \begin{cases} \leq \psi_{ij} & i \neq j \text{and} a_{ij} \neq 0 \\ 0 & \text{otherwise} \end{cases}$$

denotes the uncertainty of a_{ij} , which might be caused by actuator bias, for specified positive constants ψ_{ij}, and $w_i(t) \in L_2[0,\infty)$ is the external disturbance that might be caused by measurement/calculation errors. Here, it should be noted that there is no restricted condition imposed on the parameter k_0 and it might be positive, zero or negative.

A natural way to combine the relative information is to define output functions $z_i(t) = [z_{i1}(t), z_{i2}(t)]^T \in R^2$ for $i \in I$ computed from an average of the relative displacements and velocities of all agents as follows

$$\begin{aligned} z_{i1}(t) &= \frac{1}{n}\sum_{j=1}^{n}[x_i(t) - x_j(t)] = x_i(t) - \frac{1}{n}\sum_{j=1}^{n} x_j(t) \\ z_{i2}(t) &= \frac{1}{n}\sum_{j=1}^{n}[v_i(t) - v_j(t)] = v_i(t) - \frac{1}{n}\sum_{j=1}^{n} v_j(t) \end{aligned}$$

It is clear that consensus can be achieved if and only if

$$\lim_{t \to +\infty} z_i(t) = 0, \quad i = 1, \ldots, n$$

Denote

$$\begin{aligned} \xi &= [x_1, v_1, x_2, v_2, \ldots, x_n, v_n]^T \in \Re^{2n} \\ A &= \begin{bmatrix} 0 & 1 \\ 0 & k_0 \end{bmatrix} \in \Re^{2\times 2}, B = \begin{bmatrix} 0 & 1 \\ k_1 & k_2 \end{bmatrix} \in \Re^{2\times 2}, \\ B_2 &= \begin{bmatrix} 0 \\ 1 \end{bmatrix} \in \Re^2 \\ C &= \begin{bmatrix} \frac{n-1}{n} & -\frac{1}{n} & \cdots & -\frac{1}{n} \\ -\frac{1}{n} & \frac{n-1}{n} & \ddots & -\frac{1}{n} \\ \vdots & \ddots & \ddots & \vdots \\ -\frac{1}{n} & -\frac{1}{n} & \cdots & \frac{n-1}{n} \end{bmatrix} \in \Re^{n\times n} \end{aligned}$$

With protocol (6.128), the network dynamics are

$$\begin{aligned}\dot{\xi}(t) &= [I_n \otimes A - (L+\Delta L) \otimes B_1]\xi(t) + (I_n \otimes B_2)w(t) \\ z(t) &= (C \otimes I_2)\xi(t)\end{aligned} \tag{6.129}$$

where $w(t) = [w_1(t), \ldots, w_n(t)]^T \in \Re^n, z(t) = [z_1(t), \ldots, z_n(t)]^T \in \Re^{2n}, L$ is the Laplacian of the graph G and $\Delta L \in \Re^{n\times n}$ is the uncertainty Laplacian associated with the elements $\Delta a_{ij}(t)$.

By **Lemma** 1.2, ΔL can be transformed into $\Delta L = E_1\Sigma(t)E_2$, where $E_1 \in \Re^{n\times|E|}, E_2 \in \Re^{|E|\times n}$ are specified constant matrices and $\Sigma(t) \in \Re^{|E|\times|E|}$ is a diagonal matrix whose diagonal elements are the uncertainties of the edges, that is the non-zero $\Delta a_{ij}(t)$. It is easy to see that DL can be rewritten as $E_1\Sigma(t)E_2 = (E_1\Sigma_1)\tilde{\Sigma}(t)(\Sigma_2E_2)$, where Σ_1 and Σ_2 are adopted to validate $\tilde{\Sigma}(t)^T\tilde{\Sigma}(t) \leq I$. Therefore without loss of generality, we assume that $\Sigma^T(t)\Sigma(t) \leq I$, that is $\psi_{ij} = 1$ for all $i = j$.

Define the following H_∞ performance index

$$J = \int_0^\infty [z^T(t)z(t) - \gamma^2 w^T(t)w(t)]dt \tag{6.130}$$

where γ is a given positive constant.

In the sequel, we focus on robust H_∞ consensus problems for second-order multiagent systems and find proper values for the parameters k_0, k_1 and k_2 to make all agents reach consensus while satisfying the H_∞ performance index $J < 0$. However, due to the coupling of the two states of each agent, it is much harder to analyze the dynamics of the second-order multiagent systems, especially when the communication graph is directed and the uncertainties are included. The approach adopted is to reduce the dimension of the whole system by separating out the agreement dynamics. A detailed discussion will be made in the following section.

6.5.2 Analytic results

Before presenting the main results, we need to first introduce some lemmas [16].

Lemma 6.9
Consider the matrix C. The following statements hold.

1. *The eigenvalues of C are 1 with multiplicity $n-1$ and 0 with multiplicity 1. The vectors 1_n^T and 1_n are the left and the right eigenvectors of C associated with the zero eigenvalue, respectively.*

2. *There exists an orthogonal matrix $U \in \Re^{n\times n}$ such that*

$$U^TCU = \begin{bmatrix} I_{n-1} & 0 \\ 0 & 0 \end{bmatrix}$$

and the last column is $1_n/\sqrt{n}$. Let $\Xi_1 \in \Re^{n\times n}$ be the Laplacian of any directed graph, then $U^T\Xi_1 U = \begin{bmatrix} \vartheta_1 & 0 \end{bmatrix}, \vartheta_1 \in \Re^{n\times(n-1)}$

For convenience, denote

$$U = \begin{bmatrix} U_1 & \bar{U}_1 \end{bmatrix}$$

where $\bar{U}_1 = 1_n/\sqrt{n}$ is the last column of U and $U_1 \in \Re^{n\times(n-1)}$ is the rest part.

Theorem 6.9

Consider a directed network of agents with fixed topology. The multiagent system (6.129) reach consensus while satisfying the H_∞ performance index $J<0$ for a given constant $\gamma>0$, if there exists a symmetric positive-definite matrix $P\in\Re^{(2n-2)\times(2n-2)}$ and a scalar $\mu>0$ satisfying 6.131, where $\bar{L} = U_1^T L U_1$ and $\bar{E} = (U_1^T E_2^T E_2 U_1)\otimes I_2$.

$$\begin{bmatrix} \begin{matrix} P(I_{n-1}\otimes A-\bar{L}\otimes B_1)+ \\ (I_{n-1}\otimes A-\bar{L}\otimes B_1)^T P+ \\ \mu\bar{E}+I_{2n-2} \end{matrix} & P[(U_1^T E_1)\otimes B_1] & P(U_1^T\otimes B_2) \\ [(E_1^T U_1)\otimes B_1^T]P & -\mu I & 0 \\ (U_1\otimes B_2^T)P & 0 & -\gamma^2 I \end{bmatrix} < 0 \quad (6.131)$$

Proof: Let

$$\begin{aligned} W(t) &= \frac{1}{n}\sum_{i=1}^{n}\int_0^t e^{A(t-s)}B_2 w_i(s)ds \\ \hat{\xi}(t) &= \xi(t) - 1_n\otimes W(t), \\ \delta(t) &= (U_1\otimes I_2)^T\hat{\xi}(t), \\ \bar{\delta}(t) &= (\bar{U}_1\otimes I_2)^T\hat{\xi}(t) \end{aligned} \quad (6.132)$$

where $W(t)$ describes the average effect of external disturbances on each agent; $\hat{\xi}(t)$ describes the states of all agents, which takes out the average of external disturbances; $\bar{\delta}(t)$ describes the average states of all agents; and $\delta(t)$ depicts the disagreement states of all agents.

Premultiplying the left-hand side of system (6.129) with the matrix $(U\otimes I_2)^T$ yields

$$\begin{aligned} (U\otimes I_2)^T\dot{\hat{\xi}}(t) &= \begin{bmatrix} \dot{\delta}(t) \\ \dot{\bar{\delta}}(t) \end{bmatrix} + (U\otimes I_2)^T(I_n\otimes\dot{W}(t)) \\ &= \begin{bmatrix} \dot{\delta}(t) \\ \dot{\bar{\delta}}(t) \end{bmatrix} + \begin{bmatrix} \frac{1}{\sqrt{n}}\sum_{i=1}^n\int_0^t e^{A(t-s)}B_2 w_i(s)ds \\ +\frac{1}{\sqrt{n}}\sum_{i=1}^n B_2 w_i(t) \end{bmatrix} \quad (6.133) \\ &= \begin{bmatrix} \dot{\delta}(t) \\ \dot{\bar{\delta}}(t) \end{bmatrix} + \begin{bmatrix} 0 \\ \sqrt{n}AW(t)+\frac{1}{\sqrt{n}}\sum_{i=1}^n B_2 w_i(t) \end{bmatrix} \end{aligned}$$

Note that $L1_n = 0$ and $\Delta L 1_n = 0$. Then, premultiplying the right-hand side of system (6.129) with the matrix $(U \otimes I_2)^T$ yields

$$
\begin{aligned}
(U\otimes I_2)^T \dot{\xi}(t) &= (U\otimes I_2)^T (I_n \otimes A)(\hat{\xi}(t) + 1_n \otimes W(t)) \\
&\quad -(U\otimes I_2)^T[(L+\Delta L)\otimes B_1](\hat{\xi}(t) \\
&\quad +1_n \otimes W(t)) + (U^T \otimes B_2)w(t) \\
&= (U\otimes I_2)^T (I_n \otimes A)(U\otimes I_2)\begin{bmatrix} \delta(t) \\ \bar{\delta}(t) \end{bmatrix} \\
&\quad -(U\otimes I_2)^T[(L+\Delta L)\otimes B_1](U\otimes I_2)\begin{bmatrix} \delta(t) \\ \bar{\delta}(t) \end{bmatrix} \\
&\quad +(U\otimes I_2)^T (I_n \otimes A)(1_n \otimes W(t)) \\
&\quad +(U^T \otimes B_2)w(t) \\
&= \begin{bmatrix} I_{n-1}\otimes A & 0 \\ 0 & A \end{bmatrix}\begin{bmatrix} \delta(t) \\ \bar{\delta}(t) \end{bmatrix} \\
&\quad -\begin{bmatrix} (U_1^T L U_1 + U_1^T \Delta L U_1)\otimes B_1 & 0 \\ (\bar{U}_1^T L U_1 + \bar{U}_1^T \Delta L U_1)\otimes B_1 & 0 \end{bmatrix}\begin{bmatrix} \delta(t) \\ \bar{\delta}(t) \end{bmatrix} \\
&\quad +\begin{bmatrix} (U^T \otimes B_2)w(t) \\ \sqrt{n}AW(t) + B_2 \frac{1}{\sqrt{n}} \sum_{i=1}^n w_i(t) \end{bmatrix} \qquad (6.134)
\end{aligned}
$$

Denote $\overline{\Delta L} = U_1^T \Delta L U_1$. Then, by (6.133) and (6.134), it is easy to see that

$$
\begin{aligned}
\dot{\delta}(t) &= [I_{n-1}\otimes A - (\bar{L} + \bar{\Delta L})\otimes B_1]\delta(t) + (U_1^T \otimes B_2)w(t) \\
\dot{\bar{\delta}}(t) &= [(\bar{U}_1^T L U_1 + \bar{U}_1^T \Delta L U_1)\otimes B_1]\delta(t) + A\bar{\delta}(t) \qquad (6.135)
\end{aligned}
$$

From (6.135), it is clear that $\delta(t)$ is independent of $\bar{\delta}(t)$ and $\bar{\delta}(t)$ is dependent on $\delta(t)$. Also, by **Lemma** 6.9

$$
\begin{aligned}
z(t) &= (C\otimes I_2)\xi(t) = (C\otimes I_2)(U\otimes I_2)(U\otimes I_2)^T \xi(t) \\
&= diag\{U_1 \otimes I_2, 0\}\begin{bmatrix} \delta(t) \\ \bar{\delta}(t) \end{bmatrix} \qquad (6.136)
\end{aligned}
$$

It follows that $\lim_{t\to\infty} z(t) = 0$ when $\lim_{t\to\infty} \delta(t) = 0$. So, whether the multiagent system (6.129) can reach consensus is only related to the component $\delta(t)$. To investigate the $\mathcal{H}_\infty$ performance of the multiagent system (6.129), we can study the following system

$$
\begin{aligned}
\dot{\delta}(t) &= [I_{n-1}\otimes A - (\bar{L} + \bar{\Delta L})\otimes B_1]\delta(t) + (U_1^T \otimes B_2)w(t) \\
z(t) &= (U_1 \otimes I_2)\delta(t) \qquad (6.137)
\end{aligned}
$$

Define a Lyapunov function for system (6.137) as follows

$$V(t) = \delta^T(t) P \delta(t)$$

where $P \in \Re^{2(n-1)\times 2(n-1)}$ is a symmetric positive-definite matrix.

Calculating $\dot{V}(t)$ along the solution of system (6.137), it follows that

$$\begin{aligned}\dot{V}(t) &= 2\delta^T(t)P\dot{\delta}(t) \\ &= 2\delta^T(t)P[I_{n-1}\otimes A-(\bar{L}+\Delta\bar{L})\otimes B_1]\delta(t) \\ &+ 2\delta^T(t)P(U_1^T\otimes B_2)w(t)\end{aligned}$$

For any $x,y\in\Re^n$ and any symmetric positive-definite matrix $R\in\Re^{n\times n}$,

$$2x^Ty\le x^TR^{-1}x+y^TRy$$

And since $\Sigma^T(t)\Sigma(t)\le I_n$, it follows that

$$\begin{aligned}&- 2\delta^T(t)P(\Delta\bar{L}\otimes B_1)\delta(t) \\ &\le \delta^T(t)P(U_1^TE_1\otimes B_1)\left(\frac{1}{\mu}I_{2n}\right)(U_1^TE_1\otimes B_1)^TP\delta(t) \\ &\quad+\delta^T(t)[(U_1^TE_2^T\Sigma^T)\otimes I_2](\mu I_{2n})[(\Sigma E_2U_1)\otimes I_2]\delta(t) \\ &\le \frac{1}{\mu}\delta^T(t)P(U_1^TE_1\otimes B_1)(U_1^TE_1\otimes B_1)^TP\delta(t) \\ &\quad+\mu\delta^T(t)\bar{E}\delta(t)\end{aligned}$$

Consequently

$$\begin{aligned}\dot{V}(t) \le\ & 2\delta^T(t)P(I_{n-1}\otimes A-\bar{L}\otimes B_1)\delta(t) \\ &+2\delta^T(t)P(U_1^T\otimes B_2)w(t) \\ &+\frac{1}{\mu}\delta^T(t)P(U_1^TE_1\otimes B_1)(U_1^TE_1\otimes B_1)^TP\delta(t) \\ &+\mu\delta^T(t)\bar{E}\delta(t)\end{aligned}$$

Define the following cost performance index

$$J_T=\int_0^T[z^T(t)z(t)-\gamma^2w^T(t)w(t)]dt$$

where $T>0$ and $w(t)\in L_2[0,\infty)$. It is clear that $J=\lim_{T\to+\infty}J_T$. According to the linear superposition theorem, the response of a linear system can be decomposed into zero input response and zero state response. The former is caused by the non-zero initial condition, while the latter is caused by the external input. So, to analyse the effects of the external disturbance $w(t)$ on system (6.137), suppose that all agents start from the consensus state, that is $\delta(0)=0$. Clearly, $V(0)=0$. Then, it follows that

$$J_T = \int_0^T[z^T(t)z(t)-\gamma^2w^T(t)w(t)]dt$$

$$
\begin{aligned}
&= \int_0^T [z^T(t)z(t) - \gamma^2 w^T(t)w(t) + \dot{V}(t)]dt - (V(T) - V(0)) \\
&\leq \int_0^T [\eta^T(t)M\eta(t)]dt - V(T)
\end{aligned}
$$

where $\eta(t) = [\delta^T(t) \quad w^T(t)]^T$ and

$$
M = \begin{bmatrix} \begin{array}{c} P(I_{n-1} \otimes A - \bar{L} \otimes B_1) + (I_{n-1} \otimes A - \bar{L} \otimes B_1)^T P \\ +\frac{1}{\mu}P[(U_1^T E_1 E_1^T U_1) \otimes (B_1 B_1^T)]P \\ +\mu\bar{E} + I_{2n-2} \end{array} & P(U_1^T \otimes B_2) \\ (U_1 \otimes B_2^T)P & -\gamma^2 I \end{bmatrix} < 0
$$

By the Schur complements, $M < 0$ holds if and only if (6.131) holds. Note that $V(T) \geq 0$. Then, $J_T < 0$ when (6.131) holds. Let $T \to +\infty$. It follows that $J < 0$, that is $\int_0^\infty z^T(t)z(t)dt < \int_0^\infty \gamma^2 w^T(t)w(t)dt$. This completes the proof.

Remark 6.22 *Transformation (6.132) plays a key role in our analysis. Applying (6.132), the agreement component is separated out from the dynamics of the multi-agent system (6.129) and an equivalent system is obtained which describes the disagreement dynamics of (6.129). Moreover, it is shown that the agreement dynamics $\bar{\delta}(t)$ is independent of the external disturbance $w(t)$ but completely dependent on the disagreement dynamics $\delta(t)$.* ■

Remark 6.23 *It should be noted that a necessary condition for condition (6.131) is that the graph G has spanning trees. In fact, condition (6.131) implies that $P(I_{n-1} \otimes A - \bar{L} \otimes B_1) + (I_{n-1} \otimes A - \bar{L} \otimes B_1)^T P < 0$. Hence, $I_{n-1} \otimes A - \bar{L} \otimes B_1$ is Hurwitz. If the graph has no spanning trees, $\bar{L}$ must have zero eigenvalues, which implies $I_{n-1} \otimes A - \bar{L} \otimes B_1$ has zero eigenvalues and yields a contradiction.* ■

Condition (6.131) is a bilinear matrix inequality which can easily be solved, when the number of the agents in the network, n, is not too large. However, when n is very large, it becomes almost impossible to solve. In this case, we can consider assigning a specified form to the matrix P. In the following, discussion will be made about this on undirected graphs.

By the Schur complements, condition (6.131) is equivalent to

$$
\begin{aligned}
&P(I_{n-1} \otimes A - \bar{L} \otimes B_1) + (I_{n-1} \otimes A - \bar{L} \otimes B_1)^T P \\
&+\frac{1}{\mu}P[(U_1^T E_1 E_1^T U_1) \otimes (B_1 B_1^T)]P + \mu\bar{E} + I_{2n-2} \\
&+\gamma^{-2}P(I_{n-1} \otimes (B_2 B_2^T))P < 0
\end{aligned} \tag{6.138}
$$

Note that E_1 and E_2 are constant matrices. Denote λ_{E_1} and λ_{E_2} as the largest eigenvalues of the matrices $U_1^T E_1 E_1^T U_1$ and $U_1^T E_2^T E_2 U_1$, respectively. Then (6.138) holds if

$$\begin{aligned} & P(I_{n-1} \otimes A - \bar{L} \otimes B_1) + (I_{n-1} \otimes A - \bar{L} \otimes B_1)^T P \\ & + \frac{1}{\mu} P[I_{n-1} \otimes (\lambda_{E_1} B_1 B_1^T)]P + (\mu \lambda_{E_2} + 1) I_{2n-2} \\ & + \gamma^{-2} P(I_{n-1} \otimes (B_2 B_2^T))P < 0 \end{aligned} \tag{6.139}$$

From **Remark** 6.23, the graph has spanning trees under condition (6.131). By **Lemma** 1.1, the eigenvalues of the Laplacian L can be denoted as $0 = \lambda_1 < \lambda_2 \leq \cdots \leq \lambda_n$. Moreover, from matrix theory, the matrices L and $U^T LU$ have the same eigenvalues. Then, the eigenvalues of $\bar{L}$ are $\lambda_2, \lambda_3, \ldots, \lambda_n$ by **Lemma** 6.9. There must be an orthogonal matrix $H \in \Re^{(n-1)\times(n-1)}$ such that $H^T \bar{L} H = diag\{\lambda_2, \lambda_3, \ldots, \lambda_n\}$. Take $P = I_{n-1} \otimes \bar{P}$, where $\bar{P} \in \Re^{2\times 2}$ is an undermined positive-definite matrix. Pre- and post-multiplying the left-hand side of (6.139) with $H^T \otimes I_2$ and $H \otimes I_2$ yields

$$\begin{aligned} I_{n-1} \quad \otimes \quad & (\bar{P}A) - diag\{\lambda_2, \lambda_3, \ldots, \lambda_n\} \otimes (\bar{P}B_1) \\ & + [I_{n-1} \otimes (\bar{P}A) \otimes diag\{\lambda_2, \lambda_3, \ldots, \lambda_n\} \otimes (\bar{P}B_1)]^T \\ & + \frac{1}{\mu} I_{n-1} \otimes (\lambda_{E_1} \bar{P} B_1 B_1^T \bar{P}) + (\mu \lambda_{E_2} + 1) I_{2n-2} \\ & + \gamma^{-2} I_{n-1} \otimes (\bar{P} B_2 B_2^T \bar{P}) < 0 \end{aligned} \tag{6.140}$$

It is easy to see that (6.140) holds if and only if

$$\begin{aligned} \bar{P}A \quad - \quad & \lambda_i, [\bar{P}A - \bar{P}B_1]^T + \frac{1}{\mu} \lambda_{E_1} \bar{P} B_1 B_1^T \bar{P} \\ + \quad & (\mu \lambda_{E_2} + 1) I_2 + \gamma^{-2} \bar{P} B_2 B_2^T \bar{P} < 0 \end{aligned} \tag{6.141}$$

for $2 \leq i \leq n$. This means that if the non-zero $n-1$ eigenvalues of the Laplacian L all satisfy condition (6.141), the multiagent system (6.129) can reach consensus while satisfying the H_∞ performance index (6.130).

Remark 6.24 *As is well known, for a linear system, the asymptotic stability property is equivalent to the exponential stability property. Thus, under condition (6.131), system (6.137) is exponentially stable. That is, consensus can be achieved exponentially fast.* ▮

In **Theorem** 6.9, the case with external disturbances is discussed. For better understanding the behavior of the multiagent system (6.129), let us consider the case without external disturbances. Set $w(t) \equiv 0$. System (6.135) becomes

$$\begin{bmatrix} \dot{\delta}(t) \\ \dot{\bar{\delta}}(t) \end{bmatrix} = \begin{bmatrix} I_{n-1} \otimes A - (\bar{L} + \Delta\bar{L}) \otimes B_1 & 0 \\ (\bar{U}_1^T L U_1 + \bar{U}_1^T \Delta L U_1) \otimes B_1 & A \end{bmatrix} \begin{bmatrix} \delta(t) \\ \bar{\delta}(t) \end{bmatrix} \tag{6.142}$$

It is clear that the system matrix of (6.142) has one eigenvalue at zero and one at k_0 and its other eigenvalues all have negative real-parts under condition (6.131). And when $k_0 \geq 0$, the first component of $\bar{\delta}(t)$ tends to infinity as $t \to +\infty$. From (6.132), it is easy to see that the average position state of the multiagent system tends to infinity as $t \to +\infty$. In what follows, it will be discussed whether the states of all agents stay bounded for $k_0 < 0$. Since the component $\delta(t)$ is independent of $\bar{\delta}(t)$, then $\delta(t)$ can be denoted as

$$\delta(t) = T(t,0)\delta(0)$$

where $T(t,\cdot)$ is a continuous linear operator. Since $\delta(t)$ vanishes exponentially fast as $t \to +\infty$, there are two positive scalars r and α, for any $\Sigma(t)^T\Sigma(t) \leq I$, such that

$$\|T(t,s)\| \leq re^{-\alpha(t-s)}, \quad t \geq 0$$

Denote $\bar{\delta}(t) = [\bar{\delta}_1(t), \bar{\delta}_2(t)]^T$. From (6.142), it is easily obtained that

$$\begin{aligned}
\|\bar{\delta}_2(t)\| &\leq \int_0^t e^{k_0(t-s)}\|(\bar{U}_1^T LU_1 + \bar{U}_1^T \Delta LU_1)\| \\
&\quad \otimes [k_1 \quad k_2] re^{-\alpha s}\|\delta(0)\|ds + \|e^{k_0 t}\bar{\delta}_2(0)\| \\
&\leq r\pi_1 \int_0^t e^{k_0 t - (k_0+\alpha)}\|\delta(0)\|ds + e^{k_0 t}\|\bar{\delta}_2(0)\| \\
&= \frac{r\pi_1}{k_0+\alpha}(-e^{-\alpha t} + e^{k_0 t})\|\delta(0)\| + e^{k_0 t}\|\bar{\delta}_2(0)\| \\
\|\bar{\delta}_1(t)\| &= \|\bar{\delta}_1(0) + \int_0^t \bar{\delta}_2(s)ds\| \leq \|\bar{\delta}_1(0)\| \\
&\quad + \int_0^t \left\{\frac{r\pi_1}{k_0+\alpha}(-\tilde{e}^{-\alpha s} + e^{k_0 s})\|\delta(0)\| + e^{k_0 s}\|\bar{\delta}_2(0)\|\right\} ds \\
&= \|\bar{\delta}_1(0) + \frac{r\pi_1}{k_0+\alpha}\left[\frac{1}{\alpha}(e^{-\alpha t} - 1) + \frac{1}{k_0}(e^{k_0 t} - 1)\right]\|\delta(0)\| \\
&\quad + \frac{1}{k_0}(e^{k_0 t} - 1)\|\bar{\delta}_2(0)\|
\end{aligned}$$

where $\pi_1 = \max_t \|(\bar{U}_1^T LU_1 + \bar{U}_1^T \Delta LU_1) \otimes [k_1 \quad k_2]\|$. It is obvious that as $t \to +\infty$, each component of $\bar{\delta}(t)$ stays bounded.

$$\begin{bmatrix}
\begin{matrix} P(I_{n-1} \otimes A - \bar{L} \otimes B_1) + \\ (I_{n-1} \otimes A - \bar{L} \otimes B_1)^T P + \\ \mu \bar{E} \end{matrix} & P\left[(U_1^T E_1) \otimes B_1\right] \\
\left[(E_1^T U_1) \otimes B_1^T\right] P & -\mu I
\end{bmatrix} < 0 \tag{6.143}$$

$$\begin{bmatrix} \begin{matrix} P(I_{n-1}\otimes A-\bar{L}_\sigma\otimes B_1) \\ +(I_{n-1}\otimes A-\bar{L}_\sigma\otimes B_1)^T P \\ +\mu_\sigma \bar{E}_\sigma + I_{2n-2} \end{matrix} & P\left[(U_1^T E_{1\sigma})\otimes B_1\right] & P(U_1^T\otimes B_2) \\ \left[(E_{1\sigma}^T U_1)\otimes B_1^T\right] P & -\mu_\sigma I & 0 \\ (U_1\otimes B_2^T)P & 0 & -\gamma^2 I \end{bmatrix} < 0 \tag{6.144}$$

$$\begin{bmatrix} \begin{matrix} P(I_{n-1}\otimes A-\bar{L}_\sigma\otimes B_1) \\ +(I_{n-1}\otimes A-\bar{L}_\sigma\otimes B_1)^T P \\ +\mu_\sigma \bar{E}_\sigma \end{matrix} & P\left[(U_1^T E_{1\sigma})\otimes B_1\right] \\ \left[(E_{1\sigma}^T U_1)\otimes B_1^T\right] P & -\mu_\sigma I \end{bmatrix} < 0 \tag{6.145}$$

By repeating the same argument of the proof of **Theorem** 6.9, the following proposition can be obtained.

Proposition 6.2

Consider a directed network of agents with fixed topology in the absence of external disturbances. The multiagent system (6.129) can reach consensus if there exists a symmetric positive-definite matrix $P \in \Re^{(2n-2)\otimes(2n-2)}$ and a scalar $\mu > 0$ satisfying, (6.143)

In **Theorem** 6.9 and **Proposition** 6.2, we only discuss the case of fixed topology. In the following **Theorem** 6.10 and **Proposition** 6.3, we will discuss the case of switching topology. To this end, we need to define a switching signal $\sigma = s(t) : [0,\infty) \to P = \{1,2,\ldots,N\}$ (N denotes the total number of the graphs of all possible topologies) that determines the topology. Such a function σ has a finite number of switching times and each time interval between every two consecutive switching times is assumed to be larger than a constant.

Theorem 6.10

Consider a directed network of agents with switching topologies. The multiagent system (6.129) can reach consensus while satisfying the $\mathcal{H}_\infty$ performance index $J < 0$ for a given constant $\gamma > 0$, if there exist a common symmetric positive-definite matrix $P \in \Re^{(2n-2)\otimes(2n-2)}$ and a scalar $\mu_\sigma > 0$ for each possible communication graph G_σ satisfying (6.144) where $\bar{L}_\sigma = U_1^T L_\sigma U_1$ and $\bar{E}_\sigma = (U_1^T E_{2\sigma}^T E_{2\sigma} U_1)\otimes I_2$.

Proof: This result can be proved following the lines of the proof of *Theorem* 6.9. However, it should be emphasized that all possible $I_{n-1}\otimes A-\bar{L}_\sigma\otimes B$ should share a common Lyapunov function $V(t) = \delta^T(t)P\delta(t)$.

Remark 6.25 *As discussed previously, a necessary condition for the condition (6.133) is that each possible communication graph G_σ has spanning trees. Moreover, for undirected graphs, under condition (6.144), if each non-zero eigenvalue of all possible L_σ satisfies condition (6.141), then consensus can be achieved with desired H_∞ performance.* ∎

Similar to **Proposition** 6.2, **Proposition** 6.3 can be easily obtained for the networks with switching topologies in the absence of external disturbances.

Proposition 6.3
Consider a directed network of agents with switching topologies in the absence of external disturbances. The multiagent system (6.129) can reach consensus if there exist a common symmetric positive-definite matrix $P \in R^{(2n-2)\otimes(2n-2)}$ and a scalar $\mu_\sigma > 0$ for each possible communication graph G_σ satisfying, see (6.145)

Remark 6.26 *The agent models considered are in the form of second-order. The proposed approach is promising and all the results might be extended to high order multiagent systems with parameter uncertainties and external disturbances in the absence and presence of time delay.* ∎

6.5.3 Illustrative example 6.6

Numerical simulations will be given in order to illustrate the theoretical results obtained in the previous sections. Figure 6.23 shows three different networks, each with $n = 4$ agents. All directed graphs in this figure have spanning trees.

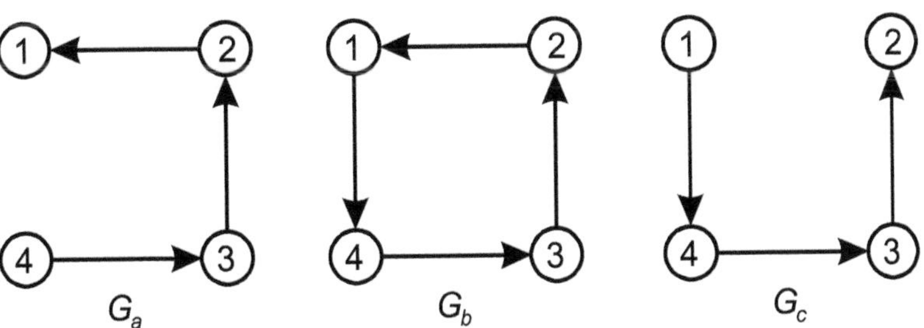

Figure 6.23: Three directed graphs

Suppose that the weight of each edge is 1, the uncertainty of each edge is

$$\Delta a_{ij} = \begin{cases} 0.01\sin[(i+j)t], & i \neq j and a_{ij} \neq 0 \\ 0 & \text{otherwise} \end{cases}$$

and the initial condition of the multiagent system is zero. Moreover, the topology of the multiagent system switches every 0.01 s in the sequence of $< G_a, G_b, G_c, G_a >$.

Choosing the performance index $\gamma = 1$, it is solved that (19) is feasible when $(k_0, k_1, k_2) = (-1, 5, 5)$, $(k_0, k_1, k_2) = (0, 5, 5)$ or $(k_0, k_1, k_2) = (0.3, 5, 5)$. According to **Theorem** 6.10, consensus can be achieved with desired H_∞ performance

$$\int_0^\infty z^T(t)z(t)dt < \int_0^\infty w^T(t)w(t)dt$$

when

$$(k_0, k_1, k_2) = (-1, 5, 5),\ (k_0, k_1, k_2) = (0, 5, 5),\ (k_0, k_1, k_2) = (0.3, 5, 5)$$

In practical situations, external disturbances usually occur in the form of pulse. So, take the external disturbance $w(t)$ as $w(t) = [1 \quad -2 \quad 0.5 \quad 3]^T \bar{\omega}(t)$, where

$$\bar{\omega}(t) = \begin{cases} 1 & 0 \neq t \leq 1 \\ 0 & \text{otherwise} \end{cases}$$

is a pulse signal. Now, simulation results are presented for the consensus problems in directed networks of second-order multiagent systems with switching topology and external disturbance w(t) for three cases:

1) $(k_0, k_1, k_2) = (-1, 5, 5)$
2) $(k_0, k_1, k_2) = (0, 5, 5)$
3) $(k_0, k_1, k_2) = (0.3, 5, 5)$

Figures 6.24–6.29 show the position and velocity trajectories of all agents. It is observed that the pulse disturbance $w(t)$ makes the multiagent system diverge from consensus in the first few seconds, but after a period of interaction between agents, the multiagent system eventually return to consensus. Specifically, for $k_0 = -1$, all agents move to a common value; for $k_0 = 0$, all agents reach consensus and move with a common constant velocity; and for $k_0 = 0.3$, all agents reach consensus and move with a common constant acceleration. This suggests that the ultimate movement of the multiagent system is heavily dependent on the parameter k_0.

Figures 6.30–6.35 describe the position error and the velocity error trajectories of all agents, that is $z_{i1}(t)$ and $z_{i2}(t)(i = 1, 2, \ldots, n)$, whereas Figs. 14–16 show the energy trajectories of the output function $z(t)$ and the disturbance $w(t)$. It is clear that the output function $z(t)$ vanishes $t \to +\infty$ and the desired H_∞ performance, $\int_0^\infty z^T(t)z(t)dt < \int_0^\infty w^T(t)w(t)dt$, is satisfied. Taken together, all simulations demonstrate that consensus can be achieved with desired $\mathcal{H}_\infty$ performance under the condition given by **Theorem** 6.10.

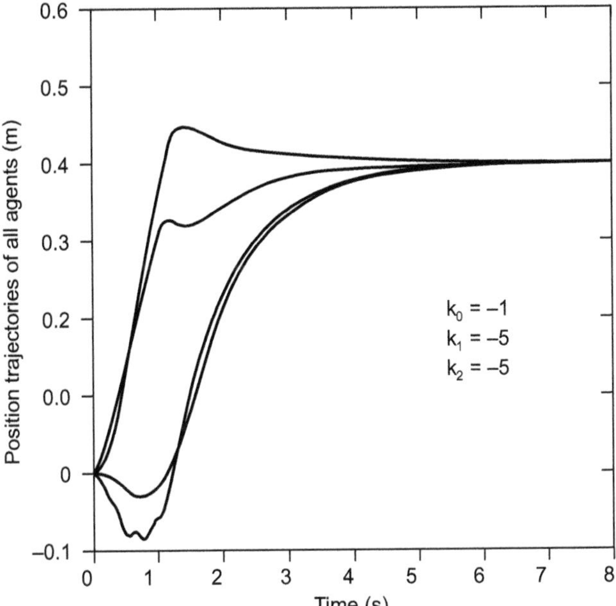

Figure 6.24: Position trajectories of all agents

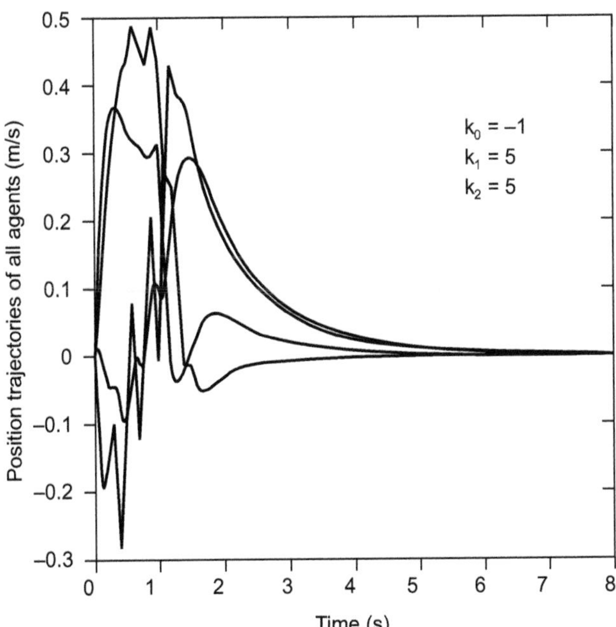

Figure 6.25: Velocity trajectories of all agents

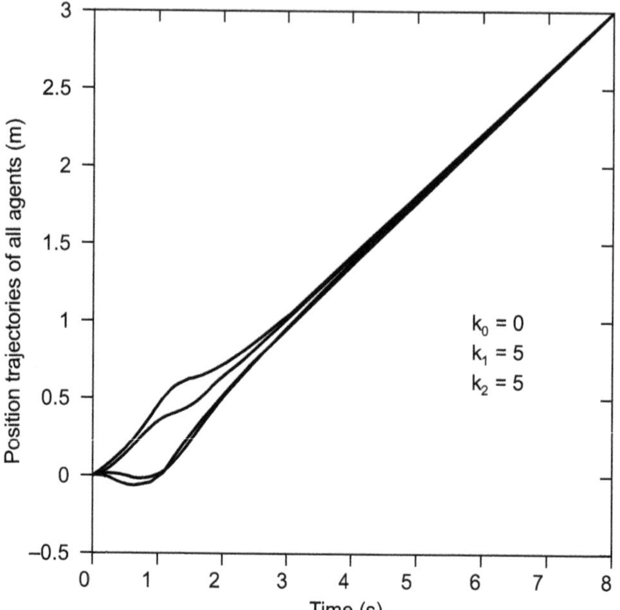

Figure 6.26: Position trajectories of all agents

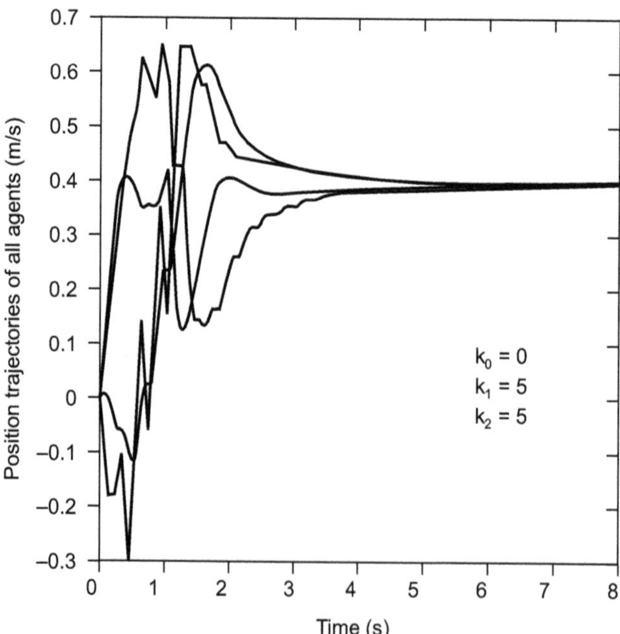

Figure 6.27: Velocity trajectories of all agents

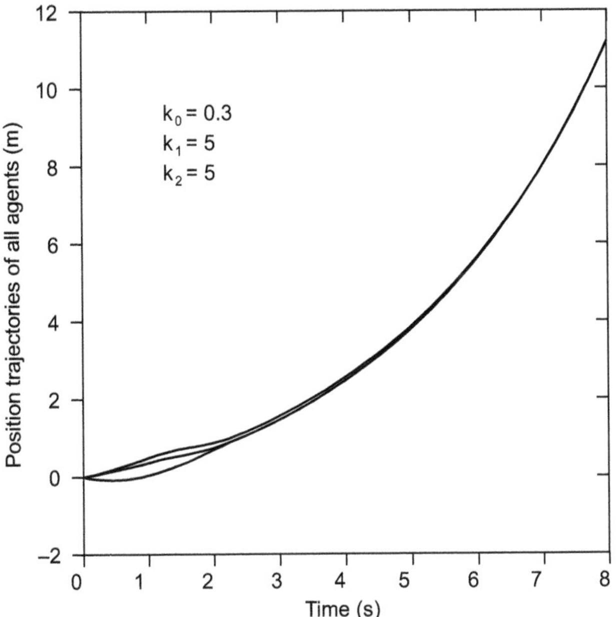

Figure 6.28: Position trajectories of all agents

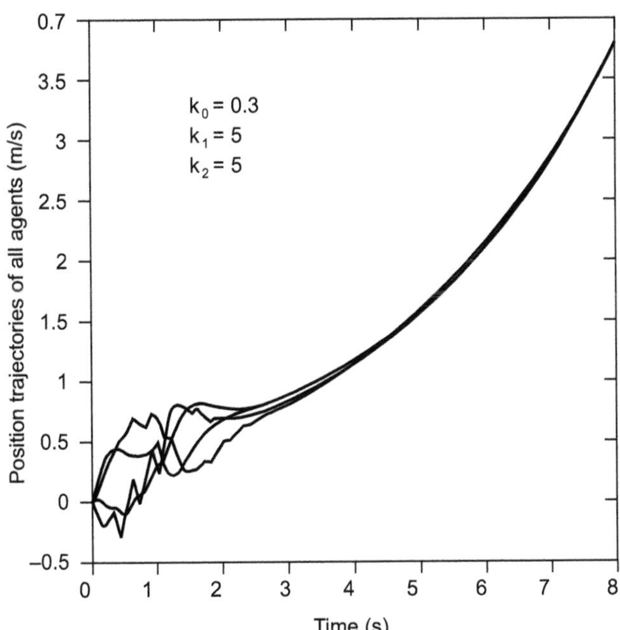

Figure 6.29: Velocity trajectories of all agents

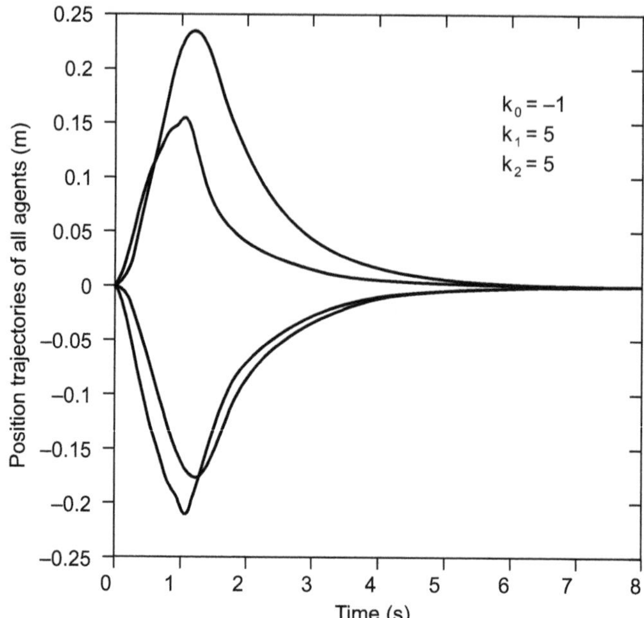

Figure 6.30: Position error trajectories of all agents

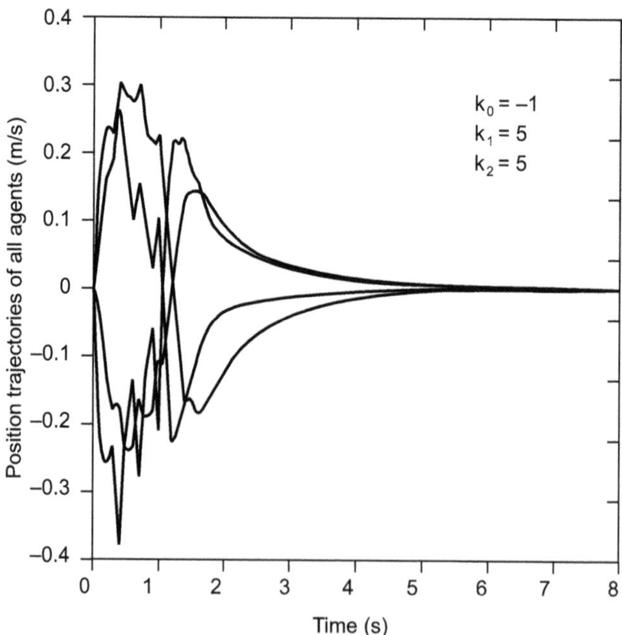

Figure 6.31: Velocity error trajectories of all agents

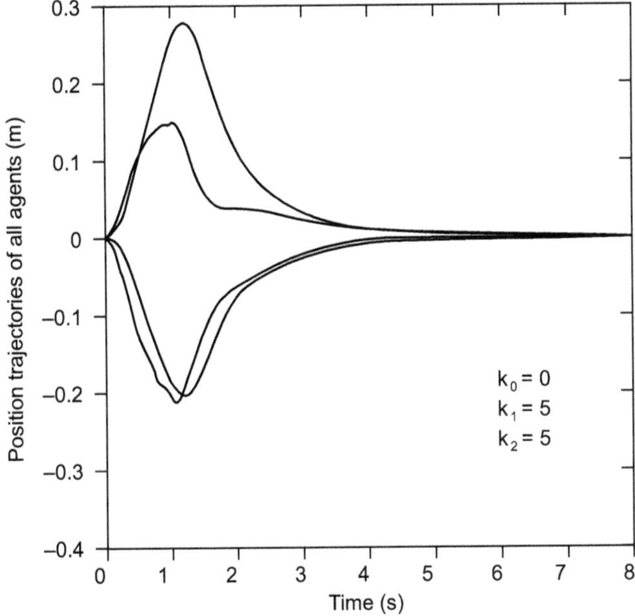

Figure 6.32: Position error trajectories of all agents

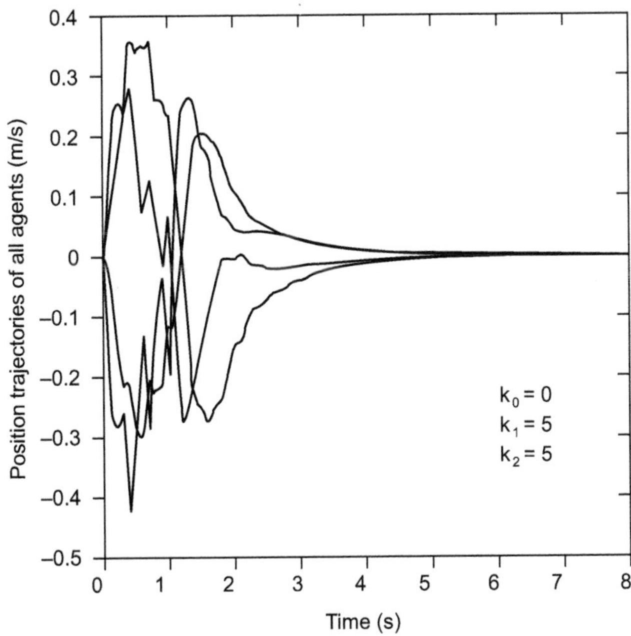

Figure 6.33: Velocity error trajectories of all agents

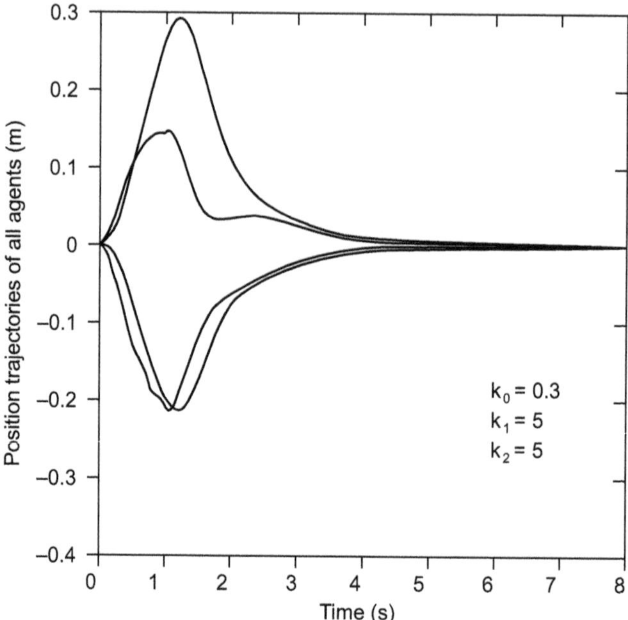

Figure 6.34: Position error trajectories of all agents

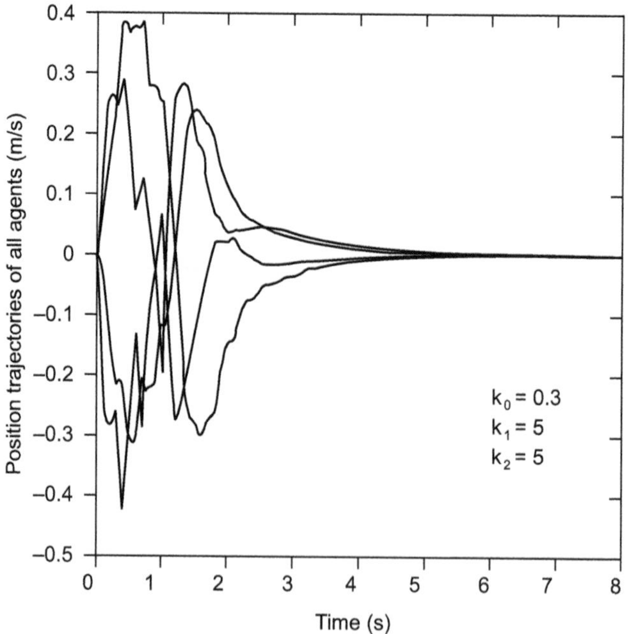

Figure 6.35: Velocity error trajectories of all agents

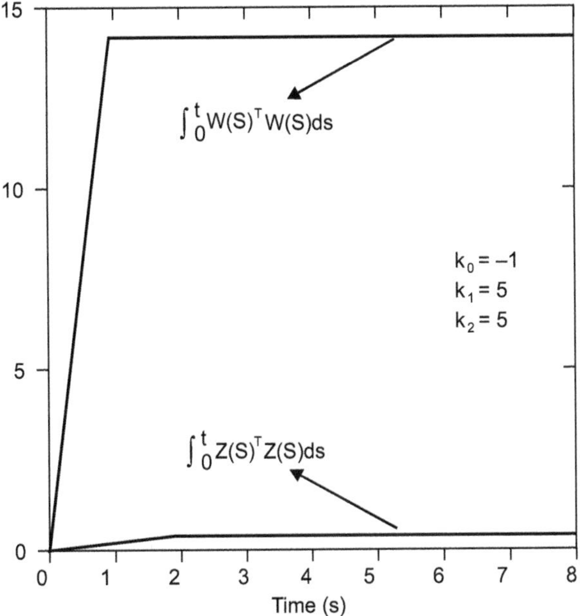

Figure 6.36: Energy trajectories of z(t) and w(t)

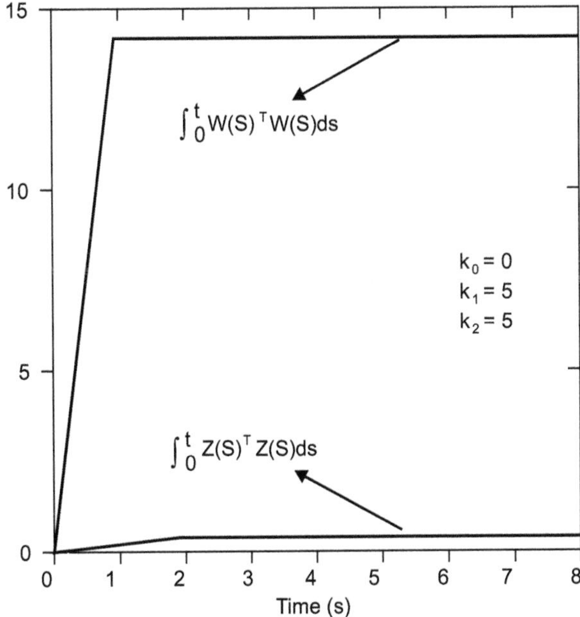

Figure 6.37: Energy trajectories of z(t) and w(t)

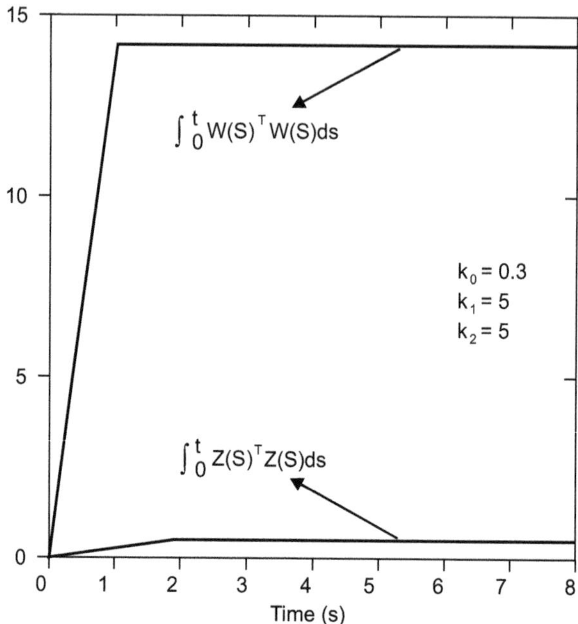

Figure 6.38: Energy trajectories of z(t) and w(t)

6.6 Notes

This Chapter initially examined the dynamic consensus of a linear or linearized multiagent system whose communication topology has a directed spanning tree. Based on the relative outputs of the neighboring agents, an observer-type protocol was adopted. It was shown, for neutrally stable agents, that there exists a protocol achieving consensus over a consensus region. This region is the entire open right-half plane if and only if each agent is stabilizable and detectable. Algorithms were developed to derive protocols to achieve consensus with or without convergence speed specification. It was established that the design procedures possess a computationally desirable decoupling property.

Next, the delayed consensus problem of a group of leaderless multiple mobile agents with neighbor-based rule was addressed. The consensus stability was guaranteed with both fixed and switched interconnection topologies of the considered multiagent system. The dynamics of each agent were second-order with time-varying delays. A Lyapunov–Razumikhin function was employed in the stability analysis. For neutrally stable agents, it was shown that there exists a protocol achieving consensus and having a consensus region that is the entire open right-half plane if and only if each agent is stabilizable and detectable.

The consensus problem with a prescribed convergence speed was later investigated. A necessary and sufficient condition was then derived for the existence of a protocol that reaches consensus with a convergence speed larger than a given positive value and, meanwhile, yields an unbounded consensus region, which means good robustness to the communication topology.

Later on, consensus problems were investigated in directed networks of second-order agents with uncertainties. Neighbor-based rules were adopted for each agent with the consideration of parameter uncertainties and external disturbances. Some conditions were derived, under which all agents asymptotically reach consensus while satisfying desired $\mathcal{H}_\infty$ performance.

To reduce the communication burden of multiagent networks, event-triggered schemes have been introduced to study the tracking problem for a class of discrete-time MAS with a time-varying reference state where the agents communicate with their local neighbours at discrete-time instants. The control actuation updates considered in this paper were event-driven, depending on certain measurement errors with respect to the states of agents and the leader. A numerical example was presented to demonstrate the effectiveness of the theoretical results.

Then, under the condition that the communication/sensing topology of a multi-vehicle system is weakly connected and contains two or more zero-in-degree and strongly connected subgraphs, the second-order controlled consensus problems have been studied. We derived the necessary and sufficient condition under which second-order controlled consensus can be achieved. The method to design the controller and the rule to choose the pinned vehicles were discussed. We also considered the variable topology case. Multiple Lyapunov functions have been employed in order to analyze the stability of the system. The second-order controlled consensus method has been applied to coordinate the movements of multiple unicycle robots.

Chapter 7

Cooperative Control of Networked Power Systems

7.1 Coordinated Model Predictive Power Flows

Microgrids (MG) are defined as smart power systems including loads, distributed generations (DGs), and energy storage systems (ESSs) (batteries, electric vehicles, hydraulic storage, etc.) grouped together within a limited geographic area [512], [513]. The main advantage that the MG offers is to enable customers both with a bidirectional communication platform and with control devices to control their energy needs and excesses. In addition, with an adequate communication structure, it is possible to shape the users load demand curves using demand response strategies [514].

MG can operate either in grid-connected or islanded mode. In grid-connected mode, the MG is connected to a highly available power grid which may act as an additional power source for the MG. In this scenario, the MG and the distribution network operator (DNO) make mutual benefits selling/purchasing powers. On the other hand, from a sustainable development viewpoint, purchasing energy from the DNO, which is mainly producing power from nonrenewable sources, should be regulated within certain limits [515], which, conversely, may affect the quality of service. In islanded mode, the MG must keep a sufficient level of distributed power generation and energy storage in order to enhance system stability and to guarantee the quality of the local load. In an islanded renewable-based MG, the power flow exchanges will bring new challenges that regard the mitigation of renewable power intermittencies, load mitigation, load mismatches, and other key problems [516]. In order to reduce the power purchased from the DNO, one interesting solution is to connect neighboring MG in a network.

7.1.1 Introduction

In this section, we provide a solution to address the power control in a network of MG, to maximize the use of available renewable energy sources (RESs) to meet loads, and to enhance the reliability of the whole network. Considering the stochastic nature of renewable power generation and loads in each MG, a challenging question is how to effectively control the power locally and among MG in an open energy market while taking into account the various MG safety constraints, the storage dynamics, and the uncertainties coming from RESs and loads.

The control and the optimization of a network of MG are still new research fields. One of the first studies in this field is the one presented in [517], where the authors proposed a smart network of MG with an optimal topology to enhance the RESs exploitation. In [518], the control approach aims at keeping the storage level in each MG around a reference value by exchanging power in a network of MG. The proposed model is defined according to a linear quadratic formulation, which provides an effective computation of the optimal solution, even for networks with a great number of MG. In [519] a method is proposed that takes care both of the MG load dispatch and of the network reconfiguration. The method uses the power-flow technique to minimize the total operating cost of a distribution network with multiple MG. The work of [520] focused on the load demand management of a network of interconnected MG. The problem is formulated as a cooperative power dispatching optimization problem, where real-time pricing is employed as a motivation for the interactions between the MG. Then, in [521], a problem of energy consumption scheduling in a distribution of connected MG is presented.

So far, there are two main approaches that can be identified for the control of a network of smart MG:

1) *decentralized* and
2) *centralized.*

On one hand, in the decentralized approach, a multiagent system (MAS) approach is frequently adopted, where each MG is related to an agent controlling some operations, such as the power flows from/to the external world [522], [523]. The main responsibility of an MG's agent is to satisfy the local demand, maximizing the power export under variable market price conditions [524]. The main challenge in the decentralized control is to establish a consensus among different agents controlling the MG.

On the other hand, in the centralized approach, which is the focus of this paper, a central controller delivers the optimal control strategy, which is communicated to each MG. The use of centralized control is very effective to control a network of MG with one owner, given that all the relevant information is gathered at a single point [525]. In addition, desired performances can be obtained as one global controller has full process knowledge and signal information which enable the coordination of decisions. Methods for solving the optimal energy management in a network of MG were reported in [526] and [527].

This section presents the control architecture and the mathematical models of a cooperative global centralized controller of a network of renewable-based MG. The model predictive control (MPC) application is highly interesting as MPC problems incorporate prediction models and operation and security constraints and enable the implementation of the future behavior of the system and its forecasts. These are attractive for renewable-based MG and load predictions [528]. At each control step, the method uses the most updated information on power generation, energy prices, and load forecasts, over a rolling horizon [529]–[534].

There is some existing work that considers a detailed comprehensive MPC approach for the optimal control of power flows in a cooperative renewable energy-based network of MG, coping with RESs intermittent and maximizing the profit of the network. This section considers a detailed comprehensive MPC approach for the optimal control of power flows in a cooperative renewable energy-based network of MG, coping with RESs intermittent and maximizing the profit of the network. The expected impact with respect to the actual operation of MG can be attained in providing more flexibility for the operation of each MG through the exchanges of power with neighboring MG, maximizing the use of renewable energy produced at the network level, exploiting the fluctuations of stochastic renewable sources and demands, and ensuring the local loads internally with a minimum interaction with the DNO.

7.1.2 System architecture

The MG is considered as a small internal grid that can be connected to other MG, and/or connected/disconnected from the DNO. Each MG integrates several units (Fig. 7.1).

1. DGs which may lead to exploit the local RESs.
2. An ESS improving the stability, the power quality, and the reliability of the supply.
3. Loads representing households demand.
4. Point of Common Connection (PCC): It can be a single, double or multi-dimensional point, depending on the number of incident connections.

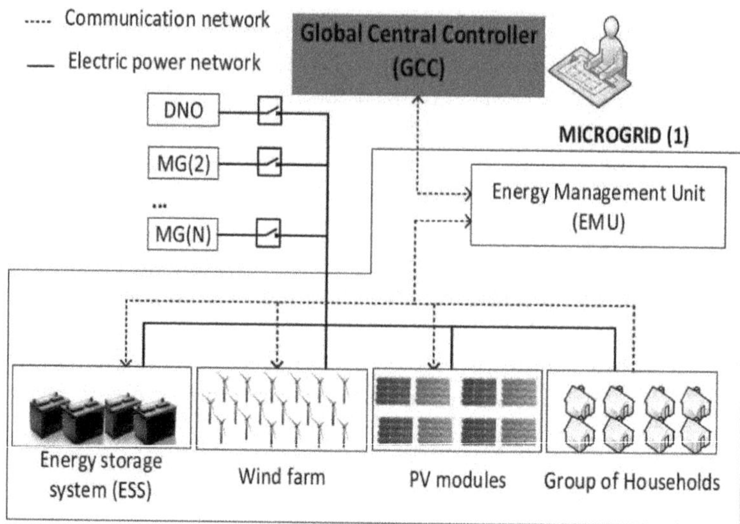

Figure 7.1: Microgrids architecture

5. Energy Management Unit (EMU): It is the interface between the global central controller (GCC) and the control unit available in the MG.

In practical cases, a residential, industrial, or commercial building integrating distributed power sources, storage systems, controllable and non-controllable loads, a building energy management system, and an advanced metering infrastructure may be considered as a MG. The steps required to model these MG components are presented hereafter.

7.1.3 Wind power generation

It is assumed that wind turbines are available in each MG. The Weibull probability distribution function (PDF) is generally used to represent the frequencies of the wind speed. It also represents the most frequent starting point of stochastic analysis, simulation, and forecasting of wind speed. Its general formulation is represented as follows [526]:

$$f(v) = \left(\frac{k}{c}\right)\left(\frac{v}{c}\right)^{k-1} exp\left(-\left(\frac{v}{c}\right)^{k}\right). \tag{7.1}$$

In the literature, several models of the output power of wind turbines are available. A simplified linear model is used. It assumes a linear dependence of the wind turbine power output on the current wind speed at the hub height.

The probabilistic power output of the wind turbine in the i-th MG is as follows [535]:

$$\bar{u}_{wt}(i,t) = \begin{cases} 0 & \bar{v}(i,t) < v_c \\ P_r\left(\hat{a} - \hat{b}\bar{v}(i,t)\right) & v_c \leq \bar{v}(i,t) \leq v_r \\ P_r & v_r \leq \bar{v}(i,t) \leq v_f \\ 0 & \bar{v}(i,t) > v_f \end{cases} \tag{7.2}$$

$$\text{with} \quad \begin{cases} \hat{a} = \frac{v_c}{v_c - v_r} \\ \hat{b} = \frac{1}{v_r - v_c}. \end{cases} \tag{7.3}$$

7.1.4 Photovoltaic module generators

It is assumed that photovoltaic (PV) modules are available in each MG. The electrical energy generated by a PV module is mostly affected by some characteristics of the site like solar irradiance, ambient temperature, as well as other characteristics of the module itself. The solar irradiation is modeled by the Beta PDF identified with historical data, to describe random phenomena. The Beta PDF is described by [536]

$$\beta(\psi) = \frac{\Gamma(\phi+\theta)}{\Gamma(\phi)\Gamma(\theta)} \times \psi^{\phi-1} \times (1-\psi)^{\theta-1}$$
$$\text{with} \quad 0 \leq \psi \leq 1,\ \theta \geq 0,\ \phi \geq 0. \tag{7.4}$$

The parameters are computed using the mean $\bar{\psi}$ and the standard deviation σ of the solar irradiance as follows:

$$\begin{cases} \theta = (1-\bar{\psi}) \times \left(\frac{\bar{\psi}\times(1+\bar{\psi})}{\sigma^2} - 1\right) \\ \phi = \frac{\bar{\psi}\times\theta}{1-\bar{\psi}}. \end{cases} \tag{7.5}$$

The probabilistic power output of the PV modules in the i-th MG is calculated as follows:

$$\bar{u}_{\text{pv}}(i,t) = S_{\text{pv}}\xi_{\text{pv}}P_f\xi_{\text{pc}}\widetilde{\psi}(i,t). \tag{7.6}$$

7.1.5 Energy storage system dynamics

Each MG has an energy storage system (ESS). So, any local shortage in supplying loads to consumers should be met either by discharging the ESS or by purchasing power from the MG neighbors or from the DNO. The function of the ESS is to participate in the balance of the electric loads and RESs power generation. The ESS capacity must be sized on the number of residences connected to the MG. We denote with $x(i,t)$ the energy storage level of the ESS of each MG at time period t. The state of charge can be expressed as

$$x(i,t+\Delta t) \quad = \quad x(i,t) + \beta_{\text{Char},i}\, u_{\text{Char}}(i,t)\Delta t - \beta_{\text{Dis},i}\, u_{\text{Dis}}(i,t)\Delta t. \tag{7.7}$$

Supposing $\Delta t = 1$ h, (7.7) can be rewritten as

$$x(i,t+1) = x(i,t) + \beta_{\text{Char},i}\, u_{\text{Char}}(i,t) - \beta_{\text{Dis},i}\, u_{\text{Dis}}(i,t).$$

7.1.6 Loads

In each period $(t,t+1)$ and for each MG, the load is assumed to be uncontrollable. Load forecasting techniques performed by each EMU can help the GCC to make important decisions for the network, such as purchasing/selling power from/to a particular MG, charging/discharging ESS and purchasing/selling power from/to the DNO. In order to provide accurate predictions for the MPC-based power scheduling for MG, appropriate weather data (such as temperature, humidity) and historical data of energy consumption, are required. At each time step, through appropriate prediction algorithms, the EMU uses measured data of previous periods to predict the loads for a future predefined horizon N_p. As the MPC process is going on, new measurements are gathered and the EMU updates parameters of the prediction model in order to include corrections and reduce the errors.

7.1.7 Energy management unit

The MG power system supports the power in grid-connected and/or MG-connected modes. The main EMU function is to optimize the MG operation in case of autonomous operation, or alternatively, to play an interface role between the MG components and the GCC. In both cases, the EMU goal is to receive and to send a control signal, such as the one for the ESS. The EMU can also disconnect the MG from other MG or/and from the DNO in case of network failure. It uses data gathered from different sensors available on-site to compute the predicted amount of power generated from RESs and the electric load demands for a few seconds, minutes or hours ahead, and send the information to the GCC.

7.1.8 Power price mechanism

A MG may be connected to the DNO, and to other MG in the network, and can send or receive power from them. Since, the power generation in the network of MG is mainly based on RESs, there are uncertainties related to power offers/demands by a given MG. Consequently, at each time period, an MG can be seller (positive balance), buyer (negative balance), or not participating (balance equals to zero). This means that seller MG may trade among buyer MG and also with the DNO in the electricity markets [537] through the GCC. Depending on the pricing mechanism, sometimes, it is expected that trading among MG may give lower costs to buyers than with the DNO.

7.2 Power Scheduling in Networked MG

7.2.1 Networked topology

The topology of the network is represented by a directed graph $G(\mathcal{M},\mathcal{L})$, where $|\mathcal{M}| = M$ denotes the cardinality of the set of MG, and $|\mathcal{L}| = L$ denotes the cardinality of the set of power links available among the MG. For a given MG, let M_i denotes the set of MG connected to the i-th MG. In a given time interval $(t,t+1)$, each MG $i \in M$ can generate a total power and must serve a group of households.

7.2.2 GCC of networked MG

The GCC is in charge of the coordination and the management of power in the network by properly allowing the optimal operation of each MG, while managing the relationship between the MG and the DNO as well as with other related MG.

The GCC aims to deliver a high-level control to generate suitable set points for all DGs, ESSs, and power exchanges, so that the total benefits of the network of MG are optimized and the predicted loads are met. The GCC reduces the effects of power variation of the RESs and loads on the MG distribution system by selling excess power to other MG or/and the DNO or, alternatively, storing the power in the local ESS. In case of excess, the GCC must decide how to distribute the excess among MG connections, DNO, and local ESS. However, in case of deficit, the GCC must decide how to fulfill the MG demand, by receiving power from other connected MG, DNO, or/and local ESS.

7.2.3 MPC-based power scheduling

The basic theory of MPC-based power scheduling strategy is that, at each time step (t), a finite horizon (N_c) optimal control sequence is computed for the ESS state, MG power exchanges, and power exchanges with the DNO for the whole network of MG. However, only the first step of control actions is applied. For example, $\bar{u}_m^*(t+k|t)$ will denote the vector of optimal power exchanged between MG at time slot $(t+k)$ predicted at time t. The method operates following a rolling horizon scheme, which means that, at the next time step $(t+1)$, new measurements of renewable resources (wind, solar), loads and prices are available, giving updates information into the future. With these updates, the optimal control routine is recalculated for the next N_c periods.

The MPC-based algorithm is implemented using the following steps.

Step 1: At $t = 1$, initialize with the actual current state of the MG, i.e., storage systems, loads, renewable energy power generation, energy price predictions.

Step 2: Compute an optimal control sequence, for the selected rolling optimization horizon (N_c), based on loads, renewable energy, and energy price predictions for the next prediction periods (N_p).

Step 3: Implement the first control period operation of the scheduling problem to all MG.

Step 4: Update the information available in each MG for the next period, i.e., ESS state, loads, renewable energy power generation, and energy price predictions. Then, move to the next sampling instant, and repeat the same algorithm.

The high-level control generates optimal set points for all DGs, ESSs, and power exchanges so as to maximize the total network profit and to meet the loads in each MG. The EMU available in each MG must guarantee that the system tracks the power reference values delivered by the GCC. The voltage and frequency stabilities are supposed to be controlled at lower level controller in each MG. In particular, in this paper, each MG is connected to the DNO, so that the frequency of each MG is maintained within some limits by the DNO.

The EMU is in charge of the forecasts for the energy prices, renewable power generation, and loads by appropriate models. It transfers the forecasts to the GCC which computes the optimal system operation and applies the first control input set points to all MG. The EMUs update the parameters of the prediction model with variations to reduce the errors and they send their update to the GCC.

7.2.4 Optimization problem formulation

In a network of MG, the primary objective is to maximize the benefits, while satisfying power balance, power generation, ESS, and energy exchange constraints. The first two terms in the objective function are related to the cost of the power sold to the DNO and the other MG, while the second two terms are related to the cost of the power purchased from the DNO and the MG.

The objective function to be maximized at each time step (t) can be formulated as follows:

$$\begin{aligned} J &= \sum_{k=1}^{N_c}\sum_{j=1}^{M} \phi(k)\cdot \overline{u}_{g,s}(j,t+k)\cdot \tilde{C}_{g,s}(j,\, t+k) \\ &+ \sum_{k=1}^{N_c}\sum_{j=1}^{M}\sum_{i,i\neq j}^{M} \tilde{\phi}_j(k)\cdot \overline{u}_{m,s}(j,i,+k)\cdot \tilde{C}_{m,s}(j,t+k) \\ &- \sum_{k=1}^{N_c}\sum_{j=1}^{M} \psi(k)\cdot \overline{u}_{g,p}(j,t+k)\cdot \tilde{C}_{g,p}(j,\, t+k) \end{aligned}$$

$$- \sum_{k=1}^{N_c}\sum_{j=1}^{M}\sum_{i,i\neq j}^{M} \widetilde{\psi}_j(k)\cdot \overline{u}_{m,p}(j,i,+k)\cdot \tilde{C}_{m,p}(i,t+k) \tag{7.8}$$

7.2.5 State equations and constraints

The energy storage state equation for each MG is given by

$$\overline{x}(i,t+k) = \overline{x}(i,t+k-1)+\beta_{\text{Char},i}\overline{u}_{\text{Char}}(i,t+k)-\beta_{\text{Dis},i}\overline{u}_{\text{Dis}}(i,t+k) \tag{7.9}$$

The stored energy in each ESS is constrained by upper and lower bounds

$$x_{i,\min} \leq \overline{x}(i,t+k) \leq x_{i,\max} \tag{7.10}$$

The power charged/discharged needs to be lower than certain maximum charging/discharging power limits

$$0 \leq \overline{u}_{\text{Char}}(i,t+k) \leq u_{\text{Char},i,\max} \tag{7.11}$$

$$0 \leq \overline{u}_{\text{Dis}}(i,t+k) \leq u_{\text{Dis},i,\max} \tag{7.12}$$

The expected wind turbine power generation in each MG is constrained between upper ($u_{wt,i,\min}$) and lower ($u_{wt,i,\max}$) bounds

$$u_{wt,i,\min} \leq \tilde{u}_{wt}(i,t+k) \leq u_{wt,i,\max} \tag{7.13}$$

The predicted PV generators power generation in each MG is constrained between upper ($u_{\text{pv},i,\min}$) and lower($u_{\text{pv},i,\max}$) bounds

$$u_{\text{pv},i,\min} \leq \tilde{u}_{\text{pv}}(i,t+k) \leq u_{\text{pv},i,\max} \tag{7.14}$$

The predicted powers sold and purchased to/from the DNO are constrained by upper and lower bounds

$$u_{g,s,\min} < \overline{u}_{g,s}(i,t+k) < u_{g,s,\max} \tag{7.15}$$

$$u_{g,p,\min} < \overline{u}_{g,p}(i,t+k) < u_{g,p,\max}. \tag{7.16}$$

The predicted power balance $\Delta\tilde{u}_{\text{bal}}(j,t+k)$ in the j-th MG and at instant $(t+k)$ is given by:

$$\begin{aligned}
\Delta\tilde{u}_{\text{bal}}(j,t+k) &= \tilde{u}_{wt}(j,t+k)+\tilde{u}_{\text{pv}}(j,t+k) \\
&\quad -\tilde{D}(j,t+k) \\
&= \sum_{i=1,i\neq j}^{M} \overline{u}_{m,s}(j,i,t+k)+\overline{u}_{g,s}(j,t+k) \\
&\quad + \beta_{\text{Char},j}\overline{u}_{\text{Char}}(j,t+k)-\beta_{\text{Dis},j}\overline{u}_{\text{Dis}}(j,t+k)
\end{aligned}$$

$$- \sum_{i=1,i\neq j}^{M} \overline{u}_{m,p}(j,i,t+k)$$
$$- \overline{u}_{g,p}(j,t+k) \tag{7.17}$$

The expected power consumed in the i-th MG $\tilde{D}(i,t+k)$ is constrained by a certain levels of acceptance, which are the bounds that the consumer is satisfied with

$$\begin{aligned} \tilde{D}(i,t+k) - \widehat{\xi}(i,t+k) &< \tilde{D}(i,t+k) \\ &< \tilde{D}(i,t+k) + \widehat{\xi}(i,t+k) \end{aligned} \tag{7.18}$$

It is assumed that each MG cannot simultaneously purchase and sell power from other grids. Consequently, each MG purchases power for negative power balance, and sells power for positive power balance

$$\begin{cases} \overline{u}_{m,s}(j,i,t+k) = 0 & \text{if } \Delta\tilde{u}_{\text{bal}}(j,t+k) < 0 \\ \overline{u}_{m,p}(j,i,t+k) = 0 & \text{if } \Delta\tilde{u}_{\text{bal}}(j,t+k) > 0 \end{cases} \tag{7.19}$$

$$\begin{cases} \overline{u}_{g,s}(i,t+k) = 0 & \text{if } \Delta\tilde{u}_{\text{bal}}(i,t+k) < 0 \\ \overline{u}_{g,p}(i,t+k) = 0 & \text{if } \Delta\tilde{u}_{\text{bal}}(i,t+k) > 0. \end{cases} \tag{7.20}$$

We should note that, as a terminology, the power purchased by the j-th MG is equal to the power sold by the i-th MG

$$\overline{u}_{mp}(j,i,t+k) = \overline{u}_{m,s}(i,j,t+k). \tag{7.21}$$

7.2.6 Case studies

The proposed example is adopted to simulate the real practices and to test models described in the previous sections. A cooperative network of five MG is considered, where each one is interconnected with four adjacent MG and with a DNO (see Fig. 7.2). It is assumed that all MG are connected to the same DNO and the power exchange can take place in both directions. The MG are assumed to be equipped with renewable generators (wind turbine and PV modules), ESSs, and inelastic loads.

The length of the prediction horizon N_p and control horizon N_c are set equal to 24h, and the control interval is 1h. The network of MG is tested under various conditions to evaluate its capabilities when operating with full and empty ESSs (case study 1), with and without prediction errors (case study 2) and finally the operation of a single MG is simulated in order to show the advantage of the proposed framework, relative to controlling a single MG (case study 3).

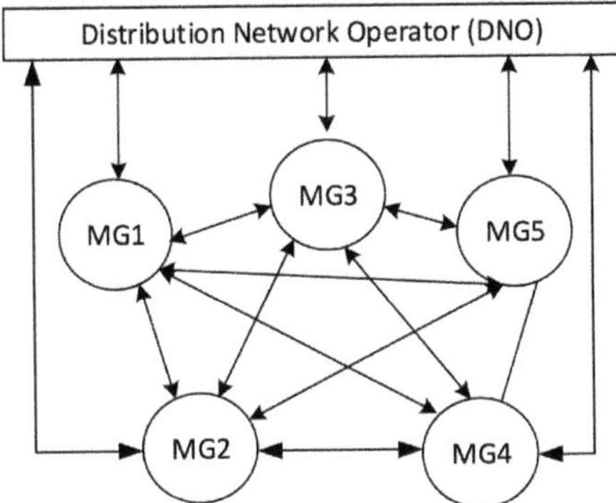

Figure 7.2: Adopted network topology

7.2.7 Simulation setup

It is supposed that the forecasts of the power generations and the loads are made by some appropriate methods. Their algebraic sum results in a predicted power balance ($\Delta\tilde{u}_{\text{bal}}$) characteristic of each MG. The forecasts of $\Delta\tilde{u}_{\text{bal}}$ are reported in Table 7.1, they are represented by independent distributed random vectors.

The expected costs of purchasing energy from the DNO ($\tilde{C}_{g,p}$) are modeled as a time of use pricing (TOU). In this section, Winter Ontario TOU prices (Nov. 1stApr. 30th) are considered and consist of: 1) off-peak prices equal to 0.072 \$/kWh from 7 P.M. to 7 A.M.; 2) mid-peak prices equal to 0.109/kWh from 11 A.M. to 5 P.M.; and 3) on-peak prices equal to 0.129 \$/kWh from 7 A.M. to 11 A.M. and from 5 P.M. to 7 P.M. [515].

The cost vectors $\tilde{C}_{m,p}$, $\tilde{C}_{m,s}$, and $\tilde{C}_{g,s}$ are modeled as constant values equal to 0.08 \$/kWh between 1 and 6A.M. and represented by independent distributed random vectors ranging between 0.075 and 0.14 \$/kWh for the rest of the day. Figure 7.3 shows the predicted costs used in the simulation.

The maximal capacity of the ESS available in each MG is supposed to be comprised between 5 and 500 kWh. For all MG, the maximal charge and discharge powers are all equal, and limited to 50% of the ESS capacity, which means that the ESS can be totally charged or discharged in 2 h. The energy exchanged (sold/purchased) with the DNO is less than 100 kWh. From an operational viewpoint, this range implies that the energy exchange for each MG with the DNO is accepted only if the constraint is satisfied.

7.2.8 Case study 1

The first case study demonstrates the capability of the network of MG under two scenarios of the initial conditions of the ESSs. For both scenarios, it is assumed that, in each MG and for each time period, the updates in the forecast of power

Table 7.1: Predicted values of $\Delta\tilde{u}_{\text{bal}}$ (kW) for the MG

	MG1	MG2	MG3	MG4	MG5
1	79.18	62.35	-0.50	-144.16	44.79
2	90.12	-141.04	-265.56	91.05	-159.36
3	-153.64	113.62	-28.08	52.47	-220.04
4	114.07	124.06	120.62	2.72	-30.73
5	12.21	-145.26	123.77	140.99	-173.89
6	-11.04	-48.40	68.76	131.67	121.79
7	-12.70	225.00	-24.41	98.10	2.49
8	139.81	-47.27	-86.78	-120.64	17.65
9	27.89	-201.11	-197.91	100.53	20.44
10	-125.26	-24.33	64.81	-96.50	157.42
11	-126.39	-11.26	-157.93	-70.63	-145.00
12	94.53	-72.88	-58.70	55.17	-71.88
13	94.78	11.43	20.85	41.00	100.59
14	21.19	-134.78	-74.61	114.09	-130.25
15	142.17	106.45	90.63	190.27	4.20
16	-39.07	-94.40	1.35	49.39	-203.43
17	-111.28	-95.46	45.52	102.85	-143.28
18	-56.59	-97.47	138.50	206.08	32.82
19	-15.78	-26.69	29.08	70.08	-48.75
20	-7.65	38.92	-221.57	29.08	11.28
21	2.49	60.25	-115.01	117.66	120.08
22	140.77	49.90	-7.45	-114.93	18.45
23	-82.55	-130.34	-100.32	-78.80	8.53
24	8.67	-32.37	-102.48	42.38	-51.72

generations, loads, and prices for the next prediction horizon (N_p) are negligible compared to the one performed in previous time step.

The first scenario considers that the initial states of the ESSs available in all MG $\overline{x}(i,0)$, $i = 1,\ldots,5$ are equal and have a value of 5 kWh. In the second scenario, the ESSs are initiated to a full charge states with a full capacity of 500 kWh.

The results showing the total ESSs and the energy exchanged (sold/purchased) during the whole time period with the DNO, according to the considered scenarios are reported in Tables 7.2 and 7.3. In scenario 1 $\overline{x}(i,0) = 5$ kWh), it may be observed that MG1 and MG4 have positive power balances with the DNO over the time horizon, while it is negative for all the others, meaning that the energy purchased is higher than the one sold to the DNO. This may be due to the low energy production and the initial starting states of the ESSs, therefore, the MG supply part of their needs from the DNO. The total energy purchased from the DNO ranges between 120 and 647 kWh, while the total energy sold to the DNO varies between 177 and 565 kWh. Furthermore, the total charging states of the ESSs reach its maximum for the second MG with a value of 492 kWh and its

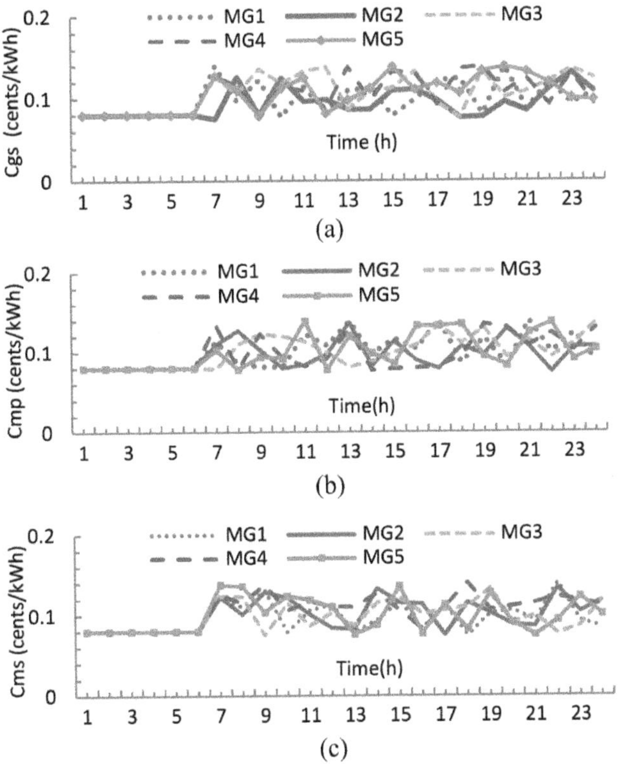

Figure 7.3: (a) Predicted costs of selling energy to the DNO, (b) purchasing energy from MG, and (c) selling energy by MG

Table 7.2: Optimal Energy Management (kWh) for the MG $\bar{x}(i,0) = 5$ kWh

Scenario 1	MG1	MG2	MG3	MG4	MG5
Energy purchased (DNO)	214	499	430	120	647
Energy sold (DNO)	218	177	231	565	223
ESS charge	333	492	461	358	359
ESS discharge	250	369	346	269	269

minimum in MG1 with a value of 333 kWh. The total discharged energy in all MG varies between 250 and 369 kWh. In scenario 1, the optimal value of the cost function is equal to 49.35 $.

In scenario 2 $\bar{x}(i,0) = 500$ kWh), the results show a positive power balance with the DNO for all MG. It is evident that MG4 is always operating in an autonomous mode without access to the DNO.

Table 7.3: Optimal Energy Management (kWh) for the MG $\bar{x}(i,0) = 500$ kWh

Scenario 2	MG1	MG2	MG3	MG4	MG5
Energy purchased (DNO)	127	300	406	0	331
Energy sold (DNO)	623	516	520	934	550
ESS charge	62	132	178	100	84
ESS discharge	459	511	546	488	475

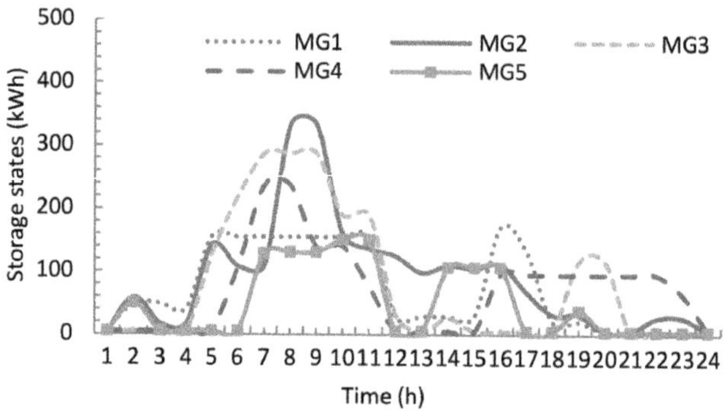

Figure 7.4: State of the ESS available in each MG

Generally, it is observed that a significant energy is discharged from the ESSs, its values range between 459 and 546 kWh, while the ESS charging states have a low variation between 62 and 178 kWh. In addition, it can be seen that a considerable energy, ranging from 516 to 934 kWh, is sold to the DNO. The optimal value of the cost function under scenario 2 presents a higher value (261 \$) than the one in scenario 1 (49.35 \$). As a conclusion, it is demonstrated that the ESS initial states considerably affect the optimal control strategy of the network and the performance of the network of MG.

In the rest of the discussion, the analysis is limited to results of scenario 1. The optimal states of different ESSs are shown in Fig. 7.4. It is reported that the ESSs show different behaviors. Their operation is strongly affected by the capacity of each ESS, the costs of power exchanges, and the optimal control strategies of the energy exchanges in the for MG. The ESSs compensate the variability of power production in each MG, covering a part of the local loads, when possible.

The optimal control of the power charge/discharge of the ESS available in each MG is reported in Fig. 7.5. Different trends can be seen and the highest power charged is observed for MG2, with a value of 250 kW. It is worth mentioning that the charged and discharged powers are limited to 50% of the capacity

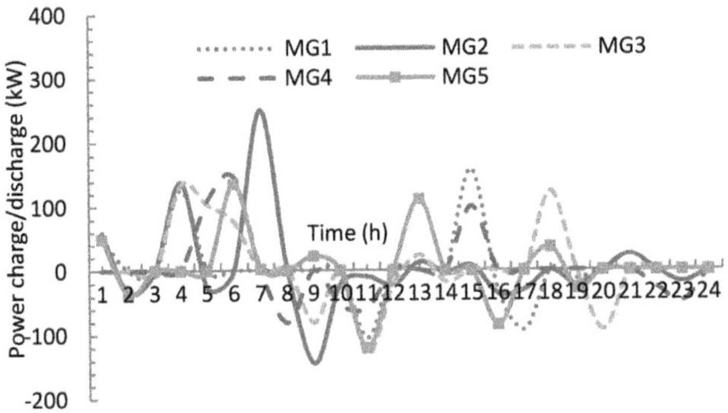

Figure 7.5: Power charge/discharge in each ESS

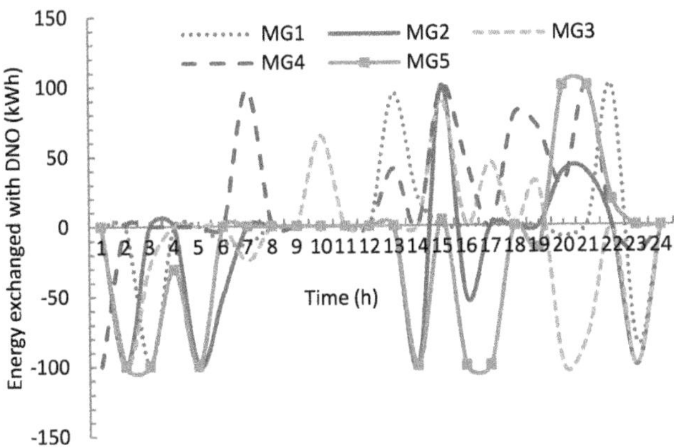

Figure 7.6: MPC-based control strategy for the DNO

of the ESS for all MG, this is in order to enhance the autonomy operation of each MG.

As a convention, positive values correspond to the energy sold while negative ones represent the energy purchased. Figure 7.6 displays the MPC-based optimal control scheduling for the energy exchanged with the DNO. It is reported that MG4 sends the maximal amount of energy to the DNO, while MG5 purchases the highest amount of energy. The sum of the energy purchased from the DNO is 1910 kWh, whereas the MG sell a total energy of 1415 kWh. The energy exchanges with the DNO are restricted to values less than 100 kWh, this is to endorse and promote the charge/discharge of the ESSs and the power exchanges among MG.

Figure 7.7 reports the optimal energy exchanges of MG1 with other MG. The MG1 purchases a total energy of 228 kWh, specifically, 103 kWh from MG4

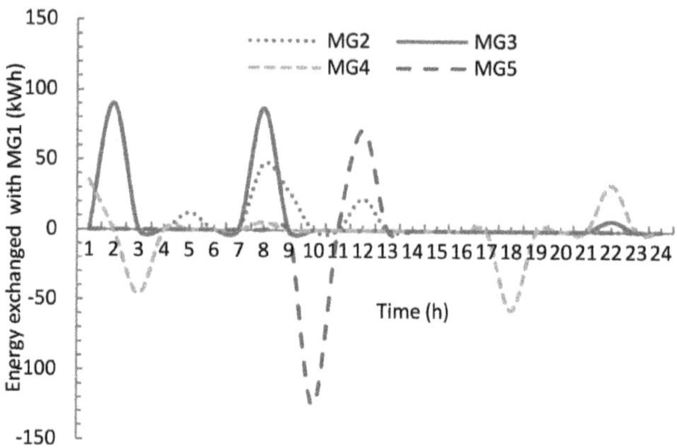

Figure 7.7: MPC-based control strategy for MG1

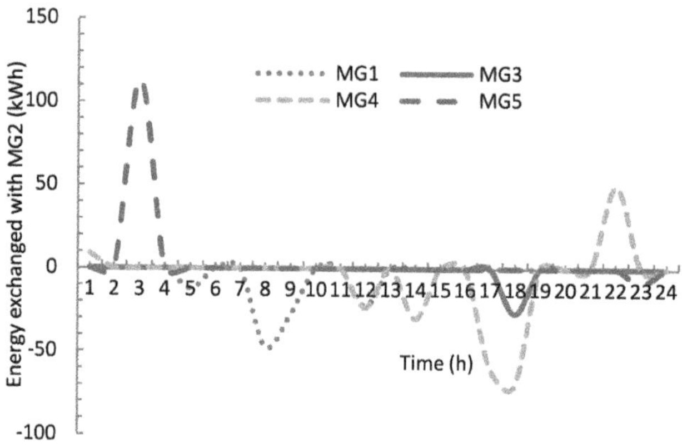

Figure 7.8: MPC-based control strategy for MG2

and 125 kWh from MG5. In addition, MG1 sells a total energy of 440 kWh. The optimal energy management of MG2 is shown in Fig. 7.8. The second MG purchases more energy than what it sells. It purchases a total of 328 kWh coming from MG1 with 110 kWh, MG3 with 27 kWh, MG4 with 183 kWh, and from MG5 with only 8 kWh. Furthermore, MG2 sells 172 kWh mainly, 59 kWh to MG4 and 113 kWh to MG5.

Figure 7.9 represents the optimal control strategy for MG3. It can be observed that, generally, and during the whole time horizon, MG3 purchases energy, mostly from MG1 (184 kWh) and MG4 (279 kWh). This remark can be justified by the high observed power deficit for MG3 (see Table 7.1). The sum of energy sold reaches a value of 58 kWh, where 27 kWh is sold to MG2 and 31 kWh to MG5. Figure 10 shows the optimal energy exchanges of MG4. From the

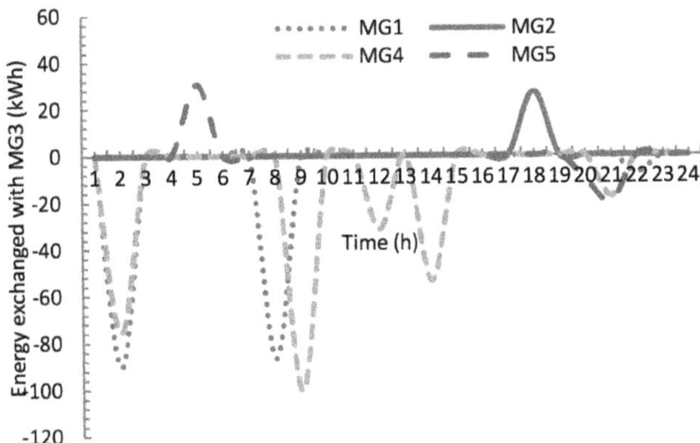

Figure 7.9: MPC-based control strategy for MG3

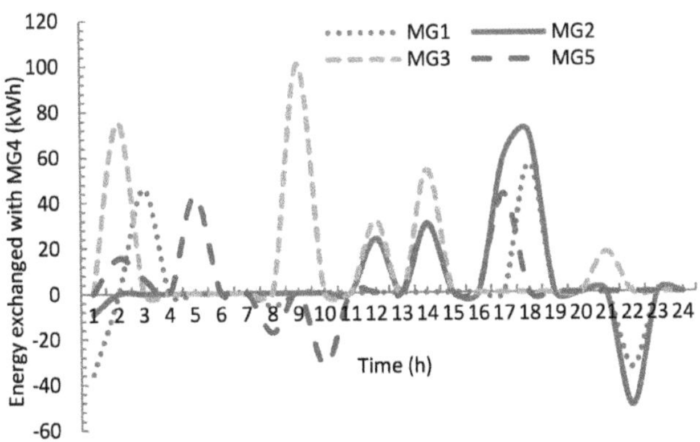

Figure 7.10: MPC-based control strategy for MG4

figure, the MG4 has the highest excess of energy, which is sold to other MG in the network. It sells a total of 706 kWh, particularly 103 kWh to MG1, 183 kWh to MG2, 279 kWh to MG3, and 141 kWh to MG5. While, the sum of the energy purchased does not exceed 183 kWh, 74 kWh coming from MG1, 59 kWh from MG2 and 50 kWh from MG5. Figure 11 reports the control strategy of energy exchanges for MG5. It purchases a total of 357 kWh, distributed as follows: 72 kWh from MG1, 113 kWh from MG2, 31 kWh from MG3 and 141 kWh from MG4. Whereas, MG5 sells 214 kWh as a total, 125 kWh to MG1, 8 kWh to MG2, 31 kWh to MG3 and 50 kWh to MG4.

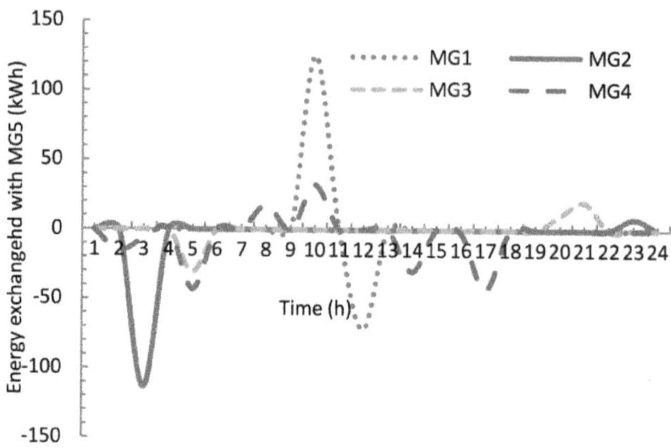

Figure 7.11: MPC-based control strategy for MG5

7.2.9 Case study 2

In this case study, the optimization problem is solved considering that the ESS initial states for $i = 1,...,5$ are equal to 5 kWh. In addition, the problem is solved taking into account an additional noise (low prediction errors) that is applied to the predicted (expected) power balance displayed in Table 7.1. This noise is represented by a normal PDF vector $N(0,1)$. The objective of this case study is to test the robustness of the proposed MPC approach under the presence of prediction errors. The MG4 is selected as an example in order to analyze and measure the effects of prediction errors on the network operation.

The ESS optimal state in MG4 is shown in Fig. 7.12. The figure displays the variation of the storage system of MG4 under the presence and the absence of a noise that is applied to the predicted power balances for the five MG in the network.

As a result, the trends demonstrate similar shapes, with a stored energy drop observed at 7 A.M., where energy stored decrease with about 60 kWh.

The optimal control of the power charge/discharge of the ESS existing in MG4 under the presence/absence of the noise is reported in Fig. 7.13. We can see that the presence of noise occasionally affects the control schedule for charging and discharging the ESS, in addition, this variation follows the original trend with some acceptable deviations when low errors occur.

The MPC-based optimal control scheduling of the total ESSs charged /discharged energy and the energy exchanged (sold/purchased) with the DNO during the time horizon in the presence of prediction errors are reported in Table 7.4. Compared to results displayed in Table 7.2 (obtained for negligible prediction errors), Table 7.4 demonstrates similar ranges for the optimal energy exchange and charge/discharge values.

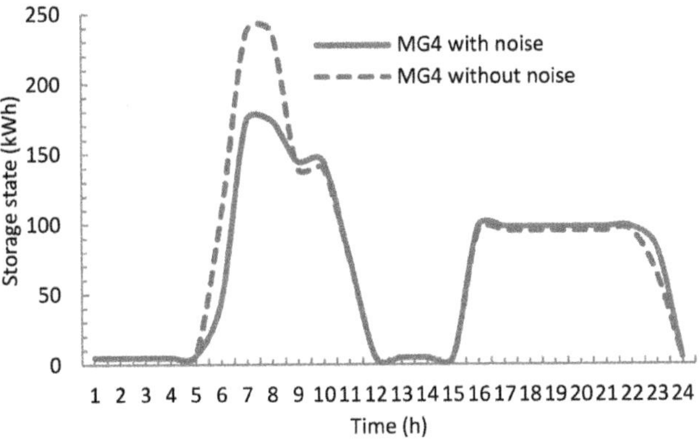

Figure 7.12: Variation of the state of ESS in MG4 under the presence of a noise

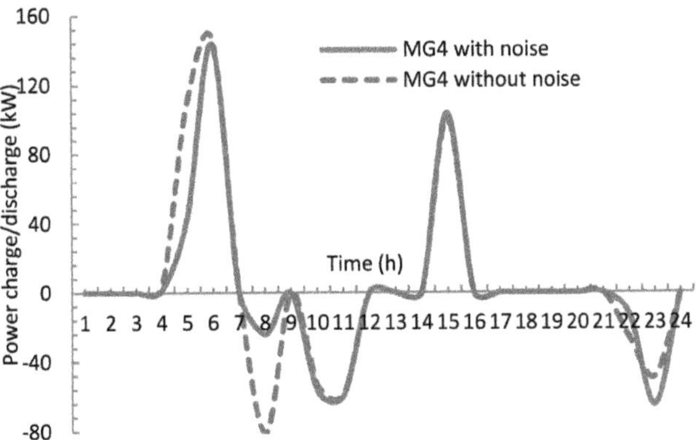

Figure 7.13: Power charged and discharged from the ESS located at MG4 under the presence and the absence of a noise

Table 7.4: Optimal Energy Management (kWh) for the MG in case of prediction errors

Scenario 1. with noise	MG1	MG2	MG3	MG4	MG5
Energy purchased (DNO)	215	492	430	115	630
Energy sold (DNO)	218	177	232	549	223
ESS charge	354	470	500	291	354
ESS discharge	265	352	375	218	266

It can be seen that for low prediction errors, such as the proposed normal PDF, the MPC-based strategy will not be strongly affected, but some variations could be observed. The optimal value of the cost function under case study 2 is equal to

51$, compared to 49.35$ obtained in scenario 1 of case study 1. As a conclusion, and in general, uncertainties in predictions should be given more attention in the optimal control scheduling using the MPC. The prediction errors depend on the prediction horizon, the duration of the prediction slot and the amount of data used to realize predictions at the first time slot.

7.2.10 Case study 3

In this case study, we analyze the performance of the proposed cooperative framework relative to control of a single MG. The aim is to evaluate the effectiveness of the cooperation among MG and how it can affect the control strategy of each MG. The single MG scenario assumes that each MG can exchange power with only the DNO. The scenario adopted has been simulated using the same data relative to case study 1 (scenario 1).

The comparison between energy purchased from the DNO in both cases of single and cooperative MG is reported in Fig. 7.14. It can be observed that the total energy purchased from the DNO is increased significantly, when we consider single MG compared to the case when a network of cooperative MG is adopted. This outcome proves that the cooperation among MG gives more flexibility for the operation of each MG by exchanging power with neighboring MG and maximizing the use of renewable energy. As an example, the optimal performance gains of MG1 and MG4 under cooperative approach are increased by 8.5% and 4.4%, respectively, compared to the single operation scenario. It is worth mentioning that the performance gain is strongly affected by the variation of the energy exchange costs.

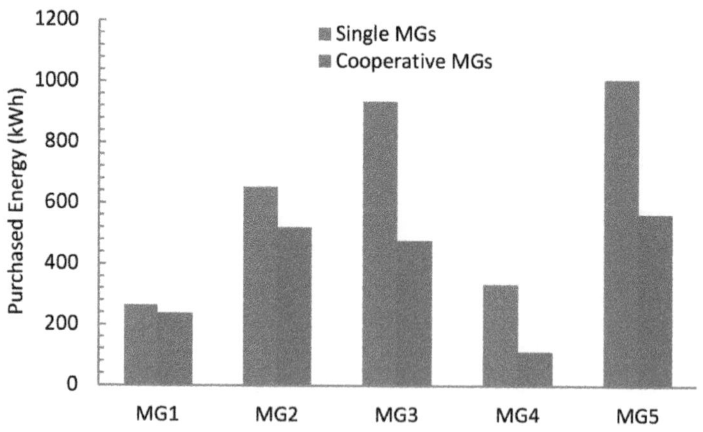

Figure 7.14: Energy purchased from the DNO under single and cooperative MG

7.3 Distributed Robust Control in Smart Microgrids

Smart power grids represent a new concept of power distribution systems, combining information communication technologies, control methodologies, and electrical power grids. On one hand, several intelligent methods based on multiagent system [538], gossip-based algorithms [539], and game theory [540] may be used for distributed controls. In a multiagent distributed configuration, the agents can interact with each other in order to reach local and/or global objectives. For example, each MG may have an agent, which can communicate information as regards its own power demand/offer and/or the allocated local demand response, and can agree on the proper power exchange policy with the other MG within a given time horizon. The main challenge in the distributed cooperative configuration is to reach a consensus among various MG' agents.

On the other hand, the robust control [541] is a technique for structuring uncertainty in the decision-making process, which may be particularly interesting for the control of a network of MG. The objective is to find the optimal solution, taking into account the occurrence of the worst scenario. In [[541] and [542], the problem of distributed decision making in a quadratic game is presented. Authors demonstrate that if there is a solution to the static minimax team problem, then linear decisions are optimal, and the linear optimal solution can be found by solving a linear matrix inequality.

7.3.1 A microgrid model

In the the sequel, an MG is modeled as an inventory system, where both the power internal production and the power internal demand are stochastic processes. As regards the former, each MG can integrate several DGs, which may lead to the exploitation of the available resources in each location in a more stable way. The MG local power production is an RES-based system, specifically based on intermittent sources, e.g., wind and solar sources. Similarly, the MG demand is taken into account as the resultant of the demand of a group of households connected to the MG. It is supposed that the MG demand has to be always fully satisfied. The inventory is represented by a given technology (e.g., a battery or an elevated water reservoir) implementing the ESS. The ESS can improve the stability, power quality, and reliability of the supply.

7.3.2 Microgrid group model

The GCM could be regarded as a model of small dispersed villages, each one with its own MG. A power link agent (PLA) is present on each power connection link connecting two MG or an MG with the MEG. A similar model was adopted in [532]. In this brief, the topology of the TCM is represented as a directed connected graph $\mathcal{G} = \{\mathcal{V}, \mathcal{E}\}$, where $\mathcal{V} = \{1 \dots V\}$ is the vertex set representing both the MG and the MEG. As a convention, the V th vertex is associated with the MEG. $\mathcal{E} = \{1 \dots E\}$ is the set of undirected power links defining the TCM topology.

The MG has power connections with other MG, and at least for one MG with the MEG. The power links also play the role of data links, as it is nowadays commonly implemented in smart power networks. Specifically, the MG network is modeled by the following power balance:

$$s(t+1) = As(t) + Bp(t)\Delta t + e(t)\Delta t \quad t = 0 \dots N-1 \tag{7.22}$$

where $s(t) \in \mathbb{R}^{V-1}$ [kWh] the state vector; its elements represent the energy stored at each MG at instant $t.p(t) \in \mathbb{R}^E$ [kW] the control vector, whose mth element represents the power flow exchanged by the mth PLA in the TCM in time interval $[t, t+\Delta t).e(t) \in \mathbb{R}^{V-1}$, [kW] power balance, whose ith element results from the algebraic sum of demand and production power components in the mth MG, in time interval $[t, t+\Delta t).A \in \mathbb{R}^{(V-1)\times(V-1)}$ diagonal matrix, whose general diagonal element α_m, $0 < \alpha_m < 1$, is the efficiency of the energy storage technology in the mth MG. $B \in \mathbb{R}^{(V-1)\times E}$ incidence matrix, where for each element $b_{i,j}$, it holds that: $b_{m,j} = -1$ if there is a link exiting the mth MG, 1 if there is a link entering the mth MG, and 0 otherwise. Δt is the discrete control time interval.

A link between two MG means that the power can be directly exchanged between them. The power exchange may take place in both the directions. As a convention, the links are directed with a positive power transfer from lower to higher grid numbers, negative in the opposite direction.

It is reasonable to suppose that

$$e(t) = w^d(t) + w(t) \tag{7.23}$$

where $w^d(t) \in \mathbb{R}^{V-1}$ is an esteem of the daily energy balance, whose elements represent a forecast of $e(t).w(t) \in \mathbb{R}^{V-1}$ is the residual error in $e(t)$. It is reasonable to suppose that $\mathbf{E}w(t) = 0$.

Let Δt have unit of measure so that $\Delta t = 1$, specifically, $\Delta t = 1$ h. Then (7.22) can be so rewritten as

$$\begin{aligned} s(t+1) =& As(t) + Bp(t) + w^d(t) + w(t) \\ t =& 0 \dots N-1 \end{aligned} \tag{1a}$$

Let $\tilde{s}(t) \in \mathbb{R}^{V-1}$ be a reference state vector, whose elements represent the optimal level of energy, which is wished at instant t in each MG, as defined either by users' specifications or by technical requirements.

Given $\tilde{e}(t)$, it is possible to compute $\tilde{p}(t) \in BBR^E$, such that

$$B\tilde{p}(t) = \tilde{s}(t+1) - A\tilde{s}(t) - w^d(t). \tag{2a}$$

The vector $\tilde{p}(t)$ is a reference control vector, whose elements represent the power desired to be exchanged on each power link in time interval $[t, t+1)$ as defined by the planning. The problem can be rewritten, taking into account the following change of variables:

$$x(t) = s(t) - \tilde{s}(t) \tag{7.24}$$

$$u(t) = p(t) - \tilde{p}(t) \tag{7.25}$$

where $x(t) \in \mathbb{R}^{V-1}$, [kWh], is the state variable, which represents the energy stored at each MG at instant t, with respect to an optimal working level $\tilde{s}(t); u(t) \in \mathbb{R}^E$, [kW] is the control variable, it represents the power exchanged between MG in time interval $[t, t+1)$, with respect to an optimal working level $\tilde{p}(t)$. Now, (1a) can be so rewritten as

$$x(t+1) = Ax(t) + Bu(t) + w(t) \quad t = 0 \dots N-1.$$

7.3.3 Problem formulation

The problem to be solved is to define the control law for each PLA in order to cooperate for a robust TCM management. The PLA can access the information on the energy level stored in the ESS of each adjacent MG. The PLA's aim is to define the power to be exchanged on its supervised power link, according to a control law which is robust against the various disturbances present in the TCM.

We should highlight that this brief focuses on a high level control of the TCM through properly coordinating power exchanged between grids. This control level typically operates in order to minimize the maximum divergence between powers to be exchanged on all the power connections, as planned by a scheduled agreement, and to minimize the maximum divergence of the energy level in each ESS, taking into account their optimal level. In order to simplify the proposed problem, the communication failures, the frequency dynamics, and the stability of the grids are not considered in this brief. The minimax control problem can be written as the following $\mathcal{P}_N$ problem:

$$\begin{aligned}
\inf_{\mu} \sup_{w \neq 0} \tilde{J}(x,u,w) &= J(x,u,w) - \gamma \sum_{t=0}^{N-1} \|w(t)\|^2 \\
&= x(N)^T Q_N x(N) \sum_{t=0}^{N-1} \left\{ \begin{bmatrix} x(t) \\ u(t) \end{bmatrix}^T Q \begin{bmatrix} x(t) \\ u(t) \end{bmatrix} \right\} \\
&- \gamma_N \sum_{t=0}^{N-1} \|w(t)\|^2
\end{aligned} \tag{7.26}$$

such that (7.3.2) and

$$y_i(t) = C_i x(t) \quad i = 1 \ldots E \ t = 0 \ldots N-1 \tag{7.27}$$

$$u_i(t) = \mu_i(y_i(t)) \quad i = 1 \ldots Et = 0 \ldots N-1 \tag{7.28}$$

where $Q_N \in \mathbb{R}^{(V-1)\times(V-1)}$ is the state cost matrix, $Q_N \succeq 0$, weighting the deviation cost from the reference state vector at instant N.

$$Q = \begin{bmatrix} Q_{xx} & Q_{xu} \\ Q_{ux} & Q_{uu} \end{bmatrix} \in \mathbb{R}^{(E+V-1)\times(E+V-1)}, Q \succeq 0$$

is the state/control cost matrix, representing the deviation cost from the reference state/control vector, respectively, at instants $t, Q_{xx} \in \mathbb{R}^{(V-1)\times(V-1)}, Q_{xu} = Q_{u,x}^T \in \mathbb{R}^{(V-1)\times E}, Q_{uu} \in \mathbb{R}^{E\times E}$, and $Q_{uu} \succ 0$.

Note that $C_i \in \mathbb{R}^{2\times 2(V-1)}$ is the information matrix for the ith PLA at each instant $t, t = 0 \ldots N-1$. It is supposed that, with no delay, at each instant t, each PLA can perfectly receive information on their own current state by the two adjacent MG. So, the elements of C_i are $c_{1,j} = 1$ and $c_{2,k} = 1$, $j < k$, where j and k are the MG adjacent to link i. The other elements of C_i are 0, otherwise. The matrix C is defined as

$$C = \begin{bmatrix} C_1 \\ C_2 \\ \ldots \\ C_E \end{bmatrix} \tag{7.29}$$

where $y_i(t) \in \mathbb{R}^2$ is the output measurement, as observed by each PLA, $u_i(t) \in \mathbb{R}^E$ is the robust control for the ith PLA, and $\mu_i(.)$ is the robust control law, minimizing the problem as a function of $y_i(t)$.

7.3.4 Robust group control

Following the team robust control theory [541], it can be shown that, in minimax team problems with a quadratic cost, linear decisions are optimal and can be found by solving a linear matrix inequality. The reader is referred to [542], with regard to the formalization of the distributed linear quadratic $\mathcal{H}_\infty$ control problem with information constraints, and to [544], where an optimal distributed controller synthesis for chain structures applied to vehicle formations is proposed. The solution of the problem is demonstrated in the following theorem:

Theorem 7.1

Let $\mathcal{P}_N$ be the problem defined by (7.3.2) and (7.26)(7.28) on $N \geq 1$ time intervals. The following statements are true.

$\mathcal{P}_N$ can be reduced to the following static problem $\bar{\mathcal{P}}_N$:

$$\begin{aligned}
\inf_{\mu}\sup_{w\neq 0} \begin{bmatrix}\bar{x}\\ \bar{u}\end{bmatrix}^T \bar{Q} \begin{bmatrix}\bar{x}\\ \bar{u}\end{bmatrix} &- \gamma_N\|\bar{x}\|^2 && (7.30)\\
y_i &= \bar{C}_i\bar{x} && (7.31)\\
\bar{u}_i &= \bar{\mu}_i(\bar{y}_i) && (7.32)
\end{aligned}$$

where

$$\bar{x} = \begin{bmatrix} w(N-1)\\ w(N-2)\\ \dots\\ w(0)\\ x(0)\end{bmatrix} \quad \bar{x}\in\mathbb{R}^{(V-1)(N+1)} \qquad (7.33)$$

$$\bar{u}_i = \begin{bmatrix} u_i(N-1)\\ u_i(N-2)\\ \dots\\ u_i(0)\end{bmatrix} \quad \bar{u}\in\mathbb{R}^{EN} \qquad (7.34)$$

$$\breve{A} = \begin{bmatrix} I_{V-1} & A & \dots & A^{N-1}\\ 0 & I_{V-1} & \dots & A^{N-2}\\ \dots & \dots & \dots & \dots\\ 0 & 0 & 0 & I_{V-1}\\ 0 & 0 & 0 & 0\end{bmatrix}$$

$$\breve{A} \in \mathbb{R}^{(N+1)(V-1)xN(V-1)} \qquad (7.35)$$

$$\bar{A} = \begin{bmatrix} I_{V-1} & A & \dots & A^{N-1} & A^N\\ 0 & I_{V-1} & \dots & A^{N-2} & A^{N-1}\\ \dots & \dots & \dots & \dots & \dots\\ 0 & 0 & 0 & I_{V-1} & A\\ 0 & 0 & 0 & 0 & I_{V-1}\end{bmatrix}$$

$$\bar{A} \in \mathbb{R}^{(V-1)(N+1)x(V-1)(N+1)} \qquad (7.36)$$

$$\bar{B} = \breve{A}diag_N(B) \quad \bar{B}\in\mathbb{R}^{(N+1)(V-1)\times EN} \qquad (7.37)$$

$$\bar{C}_i = [0_{2Nx(V-1)} \quad diag_N(C_i)]\bar{A}$$

$$\bar{C}_i \in \mathbb{R}^{2Nx(V-1)(N+1)} \qquad (7.38)$$

$$\bar{Q} = \begin{bmatrix}\bar{Q}_{xx} & \bar{Q}_{xu}\\ \bar{Q}_{ux} & \bar{Q}_{uu}\end{bmatrix}$$

$$\bar{Q} \in \mathbb{R}^{(V-1)(N+1)+EN\times(V-1)(N+1)+EN} \qquad (7.39)$$

$$\bar{Q}_{xx} = \bar{A}^T \begin{bmatrix} Q_N & 0_{(V-1)xN(V-1)}\\ 0_{N(V-1)x(V-1)} & diag_N(Q_{xx})\end{bmatrix}\bar{A} \qquad (7.40)$$

$$\bar{Q}_{uu} = \bar{B}^T \begin{bmatrix} Q_N & 0_{(V-1)xN(V-1)}\\ 0_{N(V-1)x(V-1)} & diag_N(Q_{xx})\end{bmatrix}\bar{B} + ding_N(Q_{uu}) \qquad (7.41)$$

$$\bar{Q}_{xu} = \bar{Q}_{ux}^T = \bar{A}^T \begin{bmatrix} Q_N & 0_{(V-1)xN(V-1)} \\ 0_{N(V-1)x(V-1)} & diag_N(Q_{xx}) \end{bmatrix} \bar{B} + \begin{bmatrix} 0_{(V-1)xNE} \\ diag_N(Q_{uu}) \end{bmatrix}. \quad (7.42)$$

The control law (7.28), for each PLA i, is linear, that is

$$\bar{u}_i = \bar{\mu}_i(\bar{y}_i) = \bar{K}_i \bar{C}_i \bar{x} \quad i = 1 \ldots E \quad (7.43)$$

with $\bar{K}_i \in \mathbb{R}^{2N}$.

The control law (7.28) can be computed by solving the following problem:

$$\min_{\gamma_N, K} \gamma_N \quad (7.44)$$

$$s.t.\ \bar{K} = diag(K_{1,\ldots,}K_E) = \begin{bmatrix} \bar{K}_1 & 0 & 0 & 0 \\ 0 & \bar{K}_2 & 0 & 0 \\ 0 & 0 & \ldots & 0 \\ 0 & 0 & 0 & \bar{K}_E \end{bmatrix} \quad (7.45)$$

$$\begin{pmatrix} \bar{Q}_{xx} - \gamma_N I + \bar{Q}_{xu}\bar{K}\bar{C} + \bar{C}^T\bar{K}^T\bar{Q}_{ux} & \bar{C}^T\bar{K}^T \\ \bar{K}\bar{C} & -\bar{Q}_{uu}^{-1} \end{pmatrix} \preccurlyeq 0 \quad (7.46)$$

where

$$\bar{C} = diag_N(C) \quad (7.47)$$

Proof 7.1 At the generic instant t, the state $x(t)$ can be written as

$$x(t) = A^t x(0) + \sum_{n=0}^{t-1} A^n Bu(t-n-1) + \sum_{n=0}^{t-1} A^n w(t-n-1), \quad t = 1 \ldots N. \quad (7.48)$$

For the ith PLA, the knowledge of the adjacent components of $x(t)$ is equivalent to the knowledge of the elements of $w(t-1)$ in the adjacent MG, as the ith element of $u(t-1)$ is also known.

The introduction of $\bar{x}$ and $\bar{u}_i$, as proposed in [531], allows the definition of the static problem (7.26)–(7.28), which is equivalent to $\mathcal{P}_N$. Thus, the problem has been restated in the matrix form specified in [[541] Th. 1], both of whose following statements have been shown to be true.

7.3.5 Distributed information models

It is worthwhile to underline the different information context for $\mathcal{P}_N$, when $N = 1$ and when $N > 1$. For $N = 1$, the information available to each PLA is related to the state $x(0)$, limited to the two adjacent MG to the link managed by that PLA, say $x_j(0)$ and $x_k(0)$. The control is on one step, but the procedure can be iterated with a new access to the information of the state $x_j(1)$ and $x_k(1)$ as modified by $u(0)$, as computed by the different PLA adjacent to MG j and k.

When $N > 1$, as in the previous case, each PLA i can receive information at instant $t = 0$ on the state $x_j(0)$ and $x_k(0)$, by the observation $y_i(0)$. For the following instants, $x_j(t)$ and $x_k(t)$ depend on the previous values of the control signal $\check{u}(t), \check{t} < t$, and on the noise component $w(\check{t})$. Specifically, the components $u_m(\check{t})$ that $y_i(t)$ depends on are completely determined by the structure of the matrix $[C_iA^nB]_{i,m}$ [542], and as it can be easily verified, $[C_iA^nB]_{i,m} \neq 0$ so, for the generic PLA i, it is possible to perform the control observing $w_j(t-1)$ and $w_k(t-1)$ at instant t.

7.3.6 Simulation study

In this case study, a network of $(V-1) = 2$ MG connected by $E = 3$ power connections is considered, see Fig. 7.15. The MG are assumed to be equipped with renewable generators (e.g., wind turbine and PV modules), storage devices, and loads. Each MG is interconnected with one or more adjacent MG and/or with the main electrical grid, where power can be exchanged in both the directions.

The matrixes A and B , required in (7.3.2), are given by

$$A = \begin{bmatrix} 0.99 & 0 \\ 0 & 0.95 \end{bmatrix} \tag{7.49}$$

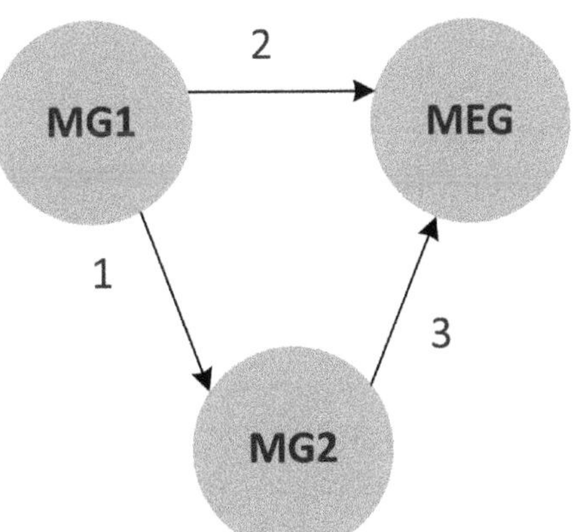

Figure 7.15: Topology of the TCM. Two MG (MG1 and MG2) are connected for power exchange, managed by a PLA defining robust power flow on link 1. MEG is the main electrical grid, with no observed state. Two additional PLAs manage the robust power exchange on link 2 and link 3

$$B = \begin{bmatrix} -1 & -1 & 0 \\ 1 & 0 & -1 \end{bmatrix} \tag{7.50}$$

The matrices for the cost function (7.26) are given by

$$Q_{xx} = 100 * I_2 \tag{7.51}$$

$$Q_{xu} = Q_{ux} = 0_{3,2} \tag{7.52}$$

$$Q_{uu} = \begin{bmatrix} 1 & 0 & 0 \\ 0 & 100 & 0 \\ 0 & 0 & 100 \end{bmatrix} \tag{7.53}$$

$$Q_N = Q = \begin{bmatrix} Q_{xx} & Q_{xu} \\ Q_{ux} & Q_{uu} \end{bmatrix} \tag{7.54}$$

The matrices C_i described in (7.27), where $i = 1 \ldots 3$ is referred to each PLA, are given by

$$C_1 = \begin{bmatrix} 1 & 0 \\ 0 & 1 \end{bmatrix} \tag{7.55}$$

$$C_2 = \begin{bmatrix} 1 & 0 \\ 0 & 0 \end{bmatrix} \tag{7.56}$$

$$C_3 = \begin{bmatrix} 0 & 0 \\ 0 & 1 \end{bmatrix} \tag{7.57}$$

The zero rows are related to the connection with the main grid, where no state is available. The state $x(t)$ is expressed in units of 100 kWh, and the control $u(t)$ in units of 100 kW. Time is discretized on time intervals of 1 h. A stochastic noise $w(t) \in \mathcal{N}(0,1)$ affects the state at each instant t.

7.3.7 Solution procedure A

In this section, the problem has been solved on one step horizon ($N = 1$). In this case, the system to be solved is

$$\begin{aligned}
\inf_{\mu} \sup_{w \neq 0} &= x(1)^T Q_N x(1) + \begin{bmatrix} x(0) \\ u(0) \end{bmatrix}^T Q \begin{bmatrix} x(0) \\ u(0) \end{bmatrix} \\
&\quad - \gamma_1 \|x(0)\|^2 - \gamma_1 \|w(0)\|^2 && (7.58) \\
\text{s.t.: } x_1(1) &= 0.99 x_1(0) - u_1(0) - u_2(0) + w_1(0) && (7.59) \\
x_2(1) &= 0.95 x_1(0) - u_1(0) - u_3(0) + w_2(0) && (7.60) \\
y_1(0) &= C_1 x(0) && (7.61) \\
y_2(0) &= C_2 x(0) && (7.62) \\
y_3(0) &= C_3 x(0) && (7.63) \\
u_1(t) &= K_1 y_1(t) && (7.64)
\end{aligned}$$

$$u_2(t) = K_2 y_2(t) \quad (7.65)$$
$$u_3(t) = K_3 y_3(t) \quad (7.66)$$

The value γ_1 is $\gamma_1 = 167.1529$. Table 7.5 shows the K_i values obtained for each PLA. The condition for asymptotical stability in the closed loop –that is the eigenvalues λ_i are such that $|\lambda_i(A+BK)| < 1$– is satisfied ($\lambda_1 = 0.0013$ and $\lambda_2 = 0.2774$).

7.3.8 Solution procedure B

The problem has been solved on six steps horizon ($N = 6$). The control law is given here for each instant $t = 0\ldots5$ by $u_i(0) = K_i(0)x(0)$ for the first time interval $[0,1)$, and by $u_i(t) = K_i(t)w(0)$, for each time interval $[t, t+1)t = 1\ldots4$. The value γ_6 is $\gamma_6 = 196.58$. Table 7.6 shows the K_i values obtained for each PLA. The condition for asymptotic stability in the closed loop is satisfied at each time interval.

7.3.9 Solution procedure C

Table 7.7 shows the γ_N values, which are obtained solving $\mathcal{P}_N$ for $1 \leq N \leq 6$. It can be observed that these values have a trend, which is dependent on the time windows that have been used. The larger the time window is, the higher is the resulting cost function. This is reasonable, as with larger time window, the control strategy has to be defined as a play against a larger number of uncertain values.

7.3.10 Solution procedure D

Two control approaches have been tested on a time horizon lasting 6 h: The first one adopts the control strategy defined by $\mathcal{P}_1$, iterating it six times; and the second one adopts the control strategy defined by $\mathcal{P}_6$.

Each of the two approaches has been tested on 10^5 different instances.

Let us define $\tilde{\gamma}_N$, the value obtained for $\tilde{J}(x,u,w)$ as defined in (7.26), for each given random instance applying the control as a solution of P_N. Figure 7.16(a) shows the distribution of $\tilde{\gamma}_6$ when the control obtained solving P_1 is iteratively

Table 7.5: K_i Values obtained for each PLA in $\mathcal{P}_1$

PLA i	$k_{i,j}(0)$	$k_{i,k}(0)$
1	$k_{1,1}(0) = 0.1552$	$k_{1,2}(0) = -0.1210$
2	$k_{2,2}(0) = 0.6783$	$k_{2,3}(0) = 0$
3	$k_{3,3}(0) = 0.7069$	$k_{3,3}(0) = 0$

Table 7.6: K_i Values obtained for each PLA in $\mathcal{P}_6$

t	PLA i	$k_{i,j}(0)$	$k_{i,k}(0)$
0	1	$k_{1,1}(0) = 0.0201$	$k_{1,2}(0) = 1.4e-06$
0	2	$k_{2,2}(0) = 0.9755$	$k_{2,3}(0) = 0$
0	3	$k_{3,1}(0) = 0.9500$	$k_{3,3}(0) = 0$
1	1	$k_{1,1}(0) = 0.0120$	$k_{1,2}(0) = -0.0107$
1	2	$k_{2,2}(0) = 0.9784$	$k_{2,3}(0) = 0$
1	3	$k_{3,1}(0) = 0.9618$	$k_{3,3}(0) = 0$
2	1	$k_{1,1}(0) = 0.0094$	$k_{1,2}(0) = -0.0122$
2	2	$k_{2,2}(0) = 0.9775$	$k_{2,3}(0) = 0$
2	3	$k_{3,1}(0) = 0.9640$	$k_{3,3}(0) = 0$
3	1	$k_{1,1}(0) = 0.0169$	$k_{1,2}(0) = -0.0083$
3	2	$k_{2,2}(0) = 0.09678$	$k_{2,3}(0) = 0$
3	3	$k_{3,1}(0) = 0.09654$	$k_{3,3}(0) = 0$
4	1	$k_{1,1}(0) = 0.0344$	$k_{1,2}(0) = -0.0237$
4	2	$k_{2,2}(0) = 0.9321$	$k_{2,3}(0) = 0$
4	3	$k_{3,1}(0) = 0.9322$	$k_{3,3}(0) = 0$
5	1	$k_{1,1}(0) = 0.1066$	$k_{1,2}(0) = -0.0977$
5	2	$k_{2,2}(0) = 0.7843$	$k_{2,3}(0) = 0$
5	3	$k_{3,1}(0) = 0.7843$	$k_{3,3}(0) = 0$

Table 7.7: γ_N Values resulting from different $\mathcal{P}_N$ solvings

N	1	2	3	4	5	6
γ_N	167.15	187.49	193.83	195.78	196.30	196.58

adopted. Figure 7.16(b) shows the distribution of $\tilde{\gamma}_6$ when the control obtained solving P_6 is adopted. The values obtained in Fig. 7.16(a) have an overall average value of 146.20, but a maximum of 239.04 has been reached for one instance. On the other hand, the values obtained in Fig. 7.16(b), although with a higher average, i.e., 175.02, as expected, respect the constraint $\tilde{\gamma}_N < \gamma_N = 196.58$ (the higher value obtained is 195.86).

Table 7.8 shows the main statistical characteristics of the control and of the state values obtained in the different random instances. It can be observed that there is not such an evident difference in the statistical characteristics of the state and control, adopting the two different strategies.

7.4 Notes

In this section, an advanced MPC approach for the high-level coordination of power exchanges in a network of MG is presented. A MPC-based algorithm is

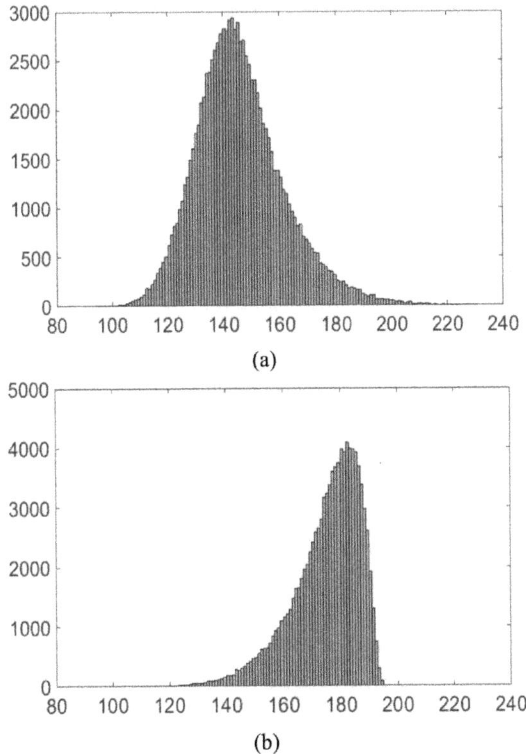

Figure 7.16: $\tilde{\gamma}$ values obtained in two different control approaches. Histogram of the $\tilde{\gamma}$ values obtained in the different control approaches both applied on a time horizon lasting 6 h. (a) Results for the $\tilde{\gamma}$ values adopting the control strategy P_1 solved on one step horizon and iterated six times. (b) $\tilde{\gamma}$ values obtained by solving control strategy P_6 solved on six steps horizon

Table 7.8: Main statistical values of the resulting state and control adopting the solution obtained solving P_1 and iterating it six times, versus the solution obtained solving P_6

	control	avg	dt.dev	max	min
x	$\mathcal{P}_1$	-0.0021	1.0179	5.0130	-4.9277
x	$\mathcal{P}_6$	6.60e-04	1.0007	4.9875	-4.8812
u	$\mathcal{P}_1$	-0.0011	0.5866	3.5361	-3.4832
u	$\mathcal{P}_6$	7.27e-04	0.7621	4.7381	-4.3674

used to determine the future scheduling of power exchanges among dispersed MG as well as the charge/discharge in each local ESS for the future time horizon. The focus of this paper is on global control of a network of MG, where the objective is to maximize the benefits at the network level. Here, each MG is a renewable-based MG, modeled as a system consisting of local loads, ESS, and locally producing power from RESs. In conclusion, it has been demonstrated that the cooperation among grids has significant advantages and benefits to each single grid operation in terms of integrating strategies to face shortage or excess of power production due to the uncontrollable RESs behavior. In addition, the uncertainties in predictions may have effects on the optimal control scheduling.

The proposed cooperation among grids may share some drawbacks with the centralized approaches, which include, among others, the failure of real-time communication with one or more grids. These issues can be taken into account, extending the current problem formulation, on a larger scale by adopting a distributed MPC control strategy. In this case, the decisions will be taken locally with a dynamic network topology, using approaches as team theory, distributed, and decentralized control.

Next, a distributed robust control problem for the power flows in a cooperative network of MG. The proposed framework attempts to contribute to the development of a new challenging and emergent problem focused on a cooperating team decision scheme for the robust control of the power flows in a TCM. The problem of a TCM has been defined in order to maximize the satisfaction of the quality of service, which is defined here as the minimization of the maximum divergence from an agreed power exchange within the TCM and with the MEG, as well as from a technical reference value of each ESS. The strength of the proposed framework comes from its capability to enable the direct incorporation of uncertainties related to RES and loads in the optimization models as well as the adoption of a distributed approach to model the power exchanges among MG.

Compared with the previous efforts on MG network operation [539], [543] that are centralized and suffer from reliability problems, the proposed approach adopts a robust distributed control design scheme to model power exchange in a TCM. This feature makes the approach more suitable for real implementation and guarantees robustness against disturbances.

Future developments and research will be devoted to the generation of the optimal solution of the control strategies using a mix of robust control and optimal average control.

Chapter 8

Dynamic Graphical Games

8.1 Constrained Graphical Games

The constrained graphical game is a special type of the standard games [545] , where the policies of the nodes are constrained and the communications between the nodes are done via a communication graph topology [546, 547]. This work brings together game theory, computational graph theory, multi-system coordination, reinforcement learning, adaptive critics, and optimal control.

The field of cooperative control has many applications in robotics, physical networks, unmanned vehicles, etc. [548]. The cooperative control problems are classified into consensus and synchronization problems. A neighbor-based controller is developed for multi-agent systems with a leader and varying communication topology in [549]. The ℓth-order model-reference problem is studied in [550], where the variable and its higher order derivatives reach the common goals. The consensus in complex networks is achieved using a distributed observer protocol [551]. The consensus problem is studied for a network of dynamic nodes with fixed and varying switching topologies in [552]. Random pinning control schemes have been used to control scale-free dynamical networks by pinning to a small number of nodes in [553].

The non-cooperative game theoretic framework is used to solve the optimal control problems for multi-agent systems [545, 554, 555]. Optimal control theory is used to derive the necessary conditions to optimize the objective functions [556]. The solution of the game's Hamilton-Jacobi (HJ) equation yields a Nash equilibrium [545, 557], which is equivalent to solving the game's Riccati equation. Markov network is used to calculate the correlated equilibrium in [558]. The games are formulated on graphs, where the agents are allowed to exchange information in [546, 547]. A near-optimal control algorithm is proposed for non-linear systems, formulating a non-zero sum game in [559]. In this algorithm, the stability of the closed loop system is shown without using initial stabilizing policies.

8.1.1 Reinforcement learning

Reinforcement Learning (RL) is one field of Machine Learning [560, 561]. It is employed to find the optimal control solutions for dynamical systems in [561, 562]. The RL approaches are designed to select the policies that minimize the objective function in dynamic learning environments [560, 561]. The RL approaches are implemented using two-step approaches, known as value and policy iteration techniques [563, 564, 565, 566]. Value and policy iteration solutions are developed for multi-agent systems formulating graphical games in [547], [567]. RL approaches are used in [568] to implement the approximate Dual Heuristic Programming (DHP) solutions for graphical games. The reward shaping is used to direct the agent's exploration by adding additional rewards to those obtained in the learning environment [569]. It is shown that the potential based reward shaping does not change the true Pareto front in the single and multi-objective RL solutions [569]. Integral Reinforcement Learning (IRL) is developed in order to solve the optimal control problem for a single agent system in [566]. An IRL-H_∞-based controller is developed for a flux-switching permanent magnet (FSPM) machine in a hostile environment in [570]. An IRL-based automatic voltage regulator for power systems is developed in [571]. This controller does not need to know the full dynamics of the model. An integral Q-Learning load frequency controller is developed for the power systems in [572]. An off-policy IRL optimal control tracking algorithm is proposed for a Lorenz chaotic system in [573]. Another off-policy RL control algorithm is developed for a rotational / translational actuator nonlinear benchmark problem in [574]. A similar algorithm is developed for a two-link manipulator in [575]. An IRL approach is proposed to solve a nonlinear optimal control problem with input-affine dynamics in [576]. Multi-Agent Reinforcement Learning (MARL) techniques have gained interest in industrial applications like robotic assembly lines, resource allocation and management, data mining, and decision support systems [577, 578, 579, 580]. MARL approaches have been developed for discrete-time systems in [581, 582]. The convergence for each node relies on the convergence of all the other nodes simultaneously. An off-policy RL algorithm is proposed to solve a cooperative control problem using a game's theoretic frame-work in [583], where a behavioral policy is used for learning purposes. A residual gradient Fuzzy-RL approach is used to solve the pursuit-evasion games in [584], where it outperformed the Q-learning solutions [584].

Adaptive critics are employed to implement the value and policy iteration solutions for the optimal control problems in [585]. The adaptive critics' approaches use actor-critic neural network structures to approximate the RL solutions [561], [585]. The critic weights are updated based on the assessment of the actions applied to the dynamic environment. The goal of the assessment is to optimize a utility function. On the other hand, the actor weights are updated using knowledge about the critic assessment and the dynamic behavior of the system [561]. Adaptive critics are used to implement the Approximate Dynamic Programming (ADP) solutions for the optimal control problems. A summary on the robustness of the ADP control strategies for the nonlinear optimal control problems has been introduced in [586]. It highlighted the stabilization conditions of nonlinear systems and the stability of interconnected systems under uncertainties. In addition, the ADP approaches considered therein, were applied to practical examples in order to show their usefulness. The RL solutions for the optimal control problem are implemented using actor-critic neural networks in [563, 564, 585]. Online and offline policy iteration approaches are used to solve the nonzero-sum games for a class of nonlinear systems, where the actor-critic neural networks' approximation errors are shown to be bounded [587]. A critic neural network is proposed for each agent of a multi-agent system in order to solve the non-zero sum game in [559]. The actor network structure was not needed in this ADP solution. Also, adaptive critics were used to implement the graphical game's solution using the concept of behavioral policy in [583]. This section contributes to the solution framework of the differential games on graphs, where a novel adaptive learning solution based on IRL is proposed in order to solve the game with constrained polices.

8.1.2 Synchronization control problem

Each node i in the graph Ω has the following uniform dynamics [546, 547]

$$\dot{\pi}_i = A\,\pi_i + B_i\,u_i, \tag{8.1}$$

where $\pi_i \in R^n$ and $u_i \in R^{m_i}$ are the states and policy for each node i. A and B_i are the physical parameters for each node i. The input control signals $u_i \in R^{m_i}, \forall i$ are of the saturated and nonlinear type. The objective of the synchronization problem is to select the policies such that the nodes are able to synchronize to the leader node's dynamics. The leader node is an autonomous command generator that generates the desired trajectory, where the follower nodes do not affect the leader's dynamics [590, 591].

The dynamics of the leader node $\pi_0 \in R^n$ are given by:

$$\dot{\pi}_0 = A\,\pi_0. \tag{8.2}$$

The competitive behavior for each node i is restricted by the graph topology. Synchronization among nodes is achieved using pinning ideas [553], [592], where the leader communicates with a small number of nodes [593]. This competitive behavior is described by the following error protocol

$$\theta_i = \sum_{j \in N_i} c_{ij} \left(\pi_i - \pi_j\right) + \gamma_i \left(\pi_i - \pi_0\right), \tag{8.3}$$

where $\theta_i \in R^n$ and $\gamma_i > 0$ are the local tracking error and the pinning gain for node i, respectively.

In order to analyze the collective behavior of the nodes, the global tracking error vector is given by

$$\theta = \left(\left(L + \Gamma\right) \otimes I_n \right) \left(\pi - \underline{\pi}_0\right), \tag{8.4}$$

where $\pi = \left[\begin{array}{cccc} \pi_1^T & \pi_2^T & .. & \pi_N^T \end{array} \right]^T \in R^{nN}$ is global vector of the nodes' states, $\theta \in R^{nN}$ is the global vector of the tracking error states, $\otimes$ is the Kronecker product symbol, and $\underline{\pi}_0 = \underline{I}\pi_0 \in R^{nN}$, with $\underline{I} = \underline{1} \otimes I_n \in R^{nN \times n}$ and $\underline{1} \in R^N$ is a vector of ones. $\Gamma \in R^{N \times N}$ is a matrix with diagonal entries of the pinning gains γ_i, $\forall i$.

Let the minimum singular value of $(L + \Gamma)$ be non-zero (*i.e., the graph is strongly connected*) and the leader is pinned to few number of nodes, then, the vector $(\pi - \underline{\pi}_0)$ is bounded or $\lim_{t \to \infty} \|(\pi_i - \pi_0)\| = 0, \forall i$. The local error dynamics are given by

$$\dot{\theta}_i = A\,\theta_i + \left(o_i + \gamma_i\right) B_i\, u_i - \sum_{j \in N_i} c_{ij} B_j\, u_j. \tag{8.5}$$

The dynamic model (8.5) shows the competitive behavior for each node i. This behavior depends on the control efforts of node i and those of its neighbors. The optimal control problem would select the policies u_i, $\forall i$ to guarantee asymptotic stability of the tracking error system (8.5).

8.1.3 Performance evaluation of the game

The nodes interacting on graphs with constrained control inputs form constrained graphical games. The errors (8.5) represent interactive and coupled dynamic systems. Therefore, a performance index is developed to reflect the coupling and the constrained properties of the graphical game such that

$$\begin{aligned} J_i(\bar{\theta}_i(t_o), \{u_i, u_{-i}\}_{t_o \geq 0}) &= \int_{t_o}^{\infty} U_i(\theta_i, u_i, u_{-i})\, dt \\ &= \tfrac{1}{2} \int_{t_o}^{\infty} (\theta_i^T Q_{ii} \theta_i + 2 \int_0^{u_i} (\Phi^{-1}(v_i))^T R_{ii} dv_i) + \\ &\quad \textstyle\sum_{j \in N_i} u_j^T R_{ij} u_j) dt, \end{aligned} \tag{8.6}$$

where $Q_{ii} \geq 0$, $R_{ii} > 0$, and $R_{ij} > 0$ are symmetric weighting matrices, U_i is the utility function, $\bar{\theta}_i$ is a local vector of the states of node i and those of its neighbors, $\Phi : R^n \to R^{m_i}$ is a bounded, integrable, one-to-one, real-analytic globally

Lipschitz continuous function, $u_{-i} = \{u_j | j \in N_i\}$ are the control policies of the neighbors of node i, and $u_{\bar{i}} = \{u_j | j \in N,\ j \neq i\}$ are all the policies except that of node i.

Herein, a brief comparison between the standard differential game and the constrained graphical game is introduced. The structure of the constrained graphical games is a subtype of the standard differential games [545]. The dynamics vector of the standard N-player differential game is given by

$$\dot{\chi} = F\chi + \sum_{i=1}^{N} B^i u_i, \tag{8.7}$$

where $\chi \in R^{\tilde{N}}$ is a global vector of the states and $u_i \in R^{m_i}$is the policy for each node i.

The standard game is evaluated for each node i using the following global performance measure index

$$\tilde{J}_i(\{\chi, u_i\}_{t \geq 0}) = \tfrac{1}{2} \int_{t=0}^{\infty} (\chi^T \hat{Q}_{ii} \chi + \sum_{j \in N} u_j^T \hat{R}_{ij} u_j) d\tau, \tag{8.8}$$

where $\hat{Q}_{ii} \geq 0 \in R^{\tilde{N} \times \tilde{N}}$ and $\hat{R}_{ij} > 0 \in R^{m_j \times m_j}$ are symmetric time-invariant weighting matrices.

For the standard differential game, both the performance measure index (8.8) and the dynamics (8.7) use global information (all policies and states of the nodes). On the other hand, the constrained graphical game takes into account the interactions between the nodes within the graph structure to solve the game. The measure index (8.6) evaluates the local interactions for each node i. This means that it depends on node's i states, its constrained control input, and the constrained control inputs of its neighbors. This is a main technical difference between the index (8.6) of the constrained graphical game and the global index (8.8) of the standard games. Index (8.6) motivates distributed solution forms for the constrained game. Moreover, this local structure relaxes the global reachability conditions imposed by the standard form of the differential game [545]. The standard game employs a centralized form of the Riccati equation, where global reachability conditions are required in order to find the Nash solution [545]. This is not the case for the differential graphical game, where distributed solution forms exist, provided that the graph is strongly connected (*i.e., has a spanning tree*).

8.1.4 Optimality conditions

The mathematical solution framework for the constrained graphical games is developed herein. The optimal control theory is employed to find the optimal solutions for the synchronization problem on graphs. Novel coupled Bellman equations, Hamiltonian functions, and HJB equations based on the Integral Reinforcement Learning (IRL) approaches are introduced in order to solve the constrained game. The best response solution of the constrained graphical game is given in terms of the solution to a set of coupled IRL-HJB equations.

8.1.5 Bellman equations

Given the policies (η_i, η_{-i}), the value structure $\Psi_i(\bar{\theta}_i(t_o))$ for each node i is defined on the infinite horizon such that

$$\Psi_i(\bar{\theta}_i(t_o)) \equiv \Psi_i(\bar{\theta}_i(t_o), \eta_i, \eta_{-i}) = \int_{t_o}^{\infty} U_i(\theta_i, \eta_i, \eta_{-i}) d\tau. \tag{8.9}$$

Remark 8.1 The proposed solution structure $\Psi_i(\bar{\theta}_i(t_o))$ uses the local neighborhood information available to each node i in order to solve the constrained graphical game. The introduced solution framework does not overlook the neighborhood states, which is a main concern in the solution given in [546]. This selection makes it possible to propose reliable distributed algorithms to solve the constrained graphical games. ■

Herein, a formulation based on coupled Bellman equations is developed in order to solve the graphical games with saturating inputs. This formulation relaxes the need to know the full dynamics of the nodes in order to evaluate the policies during the online implementation. The value function (8.9) is used to define the coupled IRL-Bellman equations such that

$$\begin{aligned} \Psi_i(\bar{\theta}_i(t)) - \Psi_i(\bar{\theta}_i(t+\Delta)) = \tfrac{1}{2} \textstyle\int_t^{t+\Delta} (\theta_i^T Q_{ii} \theta_i + \\ 2 \textstyle\int_0^{u_i} (\Phi^{-1}(v_i))^T R_{ii} dv_i) + \\ \textstyle\sum_{j \in N_i} u_j^T R_{ij} u_j) d\tau, \Psi_i(0) = 0. \end{aligned} \tag{8.10}$$

The IRL-Bellman equation (8.10) reflects the graph structure and the constrained nature of the game. This equation will be used in the sequel to find the online solution for the constrained graphical game.
It is required to solve for the optimal value Ψ_i^o such that

$$\Psi_i^o(\bar{\theta}_i(t)) = \min_{u_i}(\Psi_i(\bar{\theta}_i(t), u_i, u_{-i})). \tag{8.11}$$

Using means of Taylor expansion and applying the optimization principles yields

$$-\nabla_t \Psi_i^o(\bar{\theta}_i(t)) = \min_{u_i}(U_i(\theta_i, u_i, u_{-i}) + \nabla \Psi_i^o(\bar{\theta}_i(t))^T \dot{\bar{\theta}}_i), \tag{8.12}$$

where $\nabla_t = \partial(....)/\partial t$.

Thus, the optimal strategy for each node i is given by

$$u_i^o = \arg\min_{u_i}(\nabla_t \Psi_i^o(\bar{\theta}_i(t)) + U_i(\theta_i, u_i, u_{-i}) + \nabla \Psi_i^o(\bar{\theta}_i(t))^T \dot{\bar{\theta}}_i). \quad (8.13)$$

Since the infinite horizon optimal control problem yields $\nabla_t \Psi_i^o(\bar{\theta}_i(t)) = 0$, then

$$u_i^o = -\Phi(R_{ii}^{-1}([..(\gamma_i + o_i).. - c_{ji}..] \otimes B_i^T)\nabla \Psi_i^o(\bar{\theta}_i)),$$

or

$$u_i^o = -\Phi(M_i \nabla \Psi_i^o(\bar{\theta}_i)), \quad (8.14)$$

where $M_i = R_{ii}^{-1}([..(\gamma_i + o_i).. - c_{ji}..] \otimes B_i^T)$, the row vector $[..(\gamma_i + o_i).. - c_{ji}..]$ assigns the elements $(\gamma_i + o_i), c_{ji} \forall i, j$ to their respective positions in $\nabla \Psi_i^o$, and denotes the positions of the weights c_{ji} linked to each node i in the vector $[..(\gamma_i + o_i).. - c_{ji}..]$.

Substituting (8.14) into (8.12) yields the coupled IRL-Bellman optimality equation for each node i

$$\begin{aligned} \Psi_i^o(\bar{\theta}_i(t)) = \Psi_i^o(\bar{\theta}_i(t+\Delta)) + \tfrac{1}{2}\int_t^{t+\Delta}(\theta_i^T Q_{ii}\theta_i + \\ 2\int_0^{u_i^o}(\Phi^{-1}(v_i))^T R_{ii} dv_i) + \textstyle\sum_{j\in N_i} u_j^{oT} R_{ij} u_j^o) d\tau. \end{aligned} \quad (8.15)$$

8.1.6 The Hamiltonian function

The coupled Hamiltonian function is defined using the dynamics (8.5) and the cost function U_i for each node i so that

$$H_i(\bar{\theta}_i, \lambda_i, u_i, u_{-i}) = \lambda_i^T f_i(\bar{\theta}_i, \lambda_i, u_i, u_{-i}, u_{-\{-i\}}) + U_i(\theta_i, u_i, u_{-i}), \quad (8.16)$$

where λ_i is the costate or Lagrange multiplier for each node i, $u_{-\{-i\}}$ are the policies of the neighbors to the neighbors of each node i, $N_{i,j}$ is the total number of node i and its neighbors.
The equality constraint f_i is given by

$$f_i(\bar{\theta}_i, \lambda_i, u_i, u_{-i}, u_{-\{-i\}}) \equiv \dot{\bar{\theta}}_i = [\dot{\theta}_i^T .. \dot{\theta}_{-i}^T]^T \in R^{nN_{i,j}}. \quad (8.17)$$

Thus, the Hamiltonian function (8.16) is given such that

$$\begin{aligned} H_i(\bar{\theta}_i, \lambda_i, u_i, u_{-i}) = \lambda_i^T \dot{\bar{\theta}}_i + \tfrac{1}{2}(\theta_i^T Q_{ii}\theta_i + \\ 2\int_0^{u_i}(\Phi^{-1}(v_i))^T R_{ii} dv_i) + \\ \textstyle\sum_{j\in N_i} u_j^T R_{ij} u_j). \end{aligned} \quad (8.18)$$

The optimality conditions for the constrained graphical game are found by applying the optimality principles [556]. The costate variable λ_i adjoins the constraint

(8.17) to the index (8.6). An augmented performance index is used to derive the necessary optimal conditions of the constrained game. This augmented index is given by

$$J_i'(\bar{\theta}_i(t_o)) = \phi_i(\bar{\theta}_i(T)) + \int_{t_o}^{T} (U_i(\theta_i, u_i, u_{-i}) + \lambda_i^T (f_i(\bar{\theta}_i, \lambda_i, u_i, u_{-i}, u_{-\{-i\}}) - \dot{\bar{\theta}}_i))dt, \tag{8.19}$$

where the function $\phi_i(\bar{\theta}_i(T))$ depends on the state $\bar{\theta}_i(T)$ at final time T. The augmented performance index (8.19) yields

$$J_i'(\bar{\theta}_i(t_o)) = \phi_i(\bar{\theta}_i(T)) + \int_{t_o}^{T} (H_i(\bar{\theta}_i, \lambda_i, u_i, u_{-i}) - \lambda_i^T \dot{\bar{\theta}}_i)dt. \tag{8.20}$$

Applying Leibniz rule, the variation in $dJ_i'(.)$ depends on the variations in $\bar{\theta}_i$,λ_i, u_i, and u_{-i} such that

$$\begin{aligned} dJ_i' = {} & \nabla_{\bar{\theta}_i}(\phi_i)^T d\bar{\theta}_i\big|_T + \nabla_t(\phi_i)^T dt\big|_T + (H_i - \lambda_i^T \dot{\bar{\theta}}_i)dt\Big|_T \\ & - (H_i - \lambda_i^T \dot{\bar{\theta}}_i)dt\Big|_{t_o} + \int_{t_o}^{T} ((\nabla_{\bar{\theta}_i} H_i)^T \partial\bar{\theta}_i + (\nabla_{u_i} H_i)^T \partial u_i \\ & + (\nabla_{u_{-i}} H_i)^T \partial u_{-i} - \lambda_i^T \partial\dot{\bar{\theta}}_i + (\nabla_{\lambda_i} H_i - \dot{\bar{\theta}}_i)^T \partial\lambda_i)dt. \end{aligned} \tag{8.21}$$

Given that $-\int_{t_o}^{T} \lambda_i^T \partial\dot{\bar{\theta}}_i dt = -\lambda_i^T \partial\bar{\theta}_i\big|_T + \lambda_i^T \partial\bar{\theta}_i\big|_{t_o} + \int_{t_o}^{T} \dot{\lambda}_i^T \partial\bar{\theta}_i dt$. (8.21).

Then,

$$\begin{aligned} dJ_i' = {} & (\nabla_{\bar{\theta}_i}(\phi_i) - \lambda_i)^T d\bar{\theta}_i\big|_T + (\nabla_t(\phi_i) + H_i)^T dt\big|_T \\ & - (H_i)dt\big|_{t_o} + (\lambda_i^T d\bar{\theta}_i)\big|_{t_o} + \int_{t_o}^{T} ((\nabla_{\bar{\theta}_i} H_i + \dot{\lambda}_i)^T \partial\bar{\theta}_i \\ & + (\nabla_{u_i} H_i)^T \partial u_i + (\nabla_{u_{-i}} H_i)^T \partial u_{-i} + (\nabla_{\lambda_i} H_i - \dot{\bar{\theta}}_i)^T \partial\lambda_i)dt. \end{aligned} \tag{8.22}$$

According to Lagrange multiplier theory, the constrained minimum of index (8.6) is obtained when dJ_i' is zero [556]. The constrained minimum has the following conditions

$$-\dot{\lambda}_i = \nabla_{\bar{\theta}_i} H_i(\bar{\theta}_i, \lambda_i, u_i, u_{-i}), \tag{8.23}$$

$$\nabla_{u_i} H_i(\bar{\theta}_i, \lambda_i, u_i, u_{-i}) = 0, \tag{8.24}$$

$$\nabla_{\lambda_i} H_i(\bar{\theta}_i, \lambda_i, u_i, u_{-i}) = \dot{\bar{\theta}}_i, \tag{8.25}$$

$$(\nabla_{u_{-i}} H_i)^T \partial u_{-i} = 0. \tag{8.26}$$

The associated boundary conditions are listed as follows

$$(\nabla_{\bar{\theta}_i}(\phi_i) - \lambda_i)^T d\bar{\theta}_i\big|_T + (\nabla_t(\phi_i) + H_i)^T dt\big|_T = 0, \tag{8.27}$$

$$-\left(H_i(\bar{\theta}_i,\lambda_i,u_i,u_{-i})\right)dt\Big|_{t_o}=0, \tag{8.28}$$

$$(\lambda_i^T d\bar{\theta}_i)\Big|_{t_o}=0. \tag{8.29}$$

Using (8.23), the costate equation for node i is given by

$$\frac{\partial H_i}{\partial \bar{\theta}_i}=-\dot{\lambda}_i,\Rightarrow -\dot{\lambda}_i=\bar{A}_i^T\lambda_i+\bar{Q}_i\bar{\theta}_i, \tag{8.30}$$

where $\bar{Q}_i = diag\{0,..,Q_{ii},..,0\}$ and $\bar{A}_i=(I_{N_{i,j}}\otimes A)\in R^{nN_{i,j}\times nN_{i,j}}$.
The optimal policy for each node i based on the stationarity condition [556] $\partial H_i/\partial u_i = 0$ is given by

$$u_i^*=\arg\min_{u_i}(H_i(\bar{\theta}_i,\lambda_i,u_i,u_{-i})). \tag{8.31}$$

Then,

$$u_i^*=-\Phi(R_{ii}^{-1}([..(\gamma_i+o_i)..-c_{ji}..]\otimes B_i^T)\lambda_i),$$

or equivalently,

$$u_i^*=-\Phi(M_i\lambda_i). \tag{8.32}$$

Herein, the best response solutions are found for the constrained graphical game. The variations in the neighbors' policies ∂u_{-i} do not take effect during the minimization of the augmented index (8.20). Therefore, (8.26) holds. In addition, t_o, $\bar{\theta}_i(t_o)$ are fixed (*i.e.*, $dt_o=0, d\bar{\theta}_i(t_o)=0$). Therefore, (8.28) and (8.29) hold simultaneously. Moreover, free-final states are considered, so that (8.27) holds [556].

8.1.7 Coupled IRL-Hamilton-Jacobi theory

The relation between IRL-Bellman equation (8.10) and the Hamiltonian (8.16) is of great importance to the stability and Nash equilibrium results. The following theorem finds the coupled IRL-Hamilton-Jacobi equation (IRL-HJ) for the constrained game. It relates the value (8.9), the IRL-Bellman equation (8.10), and the function (8.16). This is attained using the relation between the gradient $\nabla\Psi_i(\bar{\theta}_i)=\partial\Psi_i(\bar{\theta}_i)/\partial\bar{\theta}_i$ and the difference $\Delta\Psi_i(\bar{\theta}_i(t))=\Psi_i(\bar{\theta}_i(t+\Delta))-\Psi_i(\bar{\theta}_i(t))$.

Theorem 8.1
(IRL-Hamilton-Jacobi Equation).
Given the value function $\Psi_i(\bar{\theta}_i(t))$ (8.9) *and the Hamiltonian function* (8.16), $\Psi_i(\bar{\theta}_i(t))$ *satisfies the IRL-HJ equation given by*

$$\begin{aligned}&\Psi_i(\bar{\theta}_i(t))-\Psi_i(\bar{\theta}_i(t+\Delta))+\\&\int_t^{t+\Delta}((\partial\Psi_i(\bar{\theta}_i(\tau))/\partial\bar{\theta}_i)^T\dot{\bar{\theta}}_i-\\&H_i(\bar{\theta}_i,\partial\Psi_i(\bar{\theta}_i(\tau))/\partial\bar{\theta}_i,u_i,u_{-i}))d\tau=0.\end{aligned} \tag{8.33}$$

Proof: The error dynamics constraint (8.5) yields,

$$\dot{\bar{\theta}}_i = f_i(\bar{\theta}_i, u_i, u_{-i}). \tag{8.34}$$

Considering the following value function expression

$$\begin{aligned} \textstyle\int_{t_o}^{\infty} \dot{\Psi}_i(\bar{\theta}_i(t))dt = \Psi_i(\bar{\theta}_i(t_\infty)) - \Psi_i(\bar{\theta}_i(t_o)) = \\ -\textstyle\int_{t_o}^{\infty} U_i(\theta_i, u_i, u_{-i})dt \end{aligned} \tag{8.35}$$

The Hamiltonian function for each node i is given by

$$H_i(\bar{\theta}_i, \lambda_i, u_i, u_{-i}) = U_i(\theta_i, u_i, u_{-i}) + \lambda_i^T f_i(\bar{\theta}_i, u_i, u_{-i}). \tag{8.36}$$

Equations (8.35) and (8.36) yield,

$$\begin{aligned} &\textstyle\int_{t_o}^{\infty} \dot{\Psi}_i(\bar{\theta}_i(t))dt = \Psi_i(\bar{\theta}_i(t_\infty)) - \Psi_i(\bar{\theta}_i(t_o)) \\ &= -\textstyle\int_{t_o}^{\infty} (U_i(\theta_i, u_i, u_{-i}) + \lambda^T (f_i(\bar{\theta}_i, u_i, u_{-i}) - \dot{\bar{\theta}}_i))dt \\ &= -\textstyle\int_{t_o}^{\infty} (H_i(\bar{\theta}_i, \lambda, u_i, u_{-i}) - \lambda_i^T \dot{\bar{\theta}}_i)dt. \end{aligned} \tag{8.37}$$

Then,

$$\int_{t_o}^{\infty} \dot{\Psi}_i(\bar{\theta}_i(t))dt = -\int_{t_o}^{\infty} (H_i(\bar{\theta}_i, \lambda, u_i, u_{-i}) - \lambda_i^T \dot{\bar{\theta}}_i)dt. \tag{8.38}$$

Taking the gradient with respect to $\dot{\bar{\theta}}_i$ yields

$$-\partial\dot{\Psi}_i(\bar{\theta}_i(t))/\partial\dot{\bar{\theta}}_i = \partial H_i(\bar{\theta}_i, \lambda, u_i, u_{-i})/\partial\dot{\bar{\theta}}_i - \partial(\lambda_i^T \dot{\bar{\theta}}_i)/\partial\dot{\bar{\theta}}_i.$$

Then,
$-\partial\Psi_i(\bar{\theta}_i(t))/\partial\bar{\theta}_i = ((\partial\lambda_i/\partial\dot{\bar{\theta}}_i)^T(\partial H_i(\bar{\theta}_i, \lambda_i, u_i, u_{-i})/\partial\lambda_i - (\dot{\bar{\theta}}_i)) - \lambda_i)$.
Since

$$(\partial H_i(\bar{\theta}_i, \lambda_i, u_i, u_{-i})/\partial\lambda_i - (\dot{\bar{\theta}}_i)) = 0.$$

Then,

$$-\partial\Psi_i(\bar{\theta}_i(t))/\partial\bar{\theta}_i = -\lambda_i,$$

or equivalently

$$\lambda_i = \nabla\Psi_i(\bar{\theta}_i(t)). \tag{8.39}$$

Together (8.10), (8.37), and (8.39) yield the IRL-HJ equation (8.33). ■

This theorem shows the relation between the costate variable λ_i and the gradient of the value function Ψ_i.

8.1.8 Coupled IRL-HJB equations

The following theorem provides the mathematical setup for a set of novel coupled IRL-HJB equations for the constrained differential games on graphs. It shows the relation between (8.15) and (8.16) on one hand and the policies given by (8.14) and (8.32) on the other hand.

Theorem 8.2
(IRL-HJB Equation).

a. *Suppose that* $0 < \Psi_i^*(\bar{\theta}_i) \in C^2$ *satisfies the (IRL-HJB) equation*

$$H_i(\bar{\theta}_i, \nabla\Psi_i^*(\bar{\theta}_i), u_i^*, u_{-i}^*) = \nabla\Psi_i^*(\bar{\theta}_i)^T \dot{\bar{\theta}}_i + \tfrac{1}{2}(\theta_i^T Q_{ii}\theta_i$$
$$+2\int_0^{u_i^*} (\Phi^{-1}(v_i))^T R_{ii} dv_i)+ \tag{8.40}$$
$$\textstyle\sum_{j\in N_i} u_j^{*T} R_{ij} u_j^*) = 0, \Psi_i^*(\mathbf{0}) = 0,$$

where

$$u_i^* = -\Phi(M_i \nabla\Psi_i^*(\bar{\theta}_i)). \tag{8.41}$$

Then, the value function $\Psi_i^*(\bar{\theta}_i)$ *satisfies* (8.15).

b. *In reference to* (8.1), *suppose that* (A, B_i) *is reachable and that the value function* $\Psi_i^*(\bar{\theta}_i)$ *satisfies* (8.15). *Then,* $\Psi_i^*(\bar{\theta}_i)$ *satisfies* (8.40).

Proof:

a. If $\Psi_i^*(\bar{\theta}_i)$ satisfies (8.40) then $H_i(\bar{\theta}_i, \nabla\Psi_i^*(\bar{\theta}_i), u_i^*, u_{-i}^*) = 0$. Theorem 8.1 yields $\Delta\Psi_i^*(\bar{\theta}_i(t)) = \int_t^{t+\Delta}(\nabla\Psi_i^*(\bar{\theta}_i)^T \dot{\bar{\theta}})d\tau$. Therefore, $\Psi_i^*(\bar{\theta}_i(t))$ satisfies (8.15).

b. Using the Hamiltonian (8.16) for arbitrary smooth function $\Psi_i(\bar{\theta}_i)$ yields

$$\begin{aligned}
&H_i(\bar{\theta}_i, \nabla\Psi_i(\bar{\theta}_i), u_i, u_{-i}) = H_i(\bar{\theta}_i, \nabla\Psi_i(\bar{\theta}_i), u_i^*, u_{-i}^*)+\\
&\int_{u_i^*}^{u_i} (\Phi^{-1}(v_i))^T R_{ii} dv_i - (\phi^{-1}(u_i^*))^T R_{ii}(u_i - u_i^*)\\
&+\tfrac{1}{2}\textstyle\sum_{j\in N_i}(u_j - u_j^*)^T R_{ij}(u_j - u_j^*)\\
&+\textstyle\sum_{j\in N_i} u_j^{*T} R_{ij}(u_j - u_j^*)\\
&-\nabla_i\Psi_i^T(\bar{\theta}_i)\textstyle\sum_{j\in N_i} c_{ij} B_j(u_j - u_j^*)\\
&-\nabla_{-i}\Psi_i^T(\bar{\theta}_i)\varepsilon_i\beta_i(\bar{u}_{-i} - \bar{u}_{-i}^*),
\end{aligned} \tag{8.42}$$

where

$$\varepsilon_i = \begin{bmatrix} (\gamma_j + o_j) & . & c_{jr} \\ \vdots & . & \vdots \\ c_{rj'} & . & (\gamma_{j'} + o_{j'}) \end{bmatrix}, \bar{u}_{-i} = \begin{bmatrix} u_j \\ \vdots \\ u_r \end{bmatrix},$$

$\beta_i = diag\{B_j,..,B_r\}, j, j' \in N_i, r \in N_j, r' \in N_{j'}, \{r,r\} \neq i, \nabla_i \Psi_i(\bar{\theta}_i)$
$= \partial \Psi_i(\bar{\theta}_i)/\partial \theta_i, \nabla_{-i}\Psi_i(\bar{\theta}_i) = \partial \Psi_i(\bar{\theta}_i)/\partial \bar{\theta}_{-i}, u_i^* = -\Phi(M_i \nabla \Psi_i(\bar{\theta}_i))$.
Now, suppose that, the value function $\Psi_i(\bar{\theta}_i) \in C^2$ satisfies (8.10). Then, the Hamiltonian function using the policies u_i, u_{-i} is given by

$$\begin{aligned}
&H_i(\bar{\theta}_i, \nabla \Psi_i^*(\bar{\theta}_i), u_i, u_{-i}) \\
&= \nabla \Psi_i^*(\bar{\theta}_i)^T \dot{\bar{\theta}}_i \quad + \tfrac{1}{2}(\theta_i^T Q_{ii} \theta_i + 2\textstyle\int_0^{u_i} (\Phi^{-1}(v_i))^T R_{ii} dv_i \\
&\quad + \textstyle\sum_{j \in N_i} u_j^T R_{ij} u_j) \\
&= \textstyle\int_{u_i^*}^{u_i} (\Phi^{-1}(v_i))^T R_{ii} dv_i - (\phi^{-1}(u_i^*))^T R_{ii}(u_i - u_i^*) \\
&\quad + \tfrac{1}{2}\textstyle\sum_{j \in N_i} (u_j - u_j^*)^T R_{ij}(u_j - u_j^*) \\
&\quad + \textstyle\sum_{j \in N_i} u_j^{*T} R_{ij}(u_j - u_j^*) \\
&\quad - \textstyle\sum_{j \in N_i} c_{ij} \nabla \Psi_i^{*T}(\bar{\theta}_i) B_j (u_j - u_j^*) \\
&\quad - \nabla_{-i} \Psi_i^{*T}(\bar{\theta}_i) \varepsilon_i \beta_i (\bar{u}_{-i} - \bar{u}_{-i}^*).
\end{aligned} \tag{8.43}$$

Bellman optimality equation (8.12) can be formulated so that
$\min_{u_i}(U_i(\theta_i, u_i, u_{-i}) + \nabla \Psi_i^*(\bar{\theta}_i)^T \dot{\bar{\theta}}_i - \nabla \Psi_i^*(\bar{\theta}_i)^T \dot{\bar{\theta}}_i + \nabla \Psi_i^o(\bar{\theta}_i)^T \dot{\bar{\theta}}_i) = 0$.
Introducing (8.43) into this equation yields
$\min_{u_i}(H_i(\bar{\theta}_i, \nabla \Psi_i^*(\bar{\theta}_i), u_i, u_{-i}) - \nabla \Psi_i^*(\bar{\theta}_i)^T \dot{\bar{\theta}}_i + \nabla \Psi_i^o(\bar{\theta}_i)^T \dot{\bar{\theta}}_i) = 0$. Applying the optimality principles yields

$$\begin{aligned}
&\min_{u_i}(\textstyle\int_{u_i^*}^{u_i} (\Phi^{-1}(v_i))^T R_{ii} dv_i - (\phi^{-1}(u_i^*))^T R_{ii}(u_i - u_i^*) \\
&+ \tfrac{1}{2}\textstyle\sum_{j \in N_i} (u_j - u_j^*)^T R_{ij}(u_j - u_j^*) \\
&+ \textstyle\sum_{j \in N_i} u_j^{*T} R_{ij}(u_j - u_j^*) \\
&- \textstyle\sum_{j \in N_i} c_{ij} \nabla \Psi_i^{*T} B_j (u_j - u_j^*) \\
&- \nabla_{-i} \Psi_i^{*T}(\bar{\theta}_i) \varepsilon_i \beta_i (\bar{u}_{-i} - \bar{u}_{-i}^*) \\
&- \nabla \Psi_i^*(\bar{\theta}_i)^T \dot{\bar{\theta}}_i + \nabla \Psi_i^o(\bar{\theta}_i)^T \dot{\bar{\theta}}_i) = 0.
\end{aligned}$$

The stationarity condition $\partial(\Psi_i^o(\bar{\theta}_i))/\partial u_i = 0$ yields the optimal policy u_i^o such that

$\partial(.)/\partial u_i = 0 \Rightarrow R_{ii}^{-1}([..(\gamma_i + o_i)..-c_{ji}..] \otimes B_i^T)$
$(\nabla \Psi_i^o(\bar{\theta}_i) - \nabla \Psi_i^*(\bar{\theta}_i)) + (\phi^{-1}(u_i^o) - \phi^{-1}(u_i^*)) = 0.$
Then,

$$-M_i(\nabla \Psi_i^o(\bar{\theta}_i) - \nabla \Psi_i^*(\bar{\theta}_i)) = (\phi^{-1}(u_i^o) - \phi^{-1}(u_i^*)). \tag{8.44}$$

The Hessians of (8.10) and (8.16) with respect to the control policies are given by $\nabla_{u_i}^2(H_i) = \partial^2 H_i/\partial u_i^2 = 1/1 - u_i^2 > 0, |u_i| < 1$ and $\nabla_{u_i}^2(\Psi_i) = \partial^2 \Psi_i/\partial u_i^2 = 1/1 - u_i^2 > 0, |u_i| < 1$. The hessians are positive, thus $u_i^* = u_i^o$. Equations (8.30) and (8.44) imply that

$$(\gamma_i + o_i) R_{ii}^{-1} B_i^T (A^T)^p (\nabla \Psi_i^o(\bar{\theta}_i) - \nabla \Psi_i^*(\bar{\theta}_i)) = 0, p = 0, 1, .., n-1$$

or equivalently,

$$\begin{aligned}&(\gamma_i + o_i)R_{ii}^{-1}B_i^T(A^T)^p(\nabla_i\Psi_i^o(\bar{\theta}_i) - \nabla_i\Psi_i^*(\bar{\theta}_i)) = 0,\\&c_{ji}R_{ii}^{-1}B_i^T(A^T)^p(\nabla_j\Psi_i^o(\bar{\theta}_i) - \nabla_j\Psi_i^*(\bar{\theta}_i)) = 0,\\&p = 0, 1, .., n-1, \forall j \in N_i.\end{aligned} \tag{8.45}$$

The reachability matrix $\mho_i$ for each node i is given by

$$\mho_i = \left[B_i A B_i A^2 B_i ... A^{n-1} B_i\right]. \tag{8.46}$$

Under the condition that, the matrix $\mho_i$ has full rank then,

$$\Psi_i^*(\bar{\theta}_i) = \Psi_i^o(\bar{\theta}_i), \forall i \Psi_i^*(\mathbf{0}) = 0, \Psi_i^o(\mathbf{0}) = 0. \tag{8.47}$$

■

Remark 8.2 *The importance of the relation between the IRL-Bellman equation* (8.10)*, Hamiltonian function* (8.16)*, and IRL-HJB equation* (8.40) *highlighted by Theorems 8.1 and 8.2 can be explained in two points. First, the IRL-Bellman optimality equation* (8.15) *is used to propose value and policy iteration solutions for the constrained game. This framework represents an easy alternative compared to the one proposed in [546], which used Hamiltonian structures to solve the differential games. The solution given in [546] will become more challenging and hard to implement if the constrained policies were considered. Second, this relation represents a very useful tool to understand the stability characteristics and provide the necessary Nash equilibrium conditions for the differential graphical game.* ■

8.1.9 Nash equilibrium solution

The non-cooperative solution of (8.11) yields the Nash equilibrium for the constrained game on graphs. The Nash solution is proven to be equivalent to solving the underlying IRL-Hamilton-Jacobi-Bellman equations (8.40) or the IRL-Bellman optimality equations (8.15). The Nash solution is given in terms of the standard Nash equilibrium condition [545], in addition to the strong connectivity requirement of the graph to sustain the reachability among the nodes.

Definition 8.1 Nash Solution for Constrained Games [545].
An N-node constrained game with a group of N optimal policies $\{u_1^*, u_2^*, ..., u_N^*\}$ has a Nash equilibrium solution if

$$J_i^* \triangleq J_i(u_i^*, u_{\bar{i}}^*) \le J_i(u_i, u_{\bar{i}}^*), \ \forall i, \tag{8.48}$$

where $u_{\bar{i}} = \{u_j | j \in N, \ j \ne i\}$ are the constrained policies of all the nodes, except that of node $\{i\}$.

The outcome $\{J_1^*,\ J_2^*,\ ...,\ J_N^*\}$ is called the Nash solution outcome for the constrained graphical game. ■

Remark 8.3 The reachability is sustained if the graph has a spanning tree *(i.e., strongly connected graph)*. ■

8.1.10 Stability analysis

The next results reveal the stability and Nash equilibrium properties for the error system (8.5), provided that all the nodes in the game use policies (8.14) and the weighting matrices of index (8.6) are properly chosen.

Theorem 8.3

(Stability and Nash Equilibrium Solution)

Suppose that the graph is strongly connected, $\Psi_i^*\ (\bar{\theta}_i)$ *satisfies* (8.15) *or* (8.40), *and each node uses the optimal policy* (8.41). *Then:*

a. *The error system* (8.5) *is asymptotically stable.*
b. $J_i^*(\bar{\theta}_i(t_o),\ u_i^*,\ u_{\bar{i}}^*) = \Psi_i^*(\ \bar{\theta}_i(t_o)\ )$ *is the optimal performance value for node i.*
c. *The nodes of the constrained games are in Nash equilibrium and the Nash outcome is* $\{J_1^*,\ J_2^*,\ ...,\ J_N^*\}$.

Proof:

a. $\Psi_i^*(\bar{\delta}_i)$ satisfies (8.15) so that

$$\begin{aligned}&\Psi_i^*(\ \bar{\theta}_i(t+\Delta)\ ) - \Psi_i^*(\ \bar{\theta}_i(t)\ ) = \\ &-\tfrac{1}{2}\textstyle\int_t^{t+\Delta}(\theta_i^T Q_{ii}\,\theta_i \\ &+2\textstyle\int_0^{u_i}(\Phi^{-1}(v_i))^T R_{ii}\,dv_i) + \sum_{j\in N_i} u_j^T R_{ij}\,u_j)d\tau.\end{aligned} \tag{8.49}$$

Theorem 8.1 and (8.49) yield

$$\begin{aligned}&\textstyle\int_t^{t+\Delta}\dot{\Psi}_i^*(\ \bar{\theta}_i(\tau)\ )\,d\tau = \int_t^{t+\Delta}(\partial\Psi_i^*(\bar{\theta}_i(\tau))/\partial\bar{\theta}_i)^T\ \dot{\bar{\delta}}_i\,d\tau = \\ &-\tfrac{1}{2}\textstyle\int_t^{t+\Delta}\left(\theta_i^T Q_{ii}\,\theta_i + 2\int_0^{u_i}(\Phi^{-1}(v_i))^T R_{ii}\,dv_i) + \sum_{j\in N_i} u_j^T R_{ij}\,u_j\right)\,d\tau.\end{aligned} \tag{8.50}$$

Equation (8.50) yields

$$\dot{\Psi}_i^*(\bar{\theta}_i(t)) = -\frac{1}{2}\left(\theta_i^T Q_{ii}\,\theta_i + 2\int_0^{u_i}(\Phi^{-1}(v_i))^T R_{ii} dv_i) + \sum_{j\in N_i} u_j^T R_{ij}\,u_j\right). \tag{8.51}$$

Therefore, Ψ_i^*, $\forall i$ are Lyapunov candidates and the error systems (8.5) are asymptotically stable. The strong connectivity ensures the reachability for all the nodes. These results guarantee synchronization of the nodes to the leader's node.

b. Equations (8.40) and (8.42) given arbitrary policies yield

$$H_i(\bar{\theta}_i,\ \nabla\Psi_i^*(\bar{\theta}_i),\ u_i,\ u_{-i}) = \nabla\Psi_i^*(\bar{\theta}_i)^T\ \dot{\bar{\theta}} + U_i(\theta_i,\ u_i,\ u_{-i})$$
$$= \int_{u_i^*}^{u_i} (\ \Phi^{-1}(v_i)\ )^T R_{ii}\, dv_i - (\ \phi^{-1}(u_i^*)\ )^T R_{ii}\ (u_i - u_i^*) +$$
$$\tfrac{1}{2}\sum_{j\in N_i} (u_j - u_j^*)^T R_{ij}\ (u_j - u_j^*) + \sum_{j\in N_i} u_j^{*T} R_{ij}\ (u_j - u_j^*) -$$
$$\sum_{j\in N_i} c_{ij}\ \nabla\Psi_i^{*T}(\bar{\theta}_i)\ B_j\ (u_j - u_j^*) - \nabla_{-i}\Psi_{-i}^{*T}(\bar{\theta}_i)\ \varepsilon_i\ \beta_i\ (\bar{u}_{-i} - \bar{u}_{-i}^*). \tag{8.52}$$

The stability results guarantee that $\bar{\theta}_i(\infty) \to 0$. Therefore, $\Psi_i^*(\ \bar{\theta}_i(\infty)\ ) = 0$ and

$$J_i(\theta_i(t_o),\ u_i,\ u_{-i}) = \Psi_i^*(\ \bar{\theta}_i(\infty)\ ) + \int_{t_o}^{\infty} U_i(\theta_i,\ u_i,\ u_{-i})\, dt. \tag{8.53}$$

Rearranging this equation yields,

$$J_i(\theta_i(t_o),\ u_i,\ u_{-i}) = \Psi_i^*(\ \bar{\theta}_i(t_o)\ ) + \int_{t_o}^{\infty} (\ U_i(\theta_i(t_o),\ u_i,\ u_{-i}) - U_i^*(\theta_i(t_o),\ u_i^*,\ u_{-i}^*)\ )\, dt. \tag{8.54}$$

Given arbitrary policies, the Hamiltonian is given by

$$H_i(\bar{\theta}_i(t),\ \nabla\Psi_i^*(\bar{\theta}_i),\ u_i,\ u_{-i}) = \nabla\Psi_i^*(\bar{\theta}_i)^T\ \dot{\bar{\theta}}_i\Big|_{u_i,u_{-i}} + U_i(\theta_i(t),\ u_i,\ u_{-i}). \tag{8.55}$$

In case of optimal policies, the Hamiltonian is given by

$$H_i(\bar{\theta}_i(t),\ \nabla\Psi_i^*(\bar{\theta}_i),\ u_i^*,\ u_{-i}^*) = \nabla\Psi_i^*(\bar{\theta}_i)^T\ \dot{\bar{\theta}}_i\Big|_{u_i^*,u_{-i}^*} + U_i^*(\theta_i(t),\ u_i^*,\ u_{-i}^*) = 0. \tag{8.56}$$

Then

$$U_i(\theta_i(t), u_i, u_{-i}) - U_i^*(\theta_i(t), u_i^*, u_{-i}^*) = H_i(\bar{\theta}_i(t),\ \nabla\Psi_i^*(\bar{\theta}_i),\ u_i,\ u_{-i}) - \nabla\Psi_i^*(\bar{\theta}_i)^T\ \dot{\bar{\theta}}_i\Big|_{u_i,u_{-i}} + \nabla\Psi_i^*(\bar{\theta}_i)^T\ \dot{\bar{\theta}}_i\Big|_{u_i^*,u_{-i}^*},$$

where

$$-\nabla\Psi_i^*(\bar{\theta}_i)^T\ \dot{\bar{\theta}}_i\Big|_{u_i,u_{-i}} + \nabla\Psi_i^*(\bar{\theta}_i)^T\ \dot{\bar{\theta}}_i\Big|_{u_i^*,u_{-i}^*} =$$
$$-\nabla\Psi_i^*(\bar{\theta}_i)^T ([..(\gamma_i + o_i).. - c_{ji}..]\ \otimes B_i^T)\ (u_i - u_i^*)$$
$$+ \sum_{j\in N_i} c_{ij}\ \nabla\Psi_i^{*T}(\bar{\theta}_i)\ B_j\ (u_j - u_j^*)$$
$$+ \nabla_{-i}\Psi_{-i}^{*T}(\bar{\theta}_i)\ \varepsilon_i\ \beta_i\ (\bar{u}_{-i} - \bar{u}_{-i}^*).$$

Then

$$
\begin{aligned}
&U_i(\theta_i,\ u_i,\ u_{-i}) - U_i^*(\theta_i,\ u_i^*,\ u_{-i}^*) = \\
&\int_{u_i^*}^{u_i} (\ \Phi^{-1}(v_i)\ )^T R_{ii}\, dv_i - (\ \phi^{-1}(u_i^*)\ )^T R_{ii}\ (u_i - u_i^*) \\
&+\tfrac{1}{2}\textstyle\sum_{j\in N_i}(u_j - u_j^*)^T R_{ij}\ (u_j - u_j^*) + \sum_{j\in N_i} u_j^{*T} R_{ij}\ (u_j - u_j^*) \\
&-\nabla_i V_i^{*T}(\bar{\theta}_i)\textstyle\sum_{j\in N_i} c_{ij} B_j\ (u_j - u_j^*) \\
&-\nabla_{-i}\Psi_i^{*T}(\bar{\theta}_i)\ \varepsilon_i\ \beta_i\ (\bar{u}_{-i} - \bar{u}_{-i}^*) \\
&-\nabla\Psi_i^*(\bar{\theta}_i)^T(\ [..(\gamma_i + o_i)..-c_{ji}..] \otimes B_i^T\ )\ (u_i - u_i^*) + \\
&\textstyle\sum_{j\in N_i} c_{ij}\ \nabla\Psi_i^{*T}(\bar{\theta}_i)\ B_j\ (u_j - u_j^*) \\
&+\nabla_{-i}\Psi_{-i}^{*T}(\bar{\theta}_i)\ \varepsilon_i\ \beta_i\ (\bar{u}_{-i} - \bar{u}_{-i}^*).
\end{aligned}
$$

Simplifying this equation yields

$$
\begin{aligned}
&U_i(\theta_i,\ u_i,\ u_{-i}) - U_i^*(\theta_i,\ u_i^*,\ u_{-i}^*) = \int_{u_i^*}^{u_i} (\Phi^{-1}(v_i))^T R_{ii}\, dv_i + \\
&\tfrac{1}{2}\textstyle\sum_{j\in N_i}(u_j - u_j^*)^T R_{ij}\ (u_j - u_j^*) + \sum_{j\in N_i} u_j^{*T} R_{ij}\ (u_j - u_j^*).
\end{aligned} \tag{8.57}
$$

Thus, the performance index of node i is given by

$$
\begin{aligned}
&J_i(\theta_i(t_o),\ u_i,\ u_{-i}) = \Psi_i^*(\ \bar{\theta}_i(t_o)\ ) + \int_{t_o}^{\infty}(\int_{u_i^*}^{u_i} (\Phi^{-1}(v_i)\ )^T R_{ii}\, dv_i \\
&+\tfrac{1}{2}\textstyle\sum_{j\in N_i}(u_j - u_j^*)^T R_{ij}\ (u_j - u_j^*) + \sum_{j\in N_i} u_j^{*T} R_{ij}\ (u_j - u_j^*)\ )\ dt.
\end{aligned} \tag{8.58}
$$

Applying the optimal control policies (equilibrium), then (8.58) yields

$$
J_i^*(\ \theta_i(t_o),\ u_i^*,\ u_{-i}^*) = \Psi_i^*(\ \bar{\theta}_i(t_o)\ ). \tag{8.59}
$$

c. Using the policies $(u_i,\ u_i^*)$, then the integrand of (8.58) is positive such that

$$
\int_{t_o}^{\infty} (\ U_i\ (\theta_i(t_o),\ u_i,\ u_{-i}^*) - U_i^*\ (\theta_i(t_o), u_i^*,\ u_{-i}^*)\ )\ dt > 0. \tag{8.60}
$$

Inequality (8.60) yields

$$
J_i^*\ (\theta_i(t_o),\ u_i^*,\ u_{\bar{i}}^*)\ \le\ J_i\ (\theta_i(t_o),\ u_i,\ u_{\bar{i}}^*). \tag{8.61}
$$

Therefore, according to *Definition 8.1*, the tuple $\{J_1^*,\ J_2^*,\ ...,\ J_N^*\}$ forms the Nash equilibrium outcome for the constrained game. ■

8.2 Value Iteration Solution and Implementation

This section introduces the online Value Iteration (VI) solution for the constrained graphical games. It does not require the knowledge of the complete dynamics of the nodes. This solution is a constrained graph version of the single-node ADP solution introduced in [563] and [564]. This is followed by the adaptive critics' implementation for the proposed solution algorithm.

8.2.1 Value iteration algorithm

The value iteration solution involves two main steps: First, value evaluation, then policy update. Each node i performs the following value iteration algorithm simultaneously.

Algorithm 1. *(VI Solution for Constrained Graphical Games).*

1: Initialize the value functions and the polices $\psi_i^0,\ u_i^0,\ \forall i$.

2: (Evaluate the Value Function).
Evaluate ψ_i^{l+1} *using the IRL-Bellman equation*

$$\psi_i^{l+1}(\bar{\theta}_i(t)) = \frac{1}{2}\int_t^{t+\Delta}(\theta_i^T Q_{ii}\,\theta_i + 2\int_0^{u_i^l}(\Phi^{-1}(v_i))^T R_{ii}\,dv_i) + \sum_{j\in N_i} u_j^{lT} R_{ij}\, u_j^l)\; d\tau + \psi_i^l(\bar{\theta}_i(t+\Delta)),\ \ \psi_i^l(0)=0,\ \forall i, \tag{8.62}$$

3: (Update Policies).

$$u_i^{l+1} = -\,\Phi\,(\,R_{ii}^{-1}([..(\gamma_i+o_i)..-c_{ji}..]\otimes B_i^T\,)\,\nabla\,\psi_i^{l+1}\,(\bar{\theta}_i). \tag{8.63}$$

4: Repeat the process until $\|\ \psi_i^{l+1}-\psi_i^l\ \|$ *converges.* ■

Remark 8.4 *The IRL-Value Iteration Algorithm 1 does not use the full dynamics in* (8.5). *It requires only the knowledge of the input control matrix* B_i *for each node i. Meanwhile, it does not use initial stabilizing policies, which is shown to be challenging for the case of multi-agent systems [546].* ■. ▌

8.2.2 Graph solution implementation

Online actor-critic neural network structures are adopted to implement the VI solution provided by *Algorithm 1*. The approximation for the value function (8.62) is introduced for each function ψ_i and it is referred to as critic structure approximation. The actor structure approximates the optimal policies for each node i (8.63). The actor-critic structures are used to implement the solution of *Algorithm 1*, as well as solving the Bellman optimality equations (8.15) simultaneously. Policies (8.63) are evaluated using only partial knowledge of the dynamics of the nodes. Updating the policies and the value functions are done simultaneously using the local information available to each node i.

The value function (8.62) for each node i is approximated by

$$C_i(\mathrm{I}_i) = \frac{1}{2}\,(\mathrm{I}_i^T\ \omega_{ic}^T\ \mathrm{I}_i), \tag{8.64}$$

where $\omega_{ic}^T \in R^{nN_{i,j}\times nN_{i,j}} \geq 0$ are the critic weights for each node i and I_i is a vector of the states of node i and the states of its neighbors.

The actor for each node i (8.63) is approximated by

$$\hat{u}_i(\mathrm{I}_i) = \omega_{ia}^T \, \mathrm{I}_i, \tag{8.65}$$

where $\omega_{ia}^T \in R^{m_i \times nN_{i,j}} \geq 0$ are the actor weights for each node i.

The policy for each node i is approximated by (8.63) such that

$$\bar{u}_i = -\,\Phi\,\left(R_{ii}^{-1}\left(\left[..(\gamma_i + o_i)..-c_{ji}..\right] \otimes B_i^T\right) \omega_{ic}^T \, I_i\right). \tag{8.66}$$

The error for the actor's approximation is given by

$$\alpha_i^{actor} = \omega_{ia}^T \, \mathrm{I}_i - \bar{u}_i. \tag{8.67}$$

Hence,

$$\bar{\alpha}_i^{error} = \frac{1}{2}\,(\alpha_i^{actor})^T\,\alpha_i^{actor}. \tag{8.68}$$

The variation in the actor weights is

$$\omega_{ia}^{(l+1)T} = \omega_{ia}^{(l)T} - \sigma_{ai}\left(\left(\omega_{ia}^{(l)T}\mathrm{I}_i - \bar{u}_i\right)\,\mathrm{I}_i^T\right), \tag{8.69}$$

where l is the iteration index and σ_{ai} is the actor learning rate.
Let the target value of the critic network for each node i be

$$\begin{aligned}\beta_i^{critic} = \tfrac{1}{2}\int_t^{t+\Delta}&(\theta_i^T Q_{ii}\,\theta_i + 2\int_0^{\hat{u}_i}(\Phi^{-1}(v_i))^T R_{ii}\,dv_i + \\ &\textstyle\sum_{j\in N_i}\hat{u}_j^T R_{ij}\,\hat{u}_j)\,d\tau + \tfrac{1}{2}(\mathrm{I}_i^T(t+\Delta)\;\omega_{ic}^T\;\mathrm{I}_i\,(t+\Delta)\,).\end{aligned} \tag{8.70}$$

The error for the critic's approximation is given by

$$\beta_i^{error} = \frac{1}{2}(\mathrm{I}_i^T(t)\;\omega_{ic}^T\;\mathrm{I}_i\,(t)\,)\;-\;\beta_i^{critic}. \tag{8.71}$$

Hence,

$$\bar{\beta}_i^{error} = \frac{1}{2}\,(\beta_i^{error})^T\;\beta_i^{error}. \tag{8.72}$$

The variation in the critic weights is governed by

$$\bar{\omega}_{ic}^{(l+1)T} = \bar{\omega}_{ic}^{(l)T} - \sigma_{ci}\left(\frac{1}{2}(\mathrm{I}_i^T(t)\;\omega_{ic}^T\,\mathrm{I}_i(t)) - \beta_i^{critic}\right) \times\;(\mathrm{I}_i(t)\,\mathrm{I}_i^T(t)), \tag{8.73}$$

where $0 < \sigma_{ci} < 1$ is the learning rate of the critic.

Remark 8.5 *The introduced IRL-Bellman formulation makes it possible to propose rigorous and easily implementable solution frameworks based on value iteration and policy iterations. The value iteration solution is implemented online using only one layer of linear neural network structures and does not use nonlinear activation functions, providing a much simpler structure compared to the one proposed in [546]. The proposed IRL solution framework resulted in simpler tuning approaches for the neural networks weights compared to those developed in [546]. Herein, the online value iteration solution considers the case of constrained inputs.*

■

8.2.3 Online actor-critic neural networks tuning

The actor-critic neural network weights are updated online using the following algorithm, which is performed simultaneously by each node i.

Algorithm 2. *Online Actor-Critic Tuning*

1. *Initialize the actor and critic weights* $\bar{\omega}_{ia}^{0}$ & $\bar{\omega}_{ic}^{0}, \forall i$.
2. *Initialize the vectors* $\mathrm{I}_i^0\left(t_0\right), \forall i$.
3. *Loop (l iteration index)* {

   3.1 *Update the critic weights using*

$$\bar{\omega}_{ic}^{(l+1)T} = \bar{\omega}_{ic}^{(l)T} - \sigma_{ci}\left(C_i^l\left(\mathrm{I}_i\left(t\right)\right) - \beta_i^{critic}\right) \times \left(\mathrm{I}_i(t)\, \mathrm{I}_i^T\left(t\right)\right),$$

   3.2 *Update the actor weights using*

$$\omega_{ia}^{(l+1)T} = \omega_{ia}^{(l)T} - \sigma_{ai}\left(\left(\omega_{ia}^{(l)T}\mathrm{I}_i - \bar{u}_i\right)\mathrm{I}_i^T\right),$$

   3.3 *End Loop on convergence of* $\left\| \omega_{ic}^{(l+1)} - \omega_{ic}^{l} \right\|, \forall i.$ ■

Remark 8.6 *The number of the actor and the critic weights for each node i depends on the graph structure* Ω *as well as the solving value function* $C_i\left(\mathrm{I}_i\right)$. *Therefore, the number of the actor* ω_{ia} *and critic* ω_{ic} *weights for each node i are* $R^{m_i \times nN_{i,j}}$ *and* $R^{nN_{i,j} \times nN_{i,j}}$, *respectively. The simple tuning laws developed herein are easier to implement than those used in [546], especially when constrained inputs are considered.* ■

8.2.4 Simulation results I

Simulation cases are designed to test the validity and robustness of the proposed *Algorithms 1 and 2*. The simulation results are judged against, 1) How the critic and actor weights converge during the learning process, and the asymptotic stability of the tracking error systems. 2) The robustness of the algorithms against the uncertainties, which are injected into the dynamics of the nodes. 3) The robustness of the proposed solution in the presence of uncertainties in the connection weights, loss of connection links, and varying the weighting matrices.

Graph Game Example and Simulation Parameters

A graphical system of four nodes is considered, as shown in Fig. 1(a). The nodes have the following information;

$$A = \begin{bmatrix} 0 & 1 \\ -1 & 0 \end{bmatrix}, B_1 = \begin{bmatrix} 1.1 \\ 0.6 \end{bmatrix}, B_2 = \begin{bmatrix} 1.3 \\ 0.7 \end{bmatrix},$$

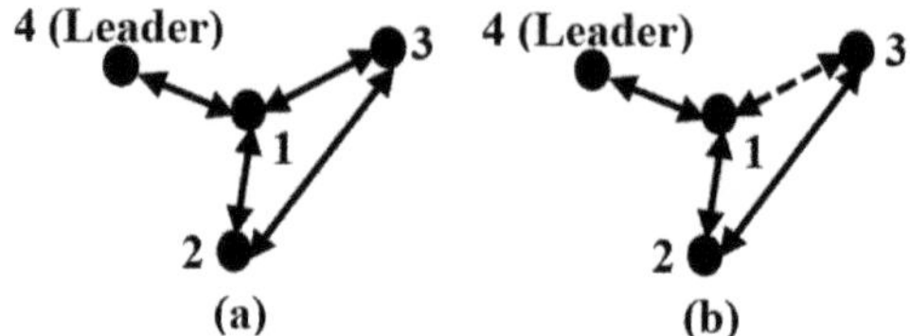

Figure 8.1: Graph example

$$B_3 = \begin{bmatrix} 1.2 \\ 0.75 \end{bmatrix}, \; B_4 = \begin{bmatrix} 1 \\ 1 \end{bmatrix}$$

The undirected graph weights are chosen such that; $(c_{ij} = c_{ji} \forall i, j, \; j \not\leq i) c_{12} = 0.9, \; c_{13} = 0.6, \; c_{14} = 0.8, c_{23} = 0.75$.
The weighting matrices Q, R are set to unity. The leader is pinned to node 4. The learning rates are $\sigma_{ai} = \sigma_{ci} = 0.001$. The saturated control input law for each node i (8.63) is given by

$$u_i = -\,2 * \tan^{-1}(\; (R_{ii}^{-1}\; ([..(\gamma_i + o_i)..-c_{ji}..] \otimes B_i^T)\; \nabla \psi_i(\bar{\theta}_i)\; /\, 2).$$

8.2.5 Simulation case 1

This simulation case tests the performance of the learning process. Figures 2 and 3 show the update of the self-critic and actor weights, respectively. The figures show the smooth convergence of the critic and actor weights. Figure 4 shows the asymptotic stability results of the tracking error dynamics, which supports the proposition of *Theorem 8.3*. It shows how the nodes synchronize their dynamics to the leader's dynamics. Figure 5 shows 3D phase-plan plot (the components of the node's states) of the nodes' dynamics. The nodes start from scattered initial states and then they synchronize to the leader's dynamics.

8.2.6 Simulation case 2

The robustness of the proposed adaptive control algorithm is tested with a white noise of Gaussian Distribution N (0,0.37) added to the dynamics of each node i. Figures 6 and 7 show the tuning of the self-critic and actor weights for all the nodes. They demonstrate that the tunings of the actor and critic weights require more iterations in order to adapt and stabilize the system against the noise. Figure 8 shows the tracking error dynamics and the dynamics of the nodes, respectively. Figure 9 shows the phase plan plot of the four nodes. The proposed algorithm is shown to be robust against the superimposed disturbances. Despite the extra time it required to compensate for the added noise, it achieved asymptotic stability and convergence.

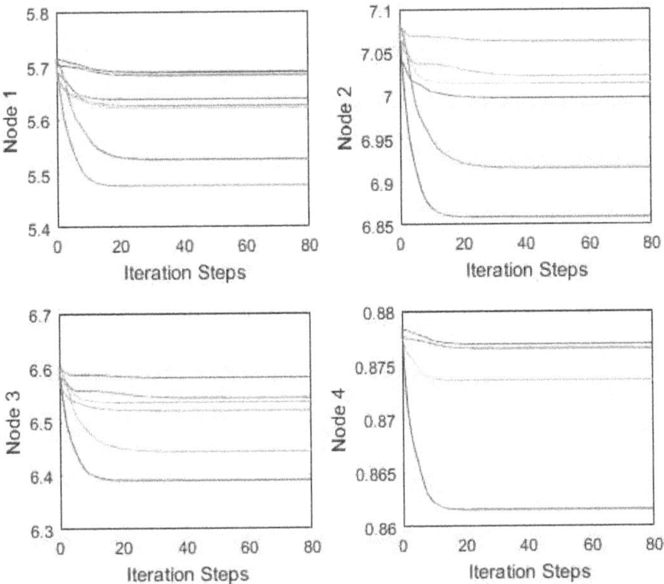

Figure 8.2: Self-critic weights update (simulation case 1)

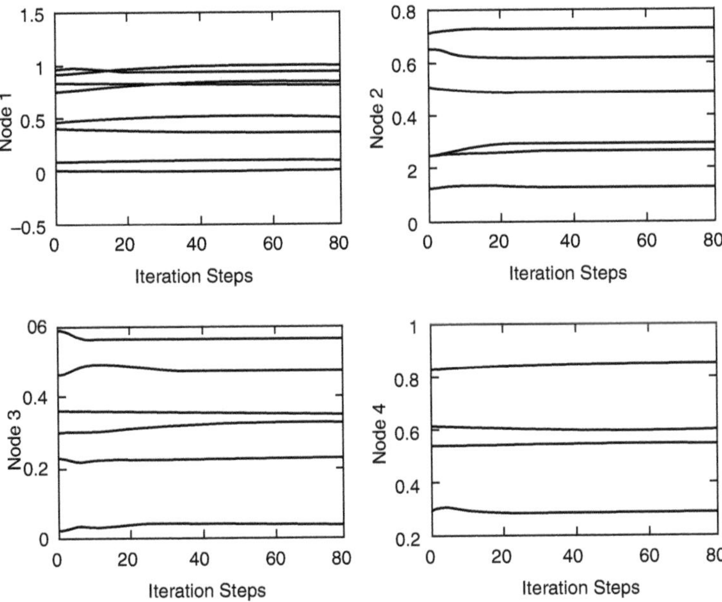

Figure 8.3: Actor weights update (simulation case 1)

8.2.7 Simulation case 3

In this simulation case, further aggressive situations are considered. The connection link between node 1 and node 3 is broken as shown in Fig. 1(b) and the

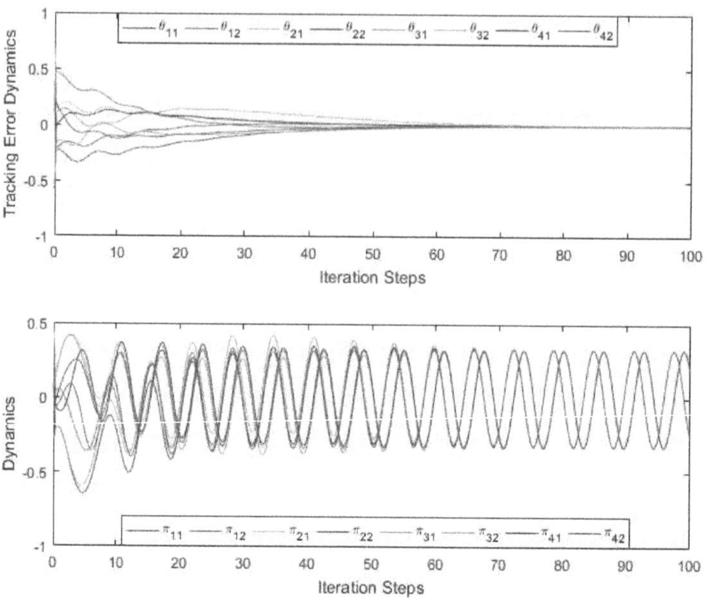

Figure 8.4: Tracking error dynamics and the nodes dynamics (simulation case 1)

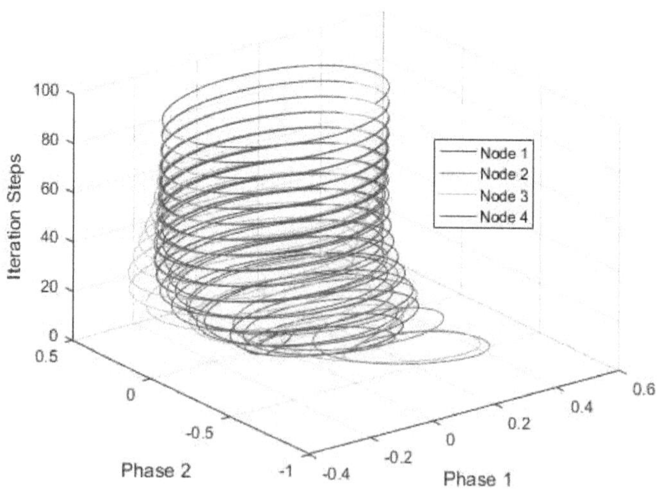

Figure 8.5: Phase plane plot (simulation case 1)

connection weights are allowed to vary by as much as 50% around their nominal values at each iteration, as shown in Fig. 10. In order to speed up the behavior of the system and test the effect of varying the weighting matrices of the graph, and

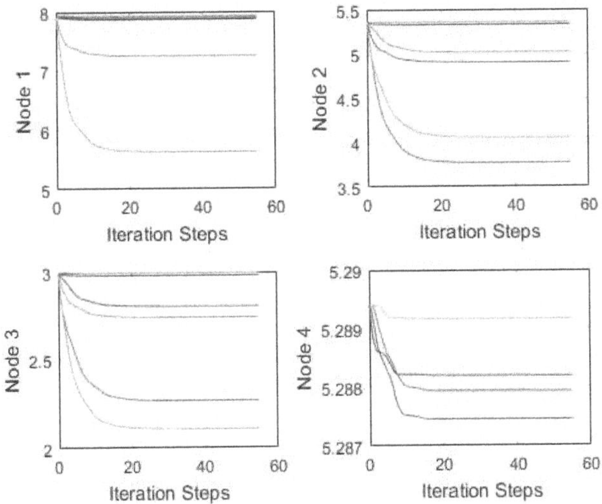

Figure 8.6: Self-critic weights update (simulation case 2)

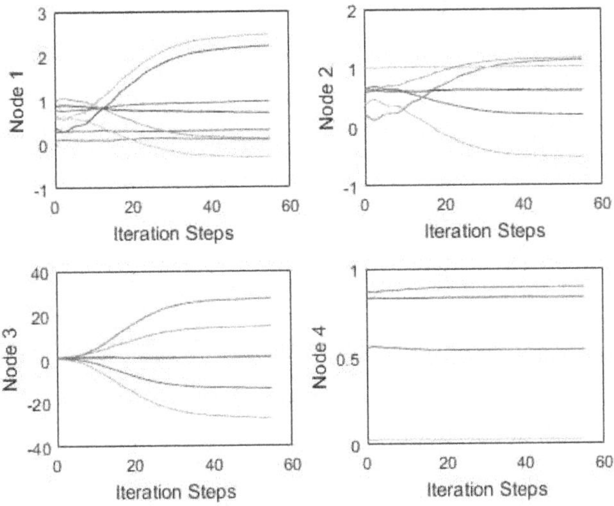

Figure 8.7: Actor weights update (simulation case 2)

to let the dynamics of the nodes synchronize to the leader's node in the shortest possible time, the weighting matrices Q are set to 10 this time. Figures 11 and 12 show that the critic and the actor weights converge smoothly irrespective of the hostile conditions. Figure 13 (tracking error dynamics and dynamics

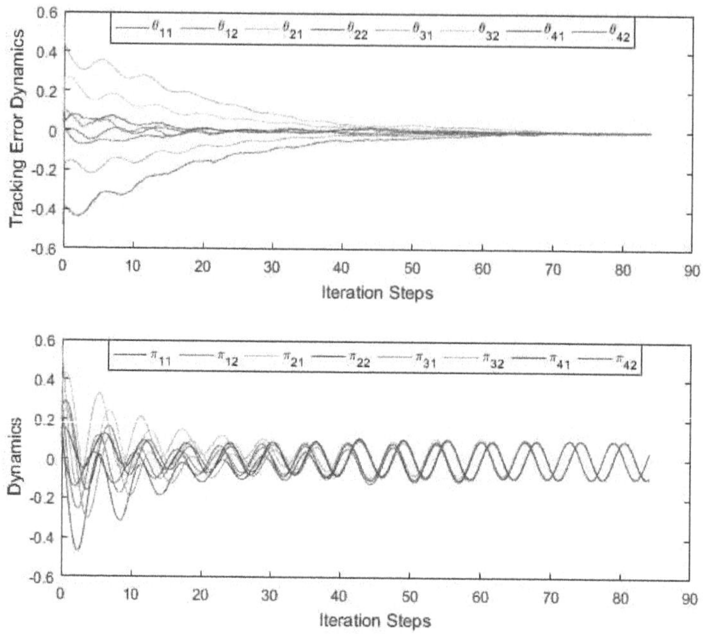

Figure 8.8: Tracking error dynamics and the nodes dynamics (simulation case 2)

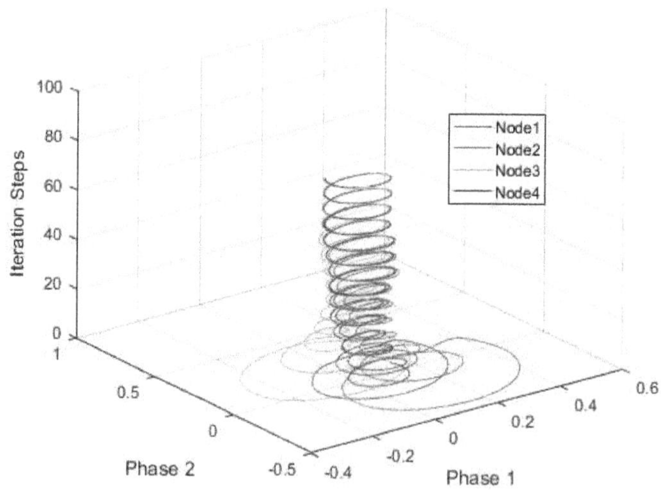

Figure 8.9: Phase plane plot (simulation case 2)

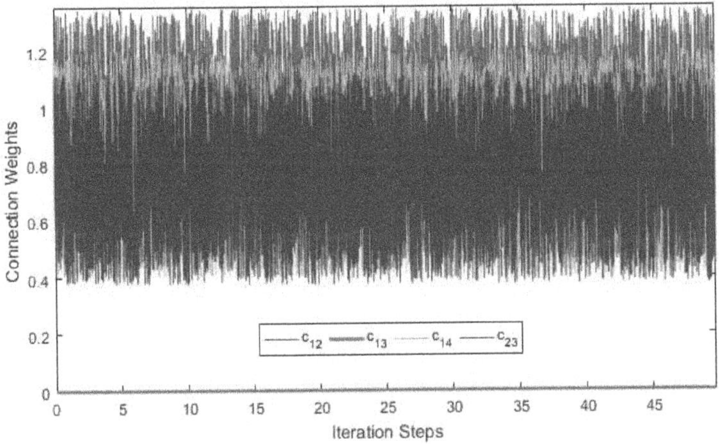

Figure 8.10: The connection weights (simulation case 3)

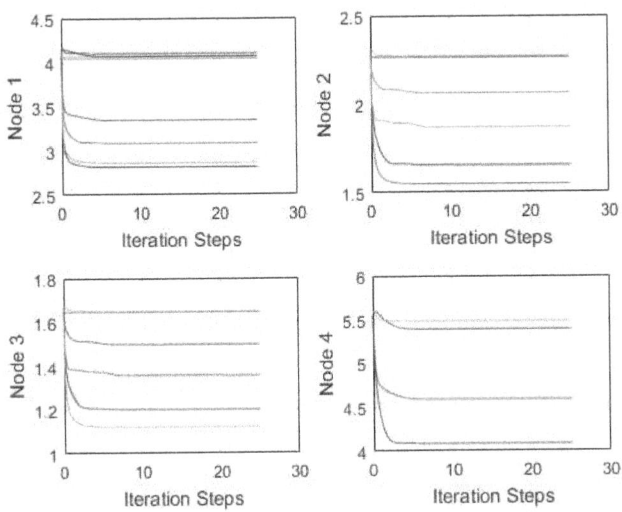

Figure 8.11: Self-critic weights update (simulation case 3)

of the nodes) shows the effect of the continuous change of the graph weights and the ability of the IRL-Algorithms to asymptotically stabilize the graph systems and synchronize the nodes' dynamics to that of the leader's. In addition, Fig. 14 shows that, with time, the adaptive learning solution was able to reject all uncertainty effects and to achieve the objectives of the optimization problem.

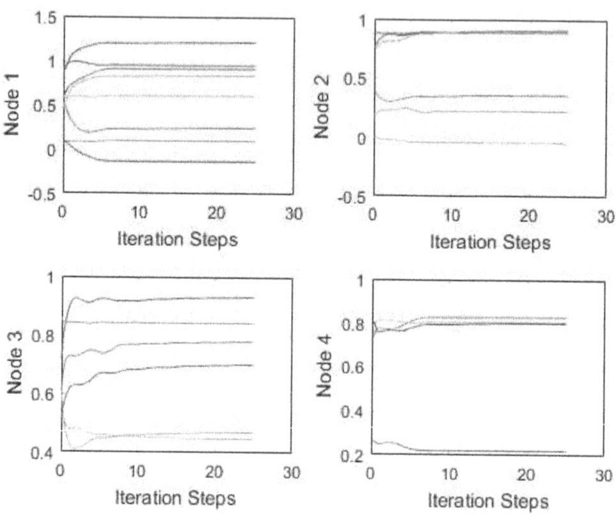

Figure 8.12: Actor weights update (simulation case 3)

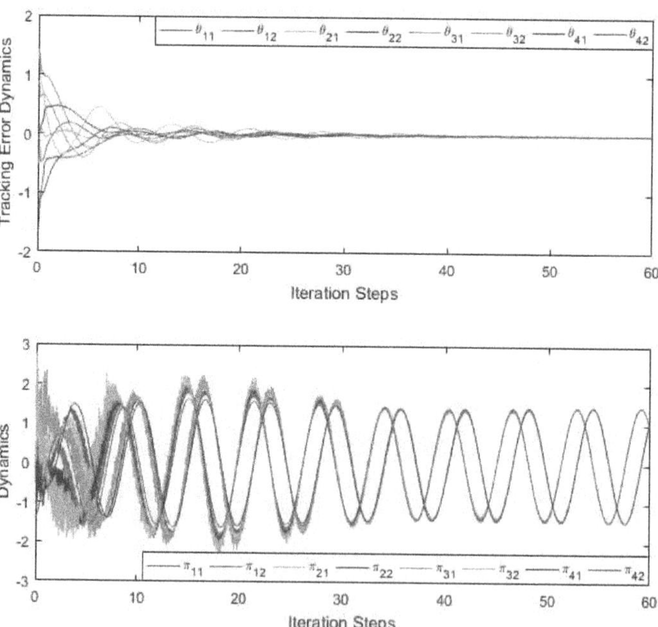

Figure 8.13: Tracking error dynamics and the nodes dynamics (simulation case 3)

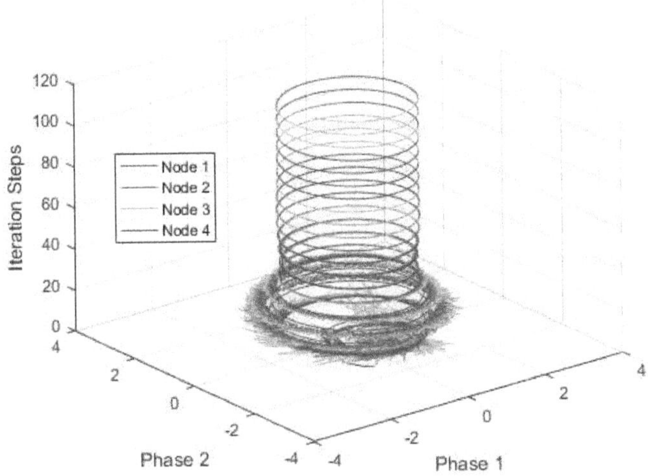

Figure 8.14: Phase plane plot (simulation case 3)

8.3 Multiagent Reinforcement Learning for Microgrids

Traditional control systems for power grids were designed to handle large production units operating under central control. The recent changes in the area of power systems, however, have significant effects on the complexity of the distribution and transmission system operation, imposing new requirements. Prominent among these changes are:

- Increase of penetration of Renewable Energy Sources (RES).
- Increase of distributed generation and storage.
- Market driven operation with prospective participation of small generation and simple consumer.
- Demand for increased Power Quality, with special focus on uninterruptible power supply and network self healing capabilities.

This paper investigates how distributed intelligence can be used to control modern power systems under the above changes. In this context, the use of distributed control appears as the natural evolution of the traditional central control, although not fully realized thus far. Consider, for example, the operation of several small SCADA systems at larger industrial or commercial installations, operating in parallel with the central SCADA of the main Distribution Management System (DMS). The complexity of the power system operation dictates the need to assign several control functions locally at lower levels.

This type of distributed monitoring and control is expected to increase as the complexity of the system increases [284].

In what follows, we focus on a future possible power system organization, called Microgrid. Microgrids consist of distributed generators (DG), together with storage devices and controllable loads (e.g., water heaters, air conditioners) that operate in Low Voltage networks. Microgrids can be operated in interconnection with the power grid, or islanded, if disconnected from the grid offering considerable control capabilities over the network operation [260]. The introduction of Microgrids in the power system introduces considerable complexity in the operation of the grid, but, at the same time, it can provide distinct benefits to the overall system performance, if managed and coordinated efficiently. Significant research is currently being carried out regarding the operation and control of Microgrids [260], [261]. The architecture proposed in this paper is based on Multi Agents System (MAS) and makes use of both artificial intelligence algorithms and traditional computational methods in order to cope with the extremely complicated and diverse problems faced in Microgrids control. Previous papers by the authors [263] and [264] have described the use of MAS to allow market participation of the micro-sources. This paper aims to propose a general distributed architecture, capable of incorporating all the functionalities of a Microgrid [266]-[267][268][269][270].

8.3.1 Microgrid control requirements

The general architecture of the Microgrid control system was presented in detail in [263], [264], [265], therefore this section provides only a brief overview. Three control levels are distinguished, as shown in Fig. 8.15.

The lower level consists of the **Local Controllers (LC)**, directly controlling the Distributed Energy Resources (DER), production and storage units, and some loads.

The **Distribution Network Operator (DNO)** is responsible for the technical operation of the medium and low voltage area, where more than one Microgrid may exist. In addition, one or more **Market Operators (MO)** are responsible for the Market Operation in the area. These two entities do not belong to the Microgrid, but they are the delegates of the grid. The main interface between the DNS/MO and the Microgrid is the *Microgrid Central Controller (MGCC)*. The *MGCC* is responsible for the optimization of the Microgrid operation, or alternatively, it simply coordinates the LCs, assuming the main responsibility in the architecture presented.

A general requirement for the Microgrid control system is adaptability and low cost, despite its complexity. Unlike centralized systems, involving large financial investments and justifying expensive studies and extended modifications of the control system to accommodate new developments, Microgrids comprise a variety of energy production or storage units (Photovoltaics, Batteries, Fuel

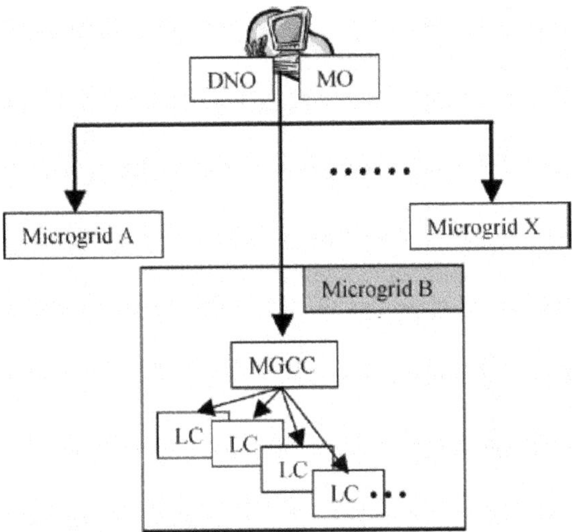

Figure 8.15: Control levels of the microgrid environment

Cells, CHP [Combined Heat Production], Diesel, Flywheels, etc.) with costs ranging from tenths to few millions of dollars [264], [265]. The owners of these units may have different goals, i.e., maximizing profits from participation in the local market to uninterrupted power supply of critical loads. Furthermore, in a small area, there might be several Microgrids of different sizes (from 1kW installed capacity to several hundreds of kWs). The low cost requirements do not only dictate cheap hardware, but mainly that the architecture should be open to new DG connections without the need for modifications or significant support from technicians or engineers. Advanced plug and play capabilities should exist in two levels. First, at the field level, the LC should be able to adapt to the requirements of the environment. Secondly, at the management level, no matter how it is implemented, the LC should be able to optimize its performance according to its goals (e.g., market participation or heat management) automatically without the presence of an operator.

8.3.2 Features of MAS technology

The main element of MAS is the agent, which is a physical entity, or a virtual one [268], [269]. In our application, the physical entity is a microsource or a controllable load and the virtual one a piece of software that coordinates the agents. The basic characteristics of agents are described next:

An agent is capable of acting in the environment, meaning that the agent is able to change its environment by its actions. For example, an agent that controls a storage unit and decides to store energy, rather than to inject it, alters the decision and the behavior of other agents.

Agents communicate with each other, this is part of their ability to act in the environment. For example, agents controlling microsources communicate with the Market Operator and the other agents in order to negotiate in the internal Microgrid market.

Agents have a certain level of autonomy. This means that they can take decisions driven by a set of tendencies without a central controller or commander. The autonomy of each agent is related to its resources, e.g., the available fuel, in case of a production unit.

Another significant characteristic of agents is that they have partial or zero representation of the environment. Each agent only knows the state of the unit or the load it controls, it can, however, be informed via conversation with the other agents about the status of the neighboring system.

Finally, an agent has a certain behavior and tends to satisfy certain objectives using its resources, skills and services. One skill could be the ability to produce or store energy and a service could be to sell power in a market. The way that the agent uses its resources, skills and services defines its behavior. As a consequence, the behavior of each agent is formed by its goals. An agent that controls a battery system aiming to provide uninterruptible supply to a load has a different behavior than a similar battery system whose goal is to maximize profits by participating in the energy market. The concept of the behavior is a significant part of the agent technology and is further analyzed in the next section. It is already obvious, however, that the MAS technology can satisfy the requirements for Microgrids control, as specified in Section II. More specifically:

- Unit autonomy. Depending on the goals of the unit owners, the various units in a Microgrid can behave mostly autonomously in a cooperative or competitive environment. On the other hand, an industrial Microgrid might be best controlled in a centralized manner, in which case, the approach presented in this paper is clearly not ideal [273].

- Reduced need for large data manipulation. The agent-based approach suggests that the information should be processed locally and the agents should exchange knowledge. In this way, the amount of information exchanged is limited and so is the demand for an expensive communication network. This feature is common to traditional distributed computing. Moreover, the Multi Agent System is characterized by the fact that agents have partial or zero representation of the environment. In our application, the agent of a unit only knows the voltage level of its own bus and, maybe, it can estimate what is happening in specific buses, but it has no information about the whole Microgrid and the design of the control system is based on this lack of information.

- Increased reliability of the control system. In case one of the controllers fails, other agents may adapt and continue the system function.
- Openness of the system. Multi Agent Systems allow any manufacturer of DER units or loads to embed a programmable agent in the controller of his equipment, according to some rules. In this way, the required plug and play capability for installing future DER units and loads can be provided.

8.3.3 A multiagent reinforcement learning method

The algorithm adopted is based on Multiagent Reinforcement Learning (RL). Reinforcement Learning is a family of iterative algorithms that allows the agent to learn a behavior through trial and error. The well-known Q-Learning algorithm is selected with the main characteristic that each agent runs its own Q-Learning for the part of the environment that it perceives, aiming, however, to optimize the overall Microgrid performance.

Q-Learning is a Reinforcement Learning algorithm [281] that does not need a model of its environment and can be used on-line. Q-learning algorithms operate by estimating the values of state-action pairs. The value $Q(s,a)$ is defined as the expected discounted sum of future payoffs obtained by taking action a from state s and following an optimal policy thereafter. Once these values have been learned, the optimal action from any state is the one with the highest Q-value. After being initialized, Q-values are estimated on the basis of experience, as follows:

- From the current state s, select an action a. This will bring an immediate payoff r, and will lead to a next state s',
- Update $Q(s,a)$ based upon this experience as follows:

$$Q(s,a) = (1-k)Q(s,a) + k(r + \gamma \max Q(s',a'))$$

where k is the learning rate and $0 < \gamma < 1$ is the discount factor.

This algorithm is guaranteed to converge to the correct Q-values with probability one, if the environment is non stochastic and depends on the current state and the action taken in it. This exploration strategy does not specify which action to select at each step. In practice, a method for action, called the Boltzmann distribution strategy, that will ensure sufficient exploration while still favouring actions with higher value estimates is usually chosen.

The main drawback of Q-learning is that it cannot operate in a stochastic environment, like the typical Microgrid environment. This means that, when an agent selects an action and the environment is stochastic, the next state of the system is unknown. For example, if an agent chooses to allow a load to operate, the consequence of this action is unknown, since the total demand is unpredictable.

Alternative learning algorithms have been investigated by the authors, including the Nash-Q learning, which is a general sum MAS reinforcement algorithm for stochastic environments. However, execution times were prohibitive, because the Nash-Q learning requires that the Q table includes the actions of the other agents as a parameter. For systems like Microgrids, the Q table becomes huge, requesting a large number of episodes for training. Other approaches, like [271], propose to forecast the decisions of other agent, however, this cannot be easily done in our case. [271] also proposes to describe the relationship connection between the system state and the environment, in order to simplify it.

The authors propose an alternative approach based on Q-learning, that takes into account the stochastic environment and the size of the problem. The core of the algorithm is based on the idea that every agent runs a separate Q learning algorithm for itself, perceiving just a state environment variable that expresses the overall state of the system. Thus, the stochastic and complex environment is considered by adding a new variable, called state transition. This variable expresses the most possible transitions of the system and describes the possible actions of the other agents of the system.

In order to understand this, let's consider that we want to have the full description of the system explicitly.

This means that we should include the selected actions of all agents in the Q table.

$$Q(s, \alpha 1, \alpha 2, \alpha 3, \ldots \alpha n) \tag{8.74}$$

$\alpha 1, \alpha 2, \alpha 3, \ldots \alpha n$ is the selected action of agent 1, agent 2... agent N. In this way, the Q table becomes huge and, moreover, the environment is still stochastic, since we still cannot predict the result of switching a load on the system state. The approach proposed in the paper replaces all actions with one single variable, called transition, that represents the final result to the environment of all actions of the agents.

$$\begin{gathered} Q(s, \underbrace{\alpha 1, \alpha 2, \alpha 3, \ldots \alpha n}) \\ Q(s, \alpha 1, \mathbf{tr}) \end{gathered} \tag{8.75}$$

As an example, we consider the following system with three states.

The states describe the power flow between the Microgrid and the upstream main grid. In state 1, the grid provides power to the Microgrid, state 2 represents the reverse power flow and state 3 represents zero power exchange. This is the system variable. Let's assume that the agent is a diesel generator and the possible actions are to produce power or not. In each state the selected action will lead to a different or the same state in the next time step, depending on the action of all the agents. Three transition variables are introduced in order to describe the most possible transitions of the system. The three transitions are:

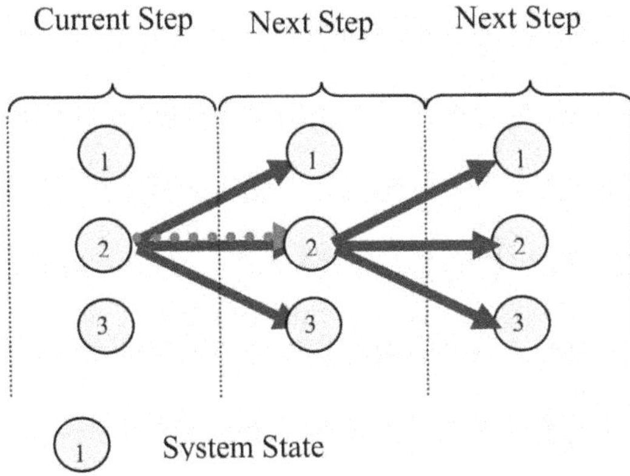

Figure 8.16: The three states of the example system

1. **System goes to State 1**
2. **System goes to State 2**
3. **System goes to State 3**

The agent learns the value of the three following cases:

1. "The agent is in State 2, selects action A and the **System goes to State 1**".
2. "The agent is in State 2, selects action A and the **System goes to State 2**".
3. "The agent is in State 2, selects action A and the **System goes to State 3**".

In this way, the agent learns what the value of its action is in all possible future states of the system and the system is no longer stochastic. This is because we are interested in whether the system sends or receives energy and not what a single load does.

It should be noted that the total number of possible transitions of the system are too many, however, we consider only the ones which are most probable. For example, if a diesel unit has no fuel, it is not expected that it will have fuel in the next state.

During the learning phase, the algorithm explores the various states and actions according to the fundamental rules of Q- learning.

The next question is how the agent uses this final knowledge that is in the Q table. Consider that the system is in the time step t and in state X. In this state, all the agents together will select which transition is the best by using the following formula.

$$Selected \text{ transition} = \underset{tr=1,2,3}{\operatorname{argmax}}\left(\sum \max_{\alpha}(Q(s,\alpha,tr))\right) \tag{8.76}$$

This formula says that, for each transition, each agent selects the action that provides the maximum Q value and they all add these values for each transition. The selected transition is the one with the higher value. In the following, the RL algorithm is applied in a typical case.

8.3.4 Critical operation in island mode

This application concerns Microgrid operation in black start or in emergency transition from grid connected to island mode. The units, after the black out, follow a simple procedure:

1. Switch off all loads
2. Launch black start units
3. Launch the other units
4. Start the MAS according to the results of the Reinforcement Learning.

It should be noted that the algorithm considers the steady state of the system and does not handle transient phenomena. The problem faced is how the system ensures power supply to the critical loads for a predefined period, e.g., 24 hours ahead. In this case, the agents have to learn to use the available resources in the most efficient way.

The main difficulty in this example is the lack of grid, which means that units significantly affect each other. For example, if a diesel unit stops, another unit should increase its production according to the control algorithms. In this way, the agents are not independent. To solve this algorithmic problem, a slack unit, i.e., a virtual storage unit, is introduced and all actual units try to set the production of this unit to zero. The virtual unit participates in the operation of the system, but provides energy only when the actual units are out of fuel or stores energy when there is a surplus of power. In an actual system, the virtual unit may be formed by the sum of the reserve power of one or more units.

In the approach presented, each agent executes a Q-Learning procedure for the part of the environment that it perceives. For the formulation of the problem, the variables that will be inserted in the Q table should be defined first. A basic goal is to minimize the size of the Q table.

The first variable is the environment state variable, which is the flow from or to the slack with three values: {Receive from the Slack, Zero Power exchange, Offer to the Slack}. The environment state variable forms a table with 24 elements, one for every hour of the schedule. The production units are characterized by one more variable, the fuel, with three values: {Low, Medium, High}. For battery units, this variable reflects the State of Charge. The transition variable is considered next, with three values: {Up, Neutral, Down}. This variable is an indication of the behaviour of the other agents and the state of the system, as explained in Section VI. The purpose of this variable is to identify the most possible next states of the system. For example, if the transition has value {Down}, the system will go to a worse state, no matter what the action of the individual agent might be. A worse state is the state where the slack constantly provides power to the system, which is an indication that the system has no fuel.

Finally, for the loads, there is a variable called Remain with values {Low, Medium, High} indicating how many hours they need to be served. To explain the use of this variable, consider as an example a water heater that is controlled by agents. The MAS should allow the device to operate only for a certain number of hours (for example 10h per day). This means that if it was just an energy market the system should block the device during the peak hours. However, please note that, according to the model of operation, when the system allows the water heater to operate this does not mean that the water heater is on, it just means that the house owner has the ability to use the devised during those hours.

Accordingly, the size of the Q table for each agent is:

- Storage Units.

  Q (Horizon {24}, Fuel{3}, Environment {3}, Transition {3}, Action {3}) = 1944 elements.

- Generation Units.

  Q (Horizon {24}, Fuel {3}, Environment {3}, Transition {3},Action {2}) = 1296 elements.

- Loads.

  Q (Horizon {24}, Environment {3}, Remain {3}, Transition {3}, Action {2}) = 1296 elements.

The agent learns the value of its action in the various states of the system. For this case study, the agents are able to act as in Table 8.1.

Table 8.1: Actions of the agents

<table>
<tr><th></th><th>Type</th><th>Actions</th></tr>
<tr><td rowspan="2">1</td><td rowspan="2">Load</td><td>On</td></tr>
<tr><td>Off</td></tr>
<tr><td rowspan="3">2</td><td rowspan="3">Storage Unit</td><td>Produce</td></tr>
<tr><td>Stop</td></tr>
<tr><td>Store</td></tr>
<tr><td rowspan="2">3</td><td rowspan="2">Production Unit</td><td>Stop</td></tr>
<tr><td>Produce</td></tr>
</table>

The intermediate reward for the algorithm is received from:

Reward=N*(TransitionReward+FinalStateReward+K)

N is a normalization parameter obtained by dividing the maximum production capacity of the unit by the total production capacity of the system. This ensures a weighted participation of all units, e.g., a 100kW unit affects the final actions more than a 1kW unit would.

- The Transition Reward has value 1/24 if the system goes to a classification level near zero power exchange, 0 if it remains at the same level and -1/24 if it goes to a power exchange status with the slack.
- The Final State reward is received in the final step and has value 1 if the system has sufficient energy for the whole period (24h) and -1 if not.
- The K parameter is different for loads or production/storage units. For production/Storage units, it indicates the remaining fuel and for load it indicates the time (in percentage that the load should be served).

This algorithm needs to be executed if there is a significant change in the system, like the installation of a new unit. This is clearly presented in Fig. 8.16. After the execution, every agent has learned what to do in case of an emergency. Consider, for example, that the system is in zero power exchange with the slack. The agents have to select among three transitions {Up, Neutral, Down}. In order to decide which transition to follow, they announce to each other the Q values for each transition in the current state. The selected transition is given by (8.76).

Selecting, for example, an "Up" transition, means that some agents have surplus power and they offer it to the system, having in mind that the selected path will lead them into a good final solution. The good solution is the one that ensures energy adequacy for the whole period (24h).

8.3.5 Simulation results II

As an example, a Microgrid system comprising the following units is considered:

- 2 diesel units of 3kW able to produce 60kWh each.
- 2 diesel units of 10kW able to produce 200kWh each
- 2 battery banks of 3kW, able to produce 50kWh each.
- 2 battery banks of 10kW, able to produce 150kWh each.
- 4 loads rated 1kW to 10kW with 200kWh total demand.

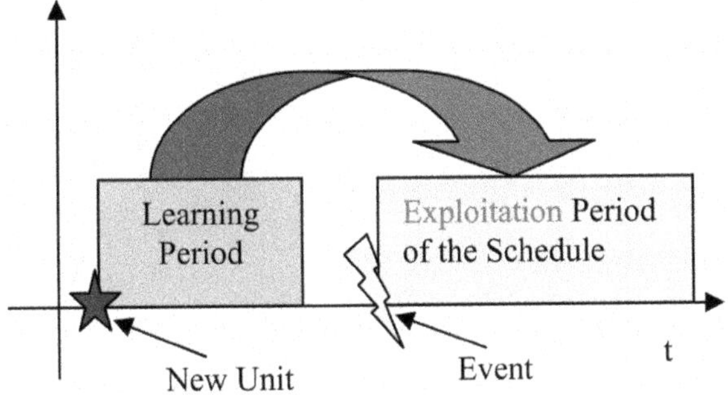

Figure 8.17: Time schedule of the algorithm

- 6 critical loads with total installed power 50kW and total demand of 600kWh
- Renewable energy sources with installed capacity 5kW and production of 50kWh.

The simulation has two parts. The first part is the training (exploration) part, in order to find the Q values. The second part is the exploitation of the algorithm, where a simple software that simulates the isolated operation was developed. Based on this program, several simulations of the operation of the system took place in order to validate whether the agents find the solution that ensures energy adequacy. Furthermore, a simple software was developed, allowing each agent to decide absolutely independently from each other in order to compare the solution with the one of the reinforcement learning algorithms.

The critical loads and the renewable energy sources participate in the simulation of the exploitation, but there is no need to train the respective agents, since they do not control their actions.

A learning rate k = 0.95 and discount factor $\gamma = 0.1$ are assumed. The algorithm converges after 20000 iterations, which means that there are no significant changes in the values of the Q table in more iterations. In order to ensure that this is the final solution, multiple runs have been made with the same schedule but with different initializations of the Q table, as well as multiple runs with the same initial Q table. Since there is no interaction between the agents during the learning period, every agent needs around 40 seconds in a single PC with 3GHz processor to complete the training.

The system learns to make the slack unit produce power as late as possible. If the slack produces power it means that some units should increase their power. If the slack unit stores power, it means that a unit should reduce its production.

In Figs. 8.17 and 8.18, results of the algorithm for some cases are presented. In the vertical axis, the Q value is presented and in the horizontal axis, the time step. Both the battery and the diesel agents appear to learn how to handle the

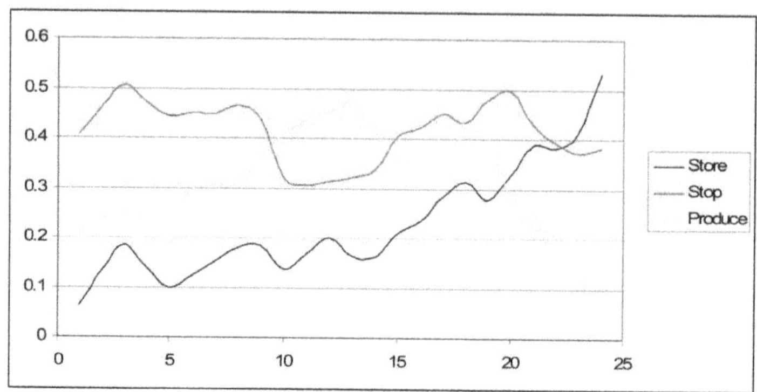

Figure 8.18: Results for restoration study case (Battery 3kW high SOC)

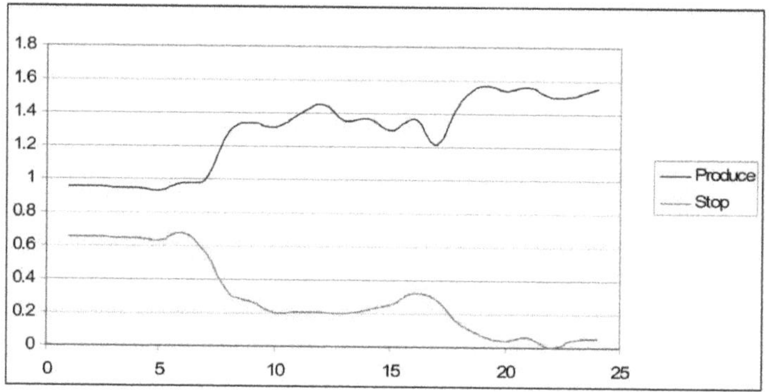

Figure 8.19: Results for restoration study case (Diesel 10kW)

island operation. Both agents behave in a conservative way at the beginning, since they do not know what will happen next and the system tries to save fuel for the next hours. However, by the time the energy adequacy is guaranteed, the agents might try to serve extra loads, like the battery in the hours between 10 and 15. However, these graphs do not provide a clear picture of what the agents learned, since the Q table is very complicated and cannot be easily presented in one chart. A clearer picture is presented in the simulation results next.

A critical parameter in this method is the proper formulation of the reward function, since it incorporates the goal of the system. It should be noted that this formulation provides increased flexibility in programming several goals.

In order to indicate the significance of the reward function formulation, several simulations considering the loads as random variables were run. This means that, if the agent controlling a load selects the "ON action, it does not mean that the load will operate in full demand. The actual demand is a random variable, constrained by the total consumption in the predefined period. Similar random operation applies for the critical loads and the renewable energy sources. The results shown next are grouped according to the State of Charge (SoC), of the battery. For each (SoC), 300 simulation episodes have been performed and two different rewards were considered. Finally, for each time step, the fine tuning of the output of the units was done by a simple algorithm based on a priority list. This was done in order to simplify the simulator. An alternative algorithm is the one presented in [265] which ensures optimal energy allocation.

In the first case, the evaluation was performed without the {TransitionReward} and the K parameter for the intermediate reward.

Table 8.2: Results of the simulation

	Battery SOC	System State	Result
1	High	Succeed	Succeed 100% (99.8%)
		Failed	0% (0.2%)
2	Medium	Succeed	77% (73%)
		Failed	23%(26%)
3	Low	Succeed	33% (25%)
		Failed	67% (75%)

As shown in Table 8.2, the system failed in several cases when the batteries where in a medium or low SoC. There are two main reasons for this:

- The system has run out of fuel.
- The overall system had enough fuel, however some of the units did not. Therefore, the maximum power of the system could not be reached.

The results in the brackets show the results of the simple algorithm in which the agents each select their own decisions independently. This is a simple benchmark that indicates that the reinforcement learning algorithm provides extra information to the system. More specifically, the cooperation between the agents provides better results.

In Table 8.3 the results obtained from a Reward function that includes the {TransitionReward} and the K parameter are shown. The operation of the system appears clearly improved. It is interesting to note, that in the latter case, when the behavior of the load the system in the failed cases was analyzed, it was seen that the failure could not be avoided. Nevertheless, the authors do not claim that the algorithm proposed finds an optimal solution in all cases. It was also shown in the previous examples that the system performance relies on the definition of the reward. In our example, formulation of the rewards was done by trial and error.

1 High Succeed 100% Failed 0%, 2 Middle Succeed 82% Failed 18%, 3 Low Succeed 42% Failed 58%.

Table 8.3: Results of the simulation

	Battery SOC	System State	Result
1	High	Succeed	Succeed 100%
		Failed	0%
2	Medium	Succeed	82%
		Failed	18%
3	Low	Succeed	42%
		Failed	58%

8.4 Notes

This section has introduced a novel solution for constrained differential games on graphs. The solution is implemented online using adaptive Integral Reinforcement Learning approaches. The graph is required to be strongly connected in order to guarantee the asymptotic convergence and synchronization of the error dynamics. A set of constrained IRL-Hamilton-Jacobi-Bellman and IRL-Bellman optimality equations are developed for differential graphical games. Solving these coupled equations yields a Nash equilibrium solution. The integral adaptive learning approach uses value iteration to solve the graphical game online, taking advantage of partial knowledge on the nodes' dynamics. The solution is implemented based on the neighborhood information available to each node. The adaptive critics implementation capitalizes on simple layers of neural network structures and tuning laws, which makes it more attractive than other complicated solution structures used for other differential graphical games. The solution is shown to be robust against uncertainties in the dynamic environment and the connection weights provided that the graph remains strongly connected.

References

[1] C.W. Reynolds, "Flocks, herds, and schools: A distributed behavioral model", *Comp. Graph*, vol. 21, no. 4, pp. 25–34, 1987.

[2] H. Yamaguchi, "A cooperative hunting behavior by mobile-robot troops", *The International J. Robotics Research*, vol. 18, no. 8, pp. 931–940, 1999.

[3] J.P. Desai, J. Ostrowski and V. Kumar, "Modeling and control of formations of nonholonomic mobile robots", *IEEE Trans. Robotics and Automation*, vol. 17, no. 6, pp. 905–908, 2001.

[4] J. Fowler and R. D'Andrea, "A formation flight experiment", *IEEE Control Systems Magazine*, vol. 23, no. 5, pp. 35–43, 2003.

[5] W. Ren and R.W. Beard, "Distributed Consensus in Multi-Vehicle Cooperative Control: Theory and Applications", *Springer*, London, 2008.

[6] D. Stilwell, B. Bishop and C. Sylvester, "Redundant manipulator techniques for partially decentralized path planning and control of a platoon of autonomous vehicles", *IEEE Trans. Systems Man and Cybernetics Part B-Cybernetics*, vol. 35, no. 4, pp. 842–848, 2005.

[7] J. Cortes, S. Martinez, T. Karatas and F. Bullo, "Coverage control for mobile sensing networks", *IEEE Trans. Robotics and Automation*, vol. 20, no. 2, pp. 243–255, 2004.

[8] I.F. Akyildiz, W. Su, Y. Sankarasubramaniam and E. Cayirci, "A survey on sensor networks", *IEEE Communications Magazine*, vol. 40, no. 8, pp. 102–114, 2002.

[9] E. Sahin, "Swarm robotics: From sources of inspiration to domains of application", *Sahin, E., Spears, W., eds.: Swarm Robotics: State-of-the-art Survey. Lecture Notes in Computer Science (LNCS 3342)*, Springer-Verlag, Berlin Heidelberg, pp. 10–20, 2005.

[10] C. Godsil and G. Royle, *Algebraic Graph Theory*, ser. Graduate Texts in Mathematics. Berlin, Germany: Springer-Verlag, 2001, vol. 207.

[11] R. Olfati-Saber, J. Alex Fax and R.M. Murray, "Consensus and cooperation in networked multi-agent systems", *Proc. the IEEE*, vol. 95, pp. 215–233, 2007.

[12] F.L. Lewis, H. Zhang, K.H. Movric and A. Das, "Cooperative Control of Multi-Agent Systems: Optimal and Adaptive Design Approaches", *Springer*, London, 2014.

[13] Y. Liu, K.M. Passino and M.M. Polycarpou, "Stability analysis of one-dimensional asynchronous swarms", *IEEE Trans. on Automatic Control*, vol. 48, no. 10, pp. 1848–1854, 2003.

[14] M.S. Mahmoud, *Distributed Control and Filtering for Industrial Systems*, IET Press, UK, December 2012.

[15] D. Angeli and P.-A. Bliman, "Convergence speed of unsteady distributed consensus: decay estimate along the settling spanning-trees", *SIAM J. Control Optimization*, vol. 48, no. 1, pp. 1–2, 2009.

[16] P. Lin, Y.M. Jia and L. Li, "Distributed robust $\mathcal{H}_\infty$ consensus control in directed networks of agents with time-delay", *Systems and Control Lett.*, vol. 57, no. 8, pp. 643–653, 2008.

[17] J. Zhou and Q. Wang, "Convergence speed in distributed consensus over dynamically switching random networks", *Automatica*, vol. 45, no. 6, 1455–461, 2009.

[18] R. Olfati-Saber and R.M. Murray, "Consensus problems in networks of agents with switching topology and time delays", *IEEE Trans. Automatic Control*, vol. 49 no. 9, pp. 1520–533, 2004.

[19] Y. Hatano and M. Mesbahi, "Agreement over random networks", *IEEE Trans. Automatic Control*, vol. 50, no. 11, pp. 1867–1872, 2005.

[20] C.W. Wu, "Synchronization and convergence of linear dynamics in random directed networks", *IEEE Trans. Automatic Control*, vol. 51, no. 7, pp. 1207–1210, 2006.

[21] M. Porfiri and D.J. Stilwell, "Consensus seeking over random weighted directed graphs", *IEEE Trans. Automatic Control*, vol. 52, no. 9, pp. 1767–1773, 2007.

[22] M. Akar and R. Shorten, "Distributed probabilistic synchronization algorithms for communication networks", *IEEE Trans. Automatic Control*, vol. 53, no. 1, pp. 389–393, 2008.

[23] A. Tahbaz-Salehi and A. Jadbabaie, "A necessary and sufficient condition for consensus over random networks", *IEEE Trans. Automatic Control*, vol. 53, no. 3, pp. 791–795, 2008.

[24] M. Huang, S. Dey, G.N. Nair and J.H. Manton, "Stochastic consensus over noisy networks with Markovian and arbitrary switches", *Automatica*, vol. 46, no. 10, pp. 1571–1583, 2010.

[25] M. Huang and J.H. Manton, "Stochastic consensus seeking with noisy and directed inter-agent communication: Fixed and randomly varying topologies", *IEEE Trans. Automatic Control*, vol. 55, no. 1, pp. 235–241, 2010.

[26] A. Tahbaz-Salehi and A. Jadbabaie, "Consensus over ergodic stationary graph processes", *IEEE Trans. Automatic Control*, vol. 55, no. 1, pp. 225–230, 2010.

[27] G. Yin, Y. Sun and L.Y. Wang, "Asymptotic properties of consensus type algorithms for networked systems with regime-switching topologies", *Automatica*, vol. 47, no. 7, pp. 1366–1378, 2011.

[28] Y. Zhang and Y.-P. Tian, "Consentability and protocol design of multiagent systems with stochastic switching topology", *Automatica*, vol. 45, no. 5, pp. 1195–1201, 2009.

[29] S. Boyd, A. Ghosh, B. Prabhakar and D. Shah, "Randomized gossip algorithms", *IEEE Trans. Information Theory*, vol. 52, no. 6, pp. 2508–2530, 2006.

[30] A.G. Dimakis, S. Kar, J.M.F. Moura, M.G. Rabbat and A. Scaglione, "Gossip algorithms for distributed signal processing", *Proc. the IEEE*, vol. 98, no. 11, pp. 1847–1864, 2010.

[31] C.-Q. Ma and J.-F. Zhang, "Necessary and sufficient conditions for consensusability of linear multiagent systems", *IEEE Trans. Automatic Control*, vol. 55, no. 5, pp. 1263–1268, 2010.

[32] W. Ren and R.W. Beard, "Consensus seeking in multi-agent systems under dynamically changing interaction topologies", *IEEE Trans. Autom. Control*, vol. 50, no. 5, pp. 655–661, May 2005.

[33] R. Olfati-Saber and R.M. Murray, "Consensus problems in networks of agents with switching topology and time–delays", *IEEE Trans. Automatic Control*, vol. 49, no. 9, pp. 1520–1533, 2004.

[34] D. Cheng, J.H. Wang and X. Hu, "An extension of LaSalle's invariance principle and its application to multi-agent consensus", *IEEE Trans. Automat. Control*, vol. 53, pp. 1765–1770, 2008.

[35] Y. Hong, L. Gao, D. Cheng and J. Hu, "Lyapunov-based approach to multi-agent systems with switching jointly connected interconnection", *IEEE Trans. Automat. Control*, vol. 52, pp. 943–948, 2007.

[36] A. Jadbabaie, J. Lin and A.S. Morse, "Coordination of groups of mobile autonomous agents using nearest neighbor rules", *IEEE Trans. Automat. Control*, vol. 48, pp. 943–948, 2003.

[37] S. Khoo, L. Xie, Z. Man and S. Zhao, "Observer-based robust finite-time cooperative consensus control for multiagent networks", *Proc. 4th IEEE Conference on Industrial Electronics and Applications*, Xi'an, pp. 1883–1888, 2009.

[38] Y. Liu, Y. Jia, J. Du and S. Yuan, "Dynamic output feedback control for consensus of multiagent systems: An H_∞ approach", *Proc. American Control Conference*, St. Louis, pp. 4470–4475, 2009.

[39] T. Namerikawa and C. Yoshioka, "Consensus control of observer-based multi-agent systems with communication delay", *Proc. SICE Annual Conference*, Tokyo, pp. 2414–2419, 2008.

[40] W. Ni and D. Cheng, "Leader-following consensus of multi-agent systems under fixed and switching topologies", *Systems Control Letter*, vol. 59, pp. 209–217, 2010.

[41] R. Olfati-Saber and R.M. Murray, "Consensus problems in networks of agents with switching topology and time-delays", *IEEE Trans. Automat. Control*, vol. 49, pp. 1520–1533, 2004.

[42] R. Olfati-Saber, J.A. Fax and R.M. Murray, "Consensus and cooperation in networked multi-agent systems", *Proc. IEEE*, vol. 95, pp. 215–233, 2007.

[43] W. Ren and R.W. Beard, "Consensus seeking in multiagent systems under dynamically changing interaction topologies", *IEEE Trans. Automat. Control*, vol. 50, pp. 655–661, 2005.

[44] J.H. Seo, H. Shima and J. Back, "Consensus of high-order linear systems using dynamic output feedback compensator: Low gain approach", *Automatica*, vol. 45, pp. 2659–2664, 2009.

[45] L. Scardovi and R. Sepulchre, "Synchronization in networks of identical linear systems", *Automatica*, vol. 45, pp. 2557–2562, 2009.

[46] J. Wang, D. Cheng and X. Hu, "Consensus of multi-agent linear dynamical systems", *Asian J. Control*, vol. 10, pp. 144–155, 2008.

[47] X. Wang and Y. Hong, "Parametrization and geometric analysis of coordination controllers for multiagent systems", *Kybernetika*, vol. 45, pp. 785–800, 2009.

[48] X. Wang, Y. Hong, J. Huang and Z. Jiang, "A distributed control approach to a robust output regulation problem for multi-agent linear systems", *IEEE Trans. Automat. Control*, vol. 55, pp. 2891–2895, 2010.

[49] X. Wang and F. Han, "Robust coordination control of switching multiagent systems via output regulation approach", *Kybernetika*, vol. 47, pp. 755–772, 2011.

[50] C. Yoshioka and T. Namerikawa, "Observer-based consensus control strategy for multiagent system with communication time delay", *Proc. 17th IEEE Int. Conference on Control Applications*, San Antonio, pp. 1037–1042, 2008.

[51] H. Zhang, F.L. Lewis and A. Das, "Optimal design for synchronization of cooperative systems: State feedback, observer and output feedback", *IEEE Trans. Automat. Control*, vol. 56, pp. 1948–1952, 2011.

[52] R.A. Horn and C.R. Johnson, *Matrix Analysis*, Cambridge Univ. Press, Cambridge, UK, 1987.

[53] M. Fiedler, "Algebraic connectivity of graphs," *Czech. Math. J.*, vol. 23, no. 98, pp. 298–305, 1973.

[54] J. Hu, G. Chen and H.X. Li, "Distributed event-triggered tracking control of leader-follower multi-agent systems with communication delays", *Kybernetika*, vol. 4, no. 4, pp. 630–643, 2011.

[55] Y. Cao, D. Stuart, W. Ren and Z. Meng, "Distributed containment control for multiple autonomous vehicles with double-integrator dynamics: Algorithms and experiments", *IEEE Trans. Control Systems Technol.* vol. 19, pp. 929–938, 2011.

[56] D.V. Dimarogonas and E. Frazzoli, "Distributed event-triggered strategies for multiagent systems", *Proc. 47th Annual Allerton Conference on Communications, Control and Computing*, Monticello, pp. 906–910, 2009.

[57] D.V. Dimarogonas and K.H. Johansson, "Event-triggered control for multi-agent systems", *Proc. IEEE CDC/CCC2009*, pp. 7131–7136, 2009.

[58] A. Eqtami, D.V. Dimarogonas and K.J. Kyriakopoulos, "Event-triggered control for discrete-time systems", *Proc. American Control Conference*, Baltimore, pp. 4719–4724, 2010.

[59] Y. Gao and L. Wang, "Asynchronous consensus of continuous-time multi-agent systems with intermittent measurements", *Int. J. Control*, vol. 83, pp. 552–562, 2010.

[60] M.S. Mahmoud, *Robust Control and Filtering for Time-Delay Systems*, Marcel Dekker Inc., New York, 2000.

[61] Y. Hong, J. Hu and L. Gao, "Tracking control for multi-agent consensus with an active leader and variable topology", *Automatica*, vol. 42, pp. 1177-1182, 2006.

[62] J. Hu, "On robust consensus of multi-agent systems with communication time-delays", *Kybernetika*, vol. 45, pp. 768–784, 2009.

[63] J. Hu and G. Feng, "Distributed tracking control of leader-follower multiagent systems under noisy measurement", *Automatica*, vol. 46, pp. 1382–1387, 2010.

[64] J. Hu and Y. Hong, "Leader-following coordination of multiagent systems with coupling time delays", *Physica A*, vol. 374, pp. 853–863, 2007.

[65] D.B. Kingston, W. Ren and R. Beard, "Consensus algorithms are input-to-state stable", *Proc. American Control Conference*, pp. 1686–1690, 2005.

[66] T. Li and J. Zhang, "Mean square average-consensus under measurement noises and fixed topologies: Necessary and sufficient conditions", *Automatica*, vol. 45, pp. 1929–1936, 2009.

[67] Z. Liu and Z. Chen, "Event-triggered average-consensus for multi-agent systems", *Proc. 29th Chinese Control Conference*, Beijing, pp. 4506–4511, 2010.

[68] Y. Liu and Y. Jia, "Consensus problem of high-order multi-agent systems with external disturbances: an $H-\infty$ analysis approach", *Int. J. Robust Nonlinear Control*, vol. 20, pp. 1579–1593, 2010.

[69] L. Moreau, "Stability of multiagent systems with time-dependent communication links", *IEEE Trans. Automat. Control*, vol. 50, pp. 169–182, 2005.

[70] G. Shi and Y. Hong, "Global target aggregation and state agreement of nonlinear multi-agent systems with switching topologies", *Automatica*, vol. 45, pp. 1165–1175, 2009.

[71] P. Tabuada, "Event-triggered real-time scheduling of stabilizing control tasks", *IEEE Trans. Automat. Control*, vol. 52, pp. 1680–1685, 2007.

[72] X. Wang, Y. Hong, J. Huang and Z. Jiang, "A distributed control approach to a robust output regulation problem for multi-agent linear systems", *IEEE Trans. Automat. Control*, vol. 55, pp. 2891–2895, 2010.

[73] X. Wang and M.D. Lemmon, "Event-triggering in distributed networked control systems", *IEEE Trans. Automat. Control* vol. 56, pp. 586–601, 2011.

[74] M.S. Mahmoud *Decentralized Systems with Design Constraints*, Springer-Verlag, UK, 2011.

[75] R.K. Khosrow and Moslehi, "Vision for a self-healing power grid," *ABB Review*, pp. 21–25, 2006.

[76] M. Mao, C. Liuchen and M. Ding, "Integration and intelligent control of micro-grids with multi-energy generations: A review," *Proc. IEEE ICSET*, pp. 777–780, 2008.

[77] G. Chicco and P. Mancarella, "Distributed multi-generation: A comprehensive view", *Renewable and Sustainable Energy Reviews*, vol. 13, pp. 535–51, 2009.

[78] R. Zamora and A.K. Srivastava, "Controls for microgrids with storage: Review, challenges, and research needs", *Renewable and Sustainable Energy Reviews*, vol. 14, pp. 2009–2018, 2010.

[79] F. Katiraei, R. Iravani, N. Hatziargyriou and A. Dimeas, "Microgrids management," *IEEE Power Energy Magazine*, vol. 6, no. 3, pp. 54–65, 2008.

[80] F. Katiraei, M. Reza Iravani and P.W. Lehn, "Micro-grid autonomous operation during and subsequent to islanding process", *IEEE Trans. Power Delivery*, vol. 20, no. 1, pp. 248–257, 2005.

[81] M.S. Mahmoud, S. Azher Hussain and M.A. Abido, "Modeling and control of microgrid: an overview", *J. the Franklin Institute*, vol. 351, no. 5, pp. 2822–2859, 2014.

[82] A.M. Bouzid, et al., "A survey on control of electric power distributed generation systems for microgrid applications", *Renewable and Sustainable Energy Reviews*, vol. 44, pp. 751–766, 2015.

[83] Y.R. Mohamed and A.A. Radwan, "Hierarchical control system for robust microgrid operation and seamless mode transfer in active distribution systems", *IEEE Trans. Smart Grid*, vol. 2, no. 2, pp. 352–362, 2011.

[84] S.K. Mazumder, M. Tahir and K. Acharya, "Pseudo-decentralized control-communication optimization framework for microgrid: A case illustration", *IEEE Proc. Transmission and Distribution Conference and Exposition (T & D)*, 2008.

[85] M.S. Mahmoud, M.S.U. Rahman and F.M. AL-Sunni, "Networked control of microgrid system of systems", *International Journal of Systems Science*, 2015.

[86] M.S. Mahmoud and O. Al-Buraiki, "Two-level control for improving the performance of Microgrid in islanded mode", *IEEE Symposium Industrial Electronics (ISIE)*, Istanbul, Turkey, pp. 254–259, June 1–4, 2014.

[87] H. Karimi, H. Nikkhajoei and R. Iravani, "Control of an electronically-coupled distributed resource unit subsequent to an islanding event", *IEEE Trans. Power Delivery*, vol. 23, no. 1, pp. 493–501, 2008.

[88] H. Karimi, E.J. Davison and R. Iravani, "Multivariable servomechanism controller for autonomous operation of a distributed generation unit: Design and performance evaluation", *IEEE Trans. Power Systems*, vol. 25, no. 2, pp. 853–865, 2010.

[89] A.G. Barto, *Reinforcement Learning: An Introduction*, MIT Press, 1998.

[90] P.J. Werbos, "Approximate dynamic programming for real-time control and neural modeling", *Handbook of intelligent control: Neural, fuzzy, and adaptive approaches*, pp. 493–525, 1992.

[91] D.P. Bertsekas and J.N. Tsitsiklis, "Neuro-dynamic programming: an overview", *IEEE Proc. Decision and Control*, vol. 1, pp. 560–564, 1995.

[92] P.J. Werbos, "A menu of designs for reinforcement learning over time", *Neural networks for control*, pp. 67–95, 1990.

[93] H. Jiayi, J. Chuanwen and X. Rong, "A review on distributed energy resources and microgrid", *Renewable and Sustainable Energy Reviews*, vol. 12, no. 9, pp. 2472–2483, 2008.

[94] R.S. Sutton and A.G. Barto, *Introduction to Reinforcement Learning*, MIT Press, 1998.

[95] F.L. Lewis and D. Vrabie, "Reinforcement learning and adaptive dynamic programming for feedback control", *IEEE Circuits and Systems Magazine*, vol. 9, no. 3, pp. 32–50, 2009.

[96] A.G. Barto, G. Andrew, R.S. Sutton and C.W. Anderson, "Neuron-like adaptive elements that can solve difficult learning control problems", *IEEE Trans. Systems, Man and Cybernetics*, vol. 5, pp. 834–846, 1983.

[97] C. Szepesvari and M.L. Littman, "A unified analysis of value-function-based reinforcement-learning algorithms", *Neural computation* vol. 11, no. 8, pp. 2017–2060, 1999.

[98] A.L. Strehl and M.L. Littman, "Online linear regression and its application to model-based reinforcement learning", *Advances in Neural Information Processing Systems*, 2008.

[99] M. Abu-Khalaf and F.L. Lewis, "Nearly optimal control laws for nonlinear systems with saturating actuators using a neural network HJB approach", *Automatica*, vol. 41, no. 5, pp. 779–791, 2005.

[100] F.L. Lewis and V.L. Syrmos, “Optimal Control”, *John Wiley & Sons*, 1995.

[101] R.H. Lasseter, “Microgrids distributed power generation”, *IEEE Power Engineering Society Winter Meeting*, vol. 1, pp. 146–149, Columbus, Ohio, Feb 2001.

[102] Om. P. Malik, “Evolution of Power Systems into Smarter Networks.” *J. Control, Automation and Electrical Systems*, vol. 24.1-2, pp. 139–147, 2013.

[103] H. Farhangi, “The path of the smart grid.” *IEEE Power and Energy Magazine*, vol. 8(1), pp. 18–28, 2010.

[104] R.H. Lasseter and P. Paigi, “Microgrid: A conceptual solution.” *IEEE 35th Annual Power Electronics Specialists Conference PESC'04*, vol. 6, 2004.

[105] L. Dobakhshari, A. Salehi, S. Azizi and A.M. Ranjbar, “Control of microgrids: aspects and prospects,” *IEEE Int. Conference Networking, Sensing and Control (ICNSC)*, 2011.

[106] M.A. Pedrasa and T. Spooner, “A survey of techniques used to control microgrid generation and storage during island operation,” *Proc. the Australian Universities Power Engineering Conference*, 2006.

[107] M.S. Mahmoud, M.F. Hassan and M.G. Darwish, *Large Scale Control Systems: Theories and Techniques*, Marcel Dekker Inc., New York, 1985.

[108] B.H. Bakken and O.S. Grande, “Automatic generation control in a deregulated power system,” *IEEE Trans. Power Electronics*, vol. 13(4), pp. 1401–1406, 1998.

[109] Y. Zhang and H. Ma, “Theoretical and experimental investigation of networked control for parallel operation of inverters,” *IEEE Trans. Industrial Electronics*, vol. 59, no. 4, pp. 1961–1970, 2012.

[110] T.L. Vandoorn et al., “Communication-based secondary control in microgrids with voltage-based droop control,” *Proc. Transmission and Distribution Conference and Exposition (T & D)*, IEEE Press, 2012.

[111] W. Zheng, H. Ma and X. He, “Modeling, analysis, and implementation of real time network controlled parallel multi-inverter systems,” *Proc. the 7th Int. Power Electronics and Motion Control Conference (IPEMC)*, vol. 2, 2012.

[112] J.C. Vasquez et al., “Hierarchical control of intelligent microgrids,” *IEEE Industrial Electronics Magazine*, vol. 4, no. 4, pp. 23–29, 2010.

[113] J.M. Guerrero et al., “Advanced control architectures for intelligent microgrids-Part I: decentralized and hierarchical control”, vol. 1, no. 1, 2012.

[114] J.M. Guerrero et al., "Advanced control architectures for intelligent microgrids-Part II: power quality, energy storage, and AC/DC microgrids," vol. 1, no. 1, 2012.

[115] M. Savaghebi et al., "Secondary control for compensation of voltage harmonics and unbalance in microgrids," *Proc. the 3rd IEEE Int. Symposium on Power Electronics for Distributed Generation Systems (PEDG)*, 2012.

[116] J.M. Guerrero et al., "Hierarchical control of droop-controlled AC and DC microgrids-A general approach toward standardization," *IEEE Trans. Industrial Electronics*, vol. 58, no. 1, pp. 158–172, 2011.

[117] J.W. Simpson-Porco, F. Dorfler and F. Bullo, "Synchronization and power sharing for droop-controlled inverters in islanded microgrids," *Automatica*, 2013.

[118] Q. Shafiee, J.C. Vasquez and J.M. Guerrero, "Distributed secondary control for islanded microgrids-A networked control systems approach," *Proc. IEEE 38th Annual Conference on Industrial Electronics—IECON'12*, 2012.

[119] G.J. Wang, C.T. Fong and K.J. Chang, "Neural-network-based self-tuning PI controller for precise motion control of PMAC motors," *IEEE Trans. Industrial Electronics*, vol 48.2, pp. 408–415, 2001.

[120] Z. Jian et al., "Modeling and control of automotive anti-lock brake systems through PI and neural network arithmetic," *Int. Conf. Electronic and Mechanical Engineering and Information Technology (EMEIT)*, vol. 4, 2011.

[121] P. Piagi and R.H. Lasseter, *Control and Design of Microgrid Components*, Final report, 2006.

[122] J.M. Guerrero et al, "Control strategy for flexible microgrid based on parallel line-interactive UPS systems", *IEEE Trans. Industrial Electronics*, vol. 56, no. 3, pp. 726–736, 2009.

[123] N. Pogaku, M. Prodanovic and T.C. Green, "Modeling, analysis and testing of autonomous operation of an inverter-based microgrid." *IEEE Trans. Power Electronics*, vol. 22, no. 2, pp. 613–625, 2007.

[124] E.A.A. Coelho, P. Cabaleiro Cortizo and P.F.D. Garcia, "Small-signal stability for parallel-connected inverters in stand-alone AC supply systems," *IEEE Trans. Industry Applications*, vol. 38, no. 2, pp. 533–542, 2002.

[125] M.C. Chandorkar, D.M. Divan and R. Adapa, "Control of parallel connected inverters in standalone ac supply systems," *IEEE Trans. Industry Applications*, vol. 29, no. 1, pp. 136–143, 1993.

[126] A. Arulampalam et al., "Control of power electronic interfaces in distributed generation microgrids," *Int. J. Electronics*, vol. 91, no. 9, pp. 503–523, 2004.

[127] H. Akagi, Y. Kanazawa and A. Nabae, "Instantaneous reactive power compensators comprising switching devices without energy storage components," *IEEE Trans. Industry Applications*, vol. 3, pp. 625–630, 1984.

[128] K.S. Narendra and K. Parthasarathy, "Identification and control of dynamical systems using neural networks," *IEEE Trans. Neural Networks*, vol. 1, no. 1, pp. 4–27, 1990.

[129] M. Soleimani-Mohseni and B. Thomas, "Neural Networks for self tuning of PI-and PID controllers," *Intelligent Systems Design and Applications (ISDA)*, 2004.

[130] T. Back, D.B. Fogel and Z. Michalewicz, *Handbook of Evolutionary Computation*, IOP Publishing Ltd., 1997.

[131] R. Storn and K. Price, "Differential evolution–a simple and efficient heuristic for global optimization over continuous spaces," *J. Global Optimization* vol. 11, no. 4, pp. 341–359, 1997.

[132] J.-P. Chiou and F. Wang, "A hybrid method of differential evolution with application to optimal control problems of a bio-process system," *Proc. IEEE Int. Conf. World Congress on Computational Intelligence and Evolutionary Computation*, 1998.

[133] L. Gao-yang and L. Ming-Nguang, "The summary of differential evolution algorithm and its improvements," *Proc. the 3rd Int. Conf. Advanced Computer Theory and Engineering (ICACTE)*, vol. 3, 2010.

[134] S. Haykin, "Neural networks: A comprehensive foundation," *Neural Networks*, vol. 2, 2004.

[135] K. Hornik, M. Stinchcombe and H. White, "Universal approximation of an unknown mapping and its derivatives using multilayer feedforward networks," *Neural networks*, vol. 3, no. 5, pp. 551–560, 1990.

[136] H. Demuth and M. Beale, "Neural network toolbox for use with Matlab", *The MathWorks Inc.*, User Guide, Natick, USA, 2000.

[137] G.W. Ng, *Application of Neural Networks to Adaptive Control of Nonlinear Systems*, Research Studies Press, New York, 1997.

[138] M.T. Hagan and M. Menhaj, "Training feedforward networks with Marquardt algorithm," *IEEE Trans. Neural Networks*, vol. 5, no. 6, pp. 989–993, 1994.

[139] Riedmiller, M. and H. Braun, "A direct adaptive method for faster back-propagation learning: The RPROP algorithm," *Proc. IEEE Int. Conf. Neural Networks*, 1993.

[140] N.A. Lynch, *Distributed Algorithms*, San Francisco, CA: Morgan Kaufman, 1997.

[141] M.H. DeGroot, "Reaching a consensus," *J. Am. Statis. Assoc.*, vol. 69, no. 345, pp. 118–121, 1974.

[142] J.A. Benediktsson and P.H. Swain, "Consensus theoretic classification methods," *IEEE Trans. Sys. Man, Cybern.*, vol. 22, no. 4, pp. 688–704, Apr. 1992.

[143] S.C. Weller and N.C. Mann, "Assessing rater performance without a gold standard using consensus theory," *Med. Decision Making*, vol. 17, no. 1, pp. 71–79, 1997.

[144] V. Borkar and P. Varaiya, "Asymptotic agreement in distributed estimation," *IEEE Trans. Autom. Control*, vol. AC-27, no. 3, pp. 650–655, Jun. 1982.

[145] J.N. Tsitsiklis, "Problems in Decentralized Decision Making and Computation," *Ph.D. dissertation, Dept. Electr. Eng. Comput. Sci., Lab. Inf. Decision Syst.*, Massachusetts Inst. Technol., Cambridge, MA, Nov. 1984.

[146] J.N. Tsitsiklis, D.P. Bertsekas and M. Athans, "Distributed asynchronous deterministic and stochastic gradient optimization algorithms," *IEEE Trans. Automatic Control*, vol. 31, no. 9, pp. 803–812, Sep. 1986.

[147] D.P. Bertsekas and J. Tsitsiklis, *Parallel and Distributed Computation*, Upper Saddle River, NJ: Prentice-Hall, 1989.

[148] R.O. Saber and R.M. Murray, "Consensus protocols for networks of dynamic agents," *Proc. Amer. Control Conf.*, pp. 951–956, 2003.

[149] R. Olfati-Saber and R.M. Murray, "Consensus problems in networks of agents with switching topology and time-delays," *IEEE Trans. Autom. Control*, vol. 49, no. 9, pp. 1520–1533, 2004.

[150] J.A. Fax, "Optimal and cooperative control of vehicle formations," *PhD dissertation, Control Dynamical Syst.*, California Inst. Technol., Pasadena, CA, 2001.

[151] J.A. Fax and R.M. Murray, "Information flow and cooperative control of vehicle formations," *IEEE Trans. Autom. Control*, vol. 49, no. 9, pp. 1465–1476, 2004.

[152] A. Jadbabaie, J. Lin and A.S. Morse, "Coordination of groups of mobile autonomous agents using nearest neighbor rules," *IEEE Trans. Autom. Control*, vol. 48, no. 6, pp. 988–1001, 2003.

[153] L. Moreau, "Stability of multiagent systems with time-dependent communication links," *IEEE Trans. Autom. Control*, vol. 50, no. 2, pp. 169–182, 2005.

[154] W. Ren and R.W. Beard, "Consensus seeking in multiagent systems under dynamically changing interaction topologies," *IEEE Trans. Autom. Control*, vol. 50, no. 5, pp. 655–661, 2005.

[155] T. Vicsek, A. Czirook, E. Ben-Jacob, I. Cohen and O. Shochet, "Novel type of phase transition in a system of self-driven particles," *Phys. Rev. Lett.*, vol. 75, no. 6, pp. 1226–1229, 1995.

[156] H. Abelson, D. Allen, D. Coore, C. Hanson, G. Homsy, J. Knight, T.F.R. Nagpal, E. Rauch, G.J. Sussman and R. Weiss, "Amorphous computing," *Commun. ACM*, vol. 43, no. 5, pp. 74–82, 2000.

[157] R. Nagpal, "Programmable self-assembly using biologically-inpired multiagent control," *Proc. 1st Int. Conf. Autonomous Agents and Multi-Agent Systems*, pp. 418–425, 2002.

[158] R. Olfati-Saber, "Flocking for multiagent dynamic systems: Algorithms and theory," *IEEE Trans. Autom. Control*, vol. 51, no. 3, pp. 401–420, 2006.

[159] M. Fiedler, "Algebraic connectivity of graphs," *Czechoslovak Math. J.*, vol. 23, no. 98, pp. 298–305, 1973.

[160] B. Mohar, "The Laplacian spectrum of graphs," in *Graph Theory, Combinatorics, and Applications*, edited by Y. Alavi, G. Chartrand, O. Ollermann and A. Schwenk, E New York: Wiley, 1991, pp. 871–898, 1991.

[161] R. Merris, "Laplacian matrices of a graph: A survey," *Linear Algebra its Appl.*, vol. 197, pp. 143–176, 1994.

[162] M. Sipser and D.A. Spielman, "Expander codes," *IEEE Trans. Inf. Theory*, vol. 42, no. 6, pp. 1710–1772, Nov. 1996.

[163] A. Lubotzky, R. Phillips and P. Sarnak, "Ramanujan graphs," *Combinatorica*, vol. 8, no. 3, pp. 261–277, 1988.

[164] Z. Lin, M. Brouke and B. Francis, "Local control strategies for groups of mobile autonomous agents," *IEEE Trans. Autom. Control*, vol. 49, no. 4, pp. 622–629, 2004.

[165] V. Blondel, J.M. Hendrickx, A. Olshevsky and J.N. Tsitsiklis, "Convergence in multiagent coordination, consensus, and flocking," *Proc. 44th IEEE Conf. Decision and Control, 2005 and 2005 Eur. Control Conf. (CDC-ECC'05)*, pp. 2996–3000, 2005.

[166] D. Bauso, L. Giarre and R. Pesenti, "Nonlinear protocols for optimal distributed consensus in networks of dynamic agents," *Systems and Control Letters*, vol. 55, no. 11, pp. 918–928, 2006.

[167] J. Cortes, "Achieving coordination tasks in finite time via nonsmooth gradient flows," *Proc. 44th IEEE Conf. Decision and Control, 2005 and 2005 Eur. Control Conf. (CDC-ECC'05)*, pp. 6376–6381, 2005.

[168] M. Mehyar, D. Spanos, J. Pongsjapan, S.H. Low and R.M. Murray, "Distributed averaging on asynchronous communication networks," *Proc. 44th IEEE Conf. Decision and Control, 2005 and 2005 Eur. Control Conf. (CDC-ECC'05)*, pp. 7446–7451, 2005.

[169] P.-A. Bliman and G. Ferrari-Trecate, "Average consensus problems in networks of agents with delayed communications," *Proc. 44th IEEE Conf. Decision and Control, 2005 and 2005 Eur. Control Conf. (CDC-ECC'05)*, pp. 7066–7071, 2005.

[170] J. Sandhu, M. Mesbahi and T. Tsukamaki, "Relative sensing networks: Observability, estimation, and the control structure," *Proc. 44th IEEE Conf. Decision and Control, 2005 and 2005 Eur. Control Conf. (CDC-ECC'05)*, pp. 6400–6405, 2005.

[171] A.V. Savkin, "Coordinated collective motion of groups of autonomous mobile robots: Analysis of Vicsek's model," *IEEE Trans. Autom. Control*, vol. 49, no. 6, pp. 981–982, 2004.

[172] N. Moshtagh, A. Jadbabaie and K. Daniilidis, "Distributed geodesic control laws for flocking of nonholonomic agents," *Proc. 44th IEEE Conf. Decision and Control, 2005 and 2005 Eur. Control Conf. (CDC-ECC'05)*, pp. 2835–2841, 2005.

[173] W. Xi, X. Tan and J.S. Baras, "A stochastic algorithm for self-organization of autonomous swarms," *Proc. 44th IEEE Conf. Decision and Control, 2005 and 2005 Eur. Control Conf. (CDC-ECC'05)*, pp. 765–770, 2005.

[174] R.A. Freeman, P. Yang and K.M. Lynch, " Distributed estimation and control of swarm formation statistics," *Proc. 2006 Am. Control Conf.*, pp. 749–755, Minneapolis, MN, 2006.

[175] R. Olfati-Saber, "Swarms on sphere: A programmable swarm with synchronous behaviors like oscillator networks," *Proc. 45th IEEE Conf. Decision and Control*, pp. 5060–5066, San Diego, CA, Dec. 2006.

[176] V.V., "Distributed Kalman filter with embedded consensus filter," *Proc. 44th IEEE Conf. Decision and Control, 2005 and 2005 Eur. Control Conf. (CDC-ECC'05)*, pp. 8179–8184, 2005.

[177] R. Olfati-Saber and J.S. Shamma, "Consensus filters for sensor networks and distributed sensor fusion," *Proc. 44th IEEE Conf. Decision and Control, 2005 and 2005 Eur. Control Conf. (CDC-ECC'05)*, pp. 6698–6703, 2005.

[178] V. Gupta, V. Hassibi and R.M. Murray, "On sensor fusion in the presence of packet-dropping communication channels," *44th IEEE Conf. Decision and Control, 2005 and 2005 Eur. Control Conf. (CDC-ECC'05)*, pp. 3547–3552, 2005.

[179] Y. Hatano and M. Mesbahi, "Agreement over random networks," *IEEE Trans. Autom. Control*, vol. 50, no. 11, pp. 1867–1872, 2005.

[180] V.M. Preciado and G.C. Verghese, "Synchronization in generalized Erdos-Renye networks of nonlinear oscillators," *Proc. 44th IEEE Conf. Decision and Control, 2005 and 2005 Eur. Control Conf. (CDC-ECC'05)*, pp. 4628–4633, 2005.

[181] R. Sepulchre, D. Paley and N. Leonard, "Collective motion and oscillator synchronization," *Proc. Block Island Workshop Cooperative Control*, Block Island, RI, Jun. 2003.

[182] A. Jadbabaie, N. Motee and M. Barahona, "On the stability of the Kuramoto model of coupled nonlinear oscillators," *Proc. 2004 Am. Control Conf.*, vol. 5, pp. 4296–4301, Jun. 2004.

[183] A. Papachristodoulou and A. Jadbabaie, "Synchronization in oscillator networks: Switching topologies and non-homogeneous delays," *Proc. 44th IEEE Conf. Decision and Control, 2005 and 2005 Eur. Control Conf. (CDC-ECC'05)*, pp. 5692–5697, 2005.

[184] N. Chopra and M.W. Spong, "On synchronization of Kuramoto oscillators," *Proc. 44th IEEE Conf. Decision and Control, 2005 and 2005 Eur. Control Conf. (CDC-ECC'05)*, pp. 3916–3922, 2005.

[185] R. Olfati-Saber, "Ultrafast consensus in small-world networks," *Proc. 2005 Am. Control Conf.*, pp. 2371–2378, June 2005.

[186] M. Cao, D.A. Spielman and A.S. Morse, "A lower bound on convergence of a distributed network consensus algorithm," *Proc. 44th IEEE Conf. Decision and Control, 2005 and 2005 Eur. Control Conf. (CDC-ECC'05)*, pp. 2356–2361.

[187] Y. Kim and M. Mesbahi, "On maximizing the second smallest eigenvalue of state-dependent graph Laplacian," *IEEE Trans. Autom. Control*, vol. 51, no. 1, pp. 116–120, Jan. 2006.

[188] L. Fang, P.J. Antsaklis and A. Tzimas, "Asynchronous consensus protocols: Preliminary results, simulations and open questions," *in 44th IEEE Conf. Decision and Control, 2005 and 2005 Eur. Control Conf. (CDC-ECC'05)*, pp. 2194–2199, 2005.

[189] M. Egerstedt and X. Hu, "Formation control with virtual leaders and reduced communications," *IEEE Trans. Robot. Autom.*, vol. 17, no. 6, pp. 947–951, 2001.

[190] R. Olfati-Saber and R.M. Murray, "Distributed cooperative control of multiple vehicle formations using structural potential functions," *presented at the 15th IFAC World Congr.*, Barcelona, Spain, Jul. 2002.

[191] V.V., "Graph rigidity and distributed formation stabilization of multivehicle systems," *in Proc. 41st IEEE Conf. Decision and Control*, pp. 2965–2971, 2002.

[192] T. Eren, W. Whiteley, A.S. Morse, P.N. Belhumeur and B.D.O. Anderson, "Sensor and network topologies of formations with direction, bearing and angle information between agents," *in Proc. 42nd IEEE Conf. Decision and Control*, pp. 3064–3069, 2003.

[193] R. Teo, D. Stipanovic and C.J. Tomlin, "Decentralize spacing control of a string of multiple vehicles over lossy datalinks," *in Proc. 42nd IEEE Conf. Decision and Control*, pp. 682–687, 2003.

[194] H.G. Tanner, G.J. Pappas and V. Kumar, "Leader-to-formation stability," *IEEE Trans. Robot. Autom.*, vol. 20, no. 3, pp. 443–455, Jun. 2004.

[195] Z. Lin, B. Francis and M. Maggiore, "Necessary and sufficient graphical conditions for formation control of unicyles," *IEEE Trans. Autom. Control*, vol. 50, no. 1, pp. 121–127, Jan. 2005.

[196] X. Xi and E.H. Abed, "Formation control with virtual leaders and reduced communications," *in 44th IEEE Conf. Decision and Control, 2005 and 2005 Eur. Control Conf. (CDC-ECC'05)*, pp. 1854–1860, 2005.

[197] D.V. Dimarogonas and K.J. Kyriakopoulos, "Formation control and collision avoidance for multiagent systems and a connection between formation infeasibility and flocking behavior," *in 44th IEEE Conf. Decision and Control, 2005 and 2005 Eur. Control Conf. (CDC-ECC'05)*, pp. 84–89, 2005.

[198] R.O. Saber, W.B. Dunbar and R.M. Murray, "Cooperative control of multivehicle systems using cost graphs and optimization," *in Proc. 2003 Am. Control Conf.*, pp. 2217–2222, 2003.

[199] T. Keviczky, G.J. Borelli and F. Balas, "A study on decentralized receding horizon control for decoupled systems," *in Proc. 2004 American Control Conf.*, pp. 4921–4926, 2004.

[200] J. Hu, M. Prandini and C. Tomlin, "Interesting conjugate points in formation constrained multiagent coordination," *in Proc. 2005 Am. Control Conf.*, pp. 1871–1876, 2005.

[201] M. Alighanbari and J.P. How, "Decentralized task assignment for unmanned aerial vehicles," *in 44th IEEE Conf. Decision and Control, 2005 and 2005 Eur. Control Conf. (CDC-ECC'05)*, pp. 5668-5673, 2005.

[202] M. Mesbahi, "On state-dependent dynamic graphs and their controllability properties," *IEEE Trans. Autom. Control*, vol. 50, no. 3, pp. 387–392, Mar. 2005.

[203] M. Ji and M. Egerstedt, "Connectedness preserving distributed coordination control over dynamic graphs," *in Proc. 2005 Am. Control Conf.*, Jun. 2005, pp. 93–98, 2005.

[204] M.M. Zavlanos and G.J. Pappas, "Controlling connectivity of dynamic graphs," *in 44th IEEE Conf. Decision and Control, 2005 and 2005 Eur. Control Conf. (CDC-ECC'05)*, Dec. 2005, pp. 6388–6393, 2005.

[205] D. Hristu and K. Morgansen, "Limited communication control," *Syst. Control Lett.*, vol. 37, pp. 193–205, Jul. 1999.

[206] E. Klavins, "Communication complexity of multirobot systems," *in Algorithmic Foundations of Robotics V, ser. Springer Tracts in Advanced Robotics, J.-D. Boissonnats, J. Burdik, K. Goldberg and S. Huchinson, eds. Budapest: Springer*, vol. 7, pp. 275–292, 2003.

[207] Martnez,F. Bullo, J. Cortes and E. Frazzoli, "On synchronous robotic networks Part I: Models, tasks, and complexity notions," *in Proc. 44th IEEE Conf. Decision and Control, 2005 and 2005 Eur. Control Conf. (CDC-ECC'05)*, pp. 2847–2852, 2005.

[208] V.V., "On synchronous robotic networks Part II: Time complexity of the rendezvous and deployment algorithms," *in Proc. 44th IEEE Conf. Decision and Control, 2005 and 2005 Eur. Control Conf. (CDC-ECC'05)*, pp. 8313–8318, 2005.

[209] V. Saligrama, M. Alanyali and O. Savas, *Asynchronous distributed detection in sensor networks*, 2005, Preprint.

[210] R. Olfati-Saber, E. Franco, E. Frazzoli and J.S. Shamma, "Belief consensus and distributed hypothesis testing in sensor networks," *presented at the Workshop on Network Embedded Sensing and Control*, Notre Dame, IN, Oct. 2005.

[211] D.P. Spanos, R. Olfati-Saber and R.M. Murray, "Approximate distributed Kalman filtering in sensor networks with quantifiable performance," *in Proc. 4th Int. Symp. Information Processing in Sensor Networks*, pp. 133–139, 2005.

[212] L. Xiao, S. Boyd and S. Lall, "A scheme for asynchronuous distributed sensor fusion based on average consensus," *in Proc. 4th Int. Symp. Information Processing in Sensor Networks*, pp. 63–70, Apr. 2005.

[213] J.-Y. Chen, G. Pandurangan and D. Xu, Robust computation of aggregates in wireless sensor networks: Distributed randomized algorithms and analysis," *in Proc. 4th Int. Symp. Information Processing in Sensor Networks*, pp. 348–355, 2005.

[214] D. Kempe, A. Dobra and J. Gehrke, "Gossip-based computation of aggregate information," *in Proc. 44th Annu. IEEE Symp. Foundations of Computer Science (FOCS'03), 2003*, vol. 3, no. 3, pp. 482–491, 2003.

[215] S. Boyd, A. Ghosh, D. Prabhakar and B. Shah, "Gossip algorithms: Design, analysis and applications," *in Proc. 24th Annu. Joint Conf. IEEE Computer and Communications Societies (INFOCOM'05)*, pp. 1653–1664, 2005.

[216] D. Fudenberg and D.K. Levine, *The Theory of Learning in Games*, Cambridge, MA: MIT Press, 1998.

[217] J.S. Shamma and G. Arslan, "Dynamic fictitious play, dynamic gradient play, and distributed convergence to Nash equilibria," *IEEE Trans. Autom. Control*, vol. 50, no. 3, pp. 312–327, Mar. 2005.

[218] R.A. Horn and C.R. Johnson, *Matrix Analysis*, Cambridge, U.K.: Cambridge Univ. Press, 1987.

[219] G. Cybenko, "Dynamic load balancing for distributed memory multiprocessors," *J. Parallel and Distributed Computing*, vol. 7, no. 2, pp. 279–301, Oct. 1989.

[220] Y. Kuramoto, *Chemical Oscillators, Waves, and Turbulance* Berlin, Germany: Springer-Verlag, 1984.

[221] R.E. Mirollo and S.H. Strogatz, "Synchronization of pulse-coupled biological oscillators," *SIAM J. Appl. Math.*, vol. 50, pp. 1645–1662, 1990.

[222] S.H. Strogatz, "From Kuramoto to Crawford: Exploring the onset of synchronization in populations of coupled oscillators," *Physica D*, vol. 143, pp. 1–20, 2000.

[223] G.B. Ermentrout and N. Kopell, "Frequency plateaus in a chain of weakly coupled oscillator," *SIAM J. Math. Anal.*, vol. 15, pp. 215–237, 1984.

[224] J. Cortes, S. Martnez, T. Karatas and F. Bullo, "Coverage control for mobile sensing networks," *IEEE Trans. Robot. Autom.*, vol. 20, no. 2, pp. 243–255, Apr. 2004.

[225] L. Xiao and S. Boyd, "Fast linear iterations for distributed averaging" *Systems & Control Letters*, vol. 52, pp. 65–78, 2004.

[226] D.J. Watts and S.H. Strogatz, "Collective dynamics of small-world networks," *Nature*, vol. 393, pp. 440–442, Jun. 1998.

[227] H. Ando, Y. Oasa, I. Suzuki and M. Yamashita, "Distributed memoryless point convergence algorithm for mobile robots with limited visibility," *IEEE Trans. Robot. Autom.*, vol. 15, no. 5, pp. 818–828, Oct. 1999.

[228] J. Lin, A.S. Morse and B.D.O. Anderson, "The multiagent rendezvous problem," *in Proc. 42nd IEEE Conf. Decision and Control*, pp. 1508–1513, 2003.

[229] J. Cortes, S. Martnez and F. Bullo, Robust rendezvous for mobile autonomous agents via proximity graphs in arbitrary dimensions," *IEEE Trans. Autom. Control*, vol. 51, no. 8, pp. 1289–1298, Aug. 2004.

[230] D. Spanos, R. Olfati-Saber and R.M. Murray, Dynamic consensus on mobile networks," *presented at the 16th IFAC World Congr.*, Prague, Czech, 2005.

[231] T. Eren, P.N. Belhumeur and A.S. Morse, Closing ranks in vehicle formations based on rigidity," *in Proc. 41st IEEE Conf. Decision and Control*, pp. 2959–2964, Dec. 2002.

[232] L. Lovasz, Random walks on graphs: A survey," *in Combinatorics, Paul Erdos is Eighty, D. Milos, V.T. Sos and T. Szony, Eds. Budapest, Hungary: Janos Bolyai Math. Soc.*, pp. 353–398, 1996.

[233] A.-L. Barabasi and R. Albert, Emergence of scaling in random networks," *Science*, vol. 286, pp. 509–512, 1999.

[234] P. Erdos and A. Renyi, On the evolution of random graphs," *Pub. Math. Inst. Hungarian Acad. Science*, vol. 5, pp. 17–61, 1960.

[235] B. Sinopoli, L. Schenato, M. Franceschetti, K. Poola, M.I. Jordan and S.S. Sastry, Kalman filtering with intermittent observations," *IEEE Trans. Autom. Control*, vol. 49, no. 9, pp. 1453–1464, Sep. 2004.

[236] R.O. Saber and R.M. Murray, Flocking with obstacle avoidance: Cooperation with limited communication in mobile networks," *in Proc. 42nd IEEE Conf. Decision and Control*, vol. 2, pp. 2022-2028, 2003.

[237] J. Wolfowitz, Products of indecomposable, aperiodic, stochastic matrices," *in Proc. Am. Math. Soc.*, vol. 15, pp. 733-736, 1963.

[238] K. Zhou and J.C. Doyle, *Essentials of Robust Control*, Upper Saddle River, NJ: Prentice Hall, 1997.

[239] M.E.J. Newman, The structure and function of complex networks," *SIAM Rev.*, vol. 45, pp. 167–256, 2003.

[240] R. Lasseter, A. Akhil, C. Marnay, J. Stephens, J. Dagle, R. Guttromson, A. Meliopoulos, R. yinger and J. Eto, "White paper on Integration of consortium Energy Resources. The CERTS Micro Grid Concept," *CERTS, CA, Rep.LBNL-50829*, Apr. 2002.

[241] Micro Grids: Large Scale integration of Micro-Generation to low Voltage Grids," *EU contact ENK5-CT-2002-00610, Technical Annex*, May 2002.

[242] M. Shahidehpour," *Restructured Electrical Power Systems: Operation, Trading, and Volatility*, Marcel Dekker, 2001.

[243] M. Shahidehpour, Market Operations in Electric Power Systems: Forecasting, Scheduling, and Risk Management," *IEEE, Wiley-Interscience*, 2002.

[244] N.D. Hatziargyriou, A.L. Dimeas, A.G. Tsikalakis, J.A. Pecas Lopes, G. Kariniotakis and J. Oyarzabal, "Management of Micro Grids in Market Environment," *IEEE*, 2005.

[245] A.L. Dimeas and N.D. Hatziargyriou, "Agent based control of Virtual Power Plants," *IEEE*, 2007.

[246] Saifur Rahman, Manisa Pipattanasompom and Yonael Teklu, "Intelligent Distributed Autonomous Power System (IDAPS)," *IEEE*, 2007.

[247] T. Nagata, H. Nakayama and H. Sasaki, "A Multi-Agent Approach to Power System Normal State Operations," *IEEE*, 2002.

[248] Vladimir S. Koritarov, "Real-World Market Representation with Agents," *IEEE Power & Energy Magazine*, 2004.

[249] Anthony J. Bagnall and George D. Smith, "A Multi agent Model of UK Market in Electricity Generation," *IEEE*, 2005.

[250] Isabel Praa, Carlos Ramos, Zita Vale and Manuel Cordeiro, MASCEM: A Multi agent System That Simulates Competitive Electricity Markets," *IEEE*, 2003.

[251] G.B. Shrestha, Song Kai and L.K. Goel "An Efficient Power Pool Simulator For The Study Of Competitive Power Market," *IEEE*, 2000.

[252] *JADE Programming and guide*, Available: http://jade.tilab.com/

[253] *FIPA standards*, Available: http://www.fipa.org/

[254] *PowerWorld Simulator*, Available: http://www.powerworld.com/

[255] *IBM Development Tool for Java-COM Bridge*, Available: http://www. alphaworks.ibm.com/

[256] Tan Ming Jin, *Intelligent Agents for Management of Engineering Systems*, NUS, 2004.

[257] F.H. Wong, *Management of Distributed Generation Using Intelligent Multi Agent System*, NUS, 2003.

[258] Farid Katiraei, Reza Iravani, Nikos Hatziargyriou and Aris Dimeas, "Micro Grids Management, control and Operation Aspects of Micro Grids," *IEEE*, 2008

[259] Peter Kadar, *Scheduling the Generation of Renewable power Sources*, AMII, 2007.

[260] *Final Report, Microgrids*, (Contract No ENK 5-CT-2002-00610). available online at Microgrids.power.ece.ntua.gr.

[261] R. Lasseter, A. Akhil, C. Marnay, J. Stephens, J. Dagle, R. Guttromson, A. Meliopoulos, R. Yinger and J. Eto, "White Paper on Integration of Distributed Energy Resources. The CERTS MicroGrid Concept," *Consortium for Electric Reliability Technology Solutions (CERTS) CA Tech. Rep. LBNL-50829*, Apr. 2002.

[262] S. Papathanassiou, D. Georgakis, N. Hatziargyriou, A. Engler and Ch. Hardt, "Operation of a prototype Microgrid system based on micro-sources equipped with fast-acting power electronics interfaces," *31th PESC 2004 Aachen*, pp. 20–25, June 2004.

[263] A. Dimeas and N.D. Hatziargyriou, "Operation of a multiagent system for microgrid control," *in IEEE Transactions on Power Systems, Digital Object Identifier 10.1109/TPWRS*, vol. 20, no. 3, pp. 1447–1455, Aug. 2005.

[264] N.D. Hatziargyriou, A. Dimeas and A. Tsikalakis, "Centralised and decentralized control of microgrids," *International Journal of distributed Energy Resources*, vol. 1, no. 3, pp. 197–212, July 2005.

[265] A. Dimeas and N.D. Hatziargyriou, "A multiAgent system for microgrids," *In Hellenic Conference on Artificial Intelligence*, pp. 447–455, 2004.

[266] Hossack J.A. Menal, J. Mc, S.D.J. Arthur and J.R. Mc Donald, "A multiagent architecture for protection engineering diagnostic assistance," *IEEE Trans. on Power Systems*, vol. 18, no. 2, pp. 639–647, May 2003.

[267] T. Nagata and H. Sasaki, "A multi-agent approach to power system restoration," *IEEE Trans. on Power Systems*, vol. 17, no. 2, pp. 457-462, 2002.

[268] T. Nagata and H. Sasaki, "Hiroshima University A Multi-Agent Approach to Power System Restoration," *Proc. ISAP 2003*, Sep. 2003.

[269] Takashi Hiyama, Masashi Kouno, Hideaki Ono and Kouichrou Furukawa, "Multi-Agent Based Wide Area Stabilization Control of Electric Power Systems," *Proc. ISAP 2003*, Sep. 2003.

[270] Zhou Ming, Ren Jianwen, Li Gengyin and Xu Xianghai, "A multi-agent based dispatching operation instructing system in electric power systems," *Power Engineering Society General Meeting 2003IEEE Publication*, vol. 1, pp. 436–440, 13–17 July 2003.

[271] S.D.J. McArthur, S.M. Strachan and G. Jahn, "The design of a multi-agent transformer condition monitoring system," *in Power Systems IEEE Transactions on, Digital*, vol. 19, no. 4, pp. 1845–1852, Nov. 2004.

[272] Peter Stone and Manuela Veloso, "Team-Partitioned Opaque-Transition Reinforcement Learning," *Minoru Asada and Hiroaki Kitano editors RoboCup-98: Robot Soccer World Cup II*, 1999.

[273] *Jade, Java Agent DEvelopment Framework*, [online] Available: *http : //jade.tilab.com.*

[274] Ygge Fredrik and Hans Akkerman, "Decentralized markets versus central control: A comparative study," *Journal of Artificial Intelligence Research 11*, pp. 301–333, October 1999.

[275] Jeffrey M. Bradshaw, *Software Agents*, MIT Press.

[276] Jacques Ferber, *Multi-Agent Systems. An introduction to Distributed Intelligence* in , Addison-Wesley.

[277] C.J. Watkins and P. Dayan, "Q-learning," *Machine Learning*, vol. 8, pp. 279–292, 1992.

[278] Tuomas W. Sandholm and Robert H. Crites, "On multiagent Q-learning in a semi-competitive domain," *Proceedings of the Workshop on Adaption and Learning in Multi-Agent Systems*, 1994, ISBN 3-540-60923-7.

[279] *NRC Fuzzy, J Toolkit,* [online] Available: *www.iit.nrc.ca/IR$_p$ublic/fuzzy/fuzzyJDocs/index.html*.

[280] Gilad Zlotkin and Jeffrey S. Rosenschein, "Negotiation and task sharing among autonomous agents in cooperative domains," *Proceedings of the Eleventh International Joint Conference on Artificial Intelligence*, pp. 912–917, August, 1989.

[281] Jeffrey S. Rosenschein and Gilad Zlotkin, "Rules of Encounter: Designing Conventions for Automated Negotiation Among Computers," *In MIT Press, Cambridge, Massachusetts*, 1994.

[282] C. Watkins, *Learning from Delayed Rewards*, Thesis, 1989.

[283] M. Littman and J. Boyan, *A Distributed Reinforcement Learning Scheme for Network Routing Tech.*, report CMU, 1993.

[284] John G. Vlachogiannis and Nikos D. Hatziargyriou, "Reinforcement Learning for Reactive Power Control IEEE Power Systems," *IEEE Transactions on*, vol. 19, no. 3, August, 2004.

[285] C.W. Gellings, M. Samotyj and B. Howe, "The future's power delivery system," *IEEE Power Energy Mag.*, vol. 2, no. 5, pp. 40–48.

[286] E.M. Davidson, S.D.J. McArthur, J.R. McDonald, T. Cumming and I. Watt, "Applying multi-agent system technology in practice: Automated management and analysis of SCADA and digital fault recorder data," *IEEE Trans. Power Syst.*, vol. 21, no. 2, pp. 559–567, May 2006.

[287] S.D.J. McArthur, S.M. Strachan and G. Jahn, "The design of a multi-agent transformer condition monitoring system," *IEEE Trans. Power Syst.*, vol. 19, no. 4, pp. 1845–1852, Nov. 2004.

[288] T. Nagata and H. Sasaki, "A multi-agent approach to power system restoration," *IEEE Trans. Power Syst.*, vol. 17, no. 2, pp. 457–462, May 2002.

[289] S.E. Widergren, J.M. Roop, R.T. Guttromson and Z. Huang, "Simulating the dynamic coupling of market and physical system operations," *Proc. IEEE Power Eng. Soc. General Meeting 2004*, pp. 748–753, 2004.

[290] D. Koesrindartoto, S. Junjie and L. Tesfatsion, "An agent-based computational laboratory for testing the economic reliability of wholesale power market designs," *Proc. IEEE Power Eng. Soc. General Meeting 2005*, pp. 931–936, 2005.

[291] A.L. Dimeas and N.D. Hatziargyriou, "Operation of a multi-agent system for microgrid control," *IEEE Trans. Power Syst.*, vol. 20, no. 3, pp. 1447–1455, Aug. 2005.

[292] A. Korbik, S.D.J. McArthur, G.W. Ault, G.M. Burt and J.R. McDonald, "Enabling active distribution networks through decentralized autonomous network management," *Proc. 18th Int. Conf. Electricity Distribution (CIRED) Turin*, 2005.

[293] D.P. Buse, P. Sun, Q.H. Wu and J. Fitch, "Agent-based substation automation," *IEEE Power Energy Mag.*, vol. 1, no. 2, pp. 50–55, Mar./Apr. 2003.

[294] S. Russell and P. Norvig, *Artificial Intelligence: A Modern Approach*, NJ, Englewood Cliffs:Prentice-Hall, 1995.

[295] P. Maes, "Artificial life meets entertainment: Life-like autonomous agents," *Commun. ACM*, vol. 38, no. 11, pp. 108–114, 1995.

[296] L.N. Foner, "Entertaining agents: A sociological case study," *Proc. 1st Int. Conf. Autonomous Agents*, 1997.

[297] B. Hayes-Roth, "An architecture for adaptive intelligent systems," *Artif. Intell.*, vol. 72, pp. 329–365, 1995.

[298] M. Wooldridge, "Intelligent Agents," *in Multi-agent Systems, MA, Cambridge:MIT Press*, pp. 3–51, Apr. 1999.

[299] S. Franklin and A. Graesser, "Is it an agent or just a program?," *Proc. 3rd Int. Workshop Agent Theories Architectures and Languages*, 1996.

[300] *Foundation for Intelligent Physical Agents, (FIPA)*, 2007.

[301] T. Wittig, N.R. Jennings and E.M. Mandan, "ARCHONA framework for intelligent co-operations," *IEE-BCS J. Intell. Syst. Eng.*, vol. 3, no. 3, pp. 168-179, 1994.

[302] IEC Energy Management System Application Program Interface (EMS-API)—Part 301: Common Information Model (CIM) Base, 2005.

[303] T. Wittig, N.R. Jennings and E.M. Mandan, Communications networks and systems in substations", *IEC Standard*, pp. 61850–61855, 2003.

[304] M. Pchouek and S. Thompson, "Agents in Industry: The best from the AAMAS 2005 Industry Track," *IEEE Intell. Syst.*, vol. 21, no. 2, pp. 86–95, Mar./Apr. 2006.

[305] M. Irving, G. Taylor and P. Hobson, "Plug in to grid computing," *IEEE Intell. Syst.*, vol. 2, no. 2, pp. 40–44, Mar./Apr. 2004.

[306] Z. Jun, "Web services provide the power to integrate," *IEEE Power Energy Mag.*, vol. 1, no. 6, pp. 40–49, Nov./Dec. 2003.

[307] M.N. Huhns, "Agents as Web services," *IEEE Internet Comput.*, vol. 6, no. 4, pp. 93–95, Jul./Aug. 2002.

[308] Proc. 11th Int. Conf. Intelligent Systems Application to Power Systems, 2001.

[309] Proc. 12th Int. Conf. Intelligent Systems Application to Power Systems, 2003.

[310] Proc. 13th Int. Conf. Intelligent Systems Application to Power Systems, 2005.

[311] S.-J. Park and J.-T. Lim, "Modelling and control of agent-based power protection system using supervisors," *Proc. Inst. Elect. Eng. Control Theory Appl.*, vol. 153, no. 1, pp. 92–98, Jan. 2006.

[312] S. Sheng, K.K. Li, W.L. Chan, Z. Xiangjun and D. Xianzhong, "Agent-based self-healing protection system," *IEEE Trans. Power Del.*, vol. 21, no. 2, pp. 610–618, Apr. 2006.

[313] D.V. Coury, J.S. Thorp, K.M. Hopkinson, K.P. Birman, "An agent-based current differential relay for use with a utility intranet," *IEEE Trans. Power Del.*, vol. 17, no. 1, pp. 47–53, Jan. 2002.

[314] C. Fukui, H. Kudo, J. Koda, K. Yabe and Y. Tomita, "A cooperative protection system with an agent model," *IEEE Trans. Power Del.*, vol. 13, no. 4, pp. 1060–1066, Oct. 1998.

[315] R. Giovanini, K. Hopkinson, D.V. Coury and J.S. Thorp, "A primary and backup cooperative protection system based on wide area agents," *IEEE Trans. Power Del.*, vol. 21, no. 3, pp. 1222–1230, Jul. 2006.

[316] S.D.J. McArthur, C.D. Booth, J.R. McDonald and I.T. McFadyen, "An agent-based anomaly detection architecture for condition monitoring," *IEEE Trans. Power Syst*, vol. 20, no. 4, pp. 1675–1682, Nov. 2005.

[317] J.A. Hossack, J. Menal, S.D.J. McArthur and J.R. McDonald, "A multiagent architecture for protection engineering diagnostic assistance," *IEEE Trans. Power Syst.*, vol. 18, no. 2, pp. 639–647, May 2003.

[318] E.E. Mangina, S.D.J. McArthur, J.R. McDonald and A. Moyes, "A multi agent system for monitoring industrial gas turbine start-up sequences," *IEEE Trans. Power Syst.*, vol. 16, no. 3, pp. 396–401, Aug. 2001.

[319] E.E. Mangina, S.D.J. McArthur and J.R. McDonald, "Reasoning with modal logic for power plant condition monitoring," *IEEE Power Eng. Rev.*, vol. 21, no. 7, pp. 58–59, Jul. 2001.

[320] B. Zhao, C.X. Guo and Y.J. Cao, "A multiagent-based particle swarm optimization approach for optimal reactive power dispatch," *IEEE Trans. Power Syst.*, vol. 20, no. 2, pp. 1070–1078, May 2005.

[321] M.M. Nordman and M. Lehtonen, "Distributed agent-based state estimation for electrical distribution networks," *IEEE Trans. Power Syst.*, vol. 20, no. 2, pp. 652–658, May 2005.

[322] M.M. Nordman and M. Lehtonen, "An agent concept for managing electrical distribution networks," *IEEE Trans. Power Del.*, vol. 20, no. 2, pp. 696–703, Apr. 2005.

[323] H.F. Wang, H. Li and H. Chen, "Coordinated secondary voltage control to eliminate voltage violations in power system contingencies," *IEEE Trans. Power Syst.*, vol. 18, no. 2, pp. 588–595, May 2003.

[324] H. Ni, G.T. Heydt and L. Mili, "Power system stability agents using robust wide area control," *IEEE Trans. Power Syst.*, vol. 17, no. 4, pp. 1123–1131, Nov. 2002.

[325] J. Jung, C.-C. Liu, S.L. Tanimoto and V. Vittal, "Adaptation in load shedding under vulnerable operating conditions," *IEEE Trans. Power Syst.*, vol. 17, no. 4, pp. 1199–1205, Nov. 2002.

[326] G.T. Heydt, C.-C. Liu, A.G. Phadke and V. Vittal, "Solution for the crisis in electric power supply," *IEEE Comput. Appl. Power*, vol. 14, no. 3, pp. 22–30, Jul. 2001.

[327] M. Amin, "Toward self-healing energy infrastructure systems," *IEEE Comput. Appl. Power*, vol. 14, no. 1, pp. 20–28, Jan. 2001.

[328] G.P. Azevedo, B. Feijo and M. Costa, "Control centers evolve with agent technology," *IEEE Comput. Appl. Power*, vol. 13, no. 3, pp. 48–53, Jul. 2000.

[329] K. Huang, S.K. Srivastava and D.A. Cartes, "Solving the information accumulation problem in mesh structured agent system," *IEEE Trans. Power Syst.*, vol. 22, no. 1, pp. 493–495, Feb. 2007.

[330] I.S. Baxevanos and D.P. Labridis, "Implementing multiagent systems technology for power distribution network control and protection management," *IEEE Trans. Power Del.*, vol. 22, no. 1, pp. 433–443, Jan. 2007.

[331] M.E. Baran and I.M. El-Markabi, "A multiagent-based dispatching scheme for distributed generators for voltage support on distribution feeders," *IEEE Trans. Power Syst.*, vol. 22, no. 1, pp. 52–59, Feb. 2007.

[332] K. Hopkinson, X. Wang, R. Giovanini, J. Thorp, K. Birman and D. Coury, "EPOCHS: A platform for agent-based electric power and communication simulation built from commercial off-the-shelf components," *IEEE Trans. Power Syst.*, vol. 21, no. 2, pp. 548–558, May 2006.

[333] J.G. Vlachogiannis, N.D. Hatziargyiou and K.Y. Lee, "Ant colony system-based algorithm for constrained load flow problem," *IEEE Trans. Power Syst.*, vol. 20, no. 3, pp. 1241–1249, Aug. 2005.

[334] V.S. Koritarov, "Real-world market representation with agents," *IEEE Power Energy Mag.*, vol. 2, no. 4, pp. 39–46, Jul. 2004.

[335] S.D.J. McArthur, E.M. Davidson, G.J.W. Dudgeon and J.R. McDonald, "Toward a model integration methodology for advanced applications in power engineering," *IEEE Trans. Power Syst.*, vol. 18, no. 3, pp. 1205–1206, Aug. 2003.

[336] M. Baran, R. Sreenath and N.R. Mahajan, "Extending EMTDC/PSCAD for simulating agent-based distributed applications," *IEEE Power Eng. Rev.*, vol. 22, no. 12, pp. 52–54, Dec. 2002.

[337] J.M. Zolezzi and H. Rudnick, "Transmission cost allocation by cooperative games and coalition formation," *IEEE Trans. Power Syst.*, vol. 17, no. 4, pp. 1008–1015, Nov. 2002.

[338] A.L. Motto and F.D. Galiana, "Equilibrium of auction markets with unit commitment: The need for augmented pricing," *IEEE Trans. Power Syst.*, vol. 17, no. 3, pp. 798–805, Aug. 2002.

[339] P. Wei, Y. Yan, Y. Ni, J. Yen and F.E. Wu, "A decentralized approach for optimal wholesale cross-border trade planning using multi-agent technology," *IEEE Trans. Power Syst.*, vol. 16, no. 4, pp. 833–838, Nov. 2001.

[340] D.W. Bunn and F.S. Oliveira, "Agent-based simulationAn application to the new electricity trading arrangements of England and Wales," *IEEE Trans. Evol. Comput.*, vol. 5, no. 5, pp. 493–503, Oct. 2001.

[341] S.-J. Huang, "Enhancement of hydroelectric generation scheduling using ant colony system based optimization approaches," *IEEE Trans. Energy Convers.*, vol. 16, no. 3, pp. 296–301, Sep. 2001.

[342] C.S.K. Yeung, A.S.Y. Poon and F.F. Wu, "Game theoretical multi-agent modelling of coalition formation for multilateral trades," *IEEE Trans. Power Syst.*, vol. 14, no. 3, pp. 929–934, Aug. 1999.

[343] V. Krishna and V.C. Ramesh, "Intelligent agents for negotiations in market games. Part I. Model," *IEEE Trans. Power Syst.*, vol. 13, no. 3, pp. 1103–1108, Aug. 1998.

[344] V. Krishna and V.C. Ramesh, "Intelligent agents for negotiations in market games. Part II. Application," *IEEE Trans. Power Syst.*, vol. 13, no. 3, pp. 1109–1114, Aug. 1998.

[345] T. Sueyoshi and G.R. Tadiparthi, "Agent-based approach to handle business complexity in U.S. wholesale power trading," *IEEE Trans. Power Syst.*, vol. 22, no. 2, pp. 532–543, May 2007.

[346] A.J. Bagnall and G.D. Smith, "A multiagent model of the UK market in electricity generation," *IEEE Trans. Evol. Comput.*, vol. 9, no. 5, pp. 522–536, Oct. 2005.

[347] J. Contreras and F.F. Wu, "Coalition formation in transmission expansion planning," *IEEE Trans. Power Syst.*, vol. 14, no. 3, pp. 1144–1152, Aug. 1999.

[348] A. Deshmukh, F. Ponci, A. Monti, M. Riva and L. Cristaldi, "Multi-agent system for diagnostics monitoring and control of electric systems," *Proc. 13th Int. Conf. Intelligent Systems Application to Power Systems*, pp. 201–206, 2005.

[349] K. Huang, D.A. Cartes and S.K. Srivastava, "A multi-agent based algorithm for mesh-structured shipboard power system reconfiguration," *Proc. 13th Int. Conf. Intelligent Systems Application to Power Systems*, pp. 188–193, 2005.

[350] *S&C Electric Company*. [Online]. Available: http://www.sandc.com/products/Energyline/IntelliTEAM, 2007.

[351] B.C. Williams, M.D. Ingham, S.H. Chung and P.H. Elliott, "Model-based programming of intelligent embedded systems and robotic space explorers," *Proc. IEEE*, vol. 91, no. 1, pp. 212–237, Jan. 2003.

[352] T.R. Gruber, "A translation approach to portable ontology specifications," *Knowl. Acquisition*, vol. 5, no. 2, pp. 199–220, 1993.

[353] M. Wooldridge and N.R. Jennings, "Pitfalls of agent oriented development," *Proc. 2nd Int. Conf. Autonomous Agents*, pp. 385–391, 1998.

[354] P. Antsaklis, Goals and challenges in cyber-physical systems research," *IEEE Transactions on Automatic Control*, vol. 59, no. 12, pp. 3117–3119, 2014.

[355] A. Arapostathis, V.S. Borkar and M.K. Ghosh, *Ergodic Control of Diffusion Processes*. Cambridge, UK: Cambridge University Press, 2012.

[356] L. Arnold, *Stochastic Differential Equations: Theory and Applications*. New York, NY: Wiley-Interscience, 1974.

[357] M. Blanke and J. Schrder, *Diagnosis and Fault-tolerant Control*, Berlin: Springer-Verlag, 2006.

[358] A. Das and F.L. Lewis, "Distributed adaptive control for synchronization of unknown nonlinear networked systems," *Automatica*, 46, pp. 2014–2021, 2010.

[359] H. Fawzi, P. Tabuada and S. Diggavi, "Secure estimation and control for cyber-physical systems under adversarial attacks," *IEEE Transactions on Automatic Control*, vol. 59, no. 6, pp. 1454–1467, 2012.

[360] C. Godsil and G. Royle, *Algebraic Graph Theory*. New York, NY: Springer, 2001.

[361] A. Gupta, C. Langbort and T. Basar, "Optimal control in the presence of an intelligent jammer with limited actions," *In Proceedings of the IEEE conference on decision and control*, pp. 1096–1101. Atlanta, GA, 2010.

[362] D. Hua, M. Kristic and R. Williams, "Stabilization of stochastic nonlinear systems driven by noise of unknown covariance," *IEEE Transactions on Automatic Control*, 48, pp. 1237–1253, 2001.

[363] I. Hwang, S. Kim, Y. Kim and C.E. Seah, "A survey of fault detection, isolation, and reconfiguration methods," *IEEE Transactions on Control Systems Technology*, vol. 18, no. 3, pp. 636–653, 2010.

[364] R.Z. Khasminskii, *Stochastic Stability of Differential Equations*. Berlin: Springer-Verlag, 2012.

[365] O. Kosut, L. Jia, R.J. Thomas and L. Tong, "Malicious data attacks on the smart grid," *IEEE Transactions on Smart Grid*, vol. 2, no. 4, pp. 645–658, 2011.

[366] E. Lavretsky and K. Wise, *Robust and Adaptive Control with Aerospace Applications*. New York, NY: Springer, 2012.

[367] Z. Li, X. Liu, W. Ren and L. Xie, "Distributed tracking control for linear multiagent systems with a leader of bounded unknown input," *IEEE Transactions on Automatic Control*, 58, pp. 518–523, 2013.

[368] M. Liu, L. Zhang, P. Shi and H.R. Karimi, "Robust control of stochastic systems against bounded disturbances with application to flight control," *IEEE Transactions on Industrial Electronics*, vol. 61, no. 3, pp. 1504–1515, 2014.

[369] M.-A. Massoumnia, G.C. Verghese and A.S. Willsky, "Failure detection and identification," *IEEE Transactions on Automatic Control*, vol. 34, no. 3, pp. 316–321, 1989.

[370] B. Oksendal, *Stochastic Differential Equations: An Introduction with Applications*. Berlin: Springer-Verlag, 1995.

[371] F. Pasqualetti, F. Dorfler and F. Bullo, "Attack detection and identification in cyber-physical systems," *IEEE Transactions on Automatic Control*, vol. 58, no. 11, pp. 2715–2729, 2013.

[372] Z. Peng, D. Wang, H. Zhang and G. Sun, "Distributed neural network control for adaptive synchronization of uncertain dynamical multiagent systems," *IEEE Transactions on Neural Networks and Learning Systems*, 25, pp. 1508–1519, 2014.

[373] L. Schenato, B. Sinopoli, M. Franceschetti, K. Poolla and S.S. Sastry, "Foundations of control and estimation over lossy networks," *Proceedings of the IEEE*, vol. 95, no. 1, pp. 163–187, 2007.

[374] K.C. Sou, H. Sandberg and K.H. Johansson, "On the exact solution to a smart grid cyber-security analysis problem," *IEEE Transactions on Smart Grid*, vol. 4, no. 2, pp. 856–865, 2013.

[375] J. Sun and Z. Geng, "Adaptive output feedback consensus tracking for linear multi-agent systems with unknown dynamics," *International Journal of Control*, 88, pp. 1735–1745, 2015.

[376] H.Q. Wang, B. Chen and C. Lin, "Adaptive neural tracking control for a class of stochastic nonlinear systems," *International Journal of Robust and Nonlinear Control*, vol. 24, no. 7, pp. 1262–1280, 2014.

[377] X. Wang and G.H. Yang, "Cooperative adaptive fault-tolerant tracking control for a class of multi-agent systems with actuator failures and mismatched parameter uncertainties," *IET Control Theory & Applications*, 9, pp. 1274–1284, 2015.

[378] D. Ye, X. Zhao and B. Cao, "Distributed adaptive fault-tolerant consensus tracking of multi-agent systems against time-varying actuator faults," *IET Control Theory & Applications*, 10, pp. 554–563, 2016.

[379] T. Yucelen and W.M. Haddad, "Low-frequency learning and fast adaptation in model reference adaptive control," *IEEE Transactions on Automatic Control*, 58(4), pp. 1080–1085, 2013.

[380] H. Zhang, T. Feng, G.H. Yang and H. Liang, "Distributed cooperative optimal control for multiagent systems on directed graphs: An inverse optimal approach," *IEEE Transactions on Cybernetics*, 45, pp. 1315–1326, 2015.

[381] H. Zhang and F.L. Lewis, "Adaptive cooperative tracking control of higher-order nonlinear systems with unknown dynamics," *Automatica*, 48, pp. 1432–1439, 2012.

[382] H. Zhang, J. Zhang, G.H. Yang and Y. Luo, "Leader-based optimal coordination control for the consensus problem of multiagent differential games via fuzzy adaptive dynamic programming," *IEEE Transactions on Fuzzy Systems*, 23, pp. 152–163, 2015.

[383] X. Zhao, P. Shi, X. Zheng and L. Zhang, "Adaptive tracking control for switched stochastic nonlinear systems with unknown actuator dead-zone," *Automatica*, 60, pp. 193–200, 2015.

[384] D. Estrin, D. Culler, K. Pister and G. Sukhatme, "Connecting the physical world with pervasive networks," *IEEE Pervasive Computing*, vol. 1, no. 1, pp. 59–69, Jan. 2002.

[385] I.A.W. Su, Y. Sankarasubramaniam and E. Cayirci, "BA survey on sensor networks," *IEEE Commun. Mag.*, vol. 40, no. 8, pp. 102–116, Aug. 2002.

[386] H. Gharavi and S.P. Kumar, eds., *Proc. IEEE, Special Issue on Sensor Networks and Applications*, vol. 91, no. 8, pp. 1151–1256, Aug. 2003.

[387] B. Warnake, M. Scott, B. Leibowitz, L. Zhou, C. Bellew, J. Chediak, J. Kahn and B.B.K. Pister, "An autonomous 16 mm3 solar-powered node for distributed wireless sensor networks," *in Proc. IEEE Int. Conf. Sensors 2002, Orlando, FL*, pp. 1510–1515, Jun. 2002.

[388] S. Roundy, D. Steingart, L. Frchette, P. Wright and J. Rabaey, "Power sources for wireless networks," *in Proc. 1st Eur. Workshop Wireless Sensor Networks (EWSN '04)*, Berlin, Germany, pp. 1–17, Jan. 2004.

[389] D. Estrin, L. Girod, G. Pottie and M. Srivastava, "Instrumenting the world with wireless sensor networks," *presented at the Int. Conf. Acoustics, Speech, and Signal Processing (ICASSP 2001)*, Salt Lake City, UT, May 2001.

[390] D. Culler, D. Estrin and M. Srivastava, "Guest Editors' Introduction: Overview of sensor networks," *IEEE Computer (Special Issue in Sensor Networks)*, vol. 37, no. 8, pp. 41–49, Aug. 2004.

[391] "B10 emerging tecnology that will change the world," *Technol. Rev.*, vol. 106, no. 1, pp. 33–49, Feb. 2003.

[392] M. Kintner-Meyer and R. Conant, "Opportunities of wireless sensors and controls for building operation," *Energ. Eng. J.*, vol. 102, no. 5, pp. 27–48, 2005.

[393] R. Szewczyk, E. Osterweil, J. Polastre, M. Hamilton, A.M. Mainwaring and D. Estrin, "Habitat monitoring with sensor networks," *Commun. ACM*, vol. 47, no. 6, pp. 34–40, 2004.

[394] M. Nekovee, "Ad hoc sensor networks on the road: The promises and challenges of vehicular ad hoc networks," *presented at the Workshop Ubiquitous Computing and e-Research*, Edinburgh, U.K., May 2005.

[395] A. Willig, K. Matheus and A. Wolisz, "Wireless technology in industrial networks," *Proc. IEEE*, vol. 93, no. 6, pp. 1130–1151, Jun. 2005.

[396] A. LaMarca, W. Brunette, D. Koizumi, M. Lease, S.B. Sigurdsson, K. Sikorski, D. Fox and G. Borriello, "Making sensor networks practical with robots," *in Pervasive '02: Proc. 1st Int. Conf. Pervasive Computing*, London, U.K., pp. 152–166, 2002.

[397] R.R. Brooks, D. Friedlander, J. Koch and S. Phoha, "Tracking multiple targets with self-organizing distributed ground sensors," *J. Parallel Distrib. Comput.*, vol. 64, pp. 874–884, 2004.

[398] A. Arora, P. Dutta, S. Bapat, V. Kulathumani, H. Zhang, V. Naik, V. Mittal, H. Cao, M. Demirbas, M. Gouda, Y. Choi, T. Herman, S. Kulkarni, U. Arumugam, M. Nesterenko, A. Vora and M. Miyashita, "A line in the sand: A wireless sensor network for target detection, classification, and tracking," *Comput. Netw.*, vol. 46, no. 5, pp. 605–634, Dec. 2004.

[399] J. Hespanha, H. Kim and S. Sastry, "Multiple-agent probabilistic pursuit-evasion games," *Proc. IEEE Int. Conf. Decision and Control*, pp. 2432–2437, 1999.

[400] R. Vidal, O. Shakernia, J. Kim, D. Shim and S. Sastry, "Probabilistic pursuit-evasion games: Theory, implementation and experimental evaluation," *IEEE Trans. Robot. Autom.*, vol. 18, no. 5, pp. 662–669, Oct. 2002.

[401] S. Thrun, W. Burgard and D. Fox, "A probabilistic approach to concurrent mapping and localization for mobile robots," *Mach. Learning Auton. Robot.* (Joint Issue), vol. 31, no. 5, pp. 1–25, 1998.

[402] L.J. Guibas, J.-C. Latombe, S.M. LaValle, D. Lin and R. Motwani, "A visibility-based pursuit-evasion problem," *Int. J. Computational Geometry Appl.*, vol. 9, no. 4/5, pp. 471–493, 1999.

[403] B. Sinopoli, C. Sharp, L. Schenato, S. Schaffert and S. Sastry, "Distributed control applications within sensor networks," *Proc. IEEE*, vol. 91, no. 8, pp. 1235–1246, Aug. 2003.

[404] S. Oh, S. Russell and S. Sastry, "Markov chain Monte Carlo data association for general multiple-target tracking problems," *presented at the 43rd IEEE Conf. Decision and Control*, Paradise Island, Bahamas, Dec. 2004.

[405] V.V., "Markov chain monte Carlo data association for multiple-target tracking," *Univ. California, Berkeley*, Tech. Rep. UCB// ERL M05/19, 2005.

[406] S. Oh, L. Schenato, P. Chen and S. Sastry, "A scalable real-time multiple-target tracking algorithm for sensor networks," *Univ. California, Berkeley*, Tech. Rep. UCB//ERL M05/9, 2005.

[407] C. Sharp, S. Schaffert, A. Woo, N. Sastry, C. Karlof, S. Sastry and D. Culler, "Design and implementation of a sensor network system for vehicle tracking and autonomous interception," *in Proc. 2nd Eur. Workshop Wireless Sensor Networks*, pp. 93–107, Jan. 2005.

[408] J. Liu, J. Liu, J. Reich, P. Cheung and F. Zhao, "Distributed group management for track initiation and maintenance in target localization applications," *in Proc. 2nd Workshop Information Processing in Sensor Networks*, pp. 113–128, Apr. 2003.

[409] J. Liu, J. Reich and F. Zhao, "Collaborative in-network processing for target tracking," *J. Applied Signal Processing*, Apr. 2003.

[410] Y. Bar-Shalom and T. Fortmann, *Tracking and Data Association.* San Diego, CA: Academic, 1988.

[411] D. Reid, "An algorithm for tracking multiple targets," *IEEE Trans. Autom. Control*, vol. AC-24, no. 6, pp. 843–854, Dec. 1979.

[412] C. Chong, S. Mori and K. Chang, "Distributed multitarget multisensor tracking," *in Multitarget-Multisensor Tracking: Advanced Applications*, Y. Bar-Shalom, Ed. Norwood, MA: Artech House, pp. 247–295, 1990.

[413] D. Li, K. Wong, Y.H. Hu and A. Sayeed, "Detection, classification and tracking of targets," *IEEE Signal Process. Mag.*, vol. 19, no. 2, pp. 17–29, Mar. 2002.

[414] F. Zhao, J. Liu, J. Liu, L. Guibas and J. Reich, Collaborative signal and information processing: An information directed approach," *Proc. IEEE*, vol. 91, no. 8, pp. 1999-1209, Aug. 2003.

[415] D. McErlean and S. Narayanan, "Distributed detection and tracking in sensor networks," *in Proc. 36th Asilomar Conf. Signal, System and Computers*, pp. 1174–1178, Nov. 2002.

[416] J. Aslam, Z. Butler, V. Crespi, G. Cybenko and D. Rus, "Tracking a moving object with a binary sensor network," *in ACM Int. Conf. Embedded Networked Sensor Systems*, pp. 150–161, 2003.

[417] W. Chen, J. Hou and L. Sha, "Dynamic clustering for acoustic target tracking in wireless sensor networks," *in Proc. of the 11th IEEE Int. Conf. Network Protocols*, pp. 284–294, Nov. 2003.

[418] M. Coates, "Distributed particle filters for sensor networks," *in Proc. 3rd Workshop Information Processing in Sensor Networks*, pp. 99–107, Apr. 2004.

[419] S. Oh and S. Sastry, "Tracking on a graph," *in Proc. 4th Int. Conf. Information Processing in Sensor Networks*, Los Angeles, CA, pp. 195–202, Apr. 2005.

[420] J. Shin, L. Guibas and F. Zhao, "A distributed algorithm for managing multi-target identities in wireless ad-hoc sensor networks," *in Proc. 2nd Workshop Information Processing in Sensor Networks*, pp. 223–238, Apr. 2003.

[421] M. Chu, S. Mitter and F. Zhao, "Distributed multiple target tracking and data association in ad hoc sensor networks," *in Proc. 6th Int. Conf. Information Fusion*, pp. 447–454, Jul. 2004.

[422] J. Liu, J. Liu, M. Chu, J. Reich and F. Zhao, "Distributed state representation for tracking problems in sensor networks," *in Proc. 3rd Workshop Information Processing in Sensor Networks*, pp. 234–242, Apr. 2004.

[423] R. Sittler, "An optimal data association problem on surveillance theory," *IEEE Trans. Military Electron.*, vol. MIL-8, pp. 125–139, Apr. 1964.

[424] J. Collins and J. Uhlmann, "Efficient gating in data association with multivariate distributed states," *IEEE Trans. Aerosp. Electron. Syst.*, vol. 28, no. 3, pp. 909–916, Jul. 1992.

[425] A. Poore, "Multidimensional assignment and multitarget tracking," *Partitioning Data Sets., ser. DIMACS Discrete Mathematics and Theoretical Computer Science*, vol. 19, pp. 169–196, 1995.

[426] J. Hill, M. Horton, R. Kling and L. Krishnamurthy, "The platforms enabling wireless sensor networks," *Commun. ACM*, vol. 47, no. 6, pp. 41–46, 2004.

[427] P. Dutta, J. Hui, J. Jeong, S. Kim, C. Sharp, J. Taneja, G. Tolle, K. Whitehouse and D. Culler, "Trio: Enabling sustainable and scalable outdoor wireless sensor network deployments," *presented at the Int. Conf. Information Processing in Sensor Networks: Special track on platform tools and design methods for network embedded sensors*, 2006.

[428] R. Burkard and R. Cela, "Linear assignment problem and extensions," *Karl-Franzens Univ. Graz*, Graz, Austria, Tech. Rep. 127, 1998.

[429] A. Nilim and L.E. Ghaoui, "Algorithms for air traffic flow management under stochastic environments," *in Proc. Am. Control Conf.*, 2004, vol. 4, pp. 3429–3434.

[430] D. Shim, H. Kim and S. Sastry, "Decentralized reflective model predictive control of multiple flying robots in dynamic environment," *presented at the IEEE Conf. Decision and Control*, Las Vegas, NV, 2003.

[431] H. Pasula, S.J. Russell, M. Ostland and Y. Ritov, "Tracking many objects with many sensors," *presented at the Int. Joint Conf. Artificial Intelligence*, Stockholm, Sweden, 1999.

[432] T. Kurien, "Issues in the design of practical multitarget tracking algorithms," *in Multitarget-Multisensor Tracking: Advanced Applications*, Y. Bar-Shalom, Ed. Norwood, MA: Artech House, 1990.

[433] S. Oh, "Multiple Target Tracking for Surveillance," *Univ. California, Berkeley*, Tech. Rep. UCB/ERL MO3/54, 2003.

[434] M. Lepetic, G. Klancar, I. Skrjanc, D. Matko and B. Potocnic, "Time optimal path planning considering acceleration limits," *Robot. Auton. Syst.*, vol. 45, pp. 199–210, 2003.

[435] A. Saccon, "Minimum time maneuver for nonholonomic car with acceleration constraints: Preliminary results," *presented at the 13th Mediterranean Conf. Control and Automation (MED)*, Limassol, Cyprus, 2005.

[436] E. Velenis and P. Tsiotras, "Optimal velocity profile generation for given acceleration limits: Receding horizon implementation," *in Proc. Am. Control Conf. (ACC05)*, Portland, OR, Jun. 2005, pp. 2147–2152.

[437] C. Belta, V. Isler and G. Pappas, "Discrete abstractions for robot motion planning and control in polygonal environments," *IEEE Trans. Robot.*, vol. 21, no. 5, pp. 864–874, Oct. 2005.

[438] P. Tabuada and G. Pappas, "Hierarchical trajectory refinement for a class of nonlinear systems," *Automatica*, vol. 41, no. 4, pp. 701–708, Apr. 2005.

[439] T. Kailath, A. Sayed and B. Hassibi, *State Space Estimation*. Upper Saddle River, NJ: Prentice-Hall, 1999.

[440] D. Lerro and Y. Bar-Shalom, "Interacting multiple model tracking with target amplitude feature," *IEEE Trans. Aerosp. Electron. Syst.*, vol. 29, no. 2, pp. 494–509, Apr. 1993.

[441] I. Beichl and F. Sullivan, "The Metropolis algorithm," *Computing Sci. Eng.*, vol. 2, no. 1, pp. 65–69, 2000.

[442] M. Jerrum and A. Sinclair, "The Markov chain Monte Carlo method: An approach to approximate counting and integration, in Approximations for NP-hard Problems," *D. Hochbaum, Ed. Boston, MA: PWS Publishing*, 1996.

[443] W. Gilks, S. Richardson and D. Spiegelhalter, eds., *Markov Chain Monte Carlo in Practice, ser. Interdisciplinary Statistics*. London, U.K.: Chapman & Hall, 1996.

[444] G. Roberts, "Markov chain concepts related to sampling algorithms", *in Markov Chain Monte Carlo in Practice, Interdisciplinary Statistics, W. Gilks, S. Richardson and D. Spiegelhalter*, eds. London, U.K.: Chapman & Hall, 1996.

[445] Z. Gao, "On discrete time optimal control: A closed-form solution," *in Proc. 2004 Am. Control Con. (ACC)*, Boston, MA, pp. 52–58, Jun. 2004.

[446] R. Zanasi and R. Morselli, "Discrete minimum time tracking problem for a chain of three integrators with bounded input," *Automatica*, vol. 39, pp. 1643–1649, 2003.

[447] E. Lee and L. Markus, *Foundations of Optimal Control Theory*. New York: Wiley, 1967.

[448] E. Ryan, *Optimal Relay and Saturation Control Synthesis*. London: Peter Peregrinus Ltd., 1982.

[449] T. Basar and G. Olsder, *Dynamic Noncooperative Game Theory*, 2nd ed. San Diego, CA: Academic Press, 1995.

[450] P. Dutta, M. Grimmer, A. Arora, S. Bibyk and D. Culler, "Design of a wireless sensor network platform for detecting rare, random, and ephemeral events," *in Proc. 4th Int. Conf. Information Processing in Sensor Networks*, pp. 497–502, Apr. 2005.

[451] X. Jiang, J. Polastr and D. Culler, "Perpetual environmentally powered sensor networks," *in Proc. 4th Int. Conf. Information Processing in Sensor Networks*, pp. 463–468, Apr. 2005.

[452] J. Polastre, R. Szewczyk and D. Culler, "Telos: Enabling ultra-low power wireless research," *in Proc. 4th Int. Conf. Information Processing in Sensor Networks*, pp. 364–369, Apr. 2005.

[453] D. Gay, P. Levis, R. von Behren, M. Welsh, E. Brewer and D. Culler, "The nesc language: A holistic approach to networked embedded systems," *in Proc. ACM SIGPLAN 2003 Conference on Programming Language Design and Implementation*, pp. 1–11, Jun. 2003.

[454] *TinyOS*, [Online]. Available: http://www.tinyos.net/.

[455] J. Hui and D. Culler, "The dynamic behavior of a data dissemination protocol for network programming at scale," *in Proc. 2nd Int. Conf. Embedded Networked Sensor Systems*, pp. 81–94, 2004.

[456] K. Whitehouse, G. Tolle, J. Taneja, C. Sharp, S. Kim, J. Jeong, J. Hui, P. Dutta and D. Culler, "Marionette: Providing an interactive environment for wireless debugging and development," *presented at the Int. Conf. Information Processing in Sensor Networks: Special track on platform tools and design methods for network embedded sensors*, 2006.

[457] G. Tolle, "A network management system for wireless sensor networks," *Master's thesis*, Univ. California, Berkeley, 2005.

[458] L. Gu, D. Jia, P. Vicaire, T. Yan, L. Luo, T. He, A. Tirumala, Q. Cao, J. Stankovic, T. Abdelzaher and B. Krogh, "Lightweight detection and classification for wireless sensor networks in realistic environments," *in Proc. SenSys*, pp. 205–217, Nov. 2005.

[459] R.W. Beard, T.W. McLain, M.A. Goodrich and E.P. Anderson, "Coordinated target assignment and intercept for unmanned air vehicles," *IEEE Transactions on Robotics and Automation*, 18, pp. 911–922, 2002.

[460] P.A. Bliman and G. Ferrari-Trecate, "Average consensus problems in networks of agents with delayed communications," *Automatica*, 44, pp. 1985–1995, 2008.

[461] J.A. Fax and R.M. Murray, "Information flow and cooperative control of vehicle formations," *IEEE Transactions on Automatic Control*, 49, pp. 1465–1475, 2004.

[462] J. Hu and Y. Hong, "Leader-following coordination of multiagent systems with coupling time delays. Physica A 374: 853-863. Hong, Y., Hu. J. and Gao. L. (2006) "Tracking control for multi-agent consensus with an active leader and variable topology," *Automatica*, 42, pp. 1177–1182, 2007.

[463] D. Jin, "Stability analysis of a double integrator swarm model related to position and velocity," *Transactions of the Institute of Measurement and Control*, 30, pp. 275–293, 2008.

[464] P. Lin and Y. Jia, "Average consensus in networks of multi-agents with both switching topology and coupling time-delay," *Physica A*, 387, pp. 303–313, 2008.

[465] P. Lin and Y. Jia, "Consensus of a class of second-order multiagent systems with time-delay and jointly-connected topologies," *IEEE Transactions on Automatic Control*, 55, pp. 778–784, 2010.

[466] C. Liu and F. Liu, "Consensus of second-order multi-agent systems with input delay," *In Chinese Control and Decision Conference*, pp. 1261–1266, 2010.

[467] Z. Meng, W. Ren, Y. Cao and Z. You, "Leaderless and leaderfollowing consensus with communication and input delays under a directed network topology," *IEEE Transactions on Systems, Man And Cybernetics-Part B: Cybernetics*, 41, pp. 75–88, 2011.

[468] R. Olfati-Saber, "Flocking for multi-agent dynamics systems: Algorithms and theory," *IEEE Transactions on Automatic Control*, 51, pp. 410–420, 2006.

[469] R. Olfati-Saber and R.M. Murray, "Consensus problems in networks of agents with switching topology and time-delays," *IEEE Transactions on Automatic Control*, 49, pp. 1520–1533, 2004.

[470] P.C. Parks and V. Hahn, *Stability Theory*, Englewood Cliffs, NJ: Prentice-Hall, 1993.

[471] W. Ren, "On consensus algorithms for double-integrator dynamics," *IEEE Transactions on Automatic Control*, 53, pp. 1503–1509, 2008.

[472] W. Ren and E. Atkins, "Second-order consensus protocols in multiple vehicle systems with local interactions," *In AIAA Guidance, Navigation and Control Conference and Exhibit*, San Francisco, CA, 2005.

[473] W. Ren and R.W. Beard, "Consensus seeking in multiagent systems under dynamically changing interaction topologies," *IEEE Transactions on Automatic Control*, 50, pp. 655–661, 2005.

[474] Y. Sun, L. Wang and G. Xie, "Average consensus in networks of dynamic agents with switching topologies and multiple timevarying delays," *System and Control Letters*, 57, pp. 175–183, 2008.

[475] J.H. Seo, H. Shim and J. Back, "Consensus of high-order linear systems using dynamic output feedback compensator: Low gain approach," *Automatica*, 45, pp. 2659–2664, 2009.

[476] Y.P. Tian and S. Liu, "Robust consensus of multi-agent systems with diverse input delays and asymmetric interconnection pertubations," *Automatica*, 45, pp. 1347–1353, 2009.

[477] L. Xiao and S. Boyd, "Fast linear iterations for distributed averaging," *Systems and Control Letters*, 53, pp. 65–78, 2004.

[478] W. Yu, G. Chen and M. Cao, "Some necessary and sufficient conditions for second-order consensus in multi-agent dynamical systems," *Automatica*, 46, pp. 1089–1095, 2010.

[479] Y. Zhang and Y. Tian, "Consentability and protocol design of multi-agent systems with stochastic switching topology," *Automatica*, 45, pp. 1195–1201, 2009.

[480] J. Zhu, Y.P. Tian and J. Kuang, "On the general consensus protocol of multi-agent systems with double integrator dynamics," *Linear Algebra and its Applications 431*, pp. 701–715, 2009.

[481] P. Ballal and F.L. Lewis, "Trust-based collaborative control for teams in communication networks," *in Proceedings of the 26th Army Science Conference*, Orlando, pp. 1–8, December 2008.

[482] J.S. Baras and P. Hovareshti, "Effects of graph topology on performance of distributed algorithms for networked control and sensing," *Workshop on Networked Distributed Systems for Intelligent Sensing and Control*, Greece 2007, pp. 1–8, June.

[483] D.S. Bernstein, *Matrix Mathematics*, NJ: Princeton University Press, 2005.

[484] N. Chopra and M.W. Spong, "Passivity-based control of multi-agent systems," *in Advances in Robot Control: From Everyday Physics to Human-like Movements*, eds. S. Kawamura and M. Svinin, Berlin: Springer-Verlag, pp. 107–134, 2006.

[485] F. Chung, *Lectures of Spectral Graph Theory*, Providence, RI: American Mathematical Society, 1997.

[486] J.A. Fax and R.M. Murray, "Information flow and cooperative control of vehicle formations", *IEEE Trans. Automatic Control*, vol. 49, pp. 1465–1476, 2004.

[487] F.R. Gantmacher, *The Theory of Matrices*, New York: Chelsea Publishing Company 1959.

[488] R. Grigoriev, M. Cross and H. Schuster, "Pinning control of spatio-temporal chaos," *Physical Review Letters*, 79, pp. 2795–2798, 1997.

[489] D.B. Gu and H.S. Hu, "Distributed network-based formation control," *International Journal of Systems Science*, 40, pp. 539–552 2009.

[490] Y. Hong, G. Chen and L. Bushnell, "Distributed observers design for leader-following control of multiagent network," *Automatic-a*, 44, pp. 846–850, 2008.

[491] Y. Hong, L. Gao, D. Chen and J. Hu, "Lyapunov-based approach to multi-agent systems with switching jointly connected interconnection," *IEEE Transactions on Automatic Control*, 52, pp. 943–948, 2007.

[492] R.A. Horn and C.R. Johnson, *Matrix Analysis*, New York: Cambridge University Press, 1985.

[493] I. Ipsen and B. Nadler, "Refined perturbation bounds for eigenvalues of hermitian and non-hermitian matrices," *SIAM Journal of Matrix Analysis Applications*, 31, pp. 40–53, 2009.

[494] A. Jadbabaie, J. Lin and A.S. Morse, "Coordination of groups of mobile autonomous agents using nearest neighbor rules," *IEEE Transactions on Automatic Control*, 48, pp. 988–1001, 2003.

[495] S. Khoo, L. Xie and Z. Man, "Robust finite-time consensus tracking algorithm for multirobot systems," *IEEE Transaction on Mechatronics*, 14, pp. 219–228, 2009.

[496] Z. Lin, B. Francis and M. Maggiore, "Necessary and sufficient graphical conditions for formation control of unicycles," *IEEE Transactions on Automatic Control*, 50, pp. 121–127, 2005.

[497] C.L. Liu and Y.P. Tian, "Formation control of multi-agents with heterogeneous communication delays," *International Journal of Systems Science*, 40, pp. 627–636, 2009.

[498] K.L. Moore and D. Lucarelli, "Decentralized adaptive scheduling using consensus variables," *International Journal of Robust and Nonlinear Control*, 17, pp. 921–940, 2007.

[499] L. Moreau, "Stability of multiagent systems with time-dependent communication links," *IEEE Transactions on Automatic Control*, 50, pp. 169–182, 2005.

[500] R. Olfati-Saber, J.A. Fax and R.M. Murray, "Consensus and cooperation in networked multiagent systems," *Proceedings of the IEEE*, 95, pp. 215–233, 2007.

[501] R. Olfati-Saber and R.M. Murray, "Consensus problems in networks of agents with switching topology and time-delays," *IEEE Transactions on Automatic Control*, 49, pp. 1520–1533, 2004.

[502] M. Porfiri and M. Bernardo, "Criteria for global pinning-controllability of complex networks", *Automatica*, vol. 44, pp. 3100–3106, 2008.

[503] Z. Qu, *Cooperative Control of Dynamical Systems*, London: Spring-Verlag, 2009.

[504] W. Ren and E. Atkins, "Distributed multivehicle coordinated control via local information exchange," *International Journal of Robust and Nonlinear Control*, 17, pp. 1002–1033, 2007.

[505] W. Ren and R.W. Beard, "Consensus seeking in multiagent systems under dynamically changing interaction topologies," *IEEE Transactions on Automatic Control*, 50, pp. 655–661, 2005.

[506] W. Ren and R.W. Beard, *Distributed Consensus in Multi-vehicle Cooperative Control: Theory and Applications*, London: Springer-Verlag, 2008.

[507] X. Wang and G. Chen, "Pinning control of scale free dynamical networks," *Physica A*, 310, pp. 521–531, 2002.

[508] J. Warfield, "Binary matrices in system modelling," *IEEE Transactions on System, Man, and Cybernetics*, 5, pp. 441–449, 1973.

[509] C.W. Wu, *Synchronization in Complex Networks Nonlinear Dynamical Systems*, Singapore: World Scientific, 2007.

[510] G. Xie and L. Wang, "Consensus control for a class of networks of dynamic agents: Switching topology," *in Proceedings of the 2006 American Control Conference*, pp. 1382–1387, 2006.

[511] J. Zhu, Y. Tian and J. Kuang, "On the general consensus protocol on multiagent systems with Double integrator Dynamics", *Linear Algebra and its Applications*, 431, pp. 701–715, 2009.

[512] Y. Zhang, N. Gatsis and G.B. Giannakis, "Robust energy management for microgrids with high penetration renewables," *IEEE Trans. Sustain. Energy*, vol. 4, no. 4, pp. 944–953, Oct. 2013.

[513] E. Dall'Anese, H. Zhu and G.B. Giannakis, "Distributed optimal power flow for smart microgrids," *IEEE Trans. Smart Grid*, vol. 4, no. 3, pp. 1464–1475, Sep. 2013.

[514] S. Salinas, M. Li and P. Li, "Multiobjective optimal energy consumption scheduling in smart grids," *IEEE Trans. Smart Grid*, vol. 4, no. 1, pp. 341–348, Mar. 2013.

[515] S.A. Arefifar, Y. Abdel-Rady, I. Mohamed and T.H.M. El-Fouly, "Supply-adequacy-based optimal construction of microgrids in smart distribution systems," *IEEE Trans. Smart Grid*, vol. 3, no. 3, pp. 1491–1502, Sep. 2012.

[516] C.H. Lo and N. Ansari, "Decentralized controls and communications for autonomous distribution networks in smart grid," *IEEE Trans. Smart Grid*, vol. 4, no. 1, pp. 66–77, Mar. 2013.

[517] M. Erol-Kantarci, B. Kantarci and H.T. Mouftah, "Reliable overlay topology design for the smart microgrid network," *IEEE Netw.*, vol. 25, no. 5, pp. 38–43, Sep./Oct. 2011.

[518] H. Dagdougui and R. Sacile, "Decentralized control of the power flows in a network of smart microgrids modeled as a team of cooperative agents," *IEEE Trans. Control Syst. Technol.*, vol. 22, no. 2, pp. 510–519, Mar. 2014.

[519] S. Tan, J.X. Xu and S.K. Panda, "Optimization of distribution network incorporating distributed generators: An integrated approach," *IEEE Trans. Power Syst.*, vol. 28, no. 3, pp. 2421–2432, Aug. 2013.

[520] M. Fathi and H. Bevrani, "Statistical cooperative power dispatching in interconnected microgrids," *IEEE Trans. Sustain. Energy*, vol. 4, no. 3, pp. 586–593, Jul. 2013.

[521] M. Fathi and H. Bevrani, "Adaptive energy consumption scheduling for connected microgrids under demand uncertainty," *IEEE Trans. Power Del.*, vol. 28, no. 3, pp. 1576–1583, Jul. 2013.

[522] C.M. Colson and M.H. Nehrir, "Algorithms for distributed decision making for multiagent microgrid power management," *Proc. IEEE Power Energy Soc. Gen. Meeting*, pp. 1–8, 2011.

[523] Z. Jiang, "Agent-based control framework for distributed energy resources microgrids," *Proc. IEEE/WIC/ACM Int. Conf. Intell. Agent Technol.*, pp. 646–652, 2006.

[524] T. Logenthiran, D. Srinivasan, A.M. Khambadkone and H.N. Aung, "Multiagent system (MAS) for short-term generation scheduling of a microgrid," *Proc. IEEE Int. Conf. Sustain. Energy Technol.*, pp. 1–6, 2010.

[525] D.E. Olivares, A. Mehrizi-Sani, A.H. Etemadi, C.A. Caizares and R. Iravani, "Trends in microgrid control," *IEEE Trans. Smart Grid*, vol. 5, no. 4, pp. 1905–1919, Jul. 2014.

[526] A. Ouammi, H. Dagdougui and R. Sacile, "Optimal control of power flows and energy local storages in a network of microgrids modeled as a system of systems," *IEEE Trans. Control Syst. Technol.*, vol. 23, no. 1, pp. 128–138, Jan. 2015.

[527] Dagdougui, A. Ouammi and R. Sacile, "Optimal control of a network of power microgrids using the Pontryagin's minimum principle," *IEEE Trans. Control Syst. Technol.*, vol. 22, no. 5, pp. 1942–1948, Sep. 2014.

[528] B. Otomega, A. Marinakis, M. Glavic and T.V. Cutsem, "Model predictive control to alleviate thermal overloads," *IEEE Trans. Power Syst.*, vol. 22, no. 3, pp. 1384–1385, Aug. 2007.

[529] A. Parisio, E. Rikos and L. Glielmo, "A model predictive control approach to microgrid operation optimization," *IEEE Trans. Control Syst. Technol.*, vol. 22, no. 5, pp. 1813–1827, Sep. 2014.

[530] G. Ferrari-Trecate et al., "Modeling and control of co-generation power plants: A hybrid system approach," *IEEE Trans. Control Syst. Technol.*, vol. 12, no. 5, pp. 694–705, Sep. 2004.

[531] R. Palma-Behnke et al., "A microgrid energy management system based on the rolling horizon strategy," *IEEE Trans. Smart Grid*, vol. 4, no. 2, pp. 996–1006, Jun. 2013.

[532] D.E. Olivares, C.A. Canizares and M. Kazerani, "A centralized energy management system for isolated microgrids," *IEEE Trans. Smart Grid*, vol. 5, no. 4, pp. 1864–1875, Jul. 2014.

[533] K.T. Tan, P.L. So, Y.C. Chu and M.Z.Q. Chen, "Coordinated control and energy management of distributed generation inverters in a microgrid," *IEEE Trans. Power Del.*, vol. 28, no. 2, pp. 704–713, Apr. 2013.

[534] A. Hooshmand, H. Malki and J. Mohammadpour, "Power flow management of microgrid networks using model predictive control," *Comput. Math. Appl.*, vol. 64, no. 5, pp. 869–876, 2012.

[535] H. Dagdougui, R. Minciardi, A. Ouammi, M. Robba and R. Sacile, "A dynamic decision model for the real time control of hybrid renewable energy production systems," *IEEE Syst. J.*, vol. 4, no. 3, pp. 323–333, Sep. 2010.

[536] S.A. Arefifar, Y. Abdel-Rady, I. Mohamed and T.H.M. El-Fouly, "Supply-adequacy-based optimal construction of microgrids in smart distribution systems," *IEEE Trans. Smart Grid*, vol. 3, no. 3, pp. 1491–1502, Sep. 2012.

[537] G.S. Kasbekar and S. Sarkar, "Pricing games among interconnected microgrids," *Proc. Power Energy Soc. Gen. Meeting*, pp. 1–8, 2012.

[538] M. Pipattanasomporn, H. Feroze and S. Rahman, "Multi-agent systems in a distributed smart grid: Design and implementation," *Proc. Power Syst. Conf. Expo. (PSCE)*, pp. 1–8, Mar. 2009.

[539] K. De Brabandere, K. Vanthournout, J. Driesen, G. Deconinck and R. Belmans, "Control of microgrids," *Proc. IEEE PES General Meeting*, pp. 1–7, Jun. 2007.

[540] N.C. Ekneligoda and W.W. Weaver, "Game-theoretic communication structures in microgrids," *IEEE Trans. Power Del.*, vol. 27, no. 4, pp. 2334–2341, Oct. 2012.

[541] A. Gattami, B. Bernhardsson and A. Rantzer, "Robust team decision theory," *IEEE Trans. Autom. Control*, vol. 57, no. 3, pp. 794–798, Mar. 2012.

[542] A. Gattami and B. Bernhardsson, "Minimax team decision problems," *Proc. Amer. Control Conf. (ACC)*, vol. 07, no. 4, pp. 766–771, Jul. 2007.

[543] H. Dagdougui and R. Sacile, "Decentralized control of the power flows in a network of smart microgrids modeled as a team of cooperative agents," *IEEE Trans. Control Syst. Technol.*, vol. 22, no. 2, pp. 510–519, Mar. 2014.

[544] O. Khorsand, A. Alam and A. Gattami, *Optimal distributed controller synthesis for chain structures: Applications to vehicle formations*, 2012, [online] Available: http://arxiv.org/abs/1204.1869.

[545] T. Baar and D.G.J. Olsder, *Dynamic Non-Cooperative Game Theory*. Philadelphia: Classics in Applied Mathematics., second ed., 1999.

[546] F.L.L.K.G. Vamvoudakis and G.R. Hudas, "Multiagent differential graphical games: Online adaptive learning solution for synchronization with optimality," *Automatica*, vol. 48, no. 8, pp. 1598–1611, 2012.

[547] K.V.S.H.M. Abouheaf, F. Lewis and R. Babuska, "Multi-agent discrete-time graphical games and reinforcement learning solutions," *Automatica*, vol. 50, no. 12, pp. 3038–3053, 2014.

[548] Z. Qu, *Cooperative Control of Dynamical Systems: Applications to Autonomous Vehicles*. Verlag: New York: Springer, 2009.

[549] J.H.Y. Hong and L. Gao, "Tracking control for multiagent consensus with an active leader and variable topology," *Automatica*, vol. 42, no. 7, pp. 1177–1182, 2006.

[550] K.M.W. Ren and Y. Chen, "High-order and model reference consensus algorithms in cooperative control of multivehicle systems," *J. Dyn. Syst., Meas., Con.,*, vol. 129, no. 5, pp. 678–688, 2007.

[551] G.C.Z. Li, Z. Duan and L. Huang, "Consensus of multiagent systems and synchronization of complex networks: A unified viewpoint," *IEEE Trans. Circ. & Syst.-I Reg. paper*, vol. 57, no. 1, pp. 213–224, 2010.

[552] R. Olfati-Saber and R.M. Murray, "Consensus problems in networks of agents with switching topology and time-delays," *IEEE Trans. Autom. Control*, vol. 49, no. 9, pp. 1520–1533, 2004.

[553] X. Wang and G. Chen, "Pinning control of scale-free dynamical networks," *Physica A*, vol. 310, no. 3-4, pp. 521–531, 2002.

[554] J.R.M.R. Gopalakrishnan and A. Wierman, "An architectural view of game theoretic control," *ACM Sig. Perf. Eval. Rev.*, vol. 38, no. 3, pp. 31–36, 2011.

[555] Y. Shoham and K. Leyton-Brown, *MultiAgent Systems: Algorithmic, Game-Theoretic, and Logical Foundations*. Cambridge Press, 2009.

[556] D.V.F.L. Lewis and V.L. Syrmos, *Optimal Control*. John Wiley, third ed., 2012.

[557] G.J.G. Freiling and H. Abou-Kandil, "On global existence of solutions to coupled matrix riccati equations in closed loop Nash games," *IEEE Trans. on Aut. Control*, vol. 41, no. 2, pp. 264–269, 2002.

[558] J.L.S. Kakade, M. Kearns and L. Ortiz, "Correlated equilibria in graphical games," *4th ACM Conf. on Elect. Comm*, pp. 42–47, 2003.

[559] C.L.Z. Huaguang and L. Yanhong, "Near-optimal control for nonzero-sum differential games of continuous-time nonlinear systems using single-network adp," *IEEE Trans. Cyb*, vol. 43, no. 1, pp. 206–216, 2013.

[560] S. Sen and G. Weiss, *Multiagent Systems: A Modern Approach to Distributed Artificial Intelligence*. Cambridge, MA: MIT Press, 1999.

[561] R.S. Sutton and A.G. Barto, *Reinforcement Learning—An Introduction.* MIT Press, Cambridge, Massachusetts, 1998.

[562] T. Dierks and S. Jagannathan, "Optimal control of affine nonlinear continuous-time systems using an online Hamilton-Jacobi-Isaacs formulation," *Proc. IEEE Conf. Dec. and Con.,*, pp. 3048–3053, 2010.

[563] P.J. Werbos, *Beyond Regression: New Tools for Prediction and Analysis in the Behavior Sciences*. PhD thesis, 1974.

[564] P.J. Werbos, *Approximate dynamic programming for real-time control and neural modeling. Handbook of Intelligent Control.* Handbook of Intelligent Control. D.A. White and D.A. Sofge, eds., New York: Van Nostrand Reinhold, 1992.

[565] D.P. Bertsekas and J.N. Tsitsiklis, *Neuro-Dynamic Programming*. Athena Scientific, MA, 1996.

[566] F.L.L.D. Vrabie, O. Pastravanu and M. Abu-Khalaf, "Adaptive optimal control for continuous-time linear systems based on policy iteration," *Automatica*, vol. 45, no. 2, pp. 477–484, 2009.

[567] M.M.M. Abouheaf, F. Lewis and D. Mikulski, "Discrete-time dynamic graphical games: Model-free reinforcement learning solution," *Con. Theory and Tech.*, vol. 13, no. 1, pp. 333–347, 2015.

[568] M. Abouheaf and F. Lewis, "Dynamic graphical games: Online adaptive learning solutions using approximate dynamic programming.," *In Frontiers of Intelligent Control and Information Processing*, pp. 1–46, 2014.

[569] S.D.P. Mannion and K. Mason, "Policy invariance under reward transformations for multi-objective reinforcement learning," *Neurocomputing*, vol. 263, pp. 60–73, 2017.

[570] Y.Y. et al., “Application of integral reinforcement learning for optimal control of a high speed flux-switching permanent magnet machine,” *IECON 2016—42nd Annual Conference of the IEEE Industrial Electronics Society,*, (Florence), pp. 2702–2707, 2016.

[571] H.O.G.L.B. Prasad and B. Tyagi, “Application of policy iteration technique based adaptive optimal control design for automatic voltage regulator of power system,” *Int. Jrn. of Elect. Pwr. & Eng. Sys.*, vol. 63, pp. 940–949, 2014.

[572] J.P.J. Lee and Y. Choi, “Integral q-learning and explorized policy iteration for adaptive optimal control of continuous-time linear systems,” *Automatica*, vol. 48, no. 11, pp. 2850–2859, 2012.

[573] R. Song and Q. Wei, “Chaotic system optimal tracking using data-based synchronous method with unknown dynamics and disturbances,” *Chinese Physics B*, vol. 26, no. 3, pp. 030505:1–8, 2017.

[574] H.-N.W.B. Luo and T. Huang, “Off-policy reinforcement learning for control design,” *IEEE trans. on cyb.*, vol. 45, no. 1, pp. 65–76, 2015.

[575] F.L.L.H. Modares and Z.P. Jiang, “H_∞ tracking control of completely unknown continuous-time systems via off-policy reinforcement learning,” *IEEE Trans. on Neur. Net. and Learn. Sys*, vol. 26, no. 10, pp. 2250–2262, 2015.

[576] J.B.P.J.Y. Lee and Y.H. Choi, “Integral reinforcement learning for continuous-time input-affine nonlinear systems with simultaneous invariant explorations,” *IEEE Transactions on Neural Networks and Learning Systems*, vol. 26, no. 5, pp. 916–932, 2015.

[577] N.K.V.P. Singh and P. Samuel, “Distributed multi-agent system-based load frequency control for multi-area power system in smart grid,” *IEEE Trans. on Indus. Elect.*, vol. 64, no. 6, pp. 5151–5160, 2017.

[578] M.Z.D. Ye and D. Sutanto, “Cloning, resource exchange, and relation adaptation: An integrative self-organization mechanism in a distributed agent network,” *IEEE Trans. on Parallel. and Dist. Sys.*, vol. 25, no. 4, pp. 887–897, 2014.

[579] K.A.S. Loscalzo, R. Wright and L. Yu, “Progressive mining of transition dynamics for autonomous control,” in *IEEE 12th Inter. Conf. on Data Mining*, pp. 990–995, 2012.

[580] B.D.S.L. Busoniu and R. Babuska, “Decentralized reinforcement learning control of a robotic manipulator,” in *9th Inter. Conf. on Con., Aut., Rob. and Vis.*, (Singapore), pp. 1–6, 2006.

[581] M.L. Littman, "Value-function reinforcement learning in markov games," *J. Cog. Sys.Res. 1*, vol. 2, no. 1, pp. 55–66, 2001.

[582] M.L.L.S. Singh, T. Jaakkola and C. Szepesvari, "Convergence results for single-step on-policy reinforcement-learning algorithms," *Machine Learning*, vol. 39, pp. 28–308, 2000.

[583] H.M.J. Li and T. Chai, "Off-policy reinforcement learning for synchronization in multiagent graphical games," *IEEE Trans. On Neur. Net. and Learn. Sys.*, vol. 28, no. 10, pp. 2434–2445, 2017.

[584] M. Awheda and H. Schwartz, "A residual gradient fuzzy reinforcement learning algorithm for differential games," *Int. Jour. On Fuzz. Sys*, vol. 19, no. 4, pp. 1058–1076, 2017.

[585] P.J. Werbos, "Neural networks for control and system identification," in *IEEE Conf. on Dec. and Con*, pp. 260–265, 1989.

[586] H.H.D. Wang and D. Liu, "Adaptive critic nonlinear robust control: A survey," *IEEE Trans. On Cyb.*, vol. 47, no. 10, pp. 3429–3451, 2017.

[587] H.J.H. Zhang and C. Luo, "Discrete-time nonzero-sum games for multiplayer using policy-iteration-based adaptive dynamic programming algorithms," *IEEE Trans. On Cyb.*, vol. 47, no. 10, pp. 3331–3340, 2017.

[588] R. B. [44] W. Ren and E. Atkins, "A survey of consensus problems in multi-agent coordination," in *Amer. Con. Conf.*, p. 1859–1864, 2005.

[589] W. Ren and R. Beard, "Consensus seeking in multiagent systems under dynamically changing interaction topologies," *IEEE Trans. Autom. Con.*, vol. 50, no. 5, pp. 655–661, 2005.

[590] F. Lewis, *Applied Optimal Control and Estimation: Digital Design and Implementation.* New Jersey: Prentice-Hall, 1992.

[591] K.H.-M.F. Lewis, H. Zhang and A. Das, *Cooperative Control of Multi-Agent Systems: Optimal and Adaptive Design Approaches.* Springer Publishing Company, Incorporated, 2014.

[592] L.X.S. Khoo and Z. Man, "Robust finite-time consensus tracking algorithm for multi-robot systems," *IEEE Trans. on Mechat*, vol. 14, pp. 219–228, 2009.

[593] X.W.X. Li and G. Chen, "Pinning a complex dynamical network to its equilibrium," *IEEE Trans. Circ. Syst. I, Reg. Paper*, vol. 51, no. 10, pp. 2074–2087, 2004.

[594] T. Apostol and I. Makai, *Mathematical Analysis*, Massachusetts: Addison-Wesley Reading, 1974.

[595] Y. Cao, Y. Li, W. Ren and Y. Chen, "Distributed coordination of networked fractional-order systems," *IEEE Trans. Syst. Man Cybern. B: Cybern.*, 40, pp. 362–370, 2010.

[596] Y. Cao, W. Ren and Y. Li, "Distributed discrete-time coordinated tracking with a time-varying reference state and limited communication," *Automatica*, 45, pp. 1299–1305, 2009.

[597] D. Dimarogonas and E. Frazzoli, "Distributed event-triggered control strategies for multi-agent systems," *47th Annual Allerton Conference on Communication, Control and Computing*, Monticello, IL, USA, pp. 906–910, 2009.

[598] L. Fang and P. Antsaklis, "Information consensus of asynchronous discrete-time multi-agent systems," *IEEE Proceedings of the 2005 American Control Conference*, Portland, USA, pp. 1883–1888, 2005.

[599] R. Horn and C. Johnson, *Matrix Analysis*, Cambridge: Cambridge University Press, 2005.

[600] J. Hu, G. Chen and H.X. Li, "Distributed event-triggered tracking control of leader-follower multi-agent systems with communication delays," *Inst. Inform. Theory Autom. AS CR*, 47, pp. 630–643, 2011.

[601] S. Khoo, L. Xie and Z. Man, "Robust finite-time consensus tracking algorithm for multirobot systems," *IEEE-ASME Trans. MECH.*, 14, pp. 219–228, 2009.

[602] P. Lin and Y. Jia, "Consensus of second-order discrete-time multi-agent systems with non-uniform time-delays and dynamically changing topologies," *Automatica*, 45, pp. 2154–2158, 2009.

[603] C. Ma and J. Zhang, "Necessary and sufficient conditions for consensusability of linear multi-agent systems," *IEEE Trans. Autom. Control*, 55, pp. 1263–1268, 2010.

[604] Z. Meng, W. Ren, Y. Cao and Z. You, "Leaderless and leader-following consensus with communication and input delays under a directed network topology," *IEEE Trans. Syst. Man Cybern. B: Cybern.*, 41, pp. 75–88, 2011.

[605] W. Ren, "Multi-vehicle consensus with a time-varying reference state," *Syst. Control Lett.*, 56, pp. 474–483, 2007.

[606] W. Ren and R. Beard, *Distributed Consensus in Multi-vehicle Cooperative Control: Theory and Applications*, Berlin: Springer, 2008.

[607] W. Ren, R. Beard and E. Atkins, "Information consensus in multivehicle cooperative control," *IEEE Control Syst. Mag.*, 27, pp. 71–82, 2007.

[608] C. Reynolds, "Flocks, herds and schools: A distributed behavioral model," *Comput. Graph.*, pp. 25–34, 1987.

[609] G. Seyboth, *Event-based Control for Multi-agent Systems*, Master's Degree Project, Stockholm, Sweden, 2010.

[610] H. Su, G. Chen, X. Wang and Z. Lin, "Adaptive second-order consensus of networked mobile agents with nonlinear dynamics," *Automatica*, 47, pp. 368–375, 2011.

[611] H. Su, X. Wang and G. Chen, "Rendezvous of multiple mobile agents with preserved network connectivity," *Syst. Control Lett.*, 59, pp. 313–322, 2010.

[612] Y. Sun and L. Wang, "Consensus of multiagent systems in directed networks with nonuniform time-varying delays," *IEEE Trans. Autom. Control*, 54, pp. 1607–1613, 2009.

[613] P. Tabuada, "Event-triggered real-time scheduling of stabilizing control tasks," *IEEE Trans. Autom. Control*, 52, pp. 1680–1685, 2007.

[614] Y. Tian and C. Liu, "Robust consensus of multi-agent systems with diverse input delays and asymmetric interconnection perturbations," *Automatica*, 45, pp. 1347–1353, 2009.

[615] T. Vicsek, A. Czirk, E. Ben-Jacob, I. Cohen and O. Shochet, "Novel type of phase transition in a system of self-driven particles," *Phys. Rev. Lett.*, 75, pp. 1226–1229, 1995.

[616] F. Xiao and L. Wang, "Consensus problems for high-dimensional multi-agent systems," *IET Control Theory Appl.*, 1, pp. 830–837, 2007.

[617] F. Xiao and L. Wang, "Asynchronous consensus in continuous-time multi-agent systems with switching topology and time-varying delays," *IEEE Trans. Autom. Control*, 53, pp. 1804–1816, 2008.

[618] G. Xie, H. Liu, L. Wang and Y. Jia, "Consensus in networked multi-agent systems via sampled control: Switching topology case," *IEEE Proceedings of the 2009 American Control Conference*, St. Louis, MO, USA, pp. 4525–4530, 2009.

[619] G. Xie, L. Wang and Y. Jia, "Consensus in networked multi-agent systems via sampled control: Fixed topology case," *IEEE Proceedings of the 2009 American Control Conference*, St. Louis, MO, USA, pp. 3902–3907, 2009.

[620] A. Ye sildirek and F.L. Lewis, "Feedback linearization using neural networks," *Automatica*, 31, pp. 1659–1664, 1995.

[621] D. Yue, E. Tian and Q. Han, "A delay system method for designing event-triggered controllers of networked control systems," *IEEE Trans. Autom. Control*, 58, pp. 475–481, 2013.

[622] Y. Zhang and Y. Tian, "Consentability and protocol design of multi-agent systems with stochastic switching topology," *Automatica*, 45, pp. 1195–1201, 2009.

[623] Y. Zhang and Y. Tian, "Consensus of data-sampled multiagent systems with random communication delay and packet loss," *IEEE Trans. Autom. Control*, 55, pp. 939-943, 2010.

Index

Milton Keynes UK
Ingram Content Group UK Ltd.
UKHW051013071024
449327UK00012B/230